FINANCIAL ENGINEERING
ADVANCED BACKGROUND SERIES

FE PRESS
New York

Financial Engineering Advanced Background Series

1. A Primer for the Mathematics of Financial Engineering, Second Edition, by Dan Stefanica. FE Press, 2011

2. Solutions Manual – A Primer for the Mathematics of Financial Engineering, Second Edition, by Dan Stefanica. FE Press, 2011

3. A Linear Algebra Primer for Financial Engineering, by Dan Stefanica. FE Press, 2014

4. Solutions Manual – A Linear Algebra Primer for Financial Engineering, by Dan Stefanica. FE Press, 2014

5. A Probability Primer for Mathematical Finance, by Elena Kosygina. FE Press, 2016

Other Titles from FE Press

1. 150 Most Frequently Asked Questions on Quant Interviews, by Dan Stefanica, Radoš Radoičić, and Tai-Ho Wang. FE Press, 2013

2. 50 Challenging Brainteasers from Quant Interviews, by Radoš Radoičić, Dan Stefanica, and Tai-Ho Wang. FE Press, 2014

3. Stochastic Calculus & Probability Quant Interview Questions, by Tai-Ho Wang, Radoš Radoičić, and Dan Stefanica. FE Press, 2014

A LINEAR ALGEBRA PRIMER

for

FINANCIAL ENGINEERING

Covariance Matrices, Eigenvectors, OLS,
and more

DAN STEFANICA

Baruch College
City University of New York

FE Press
New York

FE PRESS
New York

www.fepress.org

©Dan Stefanica 2014

All rights reserved. No part of this publication may be reproduced, stored in a retrieval system, or transmitted, in any form or by any means, electronic, mechanical, photocopying, recording, or otherwise, without the prior written permission of the publisher.

This edition first published 2014

Printed in the United States of America

ISBN-13 978-0-9797576-5-5
ISBN-10 0-9797576-5-7

To Rianna, Eric and Miriam,

my treasures

Contents

List of Tables	xi
Preface	xiii
Acknowledgments	xv

1 Vectors and matrices   1
- 1.1 Column and row vectors. Column form and row form of a matrix. . .   1
  - 1.1.1 Covariance matrix computation from time series data   7
- 1.2 Matrix rank, nullspace, and range of a matrix   10
  - 1.2.1 A one period market model   12
- 1.3 Nonsingular matrices   19
- 1.4 Diagonal matrices   22
  - 1.4.1 Converting between covariance and correlation matrices   25
- 1.5 Lower triangular and upper triangular matrices. Tridiagonal matrices.   27
- 1.6 References   30
- 1.7 Exercises   31

2 LU decomposition   37
- 2.1 The numerical solution of linear systems   37
- 2.2 Forward substitution   38
  - 2.2.1 Finding discount factors using forward substitution   41
- 2.3 Backward substitution   43
- 2.4 LU decomposition without pivoting   46
  - 2.4.1 Pseudocode and operation count for LU decomposition . . .   47
- 2.5 Linear solvers using LU decomposition without pivoting   55
  - 2.5.1 LU linear solvers for tridiagonal matrices   56
- 2.6 LU decomposition with row pivoting   61
- 2.7 Linear solvers using LU decomposition with row pivoting   69
  - 2.7.1 Solving linear systems corresponding to the same matrix   70
  - 2.7.2 Finding discount factors using the LU decomposition   73
- 2.8 Cubic spline interpolation   75

	2.8.1 Cubic spline interpolation for zero rate curves	77
2.9	References	79
2.10	Exercises	80

3 The Arrow–Debreu one period market model — 87
- 3.1 One period market models 87
- 3.2 Arbitrage–free markets 91
- 3.3 Complete markets 95
- 3.4 Risk–neutral pricing in arb–free complete markets 97
  - 3.4.1 State prices 99
- 3.5 A one period index options market model 100
- 3.6 References 104
- 3.7 Exercises 105

4 Eigenvalues and eigenvectors — 111
- 4.1 Definitions and properties 111
- 4.2 Diagonal forms 122
- 4.3 Diagonally dominant matrices 123
- 4.4 Numerical computation of eigenvalues 128
- 4.5 Eigenvalues and eigenvectors of tridiagonal symmetric matrices 128
- 4.6 References 131
- 4.7 Exercises 132

5 Symmetric matrices and symmetric positive definite matrices — 139
- 5.1 Symmetric matrices 139
- 5.2 Symmetric positive definite matrices 142
  - 5.2.1 Sylvester's Criterion 151
  - 5.2.2 Positive definiteness criteria for symmetric matrices 154
- 5.3 The diagonal form of symmetric matrices 155
- 5.4 References 157
- 5.5 Exercises 158

6 Cholesky decomposition. Efficient cubic spline interpolation. — 161
- 6.1 Cholesky decomposition 161
  - 6.1.1 Pseudocode and operation count for Cholesky decomposition . 166
- 6.2 Linear solvers for symmetric positive definite matrices 174
  - 6.2.1 Solving linear systems corresponding to the same spd matrix . 175
- 6.3 Optimal linear solvers for tridiagonal spd matrices 176
- 6.4 Efficient implementation of the cubic spline interpolation 181
  - 6.4.1 Efficient cubic spline interpolation for zero rate curves 185
- 6.5 References 186
- 6.6 Exercises 188

7 Covariance matrices. Multivariate normals. 193
- 7.1 Covariance and correlation matrices 193
- 7.2 Covariance and correlation matrix estimation from time series data . . 201
- 7.3 Linear Transformation Property 207
- 7.4 Necessary and sufficient conditions for covariance and correlation matrices 209
- 7.5 Finding normal variables with a given covariance or correlation matrix 211
  - 7.5.1 Monte Carlo simulation for basket options pricing 213
- 7.6 Multivariate normal random variables 214
- 7.7 Multivariate random variables formulation for covariance and correlation matrices 219
- 7.8 References 222
- 7.9 Exercises 223

8 Ordinary least squares (OLS). Linear regression. 227
- 8.1 Ordinary least squares 227
  - 8.1.1 Least squares for implied volatility computation 229
- 8.2 Linear regression: ordinary least squares for time series data 235
- 8.3 Ordinary least squares for random variables 237
- 8.4 The intuition behind ordinary least squares for time series data 240
- 8.5 References 244
- 8.6 Exercises 245

9 Efficient portfolios. Value at Risk. 251
- 9.1 Efficient portfolios. Markowitz portfolio theory. 251
- 9.2 Blueprints for finding efficient portfolios 255
- 9.3 Minimum variance portfolios 259
  - 9.3.1 Minimum variance portfolios and the tangency portfolio 262
- 9.4 Maximum return portfolios 265
  - 9.4.1 Maximum return portfolios and the tangency portfolio 269
- 9.5 Minimum variance portfolio with no cash position 271
- 9.6 Value at Risk (VaR). Portfolio VaR. 274
  - 9.6.1 VaR of combined portfolios and subadditivity 278
- 9.7 References 281
- 9.8 Exercises 282

10 Mathematical appendix and technical results 287
- 10.1 Numerical linear algebra tools 287
  - 10.1.1 Determinants 287
  - 10.1.2 Permutation matrices 289
  - 10.1.3 Orthogonality 291
  - 10.1.4 Quadratic forms 293

10.2 Mathematical tools 296
    10.2.1 Multivariable functions 296
    10.2.2 Lagrange multipliers 301
    10.2.3 The "Big O" notation 303
10.3 European options overview 305
10.4 Eigenvalues of symmetric matrices 307
10.5 Row rank equal to column rank 309
10.6 Technical results for the Cholesky and LU decompositions . . 311
10.7 More technical results 315
10.8 Exercises 318

Bibliography   **319**

Index   **322**

List of Tables

2.1   Pseudocode for Forward Substitution 40
2.2   Forward Substitution for lower triangular bidiagonal matrices 41
2.3   Pseudocode for Backward Substitution 45
2.4   Backward Substitution for upper triangular bidiagonal matrices 46
2.5   Pseudocode for LU decomposition without pivoting 54
2.6   Linear solver using LU decomposition without pivoting 56
2.7   LU decomposition without pivoting for tridiagonal matrices 59
2.8   Tridiagonal linear solver using LU decomposition without pivoting 59
2.9   Explicit tridiagonal linear solver using LU decomposition without pivoting 60
2.10 Pseudocode for LU decomposition with row pivoting 70
2.11 Linear solver using LU decomposition with row pivoting 71
2.12 Solution of multiple linear systems corresponding to the same matrix . . . 72
2.13 Pseudocode for the natural cubic spline interpolation 77

3.1   Dec 2012 SPX option prices on 3/9/2012 100

5.1   Necessary and sufficient conditions for spd and spsd matrices 154

6.1   Pseudocode for Cholesky decomposition 170
6.2   Linear solver using Cholesky decomposition 174
6.3   Solution of multiple linear systems corresponding to the same spd matrix 176
6.4   Cholesky decomposition for tridiagonal spd matrices 179
6.5   Tridiagonal spd linear solver using Cholesky decomposition 179
6.6   Tridiagonal spd linear solver using LU decomposition 180
6.7   Explicit tridiagonal spd linear solver with LU decomposition 181
6.8   Efficient implementation of the natural cubic spline interpolation 185

8.1   Least squares implementation 229
8.2   Dec 2012 SPX option prices on 3/9/2012 230
8.3   Pseudocode for computing implied volatility 234
8.4   Implied volatiles for SPX options 235

9.1	Pseudocode for asset allocation of minimum variance portfolio	255
9.2	Asset allocation of minimum variance portfolio from tangency portfolio	256
9.3	Pseudocode for asset allocation of maximum return portfolio	257
9.4	Asset allocation of maximum return portfolio from tangency portfolio	258

Preface

The use of quantitative methods has grown tremendously in all areas of finance, from trading to risk management, and accelerated through the financial crisis and the advent of the big data era. Many of these methods require applying linear algebra methods, for example, for solving linear systems when computing optimal asset allocations, or for computing covariance and correlation matrices from time series data.

This book covers numerical linear algebra methods required for financial engineering applications. Many of these applications are included in the book, and pseudocodes are provided for the numerical linear algebra methods.

Linear Algebra Topics

- LU and Cholesky decompositions and linear solvers
- Optimal solvers for tridiagonal symmetric positive matrices
- Linear Transformation Property
- Multivariate normal random variables
- Efficient cubic spline interpolation
- Ordinary least squares (OLS) and linear regression
- Gershgorin's theorem and diagonal dominance
- Sylvester's criterion for positive definiteness

Financial Applications

- The Arrow–Debreu one period market model
- One period index options arbitrage
- Covariance and correlation matrix estimation from time series data
- Ordinary least squares for implied volatility computation
- Minimum variance portfolios and maximum return portfolios
- Value at Risk and portfolio VaR

Every chapter concludes with exercises that are a mix of mathematical and financial questions. Some of these exercises are similar to questions frequently asked in interviews for quantitative jobs in financial institutions. A Solutions Manual to this book is forthcoming in 2014.

The book is written in a similar spirit as the best–selling "A Primer for the Mathematics of Financial Engineering" by the same author, and should accordingly be useful to a similarly large audience:

- Prospective students for financial engineering or mathematical finance programs will be able to self–study material that will prove very important in their future studies.

- Finance practitioners will find mathematical underpinnings for many methods used in practice, furthering the ability to expand upon these methods.

- Academics teaching financial engineering courses will be able to use this book as textbook, or as reference book for numerical linear algebra methods with financial applications.

As Director of the elite Financial Engineering Masters Program at Baruch College,[1] City University of New York, since its inception in 2002, the author has had the privilege of interacting with students whose knowledge and ability are exceptional. The community that evolved around the alumni, students, and faculty of the program embodies the friendliness and mutual support of everyone involved, in a highly competitive and ultimately very rewarding environment.

The material in this book has been used for the Numerical Linear Algebra with Financial Applications refresher seminars that the author has been teaching since 2004, originally to students of the Baruch MFE Program, and, recently, to a much wider audience. Studying this material before entering the program provided the students with a solid background and played an important role in making them successful graduates: over 90 percent of the graduates of the Baruch MFE Program are currently employed in the financial industry.

This is the third book in the Financial Engineering Advanced Background Series, following "A Primer for the Mathematics of Financial Engineering" and its Solutions Manual.

A *Solutions Manual* to this book is forthcoming in 2014, to be followed by a Probability Primer for Mathematical Finance.

Dan Stefanica

New York, 2014

---

[1] Baruch MFE Program web page: http://mfe.baruch.cuny.edu

Acknowledgments

As Director of the Financial Engineering Masters Program at Baruch College, it is a privilege to educate so many talented students and to contribute to launching and furthering their quant finance careers. This book is the result of interacting with many generations of students, and I am grateful to all of them.

I learned a lot from working alongside wonderful colleagues in the mathematics department. Many thanks are due to my colleagues Elena Kosygina, Andrew Lesniewski, Radoš Radoičić, Tai-Ho Wang, and Sherman Wong. Special thanks are owed to Jim Gatheral and Warren Gordon, whose contributions to the success of our program cannot be understated.

As was the case before, the title of the book was suggested by Emanuel Derman, to whom we are in debt for this.

The art for the book cover is, as always, due to the professional help of my friend Max Rumyantsev.

Many students and alumni looked over versions of the book at varying stages of completion and revision. Their help was greatly appreciated, and the book is much better thanks to them. The proofreading of the book was spearheaded by Vipul Bandari, Jing Chen, Alan Coman, Yifan Cui, Yu Gan, Ling Gu, Jun Hua, Srinivas Kannepalli, Alireza Kashef, Howard Lewis, Lanchun Liu, Ran Liu, Noam Mendel, Dru Pollini, Nikos Rachmanis, Svetlana Rafailova, Dmitry Rile, Xiaoyin Rong, Fubo Shi, Wenhui Wang, Peng Wu, Yanzhu Wu, Bo Yuan, Shixiang Zhang, He Zhao, and Wenyi Zhou.

The unwavering and wholehearted support of my family is the cornerstone of everything in my professional life. This book is a tribute to them, and nothing is more heartwarming than being able to dedicate it to them.

Thank you, my dearly beloved!

Dan Stefanica

New York, 2014

Chapter 1

Vectors and matrices.

Column vectors and row vectors. Column form and row form of a matrix.

Column-based and row-based matrix–vector and matrix–matrix multiplication.

Covariance matrix computation from time series data.

Matrix rank. Nullspace and range of a matrix. Linear independence.

A one period market model example.

Nonsingular matrices and the inverse of a matrix.

Diagonal matrices. Matrix multiplication by diagonal matrices.

Converting between covariance and correlation matrices.

Correlation matrix computation from time series data.

Lower and upper triangular matrices. Tridiagonal matrices.

1.1 Column and row vectors. Column form and row form of a matrix.

An n–dimensional vector $v \in \mathbb{R}^n$ is denoted by $v = (v_i)_{i=1:n}$ and has n components $v_i \in \mathbb{R}$, for $i = 1 : n$.[1]

The vector $v = (v_i)_{i=1:n}$ is a **column vector** of size n if

$$v = \begin{pmatrix} v_1 \\ v_2 \\ \vdots \\ v_n \end{pmatrix}. \qquad (1.1)$$

A column vector is also called an $n \times 1$ vector.

---

[1] The vectors and matrices considered here have entries which are real numbers. While complex numbers will occur naturally (for example, eigenvalues of a matrices with real entries may be complex numbers), the presentation and the notations in this book will be specific to vectors and matrices with real entries.

The vector v^t is a **row vector**[2] of size n if

$$v^t = (v_1 \ v_2 \ \ldots \ v_n). \tag{1.2}$$

A row vector is also called an $1 \times n$ vector.

Unless otherwise specified, a vector v denoted by $v = (v_i)_{i=1:n}$ is a column vector.

An $m \times n$ matrix $A = (A(j,k))_{j=1:m, k=1:n}$ has m rows and n columns. Rather than using the entry by entry notation above for the matrix A, we will use either a column–based notation (more often), or a row–based notation, both being better suited for numerical computations.

The **column form** of the matrix A is

$$A = (a_1 \mid a_2 \mid \ldots \mid a_n) = \text{col}\,(a_k)_{k=1:n}, \tag{1.3}$$

where a_k is the k-th column[3] of A, $k = 1:n$.

The **row form** of the matrix A is

$$A = \begin{pmatrix} r_1 \\ -- \\ r_2 \\ -- \\ \vdots \\ -- \\ r_m \end{pmatrix} = \text{row}\,(r_j)_{j=1:m}, \tag{1.4}$$

where r_j is the j-th row[4] of A, $j = 1:m$.

Row Vector – Column Vector multiplication:[5]

Let $v = (v_i)_{i=1:n}$ be a column vector of size n, and let $w^t = (w_1 \ w_2 \ \ldots \ w_n)$ be a row vector of size n. Then,

$$w^t v = \sum_{i=1}^{n} w_i v_i. \tag{1.5}$$

Column Vector – Row Vector multiplication:

Let $v = (v_j)_{j=1:m}$ be a column vector of size m, and let $w^t = (w_1 \ w_2 \ \ldots \ w_n)$ be a row vector of size n. Then, vw^t is an $m \times n$ matrix with the following entries:

$$(vw^t)(j,k) = v_j w_k, \quad \forall \, j = 1:m, \ k = 1:n. \tag{1.6}$$

Matrix – Column Vector multiplication:

Let $A = \text{col}\,(a_k)_{k=1:n}$ be an $m \times n$ matrix given by the column form (1.3), and let $v = (v_k)_{k=1:n}$ be a column vector of size n given by (1.1). Then,

$$Av = \sum_{k=1}^{n} v_k a_k. \tag{1.7}$$

---

[2] The notation v^t emphasizes the fact that a row vector is the transpose of a column vector; see also Definition 1.1.
[3] For every $k = 1:n$, the column vector a_k is given by $a_k = (A(j,k))_{j=1:m}$.
[4] For every $j = 1:m$, the row vector r_j is given by $r_j = (A(j,k))_{k=1:n}$.
[5] Formula (1.5) is the same as formula (5.2) for the Euclidean inner product of two vectors.

In other words, the result of the multiplication of the column vector v by the matrix A is a column vector Av which is the linear combination[6] of the columns of A with coefficients equal to the corresponding entries of v.

If $A = \text{row}\,(r_j)_{j=1:m}$ is the row form of A, then the j–th entry of the $m \times 1$ column vector Av is

$$(Av)(j) = r_j v, \quad \forall\, 1 \leq j \leq m. \tag{1.8}$$

Note that, since r_j is a $1 \times n$ row vector and v is a $n \times 1$ column vector, it follows from (1.5) that the multiplication from (1.8) can be performed.

Row Vector – Matrix multiplication:

Let $A = \text{row}\,(r_j)_{j=1:m}$ be an $m \times n$ matrix given by the row form (1.4), and let $w^t = (w_1\ w_2\ \ldots\ w_m)$ be a row vector of size m. Then,

$$w^t A = \sum_{j=1}^{m} w_j r_j. \tag{1.9}$$

In other words, the result of the multiplication of the row vector w^t by the matrix A (from the right) is a row vector $w^t A$ which is the linear combination of the rows of A with coefficients equal to the corresponding entries of w^t.

If $A = \text{col}\,(a_k)_{k=1:n}$ is the column form of A, then the k–th entry of the $1 \times n$ row vector $w^t A$ is

$$(w^t A)(k) = w^t a_k, \quad \forall\, 1 \leq k \leq n. \tag{1.10}$$

Matrix – Matrix multiplication:

(i) Let A be an $m \times n$ matrix, and let B be an $n \times p$ matrix given by $B = \text{col}\,(b_k)_{k=1:p}$. Then, AB is the $m \times p$ matrix given by

$$AB = \text{col}\,(Ab_k)_{k=1:p} = (Ab_1\ |\ Ab_2\ |\ \ldots\ |\ Ab_p). \tag{1.11}$$

The result of multiplying the matrices A and B is a matrix whose columns are the columns of B multiplied by the matrix A.

(ii) Let A be an $m \times n$ matrix given by $A = \text{row}\,(r_j)_{j=1:m}$, and let B be an $n \times p$ matrix. Then, AB is the $m \times p$ matrix given by

$$AB = \text{row}\,(r_j B)_{j=1:m} = \begin{pmatrix} r_1 B \\ -- \\ r_2 B \\ -- \\ \vdots \\ -- \\ r_m B \end{pmatrix}. \tag{1.12}$$

The result of multiplying the matrices A and B is a matrix whose rows are the rows of A multiplied by the matrix B.

---

[6] A linear combination of the vectors $w_1, w_2, \ldots, w_n$ is any sum of these vectors multiplied by real coefficients, i.e., $c_1 w_1 + c_2 w_2 + \ldots + c_n w_n$, where $c_i \in \mathbb{R}$, $i = 1:n$; see also Definition 1.5.

(iii) Let A be an $m \times n$ matrix given by $A = \text{row}(r_j)_{j=1:m}$, and let B be an $n \times p$ matrix given by $B = \text{col}(b_k)_{k=1:p}$. Then, AB is the $m \times p$ matrix whose entries are given by[7]

$$(AB)(j,k) = r_j b_k, \quad \forall\, j = 1:m,\ k = 1:p. \tag{1.13}$$

Matrix – Matrix – Matrix multiplication:

Let A be an $m \times n$ matrix given by $A = \text{row}(r_j)_{j=1:m}$, let B be an $n \times p$ matrix, and let C be a $p \times l$ matrix given by $C = \text{col}(c_k)_{k=1:l}$. Then, ABC is the $m \times l$ matrix whose entries are given by

$$(ABC)(j,k) = r_j B c_k, \quad \forall\, j = 1:m,\ k = 1:l. \tag{1.14}$$

Note that (1.14) follows from (1.13), since $BC = \text{col}(Bc_k)_{k=1:l}$; cf. (1.11).

Note that matrix multiplication is associative, i.e., $ABC = (AB)C = A(BC)$.

We emphasize again that we almost exclusively think of a matrix as either a collection of column vectors, or as a collection of row vectors, rather than as a collection of individual entries. For numerical purposes, this is an efficient way to implement matrices. Also, linear algebra proofs using the column form or the row form of a matrix are more insightful and more compact than proofs using individual entries of a matrix. Most of the proofs from this book use a vector–based approach.

Definition 1.1. *The transpose of an $n \times 1$ column vector $v = (v_i)_{i=1:n}$ is the $1 \times n$ row vector $v^t = (v_1\ v_2\ \ldots\ v_n)$. The transpose of an $1 \times n$ row vector $r = (r_1\ r_2\ \ldots\ r_n)$ is the $n \times 1$ column vector $r^t = (r_i)_{i=1:n}$.*

Note that

$$(cv)^t = cv^t, \quad \forall\, v \in \mathbb{R}^n,\ c \in \mathbb{R}. \tag{1.15}$$

Definition 1.2. *The transpose matrix A^t of an $m \times n$ matrix A is an $n \times m$ matrix given by*

$$A^t(k,j) = A(j,k), \quad \forall\, k = 1:n,\ j = 1:m. \tag{1.16}$$

Transposing a matrix switches the column form of the matrix to a row form, and the row form of the matrix to a column form as follows:

$$A = \text{col}(a_k)_{k=1:n} \iff A^t = \text{row}(a_k^t)_{k=1:n}; \tag{1.17}$$

$$A = \text{row}(r_j)_{j=1:m} \iff A^t = \text{col}(r_j^t)_{j=1:m}. \tag{1.18}$$

From (1.16), we find that, for any matrix A,

$$(A^t)^t = A, \tag{1.19}$$

and, for any matrices A and B of the same size,

$$(A+B)^t = A^t + B^t. \tag{1.20}$$

Lemma 1.1. *Let A be an $m \times n$ matrix and let v be a column vector of size n. Then,*

$$(Av)^t = v^t A^t. \tag{1.21}$$

---

[7]Note that the multiplication from (1.13) can be performed since r_j is a $1 \times n$ row vector and b_k is a $n \times 1$ column vector; see (1.5).

1.1. MATRIX COLUMN FORM AND ROW FORM

Proof. Let $A = \text{col}(a_k)_{k=1:n}$ and $v = (v_i)_{i=1:n}$. Then, $Av = \sum_{i=1}^{n} v_i a_i$, and

$$(Av)^t = \left(\sum_{i=1}^{n} v_i a_i\right)^t = \sum_{i=1}^{n} (v_i a_i)^t = \sum_{i=1}^{n} v_i a_i^t, \tag{1.22}$$

since $v_i \in \mathbb{R}$; see (1.15).

Note that $A^t = \text{row}(a_k^t)_{k=1:n}$; cf. (1.17). Then, from (1.9), it follows that

$$v^t A^t = \sum_{i=1}^{n} v_i a_i^t. \tag{1.23}$$

From (1.22) and (1.23), we conclude that $(Av)^t = v^t A^t$. □

It is very important to note that the transpose of the product of two matrices is *not* the product of the transposes of the two matrices,[8] i.e., $(AB)^t \neq A^t B^t$. Instead, the following result holds:[9]

Lemma 1.2. *Let A be an $m \times n$ matrix and let B be an $n \times p$ matrix. Then,*

$$(AB)^t = B^t A^t. \tag{1.24}$$

Proof. Recall from (1.11) that, if $B = \text{col}(b_k)_{k=1:p}$, then $AB = \text{col}(Ab_k)_{k=1:p}$. Thus, from (1.17), we obtain that

$$(AB)^t = \left(\text{col}(Ab_k)_{k=1:p}\right)^t = \text{row}\left((Ab_k)^t\right)_{k=1:p}.$$

Using (1.21), (1.12), and the fact that $B^t = \text{row}(b_k^t)_{k=1:p}$, see (1.17) we conclude that

$$(AB)^t = \text{row}(b_k^t A^t)_{k=1:p} = \left(\text{row}(b_k^t)_{k=1:p}\right) A^t = B^t A^t.$$

□

Definition 1.3. *A matrix with the same number of rows and columns is called a square matrix.*

Note that an $n \times n$ square matrix is also called a square matrix of size n.

Definition 1.4. *A square matrix is symmetric if and only if the matrix and its transpose are the same. In other words, a square matrix A of size n is symmetric if and only if $A = A^t$, i.e.,*

$$A(j,k) = A(k,j), \quad \forall\ 1 \leq j < k \leq n;$$

The product of two symmetric matrices is not necessarily a symmetric matrix, as seen in the example below.

---

[8] A similar property holds for inverses of matrices, i.e., $(AB)^{-1} \neq A^{-1} B^{-1}$. Moreover, $(AB)^{-1} = B^{-1} A^{-1}$; see Lemma 1.7 for details.

[9] The result of Lemma 1.2 extends as follows: $\left(\prod_{i=1}^{p} A_i\right)^t = \prod_{i=1}^{p} A_{p+1-i}^t$. A proof can be given by induction; see an exercise at the end of this chapter.

Example: Let $A = \begin{pmatrix} 1 & 2 \\ 2 & 1 \end{pmatrix}$ and $B = \begin{pmatrix} 2 & 1 \\ 1 & 0 \end{pmatrix}$ be two symmetric matrices. Then,

$$AB = \begin{pmatrix} 4 & 1 \\ 5 & 2 \end{pmatrix} \neq (AB)^t = \begin{pmatrix} 4 & 5 \\ 1 & 2 \end{pmatrix} \quad \square$$

The identity matrix,[10] denoted by I, is a square matrix with entries equal to 1 on the main diagonal and equal to 0 everywhere else, i.e.,

$$I = \begin{pmatrix} 1 & 0 & \cdots & 0 \\ 0 & 1 & \cdots & 0 \\ \vdots & \vdots & \ddots & \vdots \\ 0 & 0 & \cdots & 1 \end{pmatrix}.$$

The k-th column of the identity matrix is denoted by e_k. Thus,

$$e_k(i) = 0, \text{ for } 1 \leq i \neq k \leq n \quad \text{and} \quad e_k(k) = 1. \tag{1.25}$$

The column form and row form of the identity matrix I are, respectively,

$$I = \text{col}\,(e_k)_{k=1:n}\,; \quad I = \text{row}\,(e_k^t)_{k=1:n}\,;$$

cf. (1.17), since $I = I^t$.

Lemma 1.3. *(i) Let $A = \text{col}\,(a_k)_{k=1:n}$ be an $m \times n$ matrix. If e_k is the k-th column of the $n \times n$ identity matrix, then*

$$A e_k = a_k, \quad \forall\, k = 1:n, \tag{1.26}$$

and therefore $AI = A$.

(ii) Let $A = \text{row}\,(r_j)_{j=1:m}$ be an $m \times n$ matrix. If e_j is the j-th column of the $m \times m$ identity matrix, then

$$e_j^t A = r_j, \quad \forall\, j = 1:m, \tag{1.27}$$

and therefore $IA = A$.

Proof. (i) Let $A = \text{col}\,(a_k)_{k=1:n}$. Recall from (1.25) that $e_k(k) = 1$ and $e_k(i) = 0$, for $i \neq k$. From (1.7), we obtain that

$$A e_k = \sum_{i=1}^{n} e_k(i) a_i = a_k. \tag{1.28}$$

If $I = \text{col}\,(e_k)_{k=1:n}$, it follows from (1.11) and (1.28) that

$$AI = \text{col}\,(A e_k)_{k=1:n} = \text{col}\,(a_k)_{k=1:n} = A.$$

(ii) Let $A = \text{row}\,(r_j)_{j=1:m}$. Recall from (1.25) that $e_j(j) = 1$ and $e_j(i) = 0$, for $i \neq j$. From (1.9), we find that

$$e_j^t A = \sum_{i=1}^{m} e_j(i) r_i = r_j. \tag{1.29}$$

---

[10] The $n \times n$ identity matrix is sometimes denoted by I_n. We do not use this notation, but denote by I identity matrices of any size.

1.1. COVARIANCE MATRIX COMPUTATION FROM TIME SERIES DATA

If $I = \text{row}\left(e_j^t\right)_{j=1:m}$, it follows from (1.12) and (1.29) that

$$IA = \text{row}\left(e_j^t A\right)_{j=1:m} = \text{row}\left(r_j\right)_{j=1:m} = A.$$

□

1.1.1 Covariance matrix computation from time series data

Let $X_1, X_2, \ldots, X_n$ be random variables given by time series data at N data points t_i, $i = 1 : N$. In other words, the values of $X_k(t_i)$ are given for all $k = 1 : n$ and $i = 1 : N$.

Denote by $\widehat{\mu}_{X_k}$ the sample mean of the random variable X_k, for $k = 1 : n$, i.e.,

$$\widehat{\mu}_{X_k} = \frac{1}{N} \sum_{i=1}^{N} X_k(t_i).$$

The sample covariance matrix $\widehat{\Sigma}_{\mathbf{x}}$ of the n random variables $X_1, X_2, \ldots, X_n$ is the $n \times n$ square matrix with entries

$$\widehat{\Sigma}_{\mathbf{x}}(j,k) = \widehat{\text{cov}}(X_j, X_k), \quad \forall\, 1 \leq j, k \leq n, \tag{1.30}$$

where $\widehat{\text{cov}}(X_j, X_k)$ is the unbiased sample covariance of the random variables X_j and X_k given by

$$\widehat{\text{cov}}(X_j, X_k) = \frac{1}{N-1} \sum_{i=1}^{N} (X_j(t_i) - \widehat{\mu}_{X_j})(X_k(t_i) - \widehat{\mu}_{X_k}). \tag{1.31}$$

From (1.30) and (1.31), we find that

$$\widehat{\Sigma}_{\mathbf{x}}(j,k) = \frac{1}{N-1} \sum_{i=1}^{N} (X_j(t_i) - \widehat{\mu}_{X_j})(X_k(t_i) - \widehat{\mu}_{X_k}). \tag{1.32}$$

The sample covariance matrix $\widehat{\Sigma}_{\mathbf{x}}$ is symmetric since, from (1.32), it follows that

$$\widehat{\Sigma}_{\mathbf{x}}(j,k) = \frac{1}{N-1} \sum_{i=1}^{N} (X_j(t_i) - \widehat{\mu}_{X_j})(X_k(t_i) - \widehat{\mu}_{X_k})$$

$$= \frac{1}{N-1} \sum_{i=1}^{N} (X_k(t_i) - \widehat{\mu}_{X_k})(X_j(t_i) - \widehat{\mu}_{X_j})$$

$$= \widehat{\Sigma}_{\mathbf{x}}(k,j), \quad \forall\, 1 \leq j, k \leq n.$$

The sample covariance matrix can be computed efficiently by using matrix formulation for the time series data $X_k(t_i)$, $i = 1 : N$, $k = 1 : n$, as shown below.

Let $T_{\mathbf{x}}$ be the corresponding $N \times n$ matrix of time series data, i.e., let $T_{\mathbf{x}} = (T_{\mathbf{x}}(i,k))_{i=1:N, k=1:n}$ with

$$T_{\mathbf{x}}(i,k) = X_k(t_i), \quad \forall\, 1 \leq k \leq n,\ 1 \leq i \leq N. \tag{1.33}$$

Let $\overline{T}_{\mathbf{x}}$ be the $N \times n$ matrix of time series data where the sample mean of each random variable is subtracted from the corresponding time series data, i.e., let $\overline{T}_{\mathbf{x}} = (\overline{T}_{\mathbf{x}}(i,k))_{i=1:N, k=1:n}$ with

$$\overline{T}_{\mathbf{x}}(i,k) = X_k(t_i) - \widehat{\mu}_{X_k}, \quad \forall\ 1 \leq k \leq n,\ 1 \leq i \leq N. \tag{1.34}$$

Then, the sample covariance matrix $\widehat{\Sigma}_{\mathbf{x}}$ can be computed from $\overline{T}_{\mathbf{x}}$ as follows:

$$\widehat{\Sigma}_{\mathbf{x}} = \frac{1}{N-1}\ \overline{T}_{\mathbf{x}}^t \overline{T}_{\mathbf{x}}. \tag{1.35}$$

For clarity, we include an example below and the proof of (1.35).

Example: The end of day adjusted close prices for Apple, Facebook, Google, Microsoft, and Yahoo between 1/10/2013 and 1/29/2013 were:

Date	AAPL	FB	GOOG	MSFT	YHOO
1/10/2013	523.51	31.30	741.48	26.46	18.99
1/11/2013	520.30	31.72	739.99	26.83	19.29
1/14/2013	501.75	30.95	723.25	26.89	19.43
1/15/2013	485.92	30.10	724.93	27.21	19.52
1/16/2013	506.09	29.85	715.19	27.04	20.07
1/17/2013	502.68	30.14	711.32	27.25	20.13
1/18/2013	500.00	29.66	704.51	27.25	20.02
1/22/2013	504.77	30.73	702.87	27.15	19.90
1/23/2013	514.01	30.82	741.50	27.61	20.11
1/24/2013	450.50	31.08	754.21	27.63	20.44
1/25/2013	439.88	31.54	753.67	27.88	20.37
1/28/2013	449.83	32.47	750.73	27.91	20.31
1/29/2013	458.27	30.79	753.68	28.01	19.70

The time series matrix of the daily returns[11] of the five stocks above between 1/11/2013 and 1/29/2013 is

$$T_{\mathbf{x}} = \begin{pmatrix} -0.0061 & 0.0134 & -0.0020 & 0.0140 & 0.0158 \\ -0.0357 & -0.0243 & -0.0226 & 0.0022 & 0.0073 \\ -0.0315 & -0.0275 & 0.0023 & 0.0119 & 0.0046 \\ 0.0415 & -0.0083 & -0.0134 & -0.0062 & 0.0282 \\ -0.0067 & 0.0097 & -0.0054 & 0.0078 & 0.0030 \\ -0.0053 & -0.0159 & -0.0096 & 0.0000 & -0.0055 \\ 0.0095 & 0.0361 & -0.0023 & -0.0037 & -0.0060 \\ 0.0183 & 0.0029 & 0.0550 & 0.0169 & 0.0106 \\ -0.1236 & 0.0084 & 0.0171 & 0.0007 & 0.0164 \\ -0.0236 & 0.0148 & -0.0007 & 0.0090 & -0.0034 \\ 0.0226 & 0.0295 & -0.0039 & 0.0011 & -0.0029 \\ 0.0188 & -0.0517 & 0.0039 & 0.0036 & -0.0300 \end{pmatrix},$$

where, e.g., the daily return of GOOG on 1/24/2013 is

$$\frac{754.21 - 741.50}{741.50} = 0.0171 = T_{\mathbf{x}}(9,3),$$

---

[11] Unless specified otherwise, the return between times τ_1 and τ_2 of an asset with spot prices $S(\tau_1)$ and $S(\tau_2)$ will mean the percentage return, which is $\frac{S(\tau_2) - S(\tau_1)}{S(\tau_1)}$.

1.1. COVARIANCE MATRIX COMPUTATION FROM TIME SERIES DATA

and the daily return of GOOG on 1/28/2013 is

$$\frac{750.73 - 753.67}{753.67} = -0.0039 = T_{\mathbf{X}}(11,3).$$

The sample means of the returns of the five stocks are -0.0101 (AAPL), -0.0011 (FB), 0.0015 (GOOG), 0.0048 (MSFT), and 0.0032 (YHOO). By subtracting the sample mean of each column of $T_{\mathbf{X}}$ we obtain from (1.34) that

$$\overline{T}_{\mathbf{X}} = \begin{pmatrix} 0.0040 & 0.0145 & -0.0035 & 0.0092 & 0.0126 \\ -0.0255 & -0.0232 & -0.0242 & -0.0025 & 0.0041 \\ -0.0214 & -0.0264 & 0.0008 & 0.0071 & 0.0015 \\ 0.0517 & -0.0072 & -0.0150 & -0.0110 & 0.0250 \\ 0.0034 & 0.0108 & -0.0069 & 0.0030 & -0.0002 \\ 0.0048 & -0.0149 & -0.0111 & -0.0048 & -0.0086 \\ 0.0197 & 0.0371 & -0.0039 & -0.0084 & -0.0092 \\ 0.0285 & 0.0040 & 0.0534 & 0.0122 & 0.0074 \\ -0.1134 & 0.0095 & 0.0156 & -0.0041 & 0.0132 \\ -0.0134 & 0.0159 & -0.0022 & 0.0043 & -0.0066 \\ 0.0328 & 0.0306 & -0.0054 & -0.0037 & -0.0061 \\ 0.0289 & -0.0507 & 0.0024 & -0.0012 & -0.0332 \end{pmatrix}. \quad (1.36)$$

We now show that the formula (1.35) holds, i.e.,

$$\widehat{\Sigma}_{\mathbf{X}} = \frac{1}{N-1} \overline{T}_{\mathbf{X}}^t \overline{T}_{\mathbf{X}}; \quad (1.37)$$

see also Theorem 7.1 and the proof therein.

From (1.34), we find that, for any $1 \leq j, k \leq n$,

$$\overline{T}_{\mathbf{X}}(i,k) = X_k(t_i) - \widehat{\mu}_{X_k} \quad \text{and} \quad \overline{T}_{\mathbf{X}}(i,j) = X_j(t_i) - \widehat{\mu}_{X_j}, \quad \forall\, i = 1:N. \quad (1.38)$$

Then, from (1.32) and (1.38), it follows that

$$\widehat{\Sigma}_{\mathbf{X}}(j,k) = \frac{1}{N-1} \sum_{i=1}^{N} (X_j(t_i) - \widehat{\mu}_{X_j})(X_k(t_i) - \widehat{\mu}_{X_k}) \quad (1.39)$$

$$= \frac{1}{N-1} \sum_{i=1}^{N} \overline{T}_{\mathbf{X}}(i,j) \overline{T}_{\mathbf{X}}(i,k), \quad \forall\, 1 \leq j, k \leq n. \quad (1.40)$$

Let $\overline{T}_{X_k}$ be the $N \times 1$ column vector of the time series data for the random variable X_k with $\widehat{\mu}_{X_k}$ subtracted from each data value, i.e.,

$$\overline{T}_{X_k} = (X_k(t_i) - \widehat{\mu}_{X_k})_{i=1:N}.$$

The time series matrix $\overline{T}_{\mathbf{X}} = (\overline{T}_{\mathbf{X}}(i,k))_{i=1:N, k=1:n}$ has the following column form:

$$\overline{T}_{\mathbf{X}} = \text{col}\left(\overline{T}_{X_k}\right)_{k=1:n}.$$

Moreover,

$$\overline{T}_{\mathbf{X}}(i,j) = \overline{T}_{X_j}(i) \quad \text{and} \quad \overline{T}_{\mathbf{X}}(i,k) = \overline{T}_{X_k}(i), \quad \forall\, 1 \leq j, k \leq n,\; 1 \leq i \leq N,$$

and, from (1.40), we obtain that

$$\widehat{\Sigma}_{\mathbf{x}}(j,k) = \frac{1}{N-1} \sum_{i=1}^{N} \overline{T}_{X_j}(i)\overline{T}_{X_k}(i) \qquad (1.41)$$

$$= \frac{1}{N-1} \overline{T}_{X_j}^t \overline{T}_{X_k}, \quad \forall\, 1 \leq j,k \leq n, \qquad (1.42)$$

where the last equality follows from the row vector–column vector multiplication formula (1.5).

Since $\overline{T}_{\mathbf{x}} = \text{col}\left(\overline{T}_{X_k}\right)_{k=1:n}$, it follows that $\overline{T}_{\mathbf{x}}^t = \text{row}\left(\overline{T}_{X_j}^t\right)_{j=1:n}$; see (1.17). From (1.13), we obtain that the (j,k) entry of the matrix $\overline{T}_{\mathbf{x}}^t \overline{T}_{\mathbf{x}}$ is

$$(\overline{T}_{\mathbf{x}}^t \overline{T}_{\mathbf{x}})(j,k) = \overline{T}_{X_j}^t \overline{T}_{X_k}, \quad \forall\, 1 \leq j,k \leq n. \qquad (1.43)$$

Then, from (1.42) and (1.43), we conclude that

$$\widehat{\Sigma}_{\mathbf{x}}(j,k) = \frac{1}{N-1}(\overline{T}_{\mathbf{x}}^t \overline{T}_{\mathbf{x}})(j,k), \quad \forall\, 1 \leq j,k \leq n,$$

and therefore

$$\widehat{\Sigma}_{\mathbf{x}} = \frac{1}{N-1} \overline{T}_{\mathbf{x}}^t \overline{T}_{\mathbf{x}},$$

which is what we wanted to prove; see (1.37).

Example (continued):

The sample covariance matrix $\widehat{\Sigma}_{\mathbf{x}}$ of the daily returns of AAPL, FB, GOOG, MSFT, YHOO between 1/11/2013 and 1/29/2013 can be computed using formula (1.35) with $N = 12$ and $\overline{T}_{\mathbf{x}}$ given by (1.36). We find that

$$\widehat{\Sigma}_{\mathbf{x}} = \begin{pmatrix} 0.0018 & 0.0000 & -0.0001 & 0.0000 & -0.0001 \\ 0.0000 & 0.0006 & 0.0001 & 0.0000 & 0.0001 \\ -0.0001 & 0.0001 & 0.0004 & 0.0001 & 0.0000 \\ 0.0000 & 0.0000 & 0.0001 & 0.0001 & 0.0000 \\ -0.0001 & 0.0001 & 0.0000 & 0.0000 & 0.0002 \end{pmatrix}. \quad \Box \qquad (1.44)$$

More properties of covariance matrices obtained from time series data can be found in section 7.2.

1.2 Matrix rank, nullspace, and range of a matrix

Definition 1.5. *Let $w_1, w_2, \ldots, w_p$ be vectors of the same size. The vectors $w_1, w_2, \ldots, w_p$ are linearly independent if and only if the only linear combination of these vectors that is equal to 0 has all coefficients equal to 0, i.e.,*

$$\text{if } \sum_{i=1}^{p} c_i w_i = 0, \quad \text{with } c_i \in \mathbb{R}, i = 1:p, \quad \text{then } c_i = 0, \ \forall\, i = 1:p.$$

1.2. MATRIX RANK, NULLSPACE, AND RANGE OF A MATRIX

If A is an $m \times n$ matrix, the column rank of A is the largest number of linearly independent columns of A, and the row rank of A is the largest number of linearly independent rows of A. However, the column rank and the row rank of a matrix are always the same, not only for square matrices, but also for rectangular matrices; see section 10.5 for an elegant proof of this fact. Therefore, the following definition is consistent:

Definition 1.6. *The rank of a matrix A is denoted by $\mathrm{rank}(A)$ and is equal to the largest number of linearly independent columns[12] of A.*

Definition 1.7. *The nullspace of an $m \times n$ matrix A is*

$$\mathrm{Null}(A) = \{v \in \mathbb{R}^n \text{ such that } Av = 0\}.$$

The nullspace of the matrix A is also called the kernel of A and is denoted by $\mathrm{Ker}(A)$.

Definition 1.8. *The range of an $m \times n$ matrix A contains all the vectors obtained from matrix–vector multiplications involving A, i.e.,*

$$\mathrm{Range}(A) = \{u \in \mathbb{R}^m \text{ such that there exists } v \in \mathbb{R}^n \text{ with } u = Av\}. \quad (1.45)$$

Definition 1.9. *Let $w_1, w_2, \ldots, w_p$ be vectors of the same size. The space generated by $w_1, w_2, \ldots, w_p$ is made of all the linear combinations of the vectors $w_1, w_2, \ldots, w_p$, i.e.,*

$$<w_1, w_2, \ldots, w_p> \;=\; \left\{ \sum_{i=1}^{p} c_i w_i, \text{ with } c_i \in \mathbb{R}, \; i = 1:p \right\}. \quad (1.46)$$

Lemma 1.4. *Let $A = \mathrm{col}(a_k)_{k=1:n}$ be an $m \times n$ matrix. The range of the matrix A is the space generated by the column vectors of A, i.e.,*

$$\mathrm{Range}(A) \;=\; <a_1, a_2, \ldots, a_n>. \quad (1.47)$$

Proof. We prove (1.47) by double inclusion.

Let $u \in <a_1, a_2, \ldots, a_n>$. By definition (1.46), there exist $c_i \in \mathbb{R}$, $i = 1:n$, such that

$$u = \sum_{i=1}^{n} c_i a_i. \quad (1.48)$$

Denote by $v = (c_i)_{i=1:n}$ the column vector with entries equal to the coefficients from the linear combination (1.48). From (1.7), it follows that

$$Av = \sum_{i=1}^{n} v_i a_i = \sum_{i=1}^{n} c_i a_i. \quad (1.49)$$

From (1.48) and (1.49), we obtain that $u = Av$. Therefore, $u \in \mathrm{Range}(A)$, and we conclude that

$$<a_1, a_2, \ldots, a_n> \;\subseteq\; \mathrm{Range}(A). \quad (1.50)$$

---

[12] As explained above, the rank of a matrix can also be defined as the largest number of linearly independent rows of the matrix.

Let $u \in \mathrm{Range}(A)$. From (1.45), it follows that there exists a vector $v \in \mathbb{R}^n$ such that $u = Av$. Then, from (1.7) and (1.46), we obtain that

$$u = Av = \sum_{i=1}^n v_i a_i \in \; <a_1, a_2, \ldots, a_n>,$$

and therefore
$$\mathrm{Range}(A) \subseteq \; <a_1, a_2, \ldots, a_n> . \tag{1.51}$$

From (1.50) and (1.51), we conclude that $\mathrm{Range}(A) = \; <a_1, a_2, \ldots, a_n>$. □

Definition 1.10. *Let V be a vector space in $\mathbb{R}^n$. The vectors $v_1, v_2, \ldots, v_p \in V$ form a basis for V if they are linearly independent and if the space generated by the vectors $v_1, v_2, \ldots, v_p$ is equal to V, i.e., if $V = \; <v_1, v_2, \ldots, v_p>$.*

Lemma 1.5. *Any two basis of a vector space in $\mathbb{R}^n$ are made of the same number of vectors.*

The proof of this result is of no further relevance in this book and can be found, e.g., in Lax [26].

Definition 1.11. *The dimension of a vector space V from $\mathbb{R}^n$ is denoted by $\dim(V)$ and is equal to the number of vectors from a basis of V.*

While a vector space has infinitely many different basis, Definition 1.11 is consistent, since, from Lemma 1.5, it follows that the numbers of linearly independent vectors from any two different basis are equal.

1.2.1 A one period market model

In a one period market model for the evolution of the prices of financial securities, portfolio returns can be analyzed using a linear algebra framework. In this section, we present an example of this framework, which forms the basis of the Arrow–Debreu model; see Chapter 3 for details on the Arrow–Debreu model.

Consider a market with m securities. Let $S_{1t_0}, S_{2t_0}, \ldots, S_{mt_0}$ be the spot prices of the securities at time t_0, and denote by $S_{t_0} = (S_{jt_0})_{j=1:m}$ the price vector of the securities at time t_0. Note that S_{t_0} is an $m \times 1$ column vector.

Assume that, at time $\tau > t_0$, there are n possible states of the market, denoted by $\omega^1, \omega^2, \ldots, \omega^n$. Let $S_{j\tau}^{\omega^k}$ be the price at time τ of asset j if state ω^k occurs, for $1 \leq j \leq m$ and $1 \leq k \leq n$. Let

$$S_\tau^{\omega^k} = \begin{pmatrix} S_{1\tau}^{\omega^k} \\ S_{2\tau}^{\omega^k} \\ \vdots \\ S_{m\tau}^{\omega^k} \end{pmatrix}$$

be the price vector of the m assets if state ω^k occurs, for $k = 1:n$, and let

$$S_{j\tau} = \begin{pmatrix} S_{j\tau}^{\omega^1} & S_{j\tau}^{\omega^2} & \ldots & S_{j\tau}^{\omega^n} \end{pmatrix}$$

1.2. A ONE PERIOD MARKET MODEL

be the vector of all the possible prices of asset j at time τ, for $j = 1:m$. Note that $S_\tau^{\omega^k}$ is an $m \times 1$ column vector, and $S_{j\tau}$ is an $1 \times n$ row vector.

The payoff matrix M_τ is the $m \times n$ matrix made of all possible asset prices at time τ, with the j-th row of matrix M_τ corresponding to the prices of asset j, for $j = 1:m$, and the k-th column of matrix M_τ corresponding to the asset prices in state ω^k, for $k = 1:n$, i.e.,

$$M_\tau = \text{col}\left(S_\tau^{\omega^k}\right)_{k=1:n} = \left(S_\tau^{\omega^1} \mid S_\tau^{\omega^2} \mid \ldots \mid S_\tau^{\omega^n}\right); \quad (1.52)$$

$$M_\tau = \text{row}\left(S_{j\tau}\right)_{j=1:m} = \begin{pmatrix} S_{1\tau} \\ \overline{} \\ S_{2\tau} \\ \overline{} \\ \vdots \\ \overline{} \\ S_{m\tau} \end{pmatrix}. \quad (1.53)$$

Example: Consider two assets with spot prices $30 and $50, respectively. Assume that, in three months, the first asset will be worth either $34 or $24, and the second asset will be worth either $56, $51, or $46. The values of the three months at–the–money (ATM) European call and put options[13] with strike $30 on the first asset are $2.6 and $2.3, respectively, and the values of the three months ATM European call and put options with strike $50 on the second asset are $2.7 and $2.2, respectively.

Assume that the future value in three months of $1 today is $1.01.[14]

A **three months market model** with **seven securities** and **six states** can be constructed based on the information above, as follows:

Securities:
- cash;
- first asset;
- second asset;
- three months ATM call with strike $30 on the first asset;
- three months ATM put with strike $30 on the first asset;
- three months ATM call with strike $50 on the second asset;
- three months ATM put with strike $50 on the second asset.

States of the market in three months:
- first asset at $34 and second asset at $56 (state ω^1);
- first asset at $34 and second asset at $51 (state ω^2);
- first asset at $34 and second asset at $46 (state ω^3);
- first asset at $24 and second asset at $56 (state ω^4);
- first asset at $24 and second asset at $51 (state ω^5);
- first asset at $24 and second asset at $46 (state ω^6).

This is a market model with $m = 7$ securities and with $n = 6$ states.

---

[13] An at–the–money option has strike equal to the spot price. A brief overview of European options can be found in section 10.3; see also Neftci [31] and Stefanica [36].

[14] This corresponds, for continuous compounding, to a three months risk free interest rate equal to $r = 0.0398 = 3.98\%$, which can be found by solving the equation $1.01 = 1 \cdot \exp\left(r \cdot \frac{1}{4}\right)$ for r.

The price vector of the securities at time 0, corresponding to a $1 cash position and to positions equal to one unit of each of the other securities, is

$$S_0 = \begin{pmatrix} 1 \\ 30 \\ 50 \\ 2.6 \\ 2.3 \\ 2.7 \\ 2.2 \end{pmatrix}. \tag{1.54}$$

For $j = 1 : 7$, let $S_{j,1/4}$ be the vector of the six possible prices of asset j in three months. The price vectors $S_{1,1/4}$ of cash, $S_{2,1/4}$ of the first asset, and $S_{3,1/4}$ of the second asset, respectively, are

$$S_{1,1/4} = (1.01 \ 1.01 \ 1.01 \ 1.01 \ 1.01 \ 1.01); \tag{1.55}$$
$$S_{2,1/4} = (34 \ 34 \ 34 \ 24 \ 24 \ 24); \tag{1.56}$$
$$S_{3,1/4} = (56 \ 51 \ 46 \ 56 \ 51 \ 46). \tag{1.57}$$

To compute the price vectors $S_{4,1/4}, S_{5,1/4}, S_{6,1/4}, S_{7,1/4}$ of the options, note that all the options have three months maturity, and recall from (10.90) and (10.91) that the payoffs at maturity of call and put options are

$$C(T) = \max(S(T) - K, 0) = \begin{cases} S(T) - K, & \text{if } S(T) > K; \\ 0, & \text{if } S(T) \leq K; \end{cases} \tag{1.58}$$

$$P(T) = \max(K - S(T), 0) = \begin{cases} 0, & \text{if } S(T) \geq K; \\ K - S(T), & \text{if } S(T) < K. \end{cases} \tag{1.59}$$

From (1.58), we obtain that the values of the three months ATM call with strike $30 on the first asset are given by

$$C_1(1/4) = \max(S_1(1/4) - 30, 0),$$

where $S_1(1/4)$ denotes the value of the second asset in three months, and are as follows:

state ω^1 : $S_1(1/4) = 34$ and $C_1(1/4) = \max(34 - 30, 0) = 4$;
state ω^2 : $S_1(1/4) = 34$ and $C_1(1/4) = \max(34 - 30, 0) = 4$;
state ω^3 : $S_1(1/4) = 34$ and $C_1(1/4) = \max(34 - 30, 0) = 4$;
state ω^4 : $S_1(1/4) = 24$ and $C_1(1/4) = \max(24 - 30, 0) = 0$;
state ω^5 : $S_1(1/4) = 24$ and $C_1(1/4) = \max(24 - 30, 0) = 0$;
state ω^6 : $S_1(1/4) = 24$ and $C_1(1/4) = \max(24 - 30, 0) = 0$.

Thus, the vector $S_{4,1/4}$ of the six possible prices of the three months ATM call with strike $30 on the first asset is

$$S_{4,1/4} = (4 \ 4 \ 4 \ 0 \ 0 \ 0). \tag{1.60}$$

From (1.59), we obtain that the values of the three months ATM put with strike $30 on the first asset are given by

$$P_1(1/4) = \max(30 - S_1(1/4), 0),$$

1.2. A ONE PERIOD MARKET MODEL

and are as follows:

state ω^1 : $S_1(1/4) = 34$ and $P_1(1/4) = \max(30 - 34, 0) = 0$;
state ω^2 : $S_1(1/4) = 34$ and $P_1(1/4) = \max(30 - 34, 0) = 0$;
state ω^3 : $S_1(1/4) = 34$ and $P_1(1/4) = \max(30 - 34, 0) = 0$;
state ω^4 : $S_1(1/4) = 24$ and $P_1(1/4) = \max(30 - 24, 0) = 6$;
state ω^5 : $S_1(1/4) = 24$ and $P_1(1/4) = \max(30 - 24, 0) = 6$;
state ω^6 : $S_1(1/4) = 24$ and $P_1(1/4) = \max(30 - 24, 0) = 6$.

Thus, the vector $S_{5,1/4}$ of the six possible prices of the three months ATM put with strike \$30 on the first asset is

$$S_{5,1/4} = (0\ 0\ 0\ 6\ 6\ 6). \tag{1.61}$$

From (1.58), we obtain that the values of the three months ATM call with strike \$50 on the second asset are given by

$$C_2(1/4) = \max(S_2(1/4) - 50, 0),$$

where $S_2(1/4)$ denotes the value of the second asset in three months, and are as follows:

state ω^1 : $S_2(1/4) = 56$ and $C_2(1/4) = \max(56 - 50, 0) = 6$;
state ω^2 : $S_2(1/4) = 51$ and $C_2(1/4) = \max(51 - 50, 0) = 1$;
state ω^3 : $S_2(1/4) = 46$ and $C_2(1/4) = \max(46 - 50, 0) = 0$;
state ω^4 : $S_2(1/4) = 56$ and $C_2(1/4) = \max(56 - 50, 0) = 6$;
state ω^5 : $S_2(1/4) = 51$ and $C_2(1/4) = \max(51 - 50, 0) = 1$;
state ω^6 : $S_2(1/4) = 46$ and $C_2(1/4) = \max(46 - 50, 0) = 0$.

Thus, the vector $S_{6,1/4}$ of the six possible prices of the three months ATM call with strike \$50 on the second asset is

$$S_{6,1/4} = (6\ 1\ 0\ 6\ 1\ 0). \tag{1.62}$$

From (1.59), we obtain that the values of the three months ATM put with strike \$50 on the second asset are given by

$$P_2(1/4) = \max(50 - S_2(1/4), 0),$$

and are as follows:

state ω^1 : $S_2(1/4) = 56$ and $P_2(1/4) = \max(50 - 56, 0) = 0$;
state ω^2 : $S_2(1/4) = 51$ and $P_2(1/4) = \max(50 - 51, 0) = 0$;
state ω^3 : $S_2(1/4) = 46$ and $P_2(1/4) = \max(50 - 46, 0) = 4$;
state ω^4 : $S_2(1/4) = 56$ and $P_2(1/4) = \max(50 - 56, 0) = 0$;
state ω^5 : $S_2(1/4) = 51$ and $P_2(1/4) = \max(50 - 51, 0) = 0$;
state ω^6 : $S_2(1/4) = 46$ and $P_2(1/4) = \max(50 - 46, 0) = 4$.

Thus, the vector $S_{7,1/4}$ of the six possible prices of the three months ATM put with strike \$50 on the second asset is

$$S_{7,1/4} = (0\ 0\ 4\ 0\ 0\ 4). \tag{1.63}$$

Summarizing, we conclude from (1.55–1.57) and (1.60–1.63) that

$$
\begin{aligned}
S_{1,1/4} &= (1.01\ 1.01\ 1.01\ 1.01\ 1.01\ 1.01); \\
S_{2,1/4} &= (34\ 34\ 34\ 24\ 24\ 24); \\
S_{3,1/4} &= (56\ 51\ 46\ 56\ 51\ 46); \\
S_{4,1/4} &= (4\ 4\ 4\ 0\ 0\ 0); \\
S_{5,1/4} &= (0\ 0\ 0\ 6\ 6\ 6); \\
S_{6,1/4} &= (6\ 1\ 0\ 6\ 1\ 0); \\
S_{7,1/4} &= (0\ 0\ 4\ 0\ 0\ 4).
\end{aligned}
$$

The payoff matrix $M_{1/4}$ is the following 7×6 matrix:

$$
M_{1/4} = \begin{pmatrix} S_{1,1/4} \\ S_{2,1/4} \\ S_{3,1/4} \\ S_{4,1/4} \\ S_{5,1/4} \\ S_{6,1/4} \\ S_{7,1/4} \end{pmatrix} = \begin{pmatrix} 1.01 & 1.01 & 1.01 & 1.01 & 1.01 & 1.01 \\ 34 & 34 & 34 & 24 & 24 & 24 \\ 56 & 51 & 46 & 56 & 51 & 46 \\ 4 & 4 & 4 & 0 & 0 & 0 \\ 0 & 0 & 0 & 6 & 6 & 6 \\ 6 & 1 & 0 & 6 & 1 & 0 \\ 0 & 0 & 4 & 0 & 0 & 4 \end{pmatrix}; \quad (1.64)
$$

see (1.53).

Let $S_{1/4}^{\omega_i}$ be the price vector of the seven securities in three months if state ω^i occurs, for $i = 1:6$. Recall from (1.52) that

$$
M_{1/4} = \left(S_{1/4}^{\omega_1} \mid S_{1/4}^{\omega_2} \mid S_{1/4}^{\omega_3} \mid S_{1/4}^{\omega_4} \mid S_{1/4}^{\omega_5} \mid S_{1/4}^{\omega_6} \right). \quad (1.65)
$$

From (1.64) and (1.65), we obtain that

$$
S_{1/4}^{\omega_1} = \begin{pmatrix} 1.01 \\ 34 \\ 56 \\ 4 \\ 0 \\ 6 \\ 0 \end{pmatrix}; \quad S_{1/4}^{\omega_2} = \begin{pmatrix} 1.01 \\ 34 \\ 51 \\ 4 \\ 0 \\ 1 \\ 0 \end{pmatrix}; \quad S_{1/4}^{\omega_3} = \begin{pmatrix} 1.01 \\ 34 \\ 46 \\ 4 \\ 0 \\ 0 \\ 4 \end{pmatrix};
$$

$$
S_{1/4}^{\omega_4} = \begin{pmatrix} 1.01 \\ 24 \\ 56 \\ 0 \\ 6 \\ 6 \\ 0 \end{pmatrix}; \quad S_{1/4}^{\omega_5} = \begin{pmatrix} 1.01 \\ 24 \\ 51 \\ 0 \\ 6 \\ 1 \\ 0 \end{pmatrix}; \quad S_{1/4}^{\omega_6} = \begin{pmatrix} 1.01 \\ 24 \\ 46 \\ 0 \\ 6 \\ 0 \\ 4 \end{pmatrix}.
$$

Consider a portfolio made of the m securities and consisting of Θ_j units of asset j at time t_0, $j = 1:m$. The value V_{t_0} of the portfolio at time t_0 is

$$
V_{t_0} = \Theta_1 S_{1t_0} + \Theta_2 S_{2t_0} + \ldots + \Theta_m S_{mt_0},
$$

1.2. A ONE PERIOD MARKET MODEL

which can be written using the row vector–column vector multiplication formula (1.5) as

$$V_{t_0} = \Theta^t S_{t_0},$$

where $\Theta = (\Theta_j)_{j=1:m}$ is the $m \times 1$ positions vector.

We assume that the asset positions in the portfolio remain unchanged until time τ. Let

$$V_\tau = \begin{pmatrix} V_\tau^{\omega^1} & V_\tau^{\omega^2} & \cdots & V_\tau^{\omega^n} \end{pmatrix} \tag{1.66}$$

be the $1 \times n$ row vector of the possible values of the portfolio at time τ, where $V_\tau^{\omega^k}$ is the value of the portfolio if state ω^k occurs, for $k = 1:n$. Then,

$$\begin{aligned} V_\tau^{\omega^k} &= \Theta_1 S_{1\tau}^{\omega^k} + \Theta_2 S_{2\tau}^{\omega^k} + \ldots + \Theta_m S_{m\tau}^{\omega^k} \\ &= \Theta^t S_\tau^{\omega^k}, \end{aligned} \tag{1.67}$$

where (1.5) was used for deriving (1.67).

From (1.66) and (1.67), we obtain that

$$\begin{aligned} V_\tau &= \begin{pmatrix} V_\tau^{\omega^1} & V_\tau^{\omega^2} & \cdots & V_\tau^{\omega^n} \end{pmatrix} = \begin{pmatrix} \Theta^t S_\tau^{\omega^1} & \Theta^t S_\tau^{\omega^2} & \cdots & \Theta^t S_\tau^{\omega^n} \end{pmatrix} \\ &= \Theta^t \operatorname{col}\left(S_\tau^{\omega^k}\right)_{k=1:n} \\ &= \Theta^t M_\tau, \end{aligned} \tag{1.68}$$

since $M_\tau = \operatorname{col}\left(S_\tau^{\omega^k}\right)_{k=1:n}$; cf. (1.52).

Example (continued):

Consider the following portfolio in the one period market model with seven securities and six states introduced above:
- long \$10,000 cash;
- long 200 units of the first asset;
- short 100 units of the second asset;
- short 1000 three months ATM calls on the first asset;
- long 500 three months ATM calls on the second asset;
- long 600 three months ATM puts on the second asset.

The positions vector of the portfolio is

$$\Theta = \begin{pmatrix} 10000 \\ 200 \\ -100 \\ -1000 \\ 0 \\ 500 \\ 600 \end{pmatrix}.$$

The value of the portfolio at time 0 is

$$V_0 = \Theta^t S_0 = 11{,}070,$$

where the price vector S_0 of the securities at time 0 is given by (1.54).

Depending on the state of the market in three months, the possible values of the portfolio are

$$V_{1/4} = \Theta^t M_{1/4} = (10300 \; 8300 \; 10700 \; 12300 \; 10300 \; 12700),$$

where the payoff matrix $M_{1/4}$ is given by (1.64).

A derivative security is replicable in a market model with m securities and n market states at time $\tau > t_0$ if there exists a portfolio made of the m securities which has the same values at time τ as the derivative security in every state of the market at time τ. Let s_τ be the price vector at time τ of a replicable derivative security, and let $\Theta = (\Theta_j)_{j=1:m}$ be the positions vector of the replicating portfolio. If V_τ is the price vector of the replicating portfolio at time τ, then, from (1.68), we find that

$$s_\tau = V_\tau = \Theta^t M_\tau = \sum_{j=1}^m \Theta_j S_{j\tau}, \qquad (1.69)$$

where for the last equality we used (1.9) and the fact that $M_\tau = \text{row}\,(S_{j\tau})_{j=1:m}$.

In other words, a derivative security is replicable if and only if the price vector of the derivative security at time τ belongs to the space generated by the price vectors $S_{1\tau}, S_{2\tau}, \ldots, S_{m\tau}$ of the m securities at time τ; cf. Definition 1.9.

The m securities are non–redundant if no security is replicable using the other $m-1$ securities. Equivalently, the m securities are non–redundant if their price vectors at time τ are linearly independent. Otherwise, the payoff of one of the securities would be replicable by using the other $m-1$ securities, which would render the security redundant. Thus, a one period market model has no redundant securities if and only if the payoff matrix M_τ has rank equal to m, i.e., $\text{rank}(M_\tau) = m$.

Example (continued):
Recall that the price vectors in three months of the seven securities from the market model considered here are

$$\begin{aligned}
S_{1,1/4} &= (1.01 \; 1.01 \; 1.01 \; 1.01 \; 1.01 \; 1.01); \\
S_{2,1/4} &= (34 \; 34 \; 34 \; 24 \; 24 \; 24); \\
S_{3,1/4} &= (56 \; 51 \; 46 \; 56 \; 51 \; 46); \\
S_{4,1/4} &= (4 \; 4 \; 4 \; 0 \; 0 \; 0); \\
S_{5,1/4} &= (0 \; 0 \; 0 \; 6 \; 6 \; 6); \\
S_{6,1/4} &= (6 \; 1 \; 0 \; 6 \; 1 \; 0); \\
S_{7,1/4} &= (0 \; 0 \; 4 \; 0 \; 0 \; 4).
\end{aligned}$$

Note that

$$S_{5,1/4} + S_{2,1/4} - S_{4,1/4} = (30 \; 30 \; 30 \; 30 \; 30 \; 30) = \frac{30}{1.01} S_{1,1/4}. \qquad (1.70)$$

Thus, the price vectors $S_{1,1/4}$, $S_{2,1/4}$, $S_{4,1/4}$, and $S_{5,1/4}$ corresponding to cash, the first asset, the three months ATM call and the three months ATM put on the first asset, respectively, are not linearly independent.

We conclude that, e.g., the ATM put on the first asset can be replicated using cash and positions on the first asset and ATM calls on the first asset, since

$$S_{5,1/4} = \frac{30}{1.01} S_{1,1/4} - S_{2,1/4} + S_{4,1/4},$$

and therefore that the ATM put on the first asset is a redundant security.

Also, the price vectors $S_{1,1/4}$, $S_{3,1/4}$, $S_{6,1/4}$, and $S_{7,1/4}$, corresponding to cash, the second asset, the three months ATM call and the three months ATM put on the second asset, respectively, are not linearly independent, since

$$S_{7,1/4} + S_{3,1/4} - S_{6,1/4} = (50\ 50\ 50\ 50\ 50\ 50) = \frac{50}{1.01} S_{1,1/4}. \quad (1.71)$$

We conclude that, e.g., the ATM put on the second asset can be replicated using cash and positions on the second asset and ATM calls on the second asset, since

$$S_{7,1/4} = \frac{50}{1.01} S_{1,1/4} - S_{3,1/4} + S_{6,1/4},$$

and therefore that the ATM put on the second asset is a redundant security.

The redundancies above are due to the Put–Call parity,[15] which states that the values $C(t)$ and $P(t)$ of a European call and of a European put option with the same strike K and maturity T and on the same underlying asset with spot price $S(t)$ satisfy the following model independent relationship in arbitrage–free markets:

$$P(t) + S(t) - C(t) = Ke^{-r(T-t)}.$$

Thus, at maturity,
$$P(T) + S(T) - C(T) = K. \quad (1.72)$$

Then, (1.70) is a consequence of (1.72), since the vectors $S_{5,1/4}$, $S_{2,1/4}$, $S_{4,1/4}$, and $S_{1,1/4}$ are the price vectors corresponding to $P(T)$, $S(T)$, $C(T)$, and K, respectively, for the three months ATM put and call on the first asset.

Similarly, (1.71) is a consequence of (1.72), since the vectors $S_{7,1/4}$, $S_{3,1/4}$, $S_{6,1/4}$, and $S_{1,1/4}$ are the price vectors corresponding to $P(T)$, $S(T)$, $C(T)$, and K, respectively, for the three months ATM put and call on the first asset.

1.3 Nonsingular matrices

From a numerical perspective, a nonsingular matrix A is a square matrix such that any linear system of the form $Ax = b$ has a unique solution x. Solving linear systems corresponding to nonsingular matrices is often required in financial applications and is a fundamental numerical linear algebra problem.

The formal definition of a nonsingular matrix is given below:

---

[15] For more details on the Put–Call parity, see section 10.3 and section 1.9 from Stefanica [36].

Definition 1.12. *The square matrix A is nonsingular if and only if there exists another matrix, called the inverse matrix of A and denoted by A^{-1}, such that*

$$A A^{-1} = A^{-1} A = I. \tag{1.73}$$

Definition 1.13. *The square matrix A is singular if and only if the matrix A is not nonsingular.*

From (1.73), we obtain that the matrix A satisfies the definition of the inverse of the matrix A^{-1}. Thus, the inverse of the inverse of a nonsingular matrix is equal to the matrix itself, i.e.,

$$(A^{-1})^{-1} = A. \tag{1.74}$$

Note that, for Definition 1.12 to make sense, the inverse matrix of a nonsingular matrix as given by (1.73) must be unique, which is indeed the case: Assume that B_1 and B_2 are inverse matrices of a nonsingular matrix A. We will show that $B_1 = B_2$. From (1.73), we find that

$$AB_1 = B_1 A = I \quad \text{and} \quad AB_2 = B_2 A = I.$$

By multiplying $I = AB_1$ to the left by B_2 and using the fact that $B_2 A = I$, we obtain that

$$B_2 = B_2(AB_1) = (B_2 A)B_1 = IB_1 = B_1.$$

Theorem 1.1. *Let A be a square matrix of size n. The conditions below can be regarded as equivalent definitions for A to be a nonsingular matrix:*

$$A \text{ nonsingular} \iff \text{Null}(A) = \{0\} \tag{1.75}$$
$$\iff \text{Range}(A) = \mathbb{R}^n \tag{1.76}$$
$$\iff \text{rank}(A) = n. \tag{1.77}$$

Similarly, the conditions below[16] can be regarded as equivalent definitions for A to be a singular matrix:

$$A \text{ singular} \iff \text{Null}(A) \neq \{0\} \tag{1.78}$$
$$\iff \text{there exists } v \in \mathbb{R}^n,\ v \neq 0,\ \text{such that } Av = 0. \tag{1.79}$$

The proof of Theorem 1.1 is of less relevance for our purposes and can be found, e.g., in Strang [41].

A very useful equivalent characterization of a matrix being nonsingular can be given in terms of the determinant of the matrix; see section 10.1.1 for details.

Theorem 1.2. *Let A be a square matrix. Then,*

$$A \text{ nonsingular} \iff \det(A) \neq 0; \tag{1.80}$$
$$A \text{ singular} \iff \det(A) = 0. \tag{1.81}$$

---

[16] Other necessary and sufficient conditions for the matrix A to be singular are

$$A \text{ singular} \iff \text{Range}(A) \neq \mathbb{R}^n \iff \text{rank}(A) < n.$$

These conditions have less practical value, and are not included in Theorem 1.1.

1.3. NONSINGULAR MATRICES

Lemma 1.6. *Let A and B be square matrices of the same size. If $AB = I$, then A and B are nonsingular matrices, B is the inverse matrix of A (and A is the inverse matrix of B), and therefore $BA = I$.*

Proof. Recall that the determinant of the identity matrix is 1, i.e., $\det(I) = 1$; cf. (10.1). Since $AB = I$, it follows from Lemma 10.1 that $\det(A)\det(B) = 1$, and therefore both $\det(A) \neq 0$ and $\det(B) \neq 0$. From (1.80), we conclude that A and B are nonsingular matrices. Let A^{-1} be the inverse of A. Multiplying $AB = I$ to the left by A^{-1} and using the fact that $A^{-1}A = I$, we find that

$$A^{-1} = A^{-1}(AB) = (A^{-1}A)B = B.$$

We conclude that B is the inverse of A, and therefore $BA = A^{-1}A = I$. □

Lemma 1.7. *Let A and B be square matrices of the same size.*
(i) The matrix AB is nonsingular if and only if both A and B are nonsingular.
(ii) If A and B are nonsingular, then[17]

$$(AB)^{-1} = B^{-1}A^{-1}. \tag{1.82}$$

Proof. (i) From (1.80), we find that AB is nonsingular if and only if $\det(AB) \neq 0$, i.e., if and only if $\det(A)\det(B) \neq 0$; cf. (10.9). Thus, the matrix AB is nonsingular if and only if $\det(A) \neq 0$ and $\det(B) \neq 0$. Using again (1.80), we conclude that the matrix AB is nonsingular if and only if both matrices A and B are nonsingular.

(ii) If A and B are nonsingular, it follows that

$$(B^{-1}A^{-1})\,AB = B^{-1}(A^{-1}A)B = B^{-1}B = I,$$

since $A^{-1}A = I$ and $B^{-1}B = I$. From Definition 1.12, we conclude that $(AB)^{-1} = B^{-1}A^{-1}$. □

It is important to note that the inverse of the product of two matrices is not the product of the inverses, i.e.,

$$(AB)^{-1} \neq A^{-1}B^{-1}.$$

Also, note the similarity between (1.82), i.e., $(AB)^{-1} = B^{-1}A^{-1}$, and the result $(AB)^t = B^t A^t$ for the transposition of the product of two matrices; cf. (1.24).

Lemma 1.8. *Let A be a square matrix. If A is nonsingular, then A^t is a nonsingular matrix and*

$$\left(A^t\right)^{-1} = \left(A^{-1}\right)^t. \tag{1.83}$$

Proof. Note that it is enough to show that $\left(A^{-1}\right)^t A^t = I$; cf. Lemma 1.6. This follows from (1.24), since

$$\left(A^{-1}\right)^t A^t = \left(A\,A^{-1}\right)^t = I^t = I.$$

□

---

[17] Note that (1.82) extends as follows: $\left(\prod_{i=1}^{p} A_i\right)^{-1} = \prod_{i=1}^{p} A_{p+1-i}^{-1}$. A proof can be given by induction; see an exercise at the end of the chapter.

Lemma 1.9. *The inverse of a symmetric nonsingular matrix is a symmetric matrix. In other words, if A is a symmetric nonsingular matrix, then*

$$\left(A^{-1}\right)^t = A^{-1}.$$

Proof. If A is a symmetric matrix, then $A^t = A$. From (1.83), we find that

$$\left(A^{-1}\right)^t = \left(A^t\right)^{-1} = A^{-1}.$$

□

1.4 Diagonal matrices

Definition 1.14. *A square matrix is diagonal if and only if all the entries of the matrix which are not on the main diagonal are equal to 0.*
In other words, the $n \times n$ matrix D is diagonal if and only if

$$D(j,k) = 0, \quad \forall\, 1 \leq j \neq k \leq n. \tag{1.84}$$

Note that, if $d_i = D(i,i)$ for all $i = 1 : n$, then

$$D = \begin{pmatrix} d_1 & 0 & \cdots & 0 \\ 0 & d_2 & \cdots & 0 \\ \vdots & \vdots & \ddots & \vdots \\ 0 & 0 & \cdots & d_n \end{pmatrix}. \tag{1.85}$$

From (1.84) and (1.85), it follows that:

(i) any diagonal matrix is symmetric;

(ii) both the sum and the product of two diagonal matrices are diagonal matrices; see also Lemma 1.11;

(iii) any diagonal matrix is both upper triangular and lower triangular;[18] see (1.103) and (1.104).

The shorthand notation for the diagonal matrix D given by (1.85) is

$$D = \operatorname{diag}(d_k)_{k=1:n}.$$

The column form of the diagonal matrix $D = \operatorname{diag}(d_k)_{k=1:n}$ is

$$D = \operatorname{col}(d_k e_k)_{k=1:n}, \tag{1.86}$$

where e_k is the k-th column of the identity matrix of size n, for $k = 1 : n$.
The row form of the diagonal matrix $D = \operatorname{diag}(d_k)_{k=1:n}$ is

$$D = \operatorname{row}\left(d_j e_j^t\right)_{j=1:n}. \tag{1.87}$$

---

[18] An equivalent definition for a diagonal matrix is that a diagonal matrix is a matrix that is both upper triangular and lower triangular.

1.4. DIAGONAL MATRICES

Lemma 1.10. *Let A be an $m \times n$ matrix with column form $A = col(a_k)_{k=1:n}$ and row form $A = row(r_j)_{j=1:m}$.*

(i) If $D = diag(d_k)_{k=1:n}$ is a diagonal matrix of size n, then

$$AD = col(d_k a_k)_{k=1:n} = (d_1 a_1 \mid d_2 a_2 \mid \ldots \mid d_n a_n). \tag{1.88}$$

(ii) If $D = diag(d_j)_{j=1:m}$ is a diagonal matrix of size m, then

$$DA = row(d_j r_j)_{j=1:n} = \begin{pmatrix} d_1 r_1 \\ -- \\ d_2 r_2 \\ -- \\ \vdots \\ -- \\ d_n r_n \end{pmatrix}. \tag{1.89}$$

(iii) If $D_1 = diag\left(d_j^{(1)}\right)_{j=1:m}$ and $D_2 = diag\left(d_k^{(2)}\right)_{k=1:n}$ are diagonal matrices, then

$$(D_1 A D_2)(j,k) = d_j^{(1)} d_k^{(2)} A(j,k), \quad \forall\, j = 1:m,\ k = 1:n. \tag{1.90}$$

Proof. (i) Let $D = col(d_k e_k)_{k=1:n}$ be the column form of the diagonal matrix D, where e_k is the k-th column of the identity matrix of size n. Recall from (1.26) that $A e_k = a_k$, for all $k = 1:n$. Then, using (1.11), we find that

$$AD = col(A \cdot d_k e_k)_{k=1:n} = col(d_k \cdot A e_k)_{k=1:n} = col(d_k a_k)_{k=1:n}.$$

(ii) Let $D = row\left(d_j e_j^t\right)_{j=1:m}$ be the row form of the diagonal matrix D, where e_j is the j-th column of the identity matrix of size m. Recall from (1.27) that $e_j^t A = r_j$, for all $j = 1:m$. Then, using (1.12), we find that

$$DA = row\left(d_j e_j^t \cdot A\right)_{j=1:m} = row\left(d_j \cdot e_j^t A\right)_{j=1:m} = row(d_j r_j)_{j=1:m}.$$

(iii) Let

$$D_1 = row\left(d_j^{(1)} (e_j^{(1)})^t\right)_{j=1:m} \quad \text{and} \quad D_2 = col\left(d_k^{(2)} e_k^{(2)}\right)_{k=1:n}$$

be the row form of the diagonal matrix D_1 and the column form of the diagonal matrix D_2, respectively, where $e_j^{(1)}$ is the j-th column of the identity matrix of size m and $e_k^{(2)}$ is the k-th column of the identity matrix of size n.

Let $1 \leq j \leq m$ and $1 \leq k \leq n$ arbitrary. Recall from (1.14) that the entry (j,k) of the matrix $D_1 A D_2$ is

$$(D_1 A D_2)(j,k) = \left(d_j^{(1)} (e_j^{(1)})^t\right) A \left(d_k^{(2)} e_k^{(2)}\right) = d_j^{(1)} d_k^{(2)} ((e_j^{(1)})^t A e_k^{(2)}). \tag{1.91}$$

Recall from (1.26) that $A e_k^{(2)} = a_k$. Since $a_k = (A(i,k))_{i=1:m}$, we find using (1.5) that

$$(e_j^{(1)})^t A e_k^{(2)} = (e_j^{(1)})^t a_k = \sum_{i=1}^{m} e_j^{(1)}(i) A(i,k) = A(j,k), \tag{1.92}$$

since $e_j^{(1)}(i) = 0$ for any $i \neq j$ and $e_j^{(1)}(j) = 1$.
From (1.91) and (1.92), we conclude that

$$(D_1 A D_2)(j,k) = d_j^{(1)} d_k^{(2)} A(j,k), \quad \forall\ j = 1:m,\ k = 1:n.$$

□

Lemma 1.11. *The product of two diagonal matrices of the same size is a diagonal matrix. Also, products of diagonal matrices are commutative.*

In other words, if $D_1 = \text{diag}\left(d_k^{(1)}\right)_{k=1:n}$ and $D_2 = \text{diag}\left(d_k^{(2)}\right)_{k=1:n}$ are diagonal matrices, then

$$D_1 D_2 = \text{diag}\left(d_k^{(1)} d_k^{(2)}\right)_{k=1:n} \tag{1.93}$$

and $D_1 D_2 = D_2 D_1$.

Proof. Let $D_1 = \text{diag}\left(d_k^{(1)}\right)_{k=1:n}$ and $D_2 = \text{diag}\left(d_k^{(2)}\right)_{k=1:n}$ be diagonal matrices. The column form of D_1 is $D_1 = \text{col}\left(d_k^{(1)} e_k\right)_{k=1:n}$, and, using (1.88), we find that

$$\begin{aligned} D_1 D_2 &= \text{col}\left(d_k^{(2)} \cdot d_k^{(1)} e_k\right)_{k=1:n} = \text{col}\left(d_k^{(1)} d_k^{(2)} e_k\right)_{k=1:n} \\ &= \text{diag}\left(d_k^{(1)} d_k^{(2)}\right)_{k=1:n}. \end{aligned}$$

By using (1.93) for $D_1 = D_2$ and $D_2 = D_1$, we find that

$$D_2 D_1 = \text{diag}\left(d_k^{(2)} d_k^{(1)}\right)_{k=1:n} = \text{diag}\left(d_k^{(1)} d_k^{(2)}\right)_{k=1:n} = D_1 D_2,$$

and we conclude that products of diagonal matrices are commutative. □

Lemma 1.12. *(i) A diagonal matrix is nonsingular if and only if all its entries on the main diagonal are nonzero.*

In other words, the matrix $D = \text{diag}(d_k)_{k=1:n}$ is nonsingular if and only if $d_k \neq 0$ for all $k = 1:n$.

(ii) If $D = \text{diag}(d_k)_{k=1:n}$ is a nonsingular diagonal matrix, then

$$D^{-1} = \text{diag}\left(\frac{1}{d_k}\right)_{k=1:n}. \tag{1.94}$$

Proof. (i) Let $D = \text{diag}(d_k)_{k=1:n}$ be a diagonal matrix. Then, $\det(D) = \prod_{k=1}^n d_k$; cf. (10.1). From Theorem 1.2, we conclude that the matrix D is nonsingular if and only if $d_k \neq 0$ for all $k = 1:n$.

(ii) Let D^{-1} be the matrix given by (1.94); recall that $d_k \neq 0$ for all $k = 1:n$, since D is nonsingular. From (1.93), we find that

$$D\, D^{-1} = \text{diag}\left(d_k \cdot \frac{1}{d_k}\right)_{k=1:n} = \text{diag}(1)_{k=1:n} = I,$$

and therefore D^{-1} is the inverse matrix of D; cf. Lemma 1.6. □

1.4.1 Converting between covariance and correlation matrices

The covariance matrix $\Sigma_\mathbf{x}$ and the correlation matrix $\Omega_\mathbf{x}$ of n nonconstant random variables $X_1, X_2, \ldots X_n$ are the $n \times n$ matrices given by

$$\Sigma_\mathbf{x}(j,k) = \mathrm{cov}(X_j, X_k), \quad \forall\, 1 \leq j,k \leq n;$$
$$\Omega_\mathbf{x}(j,k) = \mathrm{corr}(X_j, X_k), \quad \forall\, 1 \leq j,k \leq n,$$

where $\mathrm{cov}(X_j, X_k)$ and $\mathrm{corr}(X_j, X_k)$ denote the covariance and the correlation of the random variables X_j and X_k, respectively. Recall that

$$\mathrm{cov}(X_j, X_k) = \sigma_j \sigma_k \mathrm{corr}(X_j, X_k), \quad \forall\, 1 \leq j,k \leq n,$$

where σ_j and σ_k are the standard deviations of X_j and X_k, respectively. Thus,

$$\Sigma_\mathbf{x}(j,k) = \sigma_j \sigma_k \mathrm{corr}(X_j, X_k), \quad \forall\, 1 \leq j,k \leq n.$$

Then, from (1.90), it follows that

$$\Sigma_\mathbf{x} = D_{\sigma_\mathbf{x}} \Omega_\mathbf{x} D_{\sigma_\mathbf{x}}, \tag{1.95}$$

where $D_{\sigma_\mathbf{x}}$ is the diagonal matrix given by $D_{\sigma_\mathbf{x}} = \mathrm{diag}(\sigma_i)_{i=1:n}$.

We conclude that, if the standard deviations of the n random variables are known, then the covariance matrix $\Sigma_\mathbf{x}$ can be uniquely determined from the correlation matrix $\Omega_\mathbf{x}$ by using formula (1.95).

Since $\sigma_i \neq 0$ for all $i = 1 : n$, the matrix $D_{\sigma_\mathbf{x}}$ is nonsingular and $(D_{\sigma_\mathbf{x}})^{-1} = \mathrm{diag}\left(\frac{1}{\sigma_i}\right)_{i=1:n}$; see (1.94). Then, from (1.95), we obtain that

$$\Omega_\mathbf{x} = (D_{\sigma_\mathbf{x}})^{-1} \Sigma_\mathbf{x} (D_{\sigma_\mathbf{x}})^{-1}. \tag{1.96}$$

Note that

$$D_{\sigma_\mathbf{x}} = \mathrm{diag}(\sigma_i)_{i=1:n} = \mathrm{diag}\left(\sqrt{\Sigma_\mathbf{x}(i,i)}\right)_{i=1:n}, \tag{1.97}$$

since, by definition, $\sigma_i^2 = \mathrm{cov}(X_i, X_i) = \Sigma_\mathbf{x}(i,i)$. In other words, the entries of the matrix $D_{\sigma_\mathbf{x}}$ can be obtained from the entries of $\Sigma_\mathbf{x}$.

We conclude that the correlation matrix $\Omega_\mathbf{x}$ is uniquely determined by the covariance matrix $\Sigma_\mathbf{x}$, and can be computed by using (1.96) and (1.97).

For more properties of covariance and correlation matrices, see section 7.1.

Example: Assume that the covariance matrix of three random variables is

$$\Sigma_\mathbf{x} = \begin{pmatrix} 1 & 0.1 & -0.6 \\ 0.1 & 0.25 & 0.5 \\ -0.6 & 0.5 & 4 \end{pmatrix}.$$

Note that

$$\sigma_1 = \sqrt{\Sigma_\mathbf{x}(1,1)} = 1; \quad \sigma_2 = \sqrt{\Sigma_\mathbf{x}(2,2)} = 0.5; \quad \sigma_3 = \sqrt{\Sigma_\mathbf{x}(3,3)} = 2.$$

Thus, $D_{\sigma_\mathbf{x}} = \begin{pmatrix} 1 & 0 & 0 \\ 0 & \frac{1}{2} & 0 \\ 0 & 0 & 2 \end{pmatrix}$ and $(D_{\sigma_\mathbf{x}})^{-1} = \begin{pmatrix} 1 & 0 & 0 \\ 0 & 2 & 0 \\ 0 & 0 & \frac{1}{2} \end{pmatrix}$. From (1.96), we find that the correlation matrix of the three random variables is

$$\Omega_\mathbf{x} = (D_{\sigma_\mathbf{x}})^{-1} \Sigma_\mathbf{x} (D_{\sigma_\mathbf{x}})^{-1} = \begin{pmatrix} 1 & 0.2 & -0.3 \\ 0.2 & 1 & 0.5 \\ -0.3 & 0.5 & 1 \end{pmatrix}. \quad \square$$

Example: Assume that the correlation matrix of three random variables with standard deviations $\sigma_1 = 2$, $\sigma_2 = 1$, and $\sigma_3 = 0.9$, is

$$\Omega_{\mathbf{x}} = \begin{pmatrix} 1 & 0.15 & -0.2 \\ 0.15 & 1 & 0.1 \\ -0.2 & 0.1 & 1 \end{pmatrix}.$$

Then, $D_{\sigma_{\mathbf{x}}} = \begin{pmatrix} 2 & 0 & 0 \\ 0 & 1 & 0 \\ 0 & 0 & 0.9 \end{pmatrix}$, and, from (1.95), we conclude that the covariance matrix of the three random variables is

$$\Sigma_{\mathbf{x}} = D_{\sigma_{\mathbf{x}}} \Omega_{\mathbf{x}} D_{\sigma_{\mathbf{x}}} = \begin{pmatrix} 4 & 0.3 & -0.36 \\ 0.3 & 1 & 0.09 \\ -0.36 & 0.09 & 0.81 \end{pmatrix}. \quad \square$$

Formulas similar to (1.95) and (1.96) can also be derived for sample covariance matrices and sample correlation matrices; see (1.99) and (1.100), respectively.

Denote by $\hat{\sigma}_i = \sqrt{\widehat{\mathrm{var}}(X_i)}$ the sample standard deviation of X_i, for $i = 1 : n$. Then, the sample correlation of X_j and X_k is

$$\widehat{\mathrm{corr}}(X_j, X_k) = \frac{\widehat{\mathrm{cov}}(X_j, X_k)}{\hat{\sigma}_j \hat{\sigma}_k}, \quad \forall \, 1 \leq j, k \leq n,$$

where $\widehat{\mathrm{cov}}(X_j, X_k)$ is the sample covariance of X_j and X_k given by (1.31).

The sample covariance matrix $\hat{\Sigma}_{\mathbf{x}}$ and the sample correlation matrix $\hat{\Omega}_{\mathbf{x}}$ of the random variables $X_1, X_2, \ldots X_n$ are the $n \times n$ matrices given by

$$\hat{\Sigma}_{\mathbf{x}}(j,k) = \widehat{\mathrm{cov}}(X_j, X_k), \quad \forall \, 1 \leq j, k \leq n;$$
$$\hat{\Omega}_{\mathbf{x}}(j,k) = \widehat{\mathrm{corr}}(X_j, X_k), \quad \forall \, 1 \leq j, k \leq n.$$

If

$$\hat{D}_{\sigma_{\mathbf{x}}} = \mathrm{diag}(\hat{\sigma}_i)_{i=1:n} = \mathrm{diag}\left(\sqrt{\hat{\Sigma}_{\mathbf{x}}(i,i)}\right)_{i=1:n}, \quad (1.98)$$

then,

$$\hat{\Sigma}_{\mathbf{x}} = \hat{D}_{\sigma_{\mathbf{x}}} \hat{\Omega}_{\mathbf{x}} \hat{D}_{\sigma_{\mathbf{x}}}; \quad (1.99)$$
$$\hat{\Omega}_{\mathbf{x}} = (\hat{D}_{\sigma_{\mathbf{x}}})^{-1} \hat{\Sigma}_{\mathbf{x}} (\hat{D}_{\sigma_{\mathbf{x}}})^{-1}. \quad (1.100)$$

Example (continued):
The sample covariance matrix $\hat{\Sigma}_{\mathbf{x}}$ of the daily returns of AAPL, FB, GOOG, MSFT, YHOO between 1/11/2013 and 1/29/2013 is given by (1.44). The diagonal matrix of the standard deviation of the daily returns $\hat{D}_{\sigma_{\mathbf{x}}} = \mathrm{diag}\left(\sqrt{\hat{\Sigma}_{\mathbf{x}}(i,i)}\right)_{i=1:5}$ is

$$\hat{D}_{\sigma_{\mathbf{x}}} = \begin{pmatrix} 0.0426 & 0 & 0 & 0 & 0 \\ 0 & 0.0254 & 0 & 0 & 0 \\ 0 & 0 & 0.0194 & 0 & 0 \\ 0 & 0 & 0 & 0.0072 & 0 \\ 0 & 0 & 0 & 0 & 0.0147 \end{pmatrix}. \quad (1.101)$$

From (1.100), and using (1.44) and (1.101), we find that the sample correlation matrix $\widehat{\Omega}_{\mathbf{X}}$ of the daily returns of AAPL, FB, GOOG, MSFT, YHOO between 1/11/2013 and 1/29/2013 is[19]

$$\widehat{\Omega}_{\mathbf{X}} = \begin{pmatrix} 1 & -0.0087 & -0.0736 & -0.0615 & -0.2002 \\ -0.0087 & 1 & 0.1075 & -0.0506 & 0.2929 \\ -0.0736 & 0.1075 & 1 & 0.5614 & 0.0591 \\ -0.0615 & -0.0506 & 0.5614 & 1 & 0.0250 \\ -0.2002 & 0.2929 & 0.0591 & 0.0250 & 1 \end{pmatrix} . \quad \square \quad (1.102)$$

1.5 Lower triangular and upper triangular matrices. Tridiagonal matrices.

Definition 1.15. *A square matrix is lower triangular if and only if all the entries of the matrix which are above the main diagonal are equal to 0.*
In other words, the $n \times n$ matrix L is lower triangular if and only if

$$L(j,k) = 0, \quad \forall\, 1 \leq j < k \leq n. \quad (1.103)$$

Definition 1.16. *A square matrix is upper triangular if and only if all the entries of the matrix which are below the main diagonal are equal to 0.*
In other words, the $n \times n$ matrix U is upper triangular if and only if

$$U(j,k) = 0, \quad \forall\, 1 \leq k < j \leq n. \quad (1.104)$$

From (1.103) and (1.104), it follows that the transpose of a lower triangular matrix is an upper triangular matrix and the transpose of an upper triangular matrix is a lower triangular matrix.[20]

The results below follow from (1.103) and (1.104), and can be regarded as column-based and row-based definitions for lower triangular and upper triangular matrices:

Lemma 1.13. *A square matrix of size n is lower triangular if and only if the first $k-1$ entries of the k-th column of the matrix are equal to 0, for all $k = 2 : n$.*
In other words, the $n \times n$ matrix $L = \mathrm{col}(l_k)_{k=1:n}$ is lower triangular if and only if

$$l_k(i) = 0, \quad \forall\, 1 \leq i \leq k-1, \quad \forall\, k = 2 : n. \quad (1.105)$$

A square matrix of size n is lower triangular if and only if the last $n-j$ entries of the j-th row of the matrix are equal to 0, for all $j = 1 : (n-1)$.
In other words, the $n \times n$ matrix $L = \mathrm{row}(r_j)_{j=1:n}$ is lower triangular if and only if

$$r_j(i) = 0, \quad \forall\, j+1 \leq i \leq n, \quad \forall\, j = 1 : (n-1). \quad (1.106)$$

---

[19] Note that, when computing $\widehat{D}_{\sigma_{\mathbf{X}}}$ and $\widehat{\Omega}_{\mathbf{X}}$ from (1.101) and (1.102), respectively, we used the non-truncated values for the entries of the sample covariance matrix $\widehat{\Sigma}_{\mathbf{X}}$, and not the values from (1.44) which are rounded at four decimal digits.

[20] Moreover, a matrix is lower triangular if and only if its transpose is an upper triangular matrix, and a matrix is upper triangular if and only if its transpose is a lower triangular matrix.

Lemma 1.14. *A square matrix of size n is upper triangular if and only if the last $n - k$ entries of the k-th column of the matrix are equal to 0, for all $k = 1 : (n - 1)$. In other words, the $n \times n$ matrix $U = col(u_k)_{k=1:n}$ is upper triangular if and only if*

$$u_k(i) = 0, \quad \forall \, k + 1 \leq i \leq n, \; \forall \, k = 1 : (n-1). \tag{1.107}$$

A square matrix of size n is upper triangular if and only if the first $j - 1$ entries of the j-th row of the matrix are equal to 0, for all $j = 2 : n$. In other words, the $n \times n$ matrix $U = row(r_j)_{j=1:n}$ is upper triangular if and only if

$$r_j(i) = 0, \quad \forall \, 1 \leq i \leq j - 1, \; \forall \, j = 2 : n. \tag{1.108}$$

Note that the sum of two lower triangular matrices is a lower triangular matrix, the sum of two upper triangular matrices is an upper triangular matrix, and the result of multiplying a lower triangular (or an upper triangular) matrix by a constant is a lower triangular (or, respectively, an upper triangular) matrix. Thus, any linear combination of lower triangular matrices is lower triangular and any linear combination of upper triangular matrices is upper triangular.

Lemma 1.15. *(i) The product of two lower triangular matrices is lower triangular. (ii) The product of two upper triangular matrices is upper triangular.*

Proof. (i) Let $L_1 = col\left(l_k^{(1)}\right)_{k=1:n}$ and $L_2 = col\left(l_k^{(2)}\right)_{k=1:n}$ be lower triangular matrices. Recall from (1.105) that

$$l_k^{(1)}(j) = 0, \quad 1 \leq j \leq k - 1, \; \forall \, k = 2 : n; \tag{1.109}$$

$$l_k^{(2)}(j) = 0, \quad 1 \leq j \leq k - 1, \; \forall \, k = 2 : n. \tag{1.110}$$

Recall from (1.11) that

$$L_1 L_2 = col\left(L_1 l_k^{(2)}\right)_{k=1:n}.$$

Thus, the k-th column of $L_1 L_2$ is $L_1 l_k^{(2)}$. Using (1.7) and the column form $L_1 = col\left(l_k^{(1)}\right)_{k=1:n}$ of L_1, we obtain that

$$L_1 l_k^{(2)} = \sum_{j=1}^n l_k^{(2)}(j)\, l_j^{(1)} = \sum_{j=k}^n l_k^{(2)}(j)\, l_j^{(1)}, \tag{1.111}$$

since $l_k^{(2)}(j) = 0$ for all j such that $1 \leq j \leq k - 1$; cf. (1.110).

Let i such that $1 \leq i \leq k - 1$. If $k \leq j \leq n$, then $1 \leq i \leq j - 1$ and, from (1.109), it follows that

$$l_j^{(1)}(i) = 0, \quad \forall \, k \leq j \leq n. \tag{1.112}$$

Then, from (1.111) and (1.112), we find that

$$(L_1 l_k^{(2)})(i) = \sum_{j=k}^n l_k^{(2)}(j)\, l_j^{(1)}(i) = 0, \quad \forall \, 1 \leq i \leq k - 1.$$

1.5. LOWER TRIANGULAR AND UPPER TRIANGULAR MATRICES

We conclude that the first $k-1$ entries of $L_1 l_k^{(2)}$, which is the k-th column of the matrix $L_1 L_2$, are equal to 0. Therefore, from Lemma 1.13, it follows that $L_1 L_2$ is a lower triangular matrix.

(ii) Let U_1 and U_2 be upper triangular matrices of the same size. Recall that a matrix is upper triangular if and only if its transpose is a lower triangular matrix. Thus, U_1^t and U_2^t are lower triangular matrices. The matrix $U_2^t U_1^t$ is also a lower triangular matrix, since we already proved that the product of two lower triangular matrices is lower triangular. Since $(U_1 U_2)^t = U_2^t U_1^t$, see (1.24), it follows that the transpose of the matrix $U_1 U_2$ is a lower triangular matrix. We conclude that $U_1 U_2$ is an upper triangular matrix. □

Recall from (10.3) and (10.4), respectively, that the determinant of a lower triangular matrix L is equal to the product of all its entries on the main diagonal, and the determinant of an upper triangular matrix U is equal to the product of all its entries on the main diagonal, i.e.,

$$\det(L) = \prod_{i=1}^{n} L(i,i); \qquad (1.113)$$

$$\det(U) = \prod_{i=1}^{n} U(i,i). \qquad (1.114)$$

Lemma 1.16. *(i) A lower triangular matrix L is nonsingular if and only if all its entries on the main diagonal are nonzero, i.e., if and only if*

$$L(i,i) \neq 0, \quad \forall\, i = 1:n.$$

(ii) An upper triangular matrix U is nonsingular if and only if all its entries on the main diagonal are nonzero, i.e., if and only if

$$U(i,i) \neq 0, \quad \forall\, i = 1:n.$$

Proof. These results follow from (1.113) and (1.114), and from the fact that a matrix is nonsingular if and only if its determinant is nonzero; cf. Theorem 1.2. □

Lemma 1.17. *(i) The inverse of an upper triangular matrix is upper triangular.*

(ii) The inverse of a lower triangular matrix is lower triangular.

A proof of this result can be found in Section 10.7; see Lemma 10.18.

Definition 1.17. *The $n \times n$ matrix A is banded of band m if and only if*

$$A(j,k) = 0, \quad \forall\, 1 \leq j, k \leq n \text{ with } |j-k| > m.$$

Note that a banded matrix of band 0 is a diagonal matrix, since $A(j,k) = 0$ for all j and k with $|j-k| > 0$ is equivalent to $A(j,k) = 0$ for all $j \neq k$.

Example: The positions of the entries of a 6×6 banded matrix with band 2 which could be nonzero are denoted by "×" in the matrix below:

$$\begin{pmatrix} \times & \times & \times & 0 & 0 & 0 \\ \times & \times & \times & \times & 0 & 0 \\ \times & \times & \times & \times & \times & 0 \\ 0 & \times & \times & \times & \times & \times \\ 0 & 0 & \times & \times & \times & \times \\ 0 & 0 & 0 & \times & \times & \times \end{pmatrix}. \quad \square$$

A matrix of band 1 is called a tridiagonal matrix and appears frequently in practical applications.

Definition 1.18. *The $n \times n$ matrix A is tridiagonal if and only if*

$$A(j,k) = 0, \quad \forall \ 1 \leq j, k \leq n \text{ with } |j - k| > 1,$$

or, equivalently, if and only if the only nonzero entries of A could be the main diagonal entries $A(i,i)$, for $i = 1 : n$, the upper diagonal entries $A(i, i+1)$, for $i = 1 : (n-1)$, and the lower diagonal entries $A(i, i-1)$, for $i = 2 : n$.

Example: The positions of the entries of a 6×6 tridiagonal matrix which could be nonzero are denoted by "$\times$" in the matrix below:

$$\begin{pmatrix} \times & \times & 0 & 0 & 0 & 0 \\ \times & \times & \times & 0 & 0 & 0 \\ 0 & \times & \times & \times & 0 & 0 \\ 0 & 0 & \times & \times & \times & 0 \\ 0 & 0 & 0 & \times & \times & \times \\ 0 & 0 & 0 & 0 & \times & \times \end{pmatrix}. \quad \square$$

1.6 References

Several linear algebra books are close in spirit to our approach emphasizing numerical implementation and applications: Gilbert Strang's "Introduction to Linear Algebra" [41] and "Linear Algebra and Its Applications" [40] and Peter Lax's "Linear Algebra and Its Applications" [26] are three acclaimed such texts; also, Strang's OpenCourseWare MIT videos are a remarkable resource. A classical approach to graduate level linear algebra can be found in Horn and Johnson [22].

The numerical analysis approach to linear algebra was pioneered by the classical monograph of Golub and Van Loan [18], and further solidified by Demmel [13]. The insightful numerical linear algebra textbook by Trefethen and Bau [43] presents the intuition behind numerical linear algebra methods.

Some of the exercises contained in this chapter and throughout the book are frequently asked in interviews for positions requiring quantitative skills; see Stefanica, Radoičić, and Wang [39] for more interview–style questions.

1.7 Exercises

1. Let
$$A = \begin{pmatrix} 1 & -1 & 2 & 5 & 4 \\ 3 & -2 & 1 & 4 & 2 \\ 0 & 1 & 2 & -1 & 3 \\ -5 & 4 & 2 & -4 & 3 \end{pmatrix}.$$
Show that the column rank and the row rank of A are both equal to 3.

2. Let x and y be column vectors of size n, and let I be the identity matrix of size n.

   (i) If $y^t x \neq -1$, show that
   $$(I + xy^t)^{-1} = I - \frac{1}{1 + y^t x} xy^t.$$
   In other words, show that
   $$\left(I - \frac{1}{1 + y^t x} xy^t\right)(I + xy^t) = I.$$

   (ii) Show that the matrix $I + xy^t$ is nonsingular if and only if $y^t x \neq -1$.

3. (i) Use induction to show that
   $$\left(\prod_{i=1}^{n} A_i\right)^t = \prod_{i=1}^{n} A_{n+1-i}^t$$
   for any $m_i \times n_i$ matrices A_i, $i = 1 : n$, with $n_i = m_{i+1}$ for $i = 1 : (n-1)$.

   (ii) Show that
   $$\left(\prod_{i=1}^{n} A_i\right)^{-1} = \prod_{i=1}^{n} A_{n+1-i}^{-1}$$
   for any nonsingular square matrices A_i of the same size.

4. Let $D = \text{diag}(d_i)_{i=1:n}$ be a diagonal matrix of size n with distinct diagonal entries, i.e., such that $d_j \neq d_k$, for any $1 \leq j \neq k \leq n$. If A is a square matrix of size n, show that $AD = DA$ if and only if the matrix A is diagonal.

5. Use the fact that $D_1 D_2 = D_2 D_1$ for any two diagonal matrices D_1 and D_2 of the same size to show that
   $$\prod_{i=1}^{n} D_i = \prod_{i=1}^{n} D_{p(i)},$$
   for any one-to-one function $p : \{1, 2, \ldots n\} \to \{1, 2, \ldots n\}$, where D_i, $i = 1 : n$, are diagonal matrices of the same size.

6. (i) Let A be an $n \times n$ matrix and let L be an $n \times n$ nonsingular lower triangular matrix. Show that, if LA is a lower triangular matrix, then A is lower triangular. Show that, if AL is a lower triangular matrix, then A is lower triangular.

   (ii) Let A be an $n \times n$ matrix and let U be an $n \times n$ nonsingular upper triangular matrix. Show that, if UA is an upper triangular matrix, then A is upper triangular. Show that, if AU is an upper triangular matrix, then A is upper triangular.

7. Let A be a nonsingular matrix, and let k be a positive integer. Define A^{-k} as the k-th power of the inverse matrix of A, i.e., let $A^{-k} = \left(A^{-1}\right)^k$. Show that this definition is consistent, i.e., show that
$$A^k \cdot A^{-k} = A^{-k} \cdot A^k = I.$$

8. (i) Let
$$M = \begin{pmatrix} 0 & 0 & 0 & 0 \\ 3 & 0 & 0 & 0 \\ 1 & -1 & 0 & 0 \\ -1 & 2 & 1 & 0 \end{pmatrix}.$$
Compute M^2, M^3, M^4.

   (ii) Let
$$C = I + M = \begin{pmatrix} 1 & 0 & 0 & 0 \\ 3 & 1 & 0 & 0 \\ 1 & -1 & 1 & 0 \\ -1 & 2 & 1 & 1 \end{pmatrix}.$$
Compute C^m, where $m \geq 2$ is a positive integer.

   Hint: Recall that, if A and B are square matrices of the same size such that $AB = BA$, then the following version of the binomial formula holds true:
$$(A+B)^m = \sum_{j=0}^{m} \binom{m}{j} A^j B^{m-j}, \qquad (1.115)$$
where m is a positive integer and the binomial coefficient $\binom{m}{j}$ is given by
$$\binom{m}{j} = \frac{m!}{j!\,(m-j)!},$$
where $k! = 1 \cdot 2 \cdot \ldots \cdot k$. Also, note that $A^0 = B^0 = I$.

9. Let L be an $n \times n$ lower triangular matrix with entries equal to 0 on the main diagonal, i.e., with $L(i,i) = 0$ for $i = 1:n$.

   (i) Show that $L^n = 0$;

(ii) Compute $(I+L)^m$ in terms of $L, L^2, \ldots, L^{n-1}$, where $m \geq n$ is a positive integer.

Hint: Use the binomial formula (1.115).

10. Let A and B be square matrices of the same size with nonnegative entries and such that the sum of the entries in each row is equal to 1. Show that the matrix AB has the same properties, i.e., show that all the entries of the matrix AB are nonnegative and the sum of the entries in each row of AB is equal to 1.

    Note: A matrix with nonnegative entries such that the sum of the entries in each row is equal to 1 is called a probability matrix.

11. The covariance matrix of five random variables is

$$\Sigma = \begin{pmatrix} 1 & -0.525 & 1.375 & -0.075 & -0.75 \\ -0.525 & 2.25 & 0.1875 & 0.1875 & -0.675 \\ 1.375 & 0.1875 & 6.25 & 0.4375 & -1.875 \\ -0.075 & 0.1875 & 0.4375 & 0.25 & 0.3 \\ -0.75 & -0.675 & -1.875 & 0.3 & 9 \end{pmatrix}$$

Find the correlation matrix of these random variables.

12. The correlation matrix of five random variables is

$$\Omega = \begin{pmatrix} 1 & -0.25 & 0.15 & -0.05 & -0.30 \\ -0.25 & 1 & -0.10 & -0.25 & 0.10 \\ 0.15 & -0.10 & 1 & 0.20 & 0.05 \\ -0.05 & -0.25 & 0.20 & 1 & 0.10 \\ -0.30 & 0.10 & 0.05 & 0.10 & 1 \end{pmatrix}$$

(i) Compute the covariance matrix of these random variables if their standard deviations are 0.25, 0.5, 1, 2, and 4, in this order.

(ii) Compute the covariance matrix of these random variables if their standard deviations are 4, 2, 1, 0.5, and 0.25, in this order.

13. The file *indeces-jul26-aug9-2012.xlsx* from fepress.org/nla-primer contains the July 26, 2012 – August 9, 2012 end of day values of Dow Jones, Nasdaq, and S&P 500.

    (i) Compute the daily percentage returns of the three indices over the given time period.

    (ii) Compute the covariance matrix of the daily percentage returns of the three indices.

    (iii) Compute the daily log returns of the three indices over the given time period.

    (iv) Compute the covariance matrix of the daily log returns of the three indices.

Note: The percentage return and the log return between times t_1 and t_2 of an asset with price $S(t)$ at time t are given by

$$\frac{S(t_2) - S(t_1)}{S(t_1)} \quad \text{and} \quad \ln\left(\frac{S(t_2)}{S(t_1)}\right),$$

respectively.

14. The file *indices-july2011.xlsx* from fepress.org/nla-primer contains the January 2011 – July 2011 end of day values of nine major US indeces.

    (i) Compute the sample covariance matrix of the daily percentage returns of the indeces, and the corresponding sample corelation matrix.

    Compute the sample covariance and correlation matrices for daily log returns, and compare them with the corresponding matrices for daily percentage returns.

    (ii) Compute the sample covariance matrix of the weekly percentage returns of the indeces, and the corresponding sample corelation matrix.

    Compute the sample covariance and correlation matrices for weekly log returns, and compare them with the corresponding matrices for weekly percentage returns.

    (iii) Compute the sample covariance matrix of the monthly percentage returns of the indeces, and the corresponding sample corelation matrix.

    Compute the sample covariance and correlation matrices for monthly log returns, and compare them with the corresponding matrices for monthly percentage returns.

    (iv) Comment on the differences between the sample covariance and correlation matrices for daily, weekly, and monthly returns.

15. In three months, the value of an asset with spot price \$50 will be either \$60 or \$45. The continuously compounded risk–free rate is 6%. Consider the one period market model with two securities, i.e., cash and the asset, and two states, i.e., asset value equal to \$60 and asset value equal to \$45, in three months.

    (i) Find the payoff matrix of this model.

    (ii) Is this one period market complete, i.e., is the payoff matrix nonsingular?

    (iii) How do you replicate a three months at–the–money put option on this asset, using the cash and the underlying asset?

16. In six months, the price of an asset with spot price \$40 will be either \$30, \$35, \$40, \$42, \$45, or \$50. Consider a one period market model with six states in six months corresponding to the six possible values of the asset in six months, and with the following four securities:

    - cash;

1.7. EXERCISES

- asset;
- six months at-the-money call option with strike $40 on the asset;
- six months at-the-money put option with strike $40 on the asset.

The continuously compounded risk–free interest rate is constant and equal to 6%.

(i) Find the payoff matrix of this model.

(ii) Is this one period market model complete?

(iii) Are the four securities non–redundant?

Chapter 2

LU decomposition and linear systems solutions. Discount factors computation. Cubic spline interpolation.

The numerical solution of linear systems.

Forward substitution. Backward substitution.

Finding discount factors using forward substitution.

LU decomposition without pivoting. Existence and uniqueness. Pseudocode and operation count.

Linear solvers using the LU decomposition without pivoting.

LU linear solvers for tridiagonal matrices.

LU decomposition with row pivoting. Pseudocode and operation count.

Linear solvers using the LU decomposition with row pivoting.

Solving linear systems corresponding to the same matrix.

Finding discount factors using the LU decomposition.

Cubic spline interpolation. Cubic spline interpolation for zero rate curves.

2.1 The numerical solution of linear systems

A fundamental problem in numerical analysis is solving linear systems, i.e., finding a vector x such that
$$Ax = b, \qquad (2.1)$$
where A is a square matrix and b is a column vector of size equal to the number of columns of A.

The *numerical solution* of the problem (2.1) requires finding efficient numerical algorithms to compute the vector x such that $Ax = b$, given the matrix A and the column vector b. These numerical algorithms will also address implicitly the question whether the matrix A is nonsingular, which is required for the linear system (2.1) to have a unique solution.

The numerical methods for solving linear systems are of two fundamentally different types:

- *Direct Methods:* The solution of the linear system $Ax = b$ is found by computing the LU decomposition with pivoting of the matrix A, or the Cholesky decomposition of A, if the matrix A is symmetric positive definite, and then solving two linear systems corresponding to lower triangular matrices and to upper triangular matrices.
- *Iterative Methods:* The solution of the linear system $Ax = b$ is obtained recursively. The iteration is stopped once an approximate solution with prescribed precision is found. Examples of such methods are Jacobi iteration, Gauss–Siedel iteration, and SOR (Successive Overrelaxation).

All the methods mentioned above are much more efficient from a numerical standpoint than a computation of the inverse matrix A^{-1} and finding x by using the matrix–vector multiplication $x = A^{-1}b$.

In practice, direct methods are faster for solving linear systems arising from discretizations of two dimensional problems, while iterative methods are faster for solving linear systems corresponding to three dimensional problems (or higher dimensional problems). We only discuss direct methods herein: see sections 2.4 and 2.6 for the LU decomposition, and section 6.1 for the Cholesky decomposition.

Note that linear systems corresponding to nonsingular diagonal matrices have straightforward solution. If D is a nonsingular diagonal matrix of size n, i.e., with $D(j,j) \neq 0$ for all $j = 1 : n$, see Lemma 1.12, then the solution x to $Dx = b$, where b is an $n \times 1$ vector, is given by

$$x(j) = \frac{b(j)}{D(j,j)}, \quad \forall\, j = 1 : n.$$

Linear systems corresponding to lower triangular matrices or to upper triangular matrices can also be solved directly, by using the Forward Substitution, if the matrix is lower triangular, or by using the Backward Substitution, if the matrix is upper triangular; see section 2.2 and section 2.3, respectively.

2.2 Forward substitution

Let L be a nonsingular lower triangular matrix of size n, i.e., assume that

$$L(j,k) = 0, \; \forall\, 1 \leq j < k \leq n; \quad L(i,i) \neq 0, \; \forall\, 1 \leq i \leq n; \tag{2.2}$$

see Lemma 1.16. Let b be an $n \times 1$ column vector, and let x be the $n \times 1$ vector which is the unique solution to the linear system $Lx = b$.

Forward Substitution is a numerical algorithm designed to compute the entries of x efficiently, and is detailed below.

By multiplying the first row of L by x, and using the fact that $L(1,k) = 0$ for all $k = 2 : n$, since L is lower triangular, see (2.2), we obtain that

$$\sum_{k=1}^{n} L(1,k)x(k) = L(1,1)x(1) = b(1),$$

2.2. FORWARD SUBSTITUTION

and therefore
$$x(1) = \frac{b(1)}{L(1,1)}; \tag{2.3}$$

note that $L(1,1) \neq 0$, since L is nonsingular.

Moving forward to computing $x(2)$, multiply the second row of L by x, and use the fact that $L(2,k) = 0$ for all $k = 3 : n$, since L is lower triangular, see (2.2), to obtain that

$$\sum_{k=1}^{n} L(2,k)x(k) = L(2,1)x(1) + L(2,2)x(2) = b(2). \tag{2.4}$$

By solving (2.4) for $x(2)$, we find that

$$x(2) = \frac{b(2) - L(2,1)x(1)}{L(2,2)}; \tag{2.5}$$

note that $L(2,2) \neq 0$, since L is nonsingular. Since the value of $x(1)$ is known from (2.3), the value of $x(2)$ can be computed from (2.5).

It is important to note that formula (2.3) for $x(1)$ is never substituted into the formula (2.5) for $x(2)$ in order to obtain a closed formula for $x(2)$ in terms of the entries of the matrix L. The numerical value of $x(2)$ is computed directly by substituting into (2.5) the numerical value for $x(1)$ already determined from (2.3).

We continue to move forward until all the entries of x are computed, as follows: Assume that the values of $x(1)$, $x(2)$, ..., $x(j-1)$ have been computed, where $2 \leq j \leq n$. To compute $x(j)$, multiply the j-th row of L by x, and use the fact that $L(j,k) = 0$ for all $k = (j+1) : n$, since L is lower triangular, to obtain that

$$\sum_{k=1}^{n} L(j,k)x(k) = \sum_{k=1}^{j} L(j,k)x(k) = b(j).$$

Thus,
$$L(j,j)x(j) + \sum_{k=1}^{j-1} L(j,k)x(k) = b(j). \tag{2.6}$$

By solving (2.6) for $x(j)$, we find that

$$x(j) = \frac{b(j) - \sum_{k=1}^{j-1} L(j,k)x(k)}{L(j,j)}; \tag{2.7}$$

note that $L(j,j) \neq 0$, since L is nonsingular. Thus, given $x(1)$, $x(2)$, ..., $x(j-1)$, the value for $x(j)$ can be computed using (2.7).

The pseudocode for Forward Substitution can be found in Table 2.1.

The efficiency and running time of algorithms can be estimated by computing the operation count of the algorithm. Throughout this book, we will count each arithmetic operation, e.g., addition, multiplication, to obtain the operation count.

Lemma 2.1. *The operation count for the Forward Substitution algorithm applied to a lower triangular matrix of size n is*

$$n^2 + O(n). \tag{2.8}$$

Table 2.1: Pseudocode for Forward Substitution

> Function Call:
> $x = $ forward_subst(L,b)
>
> Input:
> $L = $ nonsingular lower triangular matrix of size n
> $b = $ column vector of size n
>
> Output:
> $x = $ solution to $Lx = b$
>
> $x(1) = \frac{b(1)}{L(1,1)}$;
> for $j = 2 : n$
>   sum $= 0$;
>   for $k = 1 : (j-1)$
>   sum $=$ sum $+ L(j,k)x(k)$;
>   end
> $x(j) = \frac{b(j)-\text{sum}}{L(j,j)}$;
> end

Proof. Computing $x(1)$ requires 1 operation. At step j, the "for" loop

> for $k = 1 : (j-1)$
>   sum $=$ sum $+ L(j,k)x(k)$;
> end

to compute the term sum requires $2(j-1)$ operations. Thus, the "for" loop

> for $j = 2 : n$
>   sum $= 0$;
>   for $k = 1 : (j-1)$
>   sum $=$ sum $+ L(j,k)x(k)$;
>   end
> $x(j) = \frac{b(j)-\text{sum}}{L(j,j)}$;
> end

to compute $x(j)$ requires $2(j-1) + 2 = 2j$ operations.

Then, the total number of operations required by the Forward Substitution is

$$1 + \sum_{j=2}^{n} 2j = \sum_{j=1}^{n} 2j - 1 = 2\frac{n(n+1)}{2} - n = n^2 + n - 1 = n^2 + O(n), \quad (2.9)$$

see (10.78), since $\sum_{j=1}^{n} j = \frac{n(n+1)}{2}$; see, e.g., section 10.3.1 from Stefanica [36]. □

We conclude this section with the Forward Substitution pseudocode corresponding to a lower triangular bidiagonal matrix, see Table 2.2, which will be used for solving linear systems corresponding to tridiagonal matrices; cf. section 2.5.1 and section 6.3.

Let L be an $n \times n$ lower triangular bidiagonal matrix, i.e., a matrix whose only nonzero entries could be the main diagonal entries $L(j,j)$, for $j = 1 : n$, and the

2.2. FINDING DISCOUNT FACTORS

lower diagonal entries $L(j, j-1)$, for $j = 2 : n$. Then, the recursion formula (2.7) simplifies to
$$x(j) = \frac{b(j) - L(j, j-1)x(j-1)}{L(j,j)},$$
which corresponds to the reduced version of the Forward Substitution pseudocode from Table 2.1 included in Table 2.2.

Table 2.2: Forward Substitution for lower triangular bidiagonal matrices

---

Function Call:
$x = $ forward_subst_bidiag(L,b)

Input:
$L = $ nonsingular lower triangular bidiagonal matrix of size n
$b = $ column vector of size n

Output:
$x = $ solution to $Lx = b$

$x(1) = \frac{b(1)}{L(1,1)}$;
for $j = 2 : n$
  $x(j) = \frac{b(j) - L(j,j-1)x(j-1)}{L(j,j)}$;
end

The operation count for the Forward Substitution for lower triangular bidiagonal matrices is
$$1 + 3(n-1) = 3n - 2. \tag{2.10}$$

2.2.1 Finding discount factors using forward substitution

The value of a bond is equal to the sum of the present values of all its future cash flows. Therefore, known prices of several bonds provide information regarding the discount factors corresponding to all the cash flow dates of the bonds.

If the number of cash flow dates is higher than the number of bonds, then there is not enough information to uniquely determine the discount factors. If the number of bonds is higher than the number of cash flow dates, there is a redundancy of data and arbitrage opportunities may exist.

However, if the number of cash flow dates is equal to the number of bonds, and if there are no redundancies (i.e., if no bond can be synthesized by taking positions in the other bonds), then it is possible to uniquely identify the discount factors corresponding to the cash flow dates (and the corresponding values of the zero rates) from the bond prices.

In this section, we present an example where the discount factors can be computed using forward substitution. A more general example requiring LU decomposition for computing the discount factors can be found in section 2.7.2.

Recall that the value of a bond is equal to the sum of the present value of all its future cash flows. In other words, if B is the value of a bond with future cash flows

c_i to be paid at times t_i, and if $\text{Disc}(t_i)$ are the discount factors corresponding to time t_i, for $i = 1 : n$, then

$$B = \sum_{i=1}^{n} c_i \text{Disc}(t_i). \qquad (2.11)$$

Note that the discount factor $\text{Disc}(t_i)$ at time t_i is uniquely determined by the risk–free zero rate $r(0, t_i)$ at time t_i. For example, if interest is continuously compounded (which is assumed to be the case throughout the book, unless otherwise specified), then

$$\text{Disc}(t_i) = e^{-t_i r(0, t_i)} = \exp\left(-t_i r(0, t_i)\right). \qquad (2.12)$$

For the example below, recall that an annual coupon bond with face value $100, coupon rate C, and maturity T (measured in years) pays the holder of the bond a coupon payment equal to $C \cdot 100$ every year, except at maturity. The final payment at maturity T is equal to the face value of the bond plus one coupon payment, i.e., $(1 + C)100$. For example, an annual coupon bond with 15 months to maturity and coupon rate 5%, i.e., $C = 0.05$, has two cash flow dates, in 3 and in 15 months, corresponding to $t_1 = \frac{3}{12} = \frac{1}{4}$, and $t_2 = \frac{15}{12} = \frac{5}{4}$, respectively. The corresponding cash flows are $c_1 = 5$ and $c_2 = 105$.

Example: The prices of the following annual coupon bonds with face value $100 are given:

Bond Maturity	Coupon Rate	Bond Price
1 year	0	$98
2 years	6%	$104
3 years	8%	$111
4 years	5%	$102

The cash flows and the cash flow dates of the bonds are recorded in the table below:

Maturity	Cash Flow & Date
1 year	$100 in 1 year
2 years	$6 in 1 year
	$106 in 2 years
3 years	$8 in 1 year
	$8 in 2 years
	$108 in 3 years
4 years	$5 in 1 year
	$5 in 2 years
	$5 in 3 years
	$105 in 4 years

Note that the four bonds have exactly four cash flow dates, i.e., 1 year, 2 years, 3 years, and 4 years. For $i = 1 : 4$, denote by d_i the discount factor corresponding to time equal to i years. Using formula (2.11) for the values of the bonds, we find that

$$98 = 100 d_1;$$
$$104 = 6 d_1 + 106 d_2;$$
$$111 = 8 d_1 + 8 d_2 + 108 d_3;$$
$$102 = 5 d_1 + 5 d_2 + 5 d_3 + 105 d_4.$$

2.3. BACKWARD SUBSTITUTION

This linear system can be written in matrix notation as $Ld = b$, where L is a lower triangular matrix, and d and b are column vectors given by

$$L = \begin{pmatrix} 100 & 0 & 0 & 0 \\ 6 & 106 & 0 & 0 \\ 8 & 8 & 108 & 0 \\ 5 & 5 & 5 & 105 \end{pmatrix} ; \quad d = \begin{pmatrix} d_1 \\ d_2 \\ d_3 \\ d_4 \end{pmatrix} ; \quad b = \begin{pmatrix} 98 \\ 104 \\ 111 \\ 102 \end{pmatrix}.$$

The solution of the linear system $Ld = b$ is found using forward substitution,[1] i.e.,

$$d = \text{forward\_subst}(L, b) = \begin{pmatrix} 0.98 \\ 0.9257 \\ 0.8866 \\ 0.8385 \end{pmatrix}.$$

Formula (2.12) can be used to find the corresponding continuously compounded zero rates:

$$d_1 = \text{Disc}(1) = e^{-r(0,1)} \iff r(0,1) = -\ln(d_1) = 0.0202 = 2.02\%;$$

$$d_2 = \text{Disc}(2) = e^{-2r(0,2)} \iff r(0,2) = -\frac{\ln(d_2)}{2} = 0.0386 = 3.86\%;$$

$$d_3 = \text{Disc}(3) = e^{-3r(0,3)} \iff r(0,3) = -\frac{\ln(d_3)}{3} = 0.0401 = 4.01\%;$$

$$d_4 = \text{Disc}(4) = e^{-4r(0,4)} \iff r(0,4) = -\frac{\ln(d_4)}{4} = 0.0440 = 4.40\%. \quad \square$$

2.3 Backward substitution

Let U be a nonsingular upper triangular matrix of size n, i.e., assume that

$$U(j, k) = 0, \ \forall \ 1 \leq k < j \leq n; \quad U(i, i) \neq 0, \ \forall \ 1 \leq i \leq n; \tag{2.13}$$

see Lemma 1.16.

Let b be an $n \times 1$ column vector, and let x be the $n \times 1$ vector which is the unique solution to the linear system $Ux = b$.

Backward substitution is a numerical algorithm designed to compute the entries of x efficiently, as detailed below.

---

[1] Without using the routine forward_subst, d_1, d_2, d_3, and d_4 can be obtained as follows:

$$d_1 = \frac{98}{100} = 0.98;$$

$$d_2 = \frac{104 - 6d_1}{106} = 0.9257;$$

$$d_3 = \frac{111 - 8d_1 - 8d_2}{108} = 0.8866;$$

$$d_4 = \frac{102 - 5d_1 - 5d_2 - 5d_3}{105} = 0.8385.$$

By multiplying the n-th row of U by x, and using the fact that $U(n,k) = 0$ for all $k = 1 : (n-1)$, since U is upper triangular, see (2.13), we obtain that

$$\sum_{k=1}^{n} U(n,k)x(k) = U(n,n)x(n) = b(n),$$

and therefore

$$x(n) = \frac{b(n)}{U(n,n)}; \qquad (2.14)$$

note that $U(n,n) \neq 0$, since U is nonsingular.

Moving backward to computing $x(n-1)$, multiply the $(n-1)$-th row of U by x, and use the fact that $U(n-1,k) = 0$ for all $k = 1 : (n-2)$, since U is upper triangular, see (2.13), to obtain that

$$\sum_{k=1}^{n} U(n-1,k)x(k) = U(n-1,n-1)x(n-1) + U(n-1,n)x(n) = b(n-1). \quad (2.15)$$

By solving (2.15) for $x(n-1)$, we find that

$$x(n-1) = \frac{b(n-1) - U(n-1,n)x(n)}{U(n-1,n-1)}; \qquad (2.16)$$

note that $U(n-1,n-1) \neq 0$, since U is nonsingular. Since the value of $x(n)$ is known from (2.14), the value of $x(n-1)$ can be computed from (2.16).

We continue to move backward until all the entries of x are computed, as follows: Assume that the values of $x(n)$, $x(n-1)$, ..., $x(j+1)$ have been computed, where $n-1 \geq j \geq 1$. To compute $x(j)$, multiply the j-th row of U by x, and use the fact that $U(j,k) = 0$ for all $k = 1 : (j-1)$, since U is upper triangular, to obtain that

$$\sum_{k=1}^{n} U(j,k)x(k) = \sum_{k=j}^{n} U(j,k)x(k) = b(j).$$

Thus,

$$U(j,j)x(j) + \sum_{k=j+1}^{n} U(j,k)x(k) = b(j). \qquad (2.17)$$

By solving (2.17) for $x(j)$, we find that

$$x(j) = \frac{b(j) - \sum_{k=j+1}^{n} U(j,k)x(k)}{U(j,j)}; \qquad (2.18)$$

note that $U(j,j) \neq 0$, since L is nonsingular. Thus, given $x(n)$, $x(n-1)$, ..., $x(j+1)$, the value for $x(j)$ can be computed using (2.18).

The pseudocode for Backward Substitution can be found in Table 2.3.

The operation count for Backward Substitution is $n^2 + O(n)$, the same as for Forward Substitution; the proof of the result below is similar to that of Lemma 2.1:

Lemma 2.2. *The operation count for the Backward Substitution algorithm applied to an upper triangular matrix of size n is*

$$n^2 + O(n). \qquad (2.19)$$

2.3. BACKWARD SUBSTITUTION

Table 2.3: Pseudocode for Backward Substitution

Function Call:
$x = \text{backward\_subst}(U,b)$

Input:
U = nonsingular upper triangular matrix of size n
b = column vector of size n

Output:
x = solution to $Ux = b$

$x(n) = \frac{b(n)}{U(n,n)}$;
for $j = (n-1) : 1$
    sum = 0;
    for $k = (j+1) : n$
        sum = sum + $U(j,k)x(k)$;
    end
    $x(j) = \frac{b(j)-\text{sum}}{U(j,j)}$;
end

The relevance of Forward Substitution and Backward Substitution is highlighted by the fact that, for a nonsingular matrix A that is not upper triangular nor lower triangular, a solution to the linear system $Ax = b$ can be found without explicitly computing A^{-1}, by using forward substitution and backward substitution, and the LU decomposition with row pivoting of A; see section 2.6 and the pseudocode from Table 2.10 for details.

We conclude this section with the Backward Substitution pseudocode corresponding to an upper triangular bidiagonal matrix, which will be used for solving linear systems corresponding to tridiagonal matrices; cf. section 2.5.1 and section 6.3.

Let U be an $n \times n$ upper triangular bidiagonal matrix, i.e., a matrix whose only nonzero entries could be the main diagonal entries $U(j,j)$, for $j = 1 : n$, and the upper diagonal entries $U(j, j+1)$, for $j = 1 : (n-1)$. Then, the recursion formula (2.18) simplifies to

$$x(j) = \frac{b(j) - U(j, j+1)x(j+1)}{U(j,j)},$$

which corresponds to the reduced version of the Backward Substitution pseudocode from Table 2.3 included in Table 2.4.

The operation count for the Backward Substitution for upper triangular bidiagonal matrices is

$$1 + 3(n-1) = 3n - 2. \tag{2.20}$$

Table 2.4: Backward Substitution for upper triangular bidiagonal matrices

> Function Call:
> $x = \text{backward\_subst\_bidiag}(U,b)$
>
> Input:
> U = nonsingular upper triangular bidiagonal matrix of size n
> b = column vector of size n
>
> Output:
> x = solution to $Ux = b$
>
> $x(n) = \frac{b(n)}{U(n,n)}$;
> for $j = (n-1) : 1$
> $\quad x(j) = \frac{b(j) - U(j,j+1)x(j+1)}{U(j,j)}$;
> end

2.4 LU decomposition without pivoting

The LU decomposition of a matrix provides a computationally efficient way for solving linear systems; see section 2.5 for details. While the LU decomposition without pivoting does not exist for every nonsingular matrix, it is often used in practice, e.g., for tridiagonal matrices; see section 2.5.1. Moreover, the LU decomposition without pivoting contains the main idea for the recursive algorithm behind both the LU decomposition with row pivoting, which exists for all nonsingular matrices,[2] and the Cholesky decomposition; see section 2.6 and section 6.1, respectively.

Definition 2.1. *The LU decomposition without pivoting of a nonsingular square matrix A consists of finding a lower triangular matrix L with all entries on the main diagonal equal to 1 and a nonsingular upper triangular matrix U such that*

$$A = LU.$$

The L and U matrices are called the LU factors of A.

Note that requiring the diagonal entries of the matrix L to be equal to 1 is necessary for the uniqueness of the LU decomposition: The $n \times n$ matrix A has n^2 entries, while the matrix L has $\frac{n(n+1)}{2}$ entries below the main diagonal and on the main diagonal, and the matrix U has $\frac{n(n+1)}{2}$ entries above the main diagonal and on the main diagonal, for a total of $\frac{n(n+1)}{2} + \frac{n(n+1)}{2} = n^2 + n$ entries. These entries can be thought of as unknowns when looking for the LU decomposition of A. Thus, we have $n^2 + n$ unknowns to be found given the n^2 entries of A. Requiring the n entries of L on the main diagonal to be equal to 1 reduces the number of unknowns to n^2, which creates the framework for the LU decomposition to be unique; see Theorem 2.2.

---

[2] Note that, throughout this book, "LU decomposition" will refer to the LU decomposition without pivoting, unless otherwise specified.

2.4. LU DECOMPOSITION WITHOUT PIVOTING

Definition 2.2. *Let A be an $n \times n$ matrix. The leading principal minors of A are the determinants of the $i \times i$ matrices $A_i = A(1:i, 1:i)$ made of the i^2 upper left entries of A, for $1 \le i \le n$.*[3]

Theorem 2.1. *A matrix has an LU decomposition if and only if all the leading principal minors of the matrix are nonzero.*

Proof. The proof of this result is of no further relevance herein and can be found, e.g., in Datta [12]. □

For the LU decomposition to be consistent, it should be unique, and this is, indeed, the case:

Theorem 2.2. *If it exists, the LU decomposition without row pivoting of a matrix is unique.*

The proof of this result can be found in the technical appendix from Chapter 10; see the proof of Theorem 10.10 from section 10.6.

2.4.1 Pseudocode and operation count for LU decomposition

The L and U matrices from the LU decomposition of a matrix are computed using a recursive algorithm, one row of U and one column of L at a time.

Let A be an $n \times n$ nonsingular matrix with LU decomposition without pivoting. We are looking for an $n \times n$ lower triangular matrix L with main diagonal entries equal to 1 and for an $n \times n$ upper triangular matrix U such that

$$LU = A. \qquad (2.21)$$

Example: 4×4 matrix
For clarity, we include explicit formulations of certain formulas for 4×4 matrices. In particular, formula (2.21) is written as follows if A, L, and U are 4×4 matrices:

$$\begin{pmatrix} 1 & 0 & 0 & 0 \\ L(2,1) & 1 & 0 & 0 \\ L(3,1) & L(3,2) & 1 & 0 \\ L(4,1) & L(4,2) & L(4,3) & 1 \end{pmatrix} \begin{pmatrix} U(1,1) & U(1,2) & U(1,3) & U(1,4) \\ 0 & U(2,2) & U(2,3) & U(2,4) \\ 0 & 0 & U(3,3) & U(3,4) \\ 0 & 0 & 0 & U(4,4) \end{pmatrix}$$

$$= \begin{pmatrix} A(1,1) & A(1,2) & A(1,3) & A(1,4) \\ A(2,1) & A(2,2) & A(2,3) & A(2,4) \\ A(3,1) & A(3,2) & A(3,3) & A(3,4) \\ A(4,1) & A(4,2) & A(4,3) & A(4,4) \end{pmatrix},$$

since all the main diagonal entries of L are required to be equal to 1.

---

[3] For example, the leading principal minors of the matrix $\begin{pmatrix} 2 & -3 & 0 \\ 1 & 1 & 1 \\ -1 & 5 & -3 \end{pmatrix}$ are

$$\det(2) = 2; \quad \det\begin{pmatrix} 2 & -3 \\ 1 & 1 \end{pmatrix} = 5; \quad \det\begin{pmatrix} 2 & -3 & 0 \\ 1 & 1 & 1 \\ -1 & 5 & -3 \end{pmatrix} = -22;$$

see section 5.2.1 for more details and examples.

To compute the first row of U, we multiply the first row of L by the column k of U and use the fact that $LU = A$ to obtain that

$$U(1,k) = A(1,k), \quad \forall \, k = 1:n. \tag{2.22}$$

In particular, for $k = 1$ in (2.22), we find that

$$U(1,1) = A(1,1). \tag{2.23}$$

To compute the first column of L, we multiply the row k of L by the first column of U and obtain that $L(k,1)U(1,1) = A(k,1)$ for all $k = 2:n$, and therefore

$$L(k,1) = \frac{A(k,1)}{U(1,1)} = \frac{A(k,1)}{A(1,1)}, \quad \forall \, k = 1:n; \tag{2.24}$$

see (2.23) for the last equality. Note that the fraction from (2.24) is well defined: $A(1,1) \neq 0$ since $A(1,1)$ is the first leading principal minor of A and the matrix A has an LU decomposition; cf. Theorem 2.1 and Definition 2.1.

The other rows of U and columns of L are computed recursively, one row of U and one column of L at a time, as follows:

To compute the second row of U and the second column of L, write the matrices L and U as

$$L = \begin{pmatrix} 1 & 0 \\ L(2:n,1) & L(2:n,2:n) \end{pmatrix}, \tag{2.25}$$

$$U = \begin{pmatrix} U(1,1) & U(1,2:n) \\ 0 & U(2:n,2:n) \end{pmatrix}, \tag{2.26}$$

where $L(2:n,1) = (L(j,1))_{j=2:n}$ is an $(n-1) \times 1$ column vector; $U(1,2:n) = (U(1,k))_{k=2:n}$ is an $1 \times (n-1)$ row vector; $L(2:n,2:n) = (L(j,k))_{2 \leq j,k \leq n}$ is the $(n-1) \times (n-1)$ lower triangular matrix made of the entries from the rows $2, 3, \ldots, n$ and the columns $2, 3, \ldots, n$ of L; $U(2:n,2:n) = (U(j,k))_{2 \leq j,k \leq n}$ is the $(n-1) \times (n-1)$ upper triangular matrix made of the entries from the rows $2, 3, \ldots, n$ and the columns $2, 3, \ldots, n$ of U.

Similarly, write the matrix A as

$$A = \begin{pmatrix} A(1,1) & A(1,2:n) \\ A(2:n,1) & A(2:n,2:n) \end{pmatrix}, \tag{2.27}$$

where

$$\begin{aligned} A(1,2:n) &= (A(1,k))_{k=2:n} & \text{is an} & \quad 1 \times (n-1) \text{ row vector;} \\ A(2:n,1) &= (A(j,1))_{j=2:n} & \text{is an} & \quad (n-1) \times 1 \text{ column vector;} \\ A(2:n,2:n) &= (A(j,k))_{2 \leq j,k \leq n} & \text{is an} & \quad (n-1) \times (n-1) \text{ matrix.} \end{aligned}$$

From (2.25–2.27), it follows that $LU = A$ is equivalent to

$$\begin{pmatrix} 1 & 0 \\ L(2:n,1) & L(2:n,2:n) \end{pmatrix} \begin{pmatrix} U(1,1) & U(1,2:n) \\ 0 & U(2:n,2:n) \end{pmatrix} \tag{2.28}$$

$$= \begin{pmatrix} A(1,1) & A(1,2:n) \\ A(2:n,1) & A(2:n,2:n) \end{pmatrix}. \tag{2.29}$$

2.4. LU DECOMPOSITION WITHOUT PIVOTING

By using block matrix multiplication to multiply the rows $2:n$ of L by the columns $2:n$ of U, we obtain from (2.28–2.29) that[4]

$$L(2:n,1)\,U(1,2:n) \;+\; L(2:n,2:n)\,U(2:n,2:n) \;=\; A(2:n,2:n), \qquad (2.30)$$

and therefore

$$L(2:n,2:n)\,U(2:n,2:n) \;=\; A(2:n,2:n) \;-\; L(2:n,1)\,U(1,2:n). \qquad (2.31)$$

From (2.31), we conclude that the matrices $L(2:n,2:n)$ and $U(2:n,2:n)$ are the L and U factors from the LU decomposition of the matrix $A(2:n,2:n) - L(2:n,1)U(1,2:n)$. The first row of the matrix $U(2:n,2:n)$ (which coincides with the second row of U without its first entry which is equal to 0), and the first column of the matrix $L(2:n,2:n)$ (which coincides with the second column of L without its first entry which is equal to 0) are computed from the matrix $A(2:n,2:n) - L(2:n,1)U(1,2:n)$ the same way[5] as the first row of U and the first column of L were computed from the matrix A.

Note that, in the implementation of the LU algorithm, we will call computing the matrix $A(2:n,2:n) - L(2:n,1)U(1,2:n)$ "updating" the matrix $A(2:n,2:n)$, and will use the notation

$$A(2:n,2:n) \;=\; A(2:n,2:n) - L(2:n,1)\,U(1,2:n), \qquad (2.32)$$

which means that we overwrite the old entries of $A(2:n,2:n)$ by the entries of $A(2:n,2:n) - L(2:n,1)U(1,2:n)$.

The algorithm continues recursively until all the rows of U and all the columns of L are computed.

Example: 4×4 matrix
For $n = 4$, we obtain that

$$A(1,2:n) \;=\; A(1,2:4) \;=\; \begin{pmatrix} A(1,2) & A(1,3) & A(1,4) \end{pmatrix};$$

$$A(2:n,1) \;=\; A(2:4,1) \;=\; \begin{pmatrix} A(2,1) \\ A(3,1) \\ A(4,1) \end{pmatrix};$$

$$A(2:n,2:n) \;=\; A(2:4,2:4) \;=\; \begin{pmatrix} A(2,2) & A(2,3) & A(2,4) \\ A(3,2) & A(3,3) & A(3,4) \\ A(4,2) & A(4,3) & A(4,4) \end{pmatrix};$$

$$L(2:n,1) \;=\; L(2:4,1) \;=\; \begin{pmatrix} L(2,1) \\ L(3,1) \\ L(4,1) \end{pmatrix};$$

$$L(2:n,2:n) \;=\; L(2:4,2:4) \;=\; \begin{pmatrix} 1 & 0 & 0 \\ L(3,2) & 1 & 0 \\ L(4,2) & L(4,3) & 1 \end{pmatrix}$$

---

[4]Since $L(2:n,1)$ is an $(n-1) \times 1$ column vector and $U(1,2:n)$ is an $1 \times (n-1)$ row vector, it follows that the result of the column vector – row vector multiplication $L(2:n,1)U(1,2:n)$ is an $(n-1) \times (n-1)$ matrix, see (1.6), which is the same size as the matrices $A(2:n,2:n)$, $L(2:n,2:n)$, and $U(2:n,2:n)$. Thus, the matrix dimensions in (2.30) are consistent.

[5]Note that this step requires division by $U(2,2)$; see also (2.24). The fact that $U(2,2) \neq 0$ and therefore the division can be performed is a consequence of the fact that the leading principal minor $\det(A(1:2,1:2))$ is nonzero; see also an exercise at the end of this chapter.

$$U(1, 2:n) = U(1, 2:4) = \begin{pmatrix} U(1,2) & U(1,3) & U(1,4) \end{pmatrix};$$

$$U(2:n, 2:n) = U(2:4, 2:4) = \begin{pmatrix} U(2,2) & U(2,3) & U(2,4) \\ 0 & U(3,3) & U(3,4) \\ 0 & 0 & U(4,4) \end{pmatrix},$$

and therefore (2.28–2.29) is written as follows if A, L, and U are 4×4 matrices:

$$\begin{pmatrix} 1 & 0 \\ L(2:4, 1) & L(2:4, 2:4) \end{pmatrix} \begin{pmatrix} U(1,1) & U(1, 2:4) \\ 0 & U(2:4, 2:4) \end{pmatrix} \quad (2.33)$$

$$= \begin{pmatrix} A(1,1) & A(1, 2:4) \\ A(2:4, 1) & A(2:4, 2:4) \end{pmatrix} \quad (2.34)$$

From (2.33–2.34), we find by block matrix multiplication the following explicit form of (2.30) for 4×4 matrices:

$$L(2:4, 1)\, U(1, 2:4) + L(2:4, 2:4)\, U(2:4, 2:4) = A(2:4, 2:4),$$

and therefore

$$L(2:4, 2:4)\, U(2:4, 2:4) = A(2:4, 2:4) - L(2:4, 1)\, U(1, 2:4). \quad (2.35)$$

The LU decomposition without pivoting algorithm can be implemented recursively as detailed below; see also the pseudocode from Table 2.5.

Let A be a matrix with LU decomposition without pivoting, and let L and U be the LU factors of A.

- Compute the first row of U and the first column of L:

> for $k = 1 : n$
> $\quad U(1, k) = A(1, k)$
> $\quad L(k, 1) = \frac{A(k,1)}{U(1,1)}$
> end

Note that, in the "for" loop above, we compute $L(1,1) = 1$, rather than requiring it.
- Update the $(n-1) \times (n-1)$ lower right part of A as follows:

$$A(2:n, 2:n) = A(2:n, 2:n) - L(2:n, 1)\, U(1, 2:n), \quad (2.36)$$

see (2.32), which can be written entry by entry as follows:

> for $j = 2 : n$
> $\quad$ for $k = 2 : n$
> $\quad\quad A(j, k) = A(j, k) - L(j, 1)U(1, k)$
> $\quad$ end
> end

Every row of U and column of L are thereafter computed recursively from the latest updated part of the matrix A; see also the 4×4 example below. For example, to compute the i-th row of U and the i-th column of L, we do the following:

- Compute the i-th row of U and the i-th column of L:

2.4. LU DECOMPOSITION WITHOUT PIVOTING

$$\boxed{\begin{array}{l}\text{for } k = i : n \\ \quad U(i,k) = A(i,k) \\ \quad L(k,i) = \frac{A(k,i)}{U(i,i)} \\ \text{end}\end{array}}$$

- Update the $(n-i) \times (n-i)$ lower right part of A as follows:

$$A(i+1:n, i+1:n) = A(i+1:n, i+1:n) \\ - L(i+1:n, i)\, U(i, i+1:n), \qquad (2.37)$$

which can be written entry by entry as follows:

$$\boxed{\begin{array}{l}\text{for } j = (i+1) : n \\ \quad \text{for } k = (i+1) : n \\ \qquad A(j,k) = A(j,k) - L(j,i)U(i,k) \\ \quad \text{end} \\ \text{end}\end{array}}$$

Further clarification on the recursive part of the LU decomposition can be found in the example below for a 4×4 matrix.

Example: Let

$$A = \begin{pmatrix} 2 & -1 & 3 & 0 \\ -4 & 5 & -7 & -2 \\ -2 & 10 & -4 & -7 \\ 4 & -14 & 8 & 10 \end{pmatrix}. \qquad (2.38)$$

Let L and U be the LU factors of A. The entries of the first row of U are given by (2.22), i.e., $U(1,k) = A(1,k)$ for $k = 1:4$:

$$U(1,1) = 2; \quad U(1,2) = -1; \quad U(1,3) = 3; \quad U(1,4) = 0.$$

The entries of the first column of L are given by (2.24), i.e., $L(k,1) = \frac{A(k,1)}{U(1,1)}$ for $k = 1:4$:

$$L(1,1) = 1; \quad L(2,1) = \frac{-4}{U(1,1)} = \frac{-4}{2} = -2; \quad L(3,1) = \frac{-2}{U(1,1)} = \frac{-2}{2} = -1;$$

$$L(4,1) = \frac{4}{U(1,1)} = \frac{4}{2} = 2.$$

Then, the current forms of L and U are

$$L = \begin{pmatrix} 1 & 0 & 0 & 0 \\ -2 & 1 & 0 & 0 \\ -1 & L(3,2) & 1 & 0 \\ 2 & L(4,2) & L(4,3) & 1 \end{pmatrix}; \quad U = \begin{pmatrix} 2 & -1 & 3 & 0 \\ 0 & U(2,2) & U(2,3) & U(2,4) \\ 0 & 0 & U(3,3) & U(3,4) \\ 0 & 0 & 0 & U(4,4) \end{pmatrix}. \\ (2.39)$$

The updated form of the 3×3 matrix $A(2:4, 2:4)$ is computed using (2.36), from $A(2:4, 2:4)$ obtained from (2.38) and with L and U given by (2.39), as follows:

$$A(2:4, 2:4) \\ = A(2:4, 2:4) - L(2:4, 1)\, U(1, 2:4)$$

$$= \begin{pmatrix} 5 & -7 & -2 \\ 10 & -4 & -7 \\ -14 & 8 & 10 \end{pmatrix} - \begin{pmatrix} -2 \\ -1 \\ 2 \end{pmatrix} (-1 \ 3 \ 0)$$

$$= \begin{pmatrix} 5 & -7 & -2 \\ 10 & -4 & -7 \\ -14 & 8 & 10 \end{pmatrix} - \begin{pmatrix} 2 & -6 & 0 \\ 1 & -3 & 0 \\ -2 & 6 & 0 \end{pmatrix}$$

$$= \begin{pmatrix} 3 & -1 & -2 \\ 9 & -1 & -7 \\ -12 & 2 & 10 \end{pmatrix}.$$

Thus, the updated form of the 3×3 matrix $A(2:4, 2:4)$ is

$$A(2:4, 2:4) = \begin{pmatrix} 3 & -1 & -2 \\ 9 & -1 & -7 \\ -12 & 2 & 10 \end{pmatrix}. \tag{2.40}$$

Then,

$$L(2:4, 2:4)\, U(2:4, 2:4) = \begin{pmatrix} 3 & -1 & -2 \\ 9 & -1 & -7 \\ -12 & 2 & 10 \end{pmatrix},$$

which can be written as

$$\begin{pmatrix} 1 & 0 & 0 \\ L(3,2) & 1 & 0 \\ L(4,2) & L(4,3) & 1 \end{pmatrix} \begin{pmatrix} U(2,2) & U(2,3) & U(2,4) \\ 0 & U(3,3) & U(3,4) \\ 0 & 0 & U(4,4) \end{pmatrix} = \begin{pmatrix} 3 & -1 & -2 \\ 9 & -1 & -7 \\ -12 & 2 & 10 \end{pmatrix}.$$

The unknown entries from the second row of U and from the second column of L can be computed from the 3×3 matrix above as follows:

$$U(2,2) = 3; \quad U(2,3) = -1; \quad U(2,4) = -2;$$

$$L(2,2) = 1; \quad L(3,2) = \frac{9}{U(2,2)} = \frac{9}{3} = 3; \quad L(4,2) = \frac{-12}{U(2,2)} = \frac{-12}{3} = -4.$$

Then, the current forms of L and U are

$$L = \begin{pmatrix} 1 & 0 & 0 & 0 \\ -2 & 1 & 0 & 0 \\ -1 & 3 & 1 & 0 \\ 2 & -4 & L(4,3) & 1 \end{pmatrix}; \quad U = \begin{pmatrix} 2 & -1 & 3 & 0 \\ 0 & 3 & -1 & -2 \\ 0 & 0 & U(3,3) & U(3,4) \\ 0 & 0 & 0 & U(4,4) \end{pmatrix}. \tag{2.41}$$

The updated form of the 2×2 matrix $A(3:4, 3:4)$ is computed using (2.37), from $A(3:4, 3:4)$ obtained from (2.40) and with L and U given by (2.41), as follows:

$$A(3:4, 3:4)$$
$$= A(3:4, 3:4) - L(3:4, 2)\, U(2, 3:4)$$
$$= \begin{pmatrix} -1 & -7 \\ 2 & 10 \end{pmatrix} - \begin{pmatrix} 3 \\ -4 \end{pmatrix} (-1 \ -2)$$
$$= \begin{pmatrix} -1 & -7 \\ 2 & 10 \end{pmatrix} - \begin{pmatrix} -3 & -6 \\ 4 & 8 \end{pmatrix}$$
$$= \begin{pmatrix} 2 & -1 \\ -2 & 2 \end{pmatrix}.$$

2.4. LU DECOMPOSITION WITHOUT PIVOTING

Thus, the updated form of the 2×2 matrix $A(3:4, 3:4)$ is

$$A(3:4, 3:4) = \begin{pmatrix} 2 & -1 \\ -2 & 2 \end{pmatrix}. \tag{2.42}$$

Then,

$$L(3:4, 3) U(3, 3:4) = \begin{pmatrix} 2 & -1 \\ -2 & 2 \end{pmatrix},$$

which can be written as

$$\begin{pmatrix} 1 & 0 \\ L(4,3) & 1 \end{pmatrix} \begin{pmatrix} U(3,3) & U(3,4) \\ 0 & U(4,4) \end{pmatrix} = \begin{pmatrix} 2 & -1 \\ -2 & 2 \end{pmatrix}.$$

The unknown entries from the third row of U and from the third column of L can be computed from the 2×2 matrix above as follows:

$$U(3,3) = 2; \quad U(3,4) = -1;$$

$$L(3,3) = 1; \quad L(4,3) = \frac{-2}{U(3,3)} = \frac{-2}{2} = -1.$$

Then, the current forms of L and U are

$$L = \begin{pmatrix} 1 & 0 & 0 & 0 \\ -2 & 1 & 0 & 0 \\ -1 & 3 & 1 & 0 \\ 2 & -4 & -1 & 1 \end{pmatrix}; \quad U = \begin{pmatrix} 2 & -1 & 3 & 0 \\ 0 & 3 & -1 & -2 \\ 0 & 0 & 2 & -1 \\ 0 & 0 & 0 & U(4,4) \end{pmatrix}. \tag{2.43}$$

The updated form of $A(4,4)$, which is a number, is computed using (2.37), from $A(4,4)$ obtained from (2.42) and with L and U given by (2.43), as follows:

$$A(4,4) = A(4,4) - L(4,3)U(3,4) = 2 - (-1) \cdot (-1) = 1,$$

which corresponds to

$$L(4,4) = 1; \quad U(4,4) = 1.$$

We conclude that the matrix A has an LU decomposition with the following L and U factors:

$$L = \begin{pmatrix} 1 & 0 & 0 & 0 \\ -2 & 1 & 0 & 0 \\ -1 & 3 & 1 & 0 \\ 2 & -4 & -1 & 1 \end{pmatrix}; \quad U = \begin{pmatrix} 2 & -1 & 3 & 0 \\ 0 & 3 & -1 & -2 \\ 0 & 0 & 2 & -1 \\ 0 & 0 & 0 & 1 \end{pmatrix}. \quad \square$$

The pseudocode for the LU decomposition without pivoting, given as a function call $[L, U] = \text{lu\_no\_pivoting}(A)$, can be found in Table 2.5.

Lemma 2.3. *The operation count for the LU decomposition without pivoting of an $n \times n$ nonsingular matrix is*

$$\frac{2}{3}n^3 + O(n^2). \tag{2.44}$$

Proof. At step i, the "for" loop

Table 2.5: Pseudocode for LU decomposition without pivoting

```
Function Call:
[L, U] = lu_no_pivoting(A)

Input:
A = nonsingular matrix of size n with LU decomposition

Output:
L = lower triangular matrix with entries 1 on main diagonal
U = upper triangular matrix
such that A = LU

for i = 1 : (n − 1)
   for k = i : n
      U(i, k) = A(i, k);           // compute row i of U
      L(k, i) = A(k, i)/U(i, i);   // compute column i of L
   end
   for j = (i + 1) : n
      for k = (i + 1) : n
         A(j, k) = A(j, k) − L(j, i)U(i, k);
      end
   end
end
L(n, n) = 1; U(n, n) = A(n, n)
```

```
for k = i : n
   U(i, k) = A(i, k)
   L(k, i) = A(k, i)/U(i, i)
end
```

to compute the i-th row of U and the i-th column of L requires $n - i + 1$ operations. Also at step i, the double "for" loop

```
for j = (i + 1) : n
   for k = (i + 1) : n
      A(j, k) = A(j, k) − L(j, i)U(i, k)
   end
end
```

to update $A(i+1:n, i+1:n)$ requires

$$\sum_{j=i+1}^{n} \sum_{k=i+1}^{n} 2 = 2(n-i)^2$$

operations.

When accounting for the outside "for" loop "for $i = 1 : (n - 1)$", see Table 2.5, we obtain that the operation count for the LU decomposition without pivoting is

$$\sum_{i=1}^{n-1} \left(2(n-i)^2 + n - i + 1 \right). \tag{2.45}$$

2.4. LINEAR SOLVERS USING LU DECOMPOSITION

Recall that

$$\sum_{l=1}^{p} l = \frac{p(p+1)}{2} \quad \text{and} \quad \sum_{l=1}^{p} l^2 = \frac{p(p+1)(2p+1)}{6}; \qquad (2.46)$$

see, e.g., section 10.3.1 from Stefanica [36].

Then, by letting $l = n - i$ in (2.45) and using (2.46) for $p = n - 1$, we obtain that

$$\begin{aligned}
\sum_{i=1}^{n-1} \left(2(n-i)^2 + n - i + 1\right) &= \sum_{l=1}^{n-1}(2l^2 + l + 1) = 2\sum_{l=1}^{n-1} l^2 + \sum_{l=1}^{n-1} l + \sum_{l=1}^{n-1} 1 \\
&= 2\frac{(n-1)n(2n-1)}{6} + \frac{(n-1)n}{2} + n - 1 \\
&= \frac{2n^3}{3} - \frac{n^2}{2} + \frac{5n}{6} - 1 \\
&= \frac{2}{3}n^3 + O(n^2);
\end{aligned}$$

see (10.79) in Section 10.2.3 for the last equality.

We conclude that the operation count for the LU decomposition without pivoting is $\frac{2}{3}n^3 + O(n^2)$. □

2.5 Linear solvers using the LU decomposition without pivoting

Let A be a nonsingular square matrix of size n, and let b be a column vector of size n. If the matrix A has an LU decomposition without pivoting $A = LU$, then, solving a linear system $Ax = b$ is equivalent to solving

$$LUx = b.$$

This is the same as solving

$$Ly = b$$

for y, which can be done using forward substitution since the matrix L is lower triangular, and then solving

$$Ux = y$$

for x, which can be done using backward substitution since the matrix U is upper triangular.

The pseudocode for solving a linear system using the LU decomposition without pivoting of a matrix can be found in Table 2.6.

The operation count for the pseudocode from Table 2.6 is as follows:
- $\frac{2}{3}n^3 + O(n^2)$ for the LU decomposition of A; cf. (2.44);
- $n^2 + O(n)$ for the forward substitution for solving $Ly = b$; cf. (2.8);
- $n^2 + O(n)$ for the backward substitution for solving $Ux = y$; cf. (2.19),

Table 2.6: Linear solver using LU decomposition without pivoting

---

Function Call:
$x = $ linear_solve_LU_no_pivoting(A,b)

Input:
$A = $ nonsingular square matrix of size n with LU decomposition
$b = $ column vector of size n

Output:
$x = $ solution to $Ax = b$

$[L, U] = $ lu_no_pivoting(A);	// LU decomposition of A
$y = $ forward_subst(L, b);	// solve $Ly = b$
$x = $ backward_subst(U, y);	// solve $Ux = y$

---

for a total operation count of

$$\left(\frac{2}{3}n^3 + O(n^2)\right) + (n^2 + O(n)) + (n^2 + O(n)) = \frac{2}{3}n^3 + O(n^2);$$

see (10.86) in Section 10.2.3 for a proof of the last equality.

2.5.1 LU linear solvers for tridiagonal matrices

Solving linear systems corresponding to tridiagonal matrices having LU decomposition is often needed for practical applications such as cubic spline interpolation and the finite difference solution of the Black–Scholes PDE. We discuss the solution to tridiagonal linear systems here, and furthermore in section 6.3 when investigating efficient linear solvers for tridiagonal symmetric positive definite matrices.

We begin by showing that the L and U factors from the LU decomposition without pivoting of a tridiagonal matrix are bidiagonal matrices.[6]

Let A be an $n \times n$ tridiagonal matrix, i.e., such that

$$A(j,k) = 0, \quad \forall\, 1 \leq j, k \leq n \text{ with } |j - k| \geq 2, \tag{2.47}$$

and assume that the matrix A has an LU decomposition without pivoting.[7] Let L and U be the LU factors of A. We will show that L is a lower triangular bidiagonal matrix, i.e., the only entries of L that can be nonzero are the main diagonal entries $L(i,i)$, for $i = 1 : n$, and the lower diagonal entries $L(i, i-1)$, for $i = 2 : n$, and that U is an upper triangular bidiagonal matrix, i.e., the only entries of U that can be nonzero are the main diagonal entries $U(i,i)$, for $i = 1 : n$, and the upper diagonal entries $U(i, i+1)$, for $i = 1 : (n-1)$.

Following step by step the LU decomposition without row pivoting from section 2.4.1, we compute the entries from the first row of U as $U(1, k) = A(1, k)$, for

---

[6]More generally, the L and U factors from the LU decomposition without pivoting of a banded matrix of band m are also banded of band m; see an exercise from the end of this chapter and Stefanica [38] for details.

[7]A strictly diagonally dominated tridiagonal matrix is an example of a tridiagonal matrix with LU decomposition without pivoting; see section 4.3.

2.5. LINEAR SOLVERS USING LU DECOMPOSITION

all $k = 1 : n$, and the entries from the first column of L as $L(k,1) = \frac{A(k,1)}{U(1,1)}$, for all $k = 1 : n$. Note that $A(1,k) = 0$ if $3 \leq k \leq n$ and $A(k,1) = 0$ if $3 \leq k \leq n$, since A is a tridiagonal matrix; cf. (2.47). Then, $U(1,k) = 0$ if $3 \leq k \leq n$ and $L(k,1) = 0$ if $3 \leq k \leq n$, and therefore the only possible nonzero entries from the first row of U and from the first column of L correspond to an upper triangular bidiagonal form for U and a lower triangular bidiagonal form for L.

Moreover, since

$$U(1, 2:n) = (U(1,2) \ 0 \ \ldots \ 0) \quad \text{and} \quad L(2:n,1) = \begin{pmatrix} L(2,1) \\ 0 \\ \vdots \\ 0 \end{pmatrix},$$

it follows that

$$L(2:n,1)\,U(1,2:n) = \begin{pmatrix} L(2,1) \\ 0 \\ \vdots \\ 0 \end{pmatrix} (U(1,2) \ 0 \ \ldots \ 0)$$

$$= \begin{pmatrix} L(2,1)U(1,2) & 0 & \ldots & 0 \\ 0 & 0 & \ldots & 0 \\ \vdots & \vdots & \ldots & \vdots \\ 0 & 0 & \ldots & 0 \end{pmatrix}.$$

Thus, updating the $(n-1) \times (n-1)$ lower right part of A as in (2.36), i.e.,

$$A(2:n, 2:n) = A(2:n, 2:n) - L(2:n,1)\,U(1, 2:n),$$

only involves changing the value of $A(2,2)$ to

$$A(2,2) = A(2,2) - L(2,1)U(1,2),$$

which preserves the tridiagonal structure of the matrix $A(2:n, 2:n)$.

The tridiagonal structure of the updated part of A and the bidiagonal structure of U and L will be further preserved as every row of U and every column of L are computed.

For example, assuming that the updated form $A(i:n, i:n)$ of the matrix A is tridiagonal after $i-1$ rows of U and $i-1$ columns of L are computed, the i-th row of U is computed as $U(i,k) = A(i,k)$, for all $k = i:n$, and the i-th column of L is computed as $L(k,i) = \frac{A(k,i)}{U(i,i)}$, for all $k = i:n$. Since $A(i:n, i:n)$ is tridiagonal, it follows that $A(i,k) = 0$ if $i+2 \leq k \leq n$, and therefore

$$U(i,k) = 0, \quad \forall\, i+2 \leq k \leq n,$$

and also that $A(k,i) = 0$ if $i+2 \leq k \leq n$, and therefore

$$L(k,i) = 0, \quad \forall\, i+2 \leq k \leq n.$$

Thus, the only possible nonzero entries from the i-th row of U and from the i-th column of L correspond to an upper triangular bidiagonal form for U and a lower triangular bidiagonal form for L.

Moreover, since

$$U(i, i+1:n) = (U(i, i+1) \ 0 \ \ldots \ 0) \quad \text{and} \quad L(i+1:n, i) = \begin{pmatrix} L(i+1, i) \\ 0 \\ \vdots \\ 0 \end{pmatrix},$$

we find that

$$L(i+1:n, i)U(i, i+1:n) = \begin{pmatrix} L(i+1, i) \\ 0 \\ \vdots \\ 0 \end{pmatrix} (U(i, i+1) \ 0 \ \ldots \ 0)$$

$$= \begin{pmatrix} L(i+1, i)U(i, i+1) & 0 & \ldots & 0 \\ 0 & 0 & \ldots & 0 \\ \vdots & \vdots & \ddots & \vdots \\ 0 & 0 & \ldots & 0 \end{pmatrix}.$$

Then, updating the $(n-i) \times (n-i)$ lower right part of A as in (2.37), i.e.,

$$A(i+1:n, i+1:n) = A(i+1:n, i+1:n) - L(i+1:n, i)\, U(i, i+1:n),$$

involves only changing the value of the $A(i+1, i+1)$ entry to

$$A(i+1, i+1) = A(i+1, i+1) - L(i+1, i)U(i, i+1),$$

which preserves the tridiagonal structure of the updated $(n-i-1) \times (n-i-1)$ matrix $A(i+1:n, i+1:n)$.

The LU decomposition routine from Table 2.5 simplifies to the routine from Table 2.7 for tridiagonal matrices with LU decomposition without pivoting.

The operation count for the tridiagonal LU decomposition without pivoting from Table 2.7 is $3n - 3$ operations: in each step of the "for" loop

```
for i = 1 : (n − 1)
    L(i, i) = 1; L(i + 1, i) = A(i + 1, i)/A(i, i);
    U(i, i) = A(i, i); U(i, i + 1) = A(i, i + 1);
    A(i + 1, i + 1) = A(i + 1, i + 1) − L(i + 1, i)U(i, i + 1);
end
```

we perform 3 operations, for a total number of operations of

$$3(n-1) = 3n - 3. \tag{2.48}$$

Thus, if A is a tridiagonal matrix with LU decomposition without pivoting, the LU decomposition $[L, U] = \text{lu\_no\_pivoting}(A)$ from the linear solver routine from Table 2.6 can be replaced by the solver $[L, U] = \text{lu\_no\_pivoting\_tridiag}(A)$ from Table 2.7.

Moreover, since the matrix L is lower triangular bidiagonal, the forward substitution $y = \text{forward\_subst}(L, b)$ from Table 2.6 can be replaced by the forward substitution $y = \text{forward\_subst\_bidiag}(L, b)$ for lower triangular bidiagonal matrices, see

2.5. LINEAR SOLVERS USING LU DECOMPOSITION

Table 2.7: LU decomposition without pivoting for tridiagonal matrices

---
Function Call:
$[L, U] = $ lu_no_pivoting_tridiag(A)

Input:
$A = $ nonsingular tridiagonal matrix of size n with LU decomposition

Output:
$L = $ lower triangular bidiagonal matrix with entries 1 on main diagonal
$U = $ upper triangular bidiagonal matrix
such that $A = LU$

for $i = 1 : (n-1)$
   $L(i,i) = 1; L(i+1,i) = A(i+1,i)/A(i,i);$
   $U(i,i) = A(i,i); U(i,i+1) = A(i,i+1);$
   $A(i+1,i+1) = A(i+1,i+1) - L(i+1,i)U(i,i+1);$
end
$L(n,n) = 1; U(n,n) = A(n,n)$

Table 2.2, and, since the matrix U is upper triangular bidiagonal, the backward substitution $x = $ backward_subst(U, y) from Table 2.6 can be replaced by the backward substitution $x = $ backward_subst_bidiag(U, y) for upper triangular bidiagonal matrices, see Table 2.4.

The resulting routine for solving linear systems corresponding to tridiagonal matrices using LU decomposition without pivoting can be found in Table 2.8.

Table 2.8: Tridiagonal linear solver using LU decomposition without pivoting

---
Function Call:
$x = $ linear_solve_LU_no_pivoting_tridiag(A,b)

Input:
$A = $ nonsingular tridiagonal matrix of size n with LU decomposition
$b = $ column vector of size n

Output:
$x = $ solution to $Ax = b$

$[L, U] = $ lu_no_pivoting_tridiag(A);   // LU decomposition of A
$y = $ forward_subst_bidiag(L, b);   // solve $Ly = b$
$x = $ backward_subst_bidiag(U, y);   // solve $Ux = y$

Using the explicit implementations of lu_no_pivoting_tridiag from Table 2.7, of forward_subst_bidiag from Table 2.2, and of backward_subst_bidiag from Table 2.4, the explicit implementation of the tridiagonal linear solver from Table 2.8 can be found in Table 2.9.

Note that, in the pseudocode from Table 2.9, the following further simplifications

Table 2.9: Explicit tridiagonal linear solver using LU decomposition without pivoting

---

Function Call:
$x = $ linear_solve_LU_no_pivoting_tridiag(A,b)

Input:
$A = $ nonsingular tridiagonal matrix of size n with LU decomposition
$b = $ column vector of size n

Output:
$x = $ solution to $Ax = b$

for $i = 1 : (n-1)$
  $L(i,i) = 1; L(i+1,i) = A(i+1,i)/A(i,i);$
  $U(i,i) = A(i,i); U(i,i+1) = A(i,i+1);$
  $A(i+1,i+1) = A(i+1,i+1) - L(i+1,i)U(i,i+1);$
end
$L(n,n) = 1; U(n,n) = A(n,n);$ // LU decomposition of A
$x(1) = b(1);$
for $j = 2 : n$
  $x(j) = b(j) - L(j,j-1)x(j-1);$
end   // forward substitution for $Ly = b$
$x(n) = \frac{y(n)}{U(n,n)};$
for $j = (n-1) : 1$
  $x(j) = \frac{y(j) - U(j,j+1)x(j+1)}{U(j,j)};$
end   // backward substitution for $Ux = y$

---

in the explicit implementation of $y = $ forward_subst_bidiag(L,b), see Table 2.2, are included:

- since $L(1,1) = 1$, $x(1) = \frac{b(1)}{L(1,1)}$ from Table 2.2 becomes $x(1) = b(1)$;
- since $L(j,j) = 1$, $x(j) = \frac{b(j) - L(j,j-1)x(j-1)}{L(j,j)}$ from Table 2.2 becomes

$$x(j) = b(j) - L(j,j-1)x(j-1).$$

Thus, the operation count for the forward substitution "for" loop

---
for $j = 2 : n$
  $x(j) = b(j) - L(j,j-1)x(j-1);$
end

---

from Table 2.9 is

$$2(n-1) = 2n - 2. \qquad (2.49)$$

The operation count for the pseudocode from Table 2.9 is as follows:
- $3n - 3$ for the LU decomposition of A; cf. (2.48);
- $2n - 2$ for the forward substitution for $Ly = b$; cf. (2.49);
- $3n - 2$ for the backward substitution for $Ux = y$; cf. (2.20),

for a total operation count of

$$(3n - 3) + (2n - 2) + (3n - 2) = 8n - 7 = 8n + O(1);$$

see (10.76) in Section 10.2.3 for a proof of the last equality.

2.6 LU decomposition with row pivoting

The LU decomposition without pivoting of a matrix has a major drawback: it does not exist for all nonsingular matrices. In fact, it does not exist even for very well conditioned matrices. For example, the matrix $A = \begin{pmatrix} 0 & 1 \\ 1 & 1 \end{pmatrix}$ does not have an LU decomposition without row pivoting. If it did, then $A = LU$ could be written as

$$\begin{pmatrix} 1 & 0 \\ L(2,1) & 1 \end{pmatrix} \begin{pmatrix} U(1,1) & U(1,2) \\ 0 & U(2,2) \end{pmatrix} = \begin{pmatrix} 0 & 1 \\ 1 & 1 \end{pmatrix}. \qquad (2.50)$$

By multiplying the matrix U by the first row of L, we find that $U(1,1) = 0$ and $U(1,2) = 1$. Thus, (2.50) becomes

$$\begin{pmatrix} 1 & 0 \\ L(2,1) & 1 \end{pmatrix} \begin{pmatrix} 0 & 1 \\ 0 & U(2,2) \end{pmatrix} = \begin{pmatrix} 0 & 1 \\ 1 & 1 \end{pmatrix}.$$

However, multiplying the second row of L by the first column of U we obtain that

$$L(2,1) \cdot 0 + 1 \cdot 0 = 1,$$

which is not possible. The reason for this is that $A(1,1) = 0$, and, since $A(1,1)$ is the first leading principal minor of A, the matrix A does not satisfy the requirement for the existence of the LU decomposition without pivoting from Theorem 2.1, i.e., that all the leading principal minors are nonzero.

However, any nonsingular matrix has an LU decomposition with row pivoting. To introduce the concept of pivoting, recall from section 10.1.2 that a permutation matrix is a matrix obtained by permuting the rows of the identity matrix, and that matrix multiplication by a permutation matrix to the left results in a corresponding permutation of the rows of the matrix. For example, the permutation matrix

$$P = \begin{pmatrix} 0 & 0 & 1 & 0 \\ 1 & 0 & 0 & 0 \\ 0 & 0 & 0 & 1 \\ 0 & 1 & 0 & 0 \end{pmatrix} \text{ has row form } P = \begin{pmatrix} e_3^t \\ e_1^t \\ e_4^t \\ e_2^t \end{pmatrix},$$

and is also denoted, using column notation, as

$$P = \begin{pmatrix} 3 \\ 1 \\ 4 \\ 2 \end{pmatrix}.$$

If A is a 4×4 matrix with row form

$$A = \begin{pmatrix} r_1 \\ r_2 \\ r_3 \\ r_4 \end{pmatrix}, \text{ then } PA = \begin{pmatrix} r_3 \\ r_1 \\ r_4 \\ r_2 \end{pmatrix}.$$

Definition 2.3. *The LU decomposition with row pivoting of a nonsingular square matrix A consists of finding a permutation matrix P, a lower triangular matrix L with all entries on the main diagonal equal to 1, and a nonsingular upper triangular matrix U such that*
$$PA = LU.$$

Theorem 2.3. *Any nonsingular matrix has an LU decomposition with row pivoting.*

A proof of this result can be found, e.g., in Datta [12].

For a given permutation matrix P, the L and U factors from $PA = LU$ are unique. However, for any nonsingular matrix A, there may be many different permutation matrices P such that the matrix PA has an LU decomposition. The algorithm described below, and whose pseudocode is included in Table 2.10, uniquely identifies the permutation matrix P and the L and U factors for the LU decomposition with row pivoting of a given nonsingular matrix A. Note that all the entries of the matrix L identified using this algorithm are less than or equal in absolute value to 1.

Let A be a nonsingular matrix. We identify a permutation matrix P and a lower triangular matrix L (with main diagonal entries equal to 1) and an upper triangular matrix U as detailed below.

- Identify the largest entry (in absolute value) in the first column vector $A(1:n,1)$ of A. Switch the corresponding row and the first row of A, and do the same for the permutation matrix P, which was initialized to be equal to the identity matrix:

> $P = 1:n$
> find i_max, the location of the largest entry from $A(1:n,1)$
> $vv = A(1,1:n); A(1,1:n) = A(i\_max,1:n); A(i\_max,1:n) = vv;$
> $cc = P(1); P(1) = P(i\_max); P(i\_max) = cc;$
> clear vv cc

- Compute the first row of U and the first column of L:

> for $k = 1:n$
> $\quad U(1,k) = A(1,k)$
> $\quad L(k,1) = \frac{A(k,1)}{U(1,1)}$
> end

- Update the $(n-1) \times (n-1)$ lower right part of A as follows:

$$A(2:n, 2:n) = A(2:n, 2:n) - L(2:n, 1)\, U(1, 2:n), \qquad (2.51)$$

which can be written entry by entry as follows:

> for $j = 2:n$
> $\quad$ for $k = 2:n$
> $\quad\quad A(j,k) = A(j,k) - L(j,1)U(1,k)$
> $\quad$ end
> end

The row permutation process as well as the computation of every row of U and column of L are done recursively from the latest updated part of the matrix A; see also the 5×5 example below. For example, to compute the i-th row of U and the i-th column of L, we do the following:

2.6. LU DECOMPOSITION WITH ROW PIVOTING

- Identify the largest entry (in absolute value) in the first column vector $A(i:n,i)$ of $A(i:n,i:n)$. Switch the corresponding row and the first row of $A(i:n,i:n)$. Switch the corresponding row and the row i of the permutation matrix P. Also, switch all the entries already computed from the corresponding row and the row i of the matrix L:

$$\boxed{\begin{array}{l} \text{find } i\_max, \text{ the location of the largest entry from } A(i:n,i) \\ vv = A(i,i:n); \; A(i,i:n) = A(i\_max,i:n); \; A(i\_max,i:n) = vv; \\ cc = P(i); \; P(i) = P(i\_max); \; P(i\_max) = cc; \\ ww = L(i,1:(i-1)); \\ L(i,1:(i-1)) = L(i\_max,1:(i-1)); \; L(i\_max,1:(i-1)) = ww; \\ \text{clear } vv \; ww \; cc \end{array}}$$

- Compute the i-th row of U and the i-th column of L:

$$\boxed{\begin{array}{l} \text{for } k = i:n \\ \quad U(i,k) = A(i,k) \\ \quad L(k,i) = \frac{A(k,i)}{U(i,i)} \\ \text{end} \end{array}}$$

- Update the $(n-i) \times (n-i)$ lower right part of A as follows:

$$A(i+1:n, i+1:n) = A(i+1:n, i+1:n) \\ - L(i+1:n, i) \, U(i, i+1:n), \qquad (2.52)$$

which can be written entry by entry as follows:

$$\boxed{\begin{array}{l} \text{for } j = (i+1):n \\ \quad \text{for } k = (i+1):n \\ \quad\quad A(j,k) = A(j,k) - L(j,i)U(i,k) \\ \quad \text{end} \\ \text{end} \end{array}}$$

Further clarification on the recursive part of the LU decomposition with row pivoting can be found in the example below for a 5×5 matrix.

Example: Let

$$A = \begin{pmatrix} 1 & 2 & -7 & -1.5 & 2 \\ 4 & 4 & 0 & -6 & -2 \\ -2 & -1 & 2 & 6 & 2.5 \\ 0 & -2 & 2 & -4 & 1 \\ 2 & 1 & 13 & -5 & 3.5 \end{pmatrix}.$$

Let L and U be the LU factors from the LU decomposition with row pivoting of A corresponding to a permutation matrix P which will be identified below, i.e., such that $PA = LU$.

The permutation matrix P is set equal to the identity matrix and will be updated as rows are switched. We will use the following notation for the row form of the permutation matrix P:

$$P = \begin{pmatrix} 1 \\ 2 \\ 3 \\ 4 \\ 5 \end{pmatrix} = \begin{pmatrix} e_1^t \\ e_2^t \\ e_3^t \\ e_4^t \\ e_5^t \end{pmatrix}.$$

We begin by identifying the largest entry, in absolute value, from the first column
$\begin{pmatrix} 1 \\ 4 \\ -2 \\ 0 \\ 2 \end{pmatrix}$
of A. That entry is 4, corresponding to the second row of A. We switch the first row and the second row of A. The new form of the matrix A is

$$A = \begin{pmatrix} 4 & 4 & 0 & -6 & -2 \\ 1 & 2 & -7 & -1.5 & 2 \\ -2 & -1 & 2 & 6 & 2.5 \\ 0 & -2 & 2 & -4 & 1 \\ 2 & 1 & 13 & -5 & 3.5 \end{pmatrix}. \quad (2.53)$$

We record the switch by permuting the first row and the second row of P as follows:

$$P = \begin{pmatrix} 1 \\ 2 \\ 3 \\ 4 \\ 5 \end{pmatrix} \quad \text{becomes} \quad P = \begin{pmatrix} 2 \\ 1 \\ 3 \\ 4 \\ 5 \end{pmatrix} = \begin{pmatrix} e_2^t \\ e_1^t \\ e_3^t \\ e_4^t \\ e_5^t \end{pmatrix}. \quad (2.54)$$

After the row permutations are done, the first row of U and the first column of L are computed as in the algorithm for LU decomposition without row pivoting.

The entries of first row of U are given by (2.22), i.e., $U(1,k) = A(1,k)$ for $k = 1:5$, where the matrix A is given by (2.53):

$$U(1,1) = 4; \quad U(1,2) = 4; \quad U(1,3) = 0; \quad U(1,4) = -6; \quad U(1,5) = -2.$$

The entries of first column of L are given by (2.24), i.e., $L(k,1) = \frac{A(k,1)}{U(1,1)}$ for $k = 1:5$, where the matrix A is given by (2.53):

$$L(1,1) = 1; \quad L(2,1) = \frac{1}{U(1,1)} = \frac{1}{4} = 0.25; \quad L(3,1) = \frac{-2}{U(1,1)} = \frac{-2}{4} = -0.5;$$

$$L(4,1) = \frac{0}{U(1,1)} = 0; \quad L(5,1) = \frac{2}{U(1,1)} = \frac{2}{4} = 0.5.$$

The current forms of L and U are

$$L = \begin{pmatrix} 1 \\ 0.25 \\ -0.5 \\ 0 \\ 0.5 \end{pmatrix}; \quad U = \begin{pmatrix} 4 & 4 & 0 & -6 & -2 \\ 0 & U(2,2) & U(2,3) & U(2,4) & U(2,5) \\ 0 & 0 & U(3,3) & U(3,4) & U(3,5) \\ 0 & 0 & 0 & U(4,4) & U(4,5) \\ 0 & 0 & 0 & U(5,4) & U(5,5) \end{pmatrix}. \quad (2.55)$$

Note that, for the current form of the matrix L, we only consider the entries of L computed so far, since the rows of L will switch as the corresponding rows of A switch.

The updated form of the 4×4 matrix $A(2:5, 2:5)$ is computed using (2.51), from $A(2:5, 2:5)$ obtained from (2.53) and with L and U given by (2.55), as follows:

$$A(2:5, 2:5)$$
$$= A(2:5, 2:5) - L(2:5, 1) U(1, 2:5)$$

2.6. LU DECOMPOSITION WITH ROW PIVOTING

$$= \begin{pmatrix} 2 & -7 & -1.5 & 2 \\ -1 & 2 & 6 & 2.5 \\ -2 & 2 & -4 & 1 \\ 1 & 13 & -5 & 3.5 \end{pmatrix} - \begin{pmatrix} 0.25 \\ -0.5 \\ 0 \\ 0.5 \end{pmatrix} (4 \ 0 \ -6 \ -2)$$

$$= \begin{pmatrix} 2 & -7 & -1.5 & 2 \\ -1 & 2 & 6 & 2.5 \\ -2 & 2 & -4 & 1 \\ 1 & 13 & -5 & 3.5 \end{pmatrix} - \begin{pmatrix} 1 & 0 & -1.5 & -0.5 \\ -2 & 0 & 3 & 1 \\ 0 & 0 & 0 & 0 \\ 2 & 0 & -3 & -1 \end{pmatrix}$$

$$= \begin{pmatrix} 1 & -7 & 0 & 2.5 \\ 1 & 2 & 3 & 1.5 \\ -2 & 2 & -4 & 1 \\ -1 & 13 & -2 & 4.5 \end{pmatrix}. \tag{2.56}$$

To compute the second row of U and the second row of L, we identify the largest entry, in absolute value, from the first column $\begin{pmatrix} 1 \\ 1 \\ -2 \\ -1 \end{pmatrix}$ of the matrix $A(2:5, 2:5)$ from (2.56). That entry is -2, corresponding to the third row of $A(2:5, 2:5)$. We switch the first row and the third row of $A(2:5, 2:5)$ from (2.56), and obtain that

$$A(2:5, 2:5) = \begin{pmatrix} -2 & 2 & -4 & 1 \\ 1 & 2 & 3 & 1.5 \\ 1 & -7 & 0 & 2.5 \\ -1 & 13 & -2 & 4.5 \end{pmatrix}. \tag{2.57}$$

Note that the first row and the third row of $A(2:5, 2:5)$ correspond to the second row and the fourth row of the matrix A. We record the switch by permuting the second row and the fourth row of the matrix P given by (2.54) as follows:

$$P = \begin{pmatrix} 2 \\ 1 \\ 3 \\ 4 \\ 5 \end{pmatrix} \quad \text{becomes} \quad P = \begin{pmatrix} 2 \\ 4 \\ 3 \\ 1 \\ 5 \end{pmatrix} = \begin{pmatrix} e_2^t \\ e_4^t \\ e_3^t \\ e_1^t \\ e_5^t \end{pmatrix}. \tag{2.58}$$

Furthermore, the second row and the fourth row from the current form of L from (2.55) are also switched. The matrix L has now the following current form:

$$L = \begin{pmatrix} 1 \\ 0.25 \\ -0.5 \\ 0 \\ 0.5 \end{pmatrix} \quad \text{becomes} \quad L = \begin{pmatrix} 1 \\ \mathbf{0} \\ -0.5 \\ \mathbf{0.25} \\ 0.5 \end{pmatrix}. \tag{2.59}$$

After the row permutations are done, the second row of U and the second column of L are computed as in the algorithm for LU decomposition without row pivoting. Note that

$$L(2:5, 2:5)\, U(2:5, 2:5) = \begin{pmatrix} -2 & 2 & -4 & 1 \\ 1 & 2 & 3 & 1.5 \\ 1 & -7 & 0 & 2.5 \\ -1 & 13 & -2 & 4.5 \end{pmatrix},$$

see (2.57), which can be written as

$$\begin{pmatrix} 1 & 0 & 0 & 0 \\ L(3,2) & 1 & 0 & 0 \\ L(4,2) & L(4,3) & 1 & 0 \\ L(5,2) & L(5,3) & L(5,4) & 1 \end{pmatrix} \begin{pmatrix} U(2,2) & U(2,3) & U(2,4) & U(2,5) \\ 0 & U(3,3) & U(3,4) & U(3,5) \\ 0 & 0 & U(4,4) & U(4,5) \\ 0 & 0 & 0 & U(5,5) \end{pmatrix}$$

$$= \begin{pmatrix} -2 & 2 & -4 & 1 \\ 1 & 2 & 3 & 1.5 \\ 1 & -7 & 0 & 2.5 \\ -1 & 13 & -2 & 4.5 \end{pmatrix}.$$

Thus, the unknown entries from the second row of U and from the second column of L can now be computed from the 4×4 matrix above as follows:

$$U(2,2) = -2; \quad U(2,3) = 2; \quad U(2,4) = -4; \quad U(2,5) = 1;$$

$$L(2,2) = 1; \quad L(3,2) = \frac{1}{U(2,2)} = -0.5; \quad L(4,2) = \frac{1}{U(2,2)} = -0.5;$$

$$L(5,2) = \frac{-1}{U(2,2)} = 0.5.$$

Then, the current forms of L and U are

$$L = \begin{pmatrix} 1 & 0 \\ 0.25 & 1 \\ -0.5 & -0.5 \\ 0 & -0.5 \\ 0.5 & 0.5 \end{pmatrix}; \quad U = \begin{pmatrix} 4 & 4 & 0 & -6 & -2 \\ 0 & -2 & 2 & -4 & 1 \\ 0 & 0 & U(3,3) & U(3,4) & U(3,5) \\ 0 & 0 & 0 & U(4,4) & U(4,5) \\ 0 & 0 & 0 & 0 & U(5,5) \end{pmatrix}. \quad (2.60)$$

The updated form of the 3×3 matrix $A(3:5, 3:5)$ is computed using (2.52), from $A(3:5, 3:5)$ obtained from (2.57) and with L and U given by (2.60), as follows:

$$A(3:5, 3:5)$$
$$= A(3:5, 3:5) - L(3:5, 2) U(2, 3:5)$$
$$= \begin{pmatrix} 2 & 3 & 1.5 \\ -7 & 0 & 2.5 \\ 13 & -2 & 4.5 \end{pmatrix} - \begin{pmatrix} -0.5 \\ -0.5 \\ 0.5 \end{pmatrix} \begin{pmatrix} 2 & -4 & 1 \end{pmatrix}$$
$$= \begin{pmatrix} 2 & 3 & 1.5 \\ -7 & 0 & 2.5 \\ 13 & -2 & 4.5 \end{pmatrix} - \begin{pmatrix} -1 & 2 & -0.5 \\ -1 & 2 & -0.5 \\ 1 & -2 & 0.5 \end{pmatrix}$$
$$= \begin{pmatrix} 3 & 1 & 2 \\ -6 & -2 & 3 \\ 12 & 0 & 4 \end{pmatrix}. \quad (2.61)$$

To compute the third row of U and the third column of L, we identify the largest entry, in absolute value, from the first column $\begin{pmatrix} 3 \\ -6 \\ 12 \end{pmatrix}$ of the matrix $A(3:5, 3:5)$ from (2.61). That entry is 12, corresponding to the third row of $A(3:5, 3:5)$. We switch the first row and the third row of $A(3:5, 3:5)$ from (2.61), and obtain that

$$A(3:5, 3:5) = \begin{pmatrix} 12 & 0 & 4 \\ -6 & -2 & 3 \\ 3 & 1 & 2 \end{pmatrix}. \quad (2.62)$$

2.6. LU DECOMPOSITION WITH ROW PIVOTING

Note that the first row and the third row of $A(3:5, 3:5)$ correspond to the third row and the fifth row of the matrix A. We record the switch by permuting the third row and the fifth row of the matrix P given by (2.58) as follows:

$$P = \begin{pmatrix} 2 \\ 4 \\ 3 \\ 1 \\ 5 \end{pmatrix} \quad \text{becomes} \quad P = \begin{pmatrix} 2 \\ 4 \\ 5 \\ 1 \\ 3 \end{pmatrix} = \begin{pmatrix} e_2^t \\ e_4^t \\ e_5^t \\ e_1^t \\ e_3^t \end{pmatrix}. \tag{2.63}$$

Furthermore, the third row and the fifth row from the current form of L from (2.60) are also switched. The matrix L has now the following current form:

$$L = \begin{pmatrix} 1 & 0 \\ 0.25 & 1 \\ -0.5 & -0.5 \\ 0 & -0.5 \\ 0.5 & 0.5 \end{pmatrix} \quad \text{becomes} \quad L = \begin{pmatrix} 1 & 0 \\ 0.25 & 1 \\ \mathbf{0.5} & \mathbf{0.5} \\ 0 & -0.5 \\ \mathbf{-0.5} & \mathbf{-0.5} \end{pmatrix}. \tag{2.64}$$

After the row permutations are done, the third row of U and the third column of L are now computed as it was done in the algorithm for LU decomposition without row pivoting. Note that

$$L(3:5, 3:5)\, U(3:5, 3:5) = \begin{pmatrix} 12 & 0 & 4 \\ -6 & -2 & 3 \\ 3 & 1 & 2 \end{pmatrix},$$

see (2.62), which can be written as

$$\begin{pmatrix} 1 & 0 & 0 \\ L(4,3) & 1 & 0 \\ L(5,3) & L(5,4) & 1 \end{pmatrix} \begin{pmatrix} U(3,3) & U(3,4) & U(3,5) \\ 0 & U(4,4) & U(4,5) \\ 0 & 0 & U(5,5) \end{pmatrix} = \begin{pmatrix} 12 & 0 & 4 \\ -6 & -2 & 3 \\ 3 & 1 & 2 \end{pmatrix}.$$

Thus, the unknown entries from the third row of U and from the third column of L can now be computed from the 3×3 matrix above as follows:

$$U(3,3) = 12; \quad U(3,4) = 0; \quad U(3,5) = 4;$$

$$L(3,3) = 1; \quad L(4,3) = \frac{-6}{U(3,3)} = \frac{-6}{12} = -0.5; \quad L(5,3) = \frac{3}{U(3,3)} = \frac{3}{12} = 0.25.$$

Then, the current forms of L and U are

$$L = \begin{pmatrix} 1 & 0 & 0 \\ 0.25 & 1 & 0 \\ -0.5 & -0.5 & 1 \\ 0 & -0.5 & -0.5 \\ 0.5 & 0.5 & 0.25 \end{pmatrix}; \quad U = \begin{pmatrix} 4 & 4 & 0 & -6 & -2 \\ 0 & -2 & 2 & -4 & 1 \\ 0 & 0 & 12 & 0 & 4 \\ 0 & 0 & 0 & U(4,4) & U(4,5) \\ 0 & 0 & 0 & 0 & U(5,5) \end{pmatrix}. \tag{2.65}$$

The updated form of the 2×2 matrix $A(4:5, 4:5)$ is computed using (2.52), from $A(4:5, 4:5)$ obtained from (2.62) and with L and U given by (2.65), as follows:

$$A(4:5, 4:5)$$
$$= A(4:5, 4:5) - L(4:5, 3)\, U(3, 4:5)$$

$$= \begin{pmatrix} -2 & 3 \\ 1 & 2 \end{pmatrix} - \begin{pmatrix} -0.5 \\ 0.25 \end{pmatrix} (0 \ 4)$$

$$= \begin{pmatrix} -2 & 3 \\ 1 & 2 \end{pmatrix} - \begin{pmatrix} 0 & -2 \\ 0 & 1 \end{pmatrix}$$

$$= \begin{pmatrix} -2 & 5 \\ 1 & 1 \end{pmatrix}.$$

To compute the fourth row of U and the fourth column of L, note that the largest entry, in absolute value, from the first column $\begin{pmatrix} -2 \\ 1 \end{pmatrix}$ of the matrix $A(4:5,4:5)$ from (2.66) is -2, which is already on the first row of $A(4:5,4:5)$.

Thus, no row pivoting is necessary, and the updated form of the 2×2 matrix $A(4:5,4:5)$ is

$$A(4:5,4:5) = \begin{pmatrix} -2 & 5 \\ 1 & 1 \end{pmatrix}. \tag{2.66}$$

The fourth row of U and the fourth column of L are computed as it was done in the algorithm for LU decomposition without row pivoting. Note that

$$L(4:5,4:5)\,U(4:5,4:5) = \begin{pmatrix} -2 & 5 \\ 1 & 1 \end{pmatrix},$$

see (2.66), which can be written as

$$\begin{pmatrix} 1 & 0 \\ L(5,4) & 1 \end{pmatrix} \begin{pmatrix} U(4,4) & U(4,5) \\ 0 & U(5,5) \end{pmatrix} = \begin{pmatrix} -2 & 5 \\ 1 & 1 \end{pmatrix}.$$

Thus, the unknown entries from the fourth row of U and from the fourth column of L can be computed from the 2×2 matrix above as follows:

$$U(4,4) = -2; \quad U(3,4) = 5;$$

$$L(5,4) = \frac{1}{U(4,4)} = \frac{1}{-2} = -0.5.$$

Then, the current forms of L and U are

$$L = \begin{pmatrix} 1 & 0 & 0 & 0 \\ 0.25 & 1 & 0 & 0 \\ -0.5 & -0.5 & 1 & 0 \\ 0 & -0.5 & -0.5 & 1 \\ 0.5 & 0.5 & 0.25 & -0.5 \end{pmatrix}; \quad U = \begin{pmatrix} 4 & 4 & 0 & -6 & -2 \\ 0 & -2 & 2 & -4 & 1 \\ 0 & 0 & 12 & 0 & 4 \\ 0 & 0 & 0 & -2 & 5 \\ 0 & 0 & 0 & 0 & U(5,5) \end{pmatrix}.$$

(2.67)

The updated form of $A(5,5)$, which is a number, is computed using (2.52), from $A(5,5)$ obtained from (2.66) and with L and U given by (2.67), as follows:

$$A(5,5) = A(5,5) - L(5,4)U(4,5) = 1 - (-0.5) \cdot 5 = 3.5,$$

which corresponds to

$$L(5,5) = 1; \quad U(5,5) = 3.5.$$

2.6. LU WITH ROW PIVOTING LINEAR SOLVERS

We conclude that the matrix A has an LU decomposition with row pivoting with permutation matrix

$$P = \begin{pmatrix} 2 \\ 4 \\ 5 \\ 1 \\ 3 \end{pmatrix} = \begin{pmatrix} e_2^t \\ e_4^t \\ e_5^t \\ e_1^t \\ e_3^t \end{pmatrix} = \begin{pmatrix} 0 & 1 & 0 & 0 & 0 \\ 0 & 0 & 0 & 1 & 0 \\ 0 & 0 & 0 & 0 & 1 \\ 1 & 0 & 0 & 0 & 0 \\ 0 & 0 & 1 & 0 & 0 \end{pmatrix},$$

see (2.63), and with the following L and U factors:

$$L = \begin{pmatrix} 1 & 0 & 0 & 0 & 0 \\ 0.25 & 1 & 0 & 0 & 0 \\ -0.5 & -0.5 & 1 & 0 & 0 \\ 0 & -0.5 & -0.5 & 1 & 0 \\ 0.5 & 0.5 & 0.25 & -0.5 & 1 \end{pmatrix}; \quad U = \begin{pmatrix} 4 & 4 & 0 & -6 & -2 \\ 0 & -2 & 2 & -4 & 1 \\ 0 & 0 & 12 & 0 & 4 \\ 0 & 0 & 0 & -2 & 5 \\ 0 & 0 & 0 & 0 & 3.5 \end{pmatrix}. \quad \square$$

The pseudocode for the LU decomposition with row pivoting, given as a function call $[P, L, U] = \text{lu\_row\_pivoting}(A)$, can be found in Table 2.10.

The operation count for the LU decomposition with row pivoting is

$$\frac{2}{3}n^3 + O(n^2),$$

the same as for the LU decomposition without pivoting.

2.7 Linear solvers using the LU decomposition with row pivoting

The LU decomposition with row pivoting of a matrix can be used to solve linear systems efficiently as follows: Let A be a nonsingular square matrix of size n, and let b be a column vector of size n. If $PA = LU$ is the LU decomposition with row pivoting of A, then, solving a linear system $Ax = b$ is equivalent to solving

$$PAx = Pb,$$

since the permutation matrix P is nonsingular. Since $PA = LU$, this is equivalent to

$$LUx = Pb.$$

This is the same as solving

$$Ly = Pb$$

for y, which can be done using forward substitution since the matrix L is lower triangular, and then solving

$$Ux = y$$

for x, which can be done using backward substitution since the matrix U is upper triangular.

Table 2.10: Pseudocode for LU decomposition with row pivoting

---

Function Call:
$[P, L, U] = $ lu_row_pivoting(A)

Input:
$A = $ nonsingular matrix of size n

Output:
$P = $ permutation matrix, stored as vector of its diagonal entries
$L = $ lower triangular matrix with entries 1 on main diagonal
$U = $ upper triangular matrix
such that $PA = LU$

$P = 1:n$; $L = I$;   // initialize P and L as identity matrices
for $i = 1:(n-1)$
  find i_max, index of largest entry in absolute value from vector $A(i:n, i)$
  $vv = A(i, i:n)$; $A(i, i:n) = A(i\_max, i:n)$; $A(i\_max, i:n) = vv$;
                                        // switch rows i and i_max of A
  $cc = P(i)$; $P(i) = P(i\_max)$; $P(i\_max) = cc$;   // update matrix P
  if $i > 1$
    $ww = L(i, 1:(i-1))$;
    $L(i, 1:(i-1)) = L(i\_max, 1:(i-1))$; $L(i\_max, 1:(i-1)) = ww$;
  end   // switch rows i and i_max of L
  for $j = i:n$
    $L(j, i) = A(j, i)/A(i, i)$;   // compute column i of L
    $U(i, j) = A(i, j)$;   // compute row i of U
  end
  for $j = (i+1):n$
    for $k = (i+1):n$
      $A(j, k) = A(j, k) - L(j, i)U(i, k)$;
    end
  end
  clear vv ww cc
end
$L(n, n) = 1$; $U(n, n) = A(n, n)$;

The pseudocode for solving a linear system using the LU decomposition with row pivoting of a matrix can be found in Table 2.11.

The operation count for the linear solver from Table 2.11 is

$$\frac{2}{3}n^3 + O(n^2),$$

the same as for the linear solver using the LU decomposition without pivoting of a matrix; see section 2.5.

2.7.1 Solving linear systems corresponding to the same matrix

In this section, we show how the LU decomposition with row pivoting of a matrix can be used to solve multiple linear systems corresponding to the same nonsingular

2.7. LU WITH ROW PIVOTING LINEAR SOLVERS

Table 2.11: Linear solver using LU decomposition with row pivoting

---

Function Call:
x = linear_solve_lu_row_pivoting(A,b)

Input:
A = nonsingular square matrix of size n with LU decomposition
b = column vector of size n

Output:
x = solution to $Ax = b$

$[P, L, U]$ = lu_row_pivoting(A);   // LU decomposition of A
y = forward_subst(L, Pb);   // solve $Ly = Pb$
x = backward_subst(U, y);   // solve $Ux = y$

---

matrix efficiently, which is often needed in practice, e.g., for the finite difference solution of the Black–Scholes PDE.

Assume that we want to solve p linear systems corresponding to an $n \times n$ nonsingular matrix A. In other words, we want to find $n \times 1$ vectors x_i, $i = 1 : p$, such that
$$Ax_i = b_i, \quad \forall \, i = 1 : p, \tag{2.68}$$
where b_i is a column vector of size n, for $i = 1 : p$.

Note that the matrix A has an LU decomposition with row pivoting, since it is nonsingular; see Theorem 2.3. One way to solve the linear systems from (2.68) would be to use the routine linear_solve_lu_row_pivoting from Table 2.11 to solve each one of the p linear systems inside a "for" loop as follows:

---

for $i = 1 : p$
    x_i = linear_solve_lu_row_pivoting(A,b_i)
end

This would require
$$p\left(\frac{2}{3}n^3 + O(n^2)\right) = \frac{2}{3}pn^3 + pO(n^2) \tag{2.69}$$
operations, since each linear solver requires $\frac{2}{3}n^3 + O(n^2)$ operations; cf. Lemma 2.3.

However, the most expensive part of x_i = linear_solve_lu_row_pivoting(A,b_i) is computing the LU decomposition with row pivoting of the matrix A, which dominates the cost of the subsequent forward substitution and backward substitution. Thus, an efficient way of solving the linear systems (2.68) is to compute the permutation matrix P and the L and U factors of A only once, outside the "for" loop, and then do the forward and backward substitutions corresponding to x_i = linear_solve_lu_row_pivoting(A,b_i) inside the "for" loop; see the pseudocode from Table 2.12 for details.

Recall that the forward substitution forward_subst(L, b_i) and the backward substitution backward_subst(U, y) require $n^2 + O(n)$ operations each; cf. (2.8) and (2.19).

Table 2.12: Solution of multiple linear systems corresponding to the same matrix

> Input:
> A = nonsingular square matrix of size n with LU decomposition
> b_i = column vectors of size n, $i = 1 : p$
>
> Output:
> x_i = solution to $Ax_i = b_i$, $i = 1 : p$
>
> $[P, L, U] = \text{lu\_row\_pivoting}(A)$;
> for $i = 1 : p$
> $y = \text{forward\_subst}(L, Pb_i)$;
> $x_i = \text{backward\_subst}(U, y)$;
> end

Thus, the operation count for solving the p linear systems using the method from Table 2.12 is

$$\frac{2}{3}n^3 + O(n^2) + p\left(n^2 + O(n) + n^2 + O(n)\right) = \frac{2}{3}n^3 + 2pn^2 + O(n^2) + pO(n),$$

which is smaller than $\frac{2}{3}pn^3 + pO(n^2)$, the operation count required by solving the p linear systems sequentially; see (2.69).

As an example of solving multiple systems corresponding to the same matrix, we show how to efficiently compute the inverse of a nonsingular matrix.

Finding the inverse of a nonsingular matrix one entry at a time requires computing the determinant of the matrix and one minor for every entry of the matrix, for a total cost of more than $n^2 \cdot n!$ operations. This is beyond regular computer power limits even for small values of n, since, from Stirling's formula, $n!$ is of the order $\frac{n^{n+1/2}}{e^n}$; for example, computing the inverse of a nonsingular 27×27 matrix using this method would require more than 10^{28} operations.

Nonetheless, the inverse of an $n \times n$ nonsingular matrix having an LU decomposition can be computed very efficiently in $\frac{8}{3}n^3 + O(n^2)$ operations as follows:

Let A be an $n \times n$ nonsingular matrix, and let $A^{-1} = \text{col}(c_k)_{k=1:n}$ be the column form of the inverse matrix of A. Then, $AA^{-1} = I$, where $I = \text{col}(e_k)_{k=1:n}$ is the identity matrix of size n. Using (1.11), we find that $AA^{-1} = \text{col}(Ac_k)_{k=1:n}$, and therefore $AA^{-1} = I$ is equivalent to

$$Ac_k = e_k, \quad \forall\, k = 1 : n,$$

which can be solved using the method from Table 2.12 as follows:

> $[P, L, U] = \text{lu\_row\_pivoting}(A)$
> for $k = 1 : n$
> $y = \text{forward\_subst}(L, Pe_k)$;
> $c_k = \text{backward\_subst}(U, y)$;
> end
> $A^{-1} = \text{col}(c_k)_{k=1:n}$

2.7. LU WITH ROW PIVOTING LINEAR SOLVERS

The operation count for computing the inverse matrix using this method is

$$\frac{2}{3}n^3 + O(n^2) + n\left(n^2 + O(n) + n^2 + O(n)\right) = \frac{8}{3}n^3 + O(n^2); \qquad (2.70)$$

see (10.88) in Section 10.2.3 for a proof of the last equality.

2.7.2 Finding discount factors using the LU decomposition

If the number of cash flow dates is equal to the number of bonds (and if there are no redundancies), then the discount factors corresponding to the cash flow dates can be uniquely determined from the bond prices by solving a linear system using LU decomposition with row pivoting; see also section 2.2.1 for an example when forward substitution is used to determine the discount factors.

For the example below, recall that a semiannual coupon bond with face value $100, coupon rate C, and maturity T pays the holder of the bond a coupon payment equal to $\frac{C}{2} \cdot 100$ every six months, except at maturity. The final payment at maturity is equal to the face value of the bond plus one coupon payment, i.e., $100 + \frac{C}{2} 100$. For example, a semiannual coupon bond with 15 months to maturity and coupon rate 5%, i.e., $C = 0.05$, has three cash flow dates, in 3, 9, and 15 months, corresponding to $t_1 = \frac{3}{12} = \frac{1}{4}$, $t_2 = \frac{9}{12} = \frac{3}{4}$, and $t_3 = \frac{15}{12} = \frac{5}{4}$, respectively. The corresponding cash flows are $c_1 = 2.5$, $c_2 = 2.5$, and $c_3 = 102.5$.

Example: The values of the following coupon bonds with face value $100 are given:

Bond Type	Coupon Rate	Bond Price
11 months semiannual	4%	$101.5
17 months annual	5%	$105.5
23 months semiannual	3%	$101
23 months annual	6%	$106.75

The cash flows and the cash flow dates of the bonds are recorded in the table below:

Bond Type	Cash Flow & Date
11 months semiannual	$2 in 5 months
	$102 in 11 months
17 months annual	$5 in 5 months
	$105 in 17 months
23 months semiannual	$1.5 in 5 months
	$1.5 in 11 months
	$1.5 in 17 months
	$101.5 in 23 months
23 months annual	$6 in 11 months
	$106 in 23 months

Note that the four bonds have exactly four cash flow dates, i.e., 5 months, 11 months, 17 months, and 23 months, and let d_1, d_2, d_3, and d_4 be the discount factors corresponding to these dates. Using the formula (2.11) for bond valuation, we find that

$$101.5 = 2d_1 + 102d_2;$$

$$105.5 = 5d_1 + 105d_3;$$
$$101 = 1.5d_1 + 1.5d_2 + 1.5d_3 + 101.5d_4;$$
$$106.75 = 6d_2 + 106d_4.$$

This linear system can be written in matrix notation as $Ax = b$, where

$$A = \begin{pmatrix} 2 & 102 & 0 & 0 \\ 5 & 0 & 105 & 0 \\ 1.5 & 1.5 & 1.5 & 101.5 \\ 0 & 6 & 0 & 106 \end{pmatrix}; \quad x = \begin{pmatrix} d_1 \\ d_2 \\ d_3 \\ d_4 \end{pmatrix}; \quad b = \begin{pmatrix} 101.5 \\ 105.5 \\ 101 \\ 106.75 \end{pmatrix}.$$

The solution of $Ax = b$ is obtained using the LU decomposition with row pivoting linear solver[8] from Table 2.11, i.e.,

$$x = \text{linear\_solve\_lu\_row\_pivoting}(A, b) = \begin{pmatrix} 0.9916 \\ 0.9757 \\ 0.9575 \\ 0.9518 \end{pmatrix}.$$

Recall that the discount factors corresponding to the cash flow dates are equal to the entries of x. Thus,

$$d_1 = \text{Disc}\left(\frac{5}{12}\right) = 0.9916; \quad d_2 = \text{Disc}\left(\frac{11}{12}\right) = 0.9757;$$

$$d_3 = \text{Disc}\left(\frac{17}{12}\right) = 0.9575; \quad d_4 = \text{Disc}\left(\frac{23}{12}\right) = 0.9518.$$

Then, formula (2.12), i.e.,

$$\text{Disc}(t_i) = \exp\left(-t_i r(0, t_i)\right),$$

can be used to find the corresponding continuously compounded zero rates, as follows:

$$d_1 = \exp\left(-\frac{5}{12} r\left(0, \frac{5}{12}\right)\right) \iff r\left(0, \frac{5}{12}\right) = -\frac{\ln(d_1)}{5/12} = 0.0202 = 2.02\%;$$

$$d_2 = \exp\left(-\frac{11}{12} r\left(0, \frac{11}{12}\right)\right) \iff r\left(0, \frac{11}{12}\right) = -\frac{\ln(d_2)}{11/12} = 0.0269 = 2.69\%;$$

---

[8] We provide more numerical details here. The permutation matrix P, lower triangular matrix L, and upper triangular matrix U from the LU decomposition with row pivoting of A are

$$P = \begin{pmatrix} 0 & 1 & 0 & 0 \\ 1 & 0 & 0 & 0 \\ 0 & 0 & 1 & 0 \\ 0 & 0 & 0 & 1 \end{pmatrix}; \quad L = \begin{pmatrix} 1 & 0 & 0 & 0 \\ 0.4 & 1 & 0 & 0 \\ 0.3 & 0.0147 & 1 & 0 \\ 0 & 0.0588 & -0.0841 & 1 \end{pmatrix};$$

$$U = \begin{pmatrix} 5 & 0 & 105 & 0 \\ 0 & 102 & -42 & 0 \\ 0 & 0 & -29.3824 & 101.5 \\ 0 & 0 & 0 & 114.5345 \end{pmatrix}.$$

Furthermore,

$$y = \text{forward\_subst}(L, Pb) = \begin{pmatrix} 105.5 \\ 59.3 \\ 68.4779 \\ 109.0197 \end{pmatrix}.$$

$$d_3 = \exp\left(-\frac{17}{12}r\left(0,\frac{17}{12}\right)\right) \iff r\left(0,\frac{17}{12}\right) = -\frac{\ln(d_3)}{17/12} = 0.0306 = 3.06\%;$$

$$d_4 = \exp\left(-\frac{23}{12}r\left(0,\frac{23}{12}\right)\right) \iff r\left(0,\frac{23}{12}\right) = -\frac{\ln(d_4)}{23/12} = 0.0257 = 2.57\%.$$

2.8 Cubic spline interpolation

Interpolating a continuous function from known values at a finite number of discrete nodes is a frequently used tool for financial applications, e.g., for inferring a zero–rate curve from known discount factors.

The continuous interpolation problem can be described in general terms as follows:

Find a continuous function $f : [x_0, x_n] \to \mathbb{R}$ such that $f(x_i) = v_i$, for all $i = 0 : n$, where $x_0 < x_1 < \ldots < x_n$, and v_i are the known values of $f(x)$ at the point x_i, for all $i = 0 : n$.

The simplest way to obtain such a function is by linear interpolation between every two points x_{i-1} and x_i, for $i = 1 : n$, resulting in the following function:

$$f(x) = \frac{(x - x_{i-1})v_i}{x_i - x_{i-1}} + \frac{(x_i - x)v_{i-1}}{x_i - x_{i-1}}, \quad \forall\ x_{i-1} \leq x \leq x_i, \ \forall\ i = 1 : n.$$

However, linear interpolation has a major drawback: the resulting function $f(x)$ is not differentiable at any point x_i, $i = 1 : (n-1)$.

The interpolation method most often used in practice is *cubic spline interpolation*, which requires the function $f(x)$ to be a polynomial of degree three (i.e., a cubic polynomial) on each interval $[x_{i-1}, x_i]$, for $i = 1 : n$, as well as to be twice differentiable on the entire interval $[x_0, x_n]$.

In other words, we are looking for a function $f(x)$ of the form

$$f(x) = f_i(x) = a_i + b_i x + c_i x^2 + d_i x^3, \quad \forall\ x_{i-1} \leq x \leq x_i, \ \forall\ i = 1 : n, \quad (2.71)$$

such that

$$f_i(x_{i-1}) = v_{i-1}, \quad \forall\ i = 1 : n; \quad (2.72)$$
$$f_i(x_i) = v_i, \quad \forall\ i = 1 : n; \quad (2.73)$$
$$f_i'(x_i) = f_{i+1}'(x_i), \quad \forall\ i = 1 : (n-1); \quad (2.74)$$
$$f_i''(x_i) = f_{i+1}''(x_i), \quad \forall\ i = 1 : (n-1). \quad (2.75)$$

Using (2.71), we can rewrite (2.72–2.75), respectively, as follows:

$$a_i + b_i x_{i-1} + c_i x_{i-1}^2 + d_i x_{i-1}^3 = v_{i-1}, \quad \forall\ i = 1 : n; \quad (2.76)$$
$$a_i + b_i x_i + c_i x_i^2 + d_i x_i^3 = v_i, \quad \forall\ i = 1 : n; \quad (2.77)$$
$$b_i + 2c_i x_i + 3d_i x_i^2 = b_{i+1} + 2c_{i+1} x_i + 3d_{i+1} x_i^2, \quad \forall\ i = 1 : (n-1); \quad (2.78)$$
$$2c_i + 6d_i x_i = 2c_{i+1} + 6d_{i+1} x_i, \quad \forall\ i = 1 : (n-1). \quad (2.79)$$

The unknowns are the coefficients a_i, b_i, c_i, d_i, $i = 1 : n$. Thus, there are $4n$ unknowns. There are n constraints corresponding to (2.76), n constraints corresponding to (2.77), $n-1$ constraints corresponding to (2.78), and $n-1$ constraints corresponding to (2.79), for a total of $4n - 2$ constraints. Two more constraints are therefore needed for a unique solution. The most common choice for these two constraints is to require that $f_1''(x_0) = 0$ and $f_n''(x_n) = 0$, i.e.,

$$2c_1 + 6d_1 x_0 = 0; \tag{2.80}$$
$$2c_n + 6d_n x_n = 0. \tag{2.81}$$

The resulting method is called the *natural cubic spline interpolation*.

Let $\overline{x}$ be the $4n \times 1$ vector of the unknowns a_i, b_i, c_i, d_i, $i = 1 : n$, given by

$$\overline{x}(4i - 3) = a_i; \quad \overline{x}(4i - 2) = b_i; \quad \overline{x}(4i - 1) = c_i; \quad \overline{x}(4i) = d_i; \quad \forall\, i = 1 : n.$$

Note that (2.76–2.81) is a linear system with $4n$ equations and $4n$ unknowns which can be expressed in matrix notation as

$$\overline{M}\overline{x} = \overline{b}, \tag{2.82}$$

where $\overline{b}$ is an $4n \times 1$ vector given by

$$\overline{b}(1) = 0; \quad \overline{b}(4n) = 0; \tag{2.83}$$

$$\overline{b}(4i - 2) = v_{i-1}; \quad \overline{b}(4i - 1) = v_i, \quad \forall\, i = 1 : n; \tag{2.84}$$

$$\overline{b}(4i) = 0; \quad \overline{b}(4i + 1) = 0, \quad \forall\, i = 1 : (n - 1), \tag{2.85}$$

and $\overline{M}$ is the $4n \times 4n$ matrix given by

$$\overline{M}(1, 3) = 2; \quad \overline{M}(1, 4) = 6x_0; \tag{2.86}$$

$$\overline{M}(4n, 4n - 1) = 2; \quad \overline{M}(4n, 4n) = 6x_n; \tag{2.87}$$

$$\overline{M}(4i - 2, 4i - 3) = 1; \quad \overline{M}(4i - 2, 4i - 2) = x_{i-1}, \quad \forall\, i = 1 : n; \tag{2.88}$$

$$\overline{M}(4i - 2, 4i - 1) = x_{i-1}^2; \quad \overline{M}(4i - 2, 4i) = x_{i-1}^3, \quad \forall\, i = 1 : n; \tag{2.89}$$

$$\overline{M}(4i - 1, 4i - 3) = 1; \quad \overline{M}(4i - 1, 4i - 2) = x_i, \quad \forall\, i = 1 : n; \tag{2.90}$$

$$\overline{M}(4i - 1, 4i - 1) = x_i^2; \quad \overline{M}(4i - 1, 4i) = x_i^3, \quad \forall\, i = 1 : n; \tag{2.91}$$

$$\overline{M}(4i, 4i - 2) = 1; \quad \overline{M}(4i, 4i - 1) = 2x_i, \quad \forall\, i = 1 : (n - 1); \tag{2.92}$$

$$\overline{M}(4i, 4i) = 3x_i^2; \quad \overline{M}(4i, 4i + 2) = -1, \quad \forall\, i = 1 : (n - 1); \tag{2.93}$$

$$\overline{M}(4i, 4i + 3) = -2x_i; \quad \overline{M}(4i, 4i + 4) = -3x_i^2, \quad \forall\, i = 1 : (n - 1); \tag{2.94}$$

$$\overline{M}(4i + 1, 4i - 1) = 2; \overline{M}(4i + 1, 4i) = 6x_i, \quad \forall\, i = 1 : (n - 1); \tag{2.95}$$

$$\overline{M}(4i + 1, 4i + 3) = -2; \quad \overline{M}(4i + 1, 4i + 4) = -6x_i, \quad \forall\, i = 1 : (n - 1). \tag{2.96}$$

2.8. CUBIC SPLINE INTERPOLATION

The matrix $\overline{M}$ is a banded matrix of band 4. Moreover, the matrix $\overline{M}$ is nonsingular for any values of the nodes x_i, $i = 0 : n$.[9]

The linear system $\overline{M}\overline{x} = \overline{b}$ from (2.82) can be solved using the LU with row pivoting solver from Table 2.11, i.e., $\overline{x}$ = linear_solve_lu_row_pivoting($\overline{M},\overline{b}$).

The cubic spline interpolation pseudocode can be found in Table 2.13.

Table 2.13: Pseudocode for the natural cubic spline interpolation

```
Input:
x_i = interpolation nodes, i = 0 : n
v_i = interpolation values, i = 0 : n

Output:
a_i, b_i, c_i, d_i = cubic polynomials coefficients, i = 1 : n

compute vector b̄ from (2.83–2.85)
compute matrix M̄ from (2.86–2.96)
x̄ = linear_solve_lu_row_pivoting(M̄,b̄)
for i = 1 : n
    a_i = x̄(4i − 3); b_i = x̄(4i − 2); c_i = x̄(4i − 1); d_i = x̄(4i);
end
```

2.8.1 Cubic spline interpolation for zero rate curves

Cubic spline interpolation is often used to obtain a continuous zero rate curve from values of the zero rate for discrete times which price correctly a set of interest rate instruments such as bonds and swaps. The zero rate curve thus obtained can then be used to price interest rate instruments with any cash flow dates.

For example, assume that the following zero rates have been determined:

Time	Zero Rate
overnight	0.50%
2 months	0.65%
6 months	0.85%
12 months	1.05%
20 months	1.20%

In other words, $r(0,0) = 0.0050$; $r\left(0, \frac{2}{12}\right) = 0.0065$; $r\left(0, \frac{6}{12}\right) = 0.0085$; $r(0,1) = 0.0105$; and $r\left(0, \frac{20}{12}\right) = 0.0120$, where $r(0,t)$ is the zero rate corresponding to time t.

We use cubic spline interpolation to find the zero rate curve $r(0,t)$ for all maturities up to 20 months, i.e., for all $0 \leq t \leq \frac{20}{12}$. Thus, $r(0,t)$ is assumed to be a cubic

---

[9] While it is difficult to see that $\overline{M}$ is nonsingular by inspecting its entries, note that the solution to the cubic spline interpolation which is given by the solution to the linear system $\overline{M}\overline{x} = \overline{b}$ is equivalent to finding a solution to the tridiagonal system $Mz = b$ from (6.82). As shown in section 6.4, the matrix M is symmetric positive definite, and therefore nonsingular, for any values of the nodes x_i, $i = 0 : n$. We conclude that the cubic spline interpolation has a unique solution for any nodes x_i, $i = 0 : n$. Thus, the linear system $\overline{M}\overline{x} = \overline{b}$ must have a unique solution, and we can therefore conclude that the matrix $\overline{M}$ is nonsingular.

polynomial on each of the intervals $\left[0, \frac{2}{12}\right]$, $\left[\frac{2}{12}, \frac{6}{12}\right]$, $\left[\frac{6}{12}, 1\right]$, and $\left[1, \frac{20}{12}\right]$. The coefficients of these cubic polynomials are obtained by solving the linear system (2.82) corresponding to the 16×16 banded matrix $\overline{M}$ given by (2.97–2.98):

$$\overline{M} = \begin{pmatrix} 0 & 0 & 2 & 0 & 0 & 0 & 0 & 0 & \cdots \\ 1 & 0 & 0 & 0 & 0 & 0 & 0 & 0 & \cdots \\ 1 & 1/6 & 1/36 & 0.0046 & 0 & 0 & 0 & 0 & \cdots \\ 0 & 1 & 1/3 & 1/12 & 0 & -1 & -1/3 & -1/12 & \cdots \\ 0 & 0 & 2 & 1 & 0 & 0 & -2 & -1 & \cdots \\ 0 & 0 & 0 & 0 & 1 & 1/6 & 1/36 & 0.0046 & \cdots \\ 0 & 0 & 0 & 0 & 1 & 0.5 & 1/4 & 1/8 & \cdots \\ 0 & 0 & 0 & 0 & 0 & 1 & 1 & 3/4 & \cdots \\ 0 & 0 & 0 & 0 & 0 & 0 & 2 & 3 & \cdots \\ 0 & 0 & 0 & 0 & 0 & 0 & 0 & 0 & \cdots \\ 0 & 0 & 0 & 0 & 0 & 0 & 0 & 0 & \cdots \\ 0 & 0 & 0 & 0 & 0 & 0 & 0 & 0 & \cdots \\ 0 & 0 & 0 & 0 & 0 & 0 & 0 & 0 & \cdots \\ 0 & 0 & 0 & 0 & 0 & 0 & 0 & 0 & \cdots \\ 0 & 0 & 0 & 0 & 0 & 0 & 0 & 0 & \cdots \\ 0 & 0 & 0 & 0 & 0 & 0 & 0 & 0 & \cdots \end{pmatrix} \quad (2.97)$$

$$\begin{pmatrix} 0 & 0 & 0 & 0 & 0 & 0 & 0 & 0 \\ 0 & 0 & 0 & 0 & 0 & 0 & 0 & 0 \\ 0 & 0 & 0 & 0 & 0 & 0 & 0 & 0 \\ 0 & 0 & 0 & 0 & 0 & 0 & 0 & 0 \\ 0 & 0 & 0 & 0 & 0 & 0 & 0 & 0 \\ 0 & 0 & 0 & 0 & 0 & 0 & 0 & 0 \\ 0 & 0 & 0 & 0 & 0 & 0 & 0 & 0 \\ 0 & -1 & -1 & -3/4 & 0 & 0 & 0 & 0 \\ 0 & 0 & -2 & -3 & 0 & 0 & 0 & 0 \\ 1 & 1/2 & 1/4 & 1/8 & 0 & 0 & 0 & 0 \\ 1 & 1 & 1 & 1 & 0 & 0 & 0 & 0 \\ 0 & 1 & 2 & 3 & 0 & -1 & -2 & -3 \\ 0 & 0 & 2 & 6 & 0 & 0 & -2 & -6 \\ 0 & 0 & 0 & 0 & 1 & 1 & 1 & 1 \\ 0 & 0 & 0 & 0 & 1 & 5/3 & 25/9 & 4.6296 \\ 0 & 0 & 0 & 0 & 0 & 0 & 2 & 10 \end{pmatrix}. \quad (2.98)$$

The resulting zero rate curve is

$$r(0,t) = \begin{cases} 0.005 + 0.0095t - 0.0171t^3, & \text{if } 0 \leq t \leq \frac{2}{12}; \\ 0.0049 + 0.0115t - 0.0122t^2 + 0.0073t^3, & \text{if } \frac{2}{12} \leq t \leq \frac{6}{12}; \\ 0.0059 + 0.0057t - 0.0006t^2 - 0.0005t^3, & \text{if } \frac{6}{12} \leq t \leq 1; \\ 0.0044 + 0.01t - 0.0049t^2 + 0.001t^3, & \text{if } 1 \leq t \leq \frac{20}{12}. \end{cases} \quad (2.99)$$

The zero rate curve $r(0,t)$ can be used, e.g., to find the value of a 13 months 3% quarterly bond with face value $100. This bond has the following cash flows:

The value of the bond, denoted by B, is obtained by adding the present value of all the future cash flows of the bond. Assuming that the zero rate $r(0,t)$ corresponds to continuous compounding, we obtain that

$$B = 0.75 \exp\left(-\frac{1}{12} r\left(0, \frac{1}{12}\right)\right) + 0.75 \exp\left(-\frac{4}{12} r\left(0, \frac{4}{12}\right)\right)$$

Date	Cash flow
1 month	$0.75
4 months	$0.75
7 months	$0.75
10 months	$0.75
13 months	$100.75

$$+\ 0.75 \exp\left(-\frac{7}{12}r\left(0, \frac{7}{12}\right)\right) + 0.75 \exp\left(-\frac{10}{12}r\left(0, \frac{10}{12}\right)\right)$$
$$+\ 100.75 \exp\left(-\frac{13}{12}r\left(0, \frac{13}{12}\right)\right).$$

From (2.99), we find that $r\left(0, \frac{1}{12}\right) = 0.005782$; $r\left(0, \frac{4}{12}\right) = 0.007648$; $r\left(0, \frac{7}{12}\right) = 0.008922$; $r\left(0, \frac{10}{12}\right) = 0.009944$; and $r\left(0, \frac{13}{12}\right) = 0.010754$.

Thus, $B = 102.5707$, i.e., the value of the bond is $102.57.

2.9 References

Detailed proofs for the existence of the LU decomposition can be found in Golub and Van Loan [18]. Trefethen and Bau [43] give an implicit constructive proof for the existence of the LU decomposition with row pivoting of a nonsingular matrix, presenting the intuition behind switching the rows of the lower triangular factor L in the LU with row pivoting algorithm. A discussion of the stability of the LU decomposition, both from a theoretical and from a practical standpoint, can be found in Higham [20].

The numerical solution of the Black–Scholes PDE using finite differences requires solving linear systems corresponding to the same tridiagonal matrix. For a classical treatment of the finite difference solution of the Black–Scholes PDE, see Wilmott [46]; further implementation details can be found in Hirsa [21].

2.10 Exercises

1. Let
$$L_1 = \begin{pmatrix} 1 & 0 & 0 & 0 \\ -1 & 2 & 0 & 0 \\ 2 & -2 & 3 & 0 \\ 2 & 2 & -3 & 4 \end{pmatrix}; \quad U_1 = \begin{pmatrix} 2 & -1 & 0 & 1 \\ 0 & -1/2 & 1/2 & 0 \\ 0 & 0 & 1/3 & -1/3 \\ 0 & 0 & 0 & -1/4 \end{pmatrix}.$$

$$L_2 = \begin{pmatrix} 1 & 0 & 0 & 0 \\ -1 & 1 & 0 & 0 \\ 2 & -1 & 1 & 0 \\ 2 & 1 & -1 & 1 \end{pmatrix}; \quad U_2 = \begin{pmatrix} 2 & -1 & 0 & 1 \\ 0 & -1 & 1 & 0 \\ 0 & 0 & 1 & -1 \\ 0 & 0 & 0 & -1 \end{pmatrix}.$$

(i) Show that $L_1 U_1 = L_2 U_2$.

(ii) Explain why this does not contradict the uniqueness of the LU decomposition of a matrix.

(iii) Show that
$$L_1 = L_2 \begin{pmatrix} 1 & 0 & 0 & 0 \\ 0 & 2 & 0 & 0 \\ 0 & 0 & 3 & 0 \\ 0 & 0 & 0 & 4 \end{pmatrix} \quad \text{and} \quad U_1 = \begin{pmatrix} 1 & 0 & 0 & 0 \\ 0 & 1/2 & 0 & 0 \\ 0 & 0 & 1/3 & 0 \\ 0 & 0 & 0 & 1/4 \end{pmatrix} U_2.$$

2. Let L_1 and L_2 be nonsingular lower triangular matrices and let U_1 and U_2 be nonsingular upper triangular matrices. If $L_1 U_1 = L_2 U_2$, show that there exists a nonsingular diagonal matrix D such that
$$L_1 = L_2 D \quad \text{and} \quad U_1 = D^{-1} U_2.$$

3. Let
$$A = \begin{pmatrix} 2 & -1 & 0 & 1 \\ -2 & 0 & 1 & -1 \\ 4 & -1 & 0 & 1 \\ 4 & -3 & 0 & 2 \end{pmatrix}.$$

(i) Show that the LU decomposition with row pivoting of the matrix A is given by $PA = LU$, where
$$P = \begin{pmatrix} 0 & 0 & 1 & 0 \\ 0 & 0 & 0 & 1 \\ 0 & 1 & 0 & 0 \\ 1 & 0 & 0 & 0 \end{pmatrix};$$

$$L = \begin{pmatrix} 1 & 0 & 0 & 0 \\ 1 & 1 & 0 & 0 \\ -0.5 & 0.25 & 1 & 0 \\ 0.5 & 0.25 & 0 & 1 \end{pmatrix};$$

$$U = \begin{pmatrix} 4 & -1 & 0 & 1 \\ 0 & -2 & 0 & 1 \\ 0 & 0 & 1 & -0.75 \\ 0 & 0 & 0 & 0.25 \end{pmatrix}.$$

(ii) Solve $Ax = b$, where $b = \begin{pmatrix} 3 \\ -1 \\ 0 \\ 2 \end{pmatrix}$.

(iii) Find A^{-1}, the inverse matrix of A.

4. Let $A = \begin{pmatrix} 2 & -1 & 3 & -1 \\ 1 & 0 & -2 & -4 \\ 3 & 1 & 1 & -2 \\ -4 & 1 & 0 & 2 \end{pmatrix}$ and $b = \begin{pmatrix} -1 \\ 0 \\ 1 \\ 2 \end{pmatrix}$.

(i) Find the LU decomposition with row pivoting of the matrix A;

(ii) Use the linear solver linear_solve_lu_row_pivoting to solve the linear system $Ax = b$.

(iii) Let $P_1 = \begin{pmatrix} 1 & 0 & 0 & 0 \\ 0 & 0 & 0 & 1 \\ 0 & 1 & 0 & 0 \\ 0 & 0 & 1 & 0 \end{pmatrix}$ and $P_2 = \begin{pmatrix} 0 & 1 & 0 & 0 \\ 0 & 0 & 0 & 1 \\ 1 & 0 & 0 & 0 \\ 0 & 0 & 1 & 0 \end{pmatrix}$ be permutation matrices, and let

$$L_1 = \begin{pmatrix} 1 & 0 & 0 & 0 \\ 0 & 1 & 0 & 0 \\ -0.6667 & -0.5833 & 1 & 0 \\ 0.3333 & -0.5833 & 0.1429 & 1 \end{pmatrix};$$

$$U_1 = \begin{pmatrix} 3 & 2 & -1 & -1 \\ 0 & -4 & 2 & 1 \\ 0 & 0 & -3.5 & -0.0833 \\ 0 & 0 & 0 & 1.9286 \end{pmatrix}.$$

Show that
$$P_1 A P_2 = L_1 U_1.$$

(iv) Use forward substitution to solve $L_1 y = P_1 b$, and use backward substitution to solve $U_1 x_1 = y$. Let $x_2 = P_2 x_1$. Show that x_2 is the same as the solution x to $Ax = b$ obtained at (ii), and explain why this happens.

Note: The LU decomposition with full pivoting of A is of the form $P_1 A P_2 = L_1 U_1$.

5. Find the LU decomposition without pivoting of the matrix
$$\begin{pmatrix} 1 & 0 & 0 & 0 & 1 \\ -1 & 1 & 0 & 0 & 1 \\ -1 & -1 & 1 & 0 & 1 \\ -1 & -1 & -1 & 1 & 1 \\ -1 & -1 & -1 & -1 & 1 \end{pmatrix}.$$

Note: This is the 5×5 version of the classic example of a matrix whose LU decomposition is unstable.

6. Let
$$A = \begin{pmatrix} 2 & -1 & 1 \\ -2 & 1 & 3 \\ 4 & 0 & -1 \end{pmatrix}.$$

   (i) Show that the 2×2 leading principal minor of A is 0, i.e., show that
$$\det \begin{pmatrix} 2 & -1 \\ -2 & 1 \end{pmatrix} = 0.$$

   (ii) Attempt to do the LU decomposition without pivoting of the matrix A, and show that the division by $U(2, 2)$ cannot be performed when trying to compute the second row of L.

   (iii) Show that the matrix A is nonsingular, and compute the LU decomposition with row pivoting of A.

7. The LU decomposition with column pivoting of an $n \times n$ nonsingular matrix A is $AP = LU$, where P is an $n \times n$ permutation matrix, L is an $n \times n$ lower triangular matrix with all entries on the main diagonal equal to 1, and U is an $n \times n$ upper triangular matrix. Write a pseudocode for solving linear systems of the form $Ax = b$ by using the LU decomposition with column pivoting of A.

8. Write the pseudocode for the forward substitution corresponding to a lower triangular banded matrix of band m, i.e., for solving $Lx = b$ where b is an $n \times 1$ vector and L is an $n \times n$ lower triangular matrix such that
$$L(j, k) = 0, \quad \forall\, 1 \leq j, k \leq n \quad \text{with} \quad j - k > m.$$
   What is the corresponding operation count?

9. Write the pseudocode for the backward substitution corresponding to an upper triangular banded matrix of band m, i.e., for solving $Ux = b$ where b is an $n \times 1$ vector and U is an $n \times n$ upper triangular matrix such that
$$U(j, k) = 0, \quad \forall\, 1 \leq j, k \leq n \quad \text{with} \quad k - j > m.$$
   What is the corresponding operation count?

10. Write the pseudocode for the LU decomposition without pivoting for banded matrices of band m. What is the corresponding operation count?

    Use the fact that the L and U factors from the LU decomposition without pivoting of a banded matrix of band m are a banded lower triangular matrix of band m and a banded upper triangular matrix of band m, respectively.

11. What is the operation count for solving a linear system corresponding to a banded matrix of band m using a linear solver based on the LU decomposition without pivoting of the matrix?

2.10. EXERCISES

12. The values of the following coupon bonds with face value $100 are given:

Bond Type	Coupon Rate	Bond Price
10 months semiannual	3%	$101.30
16 months semiannual	4%	$102.95
22 months annual	6%	$107.35
22 months semiannual	5%	$105.45

    (i) List the cash flows and cash flow dates for each bond.

    (ii) Identify the 4×4 matrix and the 4×1 right hand side vector corresponding to the linear system whose solution are the 4 months, 10 months, 16 months, and 22 months discount factors.

    (iii) Find the 4 months, 10 months, 16 months, and 22 months discount factors.

13. The values of the following coupon bonds with face value $100 are given:

Bond Type	Coupon Rate	Bond Price
6 months semiannual	0	$98.50
1 year semiannual	3%	$101.00
18 months semiannual	5%	$102.00
2 years semiannual	3%	$103.50

    (i) List the cash flows and cash flow dates for each bond.

    (ii) Find the 6 months, 1 year, 18 months, and 2 years discount factors.

14. The values of the following coupon bonds with face value $100 are given:

Bond Type	Coupon Rate	Bond Price
9 months semiannual	2%	$100.80
15 months semiannual	4%	$103.50
15 months annual	5%	$107.50
21 months semiannual	5%	$110.50

    (i) List the cash flows and cash flow dates for each bond.

    (ii) Find the 3 months, 9 months, 15 months, and 21 months discount factors.

15. The following discount factors are obtained by fitting market data:

Date	Discount Factor
2 months	99.80
5 months	99.35
11 months	98.20
15 months	97.75

    The overnight rate is 1%.

    (i) What is the linear system that has to be solved for the cubic spline interpolation of the zero rate curve?

(ii) Use cubic spline interpolation to find a zero rate curve for all times less than 15 months matching the discount factors above.

(iii) Find the value of a 13 months quarterly bond with 2.5% coupon rate.

Note: A quarterly coupon bond with face value $100, coupon rate C, and maturity T pays the holder of the bond a coupon payment equal to $\frac{C}{4} \cdot 100$ every three months, except at maturity. The final payment at maturity T is equal to the face value of the bond plus one coupon payment, i.e., $100 + \frac{C}{4} 100$.

16. Consider three assets with the following expected values, standard deviations, and correlations of their returns:

$$\begin{array}{lll} \mu_1 = 0.10; & \sigma_1 = 0.15; & \rho_{1,2} = -0.25; \\ \mu_2 = 0.15; & \sigma_2 = 0.30; & \rho_{2,3} = 0.20; \\ \mu_3 = 0.20; & \sigma_3 = 0.35; & \rho_{1,3} = 0.30. \end{array}$$

(i) Find the covariance matrix M of the returns of the three assets.

Hint: From (7.15), it follows that the covariance matrix is given by

$$M = \begin{pmatrix} \sigma_1^2 & \sigma_1\sigma_2\rho_{1,2} & \sigma_1\sigma_3\rho_{1,3} \\ \sigma_1\sigma_2\rho_{1,2} & \sigma_2^2 & \sigma_2\sigma_3\rho_{2,3} \\ \sigma_1\sigma_3\rho_{1,3} & \sigma_2\sigma_3\rho_{2,3} & \sigma_3^2 \end{pmatrix}.$$

(ii) A minimum variance portfolio with 16% expected rate of return and fully invested in the three assets (i.e., with no cash position) can be set up by investing a percentage w_i of the total value of the portfolio in asset i, with $i = 1 : 3$, where w_1, w_2, w_3 can be found by solving the following linear system:

$$\begin{pmatrix} 2M & 1 & \mu \\ 1^t & 0 & 0 \\ \mu^t & 0 & 0 \end{pmatrix} \begin{pmatrix} w \\ \lambda_1 \\ \lambda_2 \end{pmatrix} = \begin{pmatrix} 0 \\ 1 \\ \mu_P \end{pmatrix}, \qquad (2.100)$$

where $w = \begin{pmatrix} w_1 \\ w_2 \\ w_3 \end{pmatrix}$ and

$$\mu_P = 0.16; \quad \mu = \begin{pmatrix} 0.1 \\ 0.15 \\ 0.2 \end{pmatrix}; \quad 1 = \begin{pmatrix} 1 \\ 1 \\ 1 \end{pmatrix}.$$

Show that the matrices from the LU decomposition with row pivoting of the matrix on the left hand side of (2.100) are

$$P = \begin{pmatrix} 0 & 0 & 0 & 1 & 0 \\ 0 & 1 & 0 & 0 & 0 \\ 0 & 0 & 1 & 0 & 0 \\ 1 & 0 & 0 & 0 & 0 \\ 0 & 0 & 0 & 0 & 1 \end{pmatrix};$$

2.10. EXERCISES

$$L = \begin{pmatrix} 1 & 0 & 0 & 0 & 0 \\ -0.0225 & 1 & 0 & 0 & 0 \\ 0.0315 & 0.051852 & 1 & 0 & 0 \\ 0.045 & -0.333333 & 0.038067 & 1 & 0 \\ 0.1 & 0.246914 & 0.400056 & -0.482738 & 1 \end{pmatrix};$$

$$U = \begin{pmatrix} 1 & 1 & 1 & 0 & 0 \\ 0 & 0.2025 & 0.0645 & 1 & 0.15 \\ 0 & 0 & 0.210555 & 0.948148 & 0.192222 \\ 0 & 0 & 0 & 1.297240 & 0.142683 \\ 0 & 0 & 0 & 0 & -0.045059 \end{pmatrix}.$$

(iii) Find the weights of each asset in the minimum variance portfolio with 16% expected return. Find the standard deviation of the return of this portfolio.

(iv) Show that the two portfolios below have 16% expected return, and compute the standard deviation of the returns of each portfolio:

- 30% invested in asset 1, 20% invested in asset 2, 50% invested in asset 3;
- 50% invested in asset 1, 70% invested in asset 3, and short an amount equal to 20% of the value of the portfolio of asset 2.

Hint: If w_1, w_2, and w_3 denote the weights of asset 1, of asset 2, and of asset 3 in the portfolio, respectively, then the expected return of the portfolio is

$$w_1\mu_1 + w_2\mu_2 + w_3\mu_3.$$

Chapter 3

The Arrow–Debreu one period market model

Matrix setup for the one period market model.

Non–redundant securities. Replicable derivative securities.

A one period binomial model example.

Arbitrage–free markets. Necessary and sufficient conditions for arbitrage–free markets. Positive state prices.

Complete markets. Necessary and sufficient conditions for complete markets.

Risk–neutral pricing in arbitrage–free complete markets.

State prices.

A one period index options market model.

3.1 One period market models

One period market models (also called Arrow–Debreu models) are designed by selecting a fixed number m of securities and assuming that, at a future time $\tau > t_0$, where t_0 denotes the present time, there will be a finite number n of possible states of the market.

If the one period market model is arbitrage–free (i.e., if there are no portfolios with value 0 at present time t_0 and with positive values in every state of the market at time τ, see Section 3.2 for details) and complete (i.e., if any cash flow at time τ can be synthesized with a portfolio made of the m securities, see Section 3.3), then a unique no–arbitrage value can be found for every derivative security in this market. In other words, every derivative security can be priced in this market. This is also called risk–neutral pricing for arbitrage–free complete one period market models; cf. Section 3.4.

Such a model is of interest in trying to identify and exploit market arbitrages. An example of a one period market model for S&P 500 options can be found in section 3.5.

We proceed with a formal introduction of one period market models with m securities and n market states.

Consider a market with m securities. Let $S_{1t_0}, S_{2t_0}, \ldots, S_{mt_0}$ be the spot prices of the securities at time t_0, and denote by S_{t_0} the price vector of the securities at time t_0, i.e.,

$$S_{t_0} = \begin{pmatrix} S_{1t_0} \\ S_{2t_0} \\ \vdots \\ S_{mt_0} \end{pmatrix}.$$

Note that S_{t_0} is an $m \times 1$ column vector.

At time $\tau > t_0$, we assume that there are n possible states of the market, denoted by $\omega^1, \omega^2, \ldots, \omega^n$. Let $S_{j\tau}^{\omega^k}$ be the price at time τ of asset j if state ω^k occurs, for $1 \leq j \leq m$ and $1 \leq k \leq n$. Let

$$S_\tau^{\omega^k} = \begin{pmatrix} S_{1\tau}^{\omega^k} \\ S_{2\tau}^{\omega^k} \\ \vdots \\ S_{m\tau}^{\omega^k} \end{pmatrix} \tag{3.1}$$

be the price vector of the m assets if state ω^k occurs, for $k = 1:n$, and let

$$S_{j\tau} = \begin{pmatrix} S_{j\tau}^{\omega^1} & S_{j\tau}^{\omega^2} & \ldots & S_{j\tau}^{\omega^n} \end{pmatrix}$$

be the vector of all the possible prices of asset j at time τ, for $j = 1:m$. Note that $S_\tau^{\omega^k}$ is an $m \times 1$ column vector, and $S_{j\tau}$ is an $1 \times n$ row vector.

Let M_τ be the $m \times n$ payoff matrix made of the possible asset prices at time τ, with the j-th row of matrix M_τ corresponding to the prices of asset j, for $j = 1:m$, and the k-th column of matrix M_τ corresponding to the asset prices in state ω^k, for $k = 1:n$, i.e.,

$$M_\tau = \mathrm{col}\left(S_\tau^{\omega^k}\right)_{k=1:n} = \left(S_\tau^{\omega^1} \mid S_\tau^{\omega^2} \mid \ldots \mid S_\tau^{\omega^n}\right); \tag{3.2}$$

$$M_\tau = \mathrm{row}\left(S_{j\tau}\right)_{j=1:m} = \begin{pmatrix} S_{1\tau} \\ -- \\ S_{2\tau} \\ -- \\ \vdots \\ -- \\ S_{m\tau} \end{pmatrix}. \tag{3.3}$$

Definition 3.1. *Consider a market model with m securities and n market states at time $\tau > t_0$. The m securities are non–redundant if and only if their price vectors at time τ are linearly independent.*

In other words, the m securities are non–redundant if and only if the price vectors $S_{1\tau}, S_{2\tau}, \ldots, S_{m\tau}$ are linearly independent, i.e., if and only if the (row) rank of the payoff matrix M_τ is m.[1]

Note that a necessary (but not sufficient) condition for the m securities to be non-redundant is that there are at least as many states of the market at time τ as there are securities, i.e., $n \geq m$.

---
[1]Recall that the row rank and the rank of a matrix are the same; cf. Lemma 10.14.

3.1. ONE PERIOD MARKET MODELS

One Period Binomial Model Example:
In a one period binomial model for the evolution of the price of an asset, it is assumed that the price at time $\tau > t_0$ of an asset with price S_0 at time t_0 will be either uS_0 or dS_0, where $d < u$.

This corresponds to a one period market model with two securities, i.e., the asset described above and cash, and two states, i.e., state ω^1, when the price of the asset at time τ is uS_0, and state ω^2, when the price of the asset at time τ is dS_0.

Assume, without restricting the generality of the model, that the cash position at time t_0 is \$1. If r denotes the continuously compounded annualized risk–free rate of return of a deposit made at time t_0 and maturing at time τ, then the future value at time τ of \$1 at time t_0 is $e^{r(\tau-t_0)} = e^{r\delta t}$, where $\delta t = \tau - t_0$.

The price vector of the securities at time t_0 is

$$S_{t_0} = \begin{pmatrix} 1 \\ S_0 \end{pmatrix} \qquad (3.4)$$

and the payoff matrix at time τ corresponding to this one period market model is

$$M_\tau = \begin{pmatrix} e^{r\delta t} & e^{r\delta t} \\ uS_0 & dS_0 \end{pmatrix}. \qquad (3.5)$$

If, as it was assumed, $d < u$, then the two securities from the one period binomial model are nonredundant.

To see this, note that the securities are nonredundant if and only if $\mathrm{rank}(M_\tau) = 2$. Note that $\mathrm{rank}(M_\tau) = 1$ if and only if the rows of the matrix M_τ are scalar multiples of each other, i.e., if and only if there exists a constant c such that

$$(uS_0 \ dS_0) = c(e^{r\delta t} \ e^{r\delta t}) \iff \begin{cases} uS_0 = ce^{r\delta t} \\ dS_0 = ce^{r\delta t} \end{cases}$$

$$\iff u = d = \frac{ce^{r\delta t}}{S_0},$$

which contradicts the assumption that $d < u$.

We conclude that $\mathrm{rank}(M_\tau) = 2$ and therefore that the two assets are non–redundant. □

Consider a portfolio made of the m securities and consisting of Θ_j units of asset j at time t_0, $j = 1:m$. The value V_{t_0} of the portfolio at time t_0 is

$$V_{t_0} = \sum_{j=1}^{m} \Theta_j S_{jt_0} = \Theta^t S_{t_0}, \qquad (3.6)$$

where $\Theta = (\Theta_j)_{j=1:m}$ denotes the $m \times 1$ column vector of securities positions; cf. (1.5) and since $S_{t_0} = (S_{jt_0})_{j=1:m}$.

Lemma 3.1. *Consider a one period market model with m securities and n market states at time $\tau > t_0$ and with payoff matrix $M_\tau = \mathrm{row}(S_{j\tau})_{j=1:m}$. Let Θ be the positions vector at time t_0 of a portfolio made of the m securities and assume that* the asset positions in the portfolio remain unchanged until time τ. If V_τ is the $1 \times n$ row vector of the possible values of the portfolio at time τ, then

$$V_\tau = \Theta^t M_\tau = \sum_{j=1}^{m} \Theta_j S_{j\tau}. \qquad (3.7)$$

Proof. Let $V_\tau^{\omega^k}$ be the value at time τ of the portfolio if state ω^k occurs, for $k = 1:n$. Since the asset positions at time τ are Θ_j, $j = 1:m$, it follows that

$$V_\tau^{\omega^k} = \sum_{j=1}^{m} \Theta_j S_{j\tau}^{\omega^k} = \Theta^t S_\tau^{\omega^k}, \qquad (3.8)$$

where $S_{j\tau}^{\omega^k}$ is the value of asset j at time τ if state ω^k occurs, for $k = 1:n$, and $S_\tau^{\omega^k} = \left(S_{j\tau}^{\omega^k}\right)_{j=1:m}$; see (3.1). Then, from (3.8), we obtain that

$$\begin{aligned} V_\tau &= \left(V_\tau^{\omega^1} \; V_\tau^{\omega^2} \; \ldots \; V_\tau^{\omega^n}\right) = \left(\Theta^t S_\tau^{\omega^1} \; \Theta^t S_\tau^{\omega^2} \; \ldots \; \Theta^t S_\tau^{\omega^n}\right) \\ &= \Theta^t \text{col}\left(S_\tau^{\omega^k}\right)_{k=1:n} \\ &= \Theta^t M_\tau, \end{aligned}$$

since $M_\tau = \text{col}\left(S_\tau^{\omega^k}\right)_{k=1:n}$; cf. (3.2).

Using (1.9) and the row form $M_\tau = \text{row}\,(S_{j\tau})_{j=1:m}$ of the payoff matrix M_τ, see (3.3), we conclude that

$$V_\tau = \Theta^t M_\tau = \sum_{j=1}^{m} \Theta_j S_{j\tau}.$$

□

Definition 3.2. *A derivative security is replicable in a market model with m securities and n market states at time $\tau > t_0$ if there exists a portfolio made of the m securities which has the same value as the derivative security in every state of the market at time τ.*

Lemma 3.2. *Consider a market model with m securities and n market states at time $\tau > t_0$ with payoff matrix $M_\tau = \text{row}(S_{j\tau})_{j=1:m}$. Let s_τ be the price vector at time τ of a replicable derivative security, and let $\Theta = (\Theta_j)_{j=1:m}$ be the positions vector of the replicating portfolio. Then,*

$$s_\tau = \Theta^t M_\tau = \sum_{j=1}^{m} \Theta_j S_{j\tau}. \qquad (3.9)$$

We note that, if a derivative security is replicable, its value at time t_0 is not necessarily uniquely determined, unless the market is arbitrage–free; see Theorem 3.1.

Proof. By Definition 3.2, if V_τ is the price vector at time τ of the replicating portfolio of a security with price vector s_τ at time τ, then $V_\tau = s_\tau$. From (3.7), we find that

$$s_\tau = V_\tau = \Theta^t M_\tau = \sum_{j=1}^{m} \Theta_j S_{j\tau}.$$

□

From (3.9), it follows that a derivative security is replicable if and only if the price vector s_τ of the derivative security at time τ belongs to the space generated by the price vectors $S_{j\tau}$, $j = 1:m$, of the m securities at time τ.

Recall from Definition 3.1 that the m securities from a market model with m securities and n market states at time $\tau > t_0$ are non–redundant if and only if their price vectors at time τ are linearly independent. Thus, the m securities are redundant if and only if their price vectors are linearly dependent, in which case the payoff of one of the securities is replicable by using the other $m - 1$ securities. Then, from (3.9), it follows that at least one of the m redundant securities can be synthesized using a portfolio containing the other $m - 1$ securities; see section 1.2.1 for an example of a market with redundant securities.

3.2 Arbitrage–free markets

Arbitrage opportunities arise when there exist investment strategies that generate guaranteed profit (i.e., with no risk). For a one period market model with m securities and n market states, such arbitrage opportunities occur in either one of the two following instances:

(I). If there exists a portfolio with value 0 at time t_0 (i.e., with no set–up cost at time t_0), with nonnegative values in every state of the market at time τ, and with value strictly greater than 0 in at least one state of the market at time τ.

(II). If there exists a portfolio with negative value at time t_0 (i.e., with negative set–up cost at time t_0, and therefore generating a positive cash flow at time t_0) and with nonnegative values in every state of the market at time τ.

The following result gives necessary and sufficient conditions for a one period market model to be arbitrage–free:

Theorem 3.1. *A one period market model with m securities and n market states is arbitrage–free if and only if there exist positive numbers (also called state prices[2]) $Q_k > 0$, $k = 1:n$, such that*

$$S_{t_0} = M_\tau Q, \qquad (3.10)$$

where S_{t_0} is the price vector of the m securities at time t_0, M_τ is the payoff matrix at time τ, and $Q = (Q_k)_{k=1:n}$ is the $n \times 1$ column vector of state prices.

Recall that the column form of the payoff matrix M_τ is $M_\tau = \operatorname{col}\left(S_\tau^{\omega^k}\right)_{k=1:n}$; cf. (3.2). Then, from (1.7), it follows that (3.10) can be written as

$$S_{t_0} = \sum_{k=1}^{n} Q_k S_\tau^{\omega^k}. \qquad (3.11)$$

In other words, a one period market model is arbitrage–free if and only if the price vector of the securities at the initial time t_0 is a linear combination *with positive coefficients* of the price vectors of the securities in the n possible states at time τ.

---
[2] See section 3.4.1 for an explanation of this nomenclature. In a nutshell, in a complete market, Q_k is the fair price at time t_0 of a bet that state ω^k will occur at time τ, or equivalently, the price at time t_0 of state ω^k occurring at time τ.

Note that, although $Q_k > 0$ for all $k = 1 : n$, Q_k is not the probability for state ω^k to occur, since $\sum_{k=1}^{n} Q_k \neq 1$. Thus, formula (3.11) does not state that the price vector of the securities at the initial time t_0 is an expected value of the price vectors of the securities at time τ.

The proof of Theorem 3.1 involves the Fundamental Theorem of Linear Programming, which, informally speaking, states that, if a set of linear inequalities implies another set of linear inequalities, then it does so trivially, i.e., by linear combinations.

While the proof of Theorem 3.1 is beyond our scope here, we will establish the sufficiency of condition (3.10) for a non–arbitrage market model to be arbitrage–free.

Proof. (Sufficiency of condition (3.10) from Theorem 3.1.)
Assume that there exists a vector $Q = (Q_k)_{k=1:n}$ such that

$$S_{t_0} = M_\tau Q \tag{3.12}$$

and $Q_k > 0$, for all $k = 1 : n$. We will show that neither an arbitrage of type (I) nor an arbitrage of type (II) can occur.

An arbitrage of type (I) occurs if and only if there exists an $m \times 1$ positions vector Θ and a state l, $1 \leq l \leq n$, such that

$$V_{t_0} = \Theta^t S_{t_0} = 0; \quad V_\tau^{\omega^k} = \Theta^t S_\tau^{\omega^k} \geq 0, \; \forall \, k = 1 : n; \quad V_\tau^{\omega^l} = \Theta^t S_\tau^{\omega^l} > 0. \tag{3.13}$$

Recall from (3.2) that $M_\tau = \text{col}\left(S_\tau^{\omega^k}\right)_{k=1:n}$ and therefore

$$M_\tau Q = \sum_{k=1}^{n} Q_k S_\tau^{\omega^k}; \tag{3.14}$$

see (1.7). From (3.12) and (3.14), we find that

$$\begin{aligned} V_{t_0} &= \Theta^t S_{t_0} = \Theta^t M_\tau Q = \Theta^t \left(\sum_{k=1}^{n} Q_k S_\tau^{\omega^k} \right) \\ &= \sum_{k=1}^{n} Q_k \Theta^t S_\tau^{\omega^k} \\ &= \sum_{k=1}^{n} Q_k V_\tau^{\omega^k}, \end{aligned} \tag{3.15}$$

since $V_\tau^{\omega^k} = \Theta^t S_\tau^{\omega^k}$; see (3.13).

Recall from (3.13) that $V_\tau^{\omega^l} > 0$. Also, $Q_l > 0$, and, for all $1 \leq k \leq n$, $Q_k > 0$ and $V_\tau^{\omega^k} \geq 0$. Then, it follows from (3.15) that

$$V_{t_0} = \sum_{k=1}^{n} Q_k V_\tau^{\omega^k} \geq Q_l V_\tau^{\omega^l} > 0,$$

since $Q_l > 0$, which contradicts the assumption $V_{t_0} = 0$ from the no–arbitrage condition (3.13).

3.2. ARBITRAGE–FREE MARKETS

An arbitrage of type (II) occurs if and only if there exists an $m \times 1$ positions vector Θ such that

$$V_{t_0} = \Theta^t S_{t_0} < 0 \quad \text{and} \quad V_\tau^{\omega^k} = \Theta^t S_\tau^{\omega^k} \geq 0, \quad \forall\, k = 1:n. \tag{3.16}$$

Note that, since $S_{t_0} = M_\tau Q$, formula (3.15) holds, i.e.,

$$V_{t_0} = \sum_{k=1}^{n} Q_k V_\tau^{\omega^k}.$$

Then, since $Q_k > 0$ and $V_\tau^{\omega^k} \geq 0$ for all $k = 1:n$, we find that $V_{t_0} \geq 0$, which contradicts the assumption that $V_{t_0} < 0$ from the no–arbitrage condition (3.16). □

One Period Binomial Model Example (Continued):
The one period binomial model is arbitrage–free if and only if

$$d < e^{r\delta t} < u. \tag{3.17}$$

To see this, note that, from Theorem 3.1, it follows that the one period binomial model is arbitrage–free if and only if there exist $Q = \begin{pmatrix} Q_1 \\ Q_2 \end{pmatrix}$ with $Q_1 > 0$ and $Q_2 > 0$ such that

$$M_\tau Q = S_{t_0}, \tag{3.18}$$

where S_{t_0} is the price vector of the securities at time t_0 given by (3.4) and M_τ is the payoff matrix at time τ given by (3.5).

The equality (3.18) can be written as follows:

$$\begin{pmatrix} e^{r\delta t} & e^{r\delta t} \\ uS_0 & dS_0 \end{pmatrix} \begin{pmatrix} Q_1 \\ Q_2 \end{pmatrix} = \begin{pmatrix} 1 \\ S_0 \end{pmatrix} \iff \begin{cases} e^{r\delta t}Q_1 + e^{r\delta t}Q_2 = 1 \\ uS_0 Q_1 + dS_0 Q_2 = S_0 \end{cases}$$

which can be written as

$$Q_1 + Q_2 = e^{-r\delta t}; \tag{3.19}$$
$$uQ_1 + dQ_2 = 1. \tag{3.20}$$

By multiplying (3.19) by d and subtracting the resulting equation from (3.20) and solving for Q_1, we obtain that

$$Q_1 = \frac{1 - de^{-r\delta t}}{u - d} = e^{-r\delta t} \frac{e^{r\delta t} - d}{u - d}. \tag{3.21}$$

From (3.19) and (3.21), we find that

$$Q_2 = \frac{ue^{-r\delta t} - 1}{u - d} = e^{-r\delta t} \frac{u - e^{r\delta t}}{u - d}. \tag{3.22}$$

Recall that $d < u$ and therefore $u - d > 0$. Then, from (3.21) and (3.22), if follows that $Q_1 > 0$ and $Q_2 > 0$ if and only if $d < e^{r\delta t} < u$. From Theorem 3.1, we conclude that the one period binomial model is arbitrage–free if and only if $d < e^{r\delta t} < u$, which is what we wanted to show; cf. (3.17).

The intuition behind the no–arbitrage condition (3.17) is as follows: if (3.17) were not satisfied, then the following arbitrage opportunities would occur:

- If $d \geq e^{r\delta t}$, then the asset will appreciate at least at the risk free rate even if its value at time τ is dS_0, the lower of the two possible values for the asset. The arbitrage follows from a "buy low, sell high" strategy: borrowing cash and purchasing the asset is guaranteed not to lose money in either state of the market at time τ, and will have a positive payoff if the value of the asset at time τ is uS_0. This is an arbitrage opportunity of type (I).

- If $e^{r\delta t} \geq u$, then the asset will appreciate at most at the risk free rate even if its value at time τ is uS_0, the higher of the two possible values for the asset. The arbitrage follows from a "buy low, sell high" strategy: shorting the asset and investing the cash at the risk–free rate is guaranteed to not lose money in either state of the market at time τ, and will have a positive payoff if the value of the asset at time τ is dS_0. This is an arbitrage opportunity of type (I). $\square$

The result below is a special case of the no–arbitrage Law of One Price for arbitrage–free one period market models; see Stefanica [36, 37] for a general form of the Law of One Price and more applications.

Theorem 3.2. *(The Law of One Price) Consider an arbitrage–free one period market model with m securities and n market states. If two portfolios have the same value in every state of the market at time $\tau > t_0$, then they must have the same value at time t_0.*

Proof. Let V_{t_0} and W_{t_0} be the values at time t_0 of two portfolios which have the same value in every state of the market at time τ, i.e. $V_\tau^{\omega^k} = W_\tau^{\omega^k}$, for all $1 \leq k \leq n$. We will show that if the one period market model is arbitrage–free, then $V_{t_0} = W_{t_0}$.

If $V_{t_0} \neq W_{t_0}$, assume, for example, that $V_{t_0} < W_{t_0}$ and consider a portfolio with a long position in the first portfolio and a short position in the second portfolio. The value at time t_0 of this portfolio is $V_{t_0} - W_{t_0} < 0$, while its value in any state ω^k at time τ is 0, since $V_\tau^{\omega^k} - W_\tau^{\omega^k} = 0$ for all $k = 1 : n$. This is an arbitrage of type (II), which contradicts the fact that the one period market model was arbitrage–free. The contradiction comes from the assumption that $V_{t_0} \neq W_{t_0}$, and therefore we conclude that $V_{t_0} = W_{t_0}$. $\square$

The value of a replicable derivative security in an arbitrage–free market can be determined as follows:

Lemma 3.3. *Consider an arbitrage–free one period market model with m securities and n market states. Let $Q_k > 0$, $k = 1 : n$, be the state prices, and let $Q = (Q_k)_{k=1:n}$. Let s_τ be the $1 \times n$ price vector at time τ of a replicable security. The value s_{t_0} at time t_0 of the replicable security is*

$$s_{t_0} = s_\tau Q = \sum_{k=1}^{n} Q_k s_\tau^{\omega^k}, \qquad (3.23)$$

where $s_\tau^{\omega^k}$ is the value of the replicable security at time τ if state ω^k occurs.

3.3. COMPLETE MARKETS

Proof. If the derivative security is replicable, then there exists a portfolio made of the m securities which has the same values at time τ as the derivative security, regardless of the state the market is at time τ. Let Θ be the $m \times 1$ positions vector of the replicating portfolio. Then,

$$s_\tau = \Theta^t M_\tau, \qquad (3.24)$$

where M_τ is the payoff matrix of the m securities at time τ; cf. (3.9) from Lemma 3.2.

Since the market model is arbitrage–free, it follows from Theorem 3.2 that the value s_{t_0} at time t_0 of the replicable derivative security must be the same as the value $\Theta^t S_{t_0}$ of the replicating portfolio at time t_0, i.e.,

$$s_{t_0} = \Theta^t S_{t_0}, \qquad (3.25)$$

where S_{t_0} is the price vector of the m securities at time t_0.

Recall from Theorem 3.1 that

$$S_{t_0} = M_\tau Q, \qquad (3.26)$$

where $Q = (Q_k)_{k=1:n}$ is the column vector of the state prices $Q_k > 0$, $k = 1:n$.

From (3.25), (3.26), and (3.24), we conclude that

$$s_{t_0} = \Theta^t S_{t_0} = \Theta^t M_\tau Q = s_\tau Q = \sum_{k=1}^{n} Q_k s_\tau^{\omega^k}, \qquad (3.27)$$

which is what we wanted to show; cf. (3.23). Note that, for the last equality from (3.27), we used the row vector – column vector multiplication formula (1.5) and the fact that $s_\tau = (s_\tau^{\omega^1} \ldots s_\tau^{\omega^n})$ is an $1 \times n$ row vector. $\square$

3.3 Complete markets

Definition 3.3. *A one period market model with m securities and n market states at time $\tau > t_0$ is complete if and only if any cash flow at time τ can be replicated using a portfolio made of the m securities.*

In other words, the one period market model is complete if and only if, for any $1 \times n$ payoff vector C_τ, there exists an $m \times 1$ positions vector Θ such that

$$C_\tau = \Theta^t M_\tau. \qquad (3.28)$$

Theorem 3.3. *A one period market model with m securities and n market states at time $\tau > t_0$ is complete if and only if the market contains n non–redundant securities, i.e., if and only if the row rank of the payoff matrix M_τ is equal to n, the number of possible states at time τ.*

Note that a consequence of Theorem 3.3 is that a complete market must contain at least as many securities as possible states in the future, i.e., that $m \geq n$, which is an intuitive requirement.

Proof. Let $M_\tau = \text{row}\,(S_{j\tau})_{j=1:m}$ be the row form of the payoff matrix M_τ, where $S_{j\tau}$ is the price vector of asset j at time τ, $j = 1 : m$; cf. (3.3). From (1.9), it follows that

$$\Theta^t M_\tau = \sum_{j=1}^m \Theta_j S_{j\tau}. \tag{3.29}$$

Recall from (3.28) that a market is complete if and only if for any $1 \times n$ payoff vector C_τ there exists an $m \times 1$ positions vector Θ such that $C_\tau = \Theta^t M_\tau$. Then, from (3.29), we find that the market is complete if and only if

$$<S_{1\tau}, S_{2\tau}, \ldots, S_{m\tau}> \;=\; \left\{\sum_{j=1}^m \Theta_j S_{j\tau} \text{ with } \Theta_j \in \mathbb{R}, j = 1 : m\right\} \;=\; \mathbb{R}^{1 \times n},$$

i.e., if $\mathbb{R}^{1 \times n}$ is the space generated by the vectors $S_{j\tau}$, $j = 1 : m$. This happens if and only if there are exactly n linearly independent vectors among the price vectors $S_{1\tau}, S_{2\tau}, \ldots, S_{m\tau}$ of the m securities, and therefore if and only if there exist exactly n non–redundant securities. $\square$

Lemma 3.4. *A one period market model with n securities and n states at time $\tau > t_0$ is complete if and only if the payoff matrix M_τ is nonsingular.*

Proof. From Theorem 3.3, it follows a one period market model with n securities and n states is complete if and only if the matrix M_τ has row rank n, i.e., it has n linearly independent rows. Since M_τ is an $n \times n$ matrix, it follows that $\text{rank}(M_\tau) = n$, and, from Theorem 1.1, we conclude that the matrix M_τ is nonsingular. $\square$

One Period Binomial Model Example (Continued):
The one period binomial model is complete.
 To see this, recall from (3.5) that the payoff matrix at time τ corresponding to one period binomial model is

$$M_\tau = \begin{pmatrix} e^{r\delta t} & e^{r\delta t} \\ uS_0 & dS_0 \end{pmatrix}.$$

From (10.6), we obtain that

$$\det(M_\tau) = e^{r\delta t} dS_0 - e^{r\delta t} uS_0 = e^{r\delta t} S_0 (d - u),$$

and therefore $\det(M_\tau) \neq 0$, since we assumed that $d < u$.
 Then, from Theorem 1.2, it follows that the matrix M_τ is nonsingular, and, from Lemma 3.4, we conclude that the one period binomial model is complete. $\square$

3.4 Risk–neutral pricing in arbitrage–free complete markets

Theorem 3.4. *Consider an arbitrage–free complete one period market model with m securities and n market states at time $\tau > t_0$, and let $Q = (Q_k)_{k=1:n}$ be the vector of state prices.*

(i) The value V_{t_0} at time t_0 of a derivative security with payoff vector V_τ at time τ is

$$V_{t_0} = V_\tau Q = \sum_{k=1}^{n} Q_k V_\tau^{\omega^k}. \tag{3.30}$$

(ii) Assume one of the securities is cash. Assume that the risk–free rate is constant between times t_0 and τ, and denote it by r.

The value V_{t_0} at time t_0 of a derivative security is the discounted expected value of its payoff V_τ at time τ with respect to the discrete risk–neutral probability p_{RN} associated to each state of the market at time τ given by $p_{RN}(k) = e^{r\delta t} Q_k$, for all $k = 1:n$, where $\delta t = \tau - t_0$, i.e.,

$$V_{t_0} = e^{-r\delta t} \sum_{k=1}^{n} p_{RN}(k) V_\tau^{\omega^k} = e^{-r\delta t} E_{RN}[V_\tau]. \tag{3.31}$$

Proof. (i) Recall from Lemma 3.3 that the value V_{t_0} at time t_0 of any replicable security in an arbitrage–free one period market model is given by $V_{t_0} = V_\tau Q$, where V_τ is the price vector at time τ of the replicable security. Since any derivative security is replicable in a complete market, we conclude that $V_{t_0} = V_\tau Q$ for *every derivative security* in a complete and arbitrage–free one period market model.

(ii) Since $Q_k > 0$ for all $k = 1:n$, a discrete probability (called the risk–neutral probability) $p_{RN}(k)$ associated to each state ω^k of the market at time τ can be obtained as follows:

$$p_{RN}(k) = \frac{Q_k}{\sum_{i=1}^{n} Q_i}, \quad \forall \, k = 1:n. \tag{3.32}$$

Note that

$$p_{RN}(k) > 0, \; \forall \, k = 1:n; \quad \sum_{i=1}^{n} p_{RN}(k) = 1.$$

Since

$$Q_k = \left(\sum_{i=1}^{n} Q_i\right) p_{RN}(k), \tag{3.33}$$

see (3.32), it follows from (3.30) and (3.33) that

$$V_{t_0} = \sum_{k=1}^{n} Q_k V_\tau^{\omega^k} = \sum_{k=1}^{n} \left(\sum_{i=1}^{n} Q_i\right) p_{RN}(k) V_\tau^{\omega^k}$$

$$= \left(\sum_{i=1}^{n} Q_i\right) \sum_{k=1}^{n} p_{RN}(k) V_\tau^{\omega^k}. \tag{3.34}$$

Assume without restricting the generality that the first security is a $1 cash position at time t_0. Since the continuously compounded risk free rate r is constant between the times t_0 and τ, it follows that

$$S_{1t_0} = 1 \quad \text{and} \quad S_{1\tau}^{\omega^i} = e^{r\delta t}, \quad \forall\, i = 1:n. \tag{3.35}$$

Recall the no-arbitrage condition $S_{t_0} = M_\tau Q$, see (3.10), and, from (3.3), that $M_\tau = \text{row}\,(S_{j\tau})_{j=1:m}$. From (1.8), it follows that the first entry of $M_\tau Q$ is $S_{1\tau} Q$, and therefore, since $S_{t_0} = M_\tau Q$, we find that

$$S_{1t_0} = S_{1\tau} Q. \tag{3.36}$$

Since $S_{1\tau} = (S_{1\tau}^{\omega^1} \ \ldots \ S_{1\tau}^{\omega^n})$ and $Q = (Q_i)_{i=1:n}$, we obtain from (3.36) and (1.5) that

$$S_{1t_0} = \sum_{i=1}^{n} S_{1\tau}^{\omega^i} Q_i, \tag{3.37}$$

Then, from (3.37) and (3.35), it follows that

$$1 = \sum_{i=1}^{n} e^{r\delta t} Q_i = e^{r\delta t} \sum_{i=1}^{n} Q_i,$$

and therefore we obtain that

$$\sum_{i=1}^{n} Q_i = e^{-r\delta t}. \tag{3.38}$$

Then, the discrete risk–neutral probability given by (3.32) becomes

$$p_{RN}(k) = \frac{Q^k}{\sum_{i=1}^{n} Q_i} = e^{r\delta t} Q_k, \quad \forall\, k = 1:n, \tag{3.39}$$

and, from (3.34) and (3.38), we find that

$$V_{t_0} = e^{-r\delta t} \sum_{k=1}^{n} p_{RN}(k) V_\tau^{\omega^k} = e^{-r\delta t} E_{RN}\left[V_\tau\right],$$

where $E_{RN}\left[V_\tau\right] = \sum_{k=1}^{n} p_{RN}(k) V_\tau^{\omega^k}$ denotes the expected value of the payoff V_τ of the derivative security with respect to the risk–neutral distribution p_{RN}. $\square$

One Period Binomial Model Example (Continued):

In section 3.3, we showed that the one period binomial model is complete. Also, recall from (3.17), (3.21), and (3.22) that the one period binomial model is arbitrage-free if and only if $d < e^{r\delta t} < u$ and the state prices are

$$Q_1 = e^{-r\delta t}\,\frac{e^{r\delta t} - d}{u - d}; \quad Q_2 = e^{-r\delta t}\,\frac{u - e^{r\delta t}}{u - d}. \tag{3.40}$$

3.4. STATE PRICES

From (3.39) and (3.40), we find that the risk–neutral probabilities associated to each of the two states of the market at time τ are

$$p_{RN}(1) = e^{r\delta t}Q^1 = \frac{e^{r\delta t} - d}{u - d};$$

$$p_{RN}(2) = e^{r\delta t}Q^2 = \frac{u - e^{r\delta t}}{u - d}.$$

Then, we obtain from (3.31) that the value at time t_0 of a derivative security with payoffs at time τ equal to $V_\tau(1)$, if the "up" state occurs, and equal to $V_\tau(2)$, if the "down" state occurs, is

$$\begin{aligned} V_{t_0} &= e^{-r\delta t}\left(p_{RN}(1)V_\tau(1) + p_{RN}(2)V_\tau(2)\right) \\ &= e^{-r\delta t}\left(\frac{e^{r\delta t} - d}{u - d}V_\tau(1) + \frac{u - e^{r\delta t}}{u - d}V_\tau(2)\right). \quad \square \end{aligned} \qquad (3.41)$$

We conclude this section by providing further intuition on the no–arbitrage condition (3.11) for a one period market model, if the market is also complete. From the definition (3.32) of the discrete risk–neutral state probabilities at time τ, we find that

$$Q_k = \left(\sum_{i=1}^n Q_i\right) p_{RN}(k).$$

Then, the no–arbitrage condition (3.11) can be written as

$$\begin{aligned} S_{t_0} &= \sum_{k=1}^n Q_k S_\tau^{\omega^k} = \sum_{k=1}^n \left(\sum_{i=1}^n Q_i\right) p_{RN}(k) S_\tau^{\omega^k} \\ &= \left(\sum_{i=1}^n Q^i\right) \sum_{k=1}^n p_{RN}(k) S_\tau^{\omega^k} \\ &= e^{-r\delta t} \sum_{i=1}^n p_{RN}(k) S_\tau^{\omega^k}, \end{aligned} \qquad (3.42)$$

where the last equality follows from (3.38).

Thus, in a complete market, the no–arbitrage condition (3.11) states that the initial values at time t_0 of the m securities are equal to the present values of the risk–neutral expected values of the securities at time τ.

3.4.1 State prices

We can now explain why the values $Q^i > 0$, $i = 1 : n$, which appeared in the arbitrage–free condition (3.10) for a one period market model are called state prices.

Consider a derivative security paying \$1 if state ω^p occurs at time τ and 0 otherwise; this derivative security is also called an insurance contract on the state ω^p. In other words, if C_τ is the $n \times 1$ price vector of the insurance contract at time τ, then

$$C_\tau^{\omega^k} = 0, \ \forall\ 1 \leq k \neq p \leq n; \quad C_\tau^{\omega^p} = 1.$$

If the market is complete and arbitrage–free, it follows from (3.30) that the value C_{t_0} of the insurance contract at time t_0 is

$$C_{t_0} = \sum_{k=1}^{n} C_\tau^{\omega^k} Q_k = Q_p.$$

We conclude that, for any $p = 1 : n$, Q_p is the price of the insurance contract paying \$1 if state p occurs, which can also be regarded as the price at time t_0 of state ω^p occurring at time τ.

3.5 A one period index options market model

A snapshot taken on March 9, 2012, of the mid prices (i.e., the average of the bid and ask prices) and trading volumes of S&P 500 options maturing on December 22, 2012, (i.e., 12/22/2012), corresponding to a spot price of the index of 1,370, can be found in Table 3.1.

Table 3.1: Dec 2012 SPX option prices on 3/9/2012

Call Strike	Price	Volume	Put Strike	Price	Volume
C1175	225.40	250	P1175	46.60	1
C1200	205.55	215	P1200	51.55	3204
C1225	186.20	1	P1225	57.15	1401
C1250	167.50	650	P1250	63.30	104
C1275	149.15	163	P1275	70.15	56
C1300	131.70	1	P1300	77.70	150
C1325	115.25	40	P1325	86.20	200
C1350	99.55	320	P1350	95.30	10118
C1375	84.90	1002	P1375	105.30	1250
C1400	71.10	5300	P1400	116.55	1250
C1425	58.70	4	P1425	129.00	200
C1450	47.25	9050	P1450	143.20	1
C1500	29.25	1000	P1500	173.95	6
C1550	15.80	1000	P1550	210.80	9
C1575	11.10	200	P1575	230.90	0
C1600	7.90	546	P1600	252.40	9

We use a small number of these options to construct an arbitrage–free complete one period market model for the 12/22/2012 S&P options as follows:[3] We choose one call option and one put option with the same strike, with all the other options having different strikes. The strikes of the options will cover the majority of the range of strikes, and are best not to be close to each other; e.g., the strikes of the options from (3.43) are at least 50 apart. We will subsequently show that the rest of the options from Table 3.1 are accurately priced in this model.

---
[3]The author first learned of this type of one period market models for options from the regretted Salih Neftci; see also Chapter 11 from the monograph Neftci [31].

3.5. AN INDEX OPTIONS MARKET MODEL

Consider the following seven securities:[4]

$$\begin{matrix} P1200; \\ P1300; \\ P1400; \\ C1400; \\ C1450; \\ C1550; \\ C1600. \end{matrix} \quad (3.43)$$

Note that the options from (3.43) are out–of–the–money puts and out–of–the–money calls,[5] plus a put option (P1400) and a call option (C1400) struck around at–the–money; recall that the spot price of the index was $1,370$. For details on at–the–money, out–of–the–money, and in–the–money options, see Section 10.3.

The price vector of the securities from (3.43) at time t_0 is the vector of their mid prices from Table 3.1, i.e.,

$$S_{t_0} = \begin{pmatrix} 51.55 \\ 77.70 \\ 116.55 \\ 71.10 \\ 47.25 \\ 15.80 \\ 7.90 \end{pmatrix}. \quad (3.44)$$

Seven possible states of the index price on 12/22/2012 are obtained as follows: There are six option strikes corresponding to the securities above, i.e.,

$$1200, 1300, 1400, 1450, 1550, 1600.$$

The five midpoints

$$1250, 1350, 1425, 1500, 1575$$

between the strikes above will give the following five states:

$$\omega^2 : \{S(\tau) = 1250\}; \quad \omega^5 : \{S(\tau) = 1500\};$$
$$\omega^3 : \{S(\tau) = 1350\}; \quad \omega^6 : \{S(\tau) = 1575\};$$
$$\omega^4 : \{S(\tau) = 1425\},$$

where $S(\tau)$ denotes the value of the S&P 500 index on 12/22/2012. Below the lowest strike and above the highest strike we choose the following two states:[6]

$$\omega^1 : \{S(\tau) = 1000\}; \quad \omega^7 : \{S(\tau) = 1700\}.$$

---

[4] More choices of securities are discussed in exercises at the end of the chapter.

[5] The choice of out–of–the–money options is driven by the fact that options market makers only trade out–of–the–money options, which have the same implied volatilities as corresponding in–the–money options. For example, the trading volume of the out–of–the–money options (C1400 through C1600 and P1175 through P1350) from Table 3.1 is $32,359$, while the trading volume of the in–the–money options (C1175 through C1350 and P1400 through P1600) is $3,134$, about 10 times smaller.

[6] The choice of the two states below the smallest option strike and above the largest strike could influence whether the one period market model is arbitrage–free, and the overall performance of the risk–neutral pricing of the other derivative securities.

102 CHAPTER 3. THE ARROW–DEBREU ONE PERIOD MARKET MODEL

Recall from (10.90) and (10.91) that the payoffs at maturity of call and put options are, respectively,

$$C(T) = \max(S(T) - K, 0) = \begin{cases} S(T) - K, & \text{if } S(T) > K; \\ 0, & \text{if } S(T) \leq K. \end{cases} \quad (3.45)$$

$$P(T) = \max(K - S(T), 0) = \begin{cases} 0, & \text{if } S(T) \geq K; \\ K - S(T), & \text{if } S(T) < K. \end{cases} \quad (3.46)$$

Then, the payoff matrix of this one period market model is

$$M_\tau = \begin{pmatrix} 200 & 0 & 0 & 0 & 0 & 0 & 0 \\ 300 & 50 & 0 & 0 & 0 & 0 & 0 \\ 400 & 150 & 50 & 0 & 0 & 0 & 0 \\ 0 & 0 & 0 & 25 & 100 & 175 & 300 \\ 0 & 0 & 0 & 0 & 50 & 125 & 250 \\ 0 & 0 & 0 & 0 & 0 & 25 & 150 \\ 0 & 0 & 0 & 0 & 0 & 0 & 100 \end{pmatrix}. \quad (3.47)$$

For example, $M_\tau(3,3)$ is the payoff of the third security P1400, i.e., of the put option with strike 1400, if state ω^3 occurs, i.e., if $S(\tau) = 1350$, and from (3.46) we find that

$$M_\tau(3,3) = \max(1400 - S(\tau), 0) = \max(1400 - 1350, 0) = 50.$$

Similarly, $M_\tau(5,6)$ is the payoff of the fifth security C1450, i.e., of the call option with strike 1450, if state ω^6 occurs, i.e., if $S(\tau) = 1575$, and from (3.45) we find that

$$M_\tau(5,6) = \max(S(\tau) - 1450, 0) = \max(1575 - 1450, 0) = 125.$$

We now show that this model is complete and arbitrage–free.

Note that the matrix M_τ is made of a 3×3 lower triangular block and a 4×4 upper triangular block. Thus, its determinant $\det(M_\tau)$ is the product of the diagonal entries of M_τ, and therefore nonzero; see Section 10.1.1. It follows that the matrix M_τ is nonsingular, see Theorem 1.2, and, from Lemma 3.4, we conclude that this market model is complete.

To decide whether this market model is arbitrage–free, we must solve the linear system $M_\tau Q = S_{t_0}$, where M_τ and S_{t_0} are given by (3.47) and (3.44), respectively, and check whether all the entries of the vector Q are positive.

Note that, due to the block structure of the payoff matrix M_τ, solving the linear system $M_\tau Q = S_{t_0}$ amounts to a forward substitution corresponding to the 3×3 lower triangular block of the matrix M_τ for computing the first 3 entries of Q, and a backward substitution corresponding to the 4×4 upper triangular block of M_τ for computing the last 4 entries of Q, i.e.,

$$Q = \begin{pmatrix} \text{forward\_subst}\left(\begin{pmatrix} 200 & 0 & 0 \\ 300 & 50 & 0 \\ 400 & 150 & 50 \end{pmatrix}, \begin{pmatrix} 51.55 \\ 77.70 \\ 116.55 \end{pmatrix} \right) \\ \text{backward\_subst}\left(\begin{pmatrix} 25 & 100 & 175 & 300 \\ 0 & 50 & 125 & 250 \\ 0 & 0 & 25 & 150 \\ 0 & 0 & 0 & 100 \end{pmatrix}, \begin{pmatrix} 71.10 \\ 47.25 \\ 15.80 \\ 7.90 \end{pmatrix} \right) \end{pmatrix}.$$

3.5. AN INDEX OPTIONS MARKET MODEL

We obtain that
$$Q = \begin{pmatrix} 0.2578 \\ 0.0075 \\ 0.2465 \\ 0.1700 \\ 0.1550 \\ 0.1580 \\ 0.0790 \end{pmatrix}. \tag{3.48}$$

Since all the entries of Q are positive, we conclude from Theorem 3.1 that the one period market model is arbitrage–free.

We conclude that the one period options market model above is both arbitrage–free and complete.

Thus, all the other options can be priced using risk–neutral pricing; cf. Theorem 3.4. For example, the no–arbitrage value of C1300 can be obtained as follows: The payoff vector $C1300_\tau$ of the call option with strike 1300 at maturity 12/22/2012 is
$$C1300_\tau = (0 \ 0 \ 50 \ 125 \ 200 \ 275 \ 400), \tag{3.49}$$
since, e.g., $C1300_\tau(5)$ is the payoff of a call option with strike 1300 if state ω^5 occurs, i.e., if $S(\tau) = 1500$, and from (3.45) we find that
$$C1300_\tau(5) = \max(S(\tau) - 1300, 0) = \max(1500 - 1300, 0) = 200.$$

Then, from (3.30), we find that the no–arbitrage value $C1300_{model}$ of C1300 given by this one period market model is
$$C1300_{model} = C1300_\tau \ Q = \sum_{i=1}^{7} Q(i) C1300_\tau(i)$$
$$= 139.6250,$$

where $C1300_\tau$ is given by (3.49) and Q is given by (3.48). The corresponding percentage error is $\frac{139.6250 - 131.70}{131.70} = 0.0602$, i.e., 6.02% over the mid value 131.70 of C1300.

To estimate the accuracy of this one period market model, we use formula (3.30) to find the risk–neutral value of each of the $32 - 7 = 25$ options from Table 3.1 which were not chosen as securities in the model. These values are denoted by $V_{model}(i)$, for $i = 1 : 25$, and are compared to the mid prices $V_{mid}(i)$ corresponding to the same option, for $i = 1 : 25$. The percentage root–mean–squared error (RMSE) of the model is then calculated as follows:

$$\text{RMSE} = \sqrt{\frac{1}{25} \sum_{i=1}^{25} \frac{(V_{model}(i) - V_{mid}(i))^2}{V_{mid}(i)^2}}$$
$$= 0.0506 = 5.06\%;$$

In other words, the options that were not chosen to be securities in the model are priced, on average, within 5% of their mid price by using the seven options from this one period market model.

3.6 References

The Arrow–Debreu model was introduced in the seminal paper [5]; a modern exposition can be found in Avellaneda and Laurence [7].

Neftci [31] covers the one period market model as a general pricing framework for derivative securities, and presents its uses by financial engineering practitioners.

The one period binomial tree risk–neutral pricing formula (3.41) can also be obtained by using either a hedged portfolio or payoff replication; see Blyth [8] for more details. Binomial and trinomial trees are used in practice as numerical methods for pricing derivative securities, and they are implemented on many time steps. The calibration of tree models and numerical implementation details can be found in Clewlow and Strickland [11] and Wilmott [45].

3.7 Exercises

1. In three months, the value of an asset with spot price $50 will be either $60 or $40, with probability one half. What is the value of a three months at–the–money put on this asset? Assume the risk–free interest rate is zero.

2. A one period market with four securities and four states at time $\tau > t_0$ has the following price vector of spot prices at the initial time t_0:

$$S_{t_0} = \begin{pmatrix} 4 \\ 100 \\ 1 \\ -2 \end{pmatrix},$$

and the following payoff matrix at time τ:

$$M_\tau = \begin{pmatrix} 1 & 1 & 1 & 1 \\ 20 & 22 & 24 & 26 \\ -5 & -3 & -1 & 2 \\ 4 & 2 & 0 & 0 \end{pmatrix}.$$

Find an arbitrage opportunity.

3. A one period market model is made of four securities and has four states at time $\tau > t_0$. Assume that the market model is complete and that the state prices are -1, 1, 2, and 4, respectively. Find an arbitrage opportunity.

4. At time $\tau > t_0$, an asset with spot price S_0 at time t_0 will be worth either uS_0, in which case the value of $1 today would be FV_1, or dS_0, in which case the value of $1 today would be FV_2, with $d < u$. Consider the one period market model with two securities, i.e., cash and the asset, and two states, i.e., asset value at time τ equal to uS_0 and asset value at time τ equal to dS_0.

    (i) Show that the payoff matrix at time τ of this one period market model is

    $$\begin{pmatrix} FV_1 & FV_2 \\ uS_0 & dS_0 \end{pmatrix}$$

    (ii) Find necessary and sufficient conditions for the model to be complete.

    (iii) Show that this model is arbitrage–free if and only if

    $$\min\left(\frac{u}{FV_1}, \frac{d}{FV_2}\right) < 1 < \max\left(\frac{u}{FV_1}, \frac{d}{FV_2}\right). \quad (3.50)$$

    (iv) Show that, if $FV_1 = FV_2 = e^{r\delta t}$, the condition (3.50) is equivalent to the no–arbitrage condition $d < e^{r\delta t} < u$ for the classical one period binomial model.

5. In a one period trinomial model, it is assumed that the price at time $\tau > t_0$ of an asset with price S_0 at time t_0 will be either dS_0, mS_0, or uS_0, where $d < m < u$.

Consider a one period market model with two securities, i.e., the asset described above and cash, and three states, i.e., state ω^1, when the price of the asset at time τ is dS_0, state ω^2, when the price of the asset at time τ is mS_0, and state ω^3, when the price of the asset at time τ is uS_0.

(i) Show that the one period trinomial model is incomplete.

(ii) Show that the one period trinomial model is arbitrage–free if and only if

$$d < e^{r\delta t} < u,$$

where $\delta t = \tau - t_0$.

6. In three months, the value of an asset with spot price $40 will be either $32, $38, $42, or $44. The value of a three months European call option with strike $36 on this asset is $8 and the value of a three months European put option with strike $40 on this asset is $5. For simplicity, assume zero risk free rates. Consider the one period market model with the following four securities and the following four states in three months:

Securities:
- cash;
- asset;
- three months call with strike $36;
- three months put with strike $40;

Market states:
- asset price $32;
- asset price $38;
- asset price $42;
- asset price $44.

(i) Find the payoff matrix of this model, and show that the four securities are non–redundant.

(ii) Show that the one period market model is complete.

(iii) How do you replicate a bull spread made of a long position in a three months call with strike $34 and a short position in a three months call with strike $40 in this one period market?

(iv) Show that this model is not arbitrage–free, and find an arbitrage opportunity.

3.7. EXERCISES

7. Two assets have spot prices $20 and $30, respectively. Assume that, in five months, the first asset will be worth either $18 or $22, and the second asset will be worth either $28 or $32. Also, assume that the risk–free rate for five months cash deposits is 0. Consider the one period market model with the following three securities and the following four states in five months:

   Securities:
   - cash;
   - first asset;
   - second asset.

   Market states:
   - first asset at $22 and second asset at $32;
   - first asset at $22 and second asset at $28;
   - first asset at $18 and second asset at $32;
   - first asset at $18 and second asset at $28.

   (i) Show that this one period market model is arbitrage–free.

   (ii) Show that, in this one period market model, it is not possible to replicate a derivative security that pays $1 if the first state occurs (i.e., if, in five months, the first asset is worth $22 and the second asset is worth $32), and does not pay anything if any other state occurs. Conclude that the model is not complete.

   Hint: For (i), consider the case when all state prices are equal to $\frac{1}{4}$.

8. This exercise is related to the example from Chapter 1.

   Consider two assets with spot prices $30 and $50, respectively. Assume that, in three months, the first asset will be worth either $34 or $24, and the second asset will be worth either $56, $51, or $46. The value of a three months at–the–money European call option with strike $30 on the first asset is $2.5, the value of a three months at–the–money European call option with strike $50 on the second asset is $2.7, and the value of a three months European put option with strike $52 on the second asset is $4.1. Assume that the future value in three months of $1 today is $1.01. Consider the one period market model with the following six securities and the following six states in three months:

   Securities:
   - cash;
   - first asset;
   - second asset;
   - three months ATM call on the first asset;
   - three months ATM call on the second asset;
   - three months put with strike $52 on the second asset;

   Market states:

- first asset at $34 and second asset at $56;
- first asset at $34 and second asset at $51;
- first asset at $34 and second asset at $46;
- first asset at $24 and second asset at $56;
- first asset at $24 and second asset at $51;
- first asset at $24 and second asset at $46.

(i) Show that the payoff matrix for this market model is nonsingular, and conclude that the market is complete.

(ii) Compute the state prices for this model, and show that the market is arbitrage–free.

(iii) Use risk–neutral pricing to find the value of a three months call option with strike $52 on the second asset.

(iv) Use Put–Call parity to find the value of a three months call option with strike $52 on the second asset, and compare it to the value computed at (iii).

(v) What is the value of a bear spread made of a long position in a three months put option with strike $35 on the first asset and a short position in a three months put option with strike $28 on the first asset?

9. This exercise refers to the S&P 500 options prices from Table 3.1.

Consider a one period market model with the following nine securities:

$$P1200;\ P1275;\ P1350;\ P1375;\ C1375;\ C1400;\ C1450;\ C1550;\ C1600.$$

The nine states of the index price at maturity are as follows: seven states correspond to the midpoints between the strikes of the options above, i.e.,

$$\omega^2 : \{S(\tau) = 1237.50\}; \quad \omega^6 : \{S(\tau) = 1425\};$$
$$\omega^3 : \{S(\tau) = 1312.50\}; \quad \omega^7 : \{S(\tau) = 1500\};$$
$$\omega^4 : \{S(\tau) = 1362.50\}; \quad \omega^8 : \{S(\tau) = 1575\};$$
$$\omega^5 : \{S(\tau) = 1387.50\};$$

the first and last state are

$$\omega^1 : \{S(\tau) = 950\}; \quad \omega^9 : \{S(\tau) = 1675\}.$$

(i) Find the payoff matrix M_τ of this one period market model, and show that the model is complete.

(ii) Find the state prices vector Q and show that the model is arbitrage–free.

(iii) Compute the root–mean–squared error (RMSE) of this model. Comment on the precision of this nine securities model compared to the seven securities model from section 3.5.

3.7. EXERCISES

10. This problem refers to the S&P 500 options prices from Table 3.1.

    Consider a one period market model with the same seven securities as in section 3.5, i.e.,

    $$P1200;\ P1300;\ P1400;\ C1400;\ C1450;\ C1550;\ C1600.$$

    The states of this market are the midpoints of the strike, i.e.,

    $$\omega^2 : \{S(\tau) = 1250\}; \qquad \omega^5 : \{S(\tau) = 1500\};$$
    $$\omega^3 : \{S(\tau) = 1350\}; \qquad \omega^6 : \{S(\tau) = 1575\};$$
    $$\omega^4 : \{S(\tau) = 1425\};$$

    and the first and last state are

    $$\omega^1 : \{S(\tau) = 1100\}; \quad \omega^7 : \{S(\tau) = 1700\}.$$

    Show that this market model is not arbitrage–free.

Chapter 4

Eigenvalues and eigenvectors.

Eigenvalues and corresponding eigenvectors of a matrix.

The characteristic polynomial of a matrix. Eigenvalues and the roots of the characteristic polynomial. Multiplicity of eigenvalues.

Linear independent eigenvectors. The number of eigenvalues and eigenvectors of a matrix.

Diagonal forms. Diagonalizable matrices. Matrices with a full set of linearly independent eigenvectors.

Diagonally dominant matrices. Gershgorin's Theorem. Nonsingularity of strictly diagonally dominant matrices.

Eigenvalues and eigenvectors of tridiagonal symmetric matrices.

4.1 Properties and identifying eigenvalues and eigenvectors

Definition 4.1. *If A is a square matrix, then λ is an eigenvalue of A if and only if there exists a column vector $v \neq 0$ such that*

$$Av = \lambda v. \qquad (4.1)$$

The vector v is called an eigenvector corresponding to λ.

Note that, even if all the entries of the matrix A are real numbers, an eigenvalue of A may be a complex number, and the corresponding eigenvector may have complex entries.

If v is an eigenvector corresponding to the eigenvalue λ of A, then, for any constant c, the vector cv is also an eigenvector of A corresponding to λ, since

$$A(cv) = c(Av) = c(\lambda v) = \lambda(cv).$$

However, cv is not considered to be an eigenvector different than v. Only linearly independent eigenvectors count as different eigenvectors. As seen in the example below, it is possible for one eigenvalue to have more than one linearly independent eigenvector.

Example: This example is *for illustration purposes only*; in practice, the eigenvalues and the corresponding eigenvectors of a matrix are computed using numerical methods; see section 4.4 for more details.

(i) Let
$$A = \begin{pmatrix} -8 & 0 & 3 \\ 3 & -2 & -1.5 \\ -18 & 0 & 7 \end{pmatrix}.$$

We will show that[1] the matrix A has eigenvalues 1 and -2, with

$$\text{eigenvectors} \quad \begin{pmatrix} 0 \\ 1 \\ 0 \end{pmatrix} \text{ and } \begin{pmatrix} 1 \\ 0 \\ 2 \end{pmatrix} \quad \text{corresponding to } -2$$

$$\text{eigenvector} \quad \begin{pmatrix} 2 \\ -1 \\ 6 \end{pmatrix} \quad \text{corresponding to } 1.$$

Denote by λ an eigenvalue of A and by $v = (v_i)_{i=1:3}$ a corresponding eigenvector of λ. Then, $Av = \lambda v$, which can be written as the following linear system:

$$-8v_1 + 3v_3 = \lambda v_1; \tag{4.2}$$
$$3v_1 - 2v_2 - 1.5v_3 = \lambda v_2; \tag{4.3}$$
$$-18v_1 + 7v_3 = \lambda v_3. \tag{4.4}$$

By eliminating v_3 from (4.2) and (4.4), we obtain that

$$(\lambda^2 + \lambda - 2)v_1 = (\lambda + 2)(\lambda - 1)v_1 = 0.$$

Thus, either $v_1 = 0$, or $\lambda = -2$, or $\lambda = 1$.

- If $v_1 = 0$, it follows from (4.2) that $v_3 = 0$. From (4.3), we find that $-2v_2 = \lambda v_2$. Recall that $v \neq 0$, since v is an eigenvector. Thus, $v_2 \neq 0$, and therefore $\lambda = -2$. We conclude that $\lambda = -2$ is an eigenvalue of A with corresponding eigenvector

$$\begin{pmatrix} 0 \\ v_2 \\ 0 \end{pmatrix} = v_2 \begin{pmatrix} 0 \\ 1 \\ 0 \end{pmatrix}.$$

Since multiplying of an eigenvector by a constant does not change the eigenvector, we choose $v_2 = 1$ and conclude that $\begin{pmatrix} 0 \\ 1 \\ 0 \end{pmatrix}$ is an eigenvector corresponding to the eigenvalue $\lambda = -2$.

- If $\lambda = -2$, then (4.2) and (4.4) are both equivalent to $v_3 = 2v_1$, and (4.3) holds true with no further constraint on v_1, v_2, or v_3. Thus, any eigenvector corresponding to $\lambda = -2$ is of the form

$$\begin{pmatrix} v_1 \\ v_2 \\ 2v_1 \end{pmatrix} = v_1 \begin{pmatrix} 1 \\ 0 \\ 2 \end{pmatrix} + v_2 \begin{pmatrix} 0 \\ 1 \\ 0 \end{pmatrix}.$$

---

[1] A simpler way to compute the eigenvalues and the corresponding eigenvectors of the matrix A, using the characteristic polynomial of A, will be given subsequently.

4.1. DEFINITIONS AND PROPERTIES

We conclude that the eigenvalue $\lambda = -2$ has two linearly independent eigenvectors, $\begin{pmatrix} 1 \\ 0 \\ 2 \end{pmatrix}$ and $\begin{pmatrix} 0 \\ 1 \\ 0 \end{pmatrix}$.

- If $\lambda = 1$, then (4.2) and (4.4) are both equivalent to $v_3 = 3v_1$, and (4.3) is equivalent to $v_2 = -0.5v_1$. Thus, any eigenvector corresponding to $\lambda = 1$ is of the form

$$\begin{pmatrix} v_1 \\ -0.5v_1 \\ 3v_1 \end{pmatrix} = 0.5v_1 \begin{pmatrix} 2 \\ -1 \\ 6 \end{pmatrix},$$

and we conclude that the eigenvalue $\lambda = 1$ has one eigenvector, e.g., $\begin{pmatrix} 2 \\ -1 \\ 6 \end{pmatrix}$.

(ii) Similarly, it can be shown that the matrix

$$B = \begin{pmatrix} 2 & 2 & -1 \\ -7 & -4 & 2.5 \\ 2 & 4 & -1 \end{pmatrix}$$

has eigenvalues 1 and -2, and has only one linearly independent eigenvector corresponding to each eigenvalue, e.g., the eigenvector $\begin{pmatrix} 1 \\ -1 \\ 2 \end{pmatrix}$ corresponding to -2 and the eigenvector $\begin{pmatrix} 0 \\ 1 \\ 2 \end{pmatrix}$ corresponding to 1. □

Definition 4.2. *Let A be a square matrix of size n. The characteristic polynomial $P_A(t)$ of the matrix A is the polynomial of degree n given by*

$$P_A(t) = det(tI - A), \tag{4.5}$$

where I is the identity matrix of size n.

Theorem 4.1. *If A is a square matrix, then λ is an eigenvalue of A if and only if λ is a root of the characteristic polynomial $P_A(t)$ of A. i.e., if and only if*

$$det(\lambda I - A) = 0.$$

Proof. If λ is an eigenvalue of A with $v \neq 0$ a corresponding eigenvector, then $Av = \lambda v$, which can be written as $(\lambda I - A)v = 0$. From (1.78) and (1.81), it follows that

$$\begin{aligned} Av = \lambda v &\iff (\lambda I - A)v = 0 \iff v \in \text{Null}(\lambda I - A) \\ &\iff \text{Null}(\lambda I - A) \neq \{0\} \iff \lambda I - A \text{ singular matrix} \\ &\iff det(\lambda I - A) = 0. \end{aligned}$$

We conclude that λ is an eigenvalue of A if and only if $P_A(\lambda) = det(\lambda I - A) = 0$. □

The result below is a direct consequence of Theorem 4.1:

Lemma 4.1. *Let A be a square matrix of size n and let λ_i, $i = 1 : n$, be the eigenvalues of A. The characteristic polynomial $P_A(t) = \det(tI - A)$ of A can be written as*

$$P_A(t) = \prod_{i=1}^{n}(t - \lambda_i). \tag{4.6}$$

Examples: We revisit the examples from the beginning of this section, and identify the eigenvalues of the matrices by using characteristic polynomials.

(i) Let

$$A = \begin{pmatrix} -8 & 0 & 3 \\ 3 & -2 & -1.5 \\ -18 & 0 & 7 \end{pmatrix}.$$

Using formula (10.8) for computing the determinant of a 3×3 matrix, we find that the characteristic polynomial of A is

$$\begin{aligned} P_A(t) = \det(tI - A) &= \begin{vmatrix} t+8 & 0 & -3 \\ -3 & t+2 & 1.5 \\ 18 & 0 & t-7 \end{vmatrix} \\ &= (t+8)(t+2)(t-7) - (-3)(t+2)(18) = (t+2)(t^2+t-2) \\ &= (t+2)^2(t-1). \end{aligned}$$

The roots of $P_A(t)$ are $\lambda_1 = \lambda_2 = -2$ and $\lambda_3 = 1$. We identify the eigenvectors corresponding to each eigenvalue separately:

• If $\lambda = -2$, any corresponding eigenvector $v \neq 0$ is a solution to $Av = -2v$, which can be written as

$$\begin{cases} -8v_1 + 3v_3 &= -2v_1 \\ 3v_1 - 2v_2 - 1.5v_3 &= -2v_2 \\ -18v_1 + 7v_3 &= -2v_3 \end{cases} \iff \begin{cases} v_3 &= 2v_1 \\ v_3 &= 2v_1 \\ v_3 &= 2v_1 \end{cases}$$

Thus, any eigenvector corresponding to the eigenvalue $\lambda = -2$ is of the form

$$v = \begin{pmatrix} v_1 \\ v_2 \\ 2v_1 \end{pmatrix} = v_1 \begin{pmatrix} 1 \\ 0 \\ 2 \end{pmatrix} + v_2 \begin{pmatrix} 0 \\ 1 \\ 0 \end{pmatrix},$$

and we conclude that the eigenvalue $\lambda = -2$ has two linearly independent eigenvectors, e.g., $\begin{pmatrix} 1 \\ 0 \\ 2 \end{pmatrix}$ and $\begin{pmatrix} 0 \\ 1 \\ 0 \end{pmatrix}$.

• If $\lambda = 1$, any corresponding eigenvector $v \neq 0$ is a solution to $Av = v$, which can be written as

$$\begin{cases} -8v_1 + 3v_3 &= v_1 \\ 3v_1 - 2v_2 - 1.5v_3 &= v_2 \\ -18v_1 + 7v_3 &= v_3 \end{cases} \iff \begin{cases} v_3 &= 3v_1 \\ 3v_2 &= 3v_1 - 1.5v_3 \\ v_3 &= 3v_1 \end{cases}$$

$$\iff \begin{cases} v_3 &= 3v_1 \\ v_2 &= -0.5v_1 \\ v_3 &= 3v_1 \end{cases}$$

4.1. DEFINITIONS AND PROPERTIES

Thus, any eigenvector corresponding to the eigenvalue $\lambda = 1$ is of the form

$$v = \begin{pmatrix} v_1 \\ -0.5v_1 \\ 3v_1 \end{pmatrix} = 0.5v_1 \begin{pmatrix} 2 \\ -1 \\ 6 \end{pmatrix}.$$

We conclude that the eigenvalue $\lambda = 1$ has one eigenvector, e.g., $\begin{pmatrix} 2 \\ -1 \\ 6 \end{pmatrix}$.

(ii) Let

$$B = \begin{pmatrix} 2 & 2 & -1 \\ -7 & -4 & 2.5 \\ 2 & 4 & -1 \end{pmatrix}.$$

The characteristic polynomial of B is

$$P_B(t) = \det(tI - B) = \begin{vmatrix} t-2 & -2 & 1 \\ 7 & t+4 & -2.5 \\ -2 & -4 & t+1 \end{vmatrix}$$

Using formula (10.8), we find that

$$P_B(t) = t^3 + 3t^2 - 4 = (t-1)(t+2)^2.$$

The roots of the characteristic polynomial $P_B(t)$ are $\lambda_1 = \lambda_2 = -2$ and $\lambda_3 = 1$.

- If $\lambda = -2$, any corresponding eigenvector $v \neq 0$ is a solution to $Bv = -2v$, which can be written as

$$\begin{cases} 2v_1 + 2v_2 - v_3 = -2v_1 \\ -7v_1 - 4v_2 + 2.5v_3 = -2v_2 \\ 2v_1 + 4v_2 - v_3 = -2v_3 \end{cases} \iff \begin{cases} v_3 = 4v_1 + 2v_2 \\ 2.5v_3 = 7v_1 + 2v_2 \\ v_3 = -2v_1 - 4v_2 \end{cases}$$

$$\iff \begin{cases} v_3 = 4v_1 + 2v_2 \\ 5v_3 = 14v_1 + 4v_2 \\ 0 = 6v_1 + 6v_2 \end{cases} \iff \begin{cases} v_3 = 2v_1 \\ v_3 = 2v_1 \\ v_2 = -v_1 \end{cases}$$

Thus, any eigenvector corresponding to the eigenvalue $\lambda = -2$ is of the form

$$v = \begin{pmatrix} v_1 \\ -v_1 \\ 2v_1 \end{pmatrix} = v_1 \begin{pmatrix} 1 \\ -1 \\ 2 \end{pmatrix}$$

and we conclude that the eigenvalue $\lambda = -2$ has one eigenvector, e.g., $\begin{pmatrix} 1 \\ -1 \\ 2 \end{pmatrix}$.

- If $\lambda = 1$, any corresponding eigenvector $v \neq 0$ is a solution to $Bv = v$, which can be written as

$$\begin{cases} 2v_1 + 2v_2 - v_3 = v_1 \\ -7v_1 - 4v_2 + 2.5v_3 = v_2 \\ 2v_1 + 4v_2 - v_3 = v_3 \end{cases} \iff \begin{cases} v_3 = v_1 + 2v_2 \\ 5v_3 = 14v_1 + 10v_2 \\ v_3 = v_1 + 2v_2 \end{cases}$$

$$\iff \begin{cases} v_3 = v_1 + 2v_2 \\ 0 = 9v_1 \\ v_3 = v_1 + 2v_2 \end{cases} \iff \begin{cases} v_3 = 2v_2 \\ v_1 = 0 \\ v_3 = 2v_2 \end{cases}$$

Thus, any eigenvector corresponding to the eigenvalue $\lambda = 1$ is of the form

$$v = \begin{pmatrix} 0 \\ v_2 \\ 2v_2 \end{pmatrix} = v_2 \begin{pmatrix} 0 \\ 1 \\ 2 \end{pmatrix}.$$

We conclude that the eigenvalue $\lambda = 1$ has one eigenvector, e.g., $\begin{pmatrix} 0 \\ 1 \\ 2 \end{pmatrix}$. □

Example: The characteristic polynomial of the 2×2 matrix $A = \begin{pmatrix} a & b \\ c & d \end{pmatrix}$ is[2]

$$P_A(t) = t^2 - (a+d)t + ad - bc, \qquad (4.7)$$

since, from definition (4.5) and the formula (10.6) for the determinant of a 2×2 matrix, it follows that

$$\begin{aligned} P_A(t) &= \det(tI - A) = \det\begin{pmatrix} t-a & -b \\ -c & t-d \end{pmatrix} \\ &= (t-a)(t-d) - (-b)(-c) \\ &= t^2 - (a+d)t + ad - bc. \quad \square \end{aligned}$$

Examples:

(i) Let $D = \operatorname{diag}(d_i)_{i=1:n}$ be a diagonal matrix of size n. The characteristic polynomial of D is

$$P_D(t) = \det(tI - D) = \prod_{i=1}^{n}(t - d_i);$$

cf. (10.1). The roots of the polynomial $P_D(t)$, i.e., the solutions to $P_D(t) = 0$, are d_i, $i = 1:n$. We conclude that the eigenvalues of D are its diagonal entries. Note that the corresponding eigenvector for the eigenvalue d_i is e_i, the i-th column of the identity matrix, i.e.,

$$De_i = d_i e_i, \quad \forall\, i = 1:n.$$

Thus, a diagonal matrix of size n has n eigenvectors.

(ii) Let L be a lower triangular matrix of size n. The characteristic polynomial of L is

$$P_L(t) = \det(tI - L) = \prod_{i=1}^{n}(t - L(i,i));$$

cf. (10.3). The roots of $P_L(t)$, i.e., the solutions to $P_L(t) = 0$, are $L(i,i)$, $i = 1:n$. We conclude that the eigenvalues of L are its diagonal entries $L(i,i)$, $i = 1:n$. Note that the eigenvector corresponding to the eigenvalue $L(n,n)$ is e_n, the n-th column of the identity matrix. However, the eigenvector corresponding to the eigenvalue $L(i,i)$, with $1 \leq i \leq (n-1)$, is not necessarily e_i, the i-th column of the identity matrix.

---

[2] Note that (4.7) corresponds to (4.19), since the trace and determinant of the 2×2 matrix A are $\operatorname{tr}(A) = a + d$ and $\det(A) = ad - bc$, respectively.

4.1. DEFINITIONS AND PROPERTIES

(iii) Let U be an upper triangular matrix of size n. The characteristic polynomial of U is

$$P_U(t) = \det(tI - U) = \prod_{i=1}^{n}(t - U(i,i)); \qquad (4.8)$$

cf. (10.4). Since the roots of $P_U(t)$ are $U(i,i)$, $i = 1 : n$, we conclude that the eigenvalues of U are its diagonal entries $U(i,i)$, $i = 1 : n$. Note that the eigenvector corresponding to the eigenvalue $U(1,1)$ is e_1, the first column of the identity matrix. However, the eigenvector corresponding to the eigenvalue $U(i,i)$, with $2 \leq i \leq n$, is not necessarily e_i, the i-th column of the identity matrix. □

Definition 4.3. *If λ is a root of multiplicity m_λ of the characteristic polynomial $P_A(t)$ corresponding to matrix A, then, by definition, m_λ is the multiplicity of the eigenvalue λ of A.*

Theorem 4.2. *A square matrix of size n has n eigenvalues, counted with their multiplicities; some of these eigenvalues may be complex numbers.*

In other words, if A is a square matrix of size n, then

$$\sum_{\lambda \in \lambda(A)} m_\lambda = n,$$

where $\lambda(A)$ is the set of all the eigenvalues[3] of A.

As a direct consequence of Theorem 4.2, note that a square matrix of size n has at most n distinct eigenvalues.

Proof. If A is a square matrix of size n, then its characteristic polynomial $P_A(t)$ has degree n. The roots of $P_A(t)$ are the eigenvalues of A; cf. Theorem 4.1. Recall from the Fundamental Theorem of Algebra that a polynomial of degree n with real coefficients has exactly n roots when counted with their multiplicities. Note that the roots of the polynomial may be complex numbers.

From Definition 4.3 of the multiplicity of an eigenvalue, and since the sum of the multiplicities of the roots of a polynomial of degree n is equal to n, we conclude that the number of the eigenvalues of A, counted with their multiplicities, is n. □

Definition 4.4. *The number of different eigenvectors corresponding to an eigenvalue λ is equal to the largest number of linearly independent eigenvectors corresponding to λ. In other words, if $V_\lambda = \{v \text{ such that } Av = \lambda v\}$ is the space of the eigenvectors of the matrix A corresponding to λ, then the number of different eigenvectors corresponding to an eigenvalue λ is equal to $dim(V_\lambda)$, where V_λ denotes the dimension of the space V_λ; see Definition 1.11.*

Every eigenvalue has at least one corresponding eigenvector. If an eigenvalue λ has multiplicity m_λ, then there could exist at most m_λ linearly independent eigenvectors corresponding to λ. However, it might also happen that there are less than m_λ eigenvectors corresponding to λ, and therefore a matrix might have less than n linearly independent eigenvectors; see the example at the beginning of this section, as well as the example below:

---
[3] The set of all the eigenvalues of a matrix is also called the spectrum of the matrix.

Example: The $n \times n$ matrix[4]

$$A = \begin{pmatrix} d & 1 & 0 & \cdots & 0 \\ 0 & d & 1 & \ddots & \vdots \\ \vdots & \ddots & \ddots & \ddots & 0 \\ \vdots & & \ddots & \ddots & 1 \\ 0 & \cdots & \cdots & 0 & d \end{pmatrix} \quad (4.9)$$

has eigenvalue d of multiplicity n, and $\begin{pmatrix} 1 \\ 0 \\ \vdots \\ 0 \end{pmatrix}$ is the only eigenvector corresponding to d.

Answer: From (4.8) and (10.5), it follows that the characteristic polynomial of the upper triangular matrix A is

$$P_A(t) = \det(tI - A) = (t - d)^n.$$

Thus, the polynomial $P_A(t)$ has root d with multiplicity n, and we conclude that the matrix A has eigenvalue d with multiplicity n.

Let $v = (v_i)_{i=1:n}$ be an eigenvector of the matrix A corresponding to the eigenvalue d. Then, $Av = dv$, i.e.,

$$\begin{cases} dv_i + v_{i+1} = dv_i, & \forall\, i = 1:(n-1); \\ v_n = 0 \end{cases}$$

$$\iff \begin{cases} v_{i+1} = 0, & \forall\, i = 1:(n-1); \\ v_n = 0 \end{cases}$$

Thus, $v = \begin{pmatrix} v_1 \\ 0 \\ \vdots \\ 0 \end{pmatrix} = v_1 \begin{pmatrix} 1 \\ 0 \\ \vdots \\ 0 \end{pmatrix}$, and we conclude that $\begin{pmatrix} 1 \\ 0 \\ \vdots \\ 0 \end{pmatrix}$ is the only eigenvector corresponding to the eigenvalue d of the matrix A. $\square$

The number of eigenvectors of a matrix is, by definition, equal to the number of linearly independent eigenvectors of the matrix. It is important to note that eigenvectors corresponding to different eigenvalues are linearly independent; see Lemma 4.2 below:

Lemma 4.2. *The eigenvectors corresponding to different eigenvalues of a matrix are linearly independent.*

Proof. We give a proof by contradiction. Let A be a square matrix of size n, and assume that there exist eigenvectors of A, each one corresponding to a different eigenvalue of A, which are not linearly independent. Since the matrix A has a finite number (not larger than n) of different eigenvalues, there must exist a *minimal*

---

[4] A matrix of the form (4.9) is called a Jordan block.

4.1. DEFINITIONS AND PROPERTIES

number of linearly dependent eigenvectors of A with each vector corresponding to a different eigenvalue. Denote this minimal number by p.

Let $v_1, v_2, \ldots, v_p$ be p linearly dependent eigenvectors of A corresponding to p distinct eigenvalues of A denoted be $\lambda_1, \lambda_2, \ldots, \lambda_p$, i.e., such that

$$c_1 v_1 + c_2 v_2 + \ldots + c_p v_p = 0, \tag{4.10}$$

with $c_1, c_2, \ldots, c_p$ constants such that $c_i \neq 0$, for all $i = 1 : p$. By multiplying (4.10) by the matrix A to the left, we obtain that

$$c_1 A v_1 + c_2 A v_2 + \ldots + c_p A v_p = 0. \tag{4.11}$$

Note that
$$A v_i = \lambda_i v_i, \quad \forall\, i = 1 : p, \tag{4.12}$$
since v_i is an eigenvector corresponding to the eigenvalue λ_i of A.

From (4.11) and (4.12), it follows that

$$c_1 \lambda_1 v_1 + c_2 \lambda_2 v_2 + \ldots + c_p \lambda_p v_p = 0. \tag{4.13}$$

By multiplying (4.10) by λ_1, we find that

$$c_1 \lambda_1 v_1 + c_2 \lambda_1 v_2 + \ldots + c_p \lambda_1 v_p = 0, \tag{4.14}$$

and, by subtracting (4.14) from (4.13), we obtain that

$$c_2 (\lambda_2 - \lambda_1) v_2 + \ldots + c_p (\lambda_p - \lambda_1) v_p = 0. \tag{4.15}$$

The coefficients of the vectors $v_2, \ldots, v_p$ from (4.15) are nonzero, since $c_i \neq 0$, for all $i = 2 : p$, and $\lambda_i \neq \lambda_1$, for all $i = 2 : p$, since the eigenvalues $\lambda_1, \lambda_2, \ldots, \lambda_p$ are distinct.

Thus, we found $p - 1$ eigenvectors of the matrix A, i.e., $v_2, \ldots, v_p$, each one corresponding to a different eigenvalue of A, which are linearly dependent. This contradicts the fact that p denotes the *minimal number* of linearly dependent eigenvectors of A.

We conclude that eigenvectors corresponding to different eigenvalues of a matrix must be linearly independent. □

Summary: General properties of eigenvalues and eigenvectors

- A square matrix of size n has exactly n eigenvalues (possibly complex numbers), if the eigenvalues are counted with their multiplicities.

- A square matrix of size n has at most n linearly independent eigenvectors, but may have less than n linearly independent eigenvectors.

- There is at least one eigenvector and there are at most m_λ linearly independent eigenvectors (and possibly fewer) corresponding to an eigenvalue λ with multiplicity m_λ.

Note that, while the eigenvalues of a matrix with real entries may be complex numbers, all the eigenvalues of a symmetric matrix with real entries are real numbers. Moreover, symmetric matrices have a full set of eigenvectors; see section 5.1 for details.

Theorem 4.3. *(i) The matrix A is singular if and only if 0 is an eigenvalue of A.*
(ii) The matrix A is nonsingular if and only if 0 is not an eigenvalue of A.

Proof. (i) From (1.75), we find that the matrix A is singular if and only if

$$\text{Null}(A) = \{v \in \mathbb{R}^n \text{ such that } Av = 0\} \neq \{0\},$$

i.e., if and only if there exists a vector $v_0 \neq 0$ such that $Av_0 = 0$, which is equivalent to saying that 0 is an eigenvalue of A; see (4.1).

(ii) Since a matrix is nonsingular if and only if the matrix is not singular, it follows from (i) that a matrix is nonsingular if and only if 0 is not an eigenvalue of A. □

Lemma 4.3. *Let A be a nonsingular matrix, and let A^{-1} be the inverse matrix of A. If (λ, v) are an eigenvalue and a corresponding eigenvector of A, then $\left(\frac{1}{\lambda}, v\right)$ are an eigenvalue and a corresponding eigenvector of A^{-1}.*

Proof. If $v \neq 0$ is the eigenvector corresponding to the eigenvalue λ of A, then $Av = \lambda v$. Multiplying to the left by A^{-1}, we obtain that $A^{-1}Av = \lambda(A^{-1}v)$, and, using the fact that $A^{-1}Av = v$ since $A^{-1}A = I$, it follows that

$$v = \lambda \left(A^{-1}v\right). \tag{4.16}$$

Note that $\lambda \neq 0$, since A is a nonsingular matrix; cf. Theorem 4.3. Then, from (4.16), we find that

$$A^{-1}v = \frac{1}{\lambda}v.$$

Since $v \neq 0$, it follows that $\frac{1}{\lambda}$ is an eigenvalue of A^{-1} with corresponding eigenvector v. □

Lemma 4.4. *Let A be a square matrix, and let λ and v be an eigenvalue and a corresponding eigenvector of A.*

(i) Let k be a positive integer. Then, λ^k is an eigenvalue of the matrix A^k and v is a corresponding eigenvector.

(ii) Let $P(x)$ be an arbitrary polynomial. Then, $P(\lambda)$ is an eigenvalue of the matrix $P(A)$ and v is a corresponding eigenvector.

Proof. (i) We show by induction over the positive integer $k \geq 1$ that

$$A^k v = \lambda^k v, \quad \forall\, k \geq 1. \tag{4.17}$$

Formula (4.17) holds for $k = 1$, since λ and v are an eigenvalue of A and a corresponding eigenvector, and therefore $Av = \lambda v$. Assume that (4.17) holds for k, i.e., assume that $A^k v = \lambda^k v$. Then,

$$A^{k+1} v = A\left(A^k v\right) = A\left(\lambda^k v\right) = \lambda^k \cdot Av = \lambda^k \cdot \lambda v = \lambda^{k+1} v.$$

Thus, formula (4.17) is established for $k+1$ and the proof by induction of (4.17) is complete.

4.1. DEFINITIONS AND PROPERTIES

(ii) Let $P(x) = \sum_{k=0}^{p} c_k x^k$, with $c_p \neq 0$, where $p = \deg(P)$ is the degree of the polynomial $P(x)$. Using (4.17), we obtain that

$$\begin{aligned} P(A)v &= \left(\sum_{k=0}^{p} c_k A^k\right) v = \sum_{k=0}^{p} c_k \left(A^k v\right) \\ &= \sum_{k=0}^{p} c_k \left(\lambda^k v\right) = \left(\sum_{k=0}^{p} c_k \lambda^k\right) \cdot v \\ &= P(\lambda)v. \end{aligned}$$

Thus, $P(A)v = P(\lambda)v$, and we conclude that $P(\lambda)$ is an eigenvalue of the matrix $P(A)$ and v is a corresponding eigenvector. □

Lemma 4.5. *If A is a square matrix, then the matrices A and A^t have the same eigenvalues.*

Proof. Recall from Theorem 4.1 that the eigenvalues of a matrix are the roots of its characteristic polynomial. Thus, the eigenvalues of the matrix A are the roots of $P_A(x) = \det(xI - A)$, and the eigenvalues of the matrix A^t are the roots of $P_{A^t}(x) = \det(xI - A^t)$.

Since $(xI - A)^t = xI - A^t$, and using the fact that $\det((xI - A)^t) = \det(xI - A)$, see Lemma 10.2, we obtain that

$$\begin{aligned} P_A(x) &= \det(xI - A) = \det((xI - A)^t) = \det(xI - A^t) \\ &= P_{A^t}(x). \end{aligned}$$

Thus, the polynomials $P_A(t)$ and $P_{A^t}(t)$ have the same roots, and we conclude that the matrices A and A^t have the same eigenvalues. □

Definition 4.5. *Let A be a square matrix of size n. The trace of the matrix A is the sum of its main diagonal entries, i.e.,*

$$\operatorname{tr}(A) = \sum_{i=1}^{n} A(i,i). \tag{4.18}$$

Lemma 4.6. *Let A be a square matrix of size n, let $P_A(t)$ be the characteristic polynomial of A, and let λ_i, $i = 1:n$, be the eigenvalues of A. Then,*

$$P_A(t) = t^n - \operatorname{tr}(A)t^{n-1} + \ldots + (-1)^n \det(A), \tag{4.19}$$

and

$$\sum_{i=1}^{n} \lambda_i = \operatorname{tr}(A); \tag{4.20}$$

$$\prod_{i=1}^{n} \lambda_i = \det(A). \tag{4.21}$$

Proof. Recall from Lemma 4.1 that

$$\det(tI - A) = \prod_{i=1}^{n}(t - \lambda_i) \tag{4.22}$$

$$= t^n - \left(\sum_{i=1}^{n}\lambda_i\right)t^{n-1} + \ldots + (-1)^n \prod_{i=1}^{n}\lambda_i. \tag{4.23}$$

Let $t = 0$ in (4.22–4.23). Then,

$$\det(-A) = (-1)^n \det(A) = (-1)^n \prod_{i=1}^{n}\lambda_i,$$

and therefore (4.21) is established.

Note that the only terms of order $n-1$ from $\det(tI-A)$ are obtained by multiplying the main diagonal entries of $tI - A$. In other words, the coefficient of the term t^{n-1} in $\det(tI - A)$ is the same as the coefficient of the term t^{n-1} in $\prod_{i=1}^{n}(t - A(i,i))$, which is equal to $-\sum_{i=1}^{n} A(i,i) = -\mathrm{tr}(A)$; see Definition 4.5. Then, we conclude from (4.23) that $\mathrm{tr}(A) = \sum_{i=1}^{n}\lambda_i$. □

4.2 Diagonal forms

Definition 4.6. *Let A be a square matrix of size n. The matrix A has a diagonal form if and only if there exists an $n \times n$ nonsingular matrix V and an $n \times n$ diagonal matrix Λ such that*

$$A = V\Lambda V^{-1}. \tag{4.24}$$

A matrix that has a diagonal form is called a diagonalizable matrix.

Theorem 4.4. *Let A be a diagonalizable matrix, and let $A = V\Lambda V^{-1}$ be the diagonal form of A. Then, the diagonal entries of the matrix Λ are the eigenvalues of A and the columns of the matrix V are the corresponding eigenvectors of A.*

More precisely, if $\Lambda = \mathrm{diag}(\lambda_k)_{k=1:n}$ and $V = \mathrm{col}(v_k)_{k=1:n}$, then λ_k, $k = 1:n$, are the eigenvalues of A, and v_k is an eigenvector corresponding to λ_k, for $k = 1:n$, respectively.

Proof. By multiplying $A = V\Lambda V^{-1}$ to the right by V, we obtain that

$$A = V\Lambda V^{-1} \iff AV = (V\Lambda V^{-1})V \iff AV = V\Lambda, \tag{4.25}$$

since $V^{-1}V = I$. Recall from (1.11) and (1.88) that $AV = \mathrm{col}(Av_k)_{k=1:n}$ and $V\Lambda = \mathrm{col}(\lambda_k v_k)_{k=1:n}$. Then, from (4.25), we find that

$$A = V\Lambda V^{-1} \iff \mathrm{col}(Av_k)_{k=1:n} = \mathrm{col}(\lambda_k v_k)_{k=1:n}$$
$$\iff Av_k = \lambda_k v_k, \ \forall\, k = 1:n,$$

i.e., λ_k is an eigenvalue of A and v_k is a corresponding eigenvector, for $k = 1:n$.

The vectors v_k, $k = 1:n$, are linearly independent vectors since they are the columns of the nonsingular matrix V. □

4.3. DIAGONALLY DOMINANT MATRICES

The result below is an equivalent characterization of diagonalizable matrices and follows immediately from the proof of Theorem 4.4 above:

Theorem 4.5. *A square matrix of size n has a diagonal form if and only if the matrix has n linearly independent eigenvectors.*

Lemma 4.7. *Let A be a diagonalizable matrix, and let $A = V\Lambda V^{-1}$ be its diagonal form. For every positive integer p, the matrix A^p is diagonalizable and has the following diagonal form:*

$$A^p = V\Lambda^p V^{-1}. \qquad (4.26)$$

Proof. If p is a positive integer, then

$$\begin{aligned} A^p &= \left(V\Lambda V^{-1}\right)^p = \left(V\Lambda V^{-1}\right)\left(V\Lambda V^{-1}\right)\ldots\left(V\Lambda V^{-1}\right)\left(V\Lambda V^{-1}\right) \\ &= V\Lambda(V^{-1}V)\Lambda(V^{-1}V)\ldots(V^{-1}V)\Lambda V^{-1} \\ &= V\Lambda^p V^{-1}, \qquad (4.27) \end{aligned}$$

since $V^{-1}V = I$. $\square$

Lemma 4.8. *Let A be a nonsingular diagonalizable matrix, and let $A = V\Lambda V^{-1}$ be its diagonal form. Then, the inverse matrix A^{-1} is also diagonalizable and has the diagonal form $A^{-1} = V\Lambda^{-1} V^{-1}$. Moreover, for every positive integer p, the matrix A^{-p} is diagonalizable and has the following diagonal form:*

$$A^{-p} = V\Lambda^{-p} V^{-1}.$$

Proof. From Lemma 1.7, it follows that

$$A^{-1} = \left(V\Lambda V^{-1}\right)^{-1} = (V^{-1})^{-1}\Lambda^{-1} V^{-1} = V\Lambda^{-1} V^{-1}.$$

By definition, if p is a positive integer, then $A^{-p} = (A^p)^{-1}$. Using (4.26), we obtain that

$$\begin{aligned} A^{-p} &= (A^p)^{-1} = \left(V\Lambda^p V^{-1}\right)^{-1} = (V^{-1})^{-1}(\Lambda^p)^{-1} V^{-1} \\ &= V\Lambda^{-p} V^{-1}. \end{aligned}$$

$\square$

4.3 Diagonally dominant matrices

Let A be an $n \times n$ matrix, and denote by

$$R_j = \sum_{k=1:n, k \neq j} |A(j,k)| \qquad (4.28)$$

the sum of the absolute values of all the entries on the j-th row of the matrix A except for the main diagonal entry $A(j,j)$.

Definition 4.7. The $n \times n$ matrix A is weakly diagonally dominant if and only if

$$|A(j,j)| \geq R_j, \quad \forall\, j = 1 : n, \tag{4.29}$$

where R_j is given by (4.28), i.e., if and only if, for every row, the absolute value of the main diagonal entry from the row is greater than the sum of the absolute values of all the other entries in that row.

Definition 4.8. The $n \times n$ matrix A is strictly diagonally dominant if and only if

$$|A(j,j)| > R_j, \quad \forall\, j = 1 : n, \tag{4.30}$$

where R_j is given by (4.28).

Example: The $N \times N$ matrix

$$B_N = \begin{pmatrix} 2 & -1 & \cdots & 0 \\ -1 & \ddots & \ddots & \vdots \\ \vdots & \ddots & \ddots & -1 \\ 0 & \cdots & -1 & 2 \end{pmatrix}$$

is a weakly diagonally dominant matrix, since the only nonzero entries of B_N are

$$\begin{aligned} B_N(j,j) &= 2, \quad \forall\, j = 1 : N; \\ B_N(j,j-1) &= -1, \quad \forall\, j = 2 : N; \\ B_N(j,j+1) &= -1, \quad \forall\, j = 1 : (N-1), \end{aligned}$$

and therefore

$$\sum_{k=2:N} |B_N(1,k)| = |B_N(1,2)| = 1 < 2 = |B_N(1,1)|;$$

$$\sum_{k=1:(N-1)} |B_N(N,k)| = |B_N(N,N-1)| = 1 < 2 = |B_N(N,N)|;$$

$$\sum_{k=1:N, k\neq j} |B_N(j,k)| = |B_N(j,j-1)| + |B_N(j,j+1)| = 2 = |B_N(j,j)|,$$

for all $j = 2 : (N-2)$.

Then, from definition 4.7, it follows that B_N is a weakly diagonally dominant matrix. $\square$

Theorem 4.6. *(Gershgorin's Theorem.)* Let A be a square matrix of size n. For any eigenvalue λ of A, there exists an index j, with $1 \leq j \leq n$, such that

$$|\lambda - A(j,j)| \leq R_j, \tag{4.31}$$

where R_j is given by (4.28).

Note that Gershgorin's Theorem can also be stated as follows:

$$\lambda(A) \subset \bigcup_{j=1}^{n} D\left(A(j,j), R_j\right),$$

where $\lambda(A)$ is the set of all the eigenvalues of A and $D(a, R) = \{z \in \mathbb{C} \text{ such that } |z - a| \leq R\}$ is the disc of center $a \in \mathbb{C}$ and radius $R > 0$ in the complex space.

4.3. DIAGONALLY DOMINANT MATRICES

Proof. Let λ be an eigenvalue of A, and let v be a corresponding eigenvector. Let j be the index of the largest entry of v in absolute value, i.e., such that

$$|v_j| = \max_{k=1:n} |v_k|. \tag{4.32}$$

Then,

$$|v_k| \leq |v_j|, \quad \forall\ k = 1:n. \tag{4.33}$$

Since $Av = \lambda v$, it follows that

$$\sum_{k=1}^{n} A(i,k) v_k = \lambda v_i, \quad \forall\ i = 1:n. \tag{4.34}$$

By letting $i = j$ in (4.34), where j is the index of the largest entry of v in absolute value, see (4.32), we find that

$$\lambda v_j = \sum_{k=1}^{n} A(j,k) v_k = A(j,j) v_j + \sum_{k=1:n, k \neq j} A(j,k) v_k,$$

and therefore

$$(\lambda - A(j,j)) v_j = \sum_{k=1:n, k \neq j} A(j,k) v_k. \tag{4.35}$$

By taking absolute values in (4.35) and dividing by $|v_j|$, we obtain, using the notation from (4.28), that

$$\begin{aligned}
|\lambda - A(j,j)| &= \frac{\left|\sum_{k=1:n, k \neq j} A(j,k) v_k\right|}{|v_j|} \leq \frac{\sum_{k=1:n, k \neq j} |A(j,k)||v_k|}{|v_j|} \\
&= \sum_{k=1:n, k \neq j} |A(j,k)| \frac{|v_k|}{|v_j|} \\
&\leq \sum_{k=1:n, k \neq j} |A(j,k)| \\
&= R_j,
\end{aligned}$$

since $\frac{|v_k|}{|v_j|} \leq 1$; cf. (4.33). $\square$

Gershgorin's Theorem can be used to derive useful properties of diagonally dominant matrices, see Theorem 4.7 and Theorem 5.7.

Theorem 4.7. *Any strictly diagonally dominant matrix is nonsingular.*

Proof. Let λ be an eigenvalue of A. From Gershgorin's Theorem, it follows that there exists j, with $1 \leq j \leq n$, such that

$$|A(j,j) - \lambda| \leq R_j; \tag{4.36}$$

cf. (4.31), and using the fact that $|\lambda - A(j,j)| = |A(j,j) - \lambda|$. Note that $|a| - |b| \leq |a - b|$, for any $a, b \in \mathbb{C}$. Then,

$$|A(j,j)| - |\lambda| \leq |A(j,j) - \lambda|. \tag{4.37}$$

From (4.36) and (4.37), it follows that

$$|A(j,j)| - |\lambda| \leq R_j,$$

and therefore

$$|\lambda| \geq |A(j,j)| - R_j > 0,$$

since A is a strictly diagonally dominant matrix; cf. (4.30).

Thus, $|\lambda| > 0$, and therefore $\lambda \neq 0$. We conclude that any eigenvalue of the matrix A is nonzero, and therefore that the matrix A is nonsingular; cf. Theorem 4.3. $\square$

Note that, although less frequently used in practice, column–based versions of Gershgorin's Theorem and of Theorem 4.7 also hold, and are based on the fact that a square matrix and its transpose have the same eigenvalues; see Lemma 4.5. We only provide a version of Theorem 4.7 here; see Theorem 4.8.

Definition 4.9. *The $n \times n$ matrix A is strictly column diagonally dominant if and only if*

$$|A(k,k)| > \sum_{j=1:n, j \neq k} |A(j,k)|, \quad \forall \, k = 1:n, \tag{4.38}$$

i.e., if and only if, for every column, the absolute value of the main diagonal entry from the column is strictly greater than the sum of the absolute values of all the other entries in that column.

Note that, unless otherwise specified, diagonal dominance will refer to the "row" diagonal dominance introduced in Definitions 4.7 and 4.8.

Lemma 4.9. *If A is a strictly column diagonally dominant matrix, then its transpose A^t is a strictly diagonally dominant matrix.*

Proof. Let A be a strictly column diagonally dominant matrix. From (4.38), it follows that

$$|A(k,k)| > \sum_{j=1:n, j \neq k} |A(j,k)|, \tag{4.39}$$

for all $k = 1:n$. By switching the indices j and k in the inequality (4.38), we find that

$$|A(j,j)| > \sum_{k=1:n, k \neq j} |A(k,j)|, \tag{4.40}$$

for all $j = 1:n$. Note that

$$\sum_{k=1:n, k \neq j} |A(k,j)| = \sum_{k=1:n, k \neq j} |A^t(j,k)|, \tag{4.41}$$

since, by definition, $A^t(j,k) = A(k,j)$ for all $1 \leq j, k \leq n$. Since $A(j,j) = A^t(j,j)$, it follows from (4.40) and (4.41) that

$$|A^t(j,j)| > \sum_{k=1:n, k \neq j} |A^t(j,k)|.$$

Then, from Definition 4.8, we find that the matrix A^t is strictly diagonally dominant. $\square$

4.3. DIAGONALLY DOMINANT MATRICES

Theorem 4.8. *Any strictly column diagonally dominant matrix is nonsingular.*

Proof. Let A be a strictly column diagonally dominant matrix. From Lemma 4.9, it follows that the matrix A^t is strictly diagonally dominant. Thus, the matrix A^t is nonsingular, see Theorem 4.7, and therefore 0 is not an eigenvalue of A^t. Since A and A^t have the same eigenvalues, see Lemma 4.5, we conclude that 0 is not an eigenvalue of A, and therefore that A is a nonsingular matrix. □

Example: Show that the following matrices are nonsingular:

$$A_1 = \begin{pmatrix} 3 & 1 & -1 & 0 \\ 2 & -4 & 1 & 0.5 \\ -2 & 1 & 5 & 0.5 \\ 0 & 2 & 0 & -2.5 \end{pmatrix};$$

$$A_2 = \begin{pmatrix} -4 & 3 & -1 & 1 \\ -1 & -5 & 1 & 4 \\ 1 & -1 & 3 & 0 \\ 0.5 & 0 & 0.5 & -6 \end{pmatrix}.$$

Answer: (i) The matrix A_1 is strictly diagonally dominant, since, for every row of A_1, the absolute value of the main diagonal entry from the row is greater than the sum of the absolute values of all the other entries in that row:

$$\begin{aligned} 3 &> 1 + |-1| = 2; \\ |-4| = 4 &> 2 + 1 + 0.5 = 3.5; \\ 5 &> |-2| + 1 + 0.5 = 3.5; \\ |-2.5| = 2.5 &> 2. \end{aligned}$$

Then, from Theorem 4.7, it follows that A_1 is a nonsingular matrix.

(ii) The matrix A_2 is strictly column diagonally dominant, since, for every column of the matrix A_2, the absolute value of the main diagonal entry from the column is strictly greater than the sum of the absolute values of all the other entries in that column:

$$\begin{aligned} |-4| = 4 &> |-1| + 1 + 0.5 = 2.5; \\ |-5| = 5 &> 3 + |-1| = 4; \\ 3 &> |-1| + 1 + 0.5 = 2.5; \\ |-6| = 6 &> 1 + 4 = 5. \end{aligned}$$

Then, from Theorem 4.8, it follows that A_2 is a nonsingular matrix.

Note that Theorem 4.7 cannot be used to show that the matrix A_2 is nonsingular, since A_2 is not strictly diagonally dominant: for the first row of A_2, we find that

$$|-4| = 4 < 3 + |-1| + 1 = 5. \quad \square$$

4.4 Numerical computation of eigenvalues

Computing the eigenvalues of a matrix is a fundamental numerical linear algebra problem, which further highlights the difference between numerical linear algebra and classical linear algebra. For example, computing the roots of the characteristic polynomial of a matrix to obtain its eigenvalues would be inefficient and prone to large errors since polynomial root computation is an ill-conditioned problem.

The methods used in practice for computing eigenvalues are iterative methods that find approximations of the eigenvalues of the matrix to desired tolerance. The simplest such method is the Power Method which works best for symmetric positive definite matrices whose largest eigenvalue has multiplicity 1, and the related Inverse Power Method and Inverse Power Method with shifts. These methods are generally slowly convergent.

Efficient eigenvalue algorithms are variants of the QR Algorithm, which was named one of the top ten algorithms of the 20-th century.[5] Based on the QR decomposition of a matrix as the product of an orthogonal matrix Q and an upper triangular matrix R, the matrix A is iteratively transformed into $A_i = QR$ and then $A_{i+1} = RQ$, until convergence to an upper triangular matrix (or to a diagonal matrix, if the matrix A is symmetric) is achieved. More details on QR algorithms and their implementations can be found, e.g., in Demmel [13] and in Trefethen and Bau [43].

4.5 Eigenvalues and eigenvectors of tridiagonal symmetric matrices

Let

$$B_N = \begin{pmatrix} 2 & -1 & \ldots & 0 \\ -1 & \ddots & \ddots & \vdots \\ \vdots & \ddots & \ddots & -1 \\ 0 & \ldots & -1 & 2 \end{pmatrix} \qquad (4.42)$$

be the $N \times N$ tridiagonal symmetric matrix whose only nonzero entries are

$$\begin{aligned} B_N(i,i) &= 2, \ \forall\, i = 1:N; \\ B_N(i,i-1) &= -1, \ \forall\, i = 2:N; \\ B_N(i,i+1) &= -1, \ \forall\, i = 1:(N-1). \end{aligned}$$

The matrix B_N appears often in practical applications, e.g., in the finite difference solution of second order differential equations.

In this section, we find the eigenvalues and eigenvectors of the matrix B_N, and then use them to compute the eigenvalues and eigenvectors of tridiagonal symmetric matrices having the more general form (4.49). Note that, since the matrix B_N is symmetric, all its eigenvalues are real numbers; cf. Theorem 5.1.

Lemma 4.10. *The matrix B_N has the following N different eigenvalues:*

$$\mu_j = 2\left(1 - \cos\left(\frac{j\pi}{N+1}\right)\right), \quad \text{for } j = 1:N. \qquad (4.43)$$

---

[5] See Cipra [10] at http://www.siam.org/pdf/news/637.pdf

4.5. EIGENVALUES OF TRIDIAGONAL SYMMETRIC MATRICES

For every $j = 1 : N$, the eigenvalue μ_j has a corresponding $N \times 1$ eigenvector v_j with the following entries:

$$v_j(i) = \sin\left(\frac{ij\pi}{N+1}\right), \quad \forall\, i = 1 : N. \tag{4.44}$$

Proof. We will show that

$$B_N v_j = \mu_j v_j, \quad \forall\, j = 1 : N. \tag{4.45}$$

Since the $N \times N$ matrix B_N has exactly N eigenvalues, counted with their multiplicities, see Theorem 4.2, we can then conclude from (4.45) that μ_j, $j = 1 : N$, are all the eigenvalues of B_N, and v_j, $j = 1 : N$, are all the eigenvectors of B_N.

Let $2 \leq i \leq N - 1$. Note that

$$(B_N v_j)(i) = 2v_j(i) - v_j(i-1) - v_j(i+1),$$

which, using (4.44), can be written as

$$(B_N v_j)(i) = 2\sin\left(\frac{ij\pi}{N+1}\right) - \sin\left(\frac{(i-1)j\pi}{N+1}\right) - \sin\left(\frac{(i+1)j\pi}{N+1}\right), \tag{4.46}$$

for all $i = 2 : (N-1)$.

If we let $i = 1$ in the right hand side of (4.46), we find that

$$2\sin\left(\frac{j\pi}{N+1}\right) - \sin\left(\frac{2j\pi}{N+1}\right) - \sin(0) = 2v_j(1) - v_j(2)$$
$$= (B_N v_j)(1), \tag{4.47}$$

since $\sin(0) = 0$.

For $i = N$ in the right hand side of (4.46), we find that

$$2\sin\left(\frac{Nj\pi}{N+1}\right) - \sin\left(\frac{(N-1)j\pi}{N+1}\right) - \sin(j\pi) = 2v_j(N) - v_j(N-1)$$
$$= (B_N v_j)(N), \tag{4.48}$$

since $\sin(j\pi) = 0$ for any integer j.

From (4.47) and (4.48), we conclude that formula (4.46) also holds for $i = 1$ and $i = N$, and therefore

$$(B_N v_j)(i) = 2\sin\left(\frac{ij\pi}{N+1}\right) - \sin\left(\frac{(i-1)j\pi}{N+1}\right) - \sin\left(\frac{(i+1)j\pi}{N+1}\right), \quad \forall\, i = 1 : N.$$

Then,

$$\begin{aligned}
(B_N v_j)(i) &= 2\sin\left(\frac{ij\pi}{N+1}\right) \\
&\quad - \left(\sin\left(\frac{ij\pi}{N+1} - \frac{j\pi}{N+1}\right) + \sin\left(\frac{ij\pi}{N+1} + \frac{j\pi}{N+1}\right)\right) \\
&= 2\sin\left(\frac{ij\pi}{N+1}\right) - 2\sin\left(\frac{ij\pi}{N+1}\right)\cos\left(\frac{j\pi}{N+1}\right) \\
&= 2\sin\left(\frac{ij\pi}{N+1}\right)\left(1 - \cos\left(\frac{j\pi}{N+1}\right)\right) \\
&= 2v_j(i)\left(1 - \cos\left(\frac{j\pi}{N+1}\right)\right) \\
&= \mu_j v_j(i), \quad \forall\, i = 1 : N;
\end{aligned}$$

for the second equality above we used the fact that
$$\sin(x-y) + \sin(x+y) = 2\sin(x)\cos(y)$$
with $x = \frac{ij\pi}{N+1}$ and $y = \frac{j\pi}{N+1}$.

We conclude that
$$B_N v_j = \mu_j v_j, \quad \forall\, j = 1:n,$$
which is what we wanted to show; cf. (4.45). $\square$

Let T_N be the $N \times N$ tridiagonal symmetric matrix given by

$$T_N = \begin{pmatrix} d & -a & \cdots & 0 \\ -a & \ddots & \ddots & \vdots \\ \vdots & \ddots & \ddots & -a \\ 0 & \cdots & -a & d \end{pmatrix}. \qquad (4.49)$$

Note that, for $d = 2$ and $a = 1$, it follows that $T_N = B_N$; cf. (4.42).

Lemma 4.11. *The matrix T_N has the following N different eigenvalues:*

$$\lambda_j = d - 2a\cos\left(\frac{\pi j}{N+1}\right), \quad \text{for } j = 1:N. \qquad (4.50)$$

For every $j = 1:N$, the eigenvalue λ_j has a corresponding $N \times 1$ eigenvector v_j with the following entries:

$$v_j(i) = \sin\left(\frac{ij\pi}{N+1}\right), \quad \forall\, i = 1:N. \qquad (4.51)$$

Proof. Note that

$$T_N = \begin{pmatrix} d-2a & 0 & \cdots & 0 \\ 0 & \ddots & \ddots & \vdots \\ \vdots & \ddots & \ddots & 0 \\ 0 & \cdots & 0 & d-2a \end{pmatrix} + \begin{pmatrix} 2a & -a & \cdots & 0 \\ -a & \ddots & \ddots & \vdots \\ \vdots & \ddots & \ddots & -a \\ 0 & \cdots & -a & 2a \end{pmatrix}$$
$$= (d-2a)I + aB_N.$$

Let μ_j and v_j be an eigenvalue and a corresponding eigenvector of B_N given by (4.43) and by (4.44), respectively. Then, $B_N v_j = \mu_j v_j$, and therefore

$$\begin{aligned} T_N v_j &= ((d-2a)I + aB_N)v_j \\ &= (d-2a)v_j + a\mu_j v_j \\ &= (d-2a+a\mu_j)v_j. \end{aligned}$$

In other words,
$$\lambda_j = d - 2a + a\mu_j \qquad (4.52)$$
is an eigenvalue of T_N with corresponding eigenvector v_j.

Recall from (4.43) that the matrix B_N has the following N eigenvalues:

$$\mu_j = 2 - 2\cos\left(\frac{j\pi}{N+1}\right), \quad \text{for} \quad j = 1 : N.$$

Then, from (4.52), it follows that

$$\begin{aligned}\lambda_j &= d - 2a + a\mu_j = d - a(2 - \mu_j) \\ &= d - 2a\cos\left(\frac{\pi j}{N+1}\right).\end{aligned} \quad (4.53)$$

We conclude that, for $j = 1 : N$, λ_j given by (4.53) are eigenvalues of the matrix T_N with corresponding eigenvectors v_j given by (4.44).

The $N \times N$ matrix has exactly N eigenvalues, counted with their multiplicities; cf. Theorem 4.2. We conclude that λ_j, $j = 1 : N$, are all the eigenvalues of T_N. $\square$

4.6 References

For an overview of numerical eigenvalue methods, see the monograph by Saad [34]. The QR algorithm and practical implementation details, including the Hessenberg reduction and tridiagonal and bidiagonal reduction, can be found in Demmel [13] and in Trefethen and Bau [43].

The general form of Gershgorin's theorem states that, if the union of k Gershgorin disks are disjoint from the other Gershgorin disks, then exactly k of the eigenvalues of the matrix are in the union of those k Gershgorin disks. This version of Gershgorin's theorem and extensions of it can be found in Varga [44].

The matrix

$$B_N = \begin{pmatrix} 2 & -1 & \cdots & 0 \\ -1 & \ddots & \ddots & \vdots \\ \vdots & \ddots & \ddots & -1 \\ 0 & \cdots & -1 & 2 \end{pmatrix}$$

appears in the finite difference discretization of the one dimensional Poisson equation. It has many interesting properties, which have a special symmetry about them; details can be found in the section "My Favorite Matrix" from Gil Strang's "Essays in Linear Algebra" [42].

An elegant complex analysis proof of the Fundamental Theorem of Algebra (which was used to show that an $n \times n$ matrix has exactly n eigenvalues, when counted with their multiplicities) is included, with detailed historical notes, Lax and Zalcman [27].

4.7 Exercises

1. Let A and B be square matrices of the same size. Show that, if v is an eigenvector of both A and B, then v is also an eigenvector of the matrix $M = c_1 A + c_2 B$, where c_1 and c_2 are constants. What is the eigenvalue of M corresponding to the eigenvector v?

2. Let λ and v be an eigenvalue and the corresponding eigenvector of the matrix A. Let d be a constant number, and let I be the identity matrix.

   (i) Show that v is an eigenvector of the matrix $B = dI + A + A^2$, and find the corresponding eigenvalue.

   (ii) If A is a nonsingular matrix, show that v is an eigenvector of the matrix $M = dI + A + A^{-1}$, and find the corresponding eigenvalue.

3. Let A be a 3×3 nonsingular matrix with eigenvalues -2, 1, and 3. What are the eigenvalues of $A^2 + 2I - 3A^{-1}$?

4. (i) Show that the eigenvalues of the matrix
$$A = \begin{pmatrix} 8 & -18 & -30 & -24 \\ 18 & -37 & -60 & -48 \\ -9 & 18 & 29 & 24 \\ 0 & 0 & 0 & -1 \end{pmatrix}$$
are -1, with multiplicity 3, and 2, with multiplicity 1.

   Show that $\begin{pmatrix} 0 \\ 1 \\ 1 \\ -2 \end{pmatrix}$, $\begin{pmatrix} 2 \\ 2 \\ -3 \\ 3 \end{pmatrix}$, $\begin{pmatrix} 2 \\ 1 \\ 0 \\ 0 \end{pmatrix}$ are three linearly independent eigenvectors corresponding to the eigenvalue -1, and show that there exists only one linearly independent eigenvector of the matrix A corresponding to the eigenvalue 2, e.g., $\begin{pmatrix} 1 \\ 2 \\ -1 \\ 0 \end{pmatrix}$.

   (ii) Show that the eigenvalues of the matrix
$$B = \begin{pmatrix} 10 & -20 & -32 & -26 \\ 18 & -41 & -68 & -54 \\ -14 & 19 & 26 & 23 \\ 7 & 1 & 9 & 4 \end{pmatrix}$$
are -1, with multiplicity 3, and 2, with multiplicity 1.

   Show that there exists only one linearly independent eigenvector of the matrix B corresponding to the eigenvalue -1, e.g., $\begin{pmatrix} 0 \\ -1 \\ -1 \\ 2 \end{pmatrix}$, and show that $\begin{pmatrix} 1 \\ 2 \\ -1 \\ 0 \end{pmatrix}$ is an eigenvector corresponding to the eigenvalue 2.

4.7. EXERCISES

5. Let $A = \begin{pmatrix} 2 & -1 \\ 1 & 4 \end{pmatrix}$.

    (i) What is the characteristic polynomial of A?

    (ii) Find the eigenvalues and the eigenvectors of A.

6. (i) Find the eigenvalues and the eigenvectors of the lower triangular matrix
$$L = \begin{pmatrix} 2 & 0 & 0 \\ 1 & -3 & 0 \\ -1 & 2 & -1 \end{pmatrix}.$$

    (ii) Find the eigenvalues and the eigenvectors of the upper triangular matrix
$$U = \begin{pmatrix} -2 & -1 & 3 \\ 0 & 1 & 2 \\ 0 & 0 & 3 \end{pmatrix}.$$

7. Let A be a square matrix such that $A^2 = A$. Show that any eigenvalue of A is either 0 or 1.

    Note: A matrix A with the property that $A^2 = A$ is called an **idempotent matrix**.

8. Let A be a square matrix with the property that there exists a positive integer p such that $A^p = 0$. Show that any eigenvalue of A must be equal to 0.

    Note: A matrix A with the property that $A^p = 0$ for a positive integer p is called a **nilpotent matrix**.

9. Let $v \neq 0$ be a column vector of size n, and let $A = vv^t$ be an $n \times n$ matrix.

    (i) Show that the matrix A has exactly one non-zero eigenvalue.

    (ii) Find the eigenvalues and the eigenvectors of A.

10. Find the eigenvalues and the eigenvectors of the $n \times n$ matrix
$$\begin{pmatrix} d & 1 & \cdots & 1 \\ 1 & d & \cdots & 1 \\ \vdots & \vdots & \ddots & \vdots \\ 1 & 1 & \cdots & d \end{pmatrix},$$

    where $d \in \mathbb{R}$ is a constant.

Hint: Note that

$$\begin{pmatrix} d & 1 & \cdots & 1 \\ 1 & d & \cdots & 1 \\ \vdots & \vdots & \ddots & \vdots \\ 1 & 1 & \cdots & d \end{pmatrix} = (d-1)I + \begin{pmatrix} 1 & 1 & \cdots & 1 \\ 1 & 1 & \cdots & 1 \\ \vdots & \vdots & \ddots & \vdots \\ 1 & 1 & \cdots & 1 \end{pmatrix}$$
$$= (d-1)I + \mathbf{1} \cdot \mathbf{1}^t,$$

where I is the identity matrix and $\mathbf{1} = \begin{pmatrix} 1 \\ 1 \\ \vdots \\ 1 \end{pmatrix}$.

11. (i) Let A be a symmetric matrix of size n, and let λ_i, $i = 1 : n$, be the eigenvalues of A, with corresponding eigenvectors v_i, $i = 1 : n$. What are the eigenvalues and the eigenvectors of A^2?

    (ii) Let A be a symmetric matrix of size n. Let ϕ_i, $i = 1 : n$, be the eigenvalues of the matrix A^2, with corresponding eigenvectors w_i, $i = 1 : n$. What can you say about the eigenvalues and the eigenvectors of A?

12. Let A be a square matrix of size n, and let S be a nonsingular matrix of size n.

    (i) Let λ and v be an eigenvalue and the corresponding eigenvector of A. Show that λ is also an eigenvalue of the matrix $S^{-1}AS$. What is the corresponding eigenvector?

    (ii) Show that the matrix $S^{-1}AS$ has the same characteristic polynomial as A, i.e., show that
    $$P_{S^{-1}AS}(t) = P_A(t), \ \forall \, t \in \mathbb{R}.$$

13. Let A be a square matrix with real entries. If $\lambda = a + ib$ is a complex eigenvalue of A (i.e., with $b \neq 0$), show that $\overline{\lambda} = a - ib$, the complex conjugate of λ, is also an eigenvalue of A.

14. The 2×2 matrix A has eigenvalues 1 and -2 with corresponding eigenvectors $\begin{pmatrix} -1 \\ 2 \end{pmatrix}$ and $\begin{pmatrix} 3 \\ 1 \end{pmatrix}$. If $v = \begin{pmatrix} 2 \\ -3 \end{pmatrix}$, find Av.

15. Let $A = \begin{pmatrix} -1 & 2 \\ 2 & 2 \end{pmatrix}$.

    (i) Find the eigenvalues and the eigenvectors of the matrix A.

    (ii) What is the diagonal form of A?

    (iii) Compute A^{12}.

16. Let $A = \begin{pmatrix} a & b \\ c & d \end{pmatrix}$ be a 2×2 matrix, and let

$$P_A(t) = t^2 - (a+d)t + (ad-bc)$$

be the characteristic polynomial associated to A.
Show that $P_A(A) = 0$, i.e., show that

$$A^2 - (a+d)A + (ad-bc)I = 0.$$

Note: This is the 2×2 case of the Cayley-Hamilton theorem which states that $P_A(A) = 0$ for any square matrix A.

17. Let A and B be square matrices of the same size.

(i) If A is nonsingular, show that the matrices AB and BA have the same characteristic polynomial, i.e., show that

$$\det(tI - AB) = \det(tI - BA).$$

(ii) Show that the characteristic polynomial of AB is the same as the characteristic polynomial of BA even if A is a singular matrix.

Hint: If A is a singular matrix, it is possible to find a number $\epsilon > 0$ as small as needed such that the matrix $A + \epsilon I$ is nonsingular.

(iii) Show that the matrices AB and BA have the same eigenvalues.

18. (i) Let A and B be square matrices of the same size. Show that the traces of the matrices AB and BA are equal, i.e., show that $\operatorname{tr}(AB) = \operatorname{tr}(BA)$.

(ii) Show that you cannot find two $n \times n$ matrices A and B such that

$$AB - BA = I,$$

where I is the $n \times n$ identity matrix.

19. Recall that the matrix

$$B_4 = \begin{pmatrix} 2 & -1 & 0 & 0 \\ -1 & 2 & -1 & 0 \\ 0 & -1 & 2 & -1 \\ 0 & 0 & -1 & 2 \end{pmatrix}$$

has four eigenvectors v_1, v_2, v_3, v_4 given by

$$v_j(i) = \sin\left(\frac{ij\pi}{5}\right), \quad \forall\, i = 1:4,$$

for $j = 1:4$.
Are the vectors v_1, v_2, v_3, and v_4 orthogonal and of norm 1?

20. Show that the matrix $\begin{pmatrix} 3 & -1 & -1 \\ 0 & 2 & 2 \\ 0 & 1 & 1 \end{pmatrix}$ is a weakly diagonally dominant singular matrix.

21. Show that the matrix
$$\begin{pmatrix} -5 & -1 & 0.25 & -1 \\ 2 & 4 & -1 & 3 \\ 0.5 & -2 & 3 & -1 \\ 1 & 0.5 & 0 & -6 \end{pmatrix}$$
is nonsingular.

22. Let A be an $n \times n$ matrix. For every $j = 1:n$, let
$$R_j = \sum_{k=1:n, k \neq j} |A(j,k)|,$$
and denote by D_j the disc of center $A(j,j)$ and radius R_j, i.e.,
$$D_j = \{z \in \mathbb{C} \text{ such that } |z - A(j,j)| \leq R_j\};$$
note that D_j is called a Gershgorin disk corresponding to the matrix A.

A more general form of Gershgorin's theorem states that, if a Gershgorin disk D_i is disjoint from the union of the other $n-1$ Gershgorin disks of A, then exactly one eigenvalue of the matrix A is in the disk D_i.

Use this result to show that all the eigenvalues of the matrix
$$\begin{pmatrix} -4 & 1 & 0 & -0.5 \\ 0 & 0.1 & 0 & -0.2 \\ 1 & 2 & 5 & -1 \\ 0.25 & -0.15 & 0.1 & -1 \end{pmatrix}$$
are real numbers.

23. Show that all the eigenvalues of the matrix
$$\begin{pmatrix} 2 & 0.0012 & -0.0003 & 0.0015 \\ -0.0002 & -1.25 & 0.0010 & -0.0001 \\ 0 & 0.0016 & 3 & 0.0009 \\ -0.0011 & -0.0008 & -0.0002 & -2.5 \end{pmatrix}$$
are real numbers, and find estimates for the values of the eigenvalues of the matrix with 0.005 accuracy.

24. Let A be an $n \times n$ matrix given by
$$\begin{aligned} A(i,i) &= 2, & \forall\, i = 1:n; \\ A(i, i-1) &= 1, & \forall\, i = 2:n; \\ A(j,k) &= 0, & \text{otherwise.} \end{aligned}$$
Find the eigenvalues and the eigenvectors of A.

4.7. EXERCISES

25. Let J be an $n \times n$ matrix given by

$$\begin{aligned}
A(i,i) &= a, \quad \forall\, i = 1:n; \\
A(i,i+1) &= b, \quad \forall\, i = 1:(n-1); \\
A(j,k) &= 0, \quad \text{otherwise,}
\end{aligned}$$

where $a, b \in \mathbb{R}$ are constants. Find the eigenvalues and the eigenvectors of J.

Note: The matrix J is called a Jordan block if $b = 1$.

26. The 2–norm of a symmetric matrix A is given by

$$\|A\|_2 = \max_{\lambda \text{ eigenvalue of } A} |\lambda|, \tag{4.54}$$

i.e., $\|A\|_2$ is equal to the largest absolute value of all the eigenvalues of A.

The Forward Euler finite difference discretization of the heat PDE is convergent if and only if $\|A_N\|_2 \leq 1$ for all $N \geq 2$, where A_N is the $N \times N$ matrix given by

$$A_N = \begin{pmatrix} 1-2\alpha & -\alpha & \cdots & 0 \\ -\alpha & \ddots & \ddots & \vdots \\ \vdots & \ddots & \ddots & -\alpha \\ 0 & \cdots & -\alpha & 1-2\alpha \end{pmatrix},$$

with $\alpha > 0$ a positive constant.

Show that $\|A_N\|_2 \leq 1$ for all $N \geq 2$ if and only if $0 < \alpha \leq \frac{1}{2}$.

Hint: Recall from Lemma 4.11 that the matrix

$$T_N = \begin{pmatrix} d & -a & \cdots & 0 \\ -a & \ddots & \ddots & \vdots \\ \vdots & \ddots & \ddots & -a \\ 0 & \cdots & -a & d \end{pmatrix}$$

has the following N different eigenvalues:

$$\lambda_j = d - 2a \cos\left(\frac{\pi j}{N+1}\right), \quad \text{for } j = 1:N.$$

27. The Backward Euler finite difference discretization of the heat PDE is convergent if and only if $\|A_N^{-1}\|_2 \leq 1$ for all $N \geq 2$, where

$$A_N = \begin{pmatrix} 1+2\alpha & \alpha & \cdots & 0 \\ \alpha & \ddots & \ddots & \vdots \\ \vdots & \ddots & \ddots & \alpha \\ 0 & \cdots & \alpha & 1+2\alpha \end{pmatrix},$$

with $\alpha > 0$ a positive constant.

Show that $||A_N^{-1}||_2 \leq 1$ for all $N \geq 2$ for any $\alpha > 0$.

Hint: Use (4.54) to show that, if A is a symmetric matrix, then

$$||A^{-1}||_2 = 1/(\min_{\lambda \text{ eigenvalue of } A} |\lambda|).$$

Chapter 5

Symmetric matrices and symmetric positive definite matrices

Symmetric matrices. Real eigenvalues of symmetric matrices. Orthogonality of the eigenvectors of symmetric matrices.

Symmetric positive definite matrices and symmetric positive semidefinite matrices.

Positive definiteness criteria for symmetric matrices. Sylvester's criterion.

Diagonal dominant symmetric positive definite matrices.

The diagonal form of symmetric matrices.

5.1 Symmetric matrices

Definition 5.1. *A symmetric matrix is a matrix with real entries that is equal to its transpose matrix. In other words, an $n \times n$ matrix A is symmetric if and only if $A = A^t$, i.e.,*
$$A(j,k) = A(k,j), \quad \forall\ 1 \leq j \neq k \leq n. \tag{5.1}$$

Examples: (i) Let M be an $n \times n$ square matrix. The matrix $A = M + M^t$ is a symmetric matrix, since $(M^t)^t = M$, see (1.19), and therefore
$$A^t = (M + M^t)^t = M^t + (M^t)^t = M^t + M = A.$$

(ii) Let M be an $m \times n$ matrix. The matrix $A = M^t M$ is a symmetric matrix,[1] since
$$A^t = (M^t M)^t = M^t (M^t)^t = M^t M = A. \quad \square$$

Recall from Theorem 4.2 that an $n \times n$ matrix with real entries has n eigenvalues, counted with their multiplicities, but these eigenvalues may be complex numbers. However, *all the eigenvalues of a symmetric matrix with real entries are real numbers*; see Theorem 5.1.

Moreover, recall from Lemma 4.2 that eigenvectors corresponding to different eigenvalues are linearly independent. For symmetric matrices, such eigenvectors are orthogonal; see Theorem 5.3. To state these results formally and prove them, we begin by introducing the concepts of inner product and orthogonality.

---
[1] Moreover, $M^t M$ is a symmetric positive semidefinite matrix; cf. Lemma 5.2.

Definition 5.2. *Let $u = (u_i)_{i=1:n}$ and $v = (v_i)_{i=1:n}$ be column vectors of size n, with $u_i, v_i \in \mathbb{R}$, for $i = 1 : n$. The inner product of u and v is*

$$(u, v) = v^t u, \tag{5.2}$$

which can be written explicitly as

$$(u, v) = u_1 v_1 + u_2 v_2 + \ldots + u_n v_n = \sum_{i=1}^{n} u_i v_i. \tag{5.3}$$

Note that $v^t u = \sum_{i=1}^{n} u_i v_i = u^t v$, see (1.5), and therefore

$$(u, v) = v^t u = u^t v = (v, u), \quad \forall\, u, v \in \mathbb{R}^n. \tag{5.4}$$

The inner product $(\cdot, \cdot)$ from (5.2) is bilinear; in particular, note that

$$(u_1 + u_2, v) = (u_1, v) + (u_2, v), \quad \forall\, u_1, u_2, v \in \mathbb{R}^n; \tag{5.5}$$
$$(u, v_1 + v_2) = (u, v_1) + (u, v_2), \quad \forall\, u, v_1, v_2 \in \mathbb{R}^n; \tag{5.6}$$
$$(cu, v) = (u, cv) = c(u, v), \quad \forall\, u, v \in \mathbb{R}^n,\ c \in \mathbb{R}. \tag{5.7}$$

Definition 5.3. *The norm of a vector $v \in \mathbb{R}^n$ is defined as $||v|| = \sqrt{(v, v)} = \sqrt{v^t v}$. If $v = (v_i)_{i=1:n}$, then*

$$||v||^2 = (v, v) = v^t v = \sum_{i=1}^{n} v_i^2. \tag{5.8}$$

The inner product from (5.2) and the norm from (5.8) are also called the Euclidean inner product and the Euclidean norm of a vector, respectively.

Theorem 5.1. *Any eigenvalue of a symmetric matrix is a real number.*

Proof. An elegant proof of Theorem 5.1 involves an extension of the Euclidean inner product (5.2) to complex numbers and can be found in section 10.4. □

Lemma 5.1. *Let A be an $m \times n$ matrix, and let B be an $n \times m$ matrix. Let u and v be column vectors of size n and m, respectively. Then,*

$$(Au, v) = (u, A^t v); \tag{5.9}$$
$$(u, Bv) = (B^t u, v). \tag{5.10}$$

Proof. Recall from (1.21) that $(Bv)^t = v^t B^t$ and $(A^t v)^t = v^t (A^t)^t = v^t A$, since $(A^t)^t = A$; cf. (1.19). Then, using (5.2), we find that

$$(Au, v) = v^t A u = (v^t A) u = (A^t v)^t u = (u, A^t v);$$
$$(u, Bv) = (Bv)^t u = v^t B^t u = v^t (B^t u) = (B^t u, v).$$

□

5.1. SYMMETRIC MATRICES

Definition 5.4. *Two vectors of the same size are orthogonal if and only if their inner product is equal to 0. In other words, the vectors u and v are orthogonal if and only if*
$$(u, v) = v^t u = 0,$$
or, equivalently, if and only if
$$(v, u) = u^t v = 0;$$
see (5.4).

Definition 5.5. *A square matrix is orthogonal if and only if any two different columns of the matrix are orthogonal and the norm of every column is equal to 1.*

Theorem 5.2. *A square matrix is orthogonal if and only if its transpose matrix is also its inverse matrix. In other words, the matrix Q is orthogonal if and only if*
$$Q^t Q = Q Q^t = I, \tag{5.11}$$
i.e., if and only if $Q^t = Q^{-1}$.

Proof. The proof of Theorem 5.2 can be found in section 10.1.3; see Theorem 10.2. □

Theorem 5.3. *Eigenvectors corresponding to different eigenvalues of a symmetric matrix are orthogonal.*

Proof. Let A be a symmetric matrix, and let $\lambda_1 \neq \lambda_2$ be two different eigenvalues of A with corresponding eigenvectors v_1 and v_2. Then,
$$A v_1 = \lambda_1 v_1 \quad \text{and} \quad A v_2 = \lambda_2 v_2, \tag{5.12}$$
and, using (5.7), we obtain that
$$(A v_1, v_2) = (\lambda_1 v_1, v_2) = \lambda_1 (v_1, v_2) \tag{5.13}$$
$$(v_1, A v_2) = (v_1, \lambda_2 v_2) = \lambda_2 (v_1, v_2). \tag{5.14}$$

Note that, since the matrix A is symmetric and therefore $A^t = A$, it follows from (5.9) that
$$(A v_1, v_2) = (v_1, A^t v_2) = (v_1, A v_2). \tag{5.15}$$

Then, from (5.15) and using (5.13) and (5.14), we obtain that
$$\lambda_1 (v_1, v_2) = \lambda_2 (v_1, v_2).$$

Thus, $(\lambda_1 - \lambda_2)(v_1, v_2) = 0$, and, since $\lambda_1 \neq \lambda_2$, we conclude that $(v_1, v_2) = 0$, i.e., the eigenvectors v_1 and v_2 are orthogonal. □

Theorem 5.4. *Any symmetric matrix is diagonalizable.*

More precisely, if A is a symmetric matrix, then there exists an orthogonal matrix Q and a diagonal matrix Λ such that[2]
$$A = Q \Lambda Q^t. \tag{5.16}$$

---
[2] The transpose of an orthogonal matrix is also the inverse of the orthogonal matrix, i.e., $Q^t = Q^{-1}$; see Theorem 5.2. Then, from (5.16), it follows that $A = Q\Lambda Q^t = Q\Lambda Q^{-1}$, which is the diagonal form of A.

Note that, from Theorem 4.4, it follows that the diagonal entries of the matrix Λ are the eigenvalues of the matrix A and the columns of the matrix Q are the corresponding eigenvectors of A.

Proof. A proof of this result can be found in Section 5.3; see Theorem 5.9. □

Theorem 5.5. *Any symmetric matrix of size n has a full set of n orthogonal eigenvectors.*

Proof. Let A be a symmetric matrix of size n. From Theorem 5.4, it follows that the matrix A has a diagonal form $A = Q\Lambda Q^t$, where $Q = \text{col}(v_k)_{k=1:n}$ is an $n \times n$ orthogonal matrix and $\Lambda = \text{diag}(\lambda_k)_{k=1:n}$ is a diagonal matrix of size n. Then, from Theorem 4.4, we obtain that v_k, $k = 1 : n$, are n orthogonal eigenvectors of A corresponding to the eigenvalues λ_k, $k = 1 : n$, of A, respectively. □

5.2 Symmetric positive definite matrices

Many matrices occurring in practical applications, e.g., when computing covariance and correlation matrices or for least squares solutions are symmetric positive definite or symmetric positive semidefinite; cf. Chapter 7 and Chapter 8. In this section, we present several equivalent properties of such matrices.

Definition 5.6. *Let A be a symmetric matrix of size n. The matrix A is symmetric positive definite (spd) if and only if* [3]

$$x^t A x > 0, \quad \forall\, x \in \mathbb{R}^n, \ x \neq 0. \tag{5.17}$$

An equivalent way to state condition (5.17) is as follows:

$$x^t A x \geq 0, \ \forall\, x \in \mathbb{R}^n \quad \text{and} \quad x^t A x = 0 \iff x = 0. \tag{5.18}$$

Note that $x^t A x$ *is a number*, since it is the product of a row vector, a matrix, and a column vector; see also Section 10.1.4.

Definition 5.7. *Let A be a symmetric matrix of size n. The matrix A is symmetric positive semidefinite (spsd) if and only if*

$$x^t A x \geq 0, \quad \forall\, x \in \mathbb{R}^n. \tag{5.19}$$

Definition 5.8. *Let A be a symmetric matrix of size n. The matrix A is negative definite if and only if the matrix $-A$ is symmetric positive definite, i.e.,*

$$x^t A x < 0, \quad \forall\, x \in \mathbb{R}^n, \ x \neq 0.$$

The matrix A is negative semidefinite if and only if the matrix $-A$ is symmetric positive semidefinite, i.e.,

$$x^t A x \leq 0, \quad \forall\, x \in \mathbb{R}^n.$$

---
[3]Note that $x^t A x$ is the quadratic form corresponding to matrix A; see section 10.1.4 for properties of quadratic forms.

5.2. SYMMETRIC POSITIVE DEFINITE MATRICES

Lemma 5.2. *Let M be an $m \times n$ matrix.*

(i) The matrix $M^t M$ is an $n \times n$ symmetric positive semidefinite matrix.

(ii) The matrix $M^t M$ is symmetric positive definite if and only if the columns of M are linearly independent.[4]

Proof. Note that the matrix $M^t M$ is symmetric, since

$$(M^t M)^t = M^t (M^t)^t = M^t M.$$

(i) Let $x = (x_i)_{i=1:n}$ be a column vector in $\mathbb{R}^n$. Then,

$$x^t M^t M x = (Mx)^t M x = (Mx, Mx) = ||Mx||^2. \tag{5.20}$$

Since $||Mx||^2 \geq 0$, it follows from (5.20) that

$$x^t M^t M x \geq 0, \quad \forall\, x \in \mathbb{R}^n, \tag{5.21}$$

and therefore that the matrix $M^t M$ is symmetric positive semidefinite; cf. Definition 5.6.

(ii) Let $M = \mathrm{col}\,(m_k)_{k=1:n}$. From (5.20), it follows that

$$x^t M^t M x = 0 \iff ||Mx||^2 = 0 \iff Mx = 0 \iff \sum_{k=1}^{n} x_k m_k = 0,$$

where the matrix–vector multiplication formula (1.7) was used for the last equivalence.

Thus, there exists a vector $x \neq 0$ such that $x^t M^t M x = 0$ if and only if the columns of the matrix M are not linearly independent. Since $x^t M^t M x \geq 0$ for all $x \in \mathbb{R}^n$, see (5.21), we conclude from Definition 5.6 that the matrix $M^t M$ is symmetric positive definite if and only if the columns of M are linearly independent. □

Note that symmetric positive semidefinite matrices of the from $M^t M$ appear often in practical applications such as finding covariance matrices from time series data, solving least square problems, and doing linear regression; see Chapter 7 and Chapter 8.

Example: Show that the $N \times N$ matrix

$$B_N = \begin{pmatrix} 2 & -1 & \cdots & 0 \\ -1 & \ddots & \ddots & \vdots \\ \vdots & \ddots & \ddots & -1 \\ 0 & \cdots & -1 & 2 \end{pmatrix}$$

is symmetric positive definite.[5]

---

[4] A necessary (but not sufficient) condition for the $m \times n$ matrix M to have linearly independent columns is that it cannot have more columns than rows, i.e., $n \leq m$.

[5] Another proof of this fact can be given using the fact that a matrix is symmetric positive definite if and only if all its eigenvalues are positive; see Theorem 5.6 and the example thereafter.

Solution: Recall from (10.20) that

$$x^t B_N x = \sum_{1 \leq j,k \leq N} B_N(j,k) x_j x_k,$$

and therefore

$$\begin{aligned}
x^t B_N x &= \sum_{i=1}^{N} 2x_i^2 - \sum_{i=2}^{N} x_{i-1}x_i - \sum_{i=1}^{N-1} x_i x_{i+1} \\
&= 2\sum_{i=1}^{N} x_i^2 - 2\sum_{i=1}^{N-1} x_i x_{i+1} \\
&= x_1^2 + \sum_{i=1}^{N-1} x_{i+1}^2 + \sum_{i=1}^{N-1} x_i^2 + x_N^2 - 2\sum_{i=1}^{N-1} x_i x_{i+1} \\
&= x_1^2 + \sum_{i=1}^{N-1} (x_i^2 - 2x_i x_{i+1} + x_{i+1}^2) + x_N^2 \\
&= x_1^2 + \sum_{i=1}^{N-1} (x_i - x_{i+1})^2 + x_N^2 \\
&\geq 0, \ \forall x \in \mathbb{R}^N.
\end{aligned}$$

Moreover,

$$\begin{aligned}
x^t B_N x = 0 &\iff x_1^2 + \sum_{i=1}^{N-1}(x_i - x_{i+1})^2 + x_N^2 = 0 \\
&\iff x_1 = 0;\ x_N = 0;\ x_i = x_{i+1},\ \forall\, i = 1:(N-1) \\
&\iff x_i = 0,\ \forall\, i = 1:N \\
&\iff x = 0.
\end{aligned}$$

We conclude that $x^t B_N x > 0$ for all $x \in \mathbb{R}^N$, $x \neq 0$, and therefore that B_N is a symmetric positive definite matrix; cf. (5.17). □

Several equivalent ways to characterize symmetric positive matrices are presented below. A summary of these conditions and comments on their practical applicability can be found in Section 5.2.2.

Theorem 5.6. *(i) A symmetric matrix is symmetric positive semidefinite if and only if all the eigenvalues of the matrix are greater than or equal to zero.*

(ii) A symmetric matrix is symmetric positive definite if and only if all the eigenvalues of the matrix are strictly greater than zero.

Proof. Let A be a symmetric matrix of size n. Recall from Theorem 5.5 that any symmetric matrix of size n has a full set of n orthogonal eigenvectors. Let $v_1, v_2, \ldots, v_n$ be n orthogonal eigenvectors of A of norm 1, and let $\lambda_1, \lambda_2, \ldots, \lambda_n$ be the corresponding eigenvalues. If $Q = \mathrm{col}\,(v_k)_{k=1:n}$ and $\Lambda = \mathrm{diag}(\lambda_k)_{k=1:n}$, the diagonal form of A is

$$A = Q \Lambda Q^t, \tag{5.22}$$

5.2. SYMMETRIC POSITIVE DEFINITE MATRICES

where Q is an orthogonal matrix; cf. Theorem 5.4. Let $x \in \mathbb{R}^n$. From (5.22), it follows that

$$x^t A x = x^t Q \Lambda Q^t x = (Q^t x)^t \Lambda (Q^t x) = y^t \Lambda y, \tag{5.23}$$

where $y = Q^t x$. If $y = (y_i)_{i=1:n}$, we find from (5.23) that

$$x^t A x = y^t \Lambda y = \sum_{i=1}^{n} \lambda_i y_i^2. \tag{5.24}$$

We now prove each part of the theorem by double implication.

(i) "If A is a symmetric positive semidefinite matrix, then all the eigenvalues of A are greater than or equal to zero."

Assume that there exists an eigenvalue λ_j of A such that $\lambda_j < 0$, and let $w_j \neq 0$ be an eigenvector corresponding to λ_j. Then, $A w_j = \lambda_j w_j$ and

$$w_j^t A w_j = w_j^t (\lambda_j w_j) = \lambda_j \cdot w_j^t w_j = \lambda_j \|w_j\|^2 < 0,$$

since $\lambda_j < 0$ and $w_j \neq 0$. This contradicts the property (5.19) of a positive semidefinite matrix.

We conclude that, if A is symmetric positive semidefinite, then all its eigenvalues must be greater than or equal to zero.

(i) "If all the eigenvalues of A are greater than or equal to zero, then A is a symmetric positive semidefinite matrix."

Assume that $\lambda_i \geq 0$, for all $i = 1:n$. Let $x \in \mathbb{R}^n$ and let $y = Q^t x$. If $y = (y_i)_{i=1:n}$, it follows from (5.24) that

$$x^t A x = y^t \Lambda y = \sum_{i=1}^{n} \lambda_i y_i^2. \tag{5.25}$$

Since $\lambda_i \geq 0$ for all $i = 1:n$, it follows from (5.25) that $x^t A x \geq 0$ for any $x \in \mathbb{R}^n$, and, from Definition 5.7, we conclude that A is a symmetric positive semidefinite matrix.

(ii) "If A is a symmetric positive definite matrix, then all the eigenvalues of A are strictly greater than zero."

Assume that there exists an eigenvalue λ_j of A such that $\lambda_j \leq 0$, and let $w_j \neq 0$ be an eigenvector corresponding to λ_j. Then, $A w_j = \lambda_j w_j$ and

$$w_j^t A w_j = w_j^t (\lambda_j w_j) = \lambda_j \cdot w_j^t w_j = \lambda_j \|w_j\|^2 \leq 0,$$

since $\lambda_j \leq 0$. This contradicts the property (5.17) of a positive definite matrix, since $w_j \neq 0$.

We conclude that, if the matrix A is symmetric positive definite, then all its eigenvalues must be strictly greater than zero.

(ii) "If all the eigenvalues of A are strictly greater than zero, then A is a symmetric positive definite matrix."

Assume that $\lambda_i > 0$, for all $i = 1:n$. Let $x \in \mathbb{R}^n$ and let $y = Q^t x$. If $y = (y_i)_{i=1:n}$, it follows from (5.24) that

$$x^t A x = y^t \Lambda y = \sum_{i=1}^{n} \lambda_i y_i^2 \geq 0. \tag{5.26}$$

Since $\lambda_i > 0$ for all $i = 1:n$, it follows from (5.26) that $x^t A x = 0$ if and only if $y_i = 0$ for all $i = 1:n$, i.e., if and only if $y = 0$. Recall that $y = Q^t x$, where Q is an orthogonal matrix. Thus,

$$x^t A x = 0 \iff y = 0 \iff Q^t x = 0 \iff Q(Q^t x) = 0 \iff x = 0,$$

since Q is a nonsingular matrix and $QQ^t = I$; see (5.11).

We conclude that $x^t A x > 0$ for any $x \neq 0$, and, from (5.17) of Definition 5.6, it follows that A is a symmetric positive definite matrix. $\square$

The following result is a simple consequence of Theorem 5.6:

Lemma 5.3. *Any symmetric positive definite matrix is nonsingular.*

Proof. Let A be a symmetric positive definite matrix. From Theorem 5.6, we obtain that all the eigenvalues of A are strictly greater than zero. Thus, 0 is not an eigenvalue of the matrix A, and, from Theorem 4.3, we conclude that the matrix A is nonsingular. $\square$

Lemma 5.4. *The inverse of a symmetric positive definite matrix is also symmetric positive definite.*

Proof. Let A be a symmetric positive definite matrix. Recall from Lemma 5.3 that the matrix A is nonsingular, and let A^{-1} be the inverse matrix of A. From Lemma 4.3, it follows that, if μ is an eigenvalue of A, then $\frac{1}{\mu}$ is an eigenvalue of A^{-1}. Note that all the eigenvalues of A are strictly greater than zero, since A is symmetric positive definite; cf. Theorem 5.6. Then, $\mu > 0$, and therefore $\frac{1}{\mu} > 0$.

In other words, all the eigenvalues of the symmetric matrix A^{-1} are positive, and, from Theorem 5.6, we conclude that A^{-1} is a symmetric positive definite matrix. $\square$

In the example below, we find necessary and sufficient conditions for a 2×2 symmetric matrix to be symmetric positive definite and symmetric positive semidefinite, by using the eigenvalue related criterion from Theorem 5.6. A proof of the same results using Sylvester's criterion is given in Lemma 5.5, and is extended to 3×3 matrices in Lemma 5.6.

Example: (i) The matrix $\begin{pmatrix} a & b \\ b & d \end{pmatrix}$ is symmetric positive definite if and only if $a > 0$ and $ad > b^2$.

(ii) The matrix $\begin{pmatrix} a & b \\ b & d \end{pmatrix}$ is symmetric positive semidefinite if and only if $a \geq 0$, $d \geq 0$, and $ad \geq b^2$.

Solution: Let $A = \begin{pmatrix} a & b \\ b & d \end{pmatrix}$. The characteristic polynomial of the matrix A is

$$P_A(t) = \det(tI - A) = t^2 - (a + d)t + ad - b^2. \tag{5.27}$$

5.2. SYMMETRIC POSITIVE DEFINITE MATRICES

Recall from Lemma 4.1 that

$$P_A(t) = (t - \lambda_1)(t - \lambda_2) = t^2 - (\lambda_1 + \lambda_2)t + \lambda_1\lambda_2, \tag{5.28}$$

where λ_1 and λ_2 are the eigenvalues of A. Since A is a symmetric matrix with real entries, it follows that λ_1 and λ_2 are real numbers; cf. Theorem 5.3. From (5.27) and (5.28), we obtain that

$$\lambda_1 + \lambda_2 = a + d; \quad \lambda_1\lambda_2 = ad - b^2. \tag{5.29}$$

(i) From Theorem 5.6 (i), it follows that

$$A \text{ symmetric positive definite} \iff (\lambda_1 > 0 \text{ and } \lambda_2 > 0). \tag{5.30}$$

Note that two real numbers are positive if and only if both their product and their sum are positive. From (5.29), we find that

$$\begin{aligned}(\lambda_1 > 0 \text{ and } \lambda_2 > 0) &\iff (\lambda_1 + \lambda_2 > 0 \text{ and } \lambda_1\lambda_2 > 0) \\ &\iff (a + d > 0 \text{ and } ad > b^2).\end{aligned} \tag{5.31}$$

Note that, if $ad > b^2$, then $ad > 0$, and therefore a and d must have the same sign and be nonzero. Thus,

$$(a + d > 0 \text{ and } ad > b^2) \iff (a > 0 \text{ and } ad > b^2). \tag{5.32}$$

From (5.31) and (5.32), it follows that

$$(\lambda_1 > 0 \text{ and } \lambda_2 > 0) \iff (a > 0 \text{ and } ad > b^2), \tag{5.33}$$

and, from (5.30) and (5.33), we conclude that the matrix A is symmetric positive definite if and only if $a > 0$ and $ad > b^2$.

(ii) From Theorem 5.6 (ii), it follows that

$$A \text{ symmetric positive semidefinite} \iff (\lambda_1 \geq 0 \text{ and } \lambda_2 \geq 0). \tag{5.34}$$

Note that two real numbers are greater than or equal to 0 if and only if both their product and their sum are greater than or equal to 0. From (5.29), we find that

$$\begin{aligned}(\lambda_1 \geq 0 \text{ and } \lambda_2 \geq 0) &\iff (\lambda_1 + \lambda_2 \geq 0 \text{ and } \lambda_1\lambda_2 \geq 0) &(5.35)\\ &\iff (a + d \geq 0 \text{ and } ad \geq b^2). &(5.36)\end{aligned}$$

Note that, if $ad \geq b^2$, then $ad \geq 0$, and therefore a and d must have the same sign. Thus,

$$(a + d \geq 0 \text{ and } ad \geq b^2) \iff (a \geq 0, \ d \geq 0, \text{ and } ad \geq b^2). \tag{5.37}$$

From (5.35–5.37), it follows that

$$(\lambda_1 \geq 0 \text{ and } \lambda_2 \geq 0) \iff (a \geq 0, \ d \geq 0, \text{ and } ad \geq b^2), \tag{5.38}$$

and, from (5.34) and (5.38), we conclude that the matrix A is symmetric positive semidefinite if and only if $a \geq 0$, $d \geq 0$, and $ad \geq b^2$. □

Example: Show that the $N \times N$ matrix

$$B_N = \begin{pmatrix} 2 & -1 & \cdots & 0 \\ -1 & \ddots & \ddots & \vdots \\ \vdots & \ddots & \ddots & -1 \\ 0 & \cdots & -1 & 2 \end{pmatrix}$$

is symmetric positive definite.

Solution: Recall from Lemma 4.10 that the eigenvalues of the matrix B_N are

$$\mu_j = 2\left(1 - \cos\left(\frac{j\pi}{N+1}\right)\right), \quad \forall j = 1 : N.$$

Since $-1 \leq \cos(x) < 1$ for all $x \neq 2k\pi$, where k is an integer, we find that $\mu_j > 0$ for all $j = 1 : N$. Thus, all the eigenvalues of B_N are strictly positive, and, from Theorem 5.6, we obtain that B_N is a symmetric positive definite matrix. $\square$

Example: Show that the $N \times N$ tridiagonal symmetric matrix

$$T_N = \begin{pmatrix} d & -a & \cdots & 0 \\ -a & \ddots & \ddots & \vdots \\ \vdots & \ddots & \ddots & -a \\ 0 & \cdots & -a & d \end{pmatrix} \tag{5.39}$$

is symmetric positive definite if and only if the parameters d and a satisfy the inequality

$$d > 2|a|\cos\left(\frac{\pi}{N+1}\right). \tag{5.40}$$

Solution: The eigenvalues of the matrix T_N are

$$\lambda_j = d - 2a\cos\left(\frac{\pi j}{N+1}\right), \quad \forall j = 1 : N; \tag{5.41}$$

see Lemma 4.11. Note that

$$1 > \cos\left(\frac{\pi}{N+1}\right) > \cos\left(\frac{2\pi}{N+1}\right) > \cos\left(\frac{N\pi}{N+1}\right) > -1. \tag{5.42}$$

If $a \geq 0$, it follows from (5.41) and (5.42) that

$$\lambda_1 \leq \lambda_2 \leq \cdots \leq \lambda_N.$$

Recall from Theorem 5.6 that a symmetric matrix is symmetric positive definite if and only if all the eigenvalues of the matrix are strictly greater than zero. Then, the matrix T_N is symmetric positive definite if and only if $\lambda_1 = d - 2a\cos\left(\frac{\pi}{N+1}\right) > 0$, which is equivalent to

$$d > 2a\cos\left(\frac{\pi}{N+1}\right). \tag{5.43}$$

5.2. SYMMETRIC POSITIVE DEFINITE MATRICES

If $a < 0$, we find from (5.41) and (5.42) that

$$\lambda_1 > \lambda_2 > \ldots > \lambda_N.$$

From Theorem 5.6, it follows that T_N is a symmetric positive definite matrix if and only if $\lambda_N > 0$.

Recall that $\cos(\pi - x) = -\cos(x)$ for all $x \in \mathbb{R}$ and therefore

$$\cos\left(\frac{N\pi}{N+1}\right) = \cos\left(\pi - \frac{\pi}{N+1}\right) = -\cos\left(\frac{\pi}{N+1}\right).$$

Then,

$$\lambda_N = d - 2a\cos\left(\frac{N\pi}{N+1}\right) = d + 2a\cos\left(\frac{\pi}{N+1}\right),$$

and $\lambda_N > 0$ is equivalent to

$$d > -2a\cos\left(\frac{\pi}{N+1}\right) = 2|a|\cos\left(\frac{\pi}{N+1}\right); \quad (5.44)$$

the last equality comes from the fact that $a < 0$ and therefore $|a| = -a$.

The conditions (5.43) and (5.44) for the matrix T_N to be symmetric positive definite can be written together as

$$d > 2|a|\cos\left(\frac{\pi}{N+1}\right),$$

which is what we wanted to show; see (5.40). $\square$

Although the solutions above are elegant, they use the fact that the eigenvalues of the matrices B_N and T_N are known in advance. In practice, deciding whether a matrix is symmetric positive definite is not done by computing matrix eigenvalues numerically, which could be computationally expensive. Instead, the Cholesky decomposition algorithm is applied to the matrix: if the algorithm does not break down, then the matrix is symmetric positive definite, else it is not. The cost of applying the Cholesky algorithm to an $n \times n$ matrix, and therefore of deciding whether the matrix is symmetric positive definite, is $\frac{1}{3}n^3 + O(n^2)$; see section 6.1 for details.

Many matrices arising in practice are symmetric and weakly or strictly diagonally dominant. The results below are thus important in practical applications.

Theorem 5.7. *(i) Any strictly diagonally dominant symmetric matrix with positive entries on the main diagonal is symmetric positive definite.*
Equivalently, all the eigenvalues of a strictly diagonally dominant symmetric matrix are strictly greater than 0.

(ii) Any weakly diagonally dominant symmetric matrix with positive entries on the main diagonal is symmetric positive semidefinite.
Equivalently, all the eigenvalues of a weakly diagonally dominant symmetric matrix are greater than or equal 0.

Proof. Let λ be an eigenvalue of A. Note that λ is a real number, since A is a symmetric matrix; cf. Theorem 5.1.

From Gershgorin's Theorem, see Theorem 4.6, it follows that there exists j, with $1 \leq j \leq n$, such that

$$|A(j,j) - \lambda| \leq R_j, \tag{5.45}$$

where R_j is given by (4.28), since $|\lambda - A(j,j)| = |A(j,j) - \lambda|$.

Since $a \leq |a|$ for any $a \in \mathbb{R}$, we find from (5.45) that

$$A(j,j) - \lambda \leq |A(j,j) - \lambda| \leq R_j,$$

and therefore

$$\lambda \geq A(j,j) - R_j. \tag{5.46}$$

(i) If A is a strictly diagonally dominant matrix with positive entries on the main diagonal, then $A(j,j) = |A(j,j)|$, and, from (4.30), it follows that

$$A(j,j) > R_j. \tag{5.47}$$

From (5.46) and (5.47) we conclude that $\lambda > 0$ for any eigenvalue λ of A, and therefore that the matrix A is symmetric positive definite; cf. Theorem 5.6.

(ii) If A is a weakly diagonally dominant symmetric matrix with positive entries on the main diagonal, then $A(j,j) = |A(j,j)|$, and, from (4.29), it follows that

$$A(j,j) \geq R_j. \tag{5.48}$$

From (5.46) and (5.48), we conclude that $\lambda \geq 0$ for any eigenvalue λ of A, and therefore the matrix A is symmetric positive semidefinite; cf. Theorem 5.6. $\square$

Example: Show that the matrix

$$A_1 = \begin{pmatrix} 3 & -0.2 & 1.25 & -0.35 \\ -0.2 & 1.5 & 0.25 & 1 \\ 1.25 & 0.25 & 2.5 & 0.5 \\ -0.35 & 1 & 0.5 & 4 \end{pmatrix}$$

is symmetric positive definite.

Answer: The matrix A_1 is symmetric and all its main diagonal entries are positive. It is also strictly diagonally dominant, since, for every row of A_1, the absolute value of the main diagonal entry from the row is greater than the sum of the absolute values of all the other entries in that row:

$$\begin{aligned} 3 &> |-0.2| + 1.25 + |-0.35| = 1.8; \\ 1.5 &> |-0.2| + 0.25 + 1 = 1.45; \\ 2.5 &> 1.25 + 0.25 + 0.5 = 2; \\ 4 &> |-0.35| + 1 + 0.5 = 1.85. \end{aligned}$$

Then, from Theorem 5.7, we conclude that the matrix A_1 is symmetric positive definite. $\square$

5.2. SYMMETRIC POSITIVE DEFINITE MATRICES

5.2.1 Sylvester's Criterion

An elegant and practical way to check whether a matrix of small size is symmetric positive definite or symmetric positive semidefinite is provided by Sylvester's Criterion; see Theorem 5.8.

Definition 5.9. *Let A be an $n \times n$ matrix. The leading principal minors of A are the determinants of the $i \times i$ matrices $A_i = A(1:i, 1:i)$ made of the i^2 upper left entries of A, for $1 \leq i \leq n$.*

Definition 5.10. *Let A be an $n \times n$ matrix. The principal minors of A are the determinants of all the square matrices obtained by eliminating the same rows and columns from the matrix A.*

Note that an $n \times n$ matrix has n leading principal minors and $2^n - 1$ principal minors; see also an exercise at the end of this chapter.

Example: The matrix $\begin{pmatrix} 2 & -3 & 0 \\ 1 & 1 & 1 \\ -1 & 5 & -3 \end{pmatrix}$ has the following three leading principal minors:

$$\det(2) = 2; \quad \det\begin{pmatrix} 2 & -3 \\ 1 & 1 \end{pmatrix} = 5; \quad \det\begin{pmatrix} 2 & -3 & 0 \\ 1 & 1 & 1 \\ -1 & 5 & -3 \end{pmatrix} = -22,$$

and the following seven principal minors:

$$\det(2) = 2; \quad \det(1) = 1; \quad \det(-3) = -3;$$

$$\det\begin{pmatrix} 2 & -3 \\ 1 & 1 \end{pmatrix} = 5; \quad \det\begin{pmatrix} 2 & 0 \\ -1 & -3 \end{pmatrix} = -6; \quad \det\begin{pmatrix} 1 & 1 \\ 5 & -3 \end{pmatrix} = -8;$$

$$\det\begin{pmatrix} 2 & -3 & 0 \\ 1 & 1 & 1 \\ -1 & 5 & -3 \end{pmatrix} = -22. \quad \square$$

Theorem 5.8. *(Sylvester's Criterion.) (i) A symmetric matrix is symmetric positive definite if and only if all its leading principal minors are positive.*

(ii) A symmetric matrix is symmetric positive semidefinite if and only if all its principal minors[6] are greater than or equal to 0.

The proof of Sylvester's Criterion is technical and of no further relevance herein.

We will use Sylvester's Criterion to establish necessary and sufficient conditions for 2×2 and 3×3 matrices to be symmetric positive definite. These conditions will be further used in Section 7.4 to identify whether a given symmetric matrix can be a covariance or correlation matrix.

---

[6]Note that a symmetric matrix whose *leading* principal minors are greater than or equal to 0 is not necessarily symmetric positive semidefinite. For example, the matrix $\begin{pmatrix} 0 & 0 & 0 \\ 0 & -1 & 0 \\ 0 & 0 & 1 \end{pmatrix}$ has all leading principal minors equal to 0, but has a negative eigenvalue, -1, and therefore is not symmetric positive semidefinite.

Lemma 5.5. Let $A = \begin{pmatrix} a & b \\ b & d \end{pmatrix}$ be a 2×2 symmetric matrix.

(i) The matrix A is symmetric positive definite if and only if
$$a > 0 \quad \text{and} \quad \det(A) = ad - b^2 > 0. \tag{5.49}$$

(ii) The matrix A is symmetric positive semidefinite if and only if
$$a \geq 0; \quad d \geq 0; \quad \det(A) = ad - b^2 \geq 0. \tag{5.50}$$

Proof. (i) The leading principal minors of the matrix A are
$$\det(a) = a \quad \text{and} \quad \det(A) = ad - b^2.$$
From Sylvester's Criterion (Theorem 5.8), it follows that A is symmetric positive definite if and only if $a > 0$ and $ad - b^2 > 0$, which is the same as (5.49).

(ii) The principal minors of the matrix A are
$$\det(a) = a; \quad \det(d) = d; \quad \det(A) = ad - b^2.$$
From Sylvester's Criterion (Theorem 5.8), it follows that A is symmetric positive semidefinite if and only if $a \geq 0$, $d \geq 0$, and $ad - b^2 \geq 0$, which is the same as (5.50). □

Note that, by letting $a = d = 1$ and $b = \rho$ it follows from (5.49) and (5.50) that[7]
$$\begin{pmatrix} 1 & \rho \\ \rho & 1 \end{pmatrix} \text{ spd} \quad \Longleftrightarrow \quad -1 < \rho < 1; \tag{5.51}$$
$$\begin{pmatrix} 1 & \rho \\ \rho & 1 \end{pmatrix} \text{ spsd} \quad \Longleftrightarrow \quad -1 \leq \rho \leq 1. \tag{5.52}$$

Lemma 5.6. Let $A = \begin{pmatrix} d_1 & a & b \\ a & d_2 & c \\ b & c & d_3 \end{pmatrix}$ be a 3×3 symmetric matrix.

(i) The matrix A is symmetric positive definite if and only if
$$d_1 > 0; \quad d_1 d_2 > a^2; \quad \det(A) = d_1 d_2 d_3 + 2abc - d_3 a^2 - d_2 b^2 - d_1 c^2 > 0. \tag{5.53}$$

(ii) The matrix A is symmetric positive semidefinite if and only if
$$d_1, d_2, d_3 \geq 0; \quad d_1 d_2 \geq a^2; \quad d_1 d_3 \geq b^2; \quad d_2 d_3 \geq c^2; \tag{5.54}$$
$$\det(A) = d_1 d_2 d_3 + 2abc - d_3 a^2 - d_2 b^2 - d_1 c^2 \geq 0. \tag{5.55}$$

Proof. (i) The leading principal minors of the matrix A are
$$\det(d_1) = d_1; \tag{5.56}$$
$$\det \begin{pmatrix} d_1 & a \\ a & d_2 \end{pmatrix} = d_1 d_2 - a^2; \tag{5.57}$$
$$\det \begin{pmatrix} d_1 & a & b \\ a & d_2 & c \\ b & c & d_3 \end{pmatrix} = d_1 d_2 d_3 + 2abc - d_3 a^2 - d_2 b^2 - d_1 c^2; \tag{5.58}$$

---
[7]The matrix $\begin{pmatrix} 1 & \rho \\ \rho & 1 \end{pmatrix}$ is the correlation matrix of two random variables X_1 and X_2 with correlation $\mathrm{corr}(X_1, X_2) = \rho$, with $|\rho| < 1$.

5.2. SYMMETRIC POSITIVE DEFINITE MATRICES

see (10.6) and (10.8) for deriving (5.57) and (5.58).

From (5.56–5.58), it follows that requiring all the leading principal minors of the matrix A to be positive is equivalent to (5.53). Then, from Sylvester's Criterion (Theorem 5.8), we conclude that A is symmetric positive definite if and only if (5.53) is satisfied.

(ii) The principal minors the matrix A are

$$\det(d_1) = d_1; \quad \det(d_2) = d_2; \quad \det(d_3) = d_3; \tag{5.59}$$

$$\det\begin{pmatrix} d_1 & a \\ a & d_2 \end{pmatrix} = d_1 d_2 - a^2; \quad \det\begin{pmatrix} d_1 & b \\ b & d_3 \end{pmatrix} = d_1 d_3 - b^2; \tag{5.60}$$

$$\det\begin{pmatrix} d_2 & c \\ c & d_3 \end{pmatrix} = d_2 d_3 - c^2; \tag{5.61}$$

$$\det\begin{pmatrix} d_1 & a & b \\ a & d_2 & c \\ b & c & d_3 \end{pmatrix} = d_1 d_2 d_3 + 2abc - d_3 a^2 - d_2 b^2 - d_1 c^2; \tag{5.62}$$

From (5.59–5.62), it follows that requiring all the principal minors of the matrix A to be positive is equivalent to (5.54–5.55). Then, from Sylvester's Criterion (Theorem 5.8), we conclude that A is symmetric positive semidefinite if and only if the inequalities (5.54–5.55) are satisfied. $\square$

Note that, by letting $d_1 = d_2 = d_3 = 1$ in (5.53), it follows that

$$A = \begin{pmatrix} 1 & a & b \\ a & 1 & c \\ b & c & 1 \end{pmatrix} \quad \text{spd}$$

$$\iff a^2 < 1 \text{ and } \det(A) = 1 + 2abc - a^2 - b^2 - c^2 > 0$$
$$\iff -1 < a < 1 \text{ and } \det(A) = 1 + 2abc - a^2 - b^2 - c^2 > 0. \tag{5.63}$$

Similarly, by letting $d_1 = d_2 = d_3 = 1$ in (5.54–5.55), it follows that

$$A = \begin{pmatrix} 1 & a & b \\ a & 1 & c \\ b & c & 1 \end{pmatrix} \quad \text{spsd}$$

$$\iff a^2 \leq 1; \ b^2 \leq 1; \ c^2 \leq 1; \ \det(A) = 1 + 2abc - a^2 - b^2 - c^2 \geq 0$$
$$\iff -1 \leq a, b, c \leq 1; \text{ and } \det(A) = 1 + 2abc - a^2 - b^2 - c^2 \geq 0. \tag{5.64}$$

Note that the matrix $\begin{pmatrix} 1 & a & b \\ a & 1 & c \\ b & c & 1 \end{pmatrix}$ is the correlation matrix of three random variables X_1, X_2, and X_3 with correlations $\text{corr}(X_1, X_2) = a$, $\text{corr}(X_1, X_3) = b$, and $\text{corr}(X_2, X_3) = c$, with $-1 \leq a, b, c \leq 1$. The positive definiteness criteria above will be further used in Section 7.4 to establish possible values for a, b, and c such that the matrix $\begin{pmatrix} 1 & a & b \\ a & 1 & c \\ b & c & 1 \end{pmatrix}$ is, indeed, a correlation matrix.

5.2.2 Positive definiteness criteria for symmetric matrices

In this section, we summarize the necessary and sufficient conditions established in the previous sections for a symmetric matrix to be symmetric positive definite or symmetric positive semidefinite, i.e., the definitions 5.6 and 5.7, the eigenvalues criteria from Theorem 5.6, Sylvester's Criterion (Theorem 5.8), and we anticipate by including Cholesky decomposition criteria; cf. Theorem 6.2 from Section 6.1.

Let A be an $n \times n$ symmetric matrix. Equivalent conditions for the matrix A to be symmetric positive definite (spd) or symmetric positive semidefinite (spsd) can be found in Table 5.1.

Table 5.1: Necessary and sufficient conditions for spd and spsd matrices

A spd	$\iff$	$x^t A x > 0$, $\forall\, x \neq 0$	definition
A spsd	$\iff$	$x^t A x \geq 0$, $\forall\, x \in \mathbb{R}^n$	
A spd	$\iff$	all the eigenvalues of A are > 0	eigenvalue
A spsd	$\iff$	all the eigenvalues of A are ≥ 0	criterion
A spd	$\iff$	all the leading principal minors of A are > 0	Sylvester's
A spsd	$\iff$	all the principal minors of A are ≥ 0	criterion
A spd	$\iff$	the matrix A has Cholesky decomposition	Cholesky decomposition

We include a few comments on the practical relevance of the conditions from Table 5.1:

• From a practical standpoint, identifying whether a matrix is symmetric positive definite is done by running the Cholesky decomposition algorithm from Table 6.1 on the matrix. If the algorithms breaks down, then the matrix is not symmetric positive definite; else, the matrix is symmetric positive definite.

• Computing the eigenvalues of the matrix numerically, e.g., by using the QR algorithm, in order to find out whether all the eigenvalues of the matrix are positive, and thus establish whether the matrix is symmetric positive definite, is a lot more expensive than running the Cholesky algorithm, and potentially imprecise for matrices with very small positive eigenvalues.

• Sylvester's Criterion can be applied to establish, without using numerical methods, whether matrices of small size are symmetric positive definite or symmetric positive semidefinite.

• The criteria given by the definitions of spd and spsd matrices are rarely of practical use; one of the few such examples can be found in Section 5.2.

Note that a Cholesky–based criterion also exists for symmetric positive semidefinite, although it is of little practical importance; see section 6.5 for details.

5.3 The diagonal form of symmetric matrices

In this section, we include for completeness the proof of the fact that any symmetric matrix is diagonalizable; see Theorem 5.4. This proof is based on properties of orthogonal matrices; see section 10.1.3 for details.

Theorem 5.9. *Any symmetric matrix is diagonalizable.*

More precisely, if A is a symmetric matrix, then there exists an orthogonal matrix Q and a diagonal matrix Λ such that

$$A = Q\Lambda Q^t. \tag{5.65}$$

Note that, from Theorem 4.4, it follows that the diagonal entries of the matrix Λ are the eigenvalues of the matrix A and the columns of the matrix Q are the corresponding eigenvectors of A.

Proof. We give a proof by induction.

Any 1×1 matrix is a number, and is the same as a diagonal matrix of size 1.

Assume that any symmetric matrix of size $n - 1$ is diagonalizable. We will show that any symmetric matrix of size n is also diagonalizable.

Let A be an $n \times n$ symmetric matrix. Let λ_1 and v_1 be an eigenvalue and a corresponding eigenvector of norm 1 of the matrix A, i.e., such that $Av_1 = \lambda_1 v_1$, with $v_1 \neq 0$ and

$$||v_1||^2 = v_1^t v_1 = 1. \tag{5.66}$$

Let Q_1 be an $n \times n$ orthogonal matrix with the vector v_1 as the first column, i.e., let

$$Q_1 = (v_1 \mid q_2 \mid \ldots \mid q_n)$$

where q_i are $n \times 1$ column vectors such that

$$(v_1, q_i) = q_i^t v_1 = 0, \ \forall \, i = 2:n, \tag{5.67}$$

and $||q_i||^2 = q_i^t q_i = 1$, for $i = 2:n$.

From the matrix–matrix multiplication formula (1.11), and using the fact that $Av_1 = \lambda_1 v_1$, we find that

$$AQ_1 = (Av_1 \mid Aq_2 \mid \ldots \mid Aq_n) = (\lambda_1 v_1 \mid Aq_2 \mid \ldots \mid Aq_n).$$

Then,

$$Q_1^t A Q_1 = \begin{pmatrix} v_1^t \\ \hline q_2^t \\ \hline \vdots \\ \hline q_n^t \end{pmatrix} (\lambda_1 v_1 \mid Aq_2 \mid \ldots \mid Aq_n)$$

$$= \begin{pmatrix} \lambda_1 v_1^t v_1 & v_1^t A q_2 & \ldots & v_1^t A q_n \\ \lambda_1 q_2^t v_1 & q_2^t A q_2 & \ldots & q_2^t A q_n \\ \vdots & \vdots & \vdots & \vdots \\ \lambda_1 q_n^t v_1 & q_n^t A q_2 & \ldots & q_n^t A q_n \end{pmatrix}$$

$$= \begin{pmatrix} \lambda_1 & v_1^t A q_2 & \ldots & v_1^t A q_n \\ 0 & q_2^t A q_2 & \ldots & q_2^t A q_n \\ \vdots & \vdots & \vdots & \vdots \\ 0 & q_n^t A q_2 & \ldots & q_n^t A q_n \end{pmatrix}, \quad (5.68)$$

where (5.66) and (5.67) were used for the last equality.

Since the matrix A is symmetric, $A^t = A$, and the matrix $Q_1^t A Q_1$ is also symmetric:

$$(Q_1^t A Q_1)^t = Q_1^t A^t (Q_1^t)^t = Q_1^t A Q_1. \quad (5.69)$$

Then, from (5.68), it follows that all the entries $(1, k)$, with $2 \leq k \leq n$, from the first row of the matrix $Q_1^t A Q_1$ must also be equal to 0, i.e.,

$$Q_1^t A Q_1 = \begin{pmatrix} \lambda_1 & 0 & \ldots & 0 \\ 0 & q_2^t A q_2 & \ldots & q_2^t A q_n \\ \vdots & \vdots & \vdots & \vdots \\ 0 & q_n^t A q_2 & \ldots & q_n^t A q_n \end{pmatrix}.$$

Denote by A_{n-1} the $(n-1) \times (n-1)$ matrix made of the rows $2 : n$ and the columns $2 : n$ of the matrix $Q_1^t A Q_1$, i.e.,

$$A_{n-1} = \begin{pmatrix} q_2^t A q_2 & \ldots & q_2^t A q_n \\ \vdots & \vdots & \vdots \\ q_n^t A q_2 & \ldots & q_n^t A q_n \end{pmatrix}.$$

Then,

$$Q_1^t A Q_1 = \begin{pmatrix} \lambda_1 & 0 & \ldots & 0 \\ 0 & & & \\ \vdots & & A_{n-1} & \\ 0 & & & \end{pmatrix}. \quad (5.70)$$

Since $Q_1^t A Q_1$ is symmetric, it follows that A_{n-1} is a symmetric matrix of size $n-1$. Then, from the induction hypothesis, we obtain that A_{n-1} is diagonalizable, i.e., there exist an orthogonal matrix Q_{n-1} of size $n-1$ and a diagonal matrix Λ_{n-1} of size $n-1$ such that

$$A_{n-1} = Q_{n-1} \Lambda_{n-1} Q_{n-1}^t. \quad (5.71)$$

From (5.70) and (5.71), we obtain that

$$Q_1^t A Q_1 = \begin{pmatrix} \lambda_1 & 0 & \ldots & 0 \\ 0 & & & \\ \vdots & & A_{n-1} & \\ 0 & & & \end{pmatrix} = \begin{pmatrix} \lambda_1 & 0 & \ldots & 0 \\ 0 & & & \\ \vdots & & Q_{n-1} \Lambda_{n-1} Q_{n-1}^t & \\ 0 & & & \end{pmatrix}$$

$$= \begin{pmatrix} 1 & 0 & \ldots & 0 \\ 0 & & & \\ \vdots & & Q_{n-1} & \\ 0 & & & \end{pmatrix} \begin{pmatrix} \lambda_1 & 0 & \ldots & 0 \\ 0 & & & \\ \vdots & & \Lambda_{n-1} & \\ 0 & & & \end{pmatrix} \begin{pmatrix} 1 & 0 & \ldots & 0 \\ 0 & & & \\ \vdots & & Q_{n-1}^t & \\ 0 & & & \end{pmatrix},$$

which can be written as

$$Q_1^t A Q_1 = Q_n \Lambda_n Q_n^t, \quad (5.72)$$

where $Q_n = \begin{pmatrix} 1 & 0 & \cdots & 0 \\ 0 & & & \\ \vdots & & Q_{n-1} & \\ 0 & & & \end{pmatrix}$ and $\Lambda_n = \begin{pmatrix} \lambda_1 & 0 & \cdots & 0 \\ 0 & & & \\ \vdots & & \Lambda_{n-1} & \\ 0 & & & \end{pmatrix}$ are an orthogonal matrix of size n and a diagonal matrix of size n, respectively.

We multiply (5.72) to the left by the matrix Q_1 and to the right by the matrix Q_1^t. Since $Q_1 Q_1^t = I$, see (10.14), it follows that

$$\begin{aligned} Q_1(Q_1^t A Q_1)Q_1^t &= Q_1(Q_n \Lambda_n Q_n^t)Q_1^t \\ \iff (Q_1 Q_1^t)A(Q_1 Q_1^t) &= (Q_1 Q_n)\Lambda_n (Q_1 Q_n)^t \\ \iff A &= Q\Lambda_n Q^t, \end{aligned}$$

where $Q = Q_1 Q_n$.

Note that Q is an orthogonal matrix, since it is the product of two orthogonal matrices; cf. Lemma 10.6. Then, $Q^t = Q^{-1}$, see (10.15), and

$$A = Q\Lambda_n Q^t = Q\Lambda_n Q^{-1}$$

is the diagonal form of A. Thus, the matrix A is diagonalizable.

We conclude, by induction, that any symmetric matrix is diagonalizable. $\square$

5.4 References

An elegant proof for Sylvester's criterion can be found in Gilbert [16].

5.5 Exercises

1. Show that the matrix $\begin{pmatrix} 1 & 1 \\ 1 & 1 \end{pmatrix}$ is symmetric positive semidefinite but is not symmetric positive definite.

2. Show that a 2×2 matrix A is symmetric positive definite if and only if A is symmetric, $\operatorname{trace}(A) > 0$, and $\det(A) > 0$.

3. Let A be a symmetric positive definite matrix. Use the diagonal form of the matrix A to find a matrix B such that $B^2 = A$.

4. Show that a matrix A is symmetric positive semidefinite if and only if there exists a symmetric matrix B such that $B^2 = A$.

5. Show that the inner product of two vectors is bounded from above by the product of the norms of the vectors, i.e., show that

$$(u, v) \leq ||u||\, ||v||, \quad \forall\, u, v \in \mathbb{R}^n. \tag{5.73}$$

Hint: Use the facts that

$$||tu + v||^2 = t^2 ||u||^2 + 2t(u, v) + ||v||^2 \geq 0, \quad \forall\, t \in \mathbb{R},$$

and that a quadratic polynomial is nonnegative if and only if its discriminant is less than ot equal to 0 , i.e.,

$$at^2 + bt + c \geq 0, \forall\, t \in \mathbb{R} \iff b^2 - 4ac \leq 0,$$

where a, b, and c are fixed real numbers.

Note: The inequality (5.73) is the Cauchy–Schwarz inequality for innner products. For the Euclidean inner product and Euclidean vector norm, the inequality (5.73) becomes

$$\left(\sum_{i=1}^n u_i v_i\right)^2 \leq \left(\sum_{i=1}^n u_i^2\right)\left(\sum_{i=1}^n v_i^2\right), \quad \forall\, u_i, v_i \in \mathbb{R},\ i = 1:n,$$

which is the classical version of the Cauchy–Schwarz inequality for real numbers.

6. Let A be a symmetric positive semidefinite matrix, and let B be a symmetric matrix such that $B^2 = A$.

   (i) Show that
   $$(Ax, y) = (Bx, By), \quad \forall\, x, y \in \mathbb{R}^n, \tag{5.74}$$
   where $(\cdot, \cdot)$ denotes the Euclidean inner product.

(ii) Show that
$$(Ax,y)^2 \leq (Ax,x)(Ay,y), \quad \forall\, x,y \in \mathbb{R}^n. \tag{5.75}$$

Hint: Note that, from the Cauchy–Schwartz inequality (5.73), it follows that $(Bx, By) \leq ||Bx||\, ||By||$.

7. Let λ and v be an eigenvalue and the corresponding eigenvector of the square matrix A of size n. Let Q be an orthogonal matrix of size n. Show that λ is also an eigenvalue of the matrix $Q^t A Q$. What is a corresponding eigenvector?

8. Let Q be an orthogonal matrix of size n, and let A be a square matrix of size n. Show that the matrix $Q^t A Q$ has the same characteristic polynomial as A, i.e., show that
$$P_{Q^t A Q}(x) = P_A(x), \quad \forall\, x \in \mathbb{R}.$$

9. Let A be a symmetric positive definite matrix with diagonal form $A = Q\Lambda Q^t$, where Q is an orthogonal matrix and $\Lambda = \operatorname{diag}(\lambda_k)_{k=1:n}$ is a diagonal matrix. Recall that λ_k, $k = 1:n$, are the eigenvalues of A, and that $\lambda_k > 0$ for all $k = 1:n$, since A is symmetric positive definite.

Let
$$\Lambda^{1/2} = \operatorname{diag}\left(\sqrt{\lambda_k}\right)_{k=1:n} \quad \text{and} \quad \Lambda^{-1/2} = \operatorname{diag}\left(\frac{1}{\sqrt{\lambda_k}}\right)_{k=1:n},$$
and let $A^{1/2}$ and $A^{-1/2}$ be the matrices given by
$$A^{1/2} = Q\Lambda^{1/2} Q^t \quad \text{and} \quad A^{-1/2} = Q\Lambda^{-1/2} Q^t.$$
Show that
$$\begin{aligned}
(A^{1/2})^2 &= A; \\
(A^{-1/2})^2 &= A^{-1}; \\
(A^{1/2})^{-1} &= A^{-1/2}.
\end{aligned}$$

10. Show that an $n \times n$ matrix has $2^n - 1$ principal minors.

11. Show that the matrix
$$A = \begin{pmatrix} 1 & 0.2 & -0.2 & 0.1 \\ 0.2 & 1 & -0.25 & 0.05 \\ -0.2 & -0.25 & 1 & -0.15 \\ 0.1 & 0.05 & -0.15 & 1 \end{pmatrix}$$
is symmetric positive definite.

12. Let
$$A = \begin{pmatrix} 1 & 0.05 & 0.25 & 0.55 \\ 0.05 & 2 & 1 & 1.25 \\ 0.25 & 1 & 4 & 2.5 \\ 0.55 & 1.25 & 2.5 & 6 \end{pmatrix}.$$

(i) Show that the matrix A is not strictly diagonally dominant.

(ii) Show that the matrix A is symmetric positive definite.

13. Let A be a symmetric positive semidefinite matrix. Show that the matrix A^k is also symmetric positive semidefinite for any positive integer k.

14. Recall that any symmetric positive definite matrix is nonsingular. Let A be a symmetric positive definite matrix. Show that A^{-1} is a symmetric positive definite matrix.

15. Let A be a square matrix such that $A^2 = A$. Show that the matrix A cannot be strictly diagonally dominated unless A is the identity matrix.

16. Let A be an $n \times n$ symmetric positive definite matrix, and let M be an $n \times m$ matrix.

(i) Show that the matrix $M^t A M$ is symmetric positive semidefinite.

(ii) Show that the matrix $M^t A M$ is symmetric positive definite if and only if the columns of the matrix M are linearly independent.

Chapter 6

Cholesky decomposition. Efficient cubic spline interpolation.

The Cholesky decomposition of a matrix.

Symmetric positive definite matrices and the Cholesky decomposition.

Uniqueness of the Cholesky decomposition.

Pseudocode and operation count for the Cholesky decomposition.

Linear solvers for symmetric positive definite matrices.

Solving linear systems corresponding to the same symmetric positive definite matrix.

Optimal linear solvers for tridiagonal symmetric positive definite matrices.

The efficient implementation of the cubic spline interpolation.

Efficient cubic spline interpolation for zero rate curves.

6.1 Cholesky decomposition

A natural idea to reduce the costs of an LU decomposition for a symmetric nonsingular matrix is to obtain an LU–type decomposition where the lower and upper triangular matrices are transposes of each other. Such a decomposition, which only exists for symmetric positive definite matrices, is called the Cholesky decomposition, and is made precise below in a way that ensures its uniqueness.

Definition 6.1. *The Cholesky decomposition of a nonsingular symmetric matrix A consists of finding a nonsingular upper triangular matrix U with positive entries on the main diagonal such that*
$$A = U^t U. \tag{6.1}$$
The matrix U is called the Cholesky factor of A.

Lemma 6.1. *If a nonsingular symmetric matrix has a Cholesky decomposition, then the matrix must be symmetric positive definite.*

Proof. Let A be an $n \times n$ nonsingular symmetric matrix, and let $A = U^t U$ be the Cholesky decomposition of A, where U is an $n \times n$ upper triangular matrix. Then,
$$x^t A x = x^t U^t U x = (Ux)^t Ux = \|Ux\|^2 \geq 0, \ \forall \, x \in \mathbb{R}^n. \tag{6.2}$$

From (6.2), we find that

$$x^t A x = 0 \iff U x = 0 \iff x = 0; \tag{6.3}$$

the last equivalence comes from the fact that U is a nonsingular matrix; see Definition 6.1.

From (6.2) and (6.3), and using (5.18), we conclude that A is a symmetric positive definite matrix. □

We now show that every symmetric positive definite matrix has a Cholesky decomposition:

Theorem 6.1. *Any symmetric positive definite matrix has a Cholesky decomposition.*

Before providing a proof for Theorem 6.1, it is important to note that, from Lemma 6.1 and Theorem 6.1, the following characterization of matrices with Cholesky decomposition can be given:

Theorem 6.2. *A nonsingular symmetric matrix has a Cholesky decomposition if and only if the matrix is symmetric positive definite.*

The proof of Theorem 6.1 given below is a constructive proof that is the basis for the Cholesky decomposition pseudocode from Table 6.1. For a proof by induction, which is elegant but of less computational consequence, see Theorem 10.9 from Chapter 10 and the proof therein.

Proof of Theorem 6.1. Let A be an $n \times n$ symmetric positive definite matrix. We are looking for an $n \times n$ upper triangular matrix U with positive entries on the main diagonal such that

$$U^t U = A. \tag{6.4}$$

Example: 4×4 *matrix*

For clarity, we include explicit formulations of certain formulas for 4×4 matrices. In particular, formula (6.4) is written as follows if A and U are 4×4 matrices:

$$\begin{pmatrix} U(1,1) & 0 & 0 & 0 \\ U(1,2) & U(2,2) & 0 & 0 \\ U(1,3) & U(2,3) & U(3,3) & 0 \\ U(1,4) & U(2,4) & U(3,4) & U(4,4) \end{pmatrix} \begin{pmatrix} U(1,1) & U(1,2) & U(1,3) & U(1,4) \\ 0 & U(2,2) & U(2,3) & U(2,4) \\ 0 & 0 & U(3,3) & U(3,4) \\ 0 & 0 & 0 & U(4,4) \end{pmatrix}$$

$$= \begin{pmatrix} A(1,1) & A(1,2) & A(1,3) & A(1,4) \\ A(2,1) & A(2,2) & A(2,3) & A(2,4) \\ A(3,1) & A(3,2) & A(3,3) & A(3,4) \\ A(4,1) & A(4,2) & A(4,3) & A(4,4) \end{pmatrix}.$$

If $U^t U = A$, by multiplying the first row of U^t by the first column of U, we obtain that

$$(U(1,1))^2 = A(1,1). \tag{6.5}$$

The equation (6.5) is solvable for $U(1,1)$, since $A(1,1)$ is nonnegative: if A is symmetric positive definite, then $x^t A x > 0$ for any $x \in \mathbb{R}^n$ with $x \neq 0$; cf. (5.17). For

6.1. CHOLESKY DECOMPOSITION

$x = e_1 = (1\ 0\ \ldots\ 0)^t$, we obtain, either by direct computation or by using (10.20), that $x^t A x = e_1^t A e_1 = A(1,1) > 0$.

Note that (6.5) has two possible solutions: $U(1,1) = \sqrt{A(1,1)}$ and $U(1,1) = -\sqrt{A(1,1)}$. Since the matrix U must have positive entries on the main diagonal, see Definition 6.1, we conclude that

$$U(1,1) = \sqrt{A(1,1)}. \tag{6.6}$$

Moreover, if $U^t U = A$, then, by multiplying the first row of U^t by the column k of U, we find that

$$U(1,1)U(1,k) = A(1,k), \quad \forall\ k = 2:n. \tag{6.7}$$

From (6.7), and using (6.6), we obtain that

$$U(1,k) = \frac{A(1,k)}{U(1,1)}, \quad \forall\ k = 2:n. \tag{6.8}$$

Thus, the first row of U is computed using (6.8). The other rows of the matrix U are computed recursively as follows:

Write the matrix U as

$$U = \begin{pmatrix} U(1,1) & U(1,2:n) \\ 0 & U(2:n,2:n) \end{pmatrix}, \tag{6.9}$$

where $U(1,2:n) = (U(1,k))_{k=2:n}$ is an $1 \times (n-1)$ row vector and $U(2:n,2:n) = (U(j,k))_{2\leq j,k \leq n}$ is the $(n-1) \times (n-1)$ upper triangular matrix with positive entries on the main diagonal made of the entries from the rows $2, 3, \ldots, n$ and the columns $2, 3, \ldots, n$ of U.

Since A is a symmetric matrix, it follows that $A(2:n,1) = (A(1,2:n))^t$, the matrix A can be written as follows:

$$A = \begin{pmatrix} A(1,1) & A(1,2:n) \\ A(2:n,1) & A(2:n,2:n) \end{pmatrix} = \begin{pmatrix} A(1,1) & A(1,2:n) \\ (A(1,2:n))^t & A(2:n,2:n) \end{pmatrix}, \tag{6.10}$$

where

$$\begin{array}{ll} A(1,2:n) = (A(1,k))_{k=2:n} & \text{is an } 1 \times (n-1) \text{ row vector;} \\ A(2:n,2:n) = (A(j,k))_{2\leq j,k \leq n} & \text{is an } (n-1) \times (n-1) \text{ matrix.} \end{array}$$

From (6.9) and (6.10), it follows that $A = U^t U$ is equivalent to

$$\begin{pmatrix} A(1,1) & A(1,2:n) \\ A(2:n,1) & A(2:n,2:n) \end{pmatrix} \tag{6.11}$$

$$= \begin{pmatrix} A(1,1) & A(1,2:n) \\ (A(1,2:n))^t & A(2:n,2:n) \end{pmatrix} \tag{6.12}$$

$$= \begin{pmatrix} U(1,1) & U(1,2:n) \\ 0 & U(2:n,2:n) \end{pmatrix}^t \begin{pmatrix} U(1,1) & U(1,2:n) \\ 0 & U(2:n,2:n) \end{pmatrix}$$

$$= \begin{pmatrix} U(1,1) & 0 \\ (U(1,2:n))^t & (U(2:n,2:n))^t \end{pmatrix} \begin{pmatrix} U(1,1) & U(1,2:n) \\ 0 & U(2:n,2:n) \end{pmatrix} \tag{6.13}$$

By using block matrix multiplication to multiply the rows $2:n$ of U^t by the columns $2:n$ of U, we obtain from (6.11) and (6.13) that[1]

$$A(2:n,2:n) = (U(1,2:n))^t\, U(1,2:n) + (U(2:n,2:n))^t U(2:n,2:n), \quad (6.14)$$

and therefore

$$(U(2:n,2:n))^t U(2:n,2:n) = A(2:n,2:n) - (U(1,2:n))^t\, U(1,2:n). \quad (6.15)$$

Example: 4×4 *matrix*
For $n = 4$, we obtain that $A(1,2:n)$, $A(2:n,2:n)$, $U(1,2:n)$, and $U(2:n,2:n)$ are given by

$$A(1,2:n) = A(1,2:4) = \begin{pmatrix} A(1,2) & A(1,3) & A(1,4) \end{pmatrix};$$

$$A(2:n,2:n) = A(2:4,2:4) = \begin{pmatrix} A(2,2) & A(2,3) & A(2,4) \\ A(3,2) & A(3,3) & A(3,4) \\ A(4,2) & A(4,3) & A(4,4) \end{pmatrix};$$

$$U(1,2:n) = U(1,2:4) = \begin{pmatrix} U(1,2) & U(1,3) & U(1,4) \end{pmatrix};$$

$$U(2:n,2:n) = U(2:4,2:4) = \begin{pmatrix} U(2,2) & U(2,3) & U(2,4) \\ 0 & U(3,3) & U(3,4) \\ 0 & 0 & U(4,4) \end{pmatrix},$$

and therefore (6.12–6.13) is written as follows if A and U are 4×4 matrices:

$$\begin{pmatrix} A(1,1) & A(1,2:4) \\ (A(1,2:4))^t & A(2:4,2:4) \end{pmatrix}$$
$$= \begin{pmatrix} U(1,1) & 0 \\ (U(1,2:4))^t & (U(2:4,2:4))^t \end{pmatrix} \begin{pmatrix} U(1,1) & U(1,2:4) \\ 0 & U(2:4,2:4) \end{pmatrix}. \quad (6.16)$$

From (6.16), we find the following explicit form of (6.14) for 4×4 matrices:

$$A(2:4,2:4) = (U(1,2:4))^t\, U(1,2:4) + (U(2:4,2:4))^t U(2:4,2:4),$$

and therefore

$$(U(2:4,2:4))^t U(2:4,2:4) = A(2:4,2:4) - (U(1,2:4))^t\, U(1,2:4). \quad (6.17)$$

From (6.8), it follows that

$$U(1,2:n) = \frac{A(1,2:n)}{\sqrt{A(1,1)}},$$

and therefore

$$(U(1,2:n))^t\, U(1,2:n) = \frac{(A(1,2:n))^t A(1,2:n)}{A(1,1)}. \quad (6.18)$$

---

[1] Since $U(1,2:n)$ is an $1 \times (n-1)$ row vector, it follows that $(U(1,2:n))^t$ is an $(n-1) \times 1$ column vector, and therefore the result of the column vector – row vector multiplication $(U(1,2:n))^t U(1,2:n)$ is an $(n-1) \times (n-1)$ matrix, see (1.6), which is the same size as the matrices $A(2:n,2:n)$ and $U(2:n,2:n)$. Thus, the matrix dimensions in (6.14) are consistent.

6.1. CHOLESKY DECOMPOSITION

Then, from (6.15) and (6.18), we obtain that

$$(U(2:n,2:n))^t U(2:n,2:n) = A(2:n,2:n) - \frac{(A(1,2:n))^t A(1,2:n)}{A(1,1)}. \quad (6.19)$$

The crucial step that makes the Cholesky decomposition possible is that, if A is a symmetric positive definite matrix, then the matrix

$$A(2:n,2:n) - \frac{(A(1,2:n))^t A(1,2:n)}{A(1,1)} \quad (6.20)$$

from the right hand side of (6.19) is symmetric positive definite matrix. This result is proved in Chapter 10; see Lemma 10.17.

Then, if follows from (6.19) that the $(n-1) \times (n-1)$ matrix $U(2:n,2:n)$ is the Cholesky factor of the symmetric positive definite matrix from (6.20), and we conclude that the matrix A has a Cholesky decomposition $A = U^t U$ with Cholesky factor $U = \begin{pmatrix} U(1,1) & U(1,2:n) \\ 0 & U(2:n,2:n) \end{pmatrix}$. □

The proof above also provides the idea for the recursive implementation of the Cholesky decomposition algorithm. Once the first row of U is computed, the entries of $A(2:n,2:n)$ are updated[2] to $A(2:n,2:n) - (U(1,2:n))^t U(1,2:n)$, i.e.,

$$A(2:n,2:n) = A(2:n,2:n) - (U(1,2:n))^t U(1,2:n). \quad (6.21)$$

Then, the first row of the matrix $U(2:n,2:n)$ (which coincides with the second row of U without the first entry which is equal to 0) is computed from the matrix $A(2:n,2:n) - (U(1,2:n))^t U(1,2:n)$ in the same way as the first row of U was computed from the matrix A. The matrix $A(3:n,3:n)$ is then updated and will again be a symmetric positive definite matrix, and therefore this recursive process continues until all the rows of U are computed.

The Cholesky factor U is obtained once all its n rows are computed recursively via this algorithm; see section 6.1.1 for more details.

Theorem 6.3. *The Cholesky decomposition of a symmetric positive definite matrix is unique.*

Proof. We give a proof by contradiction. Assume that the symmetric positive definite matrix A of size n has two Cholesky decompositions, i.e., assume that

$$A = U_1^t U_1 \quad \text{and} \quad A = U_2^t U_2,$$

where U_1 and U_2 are upper triangular matrices with positive entries on the main diagonal. Then,

$$U_1^t U_1 = U_2^t U_2. \quad (6.22)$$

Note that U_1 and U_2 are nonsingular matrices, since any Cholesky factor is a nonsingular matrix; see Definition 6.1. Multiply (6.22) by $(U_2^t)^{-1}$ on the left and by U_1^{-1} on the right and obtain

$$(U_2^t)^{-1} \left(U_1^t U_1 \right) U_1^{-1} = (U_2^t)^{-1} \left(U_2^t U_2 \right) U_1^{-1}$$
$$\iff \left((U_2^t)^{-1} U_1^t \right) \cdot \left(U_1 U_1^{-1} \right) = \left((U_2^t)^{-1} U_2^t \right) \cdot \left(U_2 U_1^{-1} \right)$$
$$\iff (U_2^t)^{-1} U_1^t = U_2 U_1^{-1}, \quad (6.23)$$

---

[2]The entries of $A(2:n,2:n)$ are updated using (6.15), i.e., $A(2:n,2:n) - (U(1,2:n))^t U(1,2:n)$; formula (6.19), i.e., $A(2:n,2:n) - \frac{(A(1,2:n))^t A(1,2:n)}{A(1,1)}$, is only used for the proof of the existence of the Cholesky decomposition.

since $U_1 U_1^{-1} = I$ and $(U_2^t)^{-1} U_2^t = I$.

Recall from Lemma 1.17 that the inverse of an upper triangular matrix is upper triangular, and the inverse of a lower triangular matrix is lower triangular, and, from Lemma 1.15, that the product of two upper triangular matrices is upper triangular, and the product of two lower triangular matrices is lower triangular. Thus, the matrix U_1^{-1} is upper triangular and therefore the matrix $U_2 U_1^{-1}$ is also upper triangular. Similarly, the matrix $(U_2^t)^{-1}$ is lower triangular and therefore the matrix $(U_2^t)^{-1} U_1^t$ is also lower triangular. Since the matrices $(U_2^t)^{-1} U_1^t$ and $U_2 U_1^{-1}$ are equal, see (6.23), it follows that they must be diagonal matrices.

Let $D = \mathrm{diag}(d_j)_{j=1:n}$ be a diagonal matrix such that

$$D = (U_2^t)^{-1} U_1^t = U_2 U_1^{-1}.$$

Then, by multiplying $D = U_2 U_1^{-1}$ to the right by U_1, we find that

$$U_2 = DU_1 \tag{6.24}$$

and therefore

$$A = U_2^t U_2 = (DU_1)^t U_2 = U_1^t D^t D U_1 = U_1^t D^2 U_1, \tag{6.25}$$

where the last equality follows from the fact that $D^t = D$, since D is a diagonal matrix. Since $A = U_1^t U_1$ and U_1 is a nonsingular matrix, it follows from (6.25) that

$$U_1^t U_1 = U_1^t D^2 U_1 \iff (U_1^t)^{-1} U_1^t U_1 (U_1)^{-1} = (U_1^t)^{-1} U_1^t D^2 U_1 (U_1)^{-1}$$
$$\iff I = D^2.$$

Note that $D^2 = \mathrm{diag}(d_j^2)_{j=1:n}$, see (1.93), and therefore $I = D^2$ if and only if $d_j^2 = 1$ for all $j = 1 : n$. Thus, all the diagonal entries of D are either 1 or -1, i.e.,

$$d_j = 1 \quad \text{or} \quad d_j = -1, \quad \forall j = 1:n. \tag{6.26}$$

Recall from (6.24) that $U_2 = DU_1$. From Lemma 1.10, we obtain that the j-th row of the matrix DU_1 is equal to the j-th row of the matrix U_1 multiplied by d_j. In particular, $(DU_1)(j,j) = d_j U_1(j,j)$. Since $U_2 = DU_1$, it follows that $U_2(j,j) = d_j U_1(j,j)$, and therefore

$$d_j = \frac{U_2(j,j)}{U_1(j,j)} > 0, \quad \forall j = 1:n, \tag{6.27}$$

since, by Definition 6.1, all the main diagonal entries of U_1 and U_2 are positive.

From (6.26) and (6.27), we obtain that $d_j = 1$ for all $j = 1 : n$, and therefore the matrix $D = \mathrm{diag}(d_j)_{j=1:n}$ is equal to the identity matrix, i.e., $D = I$.

Since $D = I$, it follows from (6.24) that $U_2 = U_1$, and we conclude that the Cholesky decomposition of the matrix A is unique. $\square$

6.1.1 Pseudocode and operation count for Cholesky decomposition

Based on the proof of Theorem 6.1, the algorithm for finding the Cholesky decomposition of a symmetric positive definite matrix can be implemented recursively as detailed below; see also the pseudocode from Table 6.1.

Let A be a symmetric positive definite matrix and let U be the Cholesky factor of A.

- Compute the first row of U:

6.1. CHOLESKY DECOMPOSITION

$$\boxed{\begin{array}{l} U(1,1) = \sqrt{A(1,1)} \\ \text{for } k = 2 : n \\ \quad U(1,k) = \frac{A(1,k)}{U(1,1)} \\ \text{end} \end{array}}$$

- Update the $(n-1) \times (n-1)$ lower right part of A as follows:

$$A(2:n, 2:n) = A(2:n, 2:n) - (U(1, 2:n))^t U(1, 2:n), \qquad (6.28)$$

see (6.21), which can be written entry by entry as follows:

$$\boxed{\begin{array}{l} \text{for } j = 2 : n \\ \quad \text{for } k = j : n \\ \quad \quad A(j,k) = A(j,k) - U(1,j)U(1,k) \\ \quad \text{end} \\ \text{end} \end{array}}$$

Note that in the second "for" loop above, only the upper triangular part of the matrix is updated, i.e., we use "for $k = j : n$" instead of "for $k = 2 : n$", as was the case for the LU decomposition without pivoting, see the pseudocode from Table 2.5, since the matrix $A(2:n, 2:n) - (U(1, 2:n))^t U(1, 2:n)$ is symmetric. This accounts for the computational savings in the Cholesky decomposition compared to the LU decomposition; see Lemma 6.2 and Lemma 2.3.

Every row of U is thereafter computed recursively from the latest updated part of the matrix A; see also the 4×4 example below. For example, to compute the i-th row of U, we do the following:

- Compute the i-th row of U:

$$\boxed{\begin{array}{l} U(i,i) = \sqrt{A(i,i)} \\ \text{for } k = (i+1) : n \\ \quad U(i,k) = \frac{A(i,k)}{U(i,i)} \\ \text{end} \end{array}}$$

- Update the $(n-i) \times (n-i)$ lower right part of A as follows:

$$\begin{aligned} A(i+1:n, i+1:n) &= A(i+1:n, i+1:n) \\ &\quad - (U(i, i+1:n))^t U(i, i+1:n), \qquad (6.29) \end{aligned}$$

which can be written entry by entry as follows:

$$\boxed{\begin{array}{l} \text{for } j = (i+1) : n \\ \quad \text{for } k = j : n \\ \quad \quad A(j,k) = A(j,k) - U(i,j)U(i,k); \\ \quad \text{end} \\ \text{end} \end{array}}$$

In the second "for" loop above, only the upper triangular part of the matrix is updated, i.e., we use "for $k = j : n$" instead of "for $k = (i+1) : n$", since the matrix $A(i+1:n, i+1:n) - (U(i, i+1:n))^t U(i, i+1:n)$ is symmetric.

Further clarification on the recursive part of the Cholesky decomposition algorithm can be found in the example below for a 4×4 matrix.

Example: Let A be the following symmetric matrix:

$$A = \begin{pmatrix} 9 & -3 & 6 & -3 \\ -3 & 5 & -4 & 7 \\ 6 & -4 & 21 & 3 \\ -3 & 7 & 3 & 15 \end{pmatrix}. \tag{6.30}$$

We attempt to find the Cholesky factor U of the matrix A using the recursive method described above. If this method fails, then A is not a symmetric positive definite matrix. If the method succeeds, the Cholesky factor of A is found.

The first row of U is computed as follows: $U(1,1) = \sqrt{A(1,1)} = 3$; cf. (6.6). From (6.8), we find that $U(1,k) = \frac{A(1,k)}{U(1,1)}$ for all $k = 2:4$, and therefore

$$U(1,2) = \frac{-3}{U(1,1)} = \frac{-3}{3} = -1; \quad U(1,3) = \frac{6}{U(1,1)} = \frac{6}{3} = 2;$$

$$U(1,4) = \frac{-3}{U(1,1)} = \frac{-3}{3} = -1.$$

Then, the current form of U is

$$U = \begin{pmatrix} 3 & -1 & 2 & -1 \\ 0 & U(2,2) & U(2,3) & U(2,4) \\ 0 & 0 & U(3,3) & U(3,4) \\ 0 & 0 & 0 & U(4,4) \end{pmatrix}. \tag{6.31}$$

The updated form of the 3×3 matrix $A(2:4, 2:4)$ is computed using (6.28), from $A(2:4, 2:4)$ obtained from (6.30) and with U given by (6.31), as follows:

$$A(2:4, 2:4)$$
$$= A(2:4, 2:4) - (U(1, 2:4))^t U(1, 2:4)$$
$$= \begin{pmatrix} 5 & -4 & 7 \\ -4 & 21 & 3 \\ 7 & 3 & 15 \end{pmatrix} - \begin{pmatrix} -1 \\ 2 \\ -1 \end{pmatrix} (-1 \quad 2 \quad -1)$$
$$= \begin{pmatrix} 5 & -4 & 7 \\ -4 & 21 & 3 \\ 7 & 3 & 15 \end{pmatrix} - \begin{pmatrix} 1 & -2 & 1 \\ -2 & 4 & -2 \\ 1 & -2 & 1 \end{pmatrix}$$
$$= \begin{pmatrix} 4 & -2 & 6 \\ -2 & 17 & 5 \\ 6 & 5 & 14 \end{pmatrix}.$$

Thus, the updated form of the 3×3 matrix $A(2:4, 2:4)$ is

$$A(2:4, 2:4) = \begin{pmatrix} 4 & -2 & 6 \\ -2 & 17 & 5 \\ 6 & 5 & 14 \end{pmatrix}. \tag{6.32}$$

Then,

$$(U(2:4, 2:4))^t \, U(2:4, 2:4) = \begin{pmatrix} 4 & -2 & 6 \\ -2 & 17 & 5 \\ 6 & 5 & 14 \end{pmatrix},$$

6.1. CHOLESKY DECOMPOSITION

which can be written as

$$\begin{pmatrix} U(2,2) & 0 & 0 \\ U(2,3) & U(3,3) & 0 \\ U(2,4) & U(3,4) & U(4,4) \end{pmatrix} \begin{pmatrix} U(2,2) & U(2,3) & U(2,4) \\ 0 & U(3,3) & U(3,4) \\ 0 & 0 & U(4,4) \end{pmatrix}$$

$$= \begin{pmatrix} 4 & -2 & 6 \\ -2 & 17 & 5 \\ 6 & 5 & 14 \end{pmatrix}.$$

The unknown entries from the second row of U can be computed as the first row of the Cholesky factor of the 3×3 matrix above, as follows:

$$U(2,2) = \sqrt{4} = 2;$$

$$U(2,3) = \frac{-2}{U(2,2)} = \frac{-2}{2} = -1; \quad U(2,4) = \frac{6}{U(2,2)} = \frac{6}{2} = 3.$$

The current form of U is

$$U = \begin{pmatrix} 3 & -1 & 2 & -1 \\ 0 & 2 & -1 & 3 \\ 0 & 0 & U(3,3) & U(3,4) \\ 0 & 0 & 0 & U(4,4) \end{pmatrix}. \qquad (6.33)$$

The updated form of the 2×2 matrix $A(3:4, 3:4)$ is computed using (6.29), from $A(3:4, 3:4)$ obtained from (6.32) and with U given by (6.33), as follows:

$$A(3:4, 3:4)$$
$$= A(3:4, 3:4) - (U(2, 3:4))^t \, U(2, 3:4)$$
$$= \begin{pmatrix} 17 & 5 \\ 5 & 14 \end{pmatrix} - \begin{pmatrix} -1 \\ 3 \end{pmatrix} (-1 \quad 3)$$
$$= \begin{pmatrix} 17 & 5 \\ 5 & 14 \end{pmatrix} - \begin{pmatrix} 1 & -3 \\ -3 & 9 \end{pmatrix}$$
$$= \begin{pmatrix} 16 & 8 \\ 8 & 5 \end{pmatrix}.$$

Thus, the updated form of the 2×2 matrix $A(3:4, 3:4)$ is

$$A(3:4, 3:4) = \begin{pmatrix} 16 & 8 \\ 8 & 5 \end{pmatrix}. \qquad (6.34)$$

Then,

$$(U(3:4, 3:4))^t \, U(3:4, 3:4) = \begin{pmatrix} 16 & 8 \\ 8 & 5 \end{pmatrix},$$

which can be written as

$$\begin{pmatrix} U(3,3) & 0 \\ U(3,4) & U(4,4) \end{pmatrix} \begin{pmatrix} U(3,3) & U(3,4) \\ 0 & U(4,4) \end{pmatrix} = \begin{pmatrix} 16 & 8 \\ 8 & 5 \end{pmatrix}.$$

The unknown entries from the third row of U can be computed as the first row of the Cholesky factor of the 2×2 matrix above, as follows:

$$U(3,3) = \sqrt{16} = 4; \quad U(3,4) = \frac{8}{U(3,3)} = \frac{8}{4} = 2.$$

The current form of U is

$$U = \begin{pmatrix} 3 & -1 & 2 & -1 \\ 0 & 2 & -1 & 3 \\ 0 & 0 & 4 & 2 \\ 0 & 0 & 0 & U(4,4) \end{pmatrix}. \tag{6.35}$$

The updated form of $A(4,4)$, which is a number, is computed using (6.29), from $A(4,4)$ obtained from (6.34) and with U given by (6.35), as follows:

$$A(4,4) = A(4,4) - U(3,4)U(3,4) = 5 - 2 \cdot 2 = 1,$$

which corresponds to

$$(U(4,4))^2 = 1.$$

Thus, $U(4,4) = \sqrt{1} = 1$ since $U(4,4)$ must be positive. We conclude that A is a symmetric positive definite matrix with the following Cholesky factor:

$$U = \begin{pmatrix} 3 & -1 & 2 & -1 \\ 0 & 2 & -1 & 3 \\ 0 & 0 & 4 & 2 \\ 0 & 0 & 0 & 1 \end{pmatrix}. \quad \square$$

The pseudocode for the Cholesky decomposition can be found in Table 6.1.

Table 6.1: Pseudocode for Cholesky decomposition

Function Call:
$U = \text{cholesky}(A)$

Input:
A = symmetric positive definite matrix of size n

Output:
U = upper triangular matrix such that $U^t U = A$

for $i = 1 : (n-1)$
  $U(i,i) = \sqrt{A(i,i)}$;
  for $k = (i+1) : n$
    $U(i,k) = A(i,k)/U(i,i)$;   // compute row i of U
  end
  for $j = (i+1) : n$
    for $k = j : n$
      $A(j,k) = A(j,k) - U(i,j)U(i,k)$;
    end
  end
end
$U(n,n) = \sqrt{A(n,n)}$

Recall from Lemma 2.3 that the operation count for the LU decomposition is $\frac{2}{3}n^3 + O(n^2)$. As expected, the operation count for the Cholesky decomposition is approximately half of the operation count for the LU decomposition:

6.1. CHOLESKY DECOMPOSITION

Lemma 6.2. *The operation count for the Cholesky decomposition of an $n \times n$ symmetric positive definite matrix is*

$$\frac{1}{3}n^3 + O(n^2). \tag{6.36}$$

Proof. At step i, computing $U(i,i) = \sqrt{A(i,i)}$ and going through the "for" loop

```
for k = (i + 1) : n
    U(i, k) = A(i, k)/U(i, i)
end
```

to compute the i-th row of U requires

$$n - i + 1 \tag{6.37}$$

operations.

Also at step i, the double "for" loop

```
for j = (i + 1) : n
    for k = j : n
        A(j, k) = A(j, k) - U(i, j)U(i, k);
    end
end
```

to update $A(i+1:n, i+1:n)$ requires

$$\sum_{j=i+1}^{n} \sum_{k=j}^{n} 2 = \sum_{j=i+1}^{n} 2(n-j+1) = 2 \sum_{j=i+1}^{n} (n-j+1) \tag{6.38}$$

operations. By letting $l = n - j + 1$ in (6.38), and using the fact that $\sum_{l=1}^{p} l = \frac{p(p+1)}{2}$, see (2.46), we obtain that

$$2 \sum_{j=i+1}^{n} (n-j+1) = 2 \sum_{l=1}^{n-i} l = 2 \cdot \frac{(n-i)(n-i+1)}{2} = (n-i)(n-i+1). \tag{6.39}$$

When accounting for the outside "for" loop "for $i = 1 : (n-1)$", see Table 6.1, and for the one extra operation required for $U(n,n) = \sqrt{A(n,n)}$, we obtain using (6.37) and (6.39) that the operation count for the Cholesky decomposition is

$$1 + \sum_{i=1}^{n-1} (n-i+1) + (n-i)(n-i+1) = 1 + \sum_{i=1}^{n-1} (n-i+1)^2 \tag{6.40}$$

Recall from (2.46) that $\sum_{l=1}^{p} l^2 = \frac{p(p+1)(2p+1)}{6}$. Then, by letting $l = n - i + 1$ in (6.40), we obtain that

$$\begin{aligned}
1 + \sum_{i=1}^{n-1} (n-i+1)^2 &= 1 + \sum_{l=2}^{n} l^2 = \sum_{l=1}^{n} l^2 = \frac{n(n+1)(2n+1)}{6} \\
&= \frac{2n^3 + 3n^2 + n}{6} = \frac{n^3}{3} + \frac{n^2}{2} + \frac{n}{6} \\
&= \frac{1}{3}n^3 + O(n^2);
\end{aligned}$$

see (10.80) in Section 10.2.3 for a proof of the last equality.

Thus, the operation count for the Cholesky decomposition is $\frac{1}{3}n^3 + O(n^2)$. $\square$

We conclude this section by computing the Cholesky factors of 2×2 and 3×3 symmetric positive definite matrices.

Lemma 6.3. *The Cholesky factor of the 2×2 symmetric positive definite matrix $\begin{pmatrix} a & b \\ b & d \end{pmatrix}$ i.e., with $a > 0$ and $ad > b^2$, see (5.49), is*

$$U = \begin{pmatrix} \sqrt{a} & \frac{b}{\sqrt{a}} \\ 0 & \sqrt{\frac{ad-b^2}{a}} \end{pmatrix}. \tag{6.41}$$

Proof. We compute the Cholesky factor $U = \begin{pmatrix} U(1,1) & U(1,2) \\ 0 & U(2,2) \end{pmatrix}$ of the matrix $A = \begin{pmatrix} a & b \\ b & d \end{pmatrix}$ by using the Cholesky decomposition algorithm from Table 6.1. From (6.6) and (6.8), we find that $U(1,1) = \sqrt{A(1,1)} = \sqrt{a}$ and $U(1,2) = \frac{A(1,2)}{U(1,1)} = \frac{b}{\sqrt{a}}$. Then, from (6.15) it follows that

$$(U(2,2))^2 = A(2,2) - U(1,2) \cdot U(1,2) = d - \frac{b^2}{a} = \frac{ad-b^2}{a}.$$

Note that $\frac{ad-b^2}{a} > 0$ since $b^2 < ad$. Then, $U(2,2) = \sqrt{\frac{ad-b^2}{a}}$, since the diagonal entries of a Cholesky factor must be positive. We conclude that the Cholesky factor of the matrix A is

$$U = \begin{pmatrix} \sqrt{a} & \frac{b}{\sqrt{a}} \\ 0 & \sqrt{\frac{ad-b^2}{a}} \end{pmatrix}.$$

□

Note that, by letting $a = d = 1$ and $b = \rho$ in (6.41), where $|\rho| < 1$, we obtain that the Cholesky factor of the matrix $\begin{pmatrix} 1 & \rho \\ \rho & 1 \end{pmatrix}$ with $-1 < \rho < 1$ is

$$\begin{pmatrix} 1 & \rho \\ 0 & \sqrt{1-\rho^2} \end{pmatrix}. \tag{6.42}$$

Lemma 6.4. *The Cholesky factor of a 3×3 symmetric positive definite matrix $\begin{pmatrix} d_1 & a & b \\ a & d_2 & c \\ b & c & d_3 \end{pmatrix}$, i.e., with d_1, d_2, d_3, a, b, c satisfying the inequalities (5.53), is*

$$U = \begin{pmatrix} \sqrt{d_1} & a/\sqrt{d_1} & b/\sqrt{d_1} \\ 0 & \sqrt{d_1 d_2 - a^2}/\sqrt{d_1} & (d_1 c - ab)/\sqrt{d_1(d_1 d_2 - a^2)} \\ 0 & 0 & \sqrt{\frac{d_1 d_2 d_3 + 2abc - d_3 a^2 - d_2 b^2 - d_1 c^2}{d_1 d_2 - a^2}} \end{pmatrix}. \tag{6.43}$$

Proof. For simplicity, we only prove (6.43) for $d_1 = d_2 = d_3 = 1$, i.e., we show that the Cholesky factor of the 3×3 symmetric positive definite matrix $\begin{pmatrix} 1 & a & b \\ a & 1 & c \\ b & c & 1 \end{pmatrix}$ is

$$U = \begin{pmatrix} 1 & a & b \\ 0 & \sqrt{1-a^2} & (c-ab)/\sqrt{1-a^2} \\ 0 & 0 & \sqrt{\frac{1+2abc-a^2-b^2-c^2}{1-a^2}} \end{pmatrix}. \tag{6.44}$$

6.1. CHOLESKY DECOMPOSITION

The general proof of (6.43) follows similarly.

Let $A = \begin{pmatrix} 1 & a & b \\ a & 1 & c \\ b & c & 1 \end{pmatrix}$ be a 3×3 symmetric positive definite matrix. From (5.63), we obtain that

$$-1 < a < 1 \quad \text{and} \quad 1 + 2abc > a^2 + b^2 + c^2. \tag{6.45}$$

If $U = \begin{pmatrix} U(1,1) & U(1,2) & U(1,3) \\ 0 & U(2,2) & U(2,3) \\ 0 & 0 & U(3,3) \end{pmatrix}$ is the Cholesky factor of A, then, from the first step of the Cholesky decomposition algorithm, see (6.6) and (6.8), we find that

$$U(1,1) = \sqrt{A(1,1)} = 1; \quad U(1,2) = \frac{A(1,2)}{U(1,1)} = a; \quad U(1,3) = \frac{A(1,3)}{U(1,1)} = b.$$

Thus, the current form of U is

$$U = \begin{pmatrix} 1 & a & b \\ 0 & U(2,2) & U(2,3) \\ 0 & 0 & U(3,3) \end{pmatrix}. \tag{6.46}$$

Then, from (6.15), we find that the matrix $\begin{pmatrix} U(2,2) & U(2,3) \\ 0 & U(3,3) \end{pmatrix}$ is the Cholesky factor of the following matrix:

$$\begin{pmatrix} 1 & c \\ c & 1 \end{pmatrix} - \begin{pmatrix} a \\ b \end{pmatrix} (a\ b) = \begin{pmatrix} 1 & c \\ c & 1 \end{pmatrix} - \begin{pmatrix} a^2 & ab \\ ab & b^2 \end{pmatrix}$$

$$= \begin{pmatrix} 1-a^2 & c-ab \\ c-ab & 1-b^2 \end{pmatrix}. \tag{6.47}$$

Note that the matrix $\begin{pmatrix} 1-a^2 & c-ab \\ c-ab & 1-b^2 \end{pmatrix}$ from (6.47) satisfies the conditions (5.49) and is therefore symmetric positive definite: from (6.45), it follows that $1 - a^2 > 0$, since $-1 < a < 1$, and that

$$(1-a^2)(1-b^2) - (c-ab)^2 = 1 + 2abc - a^2 - b^2 - c^2 > 0.$$

Since $\begin{pmatrix} U(2,2) & U(2,3) \\ 0 & U(3,3) \end{pmatrix}$ is the Cholesky factor of $\begin{pmatrix} 1-a^2 & c-ab \\ c-ab & 1-b^2 \end{pmatrix}$, we obtain from (6.41) that

$$\begin{pmatrix} U(2,2) & U(2,3) \\ 0 & U(3,3) \end{pmatrix} = \begin{pmatrix} \sqrt{1-a^2} & \frac{c-ab}{\sqrt{1-a^2}} \\ 0 & \sqrt{\frac{(1-a^2)(1-b^2)-(c-ab)^2}{1-a^2}} \end{pmatrix}$$

$$= \begin{pmatrix} \sqrt{1-a^2} & (c-ab)/\sqrt{1-a^2} \\ 0 & \sqrt{\frac{1+2abc-a^2-b^2-c^2}{1-a^2}} \end{pmatrix}. \tag{6.48}$$

From (6.46) and (6.48), we conclude that the Cholesky factor of the matrix A is

$$U = \begin{pmatrix} 1 & a & b \\ 0 & \sqrt{1-a^2} & (c-ab)/\sqrt{1-a^2} \\ 0 & 0 & \sqrt{\frac{1+2abc-a^2-b^2-c^2}{1-a^2}} \end{pmatrix}, \tag{6.49}$$

which is the same as (6.44). □

6.2 Linear solvers for symmetric positive definite matrices

Using the Cholesky decomposition of a matrix is a computationally efficient way of solving linear systems corresponding to symmetric positive definite matrices.

Let A be a symmetric positive definite matrix of size n, and let b be a column vector of size n. If $A = U^t U$ is the Cholesky decomposition of A, then, solving a linear system $Ax = b$ is equivalent to solving

$$U^t U x = b.$$

This is the same as solving

$$U^t y = b$$

for y, which can be done using forward substitution since the matrix U^t is lower triangular, and then solving

$$Ux = y$$

for x, which can be done using backward substitution since the matrix U is upper triangular.

The pseudocode for solving a linear system corresponding to a symmetric positive definite matrix using the Cholesky decomposition can be found in Table 6.2.

Table 6.2: Linear solver using Cholesky decomposition

Function Call:	
$x = $ linear_solve_cholesky(A,b)	
Input:	
$A = $ symmetric positive definite matrix of size n	
$b = $ column vector of size n	
Output:	
$x = $ solution to $Ax = b$	
$U = $ cholesky(A);	// Cholesky decomposition of A
$y = $ forward_subst(U^t, b);	// solve $U^t y = b$
$x = $ backward_subst(U, y);	// solve $Ux = y$

The operation count for the linear solver from Table 6.2 is as follows:
- $\frac{1}{3}n^3 + O(n^2)$ for the Cholesky decomposition of A; cf. (6.36);
- $n^2 + O(n)$ for the forward substitution for solving $U^t y = b$; cf. (2.8);
- $n^2 + O(n)$ for the backward substitution for solving $Ux = y$; cf. (2.19),

6.2. LINEAR SOLVERS FOR SPD MATRICES

for a total operation count of

$$\left(\frac{1}{3}n^3 + O(n^2)\right) + (n^2 + O(n)) + (n^2 + O(n)) = \frac{1}{3}n^3 + O(n^2);$$

see (10.87) from Section 10.2.3 for a proof of the last equality.

6.2.1 Solving linear systems corresponding to the same spd matrix

In this section, we show how the Cholesky decomposition of a matrix can be used to solve multiple linear systems corresponding to the same symmetric positive definite matrix efficiently.

Assume that we want to solve p linear systems corresponding to an $n \times n$ symmetric positive definite matrix A. In other words, we want to find $n \times 1$ vectors x_i, $i = 1 : p$, such that

$$Ax_i = b_i, \quad \forall\, i = 1 : p, \tag{6.50}$$

where b_i is a column vector of size n, for $i = 1 : p$.

One way to solve the linear systems from (6.50) would be to use the routine linear_solve_cholesky from Table 6.2 to solve each one of the p linear systems inside a "for" loop as follows:

$$\boxed{\begin{array}{l} \text{for } i = 1 : p \\ \quad x_i = \text{linear\_solve\_cholesky}(A, b_i) \\ \text{end} \end{array}}$$

This would require

$$p\left(\frac{1}{3}n^3 + O(n^2)\right) = \frac{1}{3}pn^3 + pO(n^2) \tag{6.51}$$

operations, since each linear solver requires $\frac{1}{3}n^3 + O(n^2)$ operations; cf. Lemma 6.2.

However, the most expensive part of $x_i = \text{linear\_solve\_cholesky}(A, b_i)$ is computing the Cholesky decomposition of the matrix A, which dominates the cost of the subsequent forward substitution and backward substitution. Thus, an efficient way of solving the linear systems (6.50) is to compute the Cholesky factor U of A only once, outside the "for" loop, and then do the forward and backward substitutions for solving each linear system inside the "for" loop; see the pseudocode from Table 6.3 for details.

Recall that both the forward substitution forward_subst(U^t, b_i) and the backward substitution backward_subst(U, y) require $n^2 + O(n)$ operations; cf. (2.8) and (2.19). Thus, the operation count for solving the p linear systems using the method from Table 6.3 is

$$\frac{1}{3}n^3 + O(n^2) + p\left(n^2 + O(n) + n^2 + O(n)\right) = \frac{1}{3}n^3 + 2pn^2 + O(n^2) + pO(n),$$

which is smaller than $\frac{1}{3}pn^3 + pO(n^2)$, the operation count required by solving the p linear systems sequentially; see (6.51).

As an example of solving multiple systems corresponding to the same matrix, we show how to efficiently compute the inverse of a symmetric positive definite matrix.

Table 6.3: Solution of multiple linear systems corresponding to the same spd matrix

```
Input:
A = symmetric positive definite matrix of size n
b_i = column vectors of size n, i = 1 : p

Output:
x_i = solution to Ax_i = b_i, i = 1 : p

U = cholesky(A)
for i = 1 : p
    y = forward_subst(U^t, b_i);
    x_i = backward_subst(U, y);
end
```

Let A be a symmetric positive definite matrix of size n, and let $A^{-1} = \text{col}\,(c_k)_{k=1:n}$ be the column form of the inverse matrix of A. Then, $AA^{-1} = I$, where $I = \text{col}\,(e_k)_{k=1:n}$ is the identity matrix of size n. Using (1.11), we find that $AA^{-1} = \text{col}\,(Ac_k)_{k=1:n}$, and therefore $AA^{-1} = I$ is equivalent to

$$Ac_k = e_k, \quad \forall\, k = 1 : n,$$

which can be solved using the method from Table 6.3 as follows:

```
U = cholesky(A)
for k = 1 : n
    y = forward_subst(U^t, e_k)
    c_k = backward_subst(U, y)
end
A^{-1} = col (c_k)_{k=1:n}
```

The operation count for computing the inverse matrix using this method is

$$\frac{1}{3}n^3 + O(n^2) + n\left(n^2 + O(n) + n^2 + O(n)\right) = \frac{7}{3}n^3 + O(n^2); \qquad (6.52)$$

see (10.89) from Section 10.2.3 for a proof of the last equality.

6.3 Optimal linear solvers for tridiagonal symmetric positive definite matrices

Solving linear systems corresponding to tridiagonal symmetric positive definite matrices is often required in financial applications, e.g., for the efficient implementation of the cubic spline interpolation and for the finite difference solution of the Black–Scholes PDE; see section 6.4 and the references from section 6.5. Note that a linear system $Ax = b$ corresponding to a tridiagonal symmetric positive definite matrix A can be solved by using a linear solver based on the Cholesky decomposition of A, or by using a linear solver based on the LU decomposition of the matrix A.

6.3. LINEAR SOLVERS FOR TRIDIAGONAL SPD MATRICES

In this section, we show that, for tridiagonal symmetric positive definite matrices, the LU solver is more efficient (i.e., has a smaller operation count) than the Cholesky solver.

Cholesky linear solvers for tridiagonal spd matrices.
Let A be an $n \times n$ tridiagonal symmetric positive definite matrix. The linear system $Ax = b$ can be solved using the Cholesky decomposition based solver $x =$ linear_solve_cholesky(A,b) from Table 6.2. For an efficient implementation, the Cholesky decomposition, forward substitution, and backward substitution routines from Table 6.2 are replaced by the specialized routines for tridiagonal matrices as seen below.

We begin by showing that the Cholesky factor of a tridiagonal symmetric positive definite matrix is an upper triangular bidiagonal matrix by analyzing how the Cholesky decomposition simplifies for tridiagonal matrices.[3]

Since the symmetric positive definite matrix A is tridiagonal,[4] note that

$$A(j,k) = 0, \quad \forall\ 1 \leq j, k \leq n \text{ with } |j - k| \geq 2; \tag{6.53}$$

$$A(i, i+1) = A(i+1, i), \quad \forall\ i = 1 : (n-1).$$

Let U be the Cholesky factor of A. We will show that U is an upper triangular bidiagonal matrix, i.e., the only entries of U that can be nonzero are the main diagonal entries $U(i,i)$, for $i = 1 : n$, and the upper diagonal entries $U(i, i+1)$, for $i = 1 : (n-1)$.

Following step by step the Cholesky decomposition algorithm from section 6.1.1, we compute $U(1,1) = \sqrt{A(1,1)}$ and the first row of U as $U(1,k) = \frac{A(1,k)}{U(1,1)}$, for all $k = 2 : n$. Note that $A(1,k) = 0$ if $3 \leq k \leq n$ since A is a tridiagonal matrix; cf. (6.53). Then, $U(1,k) = 0$ if $3 \leq k \leq n$, and therefore the only possible nonzero entries from the first row of U correspond to an upper triangular bidiagonal form for U.

Moreover, since $U(1, 2 : n) = (U(1,2)\ 0\ \ldots\ 0)$, it follows that

$$(U(1, 2:n))^t U(1, 2:n) = \begin{pmatrix} U(1,2) \\ 0 \\ \vdots \\ 0 \end{pmatrix} (U(1,2)\ 0\ \ldots\ 0)$$

$$= \begin{pmatrix} (U(1,2))^2 & 0 & \ldots & 0 \\ 0 & 0 & \ldots & 0 \\ \vdots & \vdots & \ldots & \vdots \\ 0 & 0 & \ldots & 0 \end{pmatrix}.$$

Thus, updating the $(n-1) \times (n-1)$ lower right part of A as in (6.28), i.e.,

$$A(2:n, 2:n) = A(2:n, 2:n) - (U(1, 2:n))^t U(1, 2:n),$$

---

[3] More generally, the Cholesky factor of a banded matrix of band m is also banded of band m; see an exercise from the end of this chapter and Stefanica [38] for details.

[4] Note that a sufficient, although not necessary, condition for the tridiagonal symmetric matrix A to be symmetric positive definite is $|A(i,i)| > |A(i, i-1)| + |A(i, i+1)|$ for all $i = 2 : (n-1)$, $|A(1,1)| > |A(1,2)|$, and $|A(n,n)| > |A(n, n-1)|$, since in this case A is strictly diagonally dominant, and any strictly diagonally dominant symmetric matrix is symmetric positive definite; see Theorem 5.7.

only involves changing the value of $A(2,2)$ to
$$A(2,2) = A(2,2) - (U(1,2))^2,$$
which preserves the tridiagonal structure of the matrix $A(2:n, 2:n)$.

The tridiagonal structure of the updated part of A and the bidiagonal structure of U will be further preserved as every row of U is computed.

For example, assuming that the updated form $A(i:n, i:n)$ of the matrix A is tridiagonal after $i-1$ rows of U are computed, the i-th row of U is computed as follows: $U(i,i) = \sqrt{A(i,i)}$ and $U(i,k) = \frac{A(i,k)}{U(i,i)}$, for all $k = (i+1):n$. Since $A(i:n, i:n)$ is tridiagonal, it follows that $A(i,k) = 0$ if $i+2 \leq k \leq n$, and therefore
$$U(i,k) = 0, \quad \forall\, i+2 \leq k \leq n.$$
Thus, the only possible nonzero entries from the i-th row of U correspond to an upper triangular bidiagonal form for U.

Moreover, since $U(i, i+1:n) = (U(i, i+1)\ 0\ \ldots\ 0)$, we find that
$$(U(i, i+1:n))^t U(i, i+1:n) = \begin{pmatrix} U(i,i+1) \\ 0 \\ \vdots \\ 0 \end{pmatrix} (U(i,i+1)\ 0\ \ldots\ 0)$$
$$= \begin{pmatrix} (U(i,i+1))^2 & 0 & \ldots & 0 \\ 0 & 0 & \ldots & 0 \\ \vdots & \vdots & \ddots & \vdots \\ 0 & 0 & \ldots & 0 \end{pmatrix}.$$

Thus, updating the $(n-i) \times (n-i)$ lower right part of A as follows as in (6.29), i.e.,
$$A(i+1:n, i+1:n) = A(i+1:n, i+1:n) - (U(i, i+1:n))^t U(i, i+1:n),$$
involves only changing the value of $A(i+1, i+1)$ to
$$A(i+1, i+1) = A(i+1, i+1) - (U(i, i+1))^2,$$
which preserves the tridiagonal structure of the updated $(n-i-1) \times (n-i-1)$ matrix $A(i+1:n, i+1:n)$.

The Cholesky decomposition routine from Table 6.1 simplifies to the pseudocode from Table 6.4 for tridiagonal symmetric positive definite matrices.

The operation count for the tridiagonal Cholesky decomposition from Table 6.4 is $4n-3$ operations: in each step of the "for" loop

```
for i = 1 : (n − 1)
for i = 1 : (n − 1)
  U(i,i) = √A(i,i);  U(i,i+1) = A(i,i+1)/U(i,i);
  A(i+1,i+1) = A(i+1,i+1) − U(i,i+1)²;
end
```

we perform 4 operations, plus one more operation for computing $\sqrt{A(n,n)}$, for a total number of operations of
$$4(n-1) + 1 = 4n - 3. \tag{6.54}$$

6.3. LINEAR SOLVERS FOR TRIDIAGONAL SPD MATRICES

Table 6.4: Cholesky decomposition for tridiagonal spd matrices

---
Function Call:
$U = \text{cholesky\_tridiag\_spd}(A)$

Input:
$A =$ tridiagonal symmetric positive definite matrix of size n

Output:
$U =$ upper triangular bidiagonal matrix such that $U^t U = A$

for $i = 1 : (n-1)$
  $U(i,i) = \sqrt{A(i,i)};\ \ U(i,i+1) = A(i,i+1)/U(i,i);$
  $A(i+1,i+1) = A(i+1,i+1) - U(i,i+1)^2;$
end
$U(n,n) = \sqrt{A(n,n)}$

Thus, if A is a tridiagonal symmetric positive definite matrix, the Cholesky decomposition $U = \text{cholesky}(A)$ from the linear solver routine from Table 6.2 can be replaced by the tridiagonal solver $U = \text{cholesky\_tridiag\_spd}(A)$ from Table 6.4.

Moreover, since the matrix U^t is lower triangular bidiagonal, the forward substitution $y = \text{forward\_subst}(U^t, b)$ from Table 6.2 can be replaced by the forward substitution $y = \text{forward\_subst\_bidiag}(U^t, b)$, see Table 2.2, and, since the matrix U is upper triangular bidiagonal, the backward substitution $x = \text{backward\_subst}(U, y)$ from Table 6.2 can be replaced by $x = \text{backward\_subst\_bidiag}(U, y)$, see Table 2.4.

The resulting routine for solving linear systems corresponding to tridiagonal symmetric positive definite matrices using the Cholesky decomposition can be found in Table 6.5.

Table 6.5: Tridiagonal spd linear solver using Cholesky decomposition

---
Function Call:
$x = \text{linear\_solve\_cholesky\_tridiag\_spd}(A,b)$

Input:
$A =$ tridiagonal symmetric positive definite matrix of size n
$b =$ column vector of size n

Output:
$x =$ solution to $Ax = b$

$U = \text{cholesky\_tridiag\_spd}(A);$ // Cholesky decomposition of A
$y = \text{forward\_subst\_bidiag}(U^t, b);$ // solve $U^t y = b$
$x = \text{backward\_subst\_bidiag}(U, y);$ // solve $Ux = y$

The operation count for the pseudocode from Table 6.5 is as follows:
- $4n - 3$ for the Cholesky decomposition of A; cf. (6.54);

- $3n - 2$ for the forward substitution for solving $U^t y = b$; cf. (2.10);
- $3n - 2$ for the backward substitution for solving $Ux = y$; cf. (2.20),

for a total operation count of

$$(4n - 3) + (3n - 2) + (3n - 2) = 10n - 7 = 10n + O(1);$$

see (10.77) from Section 10.2.3 for a proof of the last equality.

LU linear solvers for tridiagonal spd matrices.
Recall from Sylvester's Criterion (Theorem 5.8) that all the principal minors of a symmetric positive definite matrix are positive. Then, it follows from Theorem 2.1 that the tridiagonal symmetric positive definite matrix A has an LU decomposition without pivoting, and therefore the linear system $Ax = b$ can be solved using the solver linear_solve_LU_no_pivoting_tridiag from Table 2.8; see also the explicit form from Table 2.9. The corresponding routines can be found[5] in Table 6.6, and, in explicit form, in Table 6.7.

Table 6.6: Tridiagonal spd linear solver using LU decomposition

Function Call: $x = $ linear_solve_LU_tridiag_spd(A,b)	
Input: $A =$ tridiagonal symmetric positive definite matrix of size n $b = $ column vector of size n	
Output: $x = $ solution to $Ax = b$	
$[L, U] = $ lu_no_pivoting_tridiag(A);	// LU decomposition of A
$y = $ forward_subst_bidiag(L, b);	// solve $Ly = b$
$x = $ backward_subst_bidiag(U, y);	// solve $Ux = y$

As shown in section 2.5.1, the operation count for the LU linear solver from Table 6.7 is $8n + O(1)$, which is an improvement over the $10n + O(1)$ operation count for the Cholesky linear solver from Table 6.5.

We conclude that the efficient way to solve a linear system corresponding to a tridiagonal symmetric positive definite matrix is by using the LU decomposition solver from Table 6.6 or Table 6.7, with an operation count of

$$8n + O(1). \tag{6.55}$$

---

[5]Note that the matrix U from the pseudocodes from Tables 6.6 and 6.7 is not the Cholesky factor of the matrix A, but the U factor from the LU decomposition without pivoting of A.

Table 6.7: Explicit tridiagonal spd linear solver with LU decomposition

Function Call:
$x = \text{linear\_solve\_LU\_tridiag\_spd}(A,b)$

Input:
A = tridiagonal symmetric positive definite matrix of size n
b = column vector of size n

Output:
x = solution to $Ax = b$

for $i = 1 : (n-1)$
   $L(i,i) = 1; L(i+1,i) = A(i+1,i)/A(i,i);$
   $U(i,i) = A(i,i); U(i,i+1) = A(i,i+1);$
   $A(i+1,i+1) = A(i+1,i+1) - L(i+1,i)U(i,i+1);$
end
$L(n,n) = 1; U(n,n) = A(n,n);$ // LU decomposition of A
$x(1) = b(1);$
for $j = 2 : n$
   $x(j) = b(j) - L(j, j-1)x(j-1);$
end   // forward substitution for $Ly = b$
$x(n) = \frac{y(n)}{U(n,n)};$
for $j = (n-1) : 1$
   $x(j) = \frac{y(j) - U(j, j+1)x(j+1)}{U(j,j)};$
end   // backward substitution for $Ux = y$

6.4 Efficient implementation of the cubic spline interpolation

Recall from section 2.8 that the natural cubic spline interpolation requires finding a function $f : [x_0, x_n] \to \mathbb{R}$ such that

(i) $f(x_i) = v_i$, for $i = 0 : n$, where $x_0 < x_1 < \ldots < x_n$;

(ii) $f(x)$ is a cubic polynomial on each interval $[x_{i-1}, x_i]$, for $i = 1 : n$;

(iii) $f''(x)$ exists and is continuous on $[x_0, x_n]$;

(iv) $f_1''(x_0) = f_n''(x_n) = 0$.

In other words, the natural cubic spline interpolation requires finding a function $f(x)$ of the form

$$f(x) = f_i(x) = a_i + b_i x + c_i x^2 + d_i x^3, \quad \forall\, x_{i-1} \leq x \leq x_i, \quad \forall\, i = 1 : n, \quad (6.56)$$

such that

$$f_i(x_{i-1}) = v_{i-1}, \quad \forall\, i = 1 : n; \quad (6.57)$$
$$f_i(x_i) = v_i, \quad \forall\, i = 1 : n; \quad (6.58)$$
$$f_i'(x_i) = f_{i+1}'(x_i), \quad \forall\, i = 1 : (n-1); \quad (6.59)$$

$$f_i''(x_i) = f_{i+1}''(x_i), \quad \forall\, i = 1 : (n-1); \tag{6.60}$$
$$f_1''(x_0) = f_n''(x_n) = 0. \tag{6.61}$$

In section 2.8, we found the unique values of a_i, b_i, c_i, d_i, $i = 1 : n$, satisfying the constraints (6.57–6.61) by solving a linear system corresponding to a $4n \times 4n$ banded matrix of band 4, see (2.82), using an LU decomposition based linear solver.

The efficient solution of the natural cubic spline interpolation only requires solving a linear system corresponding to an $(n-1) \times (n-1)$ tridiagonal symmetric positive definite matrix. This can be done using an LU linear solver for tridiagonal symmetric positive definite matrices, with a computational cost of $8n + O(1)$ operations; see section 6.3.

For every node x_i, denote by w_i the value of the second derivative of f at x_i, i.e., $f''(x_i) = w_i$, for $i = 0 : n$. While it follows from (6.61) that $w_0 = w_n = 0$, the values of w_i are not known a priori for $i = 1 : n-1$. The conditions (6.57–6.61) are equivalent to

$$f_i(x_{i-1}) = v_{i-1}, \quad \forall\, i = 1 : n; \tag{6.62}$$
$$f_i(x_i) = v_i, \quad \forall\, i = 1 : n; \tag{6.63}$$
$$f_i''(x_{i-1}) = w_{i-1}, \quad \forall\, i = 1 : n; \tag{6.64}$$
$$f_i''(x_i) = w_i, \quad \forall\, i = 1 : n; \tag{6.65}$$
$$w_0 = w_n = 0; \tag{6.66}$$
$$f_i'(x_i) = f_{i+1}'(x_i), \quad \forall\, i = 1 : (n-1). \tag{6.67}$$

The efficient implementation of the natural cubic spline interpolation is based on solving for the $4n$ coefficients a_i, b_i, c_i, d_i, $i = 1 : n$, in terms of w_i, $i = 1 : (n-1)$, by using the $4n$ conditions (6.62–6.65), and then use the $n-1$ conditions given by (6.67) to solve for the $n-1$ unknowns w_i, $i = 1 : (n-1)$.

Note that (6.62–6.65) can be written as follows:

$$a_i + b_i x_{i-1} + c_i x_{i-1}^2 + d_i x_{i-1}^3 = v_{i-1}, \quad \forall\, i = 1 : n; \tag{6.68}$$
$$a_i + b_i x_i + c_i x_i^2 + d_i x_i^3 = v_i, \quad \forall\, i = 1 : n; \tag{6.69}$$
$$2c_i + 6d_i x_{i-1} = w_{i-1}, \quad \forall\, i = 1 : n; \tag{6.70}$$
$$2c_i + 6d_i x_i = w_i, \quad \forall\, i = 1 : n. \tag{6.71}$$

From (6.70) and (6.71), we obtain that

$$c_i = \frac{w_{i-1} x_i - w_i x_{i-1}}{2(x_i - x_{i-1})}, \quad \forall\, i = 1 : n; \tag{6.72}$$
$$d_i = \frac{w_i - w_{i-1}}{6(x_i - x_{i-1})}, \quad \forall\, i = 1 : n. \tag{6.73}$$

Let

$$q_{i-1} = v_{i-1} - c_i x_{i-1}^2 - d_i x_{i-1}^3, \quad \forall\, i = 1 : n; \tag{6.74}$$
$$r_i = v_i - c_i x_i^2 - d_i x_i^3, \quad \forall\, i = 1 : n. \tag{6.75}$$

Then, (6.68) and (6.69) can be written as

$$a_i + b_i x_{i-1} = q_{i-1}, \quad \forall\, i = 1 : n;$$
$$a_i + b_i x_i = r_i, \quad \forall\, i = 1 : n,$$

6.4. EFFICIENT CUBIC SPLINE INTERPOLATION

and therefore

$$a_i = \frac{q_{i-1}x_i - r_i x_{i-1}}{x_i - x_{i-1}}, \quad \forall\, i = 1:n; \tag{6.76}$$

$$b_i = \frac{r_i - q_{i-1}}{x_i - x_{i-1}}, \quad \forall\, i = 1:n. \tag{6.77}$$

Summarizing, given v_i and w_i, $i = 0:n$, we obtain c_i and d_i, $i = 1:n$, from (6.72) and (6.73), and use them to compute r_i and q_{i-1}, $i = 1:n$, from (6.74) and (6.75). In turn, r_i and q_{i-1}, $i = 1:n$, are used to obtain a_i and b_i, $i = 1:n$, from (6.76) and (6.77).

Since $w_0 = w_n = 0$, see (6.66), we are left with finding the values of w_i, for $i = 1:(n-1)$. To do so, we use the condition (6.67) for the continuity of the first derivative, i.e., $f_i'(x_i) = f_{i+1}'(x_i)$, for all $i = 1:(n-1)$, which can be written as

$$b_i + 2c_i x_i + 3d_i x_i^2 = b_{i+1} + 2c_{i+1} x_i + 3d_{i+1} x_i^2, \quad \forall\, i = 1:(n-1); \tag{6.78}$$

From (6.77) and using (6.74) and (6.75), we obtain that

$$b_i = \frac{v_i - v_{i-1}}{x_i - x_{i-1}} - c_i(x_i + x_{i-1}) - d_i(x_i^2 + x_i x_{i-1} + x_{i-1}^2);$$

$$b_{i+1} = \frac{v_{i+1} - v_i}{x_{i+1} - x_i} - c_{i+1}(x_{i+1} + x_i) - d_{i+1}(x_{i+1}^2 + x_{i+1} x_i + x_i^2),$$

for all $i = 1:(n-1)$, and therefore

$$b_i + 2c_i x_i + 3d_i x_i^2$$
$$= \frac{v_i - v_{i-1}}{x_i - x_{i-1}} + c_i(x_i - x_{i-1}) + d_i(2x_i^2 - x_i x_{i-1} - x_{i-1}^2)$$
$$= \frac{v_i - v_{i-1}}{x_i - x_{i-1}} + c_i(x_i - x_{i-1}) + d_i(x_i - x_{i-1})(2x_i + x_{i-1});$$

$$b_{i+1} + 2c_{i+1} x_i + 3d_{i+1} x_i^2$$
$$= \frac{v_{i+1} - v_i}{x_{i+1} - x_i} - c_{i+1}(x_{i+1} - x_i) - d_{i+1}(x_{i+1}^2 + x_{i+1} x_i - 2x_i^2)$$
$$= \frac{v_{i+1} - v_i}{x_{i+1} - x_i} - c_{i+1}(x_{i+1} - x_i) - d_{i+1}(x_{i+1} - x_i)(x_{i+1} + 2x_i),$$

for all $i = 1:(n-1)$, which can be written using (6.72) and (6.73) in terms of w_i, $i = 0:n$, as follows:

$$b_i + 2c_i x_i + 3d_i x_i^2$$
$$= \frac{v_i - v_{i-1}}{x_i - x_{i-1}} + \frac{w_{i-1} x_i - w_i x_{i-1}}{2} + \frac{(w_i - w_{i-1})(2x_i + x_{i-1})}{6}$$
$$= \frac{v_i - v_{i-1}}{x_i - x_{i-1}} + w_{i-1} \frac{x_i - x_{i-1}}{6} + w_i \frac{x_i - x_{i-1}}{3}; \tag{6.79}$$

$$b_{i+1} + 2c_{i+1} x_i + 3d_{i+1} x_i^2$$
$$= \frac{v_{i+1} - v_i}{x_{i+1} - x_i} - \frac{w_i x_{i+1} - w_{i+1} x_i}{2} - \frac{(w_{i+1} - w_i)(2x_{i+1} + x_i)}{6}$$
$$= \frac{v_{i+1} - v_i}{x_{i+1} - x_i} - w_i \frac{x_{i+1} - x_i}{3} - w_{i+1} \frac{x_{i+1} - x_i}{6}, \tag{6.80}$$

for all $i = 1 : (n-1)$.

From (6.79) and (6.80), we obtain that the constraints (6.78) are equivalent to

$$\frac{v_i - v_{i-1}}{x_i - x_{i-1}} + w_{i-1}\frac{x_i - x_{i-1}}{6} + w_i\frac{x_i - x_{i-1}}{3}$$
$$= \frac{v_{i+1} - v_i}{x_{i+1} - x_i} - w_i\frac{x_{i+1} - x_i}{3} - w_{i+1}\frac{x_{i+1} - x_i}{6},$$

which can be written as

$$w_{i-1}\frac{x_i - x_{i-1}}{6} + w_i\frac{x_{i+1} - x_{i-1}}{3} + w_{i+1}\frac{x_{i+1} - x_i}{6} = \frac{v_{i+1} - v_i}{x_{i+1} - x_i} - \frac{v_i - v_{i-1}}{x_i - x_{i-1}},$$
(6.81)

for all $i = 1 : (n-1)$.

After multiplication by 6, the equations (6.81) can be expressed as the linear system

$$Mw = z,$$
(6.82)

where $w = (w_i)_{i=1:n-1}$ is the vector of unknowns, z is the $(n-1) \times 1$ vector given by

$$z(i) = 6\left(\frac{v_{i+1} - v_i}{x_{i+1} - x_i} - \frac{v_i - v_{i-1}}{x_i - x_{i-1}}\right), \quad \forall\, i = 1 : (n-1),$$

and M is the $(n-1) \times (n-1)$ matrix given by

$$M(i,i) = 2(x_{i+1} - x_{i-1}), \quad \forall\, i = 1 : (n-1); \quad (6.83)$$
$$M(i,i+1) = x_{i+1} - x_i, \quad \forall\, i = 1 : (n-2); \quad (6.84)$$
$$M(i,i-1) = x_i - x_{i-1}, \quad \forall\, i = 2 : (n-1). \quad (6.85)$$

The matrix M is tridiagonal. Note that M is also symmetric, since, from (6.84) and (6.85), we find that

$$M(i,i+1) = x_{i+1} - x_i = M(i+1,i), \quad \forall\, i = 1 : (n-2).$$

Moreover, the matrix M is strictly diagonally dominant, since

$$M(1,1) = 2(x_2 - x_0) > x_2 - x_1 = M(1,2);$$
$$M(n-1,n-1) = 2(x_n - x_{n-2}) > x_{n-1} - x_{n-2} = M(n-1,n-2);$$

$$|M(i,i-1)| + |M(i,i+1)| = x_{i+1} - x_{i-1} < 2(x_{i+1} - x_{i-1}) = M(i,i),$$

for all $i = 2 : (n-2)$; cf. (6.83–6.85).

From Theorem 5.7, we conclude that the matrix M is a tridiagonal symmetric positive definite matrix. Thus, the linear system $Mw = z$ from (6.82) can be solved efficiently using the LU tridiagonal spd solver from Table 6.6, i.e.,

$$w = \text{linear\_solve\_LU\_tridiag\_spd}(M, z).$$

The pseudocode for the efficient implementation of the natural cubic spline interpolation can be found in Table 6.8.

6.4. EFFICIENT CUBIC SPLINE INTERPOLATION

Table 6.8: Efficient implementation of the natural cubic spline interpolation

---

Input:
x_i = interpolation nodes, $i = 0 : n$
v_i = interpolation values, $i = 0 : n$

Output:
a_i, b_i, c_i, d_i = cubic polynomials coefficients, $i = 1 : n$

for $i = 1 : (n-1)$, $z(i) = 6\left(\frac{v_{i+1}-v_i}{x_{i+1}-x_i} - \frac{v_i-v_{i-1}}{x_i-x_{i-1}}\right)$; end
// compute vector z
for $i = 1 : (n-1)$, $M(i,i) = 2(x_{i+1} - x_{i-1})$; end
for $i = 1 : (n-2)$, $M(i,i+1) = x_{i+1} - x_i$; end
for $i = 2 : (n-1)$, $M(i,i-1) = x_i - x_{i-1}$; end
// compute tridiagonal matrix M
w = linear_solve_LU_tridiag_spd(M, z); $w_0 = 0$; $w_n = 0$
for $i = 1 : n$
$$c_i = \frac{w_{i-1}x_i - w_i x_{i-1}}{2(x_i - x_{i-1})}; \quad d_i = \frac{w_i - w_{i-1}}{6(x_i - x_{i-1})};$$
end
for $i = 1 : n$
$$q_{i-1} = v_{i-1} - c_i x_{i-1}^2 - d_i x_{i-1}^3; \quad r_i = v_i - c_i x_i^2 - d_i x_i^3;$$
end
for $i = 1 : n$
$$a_i = \frac{q_{i-1}x_i - r_i x_{i-1}}{x_i - x_{i-1}}; \quad b_i = \frac{r_i - q_{i-1}}{x_i - x_{i-1}};$$
end

6.4.1 Efficient cubic spline interpolation for zero rate curves

To illustrate the efficiency of the natural cubic spline interpolation compared to regular cubic spline interpolation, we revisit the example from section 2.8.1 of finding a continuous zero rate curve from values of the zero rate for discrete times.

Denote by $r(0,t)$ the zero rate corresponding to time t, and assume that the following zero rates are known:

$$r(0,0) = 0.0050; \quad r\left(0, \frac{2}{12}\right) = 0.0065; \quad r\left(0, \frac{6}{12}\right) = 0.0085;$$

$$r(0,1) = 0.0105; \quad r\left(0, \frac{20}{12}\right) = 0.0120.$$

Assume that $r(0,t)$ is a cubic polynomial on each of the intervals $\left[0, \frac{2}{12}\right]$, $\left[\frac{2}{12}, \frac{6}{12}\right]$, $\left[\frac{6}{12}, 1\right]$, and $\left[1, \frac{20}{12}\right]$. Following the pseudocode from Table 6.8, we solve the linear system (6.82) corresponding to the 3×3 matrix

$$M = \begin{pmatrix} 1 & 0.3333 & 0 \\ 0.3333 & 1.6667 & 0.5 \\ 0 & 0.5 & 2.3333 \end{pmatrix} \qquad (6.86)$$

to obtain the values[6]

$$w = \begin{pmatrix} 0 \\ -0.0171 \\ -0.0026 \\ -0.0039 \\ 0 \end{pmatrix} \quad (6.87)$$

for the second order derivatives of $r(0,t)$ with respect to t at the times 0, $\frac{2}{12}$, $\frac{6}{12}$, 1, and $\frac{20}{12}$. We then use the formulas (6.72), (6.73), (6.76), and (6.77) to compute the coefficients a_i, b_i, c_i, d_i, $i = 1:4$, of the cubic polynomials that are equal to the zero rate curve $r(0,t)$ on the four intervals above; see the "for" loops at the end of the pseudocode from Table 6.8.

The resulting zero rate curve is the same as the zero rate curve from (2.99), i.e.,

$$r(0,t) = \begin{cases} 0.005 + 0.0095t - 0.0171t^3, & \text{if } 0 \leq t \leq \frac{2}{12}; \\ 0.0049 + 0.0115t - 0.0122t^2 + 0.0073t^3, & \text{if } \frac{2}{12} \leq t \leq \frac{6}{12}; \\ 0.0059 + 0.0057t - 0.0006t^2 - 0.0005t^3, & \text{if } \frac{6}{12} \leq t \leq 1; \\ 0.0044 + 0.01t - 0.0049t^2 + 0.001t^3, & \text{if } 1 \leq t \leq \frac{20}{12}, \end{cases}$$

and can then be used to value other interest rate instruments with maturity less than 20 months.

Note that using the natural cubic spline interpolation required solving a 3×3 linear system, while the regular cubic spline interpolation required solving a 16×16 linear system; see (6.86) and (2.97–2.98), respectively.

6.5 References

A comprehensive analysis of the stability of the Cholesky decomposition algorithm can be found in Higham [20].

A Cholesky–type decomposition of less practical importance also exists for symmetric positive semidefinite matrices; see Higham [19] for more details:

Let A be an $n \times n$ symmetric positive semidefinite matrix of rank r (i.e., with eigenvalue 0 of multiplicity $n - r$). Then, there exists a permutation matrix P such that

$$PAP^t = \begin{bmatrix} U & B \\ \mathbf{0} & \mathbf{0} \end{bmatrix},$$

where U is an $r \times r$ upper triangular matrix with positive elements on the main diagonal, B is an $r \times (n-r)$ matrix, and $\mathbf{0}$ and $\mathbf{0}$ on the second row above denote matrices with all entries equal to 0 and of sizes $(n-r) \times r$ and $(n-r) \times (n-r)$, respectively.

Different tridiagonal linear systems solvers can be found in Hirsa [21]. Detailed presentations of the finite difference solution to the heat equation corresponding to the Black–Scholes PDE and the solution of tridiagonal symmetric positive linear systems can be found in Andersen and Piterbarg [3] and Wilmott [45].

---

[6] Note that the first and last values of w come from the natural cubic spline interpolation assumption, while the other three values of w from (6.87) come from solving the linear system (6.82).

6.5. REFERENCES

The efficient implementation of the cubic spline interpolation, complete with pseudocodes can be found in the "Numerical Recipes" compendium by Press et al. [32]. Other spline interpolation methods are surveyed in Andersen and Piterbarg [3]. Examples of cubic splines for financial applications are presented in Alexander [1] and Neftci [30].

6.6 Exercises

1. Let
$$A = \begin{pmatrix} 2 & -2 \\ -2 & 5 \end{pmatrix}.$$

   (i) Find a 2×2 matrix M such that $A = M^2$;

   (ii) Find a 2×2 matrix M such that $A = MM^t$.

2. Let $A = \begin{pmatrix} 41 & 12 \\ 12 & 34 \end{pmatrix}.$

   (i) Show that the matrix A is symmetric positive definite.

   (ii) Find a 2×2 matrix B such that $A = B^2$.

   (iii) Find a 2×2 upper triangular matrix U such that $A = U^t U$.

3. Let $A = \begin{pmatrix} 1 & -0.2 & 0.8 \\ -0.2 & 2 & 0.3 \\ 0.8 & 0.3 & 1.1 \end{pmatrix}.$

   (i) Show that the matrix A is weakly diagonally dominated, and therefore symmetric positive semidefinite.

   (ii) Use Sylvester's criterion to show that the matrix A is symmetric positive definite.

4. Let A be a symmetric positive definite matrix, and let U be the Cholesky factor of A. If V is an upper triangular matrix such that $A = V^t V$, show that there exists a diagonal matrix D whose entries on the main diagonal are either -1 or 1 such that $V = DU$.

5. Let B_N be the following $N \times N$ symmetric positive definite matrix:
$$B_N = \begin{pmatrix} 2 & -1 & \cdots & 0 \\ -1 & \ddots & \ddots & \vdots \\ \vdots & \ddots & \ddots & -1 \\ 0 & \cdots & -1 & 2 \end{pmatrix}. \tag{6.88}$$

   Let C_N be an $N \times (N+1)$ matrix with
$$\begin{aligned} C_N(i,i) &= 1, \ \forall\, i = 1:N; \\ C_N(i,i+1) &= -1, \ \forall\, i = 1:N, \end{aligned}$$
   and with all the other entries equal to 0.

   Show that $B_N = C_N C_N^t$. Why is this not the Cholesky decomposition of the matrix B_N?

6.6. EXERCISES

6. Let B_N be the $N \times N$ tridiagonal symmetric positive definite matrix given by (6.88). Show that the Cholesky factor U_N of the matrix B_N is the upper triangular bidiagonal matrix given by

$$U_N(i,i) = \sqrt{\frac{i+1}{i}}, \quad \forall\, i = 1 : N; \tag{6.89}$$

$$U_N(i,i+1) = -\sqrt{\frac{i}{i+1}}, \quad \forall\, i = 1 : (N-1). \tag{6.90}$$

7. Let B_N be the $N \times N$ tridiagonal symmetric positive definite matrix given by (6.88), and let U_N be the Cholesky factor of B_N given by (6.89–6.90).

   (i) Show that the solution to a linear system $B_N x = b$, where b and x are $N \times 1$ column vectors can be obtained by using the explicit pseudocode below:

   > Function Call:
   > $x =$ linear_solve_cholesky_B_N(b)
   >
   > Input:
   > $b = N \times 1$ column vector
   >
   > Output:
   > $x =$ solution to $B_N x = b$
   >
   > $y(1) = \frac{b(1)}{\sqrt{2}}$
   > for $i = 2 : N$
   > $\quad y(i) = \dfrac{b(i) + y(i-1)\sqrt{(i-1)/i}}{\sqrt{(i+1)/i}}$
   > end
   > $x(N) = \dfrac{y(N)\sqrt{N}}{\sqrt{N+1}}$
   > for $i = (N-1) : 1$
   > $\quad x(i) = \dfrac{y(i) + x(i+1)\sqrt{i/(i+1)}}{\sqrt{(i+1)/i}}$
   > end

   (ii) What is the operation count for the pseudocode above, and how does it compare to $8n + O(1)$, the operation count for the optimal linear solver for tridiagonal symmetric positive definite matrices?

8. Let B_N be the $N \times N$ tridiagonal symmetric positive definite matrix given by (6.88). Show that the LU factors L and U of the matrix B_N are the lower triangular bidiagonal matrix and the upper triangular bidiagonal matrix given by

$$L(i,i) = 1, \;\forall\, i = 1:N; \quad L(i+1,i) = -\frac{i}{i+1}, \;\forall\, i = 1:(N-1); \tag{6.91}$$

$$U(i,i) = \frac{i+1}{i}, \;\forall\, i = 1:N; \quad U(i,i+1) = -1, \;\forall\, i = 1:(N-1). \tag{6.92}$$

9. Let B_N be the $N \times N$ tridiagonal symmetric positive definite matrix given by (6.88), and let L and U be the LU factors of B_N given by (6.91–6.92).

(i) Show that the solution to a linear system $B_N x = b$, where b and x are $N \times 1$ column vectors can be obtained by using the explicit pseudocode below:

> Function Call:
> $x = $ linear_solve_lu_B_N(b)
>
> Input:
> $b = N \times 1$ column vector
>
> Output:
> $x = $ solution to $B_N x = b$
>
> $y(1) = b(1)$
> for $i = 2 : N$
> $\quad y(i) = b(i) + \frac{(i-1)y(i-1)}{i}$
> end
> $x(N) = \frac{Ny(N)}{N+1}$
> for $i = (N-1) : 1$
> $\quad x(i) = \frac{i(y(i)+x(i+1))}{i+1}$
> end

(ii) What is the operation count for the pseudocode above, and how does it compare to $8n + O(1)$, the operation count for the optimal linear solver for tridiagonal symmetric positive definite matrices?

10. Write an explicit optimal pseudocode for solving linear systems corresponding to the same tridiagonal symmetric positive definite matrix. In other words, write a pseudocode for solving p linear systems $Ax_i = b_i$, for $i = 1 : p$, where A is an $n \times n$ tridiagonal symmetric positive definite matrix, by using the explicit solver linear_solve_LU_tridiag_spd from Table 6.6 and the method from Table 6.3. What is the operation count for solving the p linear systems?

11. Write the pseudocode for the Cholesky decomposition of symmetric positive definite banded matrices of band m. What is the corresponding operation count?

Hint: Use (without proving) the fact that the Cholesky factor of a symmetric positive definite banded matrix of band m is a banded upper triangular matrix of band m.

12. What is the operation count for solving a linear system corresponding to a symmetric positive definite banded matrix of band m using a Cholesky linear solver?

6.6. EXERCISES

13. The following discount factors were obtained from market data:

Date	Discount Factor
2 months	0.9980
5 months	0.9935
11 months	0.9820
15 months	0.9775

The overnight rate is 0.75%.

(i) What are the corresponding 2 months, 5 months, 11 months and 15 months zero rates?

(ii) What is the tridiagonal system that must be solved in the efficient implementation of the natural cubic spline interpolation for finding the zero rate curve for all times less than 15 months?

(iii) Use the efficient implementation of the natural cubic spline interpolation to find a zero rate curve for all times less than 15 months matching the discount factors above.

(iv) Find the value of a 14 months quarterly coupon bond with 2.5% coupon rate.

Note: A quarterly coupon bond with face value $100, coupon rate C, and maturity T pays the holder of the bond a coupon payment equal to $\frac{C}{4} \cdot 100$ every three months, except at maturity. The final payment at maturity T is equal to the face value of the bond plus one coupon payment, i.e., $100 + \frac{C}{4} 100$.

Chapter 7

Covariance and correlation matrices. Linear Transformation Property. Multivariate normal random variables.

Covariance and correlation matrices. Positive definiteness of covariance and correlation matrices.

Covariance and correlation matrix estimation from time series data.

Linear Transformation Property.

Necessary and sufficient conditions for covariance and correlation matrices.

Finding normal random variables with a given covariance or correlation matrix.

Monte Carlo simulation for basket option pricing.

Multivariate normal random variables.

Multivariate random variables formulation for covariance and correlation matrices.

7.1 Covariance and correlation matrices

Let X_1, X_2, ..., X_n be n nonconstant random variables on the same probability space. Denote by μ_i and $\sigma_i \neq 0$ the mean and the standard deviation of X_i, respectively, for $i = 1:n$. The variance of X_i is

$$\sigma_i^2 \;=\; \text{var}(X_i) \;=\; E\left[(X_i - \mu_i)^2\right], \quad \forall\, i = 1:n.$$

The covariance and the correlation of the random variables X_j and X_k are

$$\text{cov}(X_j, X_k) \;=\; E\left[(X_j - \mu_j)(X_k - \mu_k)\right], \quad \forall\, 1 \leq j, k \leq n; \qquad (7.1)$$

$$\text{corr}(X_j, X_k) \;=\; \frac{\text{cov}(X_j, X_k)}{\sigma_j \sigma_k}, \quad \forall\, 1 \leq j, k \leq n. \qquad (7.2)$$

Note that

$$\text{cov}(X_i, X_i) \;=\; \text{var}(X_i), \quad \forall\, 1 \leq i \leq n; \qquad (7.3)$$

$$\text{cov}(X_j, X_k) \;=\; \text{cov}(X_k, X_j), \quad \forall\, 1 \leq j, k \leq n; \qquad (7.4)$$

$$\text{corr}(X_i, X_i) = 1, \quad \forall\, 1 \leq i \leq n; \tag{7.5}$$
$$\text{corr}(X_j, X_k) = \text{corr}(X_k, X_j), \quad \forall\, 1 \leq j,k \leq n; \tag{7.6}$$
$$-1 \leq \text{corr}(X_j, X_k) \leq 1, \quad \forall\, 1 \leq j,k \leq n. \tag{7.7}$$

For a proof of (7.7), see an exercise at the end of this chapter.

Definition 7.1. *The covariance matrix Σ_X of the random variables $X_1, X_2, \ldots, X_n$ is the $n \times n$ matrix given by*

$$\Sigma_X(j,k) = \text{cov}(X_j, X_k), \quad \forall\, 1 \leq j,k \leq n,$$

where $\text{cov}(X_j, X_k)$ denotes the covariance of the random variables X_j and X_k.

The covariance matrix $\Sigma_\mathbf{x}$ is symmetric, since

$$\Sigma_\mathbf{x}(j,k) = \text{cov}(X_j, X_k) = \text{cov}(X_k, X_j) = \Sigma_\mathbf{x}(k,j), \quad \forall\, 1 \leq j,k \leq n; \tag{7.8}$$

cf. (7.4). Also,
$$\Sigma_\mathbf{x}(i,i) = \text{var}(X_i), \quad \forall\, i = 1:n, \tag{7.9}$$

since $\text{cov}(X_i, X_i) = \text{var}(X_i)$ for all $i = 1:n$; cf. (7.3).

Definition 7.2. *The correlation matrix Ω_X of the random variables $X_1, X_2, \ldots, X_n$ is the $n \times n$ matrix given by*

$$\Omega_X(j,k) = \text{corr}(X_j, X_k), \quad \forall\, 1 \leq j,k \leq n,$$

where $\text{corr}(X_j, X_k)$ denotes the correlation between the random variables X_j and X_k.

The correlation matrix $\Omega_\mathbf{x}$ is symmetric, since

$$\Omega_\mathbf{x}(j,k) = \text{corr}(X_j, X_k) = \text{corr}(X_k, X_j) = \Omega_\mathbf{x}(k,j), \quad \forall\, 1 \leq j,k \leq n; \tag{7.10}$$

cf. (7.6). Also,
$$\Omega_\mathbf{x}(i,i) = 1, \quad \forall\, i = 1:n, \tag{7.11}$$

since, $\text{corr}(X_i, X_i) = 1$ for all $i = 1:n$; cf. (7.5).

For example, the covariance matrix and the correlation matrix of two random variables X_1 and X_2 with mean and standard deviation μ_1, σ_1, and μ_2, σ_2, respectively, and with correlation $\rho_{1,2}$, are

$$\Sigma_\mathbf{x} = \begin{pmatrix} \sigma_1^2 & \sigma_1\sigma_2\rho_{1,2} \\ \sigma_1\sigma_2\rho_{1,2} & \sigma_2^2 \end{pmatrix}; \tag{7.12}$$

$$\Omega_\mathbf{x} = \begin{pmatrix} 1 & \rho_{1,2} \\ \rho_{1,2} & 1 \end{pmatrix}. \tag{7.13}$$

The covariance matrix and the correlation matrix of three random variables X_1, X_2, X_3 with mean and variance μ_1, σ_1; μ_2, σ_2; and μ_3, σ_3, respectively, and with correlations $\text{corr}(X_1, X_2) = \rho_{1,2}$, $\text{corr}(X_1, X_3) = \rho_{1,3}$, and $\text{corr}(X_2, X_3) = \rho_{2,3}$ are

$$\Sigma_\mathbf{x} = \begin{pmatrix} \sigma_1^2 & \sigma_1\sigma_2\rho_{1,2} & \sigma_1\sigma_3\rho_{1,3} \\ \sigma_1\sigma_2\rho_{1,2} & \sigma_2^2 & \sigma_2\sigma_3\rho_{2,3} \\ \sigma_1\sigma_3\rho_{1,3} & \sigma_2\sigma_3\rho_{2,3} & \sigma_3^2 \end{pmatrix}; \tag{7.14}$$

$$\Omega_\mathbf{x} = \begin{pmatrix} 1 & \rho_{1,2} & \rho_{1,3} \\ \rho_{1,2} & 1 & \rho_{2,3} \\ \rho_{1,3} & \rho_{2,3} & 1 \end{pmatrix}. \tag{7.15}$$

7.1. COVARIANCE AND CORRELATION MATRICES

Lemma 7.1. Let Σ_X and Ω_X be the covariance and the correlation matrix of n nonconstant random variables $X_1, X_2, \ldots, X_n$. Let $\sigma_i \neq 0$ be the standard deviation of X_i, $i = 1 : n$.

(i) The covariance matrix Σ_X and the correlation matrix Ω_X are related as follows:
$$\Sigma_X = D_{\sigma_X} \Omega_X D_{\sigma_X}, \qquad (7.16)$$

where $D_{\sigma_X} = \text{diag}(\sigma_i)_{i=1:n}$.

(ii) The correlation matrix Ω_X is uniquely determined in terms of the covariance matrix Σ_X as follows:
$$\Omega_X = (D_{\sigma_X})^{-1} \Sigma_X (D_{\sigma_X})^{-1}, \qquad (7.17)$$

where $(D_{\sigma_X})^{-1} = \text{diag}\left(\frac{1}{\sigma_i}\right)_{i=1:n}$.

Proof. (i) If $D_1 = \text{diag}\left(d_j^{(1)}\right)_{j=1:n}$ and $D_2 = \text{diag}\left(d_k^{(2)}\right)_{k=1:n}$ are diagonal matrices of size n, it follows from (1.90) of Lemma 1.10 that
$$(D_1 A D_2)(j,k) = d_j^{(1)} d_k^{(2)} A(j,k), \quad \forall\, 1 \leq j,k \leq n. \qquad (7.18)$$

Using (7.18) for $A = \Omega_X$ and for $D_1 = D_2 = D_{\sigma_X} = \text{diag}(\sigma_i)_{i=1:n}$, we find that
$$\begin{aligned}(D_{\sigma_X} \Omega_X D_{\sigma_X})(j,k) &= \sigma_j \sigma_k \Omega_X(j,k) \\ &= \sigma_j \sigma_k \text{corr}(X_j, X_k) = \text{cov}(X_j, X_k) \\ &= \Sigma_X(j,k), \quad \forall\, 1 \leq j,k \leq n, \end{aligned} \qquad (7.19)$$

since $\text{cov}(X_j, X_k) = \sigma_j \sigma_k \text{corr}(X_j, X_k)$; cf. (7.2). From (7.19), we conclude that $\Sigma_X = D_{\sigma_X} \Omega_X D_{\sigma_X}$.

(ii) Since $\sigma_i \neq 0$ for all $i = 1 : n$, the matrix $D_{\sigma_X} = \text{diag}(\sigma_i)_{i=1:n}$ is nonsingular and its inverse is $(D_{\sigma_X})^{-1} = \text{diag}\left(\frac{1}{\sigma_i}\right)_{i=1:n}$; see (1.94). Then, by multiplying (7.16) from the left and from the right by $(D_{\sigma_X})^{-1}$, we obtain that
$$(D_{\sigma_X})^{-1} \Sigma_X (D_{\sigma_X})^{-1} = \left((D_{\sigma_X})^{-1} D_{\sigma_X}\right) \Omega_X \left(D_{\sigma_X}(D_{\sigma_X})^{-1}\right) = \Omega_X.$$

□

Let Σ_X and Ω_X be the covariance matrix and the correlation matrix of two random variables X_1 and X_2 given by (7.12) and (7.13), respectively. Then,

$$\begin{aligned}\Sigma_X &= \begin{pmatrix} \sigma_1 & 0 \\ 0 & \sigma_2 \end{pmatrix} \begin{pmatrix} 1 & \rho_{1,2} \\ \rho_{1,2} & 1 \end{pmatrix} \begin{pmatrix} \sigma_1 & 0 \\ 0 & \sigma_2 \end{pmatrix} \\ &= \begin{pmatrix} \sigma_1 & 0 \\ 0 & \sigma_2 \end{pmatrix} \Omega_X \begin{pmatrix} \sigma_1 & 0 \\ 0 & \sigma_2 \end{pmatrix}; \end{aligned} \qquad (7.20)$$

$$\Omega_X = \begin{pmatrix} \frac{1}{\sigma_1} & 0 \\ 0 & \frac{1}{\sigma_2} \end{pmatrix} \Sigma_X \begin{pmatrix} \frac{1}{\sigma_1} & 0 \\ 0 & \frac{1}{\sigma_2} \end{pmatrix}. \qquad (7.21)$$

Note that (7.20) and (7.21) are the special cases for 2×2 matrices of (7.16) and (7.17), respectively.

Let Σ_X and Ω_X be the covariance matrix and the correlation matrix of three random variables X_1, X_2, X_3 given by (7.15) and (7.15), respectively. Then,

$$\Sigma_X = \begin{pmatrix} \sigma_1 & 0 & 0 \\ 0 & \sigma_2 & 0 \\ 0 & 0 & \sigma_3 \end{pmatrix} \begin{pmatrix} 1 & \rho_{1,2} & \rho_{1,3} \\ \rho_{1,2} & 1 & \rho_{2,3} \\ \rho_{1,3} & \rho_{2,3} & 1 \end{pmatrix} \begin{pmatrix} \sigma_1 & 0 & 0 \\ 0 & \sigma_2 & 0 \\ 0 & 0 & \sigma_3 \end{pmatrix}$$

$$= \begin{pmatrix} \sigma_1 & 0 & 0 \\ 0 & \sigma_2 & 0 \\ 0 & 0 & \sigma_3 \end{pmatrix} \Omega_X \begin{pmatrix} \sigma_1 & 0 & 0 \\ 0 & \sigma_2 & 0 \\ 0 & 0 & \sigma_3 \end{pmatrix}; \qquad (7.22)$$

$$\Omega_X = \begin{pmatrix} \frac{1}{\sigma_1} & 0 & 0 \\ 0 & \frac{1}{\sigma_2} & 0 \\ 0 & 0 & \frac{1}{\sigma_3} \end{pmatrix} \Sigma_X \begin{pmatrix} \frac{1}{\sigma_1} & 0 & 0 \\ 0 & \frac{1}{\sigma_2} & 0 \\ 0 & 0 & \frac{1}{\sigma_3} \end{pmatrix}. \qquad (7.23)$$

Note that (7.22) and (7.23) are the special cases for 3×3 matrices of (7.16) and (7.17), respectively.

Examples: (i) Consider three random variables X_1, X_2, X_3 with covariance matrix

$$\Sigma_X = \begin{pmatrix} 9 & 2 & -6 \\ 2 & 4 & -1 \\ -6 & -1 & 16 \end{pmatrix}.$$

The standard deviations of X_1, X_2, and X_3 are

$$\sigma_1 = \sqrt{\Sigma_X(1,1)} = 3, \quad \sigma_2 = \sqrt{\Sigma_X(2,2)} = 2, \quad \text{and} \quad \sigma_3 = \sqrt{\Sigma_X(3,3)} = 4,$$

respectively. From (7.23), we find that the correlation matrix of X_1, X_2, X_3 is

$$\Omega_X = \begin{pmatrix} \frac{1}{3} & 0 & 0 \\ 0 & \frac{1}{2} & 0 \\ 0 & 0 & \frac{1}{4} \end{pmatrix} \begin{pmatrix} 9 & 2 & -6 \\ 2 & 4 & -1 \\ -6 & -1 & 16 \end{pmatrix} \begin{pmatrix} \frac{1}{3} & 0 & 0 \\ 0 & \frac{1}{2} & 0 \\ 0 & 0 & \frac{1}{4} \end{pmatrix}$$

$$= \begin{pmatrix} 1 & \frac{1}{3} & -\frac{1}{2} \\ \frac{1}{3} & 1 & -\frac{1}{8} \\ -\frac{1}{2} & -\frac{1}{8} & 1 \end{pmatrix}.$$

(ii) Consider three random variables X_1, X_2, X_3 with correlation matrix

$$\Omega_X = \begin{pmatrix} 1 & 0.5 & -0.25 \\ 0.5 & 1 & 0.25 \\ -0.25 & 0.25 & 1 \end{pmatrix},$$

and with standard deviations $\sigma_1 = 4$, $\sigma_2 = 1$, and $\sigma_3 = 6$. From (7.22), we find that the covariance matrix of X_1, X_2, X_3 is

$$\Sigma_X = \begin{pmatrix} 4 & 0 & 0 \\ 0 & 1 & 0 \\ 0 & 0 & 6 \end{pmatrix} \begin{pmatrix} 1 & 0.5 & -0.25 \\ 0.5 & 1 & 0.25 \\ -0.25 & 0.25 & 1 \end{pmatrix} \begin{pmatrix} 4 & 0 & 0 \\ 0 & 1 & 0 \\ 0 & 0 & 6 \end{pmatrix}$$

$$= \begin{pmatrix} 16 & 2 & -6 \\ 2 & 1 & 1.5 \\ -6 & 1.5 & 36 \end{pmatrix}. \quad \square$$

7.1. COVARIANCE AND CORRELATION MATRICES

We note that, if the correlation matrix of the random variables $X_1, X_2, \ldots, X_n$ is given, the covariance matrix of $X_1, X_2, \ldots, X_n$ is not uniquely determined.

Example: Let X_1, X_2 random variables with covariance matrix $\Sigma_\mathbf{X} = \begin{pmatrix} 4 & -3 \\ -3 & 9 \end{pmatrix}$, and let Y_1, Y_2 random variables with covariance matrix $\Sigma_\mathbf{Y} = \begin{pmatrix} 1 & -2 \\ -2 & 16 \end{pmatrix}$.

Then, $\sigma(X_1) = \sqrt{\Sigma_\mathbf{X}(1,1)} = 2$ and $\sigma(X_2) = \sqrt{\Sigma_\mathbf{X}(2,2)} = 3$, and, from (7.21), it follows that the correlation matrix of X_1 and X_2 is

$$\Omega_\mathbf{X} = \begin{pmatrix} \frac{1}{2} & 0 \\ 0 & \frac{1}{3} \end{pmatrix} \begin{pmatrix} 4 & -3 \\ -3 & 9 \end{pmatrix} \begin{pmatrix} \frac{1}{2} & 0 \\ 0 & \frac{1}{3} \end{pmatrix} = \begin{pmatrix} 1 & -0.5 \\ -0.5 & 1 \end{pmatrix}.$$

Similarly, $\sigma(Y_1) = \sqrt{\Sigma_\mathbf{Y}(1,1)} = 1$ and $\sigma(Y_2) = \sqrt{\Sigma_\mathbf{Y}(2,2)} = 4$, and, from (7.21), it follows that the correlation matrix of Y_1 and Y_2 is

$$\Omega_\mathbf{Y} = \begin{pmatrix} 1 & 0 \\ 0 & \frac{1}{4} \end{pmatrix} \begin{pmatrix} 1 & -2 \\ -2 & 16 \end{pmatrix} \begin{pmatrix} 1 & 0 \\ 0 & \frac{1}{4} \end{pmatrix} = \begin{pmatrix} 1 & -0.5 \\ -0.5 & 1 \end{pmatrix}.$$

Thus, X_1, X_2 and Y_1, Y_2 have the same correlation matrix, since $\Omega_\mathbf{X} = \Omega_\mathbf{Y}$, although they have different covariance matrices, since $\Sigma_\mathbf{X} \neq \Sigma_\mathbf{Y}$. □

Lemma 7.2. *The correlation matrix of random variables with standard deviation equal to 1 is equal to the covariance matrix of the random variables.*

In other words, let $\Sigma_\mathbf{X}$ and $\Omega_\mathbf{X}$ be the covariance and correlation matrix of the random variables $X_1, X_2, \ldots, X_n$, respectively. If $\Sigma_\mathbf{X}(i,i) = 1$ for all $i = 1:n$, then $\Sigma_\mathbf{X} = \Omega_\mathbf{X}$.

Proof. Recall from (7.9) that $\Sigma_\mathbf{X}(i,i) = \text{var}(X_i) = \sigma_i^2$, for all $i = 1:n$. If $\Sigma_\mathbf{X}(i,i) = 1$, it follows that $\sigma_i = 1$ for all $i = 1:n$. Then, $D_{\sigma_\mathbf{X}} = \text{diag}(\sigma_i)_{i=1:n} = I$, and, from (7.16), we obtain that $\Omega_\mathbf{X} = \Sigma_\mathbf{X}$. □

Note that the result of Lemma 7.2 can also be stated as follows: if all the entries on the main diagonal of the covariance matrix of n random variables are equal to 1, then the covariance matrix and the correlation matrix of the random variables are equal.

Lemma 7.3. *Let $\Sigma_\mathbf{X}$ be the covariance matrix of n random variables $X_1, X_2, \ldots, X_n$. Let $C^{(1)} = (c_i^{(1)})_{i=1:n}$ and $C^{(2)} = (c_i^{(2)})_{i=1:n}$ be two column vectors of size n. Then,*

$$\text{cov}\left(\sum_{i=1}^n c_i^{(1)} X_i, \sum_{i=1}^n c_i^{(2)} X_i\right) = (C^{(1)})^t \Sigma_\mathbf{X} C^{(2)} = (C^{(2)})^t \Sigma_\mathbf{X} C^{(1)}. \quad (7.24)$$

In particular, for $C^{(1)} = C^{(2)} = C = (c_i)_{i=1:n}$, it follows from (7.24) that

$$\text{var}\left(\sum_{i=1}^n c_i X_i\right) = C^t \Sigma_\mathbf{X} C. \quad (7.25)$$

Proof. Let $\mu_i = E[X_i]$, $i = 1:n$. Let

$$Y^{(1)} = \sum_{i=1}^n c_i^{(1)} X_i; \quad Y^{(2)} = \sum_{i=1}^n c_i^{(2)} X_i.$$

Then,

$$Y^{(1)} - E[Y^{(1)}] = \sum_{i=1}^n c_i^{(1)}(X_i - \mu_i);$$

$$Y^{(2)} - E[Y^{(2)}] = \sum_{i=1}^n c_i^{(2)}(X_i - \mu_i).$$

Note that (7.24) is equivalent to

$$\mathrm{cov}(Y^{(1)}, Y^{(2)}) = (C^{(1)})^t \Sigma_\mathbf{X} C^{(2)} = (C^{(2)})^t \Sigma_\mathbf{X} C^{(1)}. \tag{7.26}$$

By definition,

$$\mathrm{cov}\left(\sum_{i=1}^n c_i^{(1)} X_i, \sum_{i=1}^n c_i^{(2)} X_i\right)$$
$$= \mathrm{cov}(Y^{(1)}, Y^{(2)})$$
$$= E\left[\left(Y^{(1)} - E[Y^{(1)}]\right)\left(Y^{(2)} - E[Y^{(2)}]\right)\right]$$
$$= E\left[\left(\sum_{i=1}^n c_i^{(1)}(X_i - \mu_i)\right)\left(\sum_{i=1}^n c_i^{(2)}(X_i - \mu_i)\right)\right]$$
$$= E\left[\sum_{1 \le j,k \le n} c_j^{(1)} c_k^{(2)}(X_j - \mu_j)(X_k - \mu_k)\right]$$
$$= \sum_{1 \le j,k \le n} c_j^{(1)} c_k^{(2)} E[(X_j - \mu_j)(X_k - \mu_k)]$$
$$= \sum_{1 \le j,k \le n} c_j^{(1)} c_k^{(2)} \mathrm{cov}(X_j, X_k)$$
$$= \sum_{1 \le j,k \le n} c_j^{(1)} c_k^{(2)} \Sigma_\mathbf{X}(j,k)$$
$$= (C^{(1)})^t \Sigma_\mathbf{X} C^{(2)},$$

where, for the last equality, we used formula (10.19), i.e.,

$$y^t A x = \sum_{1 \le j,k \le n} A(j,k) x_k y_j,$$

for $A = \Sigma_\mathbf{X}$ and $x = C^{(2)}$, $y = C^{(1)}$.

Thus, the first equality of (7.24) is proven.

To show that the second equality of (7.24) holds true as well, note that

$$\left((C^{(1)})^t \Sigma_\mathbf{X} C^{(2)}\right)^t = (C^{(2)})^t \Sigma_\mathbf{X}^t C^{(1)} = (C^{(2)})^t \Sigma_\mathbf{X} C^{(1)}, \tag{7.27}$$

7.1. COVARIANCE AND CORRELATION MATRICES

since the covariance matrix $\Sigma_{\mathbf{x}}$ is symmetric, i.e., $\Sigma_{\mathbf{x}}^t = \Sigma_{\mathbf{x}}$.

Moreover, since $(C^{(1)})^t \Sigma_{\mathbf{x}} C^{(2)} \in \mathbb{R}$ is a number, it follows that

$$\left((C^{(1)})^t \Sigma_{\mathbf{x}} C^{(2)}\right)^t = (C^{(1)})^t \Sigma_{\mathbf{x}} C^{(2)}. \tag{7.28}$$

From (7.27) and (7.28), we conclude that

$$(C^{(1)})^t \Sigma_{\mathbf{x}} C^{(2)} = (C^{(2)})^t \Sigma_{\mathbf{x}} C^{(1)},$$

and therefore the second equality of (7.24) is proven.

By letting $C^{(1)} = C^{(2)} = C = (c_i)_{i=1:n}$ in (7.24), we obtain that

$$\operatorname{var}\left(\sum_{i=1}^n c_i X_i\right) = \operatorname{cov}\left(\sum_{i=1}^n c_i X_i, \sum_{i=1}^n c_i X_i\right) = C^t \Sigma_{\mathbf{x}} C.$$

$\square$

The formulas from Lemma 7.3 connecting the covariance and correlation matrix of random variables, as well as the Linear Transformation Property from section 7.3, can also be established by using matrix operations and notations for multivariate random variables. For more details, see section 7.7.

Lemma 7.4. *(i) Any covariance matrix is symmetric positive semidefinite.*

(ii) Any correlation matrix is symmetric positive semidefinite.

Proof. Let $\Sigma_{\mathbf{x}}$ and $\Omega_{\mathbf{x}}$ be the covariance and the correlation matrix of the random variables $X_1, X_2, \ldots, X_n$, respectively. Recall from (7.8) and (7.10) that $\Sigma_{\mathbf{x}}$ and $\Omega_{\mathbf{x}}$ are symmetric matrices.

(i) Let $v = (v_i)_{i=1:n} \in \mathbb{R}^n$ be an arbitrary column vector of size n. From (7.25), we find that

$$v^t \Sigma_{\mathbf{x}} v = \operatorname{var}\left(\sum_{i=1}^n v_i X_i\right) \geq 0, \tag{7.29}$$

since the variance of any random variable is nonnegative. Thus, $v^t \Sigma_{\mathbf{x}} v \geq 0$ for any $v \in \mathbb{R}^n$, and we conclude that $\Sigma_{\mathbf{x}}$ is a symmetric positive semidefinite matrix; cf. Definition 5.7.

(ii) Recall from (7.17) that

$$\Omega_{\mathbf{x}} = (D_{\sigma\mathbf{x}})^{-1} \Sigma_{\mathbf{x}} (D_{\sigma\mathbf{x}})^{-1}, \tag{7.30}$$

where $(D_{\sigma\mathbf{x}})^{-1} = \operatorname{diag}\left(\frac{1}{\sigma_i}\right)_{i=1:n}$.

Let $v \in \mathbb{R}^n$ and let

$$w = (D_{\sigma\mathbf{x}})^{-1} v. \tag{7.31}$$

Then,

$$w^t = v^t \left((D_{\sigma\mathbf{x}})^{-1}\right)^t = v^t (D_{\sigma\mathbf{x}})^{-1}, \tag{7.32}$$

since $(D_{\sigma\mathbf{x}})^{-1}$ is a diagonal matrix and therefore symmetric, i.e., $\left((D_{\sigma\mathbf{x}})^{-1}\right)^t = (D_{\sigma\mathbf{x}})^{-1}$.

From (7.29–7.32), we find that
$$\begin{aligned} v^t \Omega_{\mathbf{x}} v &= v^t (D_{\sigma \mathbf{x}})^{-1} \Sigma_{\mathbf{x}} (D_{\sigma \mathbf{x}})^{-1} v \\ &= w^t \Sigma_{\mathbf{x}} w \\ &\geq 0, \quad \forall w \in \mathbb{R}^n. \end{aligned}$$

Thus, $v^t \Omega_{\mathbf{x}} v \geq 0$ for all $v \in \mathbb{R}^n$, and we conclude that $\Omega_{\mathbf{x}}$ is a symmetric positive semidefinite matrix; cf. Definition 5.7. □

Lemma 7.5. *Let $X_1, X_2, \ldots, X_n$ be n random variables on the same probability space. The covariance matrix $\Sigma_{\mathbf{x}}$ of $X_1, X_2, \ldots, X_n$ is nonsingular if and only if there is no linear combination of the random variables $X_1, X_2, \ldots, X_n$ that would be constant, i.e., a constant random variable.*

Proof. In order to prove Lemma 7.5, it is enough to show that the matrix $\Sigma_{\mathbf{x}}$ is singular if and only if there exist constants $c_1, c_2, \ldots, c_n$, and c_0, not all equal to 0, such that
$$\sum_{i=1}^n c_i X_i + c_0 = 0,$$
which is equivalent to
$$\operatorname{var}\left(\sum_{i=1}^n c_i X_i\right) = 0, \tag{7.33}$$
since c_0 is a constant.

Let $C = (c_i)_{i=1:n}$. From (7.25) and (7.33), we obtain that
$$C^t \Sigma_{\mathbf{x}} C = 0. \tag{7.34}$$

Note that, since the constants $c_1, c_2, \ldots, c_n$, and c_0 were assumed to not be all equal to 0, it follows that the $n \times 1$ vector C is not equal to 0.

In other words, we need to show that
$$\Sigma_{\mathbf{x}} \text{ singular} \iff \text{there exists } C \neq 0 \text{ such that } C^t \Sigma_{\mathbf{x}} C = 0. \tag{7.35}$$

To prove (7.35), it is important to recall from Lemma 7.4 that $\Sigma_{\mathbf{x}}$ is a symmetric positive semidefinite matrix.[1]

If $\Sigma_{\mathbf{x}}$ is a singular matrix, it follows from Theorem 4.3 that 0 is an eigenvalue of $\Sigma_{\mathbf{x}}$. Let $C \neq 0$ be an eigenvector of $\Sigma_{\mathbf{x}}$ corresponding to the eigenvalue 0. Then, $\Sigma_{\mathbf{x}} C = 0$ and therefore $C^t \Sigma_{\mathbf{x}} C = 0$.

If there exists a vector $C \neq 0$ such that $C^t \Sigma_{\mathbf{x}} C = 0$, we obtain from Definition 5.6 that $\Sigma_{\mathbf{x}}$ is not symmetric positive definite. Then, from Theorem 5.6, it follows that 0 is an eigenvalue of $\Sigma_{\mathbf{x}}$, and we conclude from Theorem 4.3 that the matrix $\Sigma_{\mathbf{x}}$ is singular.

Thus, the equivalence (7.35) is established. □

---

[1] The equivalence (7.35) does not hold for a matrix which is not symmetric positive semidefinite matrix. For example, if $A = \begin{pmatrix} 1 & 0 \\ 0 & -1 \end{pmatrix}$ and $C = \begin{pmatrix} 1 \\ 1 \end{pmatrix}$, then $C^t A C = 0$ and A is a nonsingular matrix.

7.2 Covariance and correlation matrix estimation from time series data

Let $X_1, X_2, \ldots, X_n$ be random variables given by time series data at N data points t_i, $i = 1 : N$, with $N > n$. Denote by T_{X_k} the column vector of the time series data for the random variable X_k, for $k = 1 : n$, i.e.,

$$T_{X_k} = (X_k(t_i))_{i=1:N}, \quad \forall\, k = 1 : n, \tag{7.36}$$

and denote by

$$T_\mathbf{X} = \mathrm{col}\,(T_{X_k})_{k=1:n} \tag{7.37}$$

the $N \times n$ matrix of time series data for the n random variables.

The sample mean $\widehat{\mu}_{X_k}$ of X_k, the unbiased sample variance $\widehat{\sigma}_k^2$ of X_k, and the unbiased sample covariance $\widehat{\mathrm{cov}}(X_j, X_k)$ and sample correlation $\widehat{\mathrm{corr}}(X_j, X_k)$ of X_j and X_k are given, respectively, by

$$\widehat{\mu}_{X_k} = \frac{1}{N}\sum_{i=1}^{N} X_k(t_i), \quad \forall\, k = 1 : n; \tag{7.38}$$

$$\widehat{\sigma}_k^2 = \frac{1}{N-1}\sum_{i=1}^{N}(X_k(t_i) - \widehat{\mu}_{X_k})^2, \quad \forall\, k = 1 : n; \tag{7.39}$$

$$\widehat{\mathrm{cov}}(X_j, X_k) = \frac{1}{N-1}\sum_{i=1}^{N}(X_j(t_i) - \widehat{\mu}_{X_j})(X_k(t_i) - \widehat{\mu}_{X_k}), \quad \forall\, 1 \le j, k \le n; \tag{7.40}$$

$$\widehat{\mathrm{corr}}(X_j, X_k) = \frac{\widehat{\mathrm{cov}}(X_j, X_k)}{\widehat{\sigma}_j \widehat{\sigma}_k}, \quad \forall\, 1 \le j, k \le n. \tag{7.41}$$

The sample covariance matrix $\widehat{\Sigma}_\mathbf{X}$ and the sample correlation matrix $\widehat{\Omega}_\mathbf{X}$ of the random variables $X_1, X_2, \ldots, X_n$ are the $n \times n$ matrices given by

$$\widehat{\Sigma}_\mathbf{X}(j,k) = \widehat{\mathrm{cov}}(X_j, X_k), \quad \forall\, 1 \le j, k \le n; \tag{7.42}$$

$$\widehat{\Omega}_\mathbf{X}(j,k) = \widehat{\mathrm{corr}}(X_j, X_k), \quad \forall\, 1 \le j, k \le n. \tag{7.43}$$

The following connections between the sample covariance matrix $\widehat{\Sigma}_\mathbf{X}$ and the sample correlation matrix $\widehat{\Omega}_\mathbf{X}$ can be established as in Lemma 7.1:

$$\widehat{\Sigma}_\mathbf{X} = \widehat{D}_{\sigma \mathbf{X}}\,\widehat{\Omega}_\mathbf{X}\,\widehat{D}_{\sigma \mathbf{X}}; \tag{7.44}$$

$$\widehat{\Omega}_\mathbf{X} = (\widehat{D}_{\sigma \mathbf{X}})^{-1}\,\widehat{\Sigma}_\mathbf{X}\,(\widehat{D}_{\sigma \mathbf{X}})^{-1}, \tag{7.45}$$

where $\widehat{D}_{\sigma \mathbf{X}} = \mathrm{diag}(\widehat{\sigma}_k)_{k=1:n}$ and $(\widehat{D}_{\sigma \mathbf{X}})^{-1} = \mathrm{diag}\left(\frac{1}{\widehat{\sigma}_k}\right)_{k=1:n}$. Note that (7.44) and (7.45) can also be written as follows:

$$\widehat{\Sigma}_\mathbf{X} = \mathrm{diag}(\widehat{\sigma}_k)_{k=1:n}\,\widehat{\Omega}_\mathbf{X}\,\mathrm{diag}(\widehat{\sigma}_k)_{k=1:n}; \tag{7.46}$$

$$\widehat{\Omega}_\mathbf{X} = \mathrm{diag}\left(\frac{1}{\widehat{\sigma}_k}\right)_{k=1:n}\,\widehat{\Sigma}_\mathbf{X}\,\mathrm{diag}\left(\frac{1}{\widehat{\sigma}_k}\right)_{k=1:n}. \tag{7.47}$$

Let $\overline{T}_{X_k}$ be the column vector of the time series data for the random variable X_k normalized to mean equal to 0, i.e.,

$$\overline{T}_{X_k} = (X_k(t_i) - \widehat{\mu}_{X_k})_{i=1:N}, \tag{7.48}$$

and let
$$\overline{T}_{\mathbf{X}} = \operatorname{col}\left(\overline{T}_{X_k}\right)_{k=1:n} \tag{7.49}$$
be the mean–normalized $N \times n$ matrix of time series data for the n random variables.

Lemma 7.6. *Let $X_1, X_2, \ldots, X_n$ be n random variables given by the $N \times n$ time series data matrix $T_{\mathbf{X}}$. The sample covariance $\widehat{\operatorname{cov}}(X_j, X_k)$ and the sample correlation $\widehat{\operatorname{corr}}(X_j, X_k)$ of X_j and X_k, and the sample variance $\widehat{\sigma}_k^2$ of X_k, are given by:*

$$\widehat{\operatorname{cov}}(X_j, X_k) = \frac{1}{N-1} \overline{T}_{X_k}^t \overline{T}_{X_j} = \frac{1}{N-1} \overline{T}_{X_j}^t \overline{T}_{X_k}, \quad \forall\, 1 \leq j, k \leq n \tag{7.50}$$

$$\widehat{\sigma}_k^2 = \frac{1}{N-1} \|\overline{T}_{X_k}\|^2 = \frac{1}{N-1} \overline{T}_{X_k}^t \overline{T}_{X_k}, \quad \forall\, k = 1:n; \tag{7.51}$$

$$\widehat{\operatorname{corr}}(X_j, X_k) = \frac{\overline{T}_{X_k}^t \overline{T}_{X_j}}{\|\overline{T}_{X_j}\| \, \|\overline{T}_{X_k}\|}, \quad \forall\, 1 \leq j, k \leq n, \tag{7.52}$$

where $\overline{T}_{X_j}$ and $\overline{T}_{X_k}$ are given by (7.48).

Proof. From (7.48), we find that

$$\overline{T}_{X_k}(i) = X_k(t_i) - \widehat{\mu}_{X_k}, \quad \forall\, i = 1:N; \tag{7.53}$$
$$\overline{T}_{X_j}(i) = X_j(t_i) - \widehat{\mu}_{X_j}, \quad \forall\, i = 1:N. \tag{7.54}$$

Then, from (7.40), (7.53), and (7.54), it follows that

$$\widehat{\operatorname{cov}}(X_j, X_k) = \frac{1}{N-1} \sum_{i=1}^{N} \overline{T}_{X_j}(i) \overline{T}_{X_k}(i), \quad \forall\, 1 \leq j, k \leq n. \tag{7.55}$$

Note that
$$\sum_{i=1}^{N} \overline{T}_{X_j}(i) \overline{T}_{X_k}(i) = \overline{T}_{X_j}^t \overline{T}_{X_k} = \overline{T}_{X_k}^t \overline{T}_{X_j}; \tag{7.56}$$
see, e.g., the row vector–column vector multiplication formula (1.5).

Then, from (7.55) and (7.56), we conclude that

$$\widehat{\operatorname{cov}}(X_j, X_k) = \frac{1}{N-1} \overline{T}_{X_j}^t \overline{T}_{X_k} = \frac{1}{N-1} \overline{T}_{X_k}^t \overline{T}_{X_j}, \quad \forall\, 1 \leq j, k \leq n. \tag{7.57}$$

Moreover, from (7.39) and (7.57), it follows that

$$\widehat{\sigma}_k^2 = \widehat{\operatorname{cov}}(X_k, X_k) = \frac{1}{N-1} \overline{T}_{X_k}^t \overline{T}_{X_k} = \frac{1}{N-1} \|\overline{T}_{X_k}\|^2, \quad \forall\, k = 1:n, \tag{7.58}$$

where the last equality comes from the fact that $v^t v = \|v\|^2$; see (5.8).

From (7.58), we obtain that

$$\widehat{\sigma}_k = \frac{1}{\sqrt{N-1}} \|\overline{T}_{X_k}\|, \quad \forall\, k = 1:n, \tag{7.59}$$

and, from (7.41), (7.57), and (7.59), we conclude that

$$\widehat{\operatorname{corr}}(X_j, X_k) = \frac{\widehat{\operatorname{cov}}(X_j, X_k)}{\widehat{\sigma}_k \widehat{\sigma}_j} = \frac{\frac{1}{N-1} \overline{T}_{X_k}^t \overline{T}_{X_j}}{\frac{1}{\sqrt{N-1}} \|\overline{T}_{X_j}\| \, \frac{1}{\sqrt{N-1}} \|\overline{T}_{X_k}\|}$$

$$= \frac{\overline{T}_{X_k}^t \overline{T}_{X_j}}{\|\overline{T}_{X_j}\| \, \|\overline{T}_{X_k}\|}, \quad \forall\, 1 \leq j, k \leq n.$$

$\square$

7.2. COVARIANCE MATRIX ESTIMATION FROM TIME SERIES DATA

Theorem 7.1. *Consider n random variables $X_1, X_2, \ldots, X_n$ given by the $N \times n$ time series data matrix T_X.*

(i) The sample covariance matrix $\widehat{\Sigma}_X$ of the n random variables can be obtained from the mean-normalized matrix of time series data $\overline{T}_X$ as follows:

$$\widehat{\Sigma}_X = \frac{1}{N-1} \overline{T}_X^t \overline{T}_X. \tag{7.60}$$

(ii) The sample correlation matrix $\widehat{\Omega}_X$ of the n random variables can be obtained from $\overline{T}_X$ as follows:

$$\widehat{\Omega}_X = \operatorname{diag}\left(\frac{1}{\|\overline{T}_{X_k}\|}\right)_{k=1:n} \overline{T}_X^t \overline{T}_X \operatorname{diag}\left(\frac{1}{\|\overline{T}_{X_k}\|}\right)_{k=1:n}. \tag{7.61}$$

Proof. (i) From (7.57), we find that

$$\widehat{\Sigma}_X(j,k) = \widehat{\operatorname{cov}}(X_j, X_k) = \frac{1}{N-1} \overline{T}_{X_j}^t \overline{T}_{X_k}, \quad \forall \, 1 \le j, k \le n, \tag{7.62}$$

and, from (1.13), we obtain that the entry (j,k) of the matrix $\overline{T}_X^t \overline{T}_X$ is

$$(\overline{T}_X^t \overline{T}_X)(j,k) = \overline{T}_{X_j}^t \overline{T}_{X_k}, \quad \forall \, 1 \le j, k \le n, \tag{7.63}$$

since $\overline{T}_X = \operatorname{col}\left(\overline{T}_{X_k}\right)_{k=1:n}$, see (7.49), and $\overline{T}_X^t = \operatorname{row}\left(\overline{T}_{X_j}^t\right)_{j=1:n}$.

Then, from (7.62) and (7.63), we conclude that

$$\widehat{\Sigma}_X(j,k) = \frac{1}{N-1} (\overline{T}_X^t \overline{T}_X)(j,k), \quad \forall \, 1 \le j, k \le n,$$

and therefore that

$$\widehat{\Sigma}_X = \frac{1}{N-1} \overline{T}_X^t \overline{T}_X.$$

(ii) Recall from (7.47) that

$$\widehat{\Omega}_X = \operatorname{diag}\left(\frac{1}{\widehat{\sigma}_k}\right)_{k=1:n} \widehat{\Sigma}_X \operatorname{diag}\left(\frac{1}{\widehat{\sigma}_k}\right)_{k=1:n}, \tag{7.64}$$

where $\widehat{\sigma}_k$ is the unbiased sample variance of X_k given by (7.59), i.e.,

$$\widehat{\sigma}_k = \frac{1}{\sqrt{N-1}} \|\overline{T}_{X_k}\|, \quad \forall \, k = 1:n.$$

Note that

$$\operatorname{diag}\left(\frac{1}{\widehat{\sigma}_k}\right)_{k=1:n} = \sqrt{N-1} \operatorname{diag}\left(\frac{1}{\|\overline{T}_{X_k}\|}\right)_{k=1:n}. \tag{7.65}$$

From (7.64), and using (7.60) and (7.65), we find that

$$\begin{aligned}
\widehat{\Omega}_X &= \sqrt{N-1} \operatorname{diag}\left(\frac{1}{\|\overline{T}_{X_k}\|}\right)_{k=1:n} \left(\frac{1}{N-1} \overline{T}_X^t \overline{T}_X\right) \sqrt{N-1} \operatorname{diag}\left(\frac{1}{\|\overline{T}_{X_k}\|}\right)_{k=1:n} \\
&= \operatorname{diag}\left(\frac{1}{\|\overline{T}_{X_k}\|}\right)_{k=1:n} \overline{T}_X^t \overline{T}_X \operatorname{diag}\left(\frac{1}{\|\overline{T}_{X_k}\|}\right)_{k=1:n}.
\end{aligned}$$

$\square$

Example:[2] The file *data-DJ30-july2011-june2013.xlsx* from fepress.org/nla-primer contains the end of week and end of month adjusted closing prices for eight financial and technology Dow Jones components (AXP; BAC; JPM; CSCO; HPQ; IBM; INTC; MSFT) between July 1, 2011 and June 30, 2013. We compute the sample covariance and sample correlation matrix of the returns of the eight stocks using this data.

The weekly (percentage) returns are computed using the end of week closing prices for the eight stocks, which, using the notation from section 7.2, give the entries of the matrix T_X. After computing the mean normalized time series matrix $\overline{T}_X$ of the stock returns, the sample covariance matrix $\widehat{\Sigma}_{X,week}$ and the sample correlation matrix $\widehat{\Omega}_{X,week}$ are computed from the formulas (7.60) and (7.61), respectively.

$$\widehat{\Sigma}_{X,week} = \begin{pmatrix} 0.0010 & 0.0013 & 0.0010 & 0.0005 & 0.0007 & 0.0005 & 0.0006 & 0.0005 \\ 0.0013 & 0.0036 & 0.0021 & 0.0010 & 0.0011 & 0.0009 & 0.0009 & 0.0009 \\ 0.0010 & 0.0021 & 0.0019 & 0.0009 & 0.0011 & 0.0007 & 0.0007 & 0.0007 \\ 0.0005 & 0.0010 & 0.0009 & 0.0015 & 0.0009 & 0.0006 & 0.0005 & 0.0005 \\ 0.0007 & 0.0011 & 0.0011 & 0.0009 & 0.0034 & 0.0008 & 0.0010 & 0.0006 \\ 0.0005 & 0.0009 & 0.0007 & 0.0006 & 0.0008 & 0.0009 & 0.0005 & 0.0004 \\ 0.0006 & 0.0009 & 0.0007 & 0.0005 & 0.0010 & 0.0005 & 0.0011 & 0.0005 \\ 0.0005 & 0.0009 & 0.0007 & 0.0005 & 0.0006 & 0.0004 & 0.0005 & 0.0009 \end{pmatrix}$$

$$\widehat{\Omega}_{X,week} = \begin{pmatrix} 1 & 0.6875 & 0.6995 & 0.3727 & 0.3607 & 0.4847 & 0.5286 & 0.5497 \\ 0.6875 & 1 & 0.8068 & 0.4165 & 0.3253 & 0.4876 & 0.4517 & 0.4771 \\ 0.6995 & 0.8068 & 1 & 0.5411 & 0.4300 & 0.5338 & 0.4848 & 0.5088 \\ 0.3727 & 0.4165 & 0.5411 & 1 & 0.4002 & 0.5183 & 0.4222 & 0.4569 \\ 0.3607 & 0.3253 & 0.4300 & 0.4002 & 1 & 0.4937 & 0.5135 & 0.3233 \\ 0.4847 & 0.4876 & 0.5338 & 0.5183 & 0.4937 & 1 & 0.5482 & 0.4872 \\ 0.5286 & 0.4517 & 0.4848 & 0.4222 & 0.5135 & 0.5482 & 1 & 0.5137 \\ 0.5497 & 0.4771 & 0.5088 & 0.4569 & 0.3233 & 0.4872 & 0.5137 & 1 \end{pmatrix}$$

Note that the rows and columns in the correlation and covariance matrices herein correspond to the companies in the following order: AXP; BAC; JPM; CSCO; HPQ; IBM; INTC; MSFT.

Similarly, the monthly returns are computed using the end of monthly closing prices for the eight stocks. This gives the entries of the matrix T_X, which can be used to compute the mean normalized time series matrix $\overline{T}_X$ of the stock returns. The following sample covariance matrix and sample correlation matrix are then computed by using formulas (7.60) and (7.61), respectively:

$$\widehat{\Sigma}_{X,month} = \begin{pmatrix} 0.0030 & 0.0053 & 0.0047 & 0.0029 & 0.0039 & 0.0012 & 0.0017 & 0.0022 \\ 0.0053 & 0.0201 & 0.0125 & 0.0058 & 0.0061 & 0.0022 & 0.0020 & 0.0047 \\ 0.0047 & 0.0125 & 0.0124 & 0.0061 & 0.0049 & 0.0022 & 0.0023 & 0.0042 \\ 0.0029 & 0.0058 & 0.0061 & 0.0076 & 0.0048 & 0.0020 & 0.0025 & 0.0028 \\ 0.0039 & 0.0061 & 0.0049 & 0.0048 & 0.0193 & 0.0035 & 0.0039 & 0.0022 \\ 0.0012 & 0.0022 & 0.0022 & 0.0020 & 0.0035 & 0.0020 & 0.0012 & 0.0008 \\ 0.0017 & 0.0020 & 0.0023 & 0.0025 & 0.0039 & 0.0012 & 0.0039 & 0.0024 \\ 0.0022 & 0.0047 & 0.0042 & 0.0028 & 0.0022 & 0.0008 & 0.0024 & 0.0034 \end{pmatrix}$$

---

[2]A similar example for computing sample covariance and correlation matrices for daily returns of Apple, Facebook, Google, Microsoft, and Yahoo was included in Chapter 1. Details on computing percentage returns can also be found there.

7.2. COVARIANCE MATRIX ESTIMATION FROM TIME SERIES DATA 205

$$\widehat{\Omega}_{\mathbf{x},month} = \begin{pmatrix} 1 & 0.6843 & 0.7659 & 0.5991 & 0.5098 & 0.4781 & 0.5116 & 0.6890 \\ 0.6843 & 1 & 0.7923 & 0.4652 & 0.3100 & 0.3482 & 0.2269 & 0.5745 \\ 0.7659 & 0.7923 & 1 & 0.6304 & 0.3188 & 0.4438 & 0.3388 & 0.6493 \\ 0.5991 & 0.4652 & 0.6304 & 1 & 0.3947 & 0.5165 & 0.4610 & 0.5610 \\ 0.5098 & 0.3100 & 0.3188 & 0.3947 & 1 & 0.5544 & 0.4464 & 0.2697 \\ 0.4781 & 0.3482 & 0.4438 & 0.5165 & 0.5544 & 1 & 0.4360 & 0.3009 \\ 0.5116 & 0.2269 & 0.3388 & 0.4610 & 0.4464 & 0.4360 & 1 & 0.6733 \\ 0.6890 & 0.5745 & 0.6493 & 0.5610 & 0.2697 & 0.3009 & 0.6733 & 1 \end{pmatrix}$$

As expected, the correlations between the returns of the financial companies, and the correlations between the returns of the technology companies are generally stronger than the correlations of the returns of a financial company and a technology company. Also, all the returns, both weekly and monthly, are positively correlated with each other. □

An important issue in practice is that the sample covariance matrix of time series data may be very close to singular, which affects the performance of many algorithms, e.g., the Cholesky decomposition and linear solvers. The result of Theorem 7.2 gives necessary and sufficient conditions for the sample covariance matrix to be nonsingular, and will be used subsequently for the linear regression of time series data; see section 8.2. This result is the time series version of Lemma 7.5 for random variables.

Theorem 7.2. Let $X_1, X_2, \ldots, X_n$ be n random variables given by the $N \times n$ time series data matrix $T_\mathbf{x} = col(T_{X_k})_{k=1:n}$ at N data points, with $N > n$. The sample covariance matrix $\widehat{\Sigma}_\mathbf{x}$ is nonsingular if and only if the vectors $T_{X_1}, T_{X_2}, \ldots, T_{X_n}, \mathbf{1}$ are linearly independent, i.e.,

$$\widehat{\Sigma}_\mathbf{x} \text{ nonsingular} \iff T_{X_1}, T_{X_2}, \ldots, T_{X_n}, \mathbf{1} \text{ linearly independent}, \quad (7.66)$$

where $\mathbf{1}$ denotes the $N \times 1$ column vector with all entries equal to 1.

Proof. Recall from (7.60) that $\widehat{\Sigma}_\mathbf{x} = \frac{1}{N-1} \overline{T}_\mathbf{x}^t \overline{T}_\mathbf{x}$, where $\overline{T}_\mathbf{x} = col\left(\overline{T}_{X_k}\right)_{k=1:n}$ is the mean–normalized $N \times n$ matrix of time series data for the n random variables; see (7.48) and (7.49).

Also, recall from Lemma 5.2 that a matrix of the form $M^t M$ is symmetric positive definite if and only if the columns of M are linearly independent.

Then, we conclude that

$$\widehat{\Sigma}_\mathbf{x} \text{ nonsingular} \iff \overline{T}_{X_1}, \overline{T}_{X_2}, \ldots, \overline{T}_{X_n} \text{ linearly independent}. \quad (7.67)$$

From (7.67), it follows that, in order to prove (7.66), it is enough to show that

$$T_{X_1}, T_{X_2}, \ldots, T_{X_n}, \mathbf{1} \text{ linearly independent} \quad (7.68)$$
$$\iff \overline{T}_{X_1}, \overline{T}_{X_2}, \ldots, \overline{T}_{X_n} \text{ linearly independent}. \quad (7.69)$$

- Assume that $T_{X_1}, T_{X_2}, \ldots, T_{X_n}, \mathbf{1}$ are linearly independent. We will show that $\overline{T}_{X_1}, \overline{T}_{X_2}, \ldots, \overline{T}_{X_n}$ are linearly independent, which is equivalent to showing that, if $c_k, k = 1 : n$, are constants such that

$$\sum_{k=1}^{n} c_k \overline{T}_{X_k} = 0, \quad (7.70)$$

then $c_k = 0$ for all $k = 1 : n$.

Since $\overline{T}_{X_k} = (X_k(t_i) - \widehat{\mu}_{X_k})_{i=1:N}$ and $T_{X_k} = (X_k(t_i))_{i=1:N}$, see (7.48) and (7.36), we obtain that
$$\overline{T}_{X_k} = T_{X_k} - \widehat{\mu}_{X_k}\mathbf{1}. \tag{7.71}$$
Then, from (7.70) and (7.71), we find that
$$\begin{aligned} 0 &= \sum_{k=1}^n c_k \overline{T}_{X_k} = \sum_{k=1}^n c_k (T_{X_k} - \widehat{\mu}_{X_k}\mathbf{1}) = \sum_{k=1}^n c_k T_{X_k} - \sum_{k=1}^n c_k \widehat{\mu}_{X_k}\mathbf{1} \\ &= \sum_{k=1}^n c_k T_{X_k} - \left(\sum_{k=1}^n c_k \widehat{\mu}_{X_k}\right)\mathbf{1}, \end{aligned}$$
and, since $T_{X_1}, T_{X_2}, \ldots, T_{X_n}, \mathbf{1}$ are linearly independent, we conclude that $c_k = 0$ for all $k = 1:n$, which is what we wanted to show.

• Assume that $\overline{T}_{X_1}, \overline{T}_{X_2}, \ldots, \overline{T}_{X_n}$ are linearly independent. We will show that $T_{X_1}, T_{X_2}, \ldots, T_{X_n}, \mathbf{1}$ are linearly independent, which is equivalent to showing that, if d_k, $k = 0:n$, are constants such that
$$d_0 \mathbf{1} + \sum_{k=1}^n d_k T_{X_k} = 0, \tag{7.72}$$
then $d_k = 0$ or all $k = 0:n$.

From the definition (7.38) of $\widehat{\mu}_{X_k}$, it follows that
$$\mathbf{1}^t T_{X_k} = \sum_{i=1}^N X_k(t_i) = N\widehat{\mu}_{X_k}, \quad \forall\, k = 1:n. \tag{7.73}$$
Also, note that
$$\mathbf{1}^t \mathbf{1} = \sum_{i=1}^N 1 = N. \tag{7.74}$$
By multiplying (7.72) by $\mathbf{1}^t$ and using (7.73) and (7.74), we find that
$$N d_0 + N \sum_{k=1}^n d_k \widehat{\mu}_{X_k} = 0,$$
and therefore
$$d_0 = -\sum_{k=1}^n d_k \widehat{\mu}_{X_k}. \tag{7.75}$$
By substituting formula (7.75) for d_0 into (7.72) and using (7.71), we obtain that
$$\begin{aligned} 0 &= d_0 \mathbf{1} + \sum_{k=1}^n d_k T_{X_k} \\ &= -\left(\sum_{k=1}^n d_k \widehat{\mu}_{X_k}\right)\mathbf{1} + \sum_{k=1}^n d_k T_{X_k} \\ &= \sum_{k=1}^n d_k T_{X_k} - \sum_{k=1}^n d_k \widehat{\mu}_{X_k}\mathbf{1} \end{aligned}$$

7.2. LINEAR TRANSFORMATION PROPERTY

$$= \sum_{k=1}^{n} d_k (T_{X_k} - \widehat{\mu}_{X_k} \mathbf{1})$$

$$= \sum_{k=1}^{n} d_k \overline{T}_{X_k}.$$

Since we assumed that $\overline{T}_{X_1}, \overline{T}_{X_2}, \ldots, \overline{T}_{X_n}$ are linearly independent, we conclude that $d_k = 0$ for all $k = 0 : n$, which is what we wanted to show. □

Note that the linear independence of the time series data vectors $T_{X_1}, T_{X_2}, \ldots, T_{X_n}$ is not sufficient for the sample covariance matrix $\widehat{\Sigma}_{\mathbf{x}}$ to be nonsingular; a counterexample can be found in an exercise at the end of this chapter.

7.3 The Linear Transformation Property

Theorem 7.3. *(Linear Transformation Property.)* Let $X_1, X_2, \ldots, X_n$ be n random variables on the same probability space, and let $Y_1, Y_2, \ldots, Y_m$ be random variables given by

$$\mathbf{Y} = M\mathbf{X},$$

where M is an $m \times n$ matrix, and $\mathbf{Y} = (Y_i)_{i=1:m}$ and $\mathbf{X} = (X_i)_{i=1:n}$ denote the column vectors of the random variables Y_i, $i = 1 : m$, and X_i, $i = 1 : n$, respectively. Let $\Sigma_{\mathbf{X}}$ and $\Sigma_{\mathbf{Y}}$ be the covariance matrices of $\mathbf{X}$ and $\mathbf{Y}$, respectively. Then,

$$\Sigma_{\mathbf{Y}} = M \Sigma_{\mathbf{X}} M^t. \tag{7.76}$$

Note that (7.76) can also be written as

$$\Sigma_{M\mathbf{X}} = M \Sigma_{\mathbf{X}} M^t. \tag{7.77}$$

Proof. To prove (7.76), recall from (1.14) that, if A, B, C are matrices of sizes $m \times n$, $n \times n$, and $n \times m$, respectively, with $A = \text{row}\,(r_j)_{j=1:m}$ and $C = \text{col}\,(c_k)_{k=1:m}$, then ABC is an $m \times m$ matrix with[3]

$$(ABC)(j,k) = r_j B c_k, \quad \forall\, j = 1 : m,\ k = 1 : m. \tag{7.78}$$

Let $M = \text{row}\,(r_j)_{j=1:m}$ be the row form of M. Then, M^t is an $n \times m$ matrix with column form $M^t = \text{col}\,(r_k^t)_{k=1:m}$; see (1.18). From (7.78), it follows that

$$(M\Sigma_{\mathbf{X}} M^t)(j,k) = r_j \Sigma_{\mathbf{X}} r_k^t, \quad \forall\, j = 1 : m,\ k = 1 : m. \tag{7.79}$$

Note that, if $M = \text{row}\,(r_j)_{j=1:m}$, then $M\mathbf{X} = (r_i \mathbf{X})_{i=1:m}$; see (1.12). Since $\mathbf{Y} = M\mathbf{X}$ and $\mathbf{Y} = (Y_i)_{i=1:m}$, we find that

$$Y_i = r_i \mathbf{X}, \quad \forall\, i = 1 : m. \tag{7.80}$$

---
[3] Note that r_j is a row vector, and therefore the row vector–matrix–column vector multiplication from (7.78) is well defined.

If $\mathbf{X} = (X_i)_{i=1:n}$ denotes the column vector of the random variables X_i, $i = 1:n$, then formula (7.24) from Lemma 7.3 can be written as follows:

$$\operatorname{cov}\left((C^{(1)})^t\mathbf{X}, (C^{(2)})^t\mathbf{X}\right) = (C^{(1)})^t \Sigma_{\mathbf{X}} C^{(2)} = (C^{(2)})^t \Sigma_{\mathbf{X}} C^{(1)}. \tag{7.81}$$

Then, from (7.80) and using (7.81) it follows that

$$\begin{aligned} \Sigma_{\mathbf{Y}}(j,k) &= \operatorname{cov}(Y_j, Y_k) = \operatorname{cov}(r_j X, r_k X) \\ &= r_j \Sigma_{\mathbf{X}} r_k^t, \quad \forall\, 1 \leq j, k \leq m. \end{aligned} \tag{7.82}$$

From (7.79) and (7.82), we conclude that $\Sigma_{\mathbf{Y}} = M \Sigma_{\mathbf{X}} M^t$. □

Example: As a simple application of the Linear Transformation Property, let X_1, $X_2, \ldots, X_n$ be nonconstant random variables, and let $Y_1, Y_2, \ldots, Y_n$ be the random variables given by $Y_i = d_i X_i$, where $d_i \neq 0$, are constants, for $i = 1:n$. Let $\mathbf{Y} = (Y_i)_{i=1:n}$ and $\mathbf{X} = (X_i)_{i=1:n}$. Then, $\mathbf{Y} = D\mathbf{X}$, and, from the Linear Transformation Property (7.76), it follows that $\Sigma_{\mathbf{Y}} = D\Sigma_{\mathbf{X}} D^t$. Since D is a diagonal matrix, $D^t = D$, we conclude that

$$\Sigma_{\mathbf{Y}} = D\Sigma_{\mathbf{X}} D. \quad \square \tag{7.83}$$

Theorem 7.4. *Let $X_1, X_2, \ldots, X_n$ be n random variables, and let $\mathbf{X} = (X_i)_{i=1:n}$. Denote by μ_X the mean vector of $\mathbf{X}$ and by Σ_X the covariance matrix of $\mathbf{X}$. Let Y_1, $Y_2, \ldots, Y_m$ be random variables given by*

$$\mathbf{Y} = b + M\mathbf{X},$$

where $\mathbf{Y} = (Y_i)_{i=1:m}$, M is an $m \times n$ matrix, and b is an $m \times 1$ column vector. Denote by μ_Y the mean vector of $\mathbf{Y}$ and by Σ_Y the covariance matrix of $\mathbf{Y}$.
Then,

$$\mu_Y = b + M\mu_X \quad \text{and} \quad \Sigma_Y = M\Sigma_X M^t. \tag{7.84}$$

Proof. From the linearity of expectation, it follows that

$$E[M\mathbf{X}] = ME[\mathbf{X}] = M\mu_{\mathbf{X}}; \tag{7.85}$$

see (7.128). Then, from (7.85), we find that

$$\mu_{\mathbf{Y}} = E[\mathbf{Y}] = E[b + M\mathbf{X}] = b + E[M\mathbf{X}] = b + M\mu_{\mathbf{X}}.$$

Moreover, since b is a constant vector, the covariance matrix of $\mathbf{Y} = b + M\mathbf{X}$ is the same as the covariance matrix of $M\mathbf{X}$, and therefore $\Sigma_{\mathbf{Y}} = \Sigma_{M\mathbf{X}}$. Note that $\Sigma_{M\mathbf{X}} = M\Sigma_{\mathbf{X}} M^t$; see (7.77). Thus, we conclude that

$$\Sigma_{\mathbf{Y}} = \Sigma_{M\mathbf{X}} = M\Sigma_{\mathbf{X}} M^t.$$

□

The Linear Transformation Property can be used for generating normal random variables with a given correlation matrix, which can be subsequently used for Monte Carlo simulations, see section 7.5, and for establishing that any symmetric positive semidefinite matrix is the covariance matrix (or the correlation matrix, if the main diagonal entries are equal to 1) of some random variables; see section 7.4.

7.4 Necessary and sufficient conditions for covariance and correlation matrices

In Lemma 7.4, we proved that any covariance matrix is symmetric positive semidefinite. We now show, using the Linear Transformation Property, that this is a necessary and sufficient condition by finding normal random variables with covariance matrix equal to any given symmetric positive semidefinite matrix, and establish a similar result for correlation matrices.

Theorem 7.5. *(i) An $n \times n$ square matrix is the covariance matrix of n random variables if and only if the matrix is symmetric positive semidefinite.*

(ii) An $n \times n$ square matrix is the correlation matrix of n random variables if and only if the matrix is symmetric positive semidefinite and has all the entries on the main diagonal equal to 1.

Proof. (i) Recall from Lemma 7.4 that any covariance matrix is symmetric positive semidefinite.

To prove that any symmetric positive semidefinite matrix is a covariance matrix, let A be an $n \times n$ symmetric positive semidefinite matrix. We will find random variables $X_1, X_2, \ldots, X_n$ with covariance matrix $\Sigma_\mathbf{X} = A$.

Since the matrix A is symmetric, it follows from Theorem 5.4 that there exists an orthogonal matrix Q and a diagonal matrix Λ such that

$$A = Q \Lambda Q^t. \tag{7.86}$$

Recall that $\Lambda = \mathrm{diag}(\lambda_i)_{i=1:n}$, where λ_i, $i = 1 : n$, are the eigenvalues of A. Note that $\lambda_i \geq 0$, for all $i = 1 : n$, since the eigenvalues of a symmetric positive semidefinite matrix are nonnegative; see Theorem 5.6. Let $\Lambda^{1/2}$ be the diagonal matrix given by

$$\Lambda^{1/2} = \mathrm{diag}\left(\sqrt{\lambda_i}\right)_{i=1:n}. \tag{7.87}$$

Using (1.93), we find that

$$\Lambda^{1/2} \Lambda^{1/2} = \mathrm{diag}(\lambda_i)_{i=1:n} = \Lambda. \tag{7.88}$$

Let

$$M = Q \Lambda^{1/2}. \tag{7.89}$$

Then,

$$M^t = (\Lambda^{1/2})^t Q^t = \Lambda^{1/2} Q^t, \tag{7.90}$$

since $\Lambda^{1/2}$ is a diagonal matrix and therefore symmetric, i.e., $(\Lambda^{1/2})^t = \Lambda^{1/2}$. Then, from (7.89), (7.90), (7.88), and (7.86), we obtain that

$$MM^t = Q\Lambda^{1/2}\Lambda^{1/2}Q^t = Q\Lambda Q^t = A. \tag{7.91}$$

Let $Z_1, Z_2, \ldots, Z_n$ be independent standard normal variables, and let $X_1, X_2, \ldots, X_n$ be random variables[4] given by $\mathbf{X} = M\mathbf{Z}$, where M is the matrix given by (7.89), $\mathbf{X} = (X_i)_{i=1:n}$ and $\mathbf{Z} = (Z_i)_{i=1:n}$. Let $\Sigma_\mathbf{X}$ be the covariance matrix of X_1,

---

[4]Note that $X_1, X_2, \ldots, X_n$ are, in fact, normal random variables, since they are linear combinations of independent normal variables.

$X_2, \ldots, X_n$. Note that the covariance matrix $\Sigma_{\mathbf{z}}$ of $Z_1, Z_2, \ldots, Z_n$ is the identity matrix, i.e., $\Sigma_{\mathbf{z}} = I$. Then, from the Linear Transformation Property (Theorem 7.3) and using (7.91), we find that

$$\Sigma_{\mathbf{x}} = M\Sigma_{\mathbf{z}}M^t = MM^t = A.$$

In other words, we found random variables $X_1, X_2, \ldots, X_n$ with covariance matrix equal to the matrix A. We conclude that any symmetric positive semidefinite matrix is a covariance matrix.

(ii) Recall from Lemma 7.4 that any correlation matrix is symmetric positive semidefinite with main diagonal entries equal to 1; see (7.11).

To prove that any symmetric positive semidefinite matrix with main diagonal entries equal to 1 is a correlation matrix, let A be an $n \times n$ symmetric positive semidefinite with $A(i,i) = 1$ for all $i = 1 : n$. We will find random variables $X_1, X_2, \ldots, X_n$ with correlation matrix $\Omega_{\mathbf{x}} = A$.

We showed above that there exist random variables $X_1, X_2, \ldots, X_n$ with covariance matrix $\Sigma_{\mathbf{x}} = A$. Since $A(i,i) = 1$ for all $i = 1 : n$, it follows that $\Sigma_{\mathbf{x}}(i,i) = 1$ for all $i = 1 : n$, and, from Lemma 7.2, we conclude that $\Omega_{\mathbf{x}} = \Sigma_{\mathbf{x}} = A$, which is what we wanted to show. □

The method for finding normal random variables with a given covariance matrix described above requires finding the eigenvalues of the given symmetric positive semidefinite matrix. Note that this method is not used in practice if the given matrix is symmetric positive definite, in which case the Cholesky decomposition of the given covariance matrix is used; see section 7.5 for details.

Example: The 3×3 matrix

$$A = \begin{pmatrix} 1 & a & b \\ a & 1 & c \\ b & c & 1 \end{pmatrix} \qquad (7.92)$$

is a correlation matrix if and only if

$$-1 \leq a, b, c \leq 1 \quad \text{and} \quad \det(A) = 1 + 2abc - a^2 - b^2 - c^2 \geq 0. \qquad (7.93)$$

Solution: Since all the main diagonal entries of A are equal to 1, it follows from Theorem 7.5 that the matrix A is a correlation matrix if and only if it is symmetric positive semidefinite, which, according to (5.64) is equivalent to

$$-1 \leq a, b, c \leq 1 \quad \text{and} \quad \det(A) = 1 + 2abc - a^2 - b^2 - c^2 \geq 0. \quad \square \qquad (7.94)$$

Example: Find all the values of ρ such that the matrix

$$\Omega = \begin{pmatrix} 1 & 0.8 & 0.3 \\ 0.8 & 1 & \rho \\ 0.3 & \rho & 1 \end{pmatrix}$$

is a correlation matrix.

7.4. NORMAL RVS WITH A GIVEN COVARIANCE MATRIX

Solution: From (7.93), it follows that the matrix Ω is a correlation matrix if and only if $-1 \leq \rho \leq 1$ and

$$\det(\Omega) = 1 + 2 \cdot (0.8) \cdot (0.3) \cdot \rho - \rho^2 - (0.8)^2 - (0.3)^2 \geq 0,$$

which is equivalent to
$$\rho^2 - 0.48\rho - 0.27 \leq 0. \qquad (7.95)$$

Thus, ρ must be between the roots -0.332364 and 0.812364 of the quadratic equation $\rho^2 - 0.48\rho - 0.27 = 0$ corresponding to (7.95), which is equivalent to $-0.332364 \leq \rho \leq 0.812364$; note that the condition $-1 \leq \rho \leq 1$ is satisfied for all such values of ρ. We conclude that the matrix Ω is a correlation matrix if and only if

$$-0.332364 \leq \rho \leq 0.812364. \qquad \square$$

Example: Show that it is not possible to find three random variables on the same probability space with correlations 0.75, 0.75, and -0.75. In other words, show that it is not possible to find random variables X_1, X_2, X_3 such that

$$\operatorname{corr}(X_1, X_2) = 0.75; \quad \operatorname{corr}(X_1, X_3) = 0.75; \quad \operatorname{corr}(X_2, X_3) = -0.75. \qquad (7.96)$$

Solution: We give a proof by contradiction. Assume that random variables X_1, X_2, X_3 with correlations given by (7.96) exist. Then, the correlation matrix of X_1, X_2, X_3 is

$$\Sigma_{\mathbf{X}} = \begin{pmatrix} 1 & 0.75 & 0.75 \\ 0.75 & 1 & -0.75 \\ -0.75 & -0.75 & 1 \end{pmatrix},$$

which is the same as the matrix from (7.92) with $a = 0.75$, $b = 0.75$, and $c = -0.75$.

However, the condition (7.93) for the matrix $\Sigma_{\mathbf{X}}$ to be a correlation matrix is not satisfied since, for $a = 0.75$, $b = 0.75$, and $c = -0.75$, we obtain that

$$\begin{aligned} 1 + 2abc - a^2 - b^2 - c^2 &= 1 + 2(0.75)(0.75)(-0.75) \\ &\quad - (0.75)^2 - (0.75)^2 - (-0.75)^2 \\ &= 1 - 0.84375 - 1.6875 = -1.53125 \\ &< 0. \end{aligned}$$

We conclude that random variables X_1, X_2, X_3 with correlations given by (7.96) do not exist.

7.5 Finding normal variables with a given covariance or correlation matrix

Finding normal random variables with a given correlation matrix is often needed in practice, e.g., for Monte Carlo simulations; see section 7.5.1. A way to do so based on the Cholesky decomposition and the Linear Transformation Property is presented below.

Theorem 7.6. *(i) Let A be a symmetric positive definite matrix, and let U be the Cholesky factor of A. Let $Z_1, Z_2, \ldots, Z_n$ be independent standard normal variables, and let $X_1, X_2, \ldots, X_n$ be random variables given by*

$$\boldsymbol{X} = U^t \boldsymbol{Z}, \tag{7.97}$$

where $\boldsymbol{X} = (X_i)_{i=1:n}$ and $\boldsymbol{Z} = (Z_i)_{i=1:n}$. Then, $X_1, X_2, \ldots, X_n$ are normal random variables with covariance matrix $\Sigma_{\boldsymbol{X}}$ equal to the given matrix A, i.e.,

$$\Sigma_{\boldsymbol{X}} = A. \tag{7.98}$$

(ii) If A is a symmetric positive definite matrix with main diagonal entries equal to 1, then the correlation matrix $\Omega_{\boldsymbol{X}}$ of the random variables $X_1, X_2, \ldots, X_n$ given by (7.97) is equal to A, i.e.,

$$\Omega_{\boldsymbol{X}} = A. \tag{7.99}$$

Proof. Since $\boldsymbol{X} = (X_i)_{i=1:n} = U^t \boldsymbol{Z}$, it follows that

$$X_i = \sum_{k=1}^{n} U^t(i,k) Z_k.$$

Thus, X_i is a linear combination of the independent standard normal variables $Z_1, Z_2, \ldots, Z_n$, and therefore X_i is a normal random variable, for all $i = 1:n$.

If U the Cholesky factor of A, then $U^t U = A$. From the Linear Transformation Property (Theorem 7.3), we find that

$$\Sigma_{\boldsymbol{X}} = U^t \Sigma_{\boldsymbol{Z}} U = U^t U = A;$$

here, we use the fact that $\Sigma_{\boldsymbol{Z}} = I$, since $Z_1, Z_2, \ldots, Z_n$ are independent standard normal variables.

(ii) If the main diagonal entries of the matrix A are equal to 1, it follows from (7.98) that all the entries on the main diagonal of the covariance matrix $\Sigma_{\boldsymbol{X}}$ are equal to 1. From Lemma 7.2, we obtain that $\Omega_{\boldsymbol{X}} = \Sigma_{\boldsymbol{X}}$, and, from (7.98), we conclude that $\Omega_{\boldsymbol{X}} = \Sigma_{\boldsymbol{X}} = A$. □

Example: Given Z_1 and Z_2 independent standard normal variables, find two normal random variables X_1 and X_2 with variance 1 and correlation ρ, where $-1 < \rho < 1$.

Solution: Recall from (6.42) that the Cholesky factor of the matrix $\begin{pmatrix} 1 & \rho \\ \rho & 1 \end{pmatrix}$ with $-1 < \rho < 1$ is $U = \begin{pmatrix} 1 & \rho \\ 0 & \sqrt{1-\rho^2} \end{pmatrix}$. Then, it follows from Theorem 7.6 that two normal random variables X_1 and X_2 given by

$$\begin{pmatrix} X_1 \\ X_2 \end{pmatrix} = U^t \begin{pmatrix} Z_1 \\ Z_2 \end{pmatrix} = \begin{pmatrix} 1 & 0 \\ \rho & \sqrt{1-\rho^2} \end{pmatrix} \begin{pmatrix} Z_1 \\ Z_2 \end{pmatrix}$$

$$= \begin{pmatrix} Z_1 \\ \rho Z_1 + \sqrt{1-\rho^2} Z_2 \end{pmatrix} \tag{7.100}$$

have correlation matrix

$$\Omega_{\boldsymbol{X}} = \begin{pmatrix} 1 & \rho \\ \rho & 1 \end{pmatrix}.$$

7.5. MONTE CARLO SIMULATION FOR BASKET OPTIONS

We conclude that the normal random variables X_1 and X_2 have variance 1 and correlation ρ.

Also, note from (7.100) that X_1 and X_2 can be written as

$$X_1 = Z_1; \tag{7.101}$$
$$X_2 = \rho Z_1 + \sqrt{1-\rho^2} Z_2. \quad \square \tag{7.102}$$

7.5.1 Monte Carlo simulation for basket options pricing

The payoff at maturity T of a basket option on two assets is

$$\max(S_1(T) + S_2(T) - K, 0),$$

where $S_1(T)$ and $S_2(T)$ are the prices of the two assets at time T.

Assume that the assets have lognormal distributions with risk neutral drift r, volatilities σ_1 and σ_2, continuous dividends q_1 and q_2, and with correlation ρ. Then,

$$S_1(T) = S_1(0) \exp\left(\left(r - q_1 - \frac{\sigma_1^2}{2}\right)T + \sigma_1 \sqrt{T} X_1\right); \tag{7.103}$$

$$S_2(T) = S_2(0) \exp\left(\left(r - q_2 - \frac{\sigma_2^2}{2}\right)T + \sigma_2 \sqrt{T} X_2\right), \tag{7.104}$$

where X_1 and X_2 are normal random variables with variance 1 and correlation ρ.

The value of the basket option can be found using Monte Carlo simulations by finding sample values of $S_1(T)$ and $S_2(T)$ from samples of the standard normal variable which can be generated, e.g., by using the Box–Muller method.

Note that, if Z_1 and Z_2 denote two independent standard normal variables, then

$$X_1 = Z_1; \tag{7.105}$$
$$X_2 = \rho Z_1 + \sqrt{1-\rho^2} Z_2. \tag{7.106}$$

are normal random variables with variance 1 and correlation ρ; see (7.101–7.102). From (7.103–7.106), we obtain that

$$S_1(T) = S_1(0) \exp\left(\left(r - q_1 - \frac{\sigma_1^2}{2}\right)T + \sigma_1 \sqrt{T} Z_1\right); \tag{7.107}$$

$$S_2(T) = S_2(0) \exp\left(\left(r - q_2 - \frac{\sigma_2^2}{2}\right)T + \sigma_2 \sqrt{T}\left(\rho Z_1 + \sqrt{1-\rho^2} Z_2\right)\right) \tag{7.108}$$

Thus, given $z_1, z_2, \ldots, z_{2N}$ independent samples of the standard normal variable, we can obtain N samples of $S_1(T)$ and $S_2(T)$ as follows:

$$S_{1,j}(T) = S_1(0) \exp\left(\left(r - q_1 - \frac{\sigma_1^2}{2}\right)T + \sigma_1 \sqrt{T} z_{2j+1}\right);$$

$$S_{2,j}(T) = S_2(0) \exp\left(\left(r - q_2 - \frac{\sigma_2^2}{2}\right)T + \sigma_2 \sqrt{T}\left(\rho z_{2j+1} + \sqrt{1-\rho^2} z_{2j+2}\right)\right),$$

for all $j = 0 : (N-1)$, which can be used to compute the following N sample values for the basket option:

$$V_j = e^{-rT} \max(S_{1,j}(T) + S_{2,j}(T) - K, 0).$$

The average sample value

$$\widehat{V}(N) = \frac{1}{N}\sum_{j=1}^{N} V_j$$

has $O\left(\frac{1}{\sqrt{N}}\right)$ convergence to the value of the basket option; see, e.g., Glasserman [17].

7.6 Multivariate normal random variables

We begin this section with a brief review of one dimensional normal random variables.

The standard normal variable Z is the random variable with probability density function

$$f(x) = \frac{1}{\sqrt{2\pi}} e^{-\frac{x^2}{2}}, \qquad (7.109)$$

and has mean 0 and variance 1, i.e., $E[Z] = 0$ and $\text{var}(Z) = 1$.

The random variable X is a normal variable if it is of the form $X = \mu + \sigma Z$, where Z is a standard normal variable and μ and σ are real constants. Note that X has mean μ and variance σ^2, i.e., $E[X] = \mu$ and $\text{var}(X) = \sigma^2$, and is often denoted by $X \sim N(\mu, \sigma^2)$. If $\sigma \neq 0$, the probability density function of X is given by

$$f(x) = \frac{1}{\sqrt{2\pi\sigma^2}} \exp\left(-\frac{(x-\mu)^2}{2\sigma^2}\right), \qquad (7.110)$$

where $\exp(t)$ is a notation for e^t.

Definition 7.3. *The random variable* $\mathbf{Z} = \begin{pmatrix} Z_1 \\ \vdots \\ Z_n \end{pmatrix}$ *is a multivariate standard normal variable if it has a probability density function*[5] $f : \mathbb{R}^n \to \mathbb{R}$ *given by*

$$f(x) = \frac{1}{(2\pi)^{n/2}} \exp\left(-\frac{1}{2}\sum_{i=1}^{n} x_i^2\right), \qquad (7.111)$$

where $x = (x_1, x_2, \ldots, x_n)$.

The mean of $\mathbf{Z}$ is $\mu_\mathbf{Z} = \mathbf{0}$, where $\mathbf{0}$ denotes the column vector of size n with all entries equal to 0, and the covariance matrix of $\mathbf{Z}$ is the identity matrix, i.e., $\Sigma_\mathbf{Z} = I$.

Equivalently, the random variable $\mathbf{Z} = (Z_i)_{i=1:n}$ is multivariate standard normal if and only if its components $Z_1, Z_2, \ldots, Z_n$ are independent standard normal variables, since, from (7.111), we find that the probability density function of the multivariate

---

[5]Recall that $f : \mathbb{R}^n \to \mathbb{R}$ is the probability density function of a multivariate random variable $\mathbf{X} = (X_i)_{i=1:n}$ if and only if, for any $a_i \in \mathbb{R}$, $i = 1 : n$,

$$P(X_1 \leq a_1, X_2 \leq a_2, \ldots, X_n \leq a_n) = \int_{-\infty}^{a_1} \int_{-\infty}^{a_2} \cdots \int_{-\infty}^{a_n} f(s_1, s_2, \ldots, s_n) \, ds_n \ldots ds_2 ds_1.$$

standard normal variable can be written as a product of functions of the underlying variables x_i, $1 \leq i \leq n$:

$$\begin{aligned} f(x) &= \frac{1}{(2\pi)^{n/2}} \exp\left(-\frac{1}{2}\sum_{i=1}^{n} x_i^2\right) = \frac{1}{(2\pi)^{n/2}} \prod_{i=1}^{n} \exp\left(-\frac{1}{2}x_i^2\right) \\ &= \prod_{i=1}^{n} \left(\frac{1}{\sqrt{2\pi}} e^{-\frac{x_i^2}{2}}\right). \end{aligned}$$

Definition 7.4. *The random variable* $\boldsymbol{X} = \begin{pmatrix} X_1 \\ \vdots \\ X_n \end{pmatrix}$ *is a multivariate normal random variable if and only if there exists an $n \times 1$ vector b and an $n \times n$ matrix A such that*

$$\boldsymbol{X} = b + A\boldsymbol{Z}, \tag{7.112}$$

where $\boldsymbol{Z} = (Z_i)_{i=1:n}$ *is a multivariate standard normal variable.*

Denote by $\mu_{\mathbf{X}}$ and $\Sigma_{\mathbf{X}}$ the mean vector and the covariance matrix of the multivariate normal variable $\boldsymbol{X} = b + A\boldsymbol{Z}$. From (7.84) and since $\mu_{\mathbf{Z}} = \boldsymbol{0}$ and $\Sigma_{\mathbf{Z}} = I$, it follows that

$$\begin{aligned} \mu_{\mathbf{X}} &= b + AE[\boldsymbol{Z}] = b; \\ \Sigma_{\mathbf{X}} &= A\Sigma_{\mathbf{Z}}A^t = AA^t. \end{aligned}$$

A multivariate normal random variable $\boldsymbol{X}$ with mean $\mu_{\mathbf{X}}$ and covariance matrix $\Sigma_{\mathbf{X}}$ is denoted by $\boldsymbol{X} \sim N(\mu_{\mathbf{X}}, \Sigma_{\mathbf{X}})$. For example, $\boldsymbol{Z} \sim N(\boldsymbol{0}, I)$.

Note that a multivariate normal variable $\boldsymbol{X}$ can be written in the form (7.112) in infinitely many different ways. However, if

$$\boldsymbol{X} = b_1 + A_1\boldsymbol{Z}_1 = b_2 + A_2\boldsymbol{Z}_2,$$

then b_1 and b_2 must be equal since $\mu_{\mathbf{X}} = b_1 = b_2$, and $A_1 A_1^t = A_2 A_2^t$ since $\Sigma_{\mathbf{X}} = A_1 A_1^t = A_2 A_2^t$. It is important to also note that, while both $\boldsymbol{Z}_1$ and $\boldsymbol{Z}_2$ are multivariate standard normals, $\boldsymbol{Z}_1$ and $\boldsymbol{Z}_2$ are different random variables.

Definition 7.5. *If the covariance matrix Σ_X of a multivariate normal variable $\boldsymbol{X}$ is nonsingular, then $\boldsymbol{X}$ is called a nondegenerate multivariate normal variable.*

The probability density function $f : \mathbb{R}^n \to \mathbb{R}$ of a nondegenerate multivariate normal variable $\boldsymbol{X} \sim N(\mu_{\mathbf{X}}, \Sigma_{\mathbf{X}})$ is given by

$$f(x) = \frac{1}{(2\pi)^{n/2}\sqrt{\det(\Sigma_{\mathbf{X}})}} \exp\left(-\frac{1}{2}(x - \mu_{\mathbf{X}})^t(\Sigma_{\mathbf{X}})^{-1}(x - \mu_{\mathbf{X}})\right). \tag{7.113}$$

Lemma 7.7. *Let $\boldsymbol{X}$ be a nondegenerate n-dimensional multivariate normal random variable with mean vector μ_X and nonsingular covariance matrix Σ_X. Then,*

$$\boldsymbol{X} = \mu_X + U^t \boldsymbol{Z},$$

where U is the Cholesky factor of the covariance matrix Σ_X and $\boldsymbol{Z}$ is a multivariate standard normal variable.

Proof. Since $\mathbf{X} \sim N(\mu_{\mathbf{X}}, \Sigma_{\mathbf{X}})$, we need to show that
$$\mu_{\mathbf{X}} + U^t \mathbf{Z} \sim N(\mu_{\mathbf{X}}, \Sigma_{\mathbf{X}}), \tag{7.114}$$
in order to conclude that $\mathbf{X} = \mu_{\mathbf{X}} + U^t \mathbf{Z}$.

From Definition 7.4, it follows that $\mu_{\mathbf{X}} + U^t \mathbf{Z}$ is a multivariate normal random variable. Recall from Definition 6.1 that, if U is the Cholesky factor of the symmetric positive definite matrix $\Sigma_{\mathbf{X}}$, then
$$\Sigma_{\mathbf{X}} = U^t U. \tag{7.115}$$
Since $\mu_{\mathbf{Z}} = \mathbf{0}$ and $\Sigma_{\mathbf{Z}} = I$, it follows from (7.84) and (7.115) that
$$E[\mu_{\mathbf{X}} + U^t \mathbf{Z}] = \mu_{\mathbf{X}};$$
$$\Sigma_{\mu_{\mathbf{X}}+U^t\mathbf{Z}} = U^t \Sigma_{\mathbf{Z}} (U^t)^t = U^t U = \Sigma_{\mathbf{X}},$$
which is what we wanted to show; cf. (7.114). □

Example: A two dimensional multivariate normal random variable is called a *bivariate normal random variable*. We use formula (7.113) to find the probability density function of a nondegenerate bivariate normal random variable; see (7.118).

Let $\mathbf{X} = \begin{pmatrix} X_1 \\ X_2 \end{pmatrix}$ be a nondegenerate bivariate normal variable, where X_1 and X_2 are normal random variable with correlation ρ with $\rho \neq 1$ and $\rho \neq -1$, and with mean and standard deviation μ_1, σ_1, and μ_2, σ_2, respectively. Recall from (7.12) that the covariance matrix of X_1 and X_2 is
$$\Sigma_{\mathbf{X}} = \begin{pmatrix} \sigma_1^2 & \sigma_1 \sigma_2 \rho \\ \sigma_1 \sigma_2 \rho & \sigma_2^2 \end{pmatrix}.$$
Then,
$$\det(\Sigma_{\mathbf{X}}) = \sigma_1^2 \sigma_2^2 (1 - \rho^2), \tag{7.116}$$
see (10.6), and, since $\rho \neq 1$ and $\rho \neq -1$, we find from (10.7) that
$$(\Sigma_{\mathbf{X}})^{-1} = \frac{1}{\sigma_1^2 \sigma_2^2 (1-\rho^2)} \begin{pmatrix} \sigma_2^2 & -\sigma_1 \sigma_2 \rho \\ -\sigma_1 \sigma_2 \rho & \sigma_1^2 \end{pmatrix}.$$
Let $x - \mu_{\mathbf{X}} = \begin{pmatrix} x_1 - \mu_1 \\ x_2 - \mu_2 \end{pmatrix}$. From (10.20), it follows that
$$(x - \mu_{\mathbf{X}})^t (\Sigma_{\mathbf{X}})^{-1} (x - \mu_{\mathbf{X}})$$
$$= \frac{\sigma_2^2 (x_1 - \mu_1)^2 - 2\sigma_1 \sigma_2 \rho (x_1 - \mu_1)(x_2 - \mu_2) + \sigma_1^2 (x_2 - \mu_2)^2}{\sigma_1^2 \sigma_2^2 (1 - \rho^2)}$$
$$= \frac{1}{1 - \rho^2} \left(\frac{(x_1 - \mu_1)^2}{\sigma_1^2} - \frac{2\rho(x_1 - \mu_1)(x_2 - \mu_2)}{\sigma_1 \sigma_2} + \frac{(x_2 - \mu_2)^2}{\sigma_2^2} \right). \tag{7.117}$$

Using (7.116) and (7.117), we obtain that the probability density function of the bivariate normal random variable given by (7.113) can be written as follows:
$$f(x_1, x_2) = \frac{1}{2\pi \sigma_1 \sigma_2 \sqrt{1 - \rho^2}} \cdot \tag{7.118}$$
$$\exp\left(-\frac{1}{2(1 - \rho^2)} \left(\frac{(x_1 - \mu_1)^2}{\sigma_1^2} - \frac{2\rho(x_1 - \mu_1)(x_2 - \mu_2)}{\sigma_1 \sigma_2} + \frac{(x_2 - \mu_2)^2}{\sigma_2^2} \right) \right)$$

7.6. MULTIVARIATE NORMAL RANDOM VARIABLES

Lemma 7.8. *If every two components of a nondegenerate multivariate normal random variable are uncorrelated, then all the components of the multivariate normal random variable are independent.*

In other words, if $\mathbf{X} = (X_i)_{i=1:n}$ is a multivariate normal random variable and if $\mathrm{cov}(X_j, X_k) = 0$ for all $1 \leq j \neq k \leq n$, then $X_1, X_2, \ldots, X_n$ are independent normal random variables.

Proof. Since $\Sigma_{\mathbf{X}}(X_j, X_k) = \mathrm{cov}(X_j, X_k) = 0$ for all $1 \leq j \neq k \leq n$, it follows that $\Sigma_{\mathbf{X}}$ is a diagonal matrix with $\Sigma_{\mathbf{X}}(i,i) = \mathrm{var}(X_i) = \sigma_i^2$ for all $i = 1 : n$. Thus, $\Sigma_{\mathbf{X}} = \mathrm{diag}\left(\sigma_i^2\right)_{i=1:n}$ and $\Sigma_{\mathbf{X}}^{-1} = \mathrm{diag}\left(\frac{1}{\sigma_i^2}\right)_{i=1:n}$; see (1.94). From (10.25), we obtain that

$$(x - \mu_{\mathbf{X}})^t (\Sigma_{\mathbf{X}})^{-1} (x - \mu_{\mathbf{X}}) = \sum_{i=1}^n \frac{1}{\sigma_i^2}(x_i - \mu_i)^2. \tag{7.119}$$

Also, from (10.1), we find that

$$\det(\Sigma_{\mathbf{X}}) = \prod_{i=1}^n \sigma_i^2. \tag{7.120}$$

From (7.113), and using (7.119) and (7.120), it follows that the probability density function of the nondegenerate multivariate normal variable $\mathbf{X}$ is

$$\begin{aligned} f(x) &= \frac{1}{(2\pi)^{n/2} \sqrt{\prod_{i=1}^n \sigma_i^2}} \exp\left(-\frac{1}{2}\sum_{i=1}^n \frac{(x_i - \mu_i)^2}{\sigma_i^2}\right) \\ &= \prod_{i=1}^n \frac{1}{\sqrt{2\pi\sigma_i^2}} \exp\left(-\frac{(x_i - \mu_i)^2}{2\sigma_i^2}\right) \\ &= \prod_{i=1}^n f_i(x_i), \end{aligned}$$

where

$$f_i(x_i) = \frac{1}{\sqrt{2\pi\sigma_i^2}} \exp\left(-\frac{(x_i - \mu_i)^2}{2\sigma_i^2}\right). \tag{7.121}$$

Since $f(x)$ can be written as a product of functions of the underlying variables $x_1, x_2, \ldots, x_n$, we conclude that the random variables $X_1, X_2, \ldots, X_n$ are independent. Also, since the function f_i given by (7.121) is the probability density function of a normal variable with mean μ_i and variance σ_i^2, see (7.110), it follows that X_i is a normal random variable, i.e., $X_i \sim N(\mu_i, \sigma_i^2)$, for all $i = 1 : n$. $\square$

Theorem 7.7. *A random variable $\mathbf{X} = (X_i)_{i=1:n}$ is a multivariate normal random variable if and only if any linear combination of the components $X_1, X_2, \ldots, X_n$ of $\mathbf{X}$ is a normal random variable, i.e., if and only if $\sum_{i=1}^n c_i X_i$ is normal for any $c_i \in \mathbb{R}$, $i = 1 : n$.*

This result is very important for practical applications, e.g., for modeling portfolio returns, and can be regarded as an alternative definition for multivariate normal variables. Its proof is beyond our purpose here and can be found, e.g., in [24].

Theorem 7.8. Let $\mathbf{X} \sim N(\mu_\mathbf{X}, \Sigma_\mathbf{X})$ be an n–dimensional multivariate normal random variable. Let $\mathbf{Y}$ be the multivariate random variable given by

$$\mathbf{Y} = b + M\mathbf{X}, \tag{7.122}$$

where M is an $m \times n$ matrix and b is an $m \times 1$ column vector. Then, $\mathbf{Y}$ is an m-dimensional multivariate normal variable with mean $b + M\mu_\mathbf{X}$ and covariance matrix $M\Sigma_\mathbf{X} M^t$, i.e.,

$$\mathbf{Y} \sim N(b + M\mu_\mathbf{X}, M\Sigma_\mathbf{X} M^t). \tag{7.123}$$

Proof. Recall from (7.84) that if $\mathbf{Y} = b + M\mathbf{X}$, then

$$\mu_\mathbf{Y} = b + M\mu_\mathbf{X} \quad \text{and} \quad \Sigma_\mathbf{Y} = M\Sigma_\mathbf{X} M^t.$$

Thus, in order to establish (7.123), it is enough to show that $\mathbf{Y}$ is multivariate normal. We do so by showing that any linear combination of the components $Y_1, Y_2, \ldots, Y_m$ of $\mathbf{Y}$ is a normal random variable; see Theorem 7.7.

Let $\sum_{j=1}^{m} c_j Y_j$ be a linear combination of $Y_1, Y_2, \ldots, Y_m$, where $c_j, j = 1 : m$, are arbitrary constants. Let $C = (c_j)_{j=1:m}$ be the corresponding $m \times 1$ column vector. From (1.6), we find that

$$\sum_{j=1}^{m} c_j Y_j = C^t \mathbf{Y}, \tag{7.124}$$

and therefore, from (7.122) and (7.124), we obtain that

$$\begin{aligned}
\sum_{j=1}^{m} c_j Y_j &= C^t \mathbf{Y} = C^t(b + M\mathbf{X}) = C^t b + C^t M \mathbf{X} \\
&= C^t b + (M^t C)^t \mathbf{X} \\
&= \widetilde{c} + \widetilde{C}^t \mathbf{X} \\
&= \widetilde{c} + \sum_{i=1}^{n} \widetilde{c}_i X_i,
\end{aligned} \tag{7.125}$$

where $\widetilde{c} = C^t b$ and $\widetilde{C} = M^t C = (\widetilde{c}_i)_{i=1:n}$.

Since $\mathbf{X}$ is a multivariate normal random variable, any linear combination of $X_1, X_2, \ldots, X_n$ is a normal random variable; cf. Theorem 7.7. Thus, from (7.125), it follows that any linear combination of $Y_1, Y_2, \ldots, Y_n$ is also a normal random variable, and we conclude, using Theorem 7.7, that $\mathbf{Y}$ is a multivariate normal random variable. □

Lemma 7.9. Let $\mathbf{Z} \sim N(\mathbf{0}, I)$ be an n–dimensional multivariate standard normal variable, and let Q be an $n \times n$ orthogonal matrix. Then, $Q\mathbf{Z}$ is also an n–dimensional multivariate standard normal variable, i.e., $Q\mathbf{Z} \sim N(\mathbf{0}, I)$.

Proof. Note that, if $\mathbf{Z} \sim N(0, I)$, then $\mu_\mathbf{Z} = 0$ and $\Sigma_\mathbf{Z} = I$. From (7.123), it follows that

$$Q\mathbf{Z} \sim N(\mathbf{0}, Q\Sigma_\mathbf{Z} Q^t) = N(\mathbf{0}, QQ^t) = N(\mathbf{0}, I),$$

since $QQ^t = I$ for any orthogonal matrix Q; cf. (10.14). □

7.7 Multivariate random variables formulation for covariance and correlation matrices

The formulas from section 7.1 connecting the covariance and correlation matrix of random variables, as well as the Linear Transformation Property from section 7.3, can be established in an elegant way by using multivariate random variables.

Let $X_1, X_2, \ldots, X_n$ be random variables on the same probability space, and let $\mathbf{X}$ be the n–dimensional multivariate random variable

$$\mathbf{X} = \begin{pmatrix} X_1 \\ X_2 \\ \vdots \\ X_n \end{pmatrix}. \tag{7.126}$$

The expected value $\mu_\mathbf{X}$ of $\mathbf{X}$ is

$$\mu_\mathbf{X} = E[\mathbf{X}] = \begin{pmatrix} E[X_1] \\ E[X_2] \\ \vdots \\ E[X_n] \end{pmatrix} = \begin{pmatrix} \mu_1 \\ \mu_2 \\ \vdots \\ \mu_n \end{pmatrix},$$

where $\mu_i = E[X_i]$ for all $i = 1 : n$.

Similarly, if $\mathbf{X} = (X_{j,k})_{1 \leq j \leq m, 1 \leq k \leq n}$ is a multivariate random variable taking values in $\mathbb{R}^{m \times n}$, where $X_{j,k}$ are univariate random variables on the same probability space, for all $1 \leq j \leq m$, $1 \leq k \leq n$, then $E[\mathbf{X}] = (E[X_{j,k}])_{1 \leq j \leq m, 1 \leq k \leq n}$.

The general result from Lemma 7.10 follows from the linearity of expected values of random variables and will be used repeatedly:

Lemma 7.10. *Let $\mathbf{X}$ be an $m \times n$ multivariate random variable. Let A and B be matrices of sizes $p \times m$ and $n \times q$, respectively, with constant real entries. Then,*

$$E[A\mathbf{X}B] = A\, E[\mathbf{X}]\, B. \tag{7.127}$$

The result below is comprised of particular cases of (7.127) which will be used subsequently.

Lemma 7.11. *Let $\mathbf{X}$ be an n–dimensional multivariate random variable. Let M be an $m \times n$ matrix with constant entries and let C be an $n \times 1$ column vector with constant entries. Then,*[6]

$$E[M\mathbf{X}] = M E[\mathbf{X}]; \tag{7.128}$$
$$E[C^t \mathbf{X}] = C^t E[\mathbf{X}]; \tag{7.129}$$
$$E[\mathbf{X} C^t] = E[\mathbf{X}] C^t. \tag{7.130}$$

The covariance matrix of the random variables $X_1, X_2, \ldots, X_n$ can be expressed compactly using the multivariate random variable $\mathbf{X}$ given by (7.126) as follows:

Lemma 7.12. *Let Σ_X be the covariance matrix of the random variables $X_1, X_2, \ldots, X_n$. Then,*

$$\Sigma_X = E\left[(\mathbf{X} - E[\mathbf{X}])(\mathbf{X} - E[\mathbf{X}])^t\right], \tag{7.131}$$

where $\mathbf{X} = (X_i)_{i=1:n}$ is the corresponding multivariate random variable.

---
[6] In formula (7.130), $\mathbf{X}C^t$ is an $n \times n$ matrix since $\mathbf{X}$ is an $n \times 1$ column vector and C^t is an $1 \times n$ row vector; cf. (1.6).

Proof. Note that $\mathbf{X} - E[\mathbf{X}]$ is an $n \times 1$ column vector and $(\mathbf{X} - E[\mathbf{X}])^t$ is an $1 \times n$ row vector. Then, from (1.6), it follows that $(\mathbf{X} - E[\mathbf{X}])(\mathbf{X} - E[\mathbf{X}])^t$ is the $n \times n$ matrix whose (j,k) entry is $(X_j - \mu_j)(X_k - \mu_k)$, for all $1 \leq j, k \leq n$. Thus, the (j,k)-th entry of the matrix $E\left[(\mathbf{X} - E[\mathbf{X}])(\mathbf{X} - E[\mathbf{X}])^t\right]$ is

$$E[(X_j - \mu_j)(X_k - \mu_k)] = \text{cov}(X_j, X_k), \tag{7.132}$$

which is the same as the (j,k)-th entry of the covariance matrix $\Sigma_{\mathbf{X}}$; see Definition 7.1.

We conclude that $\Sigma_{\mathbf{X}} = E\left[(\mathbf{X} - E[\mathbf{X}])(\mathbf{X} - E[\mathbf{X}])^t\right]$. □

The formulas for the variance and the covariance of linear combinations of random variables from Lemma 7.3 can be proved by using multivariate random variable and the formula (7.131) for the covariance matrix as seen below:

Lemma 7.13. *(Same as Lemma 7.3.) Let $X_1, X_2, \ldots, X_n$ be random variables on the same probability space. Then,*

$$\text{cov}\left(\sum_{i=1}^n c_i^{(1)} X_i, \sum_{i=1}^n c_i^{(2)} X_i\right) = (C^{(1)})^t \Sigma_{\mathbf{X}} C^{(2)} = (C^{(2)})^t \Sigma_{\mathbf{X}} C^{(1)}, \tag{7.133}$$

where $C^{(1)} = (c_i^{(1)})_{i=1:n}$ and $C^{(2)} = (c_i^{(2)})_{i=1:n}$ are two column vectors of size n with real entries, and $\Sigma_{\mathbf{X}}$ is the covariance matrix of the random variables $X_1, X_2, \ldots, X_n$.

Proof. Let $\mathbf{X} = (X_i)_{i=1:n}$ be an $n \times 1$ multivariate random variable. Note that

$$\sum_{i=1}^n c_i^{(1)} X_i = (C^{(1)})^t \mathbf{X} \quad \text{and} \quad \sum_{i=1}^n c_i^{(2)} X_i = (C^{(2)})^t \mathbf{X}.$$

Then, using (7.132), we obtain that

$$\begin{aligned}
&\text{cov}\left(\sum_{i=1}^n c_i^{(1)} X_i, \sum_{i=1}^n c_i^{(2)} X_i\right) \\
&= \text{cov}\left((C^{(1)})^t \mathbf{X}, (C^{(2)})^t \mathbf{X}\right) \\
&= E\left[\left((C^{(1)})^t \mathbf{X} - E\left[(C^{(1)})^t \mathbf{X}\right]\right)\left((C^{(2)})^t \mathbf{X} - E\left[(C^{(2)})^t \mathbf{X}\right]\right)^t\right].
\end{aligned} \tag{7.134}$$

Using (7.129), we find that

$$(C^{(1)})^t \mathbf{X} - E\left[(C^{(1)})^t \mathbf{X}\right] = (C^{(1)})^t \mathbf{X} - (C^{(1)})^t E[\mathbf{X}] = (C^{(1)})^t (\mathbf{X} - E[\mathbf{X}]); \tag{7.135}$$

$$\left((C^{(2)})^t \mathbf{X} - E\left[(C^{(2)})^t \mathbf{X}\right]\right)^t = \left((C^{(2)})^t (\mathbf{X} - E[\mathbf{X}])\right)^t = (\mathbf{X} - E[\mathbf{X}])^t C^{(2)}. \tag{7.136}$$

From (7.134–7.136) and using (7.127), we conclude that

$$\begin{aligned}
\text{cov}\left(\sum_{i=1}^n c_i^{(1)} X_i, \sum_{i=1}^n c_i^{(2)} X_i\right) &= E\left[(C^{(1)})^t (\mathbf{X} - E[\mathbf{X}])(\mathbf{X} - E[\mathbf{X}])^t C^{(2)}\right] \\
&= (C^{(1)})^t E\left[(\mathbf{X} - E[\mathbf{X}])(\mathbf{X} - E[\mathbf{X}])^t\right] C^{(2)} \\
&= (C^{(1)})^t \Sigma_{\mathbf{X}} C^{(2)},
\end{aligned}$$

7.7. REFERENCES

since $\Sigma_\mathbf{X} = E\left[(\mathbf{X} - E[\mathbf{X}])(\mathbf{X} - E[\mathbf{X}])^t\right]$; see (7.131).

Since $(C^{(1)})^t \Sigma_\mathbf{X} C^{(2)}$ is a number, it follows that

$$(C^{(1)})^t \Sigma_\mathbf{X} C^{(2)} = \left((C^{(1)})^t \Sigma_\mathbf{X} C^{(2)}\right)^t;$$

see also (7.28). Thus,

$$(C^{(1)})^t \Sigma_\mathbf{X} C^{(2)} = (C^{(2)})^t \Sigma_\mathbf{X}^t ((C^{(1)})^t)^t = (C^{(2)})^t \Sigma_\mathbf{X} C^{(1)},$$

since $\Sigma_\mathbf{X}$ is a symmetric matrix and therefore $\Sigma_\mathbf{X}^t = \Sigma_\mathbf{X}$. $\square$

Theorem 7.9. *(Linear Transformation Property; see also Theorem 7.3.)* Let $\mathbf{X}$ be an $n \times 1$ multivariate random variable, and let M be an $m \times n$ matrix with constant entries. If $\mathbf{Y}$ is the $m \times 1$ multivariate random variable given by

$$\mathbf{Y} = M\mathbf{X}, \tag{7.137}$$

then

$$\Sigma_\mathbf{Y} = M \Sigma_\mathbf{X} M^t, \tag{7.138}$$

where $\Sigma_\mathbf{X}$ and $\Sigma_\mathbf{Y}$ are the covariance matrices of $\mathbf{X}$ and of $\mathbf{Y}$, respectively.

Proof. From (7.131) and (7.137), it follows that

$$\begin{aligned}\Sigma_\mathbf{Y} &= E\left[(\mathbf{Y} - E[\mathbf{Y}])(\mathbf{Y} - E[\mathbf{Y}])^t\right] \\ &= E\left[(M\mathbf{X} - E[M\mathbf{X}])(M\mathbf{X} - E[M\mathbf{X}])^t\right]. \end{aligned} \tag{7.139}$$

From (7.128), we find that

$$M\mathbf{X} - E[M\mathbf{X}] = M\mathbf{X} - ME[\mathbf{X}] = M(\mathbf{X} - E[\mathbf{X}]), \tag{7.140}$$

and therefore

$$(M\mathbf{X} - E[M\mathbf{X}])^t = (M(\mathbf{X} - E[\mathbf{X}]))^t = (\mathbf{X} - E[\mathbf{X}])^t M^t. \tag{7.141}$$

From (7.139–7.141), and using (7.127), we obtain that

$$\begin{aligned}\Sigma_\mathbf{Y} &= E\left[M(\mathbf{X} - E[\mathbf{X}])(\mathbf{X} - E[\mathbf{X}])^t M^t\right] \\ &= M\, E\left[(\mathbf{X} - E[\mathbf{X}])(\mathbf{X} - E[\mathbf{X}])^t\right]\, M^t \\ &= M \Sigma_\mathbf{X} M^t,\end{aligned}$$

since $\Sigma_\mathbf{X} = E\left[(\mathbf{X} - E[\mathbf{X}])(\mathbf{X} - E[\mathbf{X}])^t\right]$; cf. (7.131). $\square$

7.8 References

Details on the Linear Transformation Property and its applications to Monte Carlo methods can be found in Andersen and Piterbarg [3].

An important practical issue is that, for large data sets, the covariance matrix of time series data may be very close to singular, or some eigenvalues may be very small and negative; see Lai and Xing [25] for practical ways to overcome this issue.

Three different ways for finding all the values of a parameter ρ such that a matrix is a correlation matrix can be found in Stefanica, Radoičić, and Wang [39].

For a comprehensive presentation of multivariate normal random variables, see Jacod and Protter [24].

7.9 Exercises

1. Let X_1 and X_2 be random variables with correlation matrix $\begin{pmatrix} 1 & \rho \\ \rho & 1 \end{pmatrix}$, where $-1 \leq \rho \leq 1$. Let $Y_1 = X_1$ and $Y_2 = -X_2$. Show that the correlation matrix of Y_1 and Y_2 is $\begin{pmatrix} 1 & -\rho \\ -\rho & 1 \end{pmatrix}$.

2. What is the correlation matrix of three random variables whose covariance matrix is $\begin{pmatrix} 1 & 0.36 & -1.44 \\ 0.36 & 4 & 0.80 \\ -1.44 & 0.80 & 9 \end{pmatrix}$?

3. Find all the values of ρ such that the matrix $\begin{pmatrix} 1 & 0.6 & -0.3 \\ 0.6 & 1 & \rho \\ -0.3 & \rho & 1 \end{pmatrix}$ is a correlation matrix.

4. Let X_1, X_2, X_3 be random variables such that
$$\mathrm{corr}(X_1, X_3) = 0.3; \quad \mathrm{corr}(X_2, X_3) = 0.1.$$
Find upper and lower bounds for $\rho = \mathrm{corr}(X_1, X_2)$.

5. Consider three random variables with pairwise correlation ρ, i.e., such that the correlation between any two of the random variables is ρ. What is the smallest possible value for ρ?

6. Let X_1, X_2, X_3, X_4 be random variables such that
$$\mathrm{corr}(X_1, X_3) = 0.3; \quad \mathrm{corr}(X_1, X_4) = 0.2; \quad \mathrm{corr}(X_2, X_3) = 0.1;$$
$$\mathrm{corr}(X_2, X_4) = -0.1; \quad \mathrm{corr}(X_3, X_4) = -0.2.$$
Find upper and lower bounds for $\rho = \mathrm{corr}(X_1, X_2)$.

7. Assume that all the entries of an $n \times n$ correlation matrix which are not on the main diagonal are equal to q. Find upper and lower bounds on the possible values of q.

8. Show that the matrix $\begin{pmatrix} 1 & 0.1 & 0.2 \\ 0.1 & 1 & -0.3 \\ 0.2 & -0.3 & 1 \end{pmatrix}$ is a correlation matrix, and find its Cholesky factor.

9. Show that it is not possible to find three random variables on the same probability space with correlations 0.8, 0.7, and -0.5.

10. Consider three random variables given by the following time series data at five data points:

$$\begin{pmatrix} 0.25 & -0.50 & 1.50 \\ 1 & -1 & 1.25 \\ -0.50 & -0.25 & 2 \\ 0 & 0.50 & 0.75 \\ -1 & 0.75 & 1.50 \end{pmatrix}.$$

(i) Show that the time series vectors $\begin{pmatrix} 0.25 \\ 1 \\ -0.50 \\ 0 \\ -1 \end{pmatrix}, \begin{pmatrix} -0.50 \\ -1 \\ -0.25 \\ 0.50 \\ 0.75 \end{pmatrix}, \begin{pmatrix} 1.50 \\ 1.25 \\ 2 \\ 0.75 \\ 1.50 \end{pmatrix}$ of the three random variables are linearly independent.

(ii) Show that the vectors $\begin{pmatrix} 0.25 \\ 1 \\ -0.50 \\ 0 \\ -1 \end{pmatrix}, \begin{pmatrix} -0.50 \\ -1 \\ -0.25 \\ 0.50 \\ 0.75 \end{pmatrix}, \begin{pmatrix} 1.50 \\ 1.25 \\ 2 \\ 0.75 \\ 1.50 \end{pmatrix}, \begin{pmatrix} 1 \\ 1 \\ 1 \\ 1 \\ 1 \end{pmatrix}$ are not linearly independent.

(iii) Compute the sample covariance matrix of the three random variables and show that it is singular.

Note: This is an example of random variables with linearly independent time series data whose sample covariance matrix is singular. Recall that the necessary and sufficient condition for the sample covariance matrix to be nonsingular is that the time series data column vectors *and* the column vector with all entries equal to 1 are linearly independent.

11. The file *data-DJ30-july2011-june2013.xlsx* from fepress.org/nla-primer contains the end of week and end of month closing prices for eight financial and technology Dow Jones components (AXP; BAC; JPM; CSCO; HPQ; IBM; INTC; MSFT) between July 1, 2011, and June 30, 2013.

(i) Compute the weekly and monthly log returns of these eight stocks. Recall that the log return between t_1 and t_2 of an asset with price $S(t)$ is $\ln\left(\frac{S(t_2)}{S(t_1)}\right)$.

(ii) Compute the sample covariance matrix and the sample correlation matrix of the weekly and monthly log returns of the stocks, and compare them with the sample covariance and correlation matrices of the weekly and monthly percentage returns computed in an example in this chapter.

12. Let $X_1, X_2, \ldots, X_n$ be nonconstant random variables, and let $Y_1, Y_2, \ldots, Y_n$ be the random variables given by $Y_i = d_i X_i$, $i = 1 : n$, where $d_i \neq 0$, $i = 1 : n$, are constants. Denote by $\Sigma_{\mathbf{X}}, \Omega_{\mathbf{X}}$ and $\Sigma_{\mathbf{Y}}, \Omega_{\mathbf{Y}}$ the covariance and correlation matrices of $X_1, X_2, \ldots, X_n$ and of $Y_1, Y_2, \ldots, Y_n$, respectively, and let $D = \text{diag}(d_i)_{i=1:n}$.

(i) Show that $\Sigma_{\mathbf{Y}} = D \Sigma_{\mathbf{X}} D$.

(ii) If $d_i > 0$ for all $i = 1 : n$, show that $\Omega_Y = \Omega_X$.

13. Let
$$\begin{pmatrix} X_1 \\ X_2 \\ X_3 \end{pmatrix} \sim N\left(\begin{pmatrix} 1 \\ -2 \\ 1 \end{pmatrix}, \begin{pmatrix} 1 & -1 & 0 \\ -1 & 3 & -2 \\ 0 & -2 & 3 \end{pmatrix}\right)$$
be a 3-dimensional multivariate normal random variable.
Find the probability that $X_1 + 2X_2 + 2X_3$ is positive.

14. Let
$$\begin{pmatrix} X_1 \\ X_2 \\ X_3 \end{pmatrix} \sim N\left(\begin{pmatrix} 2 \\ -1 \\ -2 \end{pmatrix}, \begin{pmatrix} 2 & 0 & 0.5 \\ 0 & 1 & -0.25 \\ 0.5 & -0.25 & 1 \end{pmatrix}\right)$$
be a 3-dimensional multivariate normal random variable, and let
$$Y_1 = X_1; \quad Y_2 = X_1 + X_2; \quad Y_3 = X_1 + X_2 + X_3.$$

(i) What are the expected value vector and the covariance matrix of $\begin{pmatrix} Y_1 \\ Y_2 \\ Y_3 \end{pmatrix}$?

(ii) Find the probability that $Y_1 + Y_2 + Y_3$ is negative.

15. Let
$$\begin{pmatrix} X_1 \\ X_2 \\ X_3 \end{pmatrix} \sim N\left(\begin{pmatrix} 1 \\ 0 \\ -2 \end{pmatrix}, \begin{pmatrix} 2 & 1 & 0.5 \\ 1 & 3 & -1.5 \\ 0.5 & -1.5 & 4 \end{pmatrix}\right)$$
be a 3-dimensional multivariate normal random variable.

(i) What are the expected value and the covariance matrix of $\begin{pmatrix} X_1 - X_2 \\ X_2 - X_3 \\ X_3 - X_1 \end{pmatrix}$?

(ii) What is the probability density function of $\begin{pmatrix} X_1 - X_2 \\ X_2 - X_3 \\ X_3 - X_1 \end{pmatrix}$?

16. Let Z_1, Z_2, Z_3 be three independent standard normal variables, and let X_1, X_2, X_3 and Y_1, Y_2, Y_3 be normal random variables given by

$$X_1 = Z_3; \quad X_2 = Z_1 + 2Z_2 - 2Z_3; \quad X_3 = -3Z_1 + Z_2 + Z_3;$$

$$Y_1 = Z_1; \quad Y_2 = -2Z_1 + \sqrt{5}Z_2; \quad Y_3 = Z_1 - \frac{1}{\sqrt{5}}Z_2 + \sqrt{9.8}Z_3.$$

Show that the covariance matrix of X_1, X_2, X_3 and the covariance matrix of Y_1, Y_2, Y_3 are equal.

CHAPTER 7. COVARIANCE MATRICES. MULTIVARIATE NORMALS.

17. Given Z_1 and Z_2 independent standard normal variables, find two normal random variables X_1 and X_2 with covariance matrix $\begin{pmatrix} 4 & -1 \\ -1 & 9 \end{pmatrix}$.

18. Given Z_1 and Z_2 independent standard normal variables, find two normal random variables X_1 and X_2 with correlation matrix $\begin{pmatrix} 1 & 0.25 \\ 0.25 & 1 \end{pmatrix}$.

19. Given Z_1, Z_2, Z_3 independent standard normal variables, find three normal random variables X_1, X_2, X_3 with covariance matrix $\begin{pmatrix} 1 & 1 & 0.5 \\ 1 & 4 & -2 \\ 0.5 & -2 & 9 \end{pmatrix}$.

20. Given Z_1, Z_2, Z_3 independent standard normal variables, find three normal random variables X_1, X_2, X_3 with correlation matrix $\begin{pmatrix} 1 & 0.3 & 0.4 \\ 0.3 & 1 & 0.5 \\ 0.4 & 0.5 & 1 \end{pmatrix}$.

Chapter 8

Ordinary least squares (OLS). Linear regression.

Ordinary least squares (OLS).

Least squares for implied volatility computation.

Linear regression: ordinary least squares for time series data.

Ordinary least squares for random variables.

The intuition behind ordinary least squares for time series data.

8.1 Ordinary least squares

Let A be an $m \times n$ matrix with more rows than columns, i.e., with $m > n$, and assume that the column vectors of the matrix A are linearly independent. Let y be a column vector of size m.

A solution $x \in \mathbb{R}^n$ to the linear system $Ax = y$ exists if and only if the vector y is a linear combination of the column vectors of A, which is rarely the case in practice.

The ordinary least squares method (OLS) provides an alternative to solving $Ax = y$ exactly, and requires finding a vector $x \in \mathbb{R}^n$ with smallest approximation error $y - Ax$, i.e., such that $||y - Ax||$ is minimal, where $||\cdot||$ denotes the Euclidean norm; see (5.8). This can be stated formally as follows:

$$\text{Given } y \in \mathbb{R}^m, \text{ find } x \in \mathbb{R}^n \text{ such that } ||y - Ax|| \text{ is minimal.} \qquad (8.1)$$

Note that we will also refer to (8.1) as solving the least squares problem

$$y \approx Ax. \qquad (8.2)$$

Problem (8.1) is equivalent to finding the global minimum point of the function $f: \mathbb{R}^n \to \mathbb{R}$ given by

$$f(x) = ||y - Ax||^2. \qquad (8.3)$$

Recall from (5.8) that $||w||^2 = (w, w) = w^t w$ for any vector w. Then,

$$\begin{aligned} ||y - Ax||^2 &= (y - Ax)^t(y - Ax) = (y^t - x^t A^t)(y - Ax) \\ &= y^t y - x^t A^t y - y^t A x + x^t A^t A x. \end{aligned} \qquad (8.4)$$

Note that
$$y^t A x = x^t A^t y \qquad (8.5)$$
since $(u, v) = (v, u)$ for any u and v and therefore
$$y^t A x = (Ax, y) = (y, Ax) = (Ax)^t y = x^t A^t y.$$

From (8.4) and (8.5), it follows that
$$\|y - Ax\|^2 = y^t y - 2x^t A^t y + x^t A^t A x. \qquad (8.6)$$

From (8.3) and (8.6), and since $y^t y = \|y\|^2$, we conclude that
$$f(x) = \|y\|^2 - 2x^t A^t y + x^t A^t A x. \qquad (8.7)$$

Recall that any minimum point x_0 of $f(x)$ must be a critical point of $f(x)$, i.e., a solution to $Df(x_0) = 0$. From (8.7), it follows that the gradient $Df(x)$ of $f(x)$ is
$$Df(x) = -2D(x^t A^t y) + D(x^t A^t A x), \qquad (8.8)$$
since $\|y\|^2$ is not a function of x and therefore $D(\|y\|^2) = 0$.

Recall from (10.44) and (10.47) the following gradient formulas:
$$D(x^t C) = C^t \qquad (8.9)$$
$$D(x^t M x) = 2(Mx)^t, \qquad (8.10)$$
for any constant column vector C and for any symmetric matrix M. Since $A^t A$ is a symmetric matrix, see Lemma 5.2, we obtain from (8.9) and (8.10) that
$$D(x^t A^t y) = (A^t y)^t; \qquad (8.11)$$
$$D(x^t A^t A x) = 2(A^t A x)^t. \qquad (8.12)$$

From (8.8), (8.11), and (8.12), it follows that
$$Df(x) = -2(A^t y)^t + 2(A^t A x)^t$$
$$= 2(A^t A x - A^t y)^t. \qquad (8.13)$$

From (8.13), we find that $Df(x_0) = 0$ if and only if
$$A^t A x_0 = A^t y. \qquad (8.14)$$

Since the columns of A are linearly independent, it follows from Lemma 5.2 that the matrix $A^t A$ is symmetric positive definite. Then, $A^t A$ is a nonsingular matrix, see Lemma 5.3, and therefore the unique solution of (8.14) is
$$x_0 = (A^t A)^{-1} A^t y. \qquad (8.15)$$

To classify the critical point x_0 given by (8.15), we compute the Hessian of $f(x)$. From (10.46) and (10.48), we obtain that $D^2(x^t A^t y) = 0$ and $D^2(x^t A^t A x) = 2(A^t A)$. Then, from (8.7), it follows that $D^2 f(x) = 2(A^t A)$, and therefore
$$D^2 f(x_0) = 2(A^t A).$$

8.1. LEAST SQUARES FOR IMPLIED VOLATILITY COMPUTATION

Since the matrix $A^t A$ is symmetric positive definite, we obtain that the Hessian $D^2 f(x_0)$ is symmetric positive definite, and therefore x_0 is a minimum point for the function $f(x)$. We conclude that the point x_0 is a global minimum point for $f(x)$, since x_0 is the only critical point of $f(x)$.

Thus, the solution to the least squares problem (8.1) is given by (8.15), i.e.,

$$x = (A^t A)^{-1} A^t y. \tag{8.16}$$

Note that the numerical value of x from (8.16) is computed by solving the linear system $(A^t A)x = A^t y$ using the Cholesky solver from Table 6.2, since $A^t A$ is a symmetric positive definite matrix; see the pseudocode from Table 8.1 for details.

Table 8.1: Least squares implementation

Function Call:
$x = $ least_squares(A,y)

Input:
$A = m \times n$ matrix; $m > n$
$y = $ column vector of size m

Output:
$x = $ solution to $\min \|y - Ax\|$

$x = $ linear_solve_cholesky$(A^t A, A^t y)$;

8.1.1 Least squares for implied volatility computation

Consider a European call or put option[1] on an underlying asset whose price is assumed to follow a lognormal model. The implied volatility of the option is the unique value of the volatility parameter σ from the lognormal model that makes the Black–Scholes value of the option equal to the market price of the option.

More precisely, if C_m and P_m are the market prices of a European call option and of a European put option, respectively, with strike K and maturity T on an underlying asset with spot price S paying dividends continuously at the rate q, and assuming that interest rates are constant and equal to r, the implied volatility σ_{imp} corresponding to the price C_m is, by definition, the solution $\sigma = \sigma_{imp}$ to

$$C_{BS}(S, K, T, \sigma, r, q) = C_m; \tag{8.17}$$

the implied volatility σ_{imp} corresponding to price P_m is the solution $\sigma = \sigma_{imp}$ to

$$P_{BS}(S, K, T, \sigma, r, q) = P_m. \tag{8.18}$$

Here, $C_{BS}(S, K, T, \sigma, r, q)$ and $P_{BS}(S, K, T, \sigma, r, q)$ are the Black–Scholes values of a call option and of a put option given by (10.93–10.96), i.e.,

$$C_{BS}(S, K, T, \sigma, r, q) = Se^{-qT} N(d_1) - Ke^{-rT} N(d_2); \tag{8.19}$$

$$P_{BS}(S, K, T, \sigma, r, q) = Ke^{-rT} N(-d_2) - Se^{-qT} N(-d_1), \tag{8.20}$$

---
[1] See Section 10.3 for a brief overview of European options.

respectively, where $N(z)$ is the cumulative distribution of the standard normal variable, i.e.,

$$N(z) = \frac{1}{\sqrt{2\pi}} \int_{-\infty}^{z} e^{-\frac{x^2}{2}} dx,$$

and

$$d_1 = \frac{\ln\left(\frac{S}{K}\right) + \left(r - q + \frac{\sigma^2}{2}\right)T}{\sigma\sqrt{T}}; \quad d_2 = d_1 - \sigma\sqrt{T}. \tag{8.21}$$

For any plain vanilla European option, the option price C_m or P_m, the maturity T, the strike K, and the spot price S of the underlying asset are known. However, a continuous dividend yield q for the underlying asset is very rarely quoted in the markets and the interest rate r could be chosen from several different discount curves. As seen below,[2] the least squares method and Put-Call parity can be used to overcome these issues and find the implied volatility using Newton's method.

As an example of how implied volatilities are computed in practice, consider the snapshot from Table 8.2 of the mid prices[3] on March 9, 2012, of the S&P 500 options (ticker symbol SPX)[4] maturing on December 22, 2012. These options are European options and therefore we can use the Black–Scholes framework. Although not needed for this method, the corresponding spot price of the index was $1,370$.

Table 8.2: Dec 2012 SPX option prices on 3/9/2012

Call Strike	Price	Put Strike	Price
C1175	225.40	P1175	46.60
C1200	205.55	P1200	51.55
C1225	186.20	P1225	57.15
C1250	167.50	P1250	63.30
C1275	149.15	P1275	70.15
C1300	131.70	P1300	77.70
C1325	115.25	P1325	86.20
C1350	99.55	P1350	95.30
C1375	84.90	P1375	105.30
C1400	71.10	P1400	116.55
C1425	58.70	P1425	129.00
C1450	47.25	P1450	143.20
C1500	29.25	P1500	173.95
C1550	15.80	P1550	210.80
C1575	11.10	P1575	230.90
C1600	7.90	P1600	252.40

Recall from Section 10.3 that the Put–Call parity states that taking a long position in a European call option and a short position in a European put option with the same strike K and maturity T is equivalent to taking a long position in a forward contract with delivery price K and maturity T, and therefore the following

---
[2]This method was implemented in 2010 in Bloomberg terminals, providing a tenfold improvement in the accuracy of implied volatility calculations over the prior method.
[3]The mid price of an option is the average of the bid price and ask price of the option.
[4]More information on SPX options can be found on the Chicago Board Options Exchange (CBOE); see http://www.cboe.com/products/indexopts/spx_spec.aspx

8.1. LEAST SQUARES FOR IMPLIED VOLATILITY COMPUTATION

relationship between the values C and P of the call and put options must hold for no–arbitrage:
$$C - P = Se^{-qT} - Ke^{-rT}. \tag{8.22}$$

Let $F = Se^{(r-q)T}$ be the forward price of the asset at time T. Then, $Se^{-qT} = Fe^{-rT}$ and the Put–Call parity (8.22) can be written as
$$C - P = Fe^{-rT} - Ke^{-rT}. \tag{8.23}$$

Denote the discount factor by
$$disc = e^{-rT}, \tag{8.24}$$

and the present value of the forward price by
$$PVF = Fe^{-rT}. \tag{8.25}$$

Then, (8.23) is the same as
$$C - P = PVF - K \cdot disc. \tag{8.26}$$

The data from Table 8.2 provides call and put options values for 16 different strikes. From (8.26), it follows that the values of PVF and $disc$ can be obtained by solving a least squares problem $y \approx Ax$, see (8.2), with $x = \begin{pmatrix} PVF \\ disc \end{pmatrix}$ and with the following 16×2 matrix A and the following 16×1 column vector y corresponding to $C - P$ for each strike:

$$A = \begin{pmatrix} 1 & -1175 \\ 1 & -1200 \\ 1 & -1225 \\ 1 & -1250 \\ 1 & -1275 \\ 1 & -1300 \\ 1 & -1325 \\ 1 & -1350 \\ 1 & -1375 \\ 1 & -1400 \\ 1 & -1425 \\ 1 & -1450 \\ 1 & -1500 \\ 1 & -1550 \\ 1 & -1575 \\ 1 & -1600 \end{pmatrix} ; \quad y = \begin{pmatrix} 178.80 \\ 154.00 \\ 129.05 \\ 104.20 \\ 79.00 \\ 54.00 \\ 29.05 \\ 4.25 \\ -20.40 \\ -45.45 \\ -70.30 \\ -95.95 \\ -144.70 \\ -195.00 \\ -219.80 \\ -244.50 \end{pmatrix}.$$

The solution $x = (A^t A)^{-1} A^t y$ to this least squares problem, see (8.16), is computed as $x = $ least_squares(A,y) by using the routine from Table 8.1. We find that
$$x = \begin{pmatrix} PVF \\ disc \end{pmatrix} = \begin{pmatrix} 1349.54 \\ 0.9964 \end{pmatrix}. \tag{8.27}$$

In order to use the values $PVF = 1349.54$ and $disc = 0.9964$ obtained above to compute implied volatilities, we first show that the Black–Scholes formulas (8.19–8.21) can be written in terms of PVF and $disc$ without any dependence on r, q, or the spot price S; see (8.35–8.37).

Recall from (8.25) that $PVF = Fe^{-rT}$. Since $F = Se^{(r-q)T}$, it follows that

$$\begin{aligned} PVF &= Fe^{-rT} = Se^{(r-q)T} \cdot e^{-rT} \\ &= Se^{-qT}. \end{aligned} \qquad (8.28)$$

Then, using (8.24) and (8.28), the Black–Scholes formulas (8.19) and (8.20) can be written as

$$C_{BS} = PVF \cdot N(d_1) - K \cdot disc \cdot N(d_2); \qquad (8.29)$$
$$P_{BS} = K \cdot disc \cdot N(-d_2) - PVF \cdot N(-d_1). \qquad (8.30)$$

Moreover,

$$\begin{aligned} \ln\left(\frac{S}{K}\right) + (r-q)T &= \ln\left(\frac{S}{K}\right) + \ln\left(e^{(r-q)T}\right) = \ln\left(\frac{S}{K} \cdot e^{(r-q)T}\right) \quad (8.31) \\ &= \ln\left(\frac{Se^{-qT}}{K} \cdot e^{rT}\right) = \ln\left(\frac{Se^{-qT}}{Ke^{-rT}}\right) \\ &= \ln\left(\frac{PVF}{K \cdot disc}\right), \end{aligned} \qquad (8.32)$$

where for (8.31) we used the facts that $\ln(e^x) = x$ for any x and $\ln(a) + \ln(b) = \ln(ab)$ for any $a, b > 0$, and for (8.32) we used (8.28) and (8.24), i.e., $Se^{-qT} = PVF$ and $e^{-rT} = disc$.

Then, from (8.21) and (8.32), we obtain that

$$d_1 = \frac{\ln\left(\frac{S}{K}\right) + (r-q)T}{\sigma\sqrt{T}} + \frac{\frac{\sigma^2}{2}T}{\sigma\sqrt{T}} = \frac{\ln\left(\frac{PVF}{K \cdot disc}\right)}{\sigma\sqrt{T}} + \frac{\sigma\sqrt{T}}{2}; \qquad (8.33)$$

$$d_2 = d_1 - \sigma\sqrt{T} = \frac{\ln\left(\frac{PVF}{K \cdot disc}\right)}{\sigma\sqrt{T}} - \frac{\sigma\sqrt{T}}{2}. \qquad (8.34)$$

From (8.29), (8.30), (8.33), and (8.34), we conclude that the Black–Scholes option values can be written as functions of PVF, $disc$, K, T, and σ as follows:

$$C_{BS}(PVF, disc, K, T, \sigma) = PVF \cdot N(d_1) - K \cdot disc \cdot N(d_2); \qquad (8.35)$$
$$P_{BS}(PVF, disc, K, T, \sigma) = K \cdot disc \cdot N(-d_2) - PVF \cdot N(-d_1), \qquad (8.36)$$

where

$$d_1 = \frac{\ln\left(\frac{PVF}{K \cdot disc}\right)}{\sigma\sqrt{T}} + \frac{\sigma\sqrt{T}}{2}; \quad d_2 = \frac{\ln\left(\frac{PVF}{K \cdot disc}\right)}{\sigma\sqrt{T}} - \frac{\sigma\sqrt{T}}{2}. \qquad (8.37)$$

Since K and T are known and PVF and $disc$ have been computed using least squares, see (8.27), we can use Newton's method to solve either

$$C_{BS}(PVF, disc, T, \sigma) = C_m \qquad (8.38)$$

or

$$P_{BS}(PVF, disc, T, \sigma) = P_m \qquad (8.39)$$

for $\sigma = \sigma_{imp}$ for every option from Table 8.2.

8.1. LEAST SQUARES FOR IMPLIED VOLATILITY COMPUTATION

For call options, we look at (8.38) as a function of only one variable, σ. Then, finding the implied volatility for a call option requires solving the nonlinear problem

$$f_C(x) = 0, \tag{8.40}$$

using Newton's method, where $x = \sigma$ and

$$f_C(x) = PVF \cdot N(d_1(x)) - K \cdot disc \cdot N(d_2(x)) - C_m, \tag{8.41}$$

with $d_1(x)$ and $d_2(x)$ given by (8.37), i.e.,

$$d_1(x) = \frac{\ln\left(\frac{PVF}{K \cdot disc}\right)}{x\sqrt{T}} + \frac{x\sqrt{T}}{2}; \quad d_2(x) = \frac{\ln\left(\frac{PVF}{K \cdot disc}\right)}{x\sqrt{T}} - \frac{x\sqrt{T}}{2}.$$

The value of x thus computed is the implied volatility σ_{imp}.

Note that differentiating the function $f_C(x)$ with respect to x is the same as computing the vega of the call option, which is equal to

$$\text{vega}_C = Se^{-qT}\sqrt{\frac{T}{2\pi}}\exp\left(-\frac{(d_1(x))^2}{2}\right); \tag{8.42}$$

see (10.101). Then, since $Se^{-qT} = PVF$, we obtain that

$$f'_C(x) = PVF\sqrt{\frac{T}{2\pi}}\exp\left(-\frac{(d_1(x))^2}{2}\right). \tag{8.43}$$

The Newton's method recursion for solving (8.40) is

$$x_{k+1} = x_k - \frac{f_C(x_k)}{f'_C(x_k)}, \tag{8.44}$$

where the functions $f_C(x)$ and $f'_C(x)$ are given by (8.41) and (8.43), respectively.

Similarly, for put options we look at (8.39) as a function of only one variable, σ. Then, finding the implied volatility for a put option requires solving the nonlinear problem

$$f_P(x) = 0, \tag{8.45}$$

where $x = \sigma$ and

$$f_P(x) = K \cdot disc \cdot N(-d_2(x)) - PVF \cdot N(-d_1(x)) - P_m, \tag{8.46}$$

with $d_1(x)$ and $d_2(x)$ given by (8.37), i.e.,

$$d_1(x) = \frac{\ln\left(\frac{PVF}{K \cdot disc}\right)}{x\sqrt{T}} + \frac{x\sqrt{T}}{2}; \quad d_2(x) = \frac{\ln\left(\frac{PVF}{K \cdot disc}\right)}{x\sqrt{T}} - \frac{x\sqrt{T}}{2}.$$

Differentiating the function $f_P(x)$ with respect to x is the same as computing the vega of the put option, which is equal to

$$\text{vega}_P = Se^{-qT}\sqrt{\frac{T}{2\pi}}\exp\left(-\frac{(d_1(x))^2}{2}\right); \tag{8.47}$$

see (10.102).

Then, since $Se^{-qT} = PVF$, we obtain that

$$f'_P(x) = PVF\sqrt{\frac{T}{2\pi}} \exp\left(-\frac{(d_1(x))^2}{2}\right). \qquad (8.48)$$

Note that $f'_P(x) = f'_C(x)$, since $\text{vega}_P = \text{vega}_C$.

The Newton's method recursion for solving (8.45) is

$$x_{k+1} = x_k - \frac{f_P(x_k)}{f'_P(x_k)}, \qquad (8.49)$$

where the functions $f_P(x)$ and $f'_P(x)$ are given by (8.46) and (8.48), respectively.

A good initial guess for Newton's method is 25% volatility, i.e., $x_0 = 0.25$, and the algorithm is stopped when two consecutive approximations in Newton's method are within 10^{-6} of each other; see the pseudocode from Table 8.3 for finding the implied volatility for both call and put options, i.e., for solving either (8.44) or (8.49).

Table 8.3: Pseudocode for computing implied volatility

Input:
V_m = option price
// $V_m = C_m$ for call implied vol; $V_m = P_m$ for put implied vol
K = strike price of the option
T = maturity of the option
PVF = present value of the forward price of the underlying asset
$disc$ = discount factor corresponding to time T
tol = tolerance for Newton's method convergence
$f_{BS}(x)$ = Black–Scholes option value; x = volatility
// $f_{BS}(x) = f_C(x)$ for calls; $f_{BS}(x) = f_P(x)$ for puts
// $f'_{BS}(x) = f'_C(x) = f'_P(x)$

Output:
x_{new} = implied volatility

$x_0 = 0.25$;   // initial guess: 25% volatility
$x_{new} = x_0$; $x_{old} = x_0 - 1$; $tol = 10^{-6}$
while ($|x_{new} - x_{old}| > tol$)
   $x_{old} = x_{new}$
   $x_{new} = x_{old} - \frac{f_{BS}(x_{old}) - V_m}{f'_{BS}(x_{old})}$
end

For the options from Table 8.2, note that the options maturity is $T = \frac{199}{252}$, i.e., the ratio of 199, the number of trading days between March 9, 2012 and December 22, 2012, and 252, the total number of trading days in a year. Using the values $PVF = 1349.54$ and $disc = 0.9964$ computed using least squares and the Newton's method from Table 8.3, we obtain the implied volatilities from Table 8.4.

A consequence of the Put–Call parity is that the theoretical values of implied volatilities of calls and puts with the same strike are equal. Note that, indeed, the implied volatilities from Table 8.4 corresponding to calls and puts with the same strike are nearly identical.

8.1. LINEAR REGRESSION FOR TIME SERIES DATA

Table 8.4: Implied volatiles for SPX options

Strike	Implied Vol Call	Implied Vol Put	Strike	Implied Vol Call	Implied Vol Put
1175	25.73%	25.72%	1375	19.69%	19.66%
1200	24.96%	24.92%	1400	18.94%	18.94%
1225	24.19%	24.16%	1425	18.26%	18.25%
1250	23.44%	23.40%	1450	17.53%	17.68%
1275	22.63%	22.65%	1500	16.34%	16.24%
1300	21.86%	21.91%	1550	15.05%	15.08%
1325	21.15%	21.20%	1575	14.48%	14.47%
1350	20.41%	20.43%	1600	14.13%	14.02%

8.2 Linear regression: ordinary least squares for time series data

Linear regression for time series data (also called ordinary least squares for time series data) requires finding the best approximation of the time series data of a random variable by a linear combination of the time series data of other random variables and a constant vector.

Let Y and $X_1, X_2, \ldots, X_n$ be random variables given by time series data at N data points t_i, $i = 1 : N$. Assume that the sample covariance matrix corresponding to the time series data for $X_1, X_2, \ldots, X_n$ is nonsingular, or, equivalently, that the column vectors of the time series data for $X_1, X_2, \ldots, X_n$ and the $N \times 1$ column vector with all entries equal to 1 are linearly independent; cf. Theorem 7.2.

We look for the best linear approximation of the time series data for Y by a linear combination of the time series data for $X_1, X_2, \ldots, X_n$ plus a constant vector, i.e., we look for constants $a, b_1, b_2, \ldots, b_n$ such that

$$\begin{pmatrix} Y(t_1) \\ Y(t_2) \\ \vdots \\ Y(t_N) \end{pmatrix} \approx \begin{pmatrix} a + \sum_{k=1}^n b_k X_k(t_1) \\ a + \sum_{k=1}^n b_k X_k(t_2) \\ \vdots \\ a + \sum_{k=1}^n b_k X_k(t_N) \end{pmatrix}$$

$$\iff \begin{pmatrix} Y(t_1) \\ Y(t_2) \\ \vdots \\ Y(t_N) \end{pmatrix} \approx \begin{pmatrix} a \\ a \\ \vdots \\ a \end{pmatrix} + \sum_{k=1}^n b_k \begin{pmatrix} X_k(t_1) \\ X_k(t_2) \\ \vdots \\ X_k(t_N) \end{pmatrix}$$

$$\iff \begin{pmatrix} Y(t_1) \\ Y(t_2) \\ \vdots \\ Y(t_N) \end{pmatrix} \approx \begin{pmatrix} 1 & X_1(t_1) & \cdots & X_n(t_1) \\ 1 & X_1(t_2) & \cdots & X_n(t_2) \\ \vdots & \vdots & \vdots & \vdots \\ 1 & X_1(t_N) & \cdots & X_n(t_N) \end{pmatrix} \begin{pmatrix} a \\ b_1 \\ \vdots \\ b_n \end{pmatrix}. \quad (8.50)$$

Denote by T_Y and T_{X_k} the column vectors of the time series data for the random variables Y and X_k, for $k = 1 : n$, respectively, i.e.,

$$T_Y = (Y(t_i))_{i=1:N}; \quad (8.51)$$

and denote by
$$T_{X_k} = (X_k(t_i))_{i=1:N}, \quad \forall\, k = 1:n, \tag{8.52}$$

$$T_{\mathbf{X}} = \text{col}\,(T_{X_k})_{k=1:n} \tag{8.53}$$

the $N \times n$ matrix of time series data for $X_1, X_2, \ldots, X_n$. Denote by $\mathbf{b} = (b_i)_{i=1:n}$ the $n \times 1$ coefficients vector, and by $\mathbf{1}$ the column vector of size N with all entries equal to 1.

Then, (8.50) can be written as follows:

$$T_Y \approx \begin{pmatrix} \mathbf{1} & T_{X_1} & \ldots & T_{X_n} \end{pmatrix} \begin{pmatrix} a \\ \mathbf{b} \end{pmatrix} = \begin{pmatrix} \mathbf{1} & T_{\mathbf{X}} \end{pmatrix} \begin{pmatrix} a \\ \mathbf{b} \end{pmatrix}. \tag{8.54}$$

Note that (8.54) is a least square problem of the form

$$y \approx Ax \quad \text{with} \quad y = T_Y;\ A = \begin{pmatrix} \mathbf{1} & T_{\mathbf{X}} \end{pmatrix}\ x = \begin{pmatrix} a \\ \mathbf{b} \end{pmatrix}. \tag{8.55}$$

Since the sample covariance matrix corresponding to the time series data for X_1, $X_2, \ldots, X_n$ is nonsingular, it follows from Theorem 7.2 that the columns of $T_{\mathbf{X}}$ and the vector $\mathbf{1}$ are linearly independent. Then, the least squares problem (8.55) has a unique solution $x = (A^t A)^{-1} A^t y$, see (8.16), and therefore

$$\begin{pmatrix} a \\ \mathbf{b} \end{pmatrix} = (A^t A)^{-1} A^t\, T_Y, \quad \text{where} \quad A = \begin{pmatrix} \mathbf{1} & T_{\mathbf{X}} \end{pmatrix}. \tag{8.56}$$

Example: For 15 consecutive trading days, the yields of the 2-year, 3-year, 5-year, and 10-year treasury bonds were, respectively:

2-year	3-year	5-year	10-year
4.69	4.58	4.57	4.63
4.81	4.71	4.69	4.73
4.81	4.72	4.70	4.74
4.79	4.78	4.77	4.81
4.79	4.77	4.77	4.80
4.83	4.75	4.73	4.79
4.81	4.71	4.72	4.76
4.81	4.72	4.74	4.77
4.83	4.76	4.77	4.80
4.81	4.73	4.75	4.77
4.82	4.75	4.77	4.80
4.82	4.75	4.76	4.80
4.80	4.73	4.75	4.78
4.78	4.71	4.72	4.73
4.79	4.71	4.71	4.73

Find a linear regression for the yield of the 3-year bond in terms of the yields of the 2-year, 5-year, and 10-year bonds.

Answer: Denote by T_2, T_3, T_5, and T_{10} the 15×1 time series column vectors for the 2-year, 3-year, 5-year, and 10-year yields from the data above, respectively. We are looking for coefficients a, b_1, b_2, b_3 corresponding to the solution to the ordinary least squares problem

$$T_3 \approx a\mathbf{1} + b_1 T_2 + b_2 T_5 + b_3 T_{10},$$

8.2. ORDINARY LEAST SQUARES FOR RANDOM VARIABLES

where **1** is the 15×1 column vector with all entries equal to 1. This can be written in least squares form as $y \approx Ax$, with

$$x = \begin{pmatrix} a \\ b_1 \\ b_2 \\ b_3 \end{pmatrix}; \quad y = T_3; \quad A = (\mathbf{1} \; T_2 \; T_5 \; T_{10});$$

in other words,

$$y = \begin{pmatrix} 4.58 \\ 4.71 \\ 4.72 \\ 4.78 \\ 4.77 \\ 4.75 \\ 4.71 \\ 4.72 \\ 4.76 \\ 4.73 \\ 4.75 \\ 4.75 \\ 4.73 \\ 4.71 \\ 4.71 \end{pmatrix}; \quad A = \begin{pmatrix} 1 & 4.69 & 4.57 & 4.63 \\ 1 & 4.81 & 4.69 & 4.73 \\ 1 & 4.81 & 4.70 & 4.74 \\ 1 & 4.79 & 4.77 & 4.81 \\ 1 & 4.79 & 4.77 & 4.80 \\ 1 & 4.83 & 4.73 & 4.79 \\ 1 & 4.81 & 4.72 & 4.76 \\ 1 & 4.81 & 4.74 & 4.77 \\ 1 & 4.83 & 4.77 & 4.80 \\ 1 & 4.81 & 4.75 & 4.77 \\ 1 & 4.82 & 4.77 & 4.80 \\ 1 & 4.82 & 4.76 & 4.80 \\ 1 & 4.80 & 4.75 & 4.78 \\ 1 & 4.78 & 4.72 & 4.73 \\ 1 & 4.79 & 4.71 & 4.73 \end{pmatrix}.$$

Recall from (8.16) that the solution to the least squares problem $y \approx Ax$ is $x = (A^t A)^{-1} A^t y$. By using the Cholesky solver linear_solve_cholesky from Table 6.2, we compute $x =$ linear_solve_cholesky($A^t A, A^t y$) with A and y given above, we obtain that

$$x = \begin{pmatrix} a \\ b_1 \\ b_2 \\ b_3 \end{pmatrix} = \begin{pmatrix} 0.0123 \\ 0.1272 \\ 0.3340 \\ 0.5298 \end{pmatrix}.$$

We conclude that the ordinary least square linear regression for the yield of the 3-year bond in terms of the yields of the 2-year, 5-year, and 10-year bonds is

$$T_3 \approx 0.0123 \cdot 1 + 0.1272 \, T_2 + 0.3340 \, T_5 + 0.5298 \, T_{10}. \quad \square$$

8.3 Ordinary least squares for random variables

The ordinary least squares problem for random variables requires finding the best approximation of a random variable by a linear combination of other random variables and a constant.

We look for the best approximation of Y by a linear combination of $X_1, X_2, \ldots, X_n$ plus a constant, i.e., we look for constants $a, b_1, b_2, \ldots, b_n$ such that

$$Y - \left(a + \sum_{i=1}^{n} b_i X_i\right) \quad \text{has mean 0 and minimal variance.}$$

Let μ_Y and μ_{X_k} be the means of Y and X_k, for $k = 1:n$, respectively, and let $\mu_\mathbf{X}$ be the $n \times 1$ column vector $\mu_\mathbf{X} = (\mu_{X_k})_{k=1:n}$.

Lemma 8.1. *Let $X_1, X_2, \ldots, X_n$ be random variables on the same probability space with nonsingular covariance matrix $\Sigma_\mathbf{X}$, and let Y be another random variable on the same probability space. The best approximation of Y by a linear combination of $X_1, X_2, \ldots, X_n$ plus a constant, i.e., such that the random variable*

$$Y - \left(a + \sum_{i=1}^n b_i X_i \right) \quad \text{has mean 0 and minimal variance,}$$

where $a, b_1, b_2, \ldots, b_n$ are constants, is given by

$$\mathbf{b} = (\Sigma_\mathbf{X})^{-1} \sigma_{Y,\mathbf{X}}. \tag{8.57}$$
$$a = \mu_Y - \mu_\mathbf{X}^t (\Sigma_\mathbf{X})^{-1} \sigma_{Y,\mathbf{X}}, \tag{8.58}$$

where $\mathbf{b} = (b_i)_{i=1:n}$ and $\sigma_{Y,\mathbf{X}} = (\text{cov}(Y, X_i))_{i=1:n}$ is the covariance vector of Y and $X_1, X_2, \ldots, X_n$.

Proof. Denote by μ_Y and μ_{X_k} the mean of Y and of X_k, respectively, for $k = 1:n$. Then,

$$E\left[Y - \left(a + \sum_{i=1}^n b_i X_i \right) \right] = \mu_Y - a - \sum_{i=1}^n b_i \mu_{X_i},$$

and therefore $E\left[Y - \left(a + \sum_{i=1}^n b_i X_i \right) \right] = 0$ if and only if

$$a = \mu_Y - \sum_{i=1}^n b_i \mu_{X_i}. \tag{8.59}$$

Note that

$$\text{var}\left(Y - (a + \sum_{i=1}^n b_i X_i) \right) = \text{var}\left((Y - \sum_{i=1}^n b_i X_i) - a \right)$$
$$= \text{var}\left(Y - \sum_{i=1}^n b_i X_i \right),$$

since $\text{var}(X - a) = \text{var}(X)$ for any random variable X and for any constant a.

Thus, we are looking for constants b_i, $i = 1:n$, such that

$$\text{var}\left(Y - \sum_{i=1}^n b_i X_i \right) \quad \text{is minimal.} \tag{8.60}$$

Recall that, for any random variables X and Y over the same probability space,

$$\text{var}(Y - X) = \text{var}(Y) - 2\text{cov}(Y, X) + \text{var}(X).$$

Then,

$$\text{var}\left(Y - \sum_{i=1}^n b_i X_i \right) = \text{var}(Y) - 2\text{cov}\left(Y, \sum_{i=1}^n b_i X_i \right) + \text{var}\left(\sum_{i=1}^n b_i X_i \right)$$
$$= \text{var}(Y) - 2 \sum_{i=1}^n b_i \text{cov}(Y, X_i) + \text{var}\left(\sum_{i=1}^n b_i X_i \right). \tag{8.61}$$

8.3. ORDINARY LEAST SQUARES FOR RANDOM VARIABLES

Let $\mathbf{b} = (b_i)_{i=1:n}$ be the coefficients column vector, and let

$$\sigma_{Y,\mathbf{x}} = (\mathrm{cov}(Y, X_i))_{i=1:n} = \begin{pmatrix} \mathrm{cov}(Y, X_1) \\ \vdots \\ \mathrm{cov}(Y, X_n) \end{pmatrix}$$

be the covariance vector of Y and $X_1, X_2, \ldots, X_n$.

From (1.5), we find that

$$\sum_{i=1}^{n} b_i \mathrm{cov}(Y, X_i) = \sigma_{Y,\mathbf{x}}^t \mathbf{b}. \tag{8.62}$$

Let $\Sigma_{\mathbf{x}}$ be the covariance matrix of the random variables $X_1, X_2, \ldots, X_n$, and recall from (7.25) that

$$\mathrm{var}\left(\sum_{i=1}^{n} b_i X_i\right) = \mathbf{b}^t \Sigma_{\mathbf{x}} \mathbf{b}. \tag{8.63}$$

From (8.61–8.63), we obtain that

$$\mathrm{var}\left(Y - \sum_{i=1}^{n} b_i X_i\right) = \mathrm{var}(Y) - 2\sigma_{Y,\mathbf{x}}^t \mathbf{b} + \mathbf{b}^t \Sigma_{\mathbf{x}} \mathbf{b}. \tag{8.64}$$

Thus, minimizing $\mathrm{var}\left(Y - \sum_{i=1}^{n} b_i X_i\right)$, see (8.60), is equivalent to finding a vector $\mathbf{b} \in \mathbb{R}^n$ such that

$$\mathrm{var}(Y) - 2\sigma_{Y,\mathbf{x}}^t \mathbf{b} + \mathbf{b}^t \Sigma_{\mathbf{x}} \mathbf{b} \quad \text{is minimal.} \tag{8.65}$$

Let $f : \mathbb{R}^n \to \mathbb{R}$ be the function given by

$$f(x) = \mathrm{var}(Y) - 2\sigma_{Y,\mathbf{x}}^t x + x^t \Sigma_{\mathbf{x}} x, \quad \forall\, x \in \mathbb{R}^n.$$

Then, solving (8.65) is equivalent to finding a minimum point for $f(x)$.

Recall from (10.43) and (10.47) the following gradient formulas:

$$D(C^t x) = C^t;$$
$$D(x^t A x) = 2(Ax)^t,$$

for any constant column vector C of size n and for any $n \times n$ symmetric matrix A.

Then, the gradient $Df(x)$ of $f(x)$ is

$$\begin{aligned} Df(x) &= D(\mathrm{var}(Y)) - 2D(\sigma_{Y,\mathbf{x}}^t x) + D(x^t \Sigma_{\mathbf{x}} x) \\ &= -2\sigma_{Y,\mathbf{x}}^t + 2(\Sigma_{\mathbf{x}} x)^t \\ &= 2(\Sigma_{\mathbf{x}} x - \sigma_{Y,\mathbf{x}})^t; \end{aligned} \tag{8.66}$$

note that $D(\mathrm{var}(Y)) = 0$ since $\mathrm{var}(Y)$ is not a function of x.

Any minimum point x_0 of $f(x)$ is also a critical point of $f(x)$, i.e., a solution to $Df(x_0) = 0$. From (8.66), we find that, if $Df(x_0) = 0$, then $\Sigma_{\mathbf{x}} x_0 = \sigma_{Y,\mathbf{x}}$, which, since we assumed that the covariance matrix $\Sigma_{\mathbf{x}}$ is nonsingular, has the unique solution

$$x_0 = (\Sigma_{\mathbf{x}})^{-1} \sigma_{Y,\mathbf{x}}. \tag{8.67}$$

To classify the critical point x_0 given by (8.67), we compute the Hessian of $f(x)$. Recall from (10.45) and (10.48), respectively, that $D^2(C^t x) = 0$ and $D^2 (x^t A x) = 2A$. Thus, $D^2 f(x) = 2\Sigma_{\mathbf{x}}$, and therefore $D^2 f(x_0) = 2\Sigma_{\mathbf{x}}$.

The covariance matrix $\Sigma_{\mathbf{x}}$ is symmetric positive definite since it is nonsingular. Then, x_0 is a local minimum point for the function $f(x)$, and since x_0 is the only critical point of the function $f(x)$, we conclude that x_0 is a global minimum point for the function $f(x)$.

Thus, the vector $\mathbf{b}$ minimizing (8.65) is $\mathbf{b} = x_0$ given by (8.67), i.e.,

$$\mathbf{b} = (\Sigma_{\mathbf{x}})^{-1} \sigma_{Y,\mathbf{x}}. \tag{8.68}$$

Let $\mu_{\mathbf{x}} = (\mu_{X_i})_{i=1:n}$. Then, from (8.59) and (8.68), we find that

$$\begin{aligned} a &= \mu_Y - \sum_{i=1}^{n} b_i \mu_i = \mu_Y - \mu_{\mathbf{x}}^t \mathbf{b} \\ &= \mu_Y - \mu_{\mathbf{x}}^t (\Sigma_{\mathbf{x}})^{-1} \sigma_{Y,\mathbf{x}}. \end{aligned} \tag{8.69}$$

From (8.68) and (8.69), we conclude that the constants $a, b_1, b_2, \ldots, b_n$ such that the random variable $Y - \left(a + \sum_{i=1}^{n} b_i X_i\right)$ has mean 0 and minimal variance are given by (8.57) and (8.58). $\square$

Note that the formulas (8.57) and (8.58) for the coefficients of ordinary least squares for random variables are the random variable versions of the formulas (8.80) and (8.81) for time series data.

8.4 The intuition behind ordinary least squares for time series data

The solution (8.56) from section 8.2 for the linear regression of time series data, while applicable in practice, lacks intuition. We provide this intuition here by expressing a and $\mathbf{b}$ from (8.56) in terms of the time series data for Y and for X_k, $k = 1 : n$, and by highlighting the connection to the solution to the ordinary least squares problem for random variables; see Lemma 8.2 and Lemma 8.1.

Let $\widehat{\mu}_Y$ and $\widehat{\mu}_{X_k}$ be the sample means of Y and X_k, for $k = 1 : n$, respectively, i.e.,

$$\widehat{\mu}_Y = \frac{1}{N} \sum_{i=1}^{N} Y(t_i) = \frac{1}{N} \mathbf{1}^t T_Y; \tag{8.70}$$

$$\widehat{\mu}_{X_k} = \frac{1}{N} \sum_{i=1}^{N} X_k(t_i) = \frac{1}{N} \mathbf{1}^t T_{X_k}, \quad \forall\, k = 1 : n, \tag{8.71}$$

where T_Y and T_{X_k} are the column vectors of the time series data for Y and X_k given by (8.51) and (8.52), respectively, and let $\widehat{\mu}_{\mathbf{x}}$ be the $n \times 1$ column vector

$$\widehat{\mu}_{\mathbf{x}} = (\widehat{\mu}_{X_k})_{k=1:n}. \tag{8.72}$$

8.4. INTUITION BEHIND OLS FOR TIME SERIES DATA

Also, let $\hat{\sigma}_{Y,\mathbf{x}}$ be the sample covariance vector of Y and $X_1, \ldots, X_n$ given by

$$\hat{\sigma}_{Y,\mathbf{x}} = \begin{pmatrix} \widehat{\text{cov}}(Y, X_1) \\ \vdots \\ \widehat{\text{cov}}(Y, X_n) \end{pmatrix}. \tag{8.73}$$

Let $\overline{T}_Y$ and $\overline{T}_{X_k}$ be the column vectors of the time series data for the random variables Y and X_k normalized to mean equal to 0, for $k = 1:n$, respectively, i.e.,

$$\overline{T}_Y = (Y(t_i) - \hat{\mu}_Y)_{i=1:N} = T_Y - \hat{\mu}_Y \mathbf{1}; \tag{8.74}$$
$$\overline{T}_{X_k} = (X_k(t_i) - \hat{\mu}_{X_k})_{i=1:N} = T_{X_k} - \hat{\mu}_{X_k} \mathbf{1}, \tag{8.75}$$

and let

$$\overline{T}_\mathbf{x} = \text{col}\left(\overline{T}_{X_k}\right)_{k=1:n}. \tag{8.76}$$

Lemma 8.2. *Let Y and $X_1, X_2, \ldots, X_n$ be random variables given by the $N \times 1$ time series data vectors T_Y and $T_{X_1}, T_{X_2}, \ldots, T_{X_n}$, respectively. Let $T_\mathbf{x} = \text{col}(T_{X_k})_{k=1:n}$. Assume that the sample covariance matrix $\hat{\Sigma}_\mathbf{x}$ corresponding to the time series data for $X_1, X_2, \ldots, X_n$ is nonsingular.*

The solution a and $\mathbf{b} = (b_i)_{i=1:n}$ to the linear regression problem

$$T_Y \approx (\mathbf{1} \ T_{X_1} \ \ldots \ T_{X_n}) \begin{pmatrix} a \\ \mathbf{b} \end{pmatrix} \tag{8.77}$$
$$= a\mathbf{1} + b_1 T_{X_1} + b_2 T_{X_2} + \ldots + b_n T_{X_n},$$

where $\mathbf{1}$ is the $N \times 1$ column vector with all entries equal to 1, is

$$\mathbf{b} = (\overline{T}_\mathbf{x}^t \overline{T}_\mathbf{x})^{-1} \overline{T}_\mathbf{x}^t \overline{T}_Y; \tag{8.78}$$
$$a = \hat{\mu}_Y - \hat{\mu}_\mathbf{x}^t (\overline{T}_\mathbf{x}^t \overline{T}_\mathbf{x})^{-1} \overline{T}_\mathbf{x}^t \overline{T}_Y, \tag{8.79}$$

where $\overline{T}_Y$ and $\overline{T}_\mathbf{x}$ are given by (8.74) and (8.76), respectively.

Moreover, (8.78) and (8.79) can be written as

$$\mathbf{b} = \left(\hat{\Sigma}_\mathbf{x}\right)^{-1} \hat{\sigma}_{Y,\mathbf{x}}. \tag{8.80}$$
$$a = \hat{\mu}_Y - \hat{\mu}_\mathbf{x}^t \left(\hat{\Sigma}_\mathbf{x}\right)^{-1} \hat{\sigma}_{Y,\mathbf{x}}, \tag{8.81}$$

where $\hat{\mu}_Y$, $\hat{\mu}_\mathbf{x}$, and $\hat{\sigma}_{Y,\mathbf{x}}$ are given by (8.70), (8.72), and (8.73), respectively, and $\hat{\Sigma}_\mathbf{x}$ is the sample covariance matrix given by (7.42).

The results of Lemma 8.2 connect the linear regression ordinary least squares solution for time series data to the ordinary least squares solution for random variables from section 8.3; see (8.57) and (8.58).

Proof. Since $\overline{T}_\mathbf{x} = \text{col}\left(\overline{T}_{X_k}\right)_{k=1:n}$, the ordinary least squares problem (8.77) can also be written as follows:

$$T_Y \approx (\mathbf{1} \ T_\mathbf{x}) \begin{pmatrix} a \\ \mathbf{b} \end{pmatrix}. \tag{8.82}$$

Recall from section 8.1 that the solution to the least squares problem $y \approx Ax$ requires solving the linear system $A^t y = A^t A x$. Problem (8.82) corresponds to

$$y \approx Ax \text{ with } y = T_Y, \ A = (\mathbf{1} \ T_\mathbf{x}), \ x = \begin{pmatrix} a \\ \mathbf{b} \end{pmatrix},$$

and therefore $A^t y = A^t A x$ can be written as

$$\begin{pmatrix} \mathbf{1}^t \\ T_\mathbf{x}^t \end{pmatrix} T_Y = \begin{pmatrix} \mathbf{1}^t \\ T_\mathbf{x}^t \end{pmatrix} (\mathbf{1} \ T_\mathbf{x}) \begin{pmatrix} a \\ \mathbf{b} \end{pmatrix}. \tag{8.83}$$

By looking only at the first row of (8.83), we obtain that

$$\begin{aligned} \mathbf{1}^t T_Y &= \mathbf{1}^t \ (\mathbf{1} \ T_\mathbf{x}) \begin{pmatrix} a \\ \mathbf{b} \end{pmatrix} = \mathbf{1}^t \ (\mathbf{1}a + T_\mathbf{x}\mathbf{b}) \\ &= \mathbf{1}^t \mathbf{1} a + \mathbf{1}^t T_\mathbf{x} \mathbf{b}. \end{aligned} \tag{8.84}$$

From (8.70), we find that
$$\mathbf{1}^t T_Y = N \widehat{\mu}_Y. \tag{8.85}$$

Also, note that
$$\mathbf{1}^t \mathbf{1} = \sum_{i=1}^{N} 1 = N. \tag{8.86}$$

Recall that $T_\mathbf{x} = \text{col}(T_{X_k})_{k=1:n}$. From (8.71), it follows that $\mathbf{1}^t T_{X_k} = N \widehat{\mu}_{X_k}$ for all $k = 1 : n$, and therefore $\mathbf{1}^t T_\mathbf{x}$ is the following row vector:

$$\begin{aligned} \mathbf{1}^t T_\mathbf{x} &= \left(\mathbf{1}^t T_{X_1} \ \mathbf{1}^t T_{X_2} \ \ldots \ \mathbf{1}^t T_{X_n}\right) \\ &= \left(N\widehat{\mu}_{X_1} \ N\widehat{\mu}_{X_2} \ \ldots \ N\widehat{\mu}_{X_n}\right) \\ &= N\left(\widehat{\mu}_{X_1} \ \widehat{\mu}_{X_2} \ \ldots \ \widehat{\mu}_{X_n}\right) \\ &= N\widehat{\mu}_\mathbf{x}^t, \end{aligned} \tag{8.87}$$

where $\widehat{\mu}_\mathbf{x}^t = (\widehat{\mu}_{X_1} \ \widehat{\mu}_{X_2} \ \ldots \ \widehat{\mu}_{X_n})$; see (8.72).

From (8.85), (8.86), and (8.87), we obtain that (8.84) can be written as

$$N\widehat{\mu}_Y = Na + N\widehat{\mu}_\mathbf{x}^t \mathbf{b}. \tag{8.88}$$

By solving (8.88) for a, we obtain that

$$a = \widehat{\mu}_Y - \widehat{\mu}_\mathbf{x}^t \mathbf{b}. \tag{8.89}$$

Note that the ordinary least squares problem (8.82) can be written as

$$T_Y \approx (\mathbf{1} \ T_\mathbf{x}) \begin{pmatrix} a \\ \mathbf{b} \end{pmatrix} = a\mathbf{1} + T_\mathbf{x}\mathbf{b}. \tag{8.90}$$

By substituting the expression (8.89) for a into (8.90), we find that

$$\begin{aligned} T_Y &\approx a\mathbf{1} + T_\mathbf{x}\mathbf{b} \\ \iff T_Y &\approx \widehat{\mu}_Y \mathbf{1} - (\widehat{\mu}_\mathbf{x}^t \mathbf{b})\mathbf{1} + T_\mathbf{x}\mathbf{b} \\ \iff T_Y - \widehat{\mu}_Y \mathbf{1} &\approx T_\mathbf{x}\mathbf{b} - (\widehat{\mu}_\mathbf{x}^t \mathbf{b})\mathbf{1}. \end{aligned} \tag{8.91}$$

8.4. INTUITION BEHIND OLS FOR TIME SERIES DATA

Recall from (8.74) that

$$T_Y - \widehat{\mu}_Y \mathbf{1} = (Y(t_i) - \widehat{\mu}_Y)_{i=1:N} = \overline{T}_Y. \tag{8.92}$$

Also,

$$\begin{aligned}
T_{\mathbf{x}}\mathbf{b} - (\widehat{\mu}_{\mathbf{x}}^t \mathbf{b})\mathbf{1} &= \sum_{k=1}^n b_k T_{X_k} - \left(\sum_{k=1}^n b_k \widehat{\mu}_{X_k}\right)\mathbf{1} \\
&= \sum_{k=1}^n b_k T_{X_k} - \sum_{k=1}^n b_k \widehat{\mu}_{X_k}\mathbf{1} \\
&= \sum_{k=1}^n b_k (T_{X_k} - \widehat{\mu}_{X_k}\mathbf{1}) \\
&= \sum_{k=1}^n b_k \overline{T}_{X_k} \tag{8.93} \\
&= \overline{T}_{\mathbf{x}}\mathbf{b}, \tag{8.94}
\end{aligned}$$

where, for (8.93), we used (8.75), and, for (8.94), we used (1.7) with $A = \overline{T}_{\mathbf{x}} = \text{col}\left(\overline{T}_{X_k}\right)_{k=1:n}$ and $v = \mathbf{b} = (b_k)_{k=1:n}$.

Thus,

$$T_{\mathbf{x}}\mathbf{b} - \widehat{\mu}_{\mathbf{x}}^t \mathbf{b}\mathbf{1} = \overline{T}_{\mathbf{x}}\mathbf{b}, \tag{8.95}$$

and, from (8.92) and (8.95), it follows that the least squares problem (8.91) can be written as

$$\overline{T}_Y \approx \overline{T}_{\mathbf{x}}\mathbf{b}. \tag{8.96}$$

Note that (8.96) is a least squares problem $y \approx Ax$ with $y = \overline{T}_Y$, $A = \overline{T}_{\mathbf{x}}$, and $x = \mathbf{b}$. Recall from (8.16) that the solution to this least squares problem is $x = (A^t A)^{-1} A^t y$, and therefore

$$\mathbf{b} = (\overline{T}_{\mathbf{x}}^t \overline{T}_{\mathbf{x}})^{-1} \overline{T}_{\mathbf{x}}^t \overline{T}_Y. \tag{8.97}$$

Note that the matrix $\overline{T}_{\mathbf{x}}^t \overline{T}_{\mathbf{x}}$ is nonsingular since the sample covariance matrix

$$\widehat{\Sigma}_{\mathbf{x}} = \frac{1}{N-1} \overline{T}_{\mathbf{x}}^t \overline{T}_{\mathbf{x}} \tag{8.98}$$

corresponding to the time series data for $X_1, X_2, \ldots, X_n$ was assumed to be nonsingular; see (7.60).

Also, note that

$$\begin{aligned}
\widehat{\text{cov}}(Y, X_k) &= \frac{1}{N-1} \sum_{i=1}^N (Y(t_i) - \widehat{\mu}_Y)(X_k(t_i) - \widehat{\mu}_{X_k}) \\
&= \frac{1}{N-1} \sum_{i=1}^N \overline{T}_Y(i)\overline{T}_{X_k}(i) \\
&= \frac{1}{N-1} \overline{T}_{X_k}^t \overline{T}_Y, \quad \forall\, k = 1:n.
\end{aligned}$$

Thus, the sample covariance vector $\widehat{\sigma}_{Y,\mathbf{x}}$ of Y and $X_1, X_2, \ldots, X_n$ is

$$\widehat{\sigma}_{Y,\mathbf{x}} = \begin{pmatrix} \widehat{\mathrm{cov}}(Y, X_1) \\ \vdots \\ \widehat{\mathrm{cov}}(Y, X_n) \end{pmatrix} = \begin{pmatrix} \frac{1}{N-1} \overline{T}_{X_1}^t \overline{T}_Y \\ \vdots \\ \frac{1}{N-1} \overline{T}_{X_n}^t \overline{T}_Y \end{pmatrix} = \frac{1}{N-1} \begin{pmatrix} \overline{T}_{X_1}^t \\ \vdots \\ \overline{T}_{X_n}^t \end{pmatrix} \overline{T}_Y$$

$$= \frac{1}{N-1} \overline{T}_{\mathbf{x}}^t \overline{T}_Y, \tag{8.99}$$

since $\overline{T}_{\mathbf{x}} = \mathrm{col}\left(\overline{T}_{X_k}\right)_{k=1:n}$, and therefore $\overline{T}_{\mathbf{x}}^t = \mathrm{row}\left((\overline{T}_{X_j})^t\right)_{j=1:n}$.

From (8.98), we obtain that $\overline{T}_{\mathbf{x}}^t \overline{T}_{\mathbf{x}} = (N-1)\widehat{\Sigma}_{\mathbf{x}}$, and therefore

$$(\overline{T}_{\mathbf{x}}^t \overline{T}_{\mathbf{x}})^{-1} = \frac{1}{N-1}\left(\widehat{\Sigma}_{\mathbf{x}}\right)^{-1}. \tag{8.100}$$

Also, from (8.99), it follows that

$$\overline{T}_{\mathbf{x}}^t \overline{T}_Y = (N-1)\widehat{\sigma}_{Y,\mathbf{x}}. \tag{8.101}$$

From (8.97), (8.100), and (8.101), we obtain that

$$\mathbf{b} = (\overline{T}_{\mathbf{x}}^t \overline{T}_{\mathbf{x}})^{-1} \overline{T}_{\mathbf{x}}^t \overline{T}_Y = \left(\widehat{\Sigma}_{\mathbf{x}}\right)^{-1} \widehat{\sigma}_{Y,\mathbf{x}}, \tag{8.102}$$

which is the same as (8.80), and, from (8.89) and (8.102), we obtain that

$$a = \widehat{\mu}_Y - \widehat{\mu}_{\mathbf{x}}^t \left(\widehat{\Sigma}_{\mathbf{x}}\right)^{-1} \widehat{\sigma}_{Y,\mathbf{x}},$$

which is the same as (8.81). □

The formulas (8.80) and (8.81) for the coefficients of ordinary least squares for time series data are the time series versions of the formulas (8.57) and (8.58).

8.5 References

The solution to a linear system associated to a least squares problem coming from linear regression with application to cartography motivated the introduction of the Cholesky decomposition by André Cholesky early in the 20-th century; cf. Brezinski [9].

A linear algebra treatment of least squares is included in Golub and Van Loan [18]. A statistical approach to least squares can be found in Lai and Xing [25].

A thorough treatment of implied volatility modeling and estimation can be found in Gatheral [15]. For details on implied volatility and its connection to Put–Call parity see Stefanica [36].

8.6 Exercises

1. Denote by x^* the solution to the ordinary least squares problem $y \approx Ax$, where A is an $m \times n$ matrix with $m > n$, y is an $m \times 1$ column vector, and x is an $n \times 1$ column vector.

   Show that x^* is the projection of the vector y onto the space generated by the columns of A, or, equivalently, show that the vector $y - Ax^*$ is orthogonal to the space generated by the columns of A. In other words, show that
   $$(y - Ax^*, Az) = 0, \quad \forall z \in \mathbb{R}^n.$$

   Note: Recall that the space generated by the columns of A is $\{Az \mid z \in \mathbb{R}^n\}$, and is also called the range of the matrix A.

2. Recall from the example from the book that, on March 9, 2012, the mid prices of the S&P 500 options maturing on December 22, 2012, were as follows:

Call Price	Strike	Put Price
225.40	1175	46.60
205.55	1200	51.55
186.20	1225	57.15
167.50	1250	63.30
149.15	1275	70.15
131.70	1300	77.70
115.25	1325	86.20
99.55	1350	95.30
84.90	1375	105.30
71.10	1400	116.55
58.70	1425	129.00
47.25	1450	143.20
29.25	1500	173.95
15.80	1550	210.80
11.10	1575	230.90
7.90	1600	252.40

   The spot price of the index corresponding to these option prices was $1,370$. For the options above, the market estimates for the annualized continuous dividend yield of the S&P 500 index and for the risk–free rate were $q = 0.0193 = 1.93\%$ and $r = 0.0015 = 0.15\%$, respectively.

   (i) Use Newton's method to compute the implied volatilities for each of the options.

   (ii) How do these values compare to the implied volatilities obtained by using ordinary least squares to compute the discount factor and the present value of the forward price?

   (iii) How do the implied volatilities of calls and puts with the same strike compare to each other?

3. On May 22, 2014, the bid and ask prices of the S&P 500 options maturing on January 17, 2015, were as follows:

Bid Price Call	Ask Price Call	Strike	Bid Price Put	Ask Price Put
431.20	434.40	1450	8.90	10.20
384.10	387.40	1500	11.60	13.10
337.90	341.20	1550	15.20	16.90
292.80	296.20	1600	19.90	21.80
228.30	231.10	1675	29.70	31.40
207.50	210.10	1700	33.60	35.50
167.60	170.00	1750	43.50	45.40
148.90	151.30	1775	49.40	51.50
130.60	132.80	1800	56.50	58.10
113.20	115.30	1825	63.60	65.70
96.80	98.60	1850	71.90	74.20
81.50	83.20	1875	81.40	83.50
67.10	69.00	1900	92.10	94.50
54.20	55.90	1925	103.80	106.30
32.80	34.50	1975	132.40	134.70
24.50	25.90	2000	149.20	151.90
12.40	13.60	2050	186.90	189.70
5.60	6.50	2100	230.00	232.40

The spot price of the index corresponding to these option prices was $1,894$.

(i) Compute the mid prices of the options, i.e., the average of the bid price and ask price of the options. Use ordinary least squares to compute the present value of the forward price PVF and the discount factor $disc$ corresponding to the mid prices of the options.

(ii) Compute the implied volatilities of these options. How do the implied volatilities of calls and puts with the same strike compare to each other?

4. Recall that the vega of an option measures the sensitivity of the price of the option to changes in volatility. In other words, for call and put options, $\text{vega}(C) = \frac{\partial C}{\partial \sigma}$ and $\text{vega}(P) = \frac{\partial P}{\partial \sigma}$.

Use the Put–Call parity

$$C - P = Se^{-qT} + Ke^{-rT}$$

to show that

$$\text{vega}(C) = \text{vega}(P).$$

5. The goal of this exercise is to derive the Black–Scholes formulas for the vegas of plain vanilla European calls and puts.

In the Black–Scholes framework, an underlying asset with spot price S follows a lognormal distribution with volatility σ and pays continuous dividends at rate q. Denote by r be the risk-free interest rate, assumed to be constant. The

8.6. EXERCISES

Black–Scholes values of a European call option and of a European put option with strike K and maturity T are

$$C_{BS}(S, K, T, \sigma, r, q) = Se^{-qT}N(d_1) - Ke^{-rT}N(d_2);$$
$$P_{BS}(S, K, T, \sigma, r, q) = Ke^{-rT}N(-d_2) - Se^{-qT}N(-d_1),$$

respectively, where

$$N(z) = \frac{1}{\sqrt{2\pi}} \int_{-\infty}^{z} e^{-\frac{x^2}{2}} dx$$

denotes the cumulative distribution of the standard normal variable, and

$$d_1 = \frac{\ln\left(\frac{S}{K}\right) + \left(r - q + \frac{\sigma^2}{2}\right)T}{\sigma\sqrt{T}}; \quad d_2 = d_1 - \sigma\sqrt{T}.$$

(i) Use Chain Rule to show that

$$\text{vega}(C) = \frac{\partial C}{\partial \sigma} = Se^{-qT} N'(d_1) \frac{\partial d_1}{\partial \sigma} - Ke^{-rT} N'(d_2) \frac{\partial d_2}{\partial \sigma}.$$

(ii) Show that

$$N'(z) = \frac{1}{\sqrt{2\pi}} e^{-\frac{z^2}{2}},$$

and use this fact to prove that

$$Se^{-qT} N'(d_1) = Ke^{-rT} N'(d_2).$$

(iii) Show that

$$\text{vega}(C) = \frac{1}{\sqrt{2\pi}} Se^{-qT} e^{-\frac{d_1^2}{2}} \sqrt{T};$$
$$\text{vega}(P) = \frac{1}{\sqrt{2\pi}} Se^{-qT} e^{-\frac{d_1^2}{2}} \sqrt{T}.$$

6. The goal of this exercise is to show that the theoretical values of the implied volatilities of plain vanilla European call and put options with the same strike and maturity are equal.

Denote by $C_{BS}(S, K, T, \sigma, r, q)$ and $P_{BS}(S, K, T, \sigma, r, q)$ the Black–Scholes values of a European call option and of a European put option, respectively, with strike K and maturity T on an underlying asset following a lognormal distribution with volatility σ, with spot price S, and paying dividends continuously at the rate q, if interest rates are constant and equal to r. Let C_m and P_m be the market prices of a call and of a put option, respectively, with parameters S, K, T, r, and q.

The implied volatility $\sigma_{imp,C}$ corresponding to the price C is the solution to

$$C_{BS}(\sigma_{imp,C}) = C_m.$$

The implied volatility $\sigma_{imp,P}$ corresponding to the price P is the solution to

$$P_{BS}(\sigma_{imp,P}) = P_m.$$

Note that, here and below, $C_{BS}(\sigma)$ and $P_{BS}(\sigma)$ are shorthand notations for $C_{BS}(S, K, T, \sigma, r, q)$ and $P_{BS}(S, K, T, \sigma, r, q)$, respectively.

(i) Use the facts that the Black–Scholes values of put and call options satisfy the Put–Call parity for any value $\sigma > 0$ of the volatility, i.e.,

$$C_{BS}(\sigma) - P_{BS}(\sigma) = Se^{-qT} - Ke^{-rT},$$

and that the market prices of put and call options satisfy the Put–Call parity as well, i.e.,

$$C_m - P_m = Se^{-qT} - Ke^{-rT},$$

to conclude that

$$P_{BS}(\sigma_{imp,P}) = P_{BS}(\sigma_{imp,C}).$$

(ii) Show that the Black–Scholes value of a put option is a strictly increasing function of volatility, and conclude that the implied volatilities corresponding to put and call options with the same strike and maturity on the same asset must be equal, i.e.,

$$\sigma_{imp,P} = \sigma_{imp,C}.$$

7. Recall the example from the book where for 15 consecutive trading days, the yields of the 2-year, 3-year, 5-year, and 10-year treasury bonds were, respectively:

2-year	3-year	5-year	10-year
4.69	4.58	4.57	4.63
4.81	4.71	4.69	4.73
4.81	4.72	4.70	4.74
4.79	4.78	4.77	4.81
4.79	4.77	4.77	4.80
4.83	4.75	4.73	4.79
4.81	4.71	4.72	4.76
4.81	4.72	4.74	4.77
4.83	4.76	4.77	4.80
4.81	4.73	4.75	4.77
4.82	4.75	4.77	4.80
4.82	4.75	4.76	4.80
4.80	4.73	4.75	4.78
4.78	4.71	4.72	4.73
4.79	4.71	4.71	4.73

Denote by T_2, T_3, T_5, and T_{10} the time series data vectors corresponding to the yield of the 2-year, 3-year, 5-year, and 10-year treasury bonds, respectively.

(i) Find the coefficients a, b_1, b_2, b_3 of the linear regression for the yield of the 3-year bond in terms of the yields of the 2-year, 5-year, and 10-year bonds, i.e., find a, b_1, b_2, b_3 corresponding to the solution to the ordinary least squares problem

$$T_3 \approx a\mathbf{1} + b_1 T_2 + b_2 T_5 + b_3 T_{10},$$

8.6. EXERCISES

where **1** is the 15×1 column vector with all entries equal to 1. Let

$$T_{3,LR} = a\mathbf{1} + b_1 T_2 + b_2 T_5 + b_3 T_{10}.$$

Find the approximation error

$$\text{error}_{LR} = ||T_3 - T_{3,LR}||$$

of the linear regression.

(ii) Compute the linear interpolation values of the 3-year yield by doing linear interpolation between the 2-year yield and the 5-year yield at each data point. Denote by $T_{3,linear\_interp}$ the time series vector of these values. In other words,

$$T_{3,linear\_interp} = \frac{2}{3}T_2 + \frac{1}{3}T_5.$$

Find the approximation error

$$\text{error}_{linear\_interp} = ||T_3 - T_{3,linear\_interp}||$$

of the linear interpolation.

(iii) Compute the cubic interpolation values of the 3-year yield by doing cubic spline interpolation between the 2-year, 5-year, and 10-year yield at each data point. Denote by $T_{3,cubic\_interp}$ the time series vector of these values.

Find the approximation error

$$\text{error}_{cubic\_interp} = ||T_3 - T_{3,cubic\_interp}||$$

of the cubic interpolation.

(iv) Compare the approximation errors from (i), (ii), and (iii), and comment on the results.

8. The file *financials2012.xlsx* from www.fepress.org/nla-primer contains the end of week adjusted closing prices for the stocks of the following financial companies: JPM; GS; MS; BAC (Bank of America); RBS; CS; UBS; RY (RBC); BCS (Barclays) between January 11, 2012, and October 15, 2012.

(i) Compute the weekly percentage returns of these stocks.

(ii) Find the linear regression of the JPM returns with respect to the returns of the other stocks. What is the approximation error of this linear regression?

(iii) Find the linear regression of the JPM returns with respect to the returns of the other American financial companies, i.e., with respect to GS, MS, and BAC. What is the approximation error of this linear regression?

(iv) Find the linear regression of the JPM stock prices with respect to the prices of the other stocks. What is the approximation error of this linear regression? How does it compare with the approximation error of the linear regression of the JPM returns computed at (ii)?

Chapter 9

Efficient portfolios. Value at Risk. Portfolio VaR.

Efficient portfolios. Markowitz Portfolio Theory.

Blueprints for finding efficient portfolios.

Minimum variance portfolios. Minimum variance portfolios and the tangency portfolio.

Maximum return portfolios. Maximum return portfolios and the tangency portfolio.

Minimum variance portfolio with no cash position.

Value at Risk (VaR). Portfolio VaR.

Subadditivity of VaR and counterexample.

9.1 Efficient portfolios. Markowitz portfolio theory.

Consider a portfolio invested in n assets and with a cash position. Let w_i be the weight of asset i in the portfolio, for $i = 1 : n$, i.e., w_i represents the proportion of the portfolio invested in asset i. Then, the weight of the cash position of the portfolio is

$$w_{cash} = 1 - \sum_{i=1}^{n} w_i. \tag{9.1}$$

Example: Consider a $80 million portfolio which is invested in three assets, as follows: a long $50 million position in asset 1, a short $20 million position in asset 2, a long $25 million position in asset 3, and with a long $25 million cash position.[1] The weights w_1, w_2, w_3, and w_{cash} of the three assets and of the cash position are:

$$w_1 = \frac{50}{80} = 0.625 = 62.50\%; \qquad w_2 = -\frac{20}{80} = -0.25 = -25\%;$$

$$w_3 = \frac{25}{80} = 0.3125 = 31.25\%; \qquad w_{cash} = \frac{25}{80} = 0.3125 = 31.25\%. \quad \square$$

---

[1] The asset position in the portfolio is $50mil + (-$20mil) + $25mil = $55mil, and therefore the cash position is $80mil - $55mil = $25mil.

We assume that it is possible to take arbitrarily large long or short positions in any of the assets, and therefore the weights w_i are not required to be positive or to be smaller than 1.

Let R be the return of the portfolio over a fixed period of time, and let $\mu_R = E[R]$ be the expected value[2] of R. Let R_i be the return (over the same period of time) of asset i, and let $\mu_i = E[R_i]$ be the expected value of R_i, for $i = 1:n$. Let r_f be the risk–free return of the cash position in the portfolio over the same period of time.

The return of the portfolio is equal to the weighted average of the returns of the assets and of the cash position, i.e.,

$$R = \sum_{i=1}^{n} w_i R_i + w_{cash} r_f; \tag{9.2}$$

for completeness, a proof of (9.2) is given at the end of this section.

By taking expected values in (9.2) and using (9.1), we find that

$$\begin{aligned}\mu_R &= \sum_{i=1}^{n} w_i \mu_i + w_{cash} r_f \\ &= \sum_{i=1}^{n} w_i \mu_i + \left(1 - \sum_{i=1}^{n} w_i\right) r_f \\ &= r_f + \sum_{i=1}^{n} w_i (\mu_i - r_f). \end{aligned} \tag{9.3}$$

Let $w = (w_i)_{i=1:n}$ be the vector of the asset weights in the portfolio, and let $\mu = (\mu_i)_{i=1:n}$ be the vector of the expected values of the returns of the n assets. Denote by $\mathbf{1}$ the $n \times 1$ column vector whose entries are all equal to 1, and let

$$\overline{\mu} = (\overline{\mu}_i)_{i=1:n} = (\mu_i - r_f)_{i=1:n} = \mu - r_f \mathbf{1} \tag{9.4}$$

be the $n \times 1$ column vector of the excess expected returns of the n assets over the risk–free rate. Then,

$$\sum_{i=1}^{n} w_i \overline{\mu}_i = \overline{\mu}^t w, \tag{9.5}$$

see (1.5), and (9.3) can be written in vector form using (9.5) as follows:

$$\begin{aligned}\mu_R &= r_f + \sum_{i=1}^{n} w_i (\mu_i - r_f) = r_f + \sum_{i=1}^{n} w_i \overline{\mu}_i \\ &= r_f + \overline{\mu}^t w. \end{aligned} \tag{9.6}$$

Also, note that (9.1) can be written in vector form using (1.5) as

$$w_{cash} = 1 - \mathbf{1}^t w. \tag{9.7}$$

Let σ_R be the standard deviation of the return R of the portfolio, and let σ_i be the standard deviation of R_i, for $i = 1:n$. Let $\rho_{j,k}$ be the correlation between the

---

[2]Throughout this book, we also refer to the expected value of the return of a portfolio as the "expected return" of the portfolio.

9.1. EFFICIENT PORTFOLIOS

returns R_j and R_k, for $1 \leq j \neq k \leq n$, and let Σ_R be the $n \times n$ covariance matrix of the returns of the n assets given by

$$\Sigma_R(j,k) = \text{cov}(R_j, R_k) = \sigma_j \sigma_k \rho_{j,k}, \quad \forall\, 1 \leq j \neq k \leq n;$$
$$\Sigma_R(i,i) = \text{var}(R_i) = \sigma_i^2, \quad \forall\, i = 1:n.$$

Since the risk–free rate r_f is a constant, we obtain from (9.2) that

$$\sigma_R^2 = \text{var}(R) = \text{var}\left(\sum_{i=1}^n w_i R_i\right),$$

and, using (7.25), we find that the variance of the return of the portfolio can be written in matrix formulation as follows:

$$\sigma_R^2 = w^t \Sigma_R w. \tag{9.8}$$

A natural assumption we make throughout this chapter is that the return of none of the assets can be replicated by using the other $n-1$ assets and cash.[3] In other words, we assume that there is no asset whose return is a linear combination of the returns of the other $n-1$ assets and the risk–free return. Note that, from Lemma 7.5, it follows that this assumption is equivalent to assuming that the covariance matrix Σ_R is nonsingular.

An important question is how should an efficient portfolio be set up?[4] In other words, what should the weights w_i, $i = 1:n$, of the assets and the weight w_{cash} of the cash position be in order to obtain a portfolio (called a minimum variance portfolio) with the smallest variance of return, given a fixed expected return, or to obtain a portfolio (called a maximum return portfolio) with the highest expected return, given a fixed variance of the return?

Minimum variance portfolio:
Given μ_P, find w_{cash} and w_i, $i = 1:n$, with $\mu_R = \mu_P$, such that σ_R^2 is minimal.

Maximum return portfolio:
Given σ_P, find w_{cash} and w_i, $i = 1:n$, with $\sigma_R^2 = \sigma_P^2$, such that μ_R is maximal.

In section 9.2, we include the solutions to the minimum variance portfolio problem and to the maximum return portfolio problem, which will be derived in sections 9.3 and 9.4, as well as the tangency portfolio formulation of these solutions. The pseudocodes for finding the efficient portfolio allocation for both the minimum variance portfolio problem and the maximum return portfolio are also included in section 9.2.

Note that the variances of asset returns and the covariance matrix for asset returns can be estimated from historical data. However, estimated expected returns accurately from historical is not feasible; see, e.g., Fabozzi and Markowitz [14] for alternative approaches to finding asset allocations for efficient portfolios.

We conclude this section by proving formula (9.2).

Let $V(0)$ be the value at time 0 of a portfolio invested in n assets and with a cash position. Let $V_i(0)$ be the value of the portfolio position in asset i at time 0, for

---
[3]Note the similarity with the non–redundancy of the securities from a one period market model; see Chapter 3.

[4]Finding efficient portfolios is one of the fundamental problems given a theoretical answer by the modern portfolio theory of Markowitz and Sharpe; see Markowitz [28] and Sharpe [35] for seminal papers.

$i = 1 : n$, and let $V_{cash}(0)$ be the value of the cash position in the portfolio at time 0. Similarly, let $V(T)$ be the value of the portfolio at time T, let $V_i(T)$ be the value of the portfolio position in asset i at time T, for $i = 1 : n$, and let $V_{cash}(T)$ be the value of the cash position in the portfolio at time T. Then,

$$V(0) = \sum_{i=1}^{n} V_i(0) + V_{cash}(0); \quad V(T) = \sum_{i=1}^{n} V_i(T) + V_{cash}(T). \qquad (9.9)$$

Note that the weight w_i of asset i in the portfolio at time 0 and the weight w_{cash} of the cash position in the portfolio at time 0 are given by

$$w_i = \frac{V_i(0)}{V(0)}, \; \forall \, i = 1 : n; \quad w_{cash} = \frac{V_{cash}(0)}{V(0)}. \qquad (9.10)$$

The return R of the portfolio between time 0 and time T and the returns R_i, $i = 1 : n$, of asset i between time 0 and time T are given by

$$R = \frac{V(T) - V(0)}{V(0)}; \quad R_i = \frac{V_i(T) - V_i(0)}{V_i(0)}, \; \forall \, i = 1 : n. \qquad (9.11)$$

The return of the cash position is equal to the risk–free return r_f, i.e.,

$$r_f = \frac{V_{cash}(T) - V_{cash}(0)}{V_{cash}(0)}. \qquad (9.12)$$

From (9.11) and (9.9), we find that

$$\begin{aligned}
R &= \frac{V(T) - V(0)}{V(0)} \\
&= \frac{1}{V(0)} \left(\sum_{i=1}^{n} V_i(T) - \sum_{i=1}^{n} V_i(0) \right) + \frac{1}{V(0)} (V_{cash}(T) - V_{cash}(0)) \\
&= \frac{1}{V(0)} \sum_{i=1}^{n} (V_i(T) - V_i(0)) + \frac{1}{V(0)} (V_{cash}(T) - V_{cash}(0)) \\
&= \sum_{i=1}^{n} \frac{V_i(T) - V_i(0)}{V(0)} + \frac{V_{cash}(T) - V_{cash}(0)}{V(0)} \\
&= \sum_{i=1}^{n} \frac{V_i(T) - V_i(0)}{V(0)} \cdot \frac{V_i(0)}{V_i(0)} + \frac{V_{cash}(T) - V_{cash}(0)}{V(0)} \cdot \frac{V_{cash}(0)}{V_{cash}(0)} \\
&= \sum_{i=1}^{n} \frac{V_i(0)}{V(0)} \frac{V_i(T) - V_i(0)}{V_i(0)} + \frac{V_{cash}(0)}{V(0)} \frac{V_{cash}(T) - V_{cash}(0)}{V_{cash}(0)} \\
&= \sum_{i=1}^{n} w_i R_i + w_{cash} r_f,
\end{aligned}$$

where formulas (9.10), (9.11), and (9.12) were used for the last equality. Thus,

$$R = \sum_{i=1}^{n} w_i R_i + w_{cash} r_f,$$

and formula (9.2) is established.

9.2 Blueprints for finding efficient portfolios

Minimum variance portfolio

The asset allocation for a portfolio invested in n assets and cash, with given expected return μ_P and smallest variance of its return can be found below:

- asset weights vector:
$$w_{min} = \frac{\mu_P - r_f}{\overline{\mu}^t \Sigma_R^{-1} \overline{\mu}} \Sigma_R^{-1} \overline{\mu}; \qquad (9.13)$$

- weight of the cash position:
$$w_{min,cash} = 1 - \mathbf{1}^t w_{min} = 1 - (\mu_P - r_f) \frac{\mathbf{1}^t \Sigma_R^{-1} \overline{\mu}}{\overline{\mu}^t \Sigma_R^{-1} \overline{\mu}}. \qquad (9.14)$$

The standard deviation of the return of the minimum variance portfolio is $\sigma_{min} = \frac{\mu_P - r_f}{\sqrt{\overline{\mu}^t \Sigma_R^{-1} \overline{\mu}}}$, and can be computed numerically as

$$\sigma_{min} = \sqrt{w_{min}^t \Sigma_R w_{min}}.$$

The asset allocation for the minimum variance portfolio can be computed using the pseudocode from Table 9.1.

Table 9.1: Pseudocode for asset allocation of minimum variance portfolio

---
Input:
$\Sigma_R = n \times n$ covariance matrix of the returns of n assets
$\mu = n \times 1$ vector of expected values of the returns of n assets
$r_f =$ risk–free rate
$\mu_P =$ required expected return of the portfolio

Output:
$w_{min} =$ asset weights vector for the minimum variance portfolio
$w_{min,cash} =$ weight of cash position for the minimum variance portfolio
$\sigma_{min} =$ standard deviation of the return of the minimum variance portfolio

$\overline{\mu} = \mu - r_f \mathbf{1}$
$x =$ linear_solve_cholesky$(\Sigma_R, \overline{\mu})$ // compute $x = \Sigma_R^{-1} \overline{\mu}$
$w_{min} = \frac{\mu_P - r_f}{\overline{\mu}^t x} x$
$w_{min,cash} = 1 - \mathbf{1}^t w_{min}$
$\sigma_{min} = \sqrt{w_{min}^t \Sigma_R w_{min}}$

Minimum variance portfolio using tangency portfolio: If

$$w_T = \frac{1}{\mathbf{1}^t \Sigma_R^{-1} \overline{\mu}} \Sigma_R^{-1} \overline{\mu}$$

is the weight of the n assets in the tangency portfolio, then the asset weights vector w_{min} and the weight $w_{min,cash}$ of the cash position given by (9.13) and (9.14) can also be computed as follows:

$$w_{min,cash} = 1 - \frac{\mu_P - r_f}{\overline{\mu}^t w_T}; \qquad (9.15)$$

$$w_{min} = (1 - w_{min,cash}) w_T. \qquad (9.16)$$

The standard deviation of the return of the minimum variance portfolio is

$$\sigma_{min} = \sqrt{w_{min}^t \Sigma_R w_{min}}.$$

The asset allocation for the minimum variance portfolio computed using the tangency portfolio can be found using the pseudocode from Table 9.2.

Table 9.2: Asset allocation of minimum variance portfolio from tangency portfolio

---

Input:
$\Sigma_R = n \times n$ covariance matrix of the returns of n assets
$\mu = n \times 1$ vector of expected values of the returns of n assets
$r_f =$ risk–free rate
$\mu_P =$ required expected return of the portfolio

Output:
$w_{min} =$ asset weights vector for the minimum variance portfolio
$w_{min,cash} =$ weight of cash position for the minimum variance portfolio
$\sigma_{min} =$ standard deviation of the return of the minimum variance portfolio

$\overline{\mu} = \mu - r_f \mathbf{1}$
$x = \text{linear\_solve\_cholesky}(\Sigma_R, \overline{\mu})$ // compute $x = \Sigma_R^{-1} \overline{\mu}$
$w_T = \frac{1}{\mathbf{1}^t x} x$
$w_{min,cash} = 1 - \frac{\mu_P - r_f}{\overline{\mu}^t w_T}$
$w_{min} = (1 - w_{min,cash}) w_T$
$\sigma_{min} = \sqrt{w_{min}^t \Sigma_R w_{min}}$

Note that the asset allocation formulas (9.13–9.14) and (9.15–9.16) will be derived in section 9.3.

9.2. BLUEPRINTS FOR EFFICIENT PORTFOLIOS

Maximum return portfolio

The asset allocation for a portfolio invested in n assets and cash, given a variance of the return $\sigma_P^2 \neq 0$ and largest expected return can be found below:

- asset weights vector:

$$w_{max} = \frac{\sigma_P}{\sqrt{\overline{\mu}^t \Sigma_R^{-1} \overline{\mu}}} \Sigma_R^{-1} \overline{\mu}; \qquad (9.17)$$

- weight of the cash position:

$$w_{max,cash} = 1 - \mathbf{1}^t w_{max} = 1 - \sigma_P \frac{\mathbf{1}^t \Sigma_R^{-1} \overline{\mu}}{\sqrt{\overline{\mu}^t \Sigma_R^{-1} \overline{\mu}}}. \qquad (9.18)$$

The expected return of the maximum return portfolio with variance of return equal to σ_P^2 is $\mu_{max} = r_f + \sigma_P \sqrt{\overline{\mu}^t \Sigma_R^{-1} \overline{\mu}}$, and can be computed numerically as

$$\mu_{max} = r_f + \overline{\mu}^t w_{max}.$$

The asset allocation for the maximum return portfolio can be computed using the pseudocode from Table 9.3.

Table 9.3: Pseudocode for asset allocation of maximum return portfolio

---

Input:
$\Sigma_R = n \times n$ covariance matrix of the returns of n assets
$\mu = n \times 1$ vector of expected values of the returns of n assets
r_f = risk–free rate
σ_P = required standard deviation of the return of the portfolio

Output:
w_{max} = asset weights vector for the maximum return portfolio
$w_{max,cash}$ = weight of cash position for the maximum return portfolio
μ_{max} = expected return of the maximum return portfolio

$\overline{\mu} = \mu - r_f \mathbf{1}$
$x = \text{linear\_solve\_cholesky}(\Sigma_R, \overline{\mu})$ // compute $x = \Sigma_R^{-1} \overline{\mu}$
$w_{max} = \frac{\sigma_P}{\sqrt{\overline{\mu}^t x}} x$
$w_{max,cash} = 1 - \mathbf{1}^t w_{max}$
$\mu_{max} = r_f + \overline{\mu}^t w_{max}$

Maximum return portfolio using tangency portfolio: If

$$w_T = \frac{1}{\mathbf{1}^t \Sigma_R^{-1} \overline{\mu}} \Sigma_R^{-1} \overline{\mu}$$

is the weight of the n assets in the tangency portfolio, then the asset weights vector w_{max} and the weight $w_{max,cash}$ of the cash position given by (9.17) and (9.18) can also be computed as follows:

$$w_{max,cash} = 1 - \frac{\sigma_P}{\sqrt{w_T^t \Sigma_R w_T}} \cdot \text{sign}(\mathbf{1}^t \Sigma_R^{-1} \overline{\mu}); \qquad (9.19)$$

$$w_{max} = (1 - w_{max,cash}) w_T; \qquad (9.20)$$

in (9.19), $\text{sign}(\mathbf{1}^t \Sigma_R^{-1} \overline{\mu}) = 1$, if $\mathbf{1}^t \Sigma_R^{-1} \overline{\mu} > 0$, and $\text{sign}(\mathbf{1}^t \Sigma_R^{-1} \overline{\mu}) = -1$, if $\mathbf{1}^t \Sigma_R^{-1} \overline{\mu} < 0$. The expected return of the maximum return portfolio is

$$\mu_{max} = r_f + \overline{\mu}^t w_{max}.$$

The asset allocation for the maximum return portfolio computed using the tangency portfolio can be found using the pseudocode from Table 9.4.

Table 9.4: Asset allocation of maximum return portfolio from tangency portfolio

---

Input:
$\Sigma_R = n \times n$ covariance matrix of the returns of n assets
$\mu = n \times 1$ vector of expected values of the returns of n assets
$r_f = $ risk–free rate
$\sigma_P = $ required standard deviation of the return of the portfolio

Output:
$w_{max} = $ asset weights vector for the maximum return portfolio
$w_{max,cash} = $ weight of cash position for the maximum return portfolio
$\mu_{max} = $ expected return of the maximum return portfolio

$\overline{\mu} = \mu - r_f \mathbf{1}$
$x = \text{linear\_solve\_cholesky}(\Sigma_R, \overline{\mu})$ // compute $x = \Sigma_R^{-1} \overline{\mu}$
$w_T = \frac{1}{\mathbf{1}^t x} x$
if $\mathbf{1}^t \Sigma_R^{-1} \overline{\mu} > 0$
    $w_{max,cash} = 1 - \frac{\sigma_P}{\sqrt{w_T^t \Sigma_R w_T}}$
else
    $w_{max,cash} = 1 + \frac{\sigma_P}{\sqrt{w_T^t \Sigma_R w_T}}$
end
$w_{max} = (1 - w_{max,cash}) w_T$
$\mu_{max} = r_f + \overline{\mu}^t w_{max}$

Note that the asset allocation formulas (9.17–9.18) and (9.19–9.20) will be derived in section 9.4.

9.3 Minimum variance portfolios

The minimum variance portfolio invested in n assets and with a cash position is the portfolio which has the smallest variance of its return of all the portfolios with a given expected return μ_P.

In other words, given μ_P, we are looking for a weights vector $w = (w_i)_{i=1:n}$ such that $\mu_R = \mu_P$ and σ_R^2 is minimal. From (9.6) and (9.8), it follows that we want to minimize $\sigma_R^2 = w^t \Sigma_R w$ subject to $\mu_R = r_f + \overline{\mu}^t w = \mu_P$, i.e.,

$$\min_{r_f + \overline{\mu}^t w = \mu_P} w^t \Sigma_R w. \qquad (9.21)$$

We use Lagrange multipliers to solve this problem; see section 10.2.2 for details. The associated Lagrangian function $F : \mathbb{R}^{n+1} \to \mathbb{R}$ is given by

$$F(w, \lambda) = w^t \Sigma_R w + \lambda(\mu_P - r_f - \overline{\mu}^t w),$$

where $\lambda \in \mathbb{R}$ is the Lagrange multiplier.[5]

Since the covariance matrix Σ_R is symmetric, we obtain from (10.47) that

$$D\left(w^t \Sigma_R w\right) = 2(\Sigma_R w)^t. \qquad (9.22)$$

Also, from (10.43), it follows that

$$D(\overline{\mu}^t w) = \overline{\mu}^t. \qquad (9.23)$$

Then,

$$\begin{aligned} D_w F(w, \lambda) &= D\left(w^t \Sigma_R w\right) + \lambda D(\mu_P - r_f - \overline{\mu}^t w) \\ &= D\left(w^t \Sigma_R w\right) - \lambda D(\overline{\mu}^t w) \\ &= 2(\Sigma_R w)^t - \lambda \overline{\mu}^t \\ &= (2\Sigma_R w - \lambda \overline{\mu})^t. \end{aligned} \qquad (9.24)$$

Also, note that

$$D_\lambda F(w, \lambda) = \frac{\partial F}{\partial \lambda}(w, \lambda) = \mu_P - r_f - \overline{\mu}^t w. \qquad (9.25)$$

From (10.67), (9.24), and (9.25), we conclude that the gradient of the Lagrangian function is

$$D_{(w,\lambda)} F(w, \lambda) = \begin{pmatrix} (D_w F(w, \lambda))^t \\ (D_\lambda F(w, \lambda))^t \end{pmatrix}^t = \begin{pmatrix} 2\Sigma_R w - \lambda \overline{\mu} \\ \mu_P - r_f - \overline{\mu}^t w \end{pmatrix}^t.$$

To find the critical point of the Lagrangian, we solve $D_{(w,\lambda)} F(w_0, \lambda_0) = 0$, which is equivalent to solving

$$2\Sigma_R w_0 = \lambda_0 \overline{\mu}; \qquad (9.26)$$
$$\overline{\mu}^t w_0 = \mu_P - r_f. \qquad (9.27)$$

---

[5] Lagrange multipliers can be used to solve this constrained optimization problem since the condition (10.66), i.e., $\text{rank}(Dg(w)) = 1$, is satisfied for the constraint function $g(w) = \mu_P - r_f - \overline{\mu}^t w$. From (10.43), we find that

$$Dg(w) = D(\mu_P - r_f - \overline{\mu}^t w) = -D(\overline{\mu}^t w) = -\overline{\mu}^t,$$

and therefore $\text{rank}(Dg(w)) = 1$.

Recall that Σ_R is a nonsingular matrix, since we assumes that the return of none of the assets can be replicated by using the other $n-1$ assets and cash; see section 9.1. Then, from (9.26), we find that

$$w_0 = \frac{\lambda_0}{2} \Sigma_R^{-1} \overline{\mu}. \tag{9.28}$$

By substituting formula (9.28) for w_0 in (9.27), we obtain that

$$\frac{\lambda_0}{2} \overline{\mu}^t \Sigma_R^{-1} \overline{\mu} = \mu_P - r_f,$$

and therefore

$$\lambda_0 = \frac{2(\mu_P - r_f)}{\overline{\mu}^t \Sigma_R^{-1} \overline{\mu}}. \tag{9.29}$$

From (9.28) and (9.29), we find that

$$w_0 = \frac{\mu_P - r_f}{\overline{\mu}^t \Sigma_R^{-1} \overline{\mu}} \Sigma_R^{-1} \overline{\mu}. \tag{9.30}$$

Let $F_0 : \mathbb{R}^n \to \mathbb{R}$ given by $F_0(w) = F(w, \lambda_0)$, where λ_0 is given by (9.29), i.e.,

$$F_0(w) = w^t \Sigma_R w + \lambda_0 (\mu_P - r_f - \overline{\mu}^t w)$$
$$= w^t \Sigma_R w + \frac{2(\mu_P - r_f)}{\overline{\mu}^t \Sigma_R^{-1} \overline{\mu}} (\mu_P - r_f - \overline{\mu}^t w).$$

Note that $D^2 \left(w^t \Sigma_R w \right) = 2\Sigma_R$, since Σ_R is a symmetric matrix, and $D^2(\overline{\mu}^t w) = 0$; cf. (10.48) and (10.45), respectively. Also, $D^2(\mu_P - r_f) = 0$, since $\mu_P - r_f$ is a constant. Thus, the Hessian of $F_0(w)$ is

$$D^2 F_0(w) = D^2(w^t \Sigma_R w) + \frac{2(\mu_P - r_f)}{\overline{\mu}^t \Sigma_R^{-1} \overline{\mu}} D^2(\mu_P - r_f - \overline{\mu}^t w)$$
$$= 2\Sigma_R.$$

Since Σ_R is a symmetric positive definite matrix, it follows that $D^2 F_0(w_0)$ is symmetric positive definite. From Theorem 10.7, we find that w_0 given by (9.30) is a constrained minimum point, and therefore $w_{min} = w_0$, i.e.,

$$w_{min} = \frac{\mu_P - r_f}{\overline{\mu}^t \Sigma_R^{-1} \overline{\mu}} \Sigma_R^{-1} \overline{\mu} \tag{9.31}$$

is the solution to the minimum variance portfolio problem (9.21).

Moreover, recall from (9.7) that the cash position $w_{min,cash}$ in a portfolio with asset weights vector w_{min} is

$$w_{min,cash} = 1 - \mathbf{1}^t w_{min}. \tag{9.32}$$

We conclude from (9.31) and (9.32) that the minimum variance portfolio with expected return μ_P is obtained for the following asset allocation:

- asset weights vector w_{min} given by

$$w_{min} = \frac{\mu_P - r_f}{\overline{\mu}^t \Sigma_R^{-1} \overline{\mu}} \Sigma_R^{-1} \overline{\mu}; \tag{9.33}$$

9.3. MINIMUM VARIANCE PORTFOLIOS

- weight $w_{min,cash}$ of the cash position given by

$$w_{min,cash} = 1 - \mathbf{1}^t w_{min} = 1 - (\mu_P - r_f)\frac{\mathbf{1}^t \Sigma_R^{-1} \overline{\mu}}{\overline{\mu}^t \Sigma_R^{-1} \overline{\mu}}. \qquad (9.34)$$

The minimum standard deviation of the return of a portfolio with given expected return μ_P is

$$\begin{aligned}
\sigma_{min} &= \sqrt{w_{min}^t \Sigma_R w_{min}} = \frac{\mu_P - r_f}{\overline{\mu}^t \Sigma_R^{-1} \overline{\mu}} \sqrt{(\Sigma_R^{-1}\overline{\mu})^t \Sigma_R (\Sigma_R^{-1}\overline{\mu})} \\
&= \frac{\mu_P - r_f}{\overline{\mu}^t \Sigma_R^{-1} \overline{\mu}} \sqrt{\overline{\mu}^t (\Sigma_R^{-1})^t (\Sigma_R \Sigma_R^{-1})\overline{\mu}} = \frac{\mu_P - r_f}{\overline{\mu}^t \Sigma_R^{-1} \overline{\mu}} \sqrt{\overline{\mu}^t \Sigma_R^{-1} \overline{\mu}} \\
&= \frac{\mu_P - r_f}{\sqrt{\overline{\mu}^t \Sigma_R^{-1} \overline{\mu}}}; \qquad (9.35)
\end{aligned}$$

here, we used the facts that $(\Sigma_R^{-1})^t = \Sigma_R^{-1}$, since Σ_R is a symmetric matrix; see Lemma 1.9. Note that $\overline{\mu}^t \Sigma_R^{-1} \overline{\mu} > 0$ since Σ_R is a symmetric positive definite matrix, and therefore Σ_R^{-1} is also symmetric positive definite; cf. Lemma 5.4.

The pseudocode for the asset allocation for the minimum variance portfolio computed using the formulas (9.33–9.35) can be found in Table 9.1.

Example: Find the $100 million minimum variance portfolio with expected return equal to 2.25% and invested in cash and four assets with expected returns equal to 2%, 1.75%, 2.5%, and 1.5%, and with the following covariance matrix of their returns:

$$\begin{pmatrix} 0.09 & 0.01 & 0.03 & -0.015 \\ 0.01 & 0.0625 & -0.02 & -0.01 \\ 0.03 & -0.02 & 0.1225 & 0.02 \\ -0.015 & -0.01 & 0.02 & 0.0576 \end{pmatrix}.$$

Assume that the risk free rate is 1%.

Answer: Let $\mu_1 = 0.02$, $\mu_2 = 0.0175$, $\mu_3 = 0.025$, $\mu_4 = 0.015$, and $r_f = 0.01$. We look for the asset and cash allocation corresponding to the minimum variance portfolio with expected return $\mu_P = 0.0225$.

Note that $\overline{\mu} = \mu - r_f \mathbf{1}$ and Σ_R are given by

$$\overline{\mu} = \begin{pmatrix} 0.01 \\ 0.0075 \\ 0.015 \\ 0.005 \end{pmatrix}; \quad \Sigma_R = \begin{pmatrix} 0.09 & 0.01 & 0.03 & -0.015 \\ 0.01 & 0.0625 & -0.02 & -0.01 \\ 0.03 & -0.02 & 0.1225 & 0.02 \\ -0.015 & -0.01 & 0.02 & 0.0576 \end{pmatrix}.$$

The vector $\Sigma_R^{-1} \overline{\mu}$ is computed by using the Cholesky decomposition to solve the linear system corresponding to the matrix Σ_R and to the right hand side $\overline{\mu}$, i.e., $\Sigma_R^{-1} \overline{\mu}$ = linear_solve_cholesky($\Sigma_R, \overline{\mu}$); see Table 6.2 and the pseudocode from Table 9.1. From (9.33) and (9.34), we find that the asset weights vector corresponding to the minimum variance portfolio is

$$w_{min} = \frac{\mu_P - r_f}{\overline{\mu}^t \Sigma_R^{-1} \overline{\mu}} \Sigma_R^{-1} \overline{\mu} = \begin{pmatrix} 0.2120 \\ 0.4888 \\ 0.3540 \\ 0.2808 \end{pmatrix},$$

and the weight of the cash position is

$$w_{min,cash} = 1 - \mathbf{1}^t w_{min} = -0.3356.$$

Thus, the $100 million minimum variance portfolio with expected return equal to 2.25% is obtained by borrowing $33.56 million and investing $21.20 million in asset 1, $48.88 million in asset 2, $35.40 million in asset 3, and $28.08 million in asset 4.

From (9.35), we find that the standard deviation of the return of the minimum variance portfolio is $\sigma_{min} = 0.1949$, i.e., 19.49%, which is smaller than the standard deviation of the returns of each of the four assets, which are $\sqrt{0.09} = 0.3 = 30\%$, $\sqrt{0.0625} = 0.25 = 25\%$, $\sqrt{0.1225} = 0.35 = 35\%$, $\sqrt{0.0576} = 0.24 = 24\%$, respectively.
□

9.3.1 Minimum variance portfolios and the tangency portfolio

It is important to note the connection between the minimum variance portfolio and a special portfolio called the tangency portfolio: in a nutshell, any minimum variance portfolio consists of a cash position that is determined to match the required expected return of the portfolio, with the rest of the portfolio invested in the tangency portfolio.

To see this, and implicitly introduce the tangency portfolio, note that the asset weights vector w_{min} given by (9.33) is a scalar multiple of the vector $\Sigma_R^{-1}\overline{\mu}$, i.e., $w_{min} = c\,\Sigma_R^{-1}\overline{\mu}$, where $c = \frac{\mu_P - r_f}{\overline{\mu}^t \Sigma_R^{-1} \overline{\mu}}$. Denote by

$$w_T = \frac{1}{\mathbf{1}^t \Sigma_R^{-1} \overline{\mu}} \Sigma_R^{-1} \overline{\mu} \qquad (9.36)$$

the asset weights vector in a portfolio with no cash, i.e., with $\mathbf{1}^t w_T = 1$, and with the n assets allocated in the same proportions as the $\Sigma_R^{-1}\overline{\mu}$ vector.

This portfolio is called the *tangency portfolio*. Note that another way of identifying the tangency portfolio is as the portfolio with the highest Sharpe ratio of all portfolios fully invested in n assets. The tangency portfolio also plays an important role in the Capital Asset Pricing Model (CAPM), where it is called the market portfolio.

From (9.36), we find that

$$\overline{\mu}^t w_T = \frac{\overline{\mu}^t \Sigma_R^{-1} \overline{\mu}}{\mathbf{1}^t \Sigma_R^{-1} \overline{\mu}},$$

and therefore

$$\frac{\mathbf{1}^t \Sigma_R^{-1} \overline{\mu}}{\overline{\mu}^t \Sigma_R^{-1} \overline{\mu}} = \frac{1}{\overline{\mu}^t w_T}. \qquad (9.37)$$

From (9.34) and (9.37), we obtain that the weight $w_{min,cash}$ of the cash position in the minimum variance portfolio can be written in terms of w_T as follows:

$$w_{min,cash} = 1 - \frac{\mu_P - r_f}{\overline{\mu}^t w_T}. \qquad (9.38)$$

Moreover, from (9.33) and (9.36), we find that

$$\begin{aligned} w_{min} &= \frac{\mu_P - r_f}{\overline{\mu}^t \Sigma_R^{-1} \overline{\mu}} \cdot \Sigma_R^{-1} \overline{\mu} \\ &= (\mu_P - r_f) \frac{\mathbf{1}^t \Sigma_R^{-1} \overline{\mu}}{\overline{\mu}^t \Sigma_R^{-1} \overline{\mu}} \cdot \frac{1}{\mathbf{1}^t \Sigma_R^{-1} \overline{\mu}} \Sigma_R^{-1} \overline{\mu} \\ &= (1 - w_{min,cash})\,w_T, \qquad (9.39) \end{aligned}$$

9.3. MIN VAR PORTFOLIO AND TANGENCY PORTFOLIO

since, from (9.34), it follows that

$$(\mu_P - r_f)\frac{\mathbf{1}^t \Sigma_R^{-1} \overline{\mu}}{\overline{\mu}^t \Sigma_R^{-1} \overline{\mu}} = 1 - w_{min,cash}.$$

From (9.38) and (9.39), we conclude that the minimum variance portfolio with expected return μ_P is obtained for the following asset allocation:

- weight $w_{min,cash}$ of the cash position given by

$$w_{min,cash} = 1 - \frac{\mu_P - r_f}{\overline{\mu}^t w_T}; \qquad (9.40)$$

- asset weights vector w_{min} given by

$$w_{min} = (1 - w_{min,cash}) w_T. \qquad (9.41)$$

The pseudocode for the asset allocation for the minimum variance portfolio computed using the formulas (9.40) and (9.41) can be found in Table 9.2.

We revisit below the example from section 9.3 and find the minimum variance portfolio by using the tangency portfolio.

Example: Find the $100 million minimum variance portfolio with expected return equal to 2.25% and invested in cash and four assets with expected returns equal to 2%, 1.75%, 2.5%, and 1.5%, and with the following covariance matrix of their returns:

$$\begin{pmatrix} 0.09 & 0.01 & 0.03 & -0.015 \\ 0.01 & 0.0625 & -0.02 & -0.01 \\ 0.03 & -0.02 & 0.1225 & 0.02 \\ -0.015 & -0.01 & 0.02 & 0.0576 \end{pmatrix}.$$

Assume that the risk free rate is 1%.

Answer: Let $\mu_1 = 0.02$, $\mu_2 = 0.0175$, $\mu_3 = 0.025$, $\mu_4 = 0.015$, and $r_f = 0.01$. We look for the assets and cash allocation corresponding to the minimum variance portfolio with expected return $\mu_P = 0.0225$.

Note that $\overline{\mu} = \mu - r_f \mathbf{1}$ and Σ_R are given by

$$\overline{\mu} = \begin{pmatrix} 0.01 \\ 0.0075 \\ 0.015 \\ 0.005 \end{pmatrix}; \quad \Sigma_R = \begin{pmatrix} 0.09 & 0.01 & 0.03 & -0.015 \\ 0.01 & 0.0625 & -0.02 & -0.01 \\ 0.03 & -0.02 & 0.1225 & 0.02 \\ -0.015 & -0.01 & 0.02 & 0.0576 \end{pmatrix}.$$

The vector $\Sigma_R^{-1} \overline{\mu} = $ linear_solve_cholesky$(\Sigma_R, \overline{\mu})$ is computed by using the Cholesky decomposition to solve the linear system corresponding to the matrix Σ_R and to the right hand side $\overline{\mu}$. From (9.36), we find that the asset weights vector of the tangency portfolio is

$$w_T = \frac{1}{\mathbf{1}^t \Sigma_R^{-1} \overline{\mu}} \Sigma_R^{-1} \overline{\mu} = \begin{pmatrix} 0.1587 \\ 0.3660 \\ 0.2650 \\ 0.2103 \end{pmatrix}.$$

From (9.40), we find that the weight of the cash position in the minimum variance portfolio is

$$w_{min,cash} = 1 - \frac{\mu_P - r_f}{\overline{\mu}^t w_T} = -0.3356,$$

and, from (9.41), we find that the asset weights vector corresponding to the minimum variance portfolio is

$$w_{min} = (1 - w_{min,cash})\, w_T = \begin{pmatrix} 0.2120 \\ 0.4888 \\ 0.3540 \\ 0.2808 \end{pmatrix}.$$

Thus, the \$100 million minimum variance portfolio with expected return equal to 2.25% is obtained by borrowing \$33.56 million and investing \$21.20 million in asset 1, \$48.88 million in asset 2, \$35.40 million in asset 3, and \$28.08 million in asset 4.

From (9.35), we find that the standard deviation of the return of the minimum variance portfolio is $\sigma_{min} = 0.1949$, i.e., 19.49%, which is smaller than the standard deviation of the returns of each of the four assets, which are $\sqrt{0.09} = 0.3 = 30\%$, $\sqrt{0.0625} = 0.25 = 25\%$, $\sqrt{0.1225} = 0.35 = 35\%$, $\sqrt{0.0576} = 0.24 = 24\%$, respectively. □

We conclude this section by deriving the formulas for the weights of the tangency portfolio made of two assets by using formula (9.36) for $n = 2$ assets.

For $n = 2$, the covariance matrix Σ_R of the returns of two assets and the vector $\overline{\mu}$ of the excess returns of the assets over the risk–free rate are

$$\Sigma_R = \begin{pmatrix} \sigma_1^2 & \sigma_1 \sigma_2 \rho_{1,2} \\ \sigma_1 \sigma_2 \rho_{1,2} & \sigma_2^2 \end{pmatrix} \quad \text{and} \quad \overline{\mu} = \begin{pmatrix} \mu_1 - r_f \\ \mu_2 - r_f \end{pmatrix}, \qquad (9.42)$$

respectively; see (7.12) and (9.4). From (10.7), we find that

$$\Sigma_R^{-1} = \frac{1}{\sigma_1^2 \sigma_2^2 (1 - \rho_{1,2}^2)} \begin{pmatrix} \sigma_2^2 & -\sigma_1 \sigma_2 \rho_{1,2} \\ -\sigma_1 \sigma_2 \rho_{1,2} & \sigma_1^2 \end{pmatrix}. \qquad (9.43)$$

From (9.42) and (9.43), we obtain that

$$\Sigma_R^{-1} \overline{\mu} = \frac{1}{\sigma_1^2 \sigma_2^2 (1 - \rho_{1,2}^2)} \begin{pmatrix} \sigma_2^2 (\mu_1 - r_f) - \sigma_1 \sigma_2 \rho_{1,2} (\mu_2 - r_f) \\ \sigma_1^2 (\mu_2 - r_f) - \sigma_1 \sigma_2 \rho_{1,2} (\mu_1 - r_f) \end{pmatrix};$$

$$1^t \Sigma_R^{-1} \overline{\mu} = \frac{\sigma_1^2 (\mu_2 - r_f) - \rho_{1,2} \sigma_1 \sigma_2 (\mu_1 + \mu_2 - 2 r_f) + \sigma_2^2 (\mu_1 - r_f)}{\sigma_1^2 \sigma_2^2 (1 - \rho_{1,2}^2)},$$

and, from (9.36), we conclude that

$$w_T = \begin{pmatrix} w_{1,T} \\ w_{2,T} \end{pmatrix} = \frac{\Sigma_R^{-1} \overline{\mu}}{1^t \Sigma_R^{-1} \overline{\mu}}$$

$$= \begin{pmatrix} \frac{\sigma_2^2 (\mu_1 - r_f) - \sigma_1 \sigma_2 \rho_{1,2} (\mu_2 - r_f)}{\sigma_1^2 (\mu_2 - r_f) - \rho_{1,2} \sigma_1 \sigma_2 (\mu_1 + \mu_2 - 2 r_f) + \sigma_2^2 (\mu_1 - r_f)} \\ \\ \frac{\sigma_1^2 (\mu_2 - r_f) - \sigma_1 \sigma_2 \rho_{1,2} (\mu_1 - r_f)}{\sigma_1^2 (\mu_2 - r_f) - \rho_{1,2} \sigma_1 \sigma_2 (\mu_1 + \mu_2 - 2 r_f) + \sigma_2^2 (\mu_1 - r_f)} \end{pmatrix}.$$

9.4 Maximum return portfolios

The maximum return portfolio invested in n assets and with a cash position is the portfolio which has the largest expected return of all the portfolios with given variance σ_P^2 of the portfolio return.

In other words, given $\sigma_P^2 \neq 0$, we are looking for a weights vector $w = (w_i)_{i=1:n}$ such that $\sigma_R^2 = \sigma_P^2$ and μ_R is maximal. From (9.6) and (9.8), it follows that we want to maximize $\mu_R = r_f + \overline{\mu}^t w$ subject to $\sigma_R^2 = w^t \Sigma_R w = \sigma_P^2$, i.e.,

$$\max_{w^t \Sigma_R w = \sigma_P^2} \left(r_f + \overline{\mu}^t w\right). \tag{9.44}$$

We use Lagrange multipliers to solve this problem; see section 10.2.2 for details. The associated Lagrangian function $F : \mathbb{R}^{n+1} \to \mathbb{R}$ is given by

$$F(w, \lambda) = r_f + \overline{\mu}^t w + \lambda(w^t \Sigma_R w - \sigma_P^2),$$

where $\lambda \in \mathbb{R}$ is the Lagrange multiplier.[6] Recall that $D(\overline{\mu}^t w) = \overline{\mu}^t$ and $D\left(w^t \Sigma_R w\right) = 2(\Sigma_R w)^t$; see (9.23) and (9.22). Then,

$$\begin{aligned} D_w F(w, \lambda) &= D(r_f + \overline{\mu}^t w) + \lambda D(w^t \Sigma_R w - \sigma_P^2) \\ &= D(\overline{\mu}^t w) + \lambda D\left(w^t \Sigma_R w\right) \\ &= \overline{\mu}^t + 2\lambda \left(\Sigma_R w\right)^t \\ &= \left(\overline{\mu} + 2\lambda \Sigma_R w\right)^t; \end{aligned} \tag{9.45}$$

$$D_\lambda F(w, \lambda) = \frac{\partial F}{\partial \lambda}(w, \lambda) = w^t \Sigma_R w - \sigma_P^2. \tag{9.46}$$

From (10.67), (9.45), and (9.46), we conclude that the gradient of the Lagrangian function is

$$D_{(w,\lambda)} F(w, \lambda) = \begin{pmatrix} (D_w F(w,\lambda))^t \\ (D_\lambda F(w,\lambda))^t \end{pmatrix}^t = \begin{pmatrix} \overline{\mu} + 2\lambda \Sigma_R w \\ w^t \Sigma_R w - \sigma_P^2 \end{pmatrix}^t.$$

To find the critical point of the Lagrangian, we solve $D_{(w,\lambda)}F(w_0, \lambda_0) = 0$, which is equivalent to solving

$$2\lambda_0 \Sigma_R w_0 = -\overline{\mu}; \tag{9.47}$$

$$\sigma_P^2 = w_0^t \Sigma_R w_0. \tag{9.48}$$

Recall that Σ_R is a nonsingular matrix, since we assumes that the return of none of the assets can be replicated by using the other $n-1$ assets and cash; see section 9.1. Then, from (9.47), we find that

$$w_0 = -\frac{1}{2\lambda_0} \Sigma_R^{-1} \overline{\mu}. \tag{9.49}$$

---

[6]Lagrange multipliers can be used to solve this constrained optimization problem, since the condition (10.66), i.e., $\text{rank}(Dg(w)) = 1$, is satisfied for the constraint function $g(w) = w^t \Sigma_R w - \sigma_P^2$. From (9.22), we find that

$$Dg(w) = D(w^t \Sigma_R w - \sigma_P^2) = 2(\Sigma_R w)^t.$$

Thus, $\text{rank}(Dg(w)) = 1$ for any vector satisfying the constraint $w^t \Sigma_R w = \sigma_P^2$, unless $\Sigma_R w = 0$. This would imply that $\sigma_P^2 = 0$, which would contradict the assumption that $\sigma_P \neq 0$.

Note that
$$(\Sigma_R^{-1})^t = \Sigma_R^{-1}, \qquad (9.50)$$
since Σ_R is a symmetric matrix; see Lemma 1.9. Then, from (9.49) and (9.50), it follows that
$$w_0^t = -\frac{1}{2\lambda_0}(\Sigma_R^{-1}\overline{\mu})^t = -\frac{1}{2\lambda_0}\overline{\mu}^t(\Sigma_R^{-1})^t = -\frac{1}{2\lambda_0}\overline{\mu}^t\Sigma_R^{-1}. \qquad (9.51)$$

By substituting the formulas (9.49) for w_0 and (9.51) for w_0^t in (9.48), we obtain that
$$\begin{aligned}\sigma_P^2 &= \frac{1}{4\lambda_0^2}(\overline{\mu}^t\Sigma_R^{-1})\Sigma_R(\Sigma_R^{-1}\overline{\mu}) = \frac{1}{4\lambda_0^2}\overline{\mu}^t\Sigma_R^{-1}(\Sigma_R\Sigma_R^{-1})\overline{\mu} \\ &= \frac{1}{4\lambda_0^2}\overline{\mu}^t\Sigma_R^{-1}\overline{\mu}.\end{aligned} \qquad (9.52)$$

Note that $\overline{\mu}^t\Sigma_R^{-1}\overline{\mu} > 0$ since Σ_R is a symmetric positive definite matrix, and therefore Σ_R^{-1} is also symmetric positive definite; cf. Lemma 5.4.

From (9.52), we find that
$$\lambda_0^2 = \frac{1}{4\sigma_P^2}\overline{\mu}^t\Sigma_R^{-1}\overline{\mu},$$
which has two solutions, i.e.,
$$\lambda_{0,1} = -\frac{1}{2\sigma_P}\sqrt{\overline{\mu}^t\Sigma_R^{-1}\overline{\mu}}; \qquad (9.53)$$
$$\lambda_{0,2} = \frac{1}{2\sigma_P}\sqrt{\overline{\mu}^t\Sigma_R^{-1}\overline{\mu}}. \qquad (9.54)$$

From (9.49), we find that the corresponding values of w_0 are
$$w_{0,1} = \frac{\sigma_P}{\sqrt{\overline{\mu}^t\Sigma_R^{-1}\overline{\mu}}}\Sigma_R^{-1}\overline{\mu}; \qquad (9.55)$$
$$w_{0,2} = -\frac{\sigma_P}{\sqrt{\overline{\mu}^t\Sigma_R^{-1}\overline{\mu}}}\Sigma_R^{-1}\overline{\mu}. \qquad (9.56)$$

Thus, the Lagrangian associated to this problem has two critical points, $(w_{0,1}, \lambda_{0,1})$ and $(w_{0,2}, \lambda_{0,2})$.

To classify the critical point $(w_{0,1}, \lambda_{0,1})$, let $F_{0,1}: \mathbb{R}^n \to \mathbb{R}$ given by $F_{0,1}(w) = F(w, \lambda_{0,1})$, where $\lambda_{0,1}$ is given by (9.53), i.e.,
$$\begin{aligned}F_{0,1}(w) &= r_f + \overline{\mu}^t w + \lambda_{0,1}(w^t\Sigma_R w - \sigma_P^2) \\ &= r_f + \overline{\mu}^t w - \frac{1}{2\sigma_P}\sqrt{\overline{\mu}^t\Sigma_R^{-1}\overline{\mu}}\,(w^t\Sigma_R w - \sigma_P^2).\end{aligned}$$

Note that $D^2(w^t\Sigma_R w) = 2\Sigma_R$, since Σ_R is a symmetric matrix, and $D^2(\overline{\mu}^t w) = 0$; cf. (10.48) and (10.45), respectively. Also, $D^2(r_f) = D^2(\sigma_P^2) = 0$. Then, the Hessian

9.4. MAXIMUM RETURN PORTFOLIOS

of $F_{0,1}(w)$ is

$$\begin{aligned} D^2 F_{0,1}(w) &= D^2(\overline{\mu}^t w) - \frac{1}{2\sigma_P}\sqrt{\overline{\mu}^t \Sigma_R^{-1}\overline{\mu}}\; D^2(w^t \Sigma_R w) \\ &= -\frac{1}{2\sigma_P}\sqrt{\overline{\mu}^t \Sigma_R^{-1}\overline{\mu}}\; 2\Sigma_R \\ &= -\frac{1}{\sigma_P}\sqrt{\overline{\mu}^t \Sigma_R^{-1}\overline{\mu}}\; \Sigma_R. \end{aligned}$$

Since Σ_R is a symmetric positive definite matrix, it follows that $-\Sigma_R$ is a negative definite matrix, see Definition 5.8, and therefore $D^2 F_{0,1}(w_0)$ is also negative definite. From Theorem 10.7, we conclude that $w_{0,1}$ is a constrained maximum point.

To classify the critical point $(w_{0,2}, \lambda_{0,2})$, let $F_{0,2}: \mathbb{R}^n \to \mathbb{R}$ given by $F_{0,2}(w) = F(w, \lambda_{0,2})$, where $\lambda_{0,2}$ is given by (9.54), i.e.,

$$\begin{aligned} F_{0,2}(w) &= r_f + \overline{\mu}^t w + \lambda_{0,2}(w^t \Sigma_R w - \sigma_P^2) \\ &= r_f + \overline{\mu}^t w + \frac{1}{2\sigma_P}\sqrt{\overline{\mu}^t \Sigma_R^{-1}\overline{\mu}}\; (w^t \Sigma_R w - \sigma_P^2). \end{aligned}$$

The Hessian of $F_{0,2}(w)$ is

$$\begin{aligned} D^2 F_{0,2}(w) &= D^2(\overline{\mu}^t w) + \frac{1}{2\sigma_P}\sqrt{\overline{\mu}^t \Sigma_R^{-1}\overline{\mu}}\; D^2(w^t \Sigma_R w) \\ &= \frac{1}{\sigma_P}\sqrt{\overline{\mu}^t \Sigma_R^{-1}\overline{\mu}}\; \Sigma_R. \end{aligned}$$

Since Σ_R is a symmetric positive definite matrix, it follows that $D^2 F_{0,2}(w_0)$ is positive definite. Then, $w_{0,2}$ is a constrained minimum point for the function $f(w)$; see Theorem 10.7.

Thus, we conclude that the maximum return portfolio problem (9.44) has one solution, $w_{max} = w_{0,1}$ given by (9.55), i.e.,

$$w_{max} = \frac{\sigma_P}{\sqrt{\overline{\mu}^t \Sigma_R^{-1}\overline{\mu}}} \Sigma_R^{-1}\overline{\mu}. \tag{9.57}$$

Moreover, recall from (9.7) that the cash position $w_{max,cash}$ in a portfolio with asset weights vector w_{max} is

$$w_{max,cash} = 1 - \mathbf{1}^t w_{max}. \tag{9.58}$$

We conclude from (9.57) and (9.58) that the maximum expected return of a portfolio with variance of return equal to σ_P^2 is obtained for the following asset allocation:

- asset weights vector w_{max} given by

$$w_{max} = \frac{\sigma_P}{\sqrt{\overline{\mu}^t \Sigma_R^{-1}\overline{\mu}}} \Sigma_R^{-1}\overline{\mu}; \tag{9.59}$$

- weight $w_{max,cash}$ of the cash position given by

$$w_{max,cash} = 1 - \mathbf{1}^t w_{max} = 1 - \sigma_P \frac{\mathbf{1}^t \Sigma_R^{-1}\overline{\mu}}{\sqrt{\overline{\mu}^t \Sigma_R^{-1}\overline{\mu}}}. \tag{9.60}$$

The maximum expected return of a portfolio with variance of return equal to σ_P^2 is

$$\mu_{max} = r_f + \overline{\mu}^t w_{max} = r_f + \sigma_P \frac{\overline{\mu}^t \Sigma_R^{-1} \overline{\mu}}{\sqrt{\overline{\mu}^t \Sigma_R^{-1} \overline{\mu}}}$$

$$= r_f + \sigma_P \sqrt{\overline{\mu}^t \Sigma_R^{-1} \overline{\mu}}. \tag{9.61}$$

The pseudocode for the asset allocation for the maximum return portfolio computed using the formulas (9.59–9.61) can be found in Table 9.3.

Example: Find the \$100 million maximum return portfolio with 27% standard deviation of return invested in cash and four assets with expected returns equal to 2%, 1.75%, 2.5%, and 1.5%, and with the following covariance matrix of their returns:

$$\begin{pmatrix} 0.09 & 0.01 & 0.03 & -0.015 \\ 0.01 & 0.0625 & -0.02 & -0.01 \\ 0.03 & -0.02 & 0.1225 & 0.02 \\ -0.015 & -0.01 & 0.02 & 0.0576 \end{pmatrix}.$$

Assume that the risk free rate is 1%.

Answer: We know that $\mu_1 = 0.02$, $\mu_2 = 0.0175$, $\mu_3 = 0.025$, $\mu_4 = 0.015$, and $r_f = 0.01$. We look for the asset and cash allocation corresponding to the maximum return portfolio with standard deviation of return equal to $\sigma_P = 0.27$.

Note that $\overline{\mu} = \mu - r_f \mathbf{1}$ and Σ_R are given by

$$\overline{\mu} = \mu - r_f \mathbf{1} = \begin{pmatrix} 0.01 \\ 0.0075 \\ 0.015 \\ 0.005 \end{pmatrix}; \quad \Sigma_R = \begin{pmatrix} 0.09 & 0.01 & 0.03 & -0.015 \\ 0.01 & 0.0625 & -0.02 & -0.01 \\ 0.03 & -0.02 & 0.1225 & 0.02 \\ -0.015 & -0.01 & 0.02 & 0.0576 \end{pmatrix}.$$

The vector $\Sigma_R^{-1} \overline{\mu}$ is computed by using the Cholesky decomposition to solve the linear system corresponding to the matrix Σ_R and to the right hand side $\overline{\mu}$, i.e., $\Sigma_R^{-1} \overline{\mu}$ = linear_solve_cholesky($\Sigma_R, \overline{\mu}$); see Table 6.2 and also the pseudocode from Table 9.3. From (9.59) and (9.60), we find that the asset weights vector corresponding to the maximum return portfolio is

$$w_{max} = \frac{\sigma_P}{\sqrt{\overline{\mu}^t \Sigma_R^{-1} \overline{\mu}}} \Sigma_R^{-1} \overline{\mu} = \begin{pmatrix} 0.2938 \\ 0.6773 \\ 0.4905 \\ 0.3891 \end{pmatrix},$$

and the weight of the cash position is

$$w_{max,cash} = 1 - \mathbf{1}^t w_{max} = -0.8507.$$

Thus, the \$100 million maximum return portfolio with 27% standard deviation of return is obtained by borrowing \$85.07 million and investing \$29.38 million in asset 1, \$67.73 million in asset 2, \$49.05 million in asset 3, and \$38.91 million in asset 4.

From (9.61), we find that the maximum expected return of this portfolio is $\mu_{max} = 0.0273$, i.e., 2.73%, which is more than 2.5%, the largest expected return of any of the four assets. □

9.4. MAX RETURN PORTFOLIO AND TANGENCY PORTFOLIO

9.4.1 Maximum return portfolios and the tangency portfolio

As was the case for the minimum variance portfolio, see section 9.3.1, any maximum return portfolio consists of a cash position that is determined to match the required variance of the portfolio return, with the rest of the portfolio invested in the tangency portfolio.

Recall from (9.36) that the asset weights vector in the tangency portfolio can be written as

$$w_T = \frac{1}{\mathbf{1}^t \Sigma_R^{-1} \overline{\mu}} \Sigma_R^{-1} \overline{\mu}, \tag{9.62}$$

where $\frac{1}{\mathbf{1}^t \Sigma_R^{-1} \overline{\mu}}$ is a constant and $\Sigma_R^{-1} \overline{\mu}$ is a vector. Then,

$$\begin{aligned} w_T^t \Sigma_R w_T &= \frac{1}{(\mathbf{1}^t \Sigma_R^{-1} \overline{\mu})^2} (\Sigma_R^{-1} \overline{\mu})^t \Sigma_R (\Sigma_R^{-1} \overline{\mu}) \\ &= \frac{1}{(\mathbf{1}^t \Sigma_R^{-1} \overline{\mu})^2} \overline{\mu}^t (\Sigma_R^{-1})^t (\Sigma_R \Sigma_R^{-1}) \overline{\mu} \\ &= \frac{1}{(\mathbf{1}^t \Sigma_R^{-1} \overline{\mu})^2} \overline{\mu}^t \Sigma_R^{-1} \overline{\mu}, \end{aligned} \tag{9.63}$$

where for (9.63) we used the facts that $(\Sigma_R^{-1})^t = \Sigma_R^{-1}$ since Σ_R^{-1} is a symmetric matrix, see Lemma 5.4, and that $\Sigma_R \Sigma_R^{-1} = I$.

By taking the square root on both sides of (9.63),[7] we find that

$$\sqrt{w_T^t \Sigma_R w_T} = \frac{1}{\mathbf{1}^t \Sigma_R^{-1} \overline{\mu}} \sqrt{\overline{\mu}^t \Sigma_R^{-1} \overline{\mu}} \cdot \operatorname{sign}(\mathbf{1}^t \Sigma_R^{-1} \overline{\mu}),$$

and therefore

$$\frac{\mathbf{1}^t \Sigma_R^{-1} \overline{\mu}}{\sqrt{\overline{\mu}^t \Sigma_R^{-1} \overline{\mu}}} = \frac{1}{\sqrt{w_T^t \Sigma_R w_T}} \cdot \operatorname{sign}(\mathbf{1}^t \Sigma_R^{-1} \overline{\mu}). \tag{9.64}$$

Then, from (9.60) and (9.64), it follows that

$$w_{max,cash} = 1 - \frac{\sigma_P}{\sqrt{w_T^t \Sigma_R w_T}} \cdot \operatorname{sign}(\mathbf{1}^t \Sigma_R^{-1} \overline{\mu}). \tag{9.65}$$

Moreover, from (9.59) and (9.62), we find that

$$\begin{aligned} w_{max} &= \frac{\sigma_P}{\sqrt{\overline{\mu}^t \Sigma_R^{-1} \overline{\mu}}} \Sigma_R^{-1} \overline{\mu} \\ &= \sigma_P \frac{\mathbf{1}^t \Sigma_R^{-1} \overline{\mu}}{\sqrt{\overline{\mu}^t \Sigma_R^{-1} \overline{\mu}}} \cdot \frac{1}{\mathbf{1}^t \Sigma_R^{-1} \overline{\mu}} \Sigma_R^{-1} \overline{\mu} \\ &= \sigma_P \frac{\mathbf{1}^t \Sigma_R^{-1} \overline{\mu}}{\sqrt{\overline{\mu}^t \Sigma_R^{-1} \overline{\mu}}} w_T \\ &= (1 - w_{max,cash}) \, w_T, \end{aligned} \tag{9.66}$$

---

[7] Note that $\overline{\mu}^t \Sigma_R^{-1} \overline{\mu} > 0$ since Σ_R is a symmetric positive definite matrix, and therefore Σ_R^{-1} is also symmetric positive definite; cf. Lemma 5.4.

since, from (9.60), it follows that

$$\sigma_P \frac{1^t \Sigma_R^{-1} \bar{\mu}}{\sqrt{\bar{\mu}^t \Sigma_R^{-1} \bar{\mu}}} = 1 - w_{max,cash}.$$

From (9.65) and (9.66), we conclude that the maximum expected return of a portfolio with variance of return equal to σ_P^2 is obtained for the following asset allocation:

- weight $w_{max,cash}$ of the cash position given by

$$w_{max,cash} = 1 - \frac{\sigma_P}{\sqrt{w_T^t \Sigma_R w_T}} \cdot \text{sign}(1^t \Sigma_R^{-1} \bar{\mu}); \qquad (9.67)$$

- asset weights vector w_{max} given by

$$w_{max} = (1 - w_{max,cash}) \, w_T. \qquad (9.68)$$

The pseudocode for the asset allocation for the maximum return portfolio computed using the formulas (9.65) and (9.66) can be found in Table 9.4.

We revisit below the example from section 9.4 and find the maximum return portfolio by using the tangency portfolio.

Example: Find the \$100 million maximum return portfolio with 27% standard deviation of return invested in cash and four assets with expected returns equal to 2%, 1.75%, 2.5%, and 1.5%, and with the following covariance matrix of their returns:

$$\begin{pmatrix} 0.09 & 0.01 & 0.03 & -0.015 \\ 0.01 & 0.0625 & -0.02 & -0.01 \\ 0.03 & -0.02 & 0.1225 & 0.02 \\ -0.015 & -0.01 & 0.02 & 0.0576 \end{pmatrix}.$$

Assume that the risk free rate is 1%.

Answer: Let $\mu_1 = 0.02$, $\mu_2 = 0.0175$, $\mu_3 = 0.025$, $\mu_4 = 0.015$, and $r_f = 0.01$. We look for the asset and cash allocation corresponding to the maximum return portfolio with standard deviation of return equal to $\sigma_P = 0.27$.

Note that $\bar{\mu} = \mu - r_f 1$ and Σ_R are given by

$$\bar{\mu} = \mu - r_f 1 = \begin{pmatrix} 0.01 \\ 0.0075 \\ 0.015 \\ 0.005 \end{pmatrix}; \quad \Sigma_R = \begin{pmatrix} 0.09 & 0.01 & 0.03 & -0.015 \\ 0.01 & 0.0625 & -0.02 & -0.01 \\ 0.03 & -0.02 & 0.1225 & 0.02 \\ -0.015 & -0.01 & 0.02 & 0.0576 \end{pmatrix}.$$

The vector $\Sigma_R^{-1} \bar{\mu} = \text{linear\_solve\_cholesky}(\Sigma_R, \bar{\mu})$ is computed by using the Cholesky decomposition to solve the linear system corresponding to the matrix Σ_R and to the right hand side $\bar{\mu}$.

From (9.62), we find that the asset weights vector of the tangency portfolio is

$$w_T = \frac{1}{1^t \Sigma_R^{-1} \bar{\mu}} \Sigma_R^{-1} \bar{\mu} = \begin{pmatrix} 0.1587 \\ 0.3660 \\ 0.2650 \\ 0.2103 \end{pmatrix}.$$

9.4. MIN VAR PORTFOLIO NO CASH POSITION

From (9.67), we find that the weight of the cash position in the maximum return portfolio is

$$w_{max,cash} = 1 - \frac{\sigma_P}{\sqrt{w_T^t \Sigma_R w_T}} \cdot \text{sign}(\mathbf{1}^t \Sigma_R^{-1} \overline{\mu}) = -0.8507,$$

and, from (9.68), we find that the asset weights vector corresponding to the maximum return portfolio is

$$w_{max} = (1 - w_{max,cash}) w_T = \begin{pmatrix} 0.2938 \\ 0.6773 \\ 0.4905 \\ 0.3891 \end{pmatrix}.$$

Thus, the \$100 million maximum return portfolio with 27% standard deviation of return is obtained by borrowing \$85.07 million and investing \$29.38 million in asset 1, \$67.73 million in asset 2, \$49.05 million in asset 3, and \$38.91 million in asset 4.

From (9.61), we find that the maximum expected return of this portfolio is $\mu_{max} = 0.0273$, i.e., 2.73%, which is more than 2.5%, the largest expected return of any of the four assets. □

9.5 Minimum variance portfolio with no cash position

In this section, we find the asset allocation for a minimum variance portfolio fully invested in n assets. Note that this is different from the minimum variance portfolio found in Section 9.3, since we now require that no cash position is being held.

Consider a portfolio fully invested in n assets. Since there is no cash position in the portfolio, it follows that $\sum_{i=1}^{n} w_i = 1$, which can be written in vector form as $\mathbf{1}^t w = 1$, where $\mathbf{1}$ is the $n \times 1$ column vector whose entries are all equal to 1.

We look for a weights vector $w = (w_i)_{i=1:n}$ such that the variance $\sigma_R^2 = w^t \Sigma_R w$ of the return of the portfolio is minimal and such that $\mathbf{1}^t w = 1$. Thus, we have to solve the following constrained minimization problem:

Find $w \in \mathbb{R}^n$ corresponding to

$$\min_{\mathbf{1}^t w = 1} w^t \Sigma_R w.$$

We use Lagrange multipliers to solve this problem.

The associated Lagrangian function $F : \mathbb{R}^{n+1} \to \mathbb{R}$ is given by

$$F(w, \lambda) = w^t \Sigma_R w + \lambda(1 - \mathbf{1}^t w),$$

where $\lambda \in \mathbb{R}$ is a Lagrange multiplier.[8]

---

[8] Note that we can use Lagrange multipliers to solve this constrained optimization problem, since the condition (10.66) is satisfied for the constraint function $g(w) = 1 - \mathbf{1}^t w$:

$$Dg(w) = D(1 - \mathbf{1}^t w) = -D(\mathbf{1}^t w) = -\mathbf{1}^t,$$

see (10.43), and therefore rank$(Dg(w)) = 1$.

Recall from (10.43) and (9.22) that $D(\mathbf{1}^t w) = \mathbf{1}^t$ and $D(w^t \Sigma_R w) = 2(\Sigma_R w)^t$. Then,

$$\begin{aligned} D_w F(w,\lambda) &= D(w^t \Sigma_R w) + \lambda D(1 - \mathbf{1}^t w) \\ &= 2(\Sigma_R w)^t - \lambda \mathbf{1}^t \\ &= (2\Sigma_R w - \lambda \mathbf{1})^t. \end{aligned} \qquad (9.69)$$

Also, note that

$$D_\lambda F(w,\lambda) = \frac{\partial F}{\partial \lambda}(w,\lambda) = 1 - \mathbf{1}^t w. \qquad (9.70)$$

From (10.67), (9.69), and (9.70) we conclude that the gradient of the Lagrangian function is

$$D_{(w,\lambda)} F(w,\lambda) = \begin{pmatrix} (D_w F(w,\lambda))^t \\ (D_\lambda F(w,\lambda))^t \end{pmatrix}^t = \begin{pmatrix} 2\Sigma_R w - \lambda \mathbf{1} \\ 1 - \mathbf{1}^t w \end{pmatrix}^t.$$

To find the critical point of the Lagrangian, we solve $D_{(w,\lambda)} F(w_0, \lambda_0) = 0$, which is equivalent to solving

$$2\Sigma_R w_0 = \lambda_0 \mathbf{1}; \qquad (9.71)$$
$$\mathbf{1}^t w_0 = 1. \qquad (9.72)$$

Recall that Σ_R is a nonsingular matrix, since we assumes that the return of none of the assets can be replicated by using the other $n-1$ assets and cash; see section 9.1. From (9.71), we find that

$$w_0 = \frac{\lambda_0}{2} \Sigma_R^{-1} \mathbf{1}. \qquad (9.73)$$

By substituting formula (9.73) for w_0 in (9.72), we obtain that

$$\frac{\lambda_0}{2} \mathbf{1}^t \Sigma_R^{-1} \mathbf{1} = 1,$$

and therefore

$$\lambda_0 = \frac{2}{\mathbf{1}^t \Sigma_R^{-1} \mathbf{1}}. \qquad (9.74)$$

From (9.73) and (9.74), we find that

$$w_0 = \frac{1}{\mathbf{1}^t \Sigma_R^{-1} \mathbf{1}} \Sigma_R^{-1} \mathbf{1}. \qquad (9.75)$$

Let $F_0 : \mathbb{R}^n \to \mathbb{R}$ given by $F_0(w) = F(w, \lambda_0)$, where λ_0 is given by (9.74), i.e.,

$$\begin{aligned} F_0(w) &= w^t \Sigma_R w + \lambda_0 (1 - \mathbf{1}^t w) \\ &= w^t \Sigma_R w + \frac{2}{\mathbf{1}^t \Sigma_R^{-1} \mathbf{1}} (1 - \mathbf{1}^t w). \end{aligned}$$

Note that $D^2(w^t \Sigma_R w) = 2\Sigma_R$ and $D^2(\mathbf{1}^t w) = 0$; cf. (10.48) and (10.45), respectively. Then, the Hessian of $F_0(w)$ is

$$\begin{aligned} D^2 F_0(w) &= D^2(w^t \Sigma_R w) + \frac{2}{\mathbf{1}^t \Sigma_R^{-1} \mathbf{1}} D^2(1 - \mathbf{1}^t w) \\ &= 2\Sigma_R. \end{aligned}$$

9.5. MIN VAR PORTFOLIO NO CASH POSITION

Since Σ_R is a symmetric positive definite matrix, it follows that $D^2 F_0(w_0)$ is symmetric positive definite. From Theorem 10.7, we find that w_0 given by (9.75) is a constrained minimum point.

We conclude that the portfolio with asset allocation $w_m = w_0$, i.e., with

$$w_m = \frac{1}{\mathbf{1}^t \Sigma_R^{-1} \mathbf{1}} \Sigma_R^{-1} \mathbf{1}, \tag{9.76}$$

is the minimum variance portfolio. Its variance is

$$\sigma_m^2 = w_m^t \Sigma_R w_m = \frac{1}{(\mathbf{1}^t \Sigma_R^{-1} \mathbf{1})^2} (\Sigma_R^{-1} \mathbf{1})^t \Sigma_R (\Sigma_R^{-1} \mathbf{1})$$

$$= \frac{1}{(\mathbf{1}^t \Sigma_R^{-1} \mathbf{1})^2} \mathbf{1}^t (\Sigma_R^{-1})^t (\Sigma_R \Sigma_R^{-1}) \mathbf{1} = \frac{1}{(\mathbf{1}^t \Sigma_R^{-1} \mathbf{1})^2} \mathbf{1}^t \Sigma_R^{-1} \mathbf{1}$$

$$= \frac{1}{\mathbf{1}^t \Sigma_R^{-1} \mathbf{1}}; \tag{9.77}$$

here, we used the fact that $(\Sigma_R^{-1})^t = \Sigma_R^{-1}$, since Σ_R is a symmetric matrix; see (9.50).

We conclude this section by deriving the asset allocation for the minimum variance portfolio made of two assets by using formula (9.76) for $n = 2$ assets.

For $n = 2$, the covariance matrix Σ_R of the returns of two assets is given by

$$\Sigma_R = \begin{pmatrix} \sigma_1^2 & \sigma_1 \sigma_2 \rho_{1,2} \\ \sigma_1 \sigma_2 \rho_{1,2} & \sigma_2^2 \end{pmatrix};$$

see (7.12). From (10.7), it follows that

$$\Sigma_R^{-1} = \frac{1}{\sigma_1^2 \sigma_2^2 (1 - \rho_{1,2}^2)} \begin{pmatrix} \sigma_2^2 & -\sigma_1 \sigma_2 \rho_{1,2} \\ -\sigma_1 \sigma_2 \rho_{1,2} & \sigma_1^2 \end{pmatrix}. \tag{9.78}$$

Let $\mathbf{1} = \begin{pmatrix} 1 \\ 1 \end{pmatrix}$. Then,

$$\Sigma_R^{-1} \mathbf{1} = \frac{1}{\sigma_1^2 \sigma_2^2 (1 - \rho_{1,2}^2)} \begin{pmatrix} \sigma_2^2 - \sigma_1 \sigma_2 \rho_{1,2} \\ \sigma_1^2 - \sigma_1 \sigma_2 \rho_{1,2} \end{pmatrix},$$

and therefore we find that

$$\mathbf{1}^t \Sigma_R^{-1} \mathbf{1} = \frac{\sigma_1^2 - 2\sigma_1 \sigma_2 \rho_{1,2} + \sigma_2^2}{\sigma_1^2 \sigma_2^2 (1 - \rho_{1,2}^2)}. \tag{9.79}$$

From (9.76) for $n = 2$, and using (9.78) and (9.79), we obtain that

$$w_m = \begin{pmatrix} w_1 \\ w_2 \end{pmatrix} = \frac{1}{\mathbf{1}^t \Sigma_R^{-1} \mathbf{1}} \Sigma_R^{-1} \mathbf{1}$$

$$= \frac{1}{\sigma_1^2 - 2\sigma_1 \sigma_2 \rho_{1,2} + \sigma_2^2} \begin{pmatrix} \sigma_2^2 - \sigma_1 \sigma_2 \rho_{1,2} \\ \sigma_1^2 - \sigma_1 \sigma_2 \rho_{1,2} \end{pmatrix}$$

$$= \begin{pmatrix} \frac{\sigma_2^2 - \sigma_1 \sigma_2 \rho_{1,2}}{\sigma_1^2 - 2\sigma_1 \sigma_2 \rho_{1,2} + \sigma_2^2} \\ \frac{\sigma_1^2 - \sigma_1 \sigma_2 \rho_{1,2}}{\sigma_1^2 - 2\sigma_1 \sigma_2 \rho_{1,2} + \sigma_2^2} \end{pmatrix}.$$

Thus, the asset allocation for the minimum variance portfolio fully invested in two assets is

$$w_1 = \frac{\sigma_2^2 - \sigma_1\sigma_2\rho_{1,2}}{\sigma_1^2 - 2\sigma_1\sigma_2\rho_{1,2} + \sigma_2^2}; \qquad (9.80)$$

$$w_2 = \frac{\sigma_1^2 - \sigma_1\sigma_2\rho_{1,2}}{\sigma_1^2 - 2\sigma_1\sigma_2\rho_{1,2} + \sigma_2^2} = 1 - w_1. \qquad (9.81)$$

From (9.77) and (9.79), we obtain that the standard deviation of the return of this portfolio is

$$\sigma_m = \frac{1}{\sqrt{\mathbf{1}^t \Sigma_R^{-1} \mathbf{1}}} = \frac{\sigma_1 \sigma_2 \sqrt{1-\rho_{1,2}^2}}{\sqrt{\sigma_1^2 - 2\sigma_1\sigma_2\rho_{1,2} + \sigma_2^2}}. \qquad (9.82)$$

9.6 Value at Risk (VaR). Portfolio VaR.

The Value at Risk (VaR) of a portfolio provides one number estimating, at a given level of confidence, how much of the portfolio value could be lost over a given time horizon. Thus, VaR depends on two parameters:

- N, the number of days in the time horizon;
- C, the confidence level.

Denote by $\text{VaR}(N,C)$ the N day $C\%$ VaR of a portfolio. Then, by definition, $\text{VaR}(N,C)$ is the largest value (dollar amount) such that the probability that the portfolio loss over the next N days is smaller than $\text{VaR}(N,C)$ is C. In other words, if $V(0)$ and $V(N)$ denote the current value of the portfolio and the value of the portfolio in N days, respectively, then

$$\text{VaR}(N,C) = \sup\{x \text{ such that } P(V(N) - V(0) \geq -x) = C\}. \qquad (9.83)$$

Example: If a portfolio has a five–day 98% VaR of $10 million, then there is a 98% probability that the portfolio will not lose more that $10 million within five days or, equivalently, the probability of the portfolio suffering losses bigger than $10 million within five days is 2%. □

If the portfolio value $V(N)$, or, equivalently, the portfolio return $\frac{V(N)-V(0)}{V(0)}$, is assumed to have a continuous probability distribution with strictly increasing probability density function, then (9.83) simplifies to:

$\text{VaR}(N,C)$ is the number given by

$$P(\,V(N) - V(0) \geq -\text{VaR}(N,C)\,) = C. \qquad (9.84)$$

Note that (9.84) is equivalent to

$$P(\,V(N) - V(0) \leq -\text{VaR}(N,C)\,) = 1 - C, \qquad (9.85)$$

which can be interpreted as follows: the probability that the loss of the portfolio over the next N days is greater than $\text{VaR}(N,C)$ is $1-C$.

9.6. VALUE AT RISK

A frequent assumption is that the return of a portfolio is normally distributed. Note that this would indeed be the case if the returns of the portfolio components have a joint multivariate normal distribution. Then, any linear combination of their returns, including the weighted average of the portfolio returns that gives the portfolio return, see (9.2), would be normally distributed; cf. Theorem 7.7.

If a portfolio is assumed to have normally distributed returns, then the formulas (9.84) and (9.85) for the N day $C\%$ VaR of the portfolio hold. If μ_{R_V} and σ_{R_V} are the annualized expected return and the standard deviation of the return of the portfolio over a small time period t, then

$$\frac{V(t) - V(0)}{V(0)} = \mu_{R_V} t + \sigma_{R_V} \sqrt{t} Z. \qquad (9.86)$$

For an N day horizon, let $t = \frac{N}{252}$ in (9.86) and obtain that

$$\frac{V(N) - V(0)}{V(0)} = \mu_{R_V} \frac{N}{252} + \sigma_{R_V} \sqrt{\frac{N}{252}} Z, \qquad (9.87)$$

where $V(N)$ is a simplified notation for $V\left(\frac{N}{252}\right)$, the value of the portfolio in N days.

From (9.85) and (9.87), it follows that[9]

$$P(\, V(N) - V(0) \leq -\text{VaR}(N, C)\,) = 1 - C$$

$$\iff P\left(\frac{V(N) - V(0)}{V(0)} \leq -\frac{\text{VaR}(N, C)}{V(0)}\right) = 1 - C \qquad (9.88)$$

$$\iff P\left(\mu_{R_V} \frac{N}{252} + \sigma_{R_V} \sqrt{\frac{N}{252}} Z \leq -\frac{\text{VaR}(N, C)}{V(0)}\right) = 1 - C$$

$$\iff P\left(\sigma_{R_V} \sqrt{\frac{N}{252}} Z \leq -\frac{\text{VaR}(N, C)}{V(0)} - \mu_{R_V} \frac{N}{252}\right) = 1 - C$$

$$\iff P\left(Z \leq -\sqrt{\frac{252}{N}} \frac{\text{VaR}(N, C)}{\sigma_{R_V} V(0)} - \sqrt{\frac{N}{252}} \frac{\mu_{R_V}}{\sigma_{R_V}}\right) = 1 - C$$

$$\iff P\left(Z \leq -\left(\sqrt{\frac{252}{N}} \frac{\text{VaR}(N, C)}{\sigma_{R_V} V(0)} + \sqrt{\frac{N}{252}} \frac{\mu_{R_V}}{\sigma_{R_V}}\right)\right) = 1 - C. \qquad (9.89)$$

Let z_C be the z-score of the standard normal distribution corresponding to C, i.e., $P(Z \leq z_C) = C$. Note that

$$z_{99} = 2.3263, \quad \text{since} \quad P(Z \leq 2.3263) = 0.99 = 99\%$$
$$z_{98} = 2.0537, \quad \text{since} \quad P(Z \leq 2.0537) = 0.98 = 98\%;$$
$$z_{95} = 1.6449, \quad \text{since} \quad P(Z \leq 1.6449) = 0.95 = 95\%;$$
$$z_{90} = 1.2816, \quad \text{since} \quad P(Z \leq 1.2816) = 0.90 = 90\%.$$

Recall that $P(Z \leq -a) = 1 - P(Z \leq a)$ for any $a \in \mathbb{R}$; see Lemma 10.19 for a proof of this result. Then,

$$P(Z \leq -z_C) = 1 - C. \qquad (9.90)$$

---

[9] The assumption that the portfolio has positive initial value, i.e., $V(0) > 0$, was made and used implicitly in (9.88).

From (9.89) and (9.90), we obtain that

$$z_C = \sqrt{\frac{252}{N}} \frac{\text{VaR}(N,C)}{\sigma_{R_V} V(0)} + \sqrt{\frac{N}{252}} \frac{\mu_{R_V}}{\sigma_{R_V}}. \qquad (9.91)$$

By solving (9.91) for $\text{VaR}(N,C)$, we find that

$$\text{VaR}(N,C) = \sqrt{\frac{N}{252}} \sigma_{R_V} z_C V(0) - \frac{N}{252} \mu_{R_V} V(0). \qquad (9.92)$$

For small values of N, e.g., for $N \leq 10$ corresponding to time horizons of less than two weeks, $\frac{N}{252}$ is much smaller[10] than $\sqrt{\frac{N}{252}}$. Thus, from (9.92), we obtain the following approximation:

$$\text{VaR}(N,C) \approx \sqrt{\frac{N}{252}} \sigma_{R_V} z_C V(0). \qquad (9.93)$$

From (9.93), it can be inferred that the Value at Risk of a portfolio with normally distributed return is proportional to the square root of the time horizon, which provides the following simple way to scale the Value at Risk of a portfolio to different time horizons and confidence levels:

$$\frac{\text{VaR}(N_2, C_2)}{\text{VaR}(N_1, C_1)} \approx \frac{z_{C_2} \sqrt{N_2}}{z_{C_1} \sqrt{N_1}},$$

which can also be written as

$$\text{VaR}(N_2, C_2) \approx \frac{z_{C_2} \sqrt{N_2}}{z_{C_1} \sqrt{N_1}} \text{VaR}(N_1, C_1). \qquad (9.94)$$

Example: What is the ten–day 99% VaR of a portfolio with a five–day 98% VaR of $10 million?

Answer: Assuming that the returns of the portfolio are normally distributed, we obtain from (9.94) that

$$\text{VaR}(10 \text{ days}, 99\%) \approx \frac{z_{99} \sqrt{10}}{z_{98} \sqrt{5}} \text{VaR}(5 \text{ days}, 98\%) = \frac{2.3263\sqrt{10}}{2.0537\sqrt{5}} \cdot \$10,000,000$$
$$= \$16,019,307. \quad \square$$

Example: Consider two assets with multivariate normal distribution of their returns. Their returns have standard deviations of 25% and 35%, and a correlation of -25%.

(i) Use formula (9.93) to find approximate values for the 10–day 98% VaR of a $100 million portfolio if the portfolio is invested in the first asset, invested in the second asset, or invested in the minimum variance portfolio fully invested in the two assets.

(ii) Assume that the returns of the two assets have expected values of 3% and 6%, respectively. Use formula (9.92) to find approximate values for the 10–day 98% VaR of a $100 million portfolio if the portfolio is invested in the first asset, invested in the

---

[10] For example, for $N = 10$, $\sqrt{\frac{N}{252}} = \sqrt{\frac{10}{252}} \approx 0.20$ and $\frac{N}{252} = \frac{10}{252} \approx 0.04$.

9.6. VALUE AT RISK

second asset, or invested in the minimum variance portfolio fully invested in the two assets.

(iii) What is the percentage difference between the VaRs obtained by using the formulas (9.93) and (9.92)?

Answer: (i) Let $\text{VaR}_1(10 \text{ days}, 98\%)$, $\text{VaR}_2(10 \text{ days}, 98\%)$, $\text{VaR}_m(10 \text{ days}, 98\%)$ be the 10–day 98% VaR of the $100 million portfolio fully invested in the first asset, fully invested in the second asset, and invested in the minimum variance portfolio fully invested in the two assets, respectively.

Let $\sigma_1 = 0.25$, $\sigma_2 = 0.35$, and $\rho_{1,2} = -0.25$ be the standard deviations and the correlation of the returns of the two assets, respectively. From (9.82), we find that the standard deviation of the return of the minimum variance portfolio fully invested in the two assets is $\sigma_m = 0.177139$.

From the approximate VaR formula (9.93), we obtain that

$$\text{VaR}_1(10 \text{ days}, 98\%) \approx \sqrt{\frac{10}{252}} \sigma_1 z_{98} \cdot \$100\text{mil} = \$10.228\text{mil};$$

$$\text{VaR}_2(10 \text{ days}, 98\%) \approx \sqrt{\frac{10}{252}} \sigma_2 z_{98} \cdot \$100\text{mil} = \$14.319\text{mil};$$

$$\text{VaR}_m(10 \text{ days}, 98\%) \approx \sqrt{\frac{10}{252}} \sigma_m z_{98} \cdot \$100\text{mil} = \$7.247\text{mil};$$

recall that $z_{98} = 2.0537$.

The VaR of the minimum variance portfolio is significantly smaller that the VaR of both the portfolio invested in the first asset, and of the portfolio invested in the second asset, which shows that portfolio diversification can be used to reduce the risk of the portfolio.

(ii) Let $\mu_1 = 0.03$ and $\mu_2 = 0.06$ be the expected values of the returns of the two assets, respectively.

Since $z_{98} = 2.0537$, we obtain from (9.92) that

$$\text{VaR}_1(10 \text{ days}, 98\%) = \sqrt{\frac{10}{252}} \sigma_1 z_{98} \cdot \$100\text{mil} - \frac{10}{252} \mu_1 \$100\text{mil} = \$10.109\text{mil};$$

$$\text{VaR}_2(10 \text{ days}, 98\%) = \sqrt{\frac{10}{252}} \sigma_2 z_{98} \cdot \$100\text{mil} - \frac{10}{252} \mu_2 \$100\text{mil} = \$14.081\text{mil}.$$

The expected value of the return of the minimum variance portfolio fully invested in the two assets is $\mu_m = w_1\mu_1 + w_2\mu_1$, where w_1 and w_2 are given by (9.80–9.81). We obtain that $\mu_m = 0.04107$, and, from (9.92), it follows that

$$\text{VaR}_m(10 \text{ days}, 98\%) = \sqrt{\frac{10}{252}} \sigma_m z_{98} \$100\text{mil} - \frac{10}{252} \mu_m \$100\text{mil} = \$7.084\text{mil}.$$

(iii) The percentage differences between the VaRs obtained by using the formulas (9.93) and (9.92) are all smaller than 2.5%, as follows:

for the portfolio fully invested in the first asset:

$$\frac{|10.228 - 10.109|}{10.228} = 0.0116 = 1.16\%.$$

for the portfolio fully invested in the second asset:

$$\frac{|14.319 - 14.081|}{14.319} = 0.0166 = 1.66\%.$$

for the minimum variance portfolio fully invested in the two assets:

$$\frac{|7.247 - 7.084|}{7.247} = 0.0225 = 2.25\%.$$

In other words, the VaRs obtained using the expected values of the returns of the two assets and the VaRs obtained using only the standard deviations of the returns are very similar. Thus, in order to estimate Value at Risk, there is no need to find the expected values of the returns of assets or portfolios, which is very difficult to do with any accuracy in practice. This is similar to option pricing in the Black–Scholes framework, where the drift of the asset (i.e., the expected value of the instantaneous return of the asset) is not needed in order to compute the Black–Scholes values of the options. □

The usefulness of Value at Risk comes from its simplicity: it is a single number that makes comparing VaRs at different times easy, and makes deteriorating trends easy to spot. However, its simplicity is also its main drawback, since VaR does not distinguish between possible sizes of the losses beyond the $1 - C$ percentile.

A coherent risk measure that distinguishes between different sizes of losses under tail events is expected shortfall, also called conditional Value at Risk (cVaR). The N days expected shortfall of a portfolio at confidence level C is the expected loss of the portfolio over the next N days conditional on the loss being greater than VaR(N,C). Expected shortfall is subadditive, unlike VaR; see section 9.6.1 for details on the subadditivity of VaR.

9.6.1 VaR of combined portfolios and subadditivity

An intuitive requirement for a risk measure is that it would decrease with portfolio diversification. Formally, this is called the subadditivity requirement for a coherent risk measure: If rm(V) denotes the risk measure of portfolio V, then this risk measure is subadditive if and only if rm$(V_1 + V_2) \leq$ rm$(V_1) +$ rm(V_2) for any two portfolios V_1 and V_2.

Value at Risk is not a coherent risk measure, as first pointed out by Artzner et al. [6]; see the example below. This has potentially very detrimental consequences for using VaR in practice. For example, it may not be true that the overall Value at Risk of a financial institution is smaller than the sum of the VaRs for different groups within the firm. Note that expected shortfall (cVar) is subadditive, and it has the further advantage of better estimating tail risk exposure.

The example below of an instance when VaR is not subadditive is adapted from Artzner et al. [6].

Assume that the changes $V_1(N) - V_1(0)$ and $V_2(N) - V_2(0)$ in the values of two given portfolios over an N day time horizon are independent and identically distributed, with probability density functions given by

$$f_1(x) = f_2(x) = \begin{cases} 0.05, & \text{if } -2 \leq x \leq 0; \\ 0.90, & \text{if } 0 < x \leq 1; \\ 0, & \text{if } 1 < x. \end{cases} \quad (9.95)$$

9.6. VAR OF COMBINED PORTFOLIOS. SUBADDITIVITY OF VAR.

Note that

$$P(V_1(N) - V_1(0) \geq 0) = \int_0^\infty f_1(x) \, dx = \int_0^1 0.9 \, dx = 0.9 = 90\%;$$

$$P(V_2(N) - V_2(0) \geq 0) = \int_0^\infty f_2(x) \, dx = \int_0^1 0.9 \, dx = 0.9 = 90\%.$$

Then, from (9.83), it follows that

$$\text{VaR}_{V_1}(N, 90\%) = \text{VaR}_{V_2}(N, 90\%) = 0, \qquad (9.96)$$

i.e., the N-day 90% VaR of both portfolios is 0.

However, we will show below that the N-day 90% VaR of the combined portfolio is 0.4966, see (9.101), which is larger than 0, the sum of the N-day 90% VaRs of each portfolio; see (9.96).

Denote by $V(N)$ the value after N days of the portfolio obtained by combining the two portfolios. Then, the change in the value of the combined portfolios is the sum of the changes in the values of each portfolio, i.e.,

$$\begin{aligned} V(N) - V(0) &= (V_1(N) + V_2(N)) - (V_1(0) + V_2(0)) \\ &= (V_1(N) - V_1(0)) + (V_2(N) - V_2(0)). \end{aligned}$$

Since $V_1(N) - V_1(0)$ and $V_2(N) - V_2(0)$ are independent with probability density functions $f_1(x)$ and $f_2(x)$ given by (9.95), if follows that the probability density function $f(x)$ of $V(N) - V(0)$ is the convolution of $f_1(x)$ and $f_2(x)$, i.e.,

$$f(x) = (f_1 * f_2)(x) = \int_{-\infty}^\infty f_1(y) f_2(x - y) \, dy;$$

see, e.g., Theorem 4.1 from Stefanica [36].

By using formula (9.95) for $f_1(y)$ and noting that $f_1(y) = 0$ if $y < -2$ and if $y > 1$, we obtain that

$$\begin{aligned} f(x) &= \int_{-2}^0 f_1(y) f_2(x - y) \, dy + \int_0^1 f_1(y) f_2(x - y) \, dy \\ &= 0.05 \int_{-2}^0 f_2(x - y) \, dy + 0.9 \int_0^1 f_2(x - y) \, dy. \qquad (9.97) \end{aligned}$$

By using the substitutions $s = x - y$ and $t = x - y$ for the first and second integral from (9.97), respectively, we find that

$$\begin{aligned} f(x) &= 0.05 \int_{x+2}^x f_2(s)\,(-ds) + 0.9 \int_x^{x-1} f_2(t)\,(-dt) \\ &= 0.05 \int_x^{x+2} f_2(s)\, ds + 0.9 \int_{x-1}^x f_2(t)\, dt. \end{aligned}$$

After further computations using (9.95) for f_2, we conclude that

$$f(x) = \begin{cases} 0, & \text{if } x < -4; \\ 0.01 + 0.0025x, & \text{if } -4 \leq x < -2; \\ 0.18 + 0.0875x, & \text{if } -2 \leq x < -1; \\ 0.09 - 0.0025x, & \text{if } -1 \leq x < 0; \\ 0.09 + 0.72x, & \text{if } 0 \leq x < 1; \\ 1.62 - 0.81x, & \text{if } 1 \leq x < 2; \\ 0, & \text{if } 2 \leq x. \end{cases}$$

Furthermore, note that

$$P\Big(V(N) - V(0) \leq -6(\sqrt{37} - 6)\Big) \tag{9.98}$$

$$= \int_{-\infty}^{-6(\sqrt{37}-6)} f(x)\, dx$$

$$= \int_{-4}^{-2} (0.01 + 0.0025x)\, dx + \int_{-2}^{-1} (0.18 + 0.0875x)\, dx$$

$$+ \int_{-1}^{-6(\sqrt{37}-6)} (0.09 - 0.0025x)\, dx$$

$$= \left(0.02 + 0.0025\left(\frac{x^2}{2}\right)\Big|_{-4}^{-2}\right) + \left(0.18 + 0.0875\left(\frac{x^2}{2}\right)\Big|_{-2}^{-1}\right)$$

$$+ \left(0.09(-6(\sqrt{37}-6)+1) - 0.0025\left(\frac{x^2}{2}\right)\Big|_{-1}^{-6(\sqrt{37}-6)}\right) \tag{9.99}$$

$$= 0.005 + 0.04875 + 0.04625$$

$$= 0.1. \tag{9.100}$$

For completeness, we include the details for the computation of (9.99) here. Let $u = -6(\sqrt{37}-6)$. Note that u is a solution to the quadratic equation $u^2 - 72u - 36 = 0$, and therefore $\frac{u^2}{2} = 36u + 18$. Then, (9.99) can be written as

$$0.09(u+1) - 0.0025\left(\frac{x^2}{2}\right)\Big|_{-1}^{u} = 0.09(u+1) - 0.0025\left(\frac{u^2}{2} - \frac{1}{2}\right)$$

$$= 0.09(u+1) - 0.0025\left(36u + 18 - \frac{1}{2}\right)$$

$$= 0.09u + 0.09 - 0.09u - 0.045 + 0.00125$$

$$= 0.04625.$$

From (9.98) and (9.100), we conclude that

$$P\Big(V(N) - V(0) \geq -(\sqrt{37}-6)\Big) = 0.9.$$

From (9.83), it follows that the N–day 90% VaR of the combined portfolio is

$$\text{VaR}_V(N, 90\%) = 6(\sqrt{37}-6) \approx 0.4966, \tag{9.101}$$

which is greater than 0, the sum of the N–day 90% VaR of each portfolio:

$$\text{VaR}_{V_1}(N, 90\%) + \text{VaR}_{V_2}(N, 90\%) = 0;$$

cf. (9.96).

In the example above, we used the definition (9.83) for Value at Risk, and not the approximate formula (9.93) which is accurate only if the change in the value of the portfolio were normally distributed. Note that, if formula (9.93) for VaR were to be used, then it can be shown that the VaR of two combined portfolios would be smaller than the sum of the VaRs of the portfolios, and it would appear that VaR is a subadditive measure; see an exercise at the end of this chapter. However, formula (9.93) only holds if the portfolio return is normally distributed, which is not the case in practice, and, in particular, is not the case for the portfolios from the example above.

9.7 References

For an overview of the latest advances in asset allocation and portfolio optimization see Fabozzi and Markowitz [14]. Advanced risk and portfolio management techniques are analyzed in depth in Meucci [29].

Efficient portfolios invested in only two assets are analyzed in detail in many books; see. e.g., Ruppert [33].

An expanded treatment of VaR can be found in Hull's risk management book [23]. An approach further tailored to practical applications can be found in Alexander [2].

Expected shortfall was introduced as a measure of risk in the seminal paper of Artzner et al. [6]. Further details on expected shortfall (cVar) and other alternatives to VaR are included in Andersen and Piterbarg [4].

9.8 Exercises

1. Two stocks trade at $100 and $60, respectively. Their three-months returns have expected values of 8% and 4%, respectively, and standard deviation of 20% and 15%, respectively. The correlation of the returns is 25%.

   (i) Consider a portfolio made of 150 shares of the first stock and 500 shares of the second stock. What are the weights of each stock in this portfolio?

   (ii) Assume that you have $500,000 to invest. Find a portfolio made of the two stocks that has a 9% expected return.

   (iii) Identify the two portfolios fully invested in the two assets that have a 14.5% standard deviation of return. What are the expected returns of the two portfolios?

2. Assume that the asset allocation for a $100 million maximum return portfolio invested in three assets is $30 million in the first asset, $10 million in the second asset, $40 million in the third asset, and $20 million in cash. What is the asset allocation of the tangency portfolio made of these three assets?

3. Consider three assets with the following expected values, standard deviations, and correlations of their returns:

$$\mu_1 = 0.08; \quad \sigma_1 = 0.25; \quad \rho_{1,2} = -0.25;$$
$$\mu_2 = 0.12; \quad \sigma_2 = 0.25; \quad \rho_{2,3} = -0.25;$$
$$\mu_3 = 0.16; \quad \sigma_3 = 0.30; \quad \rho_{1,3} = 0.25.$$

   The risk-free interest rate is 4%.

   (i) Find the asset allocation corresponding to the tangency portfolio. What are the expected value and the standard deviation of the return of the tangency portfolio?

   (ii) Find the asset allocation corresponding to the minimum variance portfolio. What are the expected value and the standard deviation of the return of the minimum variance portfolio?

4. Assume that you invest $10 million in two different assets and cash. The three-months returns of the two assets have expected values of 8% and 12%, respectively, and standard deviations of 15% and 20%, respectively. The correlation of the returns of the two assets is 25%. The risk-free interest rate is 5%.

   (i) Find the asset allocation for the tangency portfolio.

   (ii) Find the asset allocation for a minimum variance portfolio with 7% expected return, and the standard deviation of the return of this portfolio.

   (iii) Find the asset allocation for a minimum variance portfolio with 11% expected return, and the standard deviation of the return of this portfolio.

(iv) Find the asset allocation for a maximum return portfolio with 12% standard deviation of return, and the expected return of this portfolio.

(v) Find the asset allocation for a maximum return portfolio with 18% standard deviation of return, and the expected return of this portfolio.

(vi) Assume that the risk–free interest rate changes to 5.25%. How do you adjust the asset allocation of the minimum variance portfolio with 7% expected return in order to maintain a minimum variance portfolio with 7% expected return?

5. Consider two assets with three-months returns with expected values of 6% and 10%, respectively, and standard deviations of 25% and 35%, respectively. The correlation of the three-months returns of the two assets is -25%. The risk–free interest rate is 3%. Assume that you invest \$100 million in the two assets.

(i) Find the minimum variance of the return of a portfolio made of the two assets. What is the expected return of this portfolio?

(ii) What is the 10–day 98% VaR of a \$100 million portfolio, if it is invested in the first asset, invested in the second asset, or invested in the minimum variance portfolio, respectively?

6. Consider three assets with the following expected values, standard deviations, and correlations of their returns:

$$\mu_1 = 0.06; \quad \sigma_1 = 0.18; \quad \rho_{1,2} = -0.50;$$
$$\mu_2 = 0.09; \quad \sigma_2 = 0.20; \quad \rho_{2,3} = -0.25;$$
$$\mu_3 = 0.12; \quad \sigma_3 = 0.24; \quad \rho_{1,3} = 0.15.$$

The risk–free interest rate is 3%.

(i) Find the asset allocation for the tangency portfolio. What are the expected return and the standard deviation of the return of the tangency portfolio?

(ii) Find the asset allocation for a minimum variance portfolio with 10% expected return, and the standard deviation of the return of this portfolio.

(iii) Find the asset allocation for a maximum return portfolio with 20% standard deviation of return, and the expected return of this portfolio.

7. Consider five assets with the following expected values, standard deviations, and correlations of their returns:

$$\mu_1 = 0.08; \quad \sigma_1 = 0.25;$$
$$\mu_2 = 0.12; \quad \sigma_2 = 0.25;$$
$$\mu_3 = 0.16; \quad \sigma_3 = 0.30;$$
$$\mu_4 = 0.18; \quad \sigma_4 = 0.32;$$
$$\mu_5 = 0.21; \quad \sigma_5 = 0.35.$$

$$\rho_{1,2} = -0.25; \quad \rho_{1,3} = -0.25; \quad \rho_{1,4} = 0.35; \quad \rho_{1,5} = -0.10;$$
$$\rho_{2,3} = 0.30; \quad \rho_{2,4} = -0.50; \quad \rho_{2,5} = 0.10;$$
$$\rho_{3,4} = -0.30; \quad \rho_{3,5} = -0.35; \quad \rho_{4,5} = 0.65;$$

The risk-free interest rate is 5%.

(i) Find the asset allocation for a minimum variance portfolio with 17% expected return, and the standard deviation of the return of this portfolio;

(ii) Find the asset allocation for a maximum return portfolio with 30% standard deviation of return, and the expected return of this portfolio.

8. Consider four assets with the following expected returns over a fixed time period:

$$\mu_1 = 4\%;\ \mu_2 = 3.5\%;\ \mu_3 = 5\%;\ \mu_4 = 3.4\%,$$

and with the following covariance matrix of their returns over the same time period:

$$\begin{pmatrix} 0.09 & 0.01 & 0.03 & -0.015 \\ 0.01 & 0.0625 & -0.02 & -0.01 \\ 0.03 & -0.02 & 0.1225 & 0.02 \\ -0.015 & -0.01 & 0.02 & 0.0576 \end{pmatrix}.$$

Assume that the risk-free interest rate is 1%.

(i) Find the asset allocation for the tangency portfolio. Find the expected value and the standard deviation of the return of the tangency portfolio. What is the Sharpe ratio of the tangency portfolio?

(ii) Find the asset allocation for a minimum variance portfolio with 3% expected return, and the standard deviation of the return of this portfolio. What is the Sharpe ratio of this portfolio?

(iii) Find the asset allocation for a maximum return portfolio with 27% standard deviation of return, and the expected return of this portfolio. What is the Sharpe ratio of this portfolio?

(iv) Find the asset allocation for the minimum variance portfolio fully invested in the assets (i.e., with no cash position). What is the Sharpe ratio of this portfolio?

9. Consider three assets with the following expected values, standard deviations, and correlations of their returns:

$$\mu_1 = 0.05;\quad \sigma_1 = 0.15;\quad \rho_{1,2} = -0.25;$$
$$\mu_2 = 0.09;\quad \sigma_2 = 0.20;\quad \rho_{2,3} = 0.25;$$
$$\mu_3 = 0.10;\quad \sigma_3 = 0.25;\quad \rho_{1,3} = 0.50.$$

The risk-free interest rate is 2%.

(i) Find the asset allocation for a minimum variance portfolio with 8% expected return, and the standard deviation of the return of this portfolio.

(ii) Assume that the returns of the three assets have a joint multivariate normal distribution. Find the probability density function of the return of the minimum variance portfolio with 8% expected return.

9.8. EXERCISES

(iii) Find the probability that the return of the minimum variance portfolio with 8% expected return is between 7% and 9%. Also, find the probability that the return of this portfolio is below 5%, and the probability that the return of this portfolio is above 10%.

(iv) Consider a portfolio equally invested in each of the three assets. Note that the expected return of this portfolio is 8%. Find the probabilities that the return of this portfolio is between 7% and 9%, is below 5%, and is above 10%, respectively.

10. Let μ_1, σ_1 and μ_2, σ_2 be the expected values and the standard deviations of the returns of two assets over a fixed time period, respectively, and let $\rho_{1,2}$ be the correlation of the returns of the two assets over the same time period. Recall that the minimum variance portfolio fully invested in two assets is obtained by allocating

$$w_1 = \frac{\sigma_2(\sigma_2 - \rho_{1,2}\sigma_1)}{(\sigma_1^2 - 2\sigma_1\sigma_2\rho_{1,2} + \sigma_2^2)}$$

of the portfolio value to the first asset and $w_2 = 1 - w_1$ of the portfolio value to the second asset.

Show that the minimum variance portfolio has only long asset positions, i.e., $0 \leq w_1, w_2 \leq 1$, if and only if

$$\rho_{1,2} \leq \min\left(\frac{\sigma_1}{\sigma_2}, \frac{\sigma_2}{\sigma_1}\right).$$

11. (i) Show that the asset allocation for a minimum variance portfolio with expected return μ_P can also be written as follows in terms of the asset weights vector w_T of the tangency portfolio:

- asset weights vector w_{min} given by

$$w_{min} = \frac{\mu_P - r_f}{\overline{\mu}^t w_T} w_T. \tag{9.102}$$

- weight $w_{min,cash}$ of the cash position given by

$$w_{min,cash} = 1 - \mathbf{1}^t w_{min}; \tag{9.103}$$

(ii) Write a pseudocode for computing the asset allocation for a minimum variance portfolio with expected return μ_P using the formulas (9.102) and (9.103).

12. (i) Show that the asset allocation for a maximum return portfolio with variance of return equal to σ_P^2 can also be written as follows in terms of the asset weights vector w_T of the tangency portfolio:

- asset weights vector w_{max} given by

$$w_{max} = \frac{\sigma_P}{\sqrt{w_T^t \Sigma_R w_T}} \cdot \text{sign}(\mathbf{1}^t \Sigma_R^{-1} \overline{\mu}) w_T; \tag{9.104}$$

- weight $w_{max,cash}$ of the cash position equal to $1 - \mathbf{1}^t w_{max}$, i.e.,

$$w_{max,cash} = 1 - \mathbf{1}^t w_{max}. \tag{9.105}$$

(ii) Write a pseudocode for computing the asset allocation for maximum return portfolio with variance of return equal to σ_P^2 using the formulas (9.104) and (9.105).

13. Assume that the 99% two day VaR of a portfolio is $10 million. Estimate the two day 95% VaR of the portfolio and the five day 95% VaR of the portfolio.

14. Show that if two portfolios and their combined portfolio have normally distributed returns, then the VaR of the combined portfolio is smaller than the sum of the VaRs of each individual portfolio.

    In other words, if V_1, V_2, and $V = V_1 + V_2$ are portfolios with normal returns, show that
    $$\text{VaR}_V(N,C) \leq \text{VaR}_{V_1}(N,C) + \text{VaR}_{V_2}(N,C),$$
    where $\text{VaR}_V(N,C)$, $\text{VaR}_{V_1}(N,C)$, and $\text{VaR}_{V_2}(N,C)$ are the N day $C\%$ VaRs of V, V_1, and V_2, respectively.

    Hint: Recall that, for a portfolio W with normal returns,
    $$\text{VaR}_W(N,C) = \sqrt{\frac{N}{252}} \sigma_{R_W} z_C W(0) - \frac{N}{252} \mu_{R_W} W(0),$$
    and use the fact that the return R_V of the combined portfolio is the weighted average of the returns R_{V_1} and R_{V_2} of the two portfolios, i.e.,
    $$R_V = \frac{V_1(0)}{V(0)} R_{V_1} + \frac{V_2(0)}{V(0)} R_{V_2}.$$

15. Consider three assets with multivariate normal distribution of their returns. The expected values, standard deviations, and correlations of their returns are

    $$\begin{array}{lll} \mu_1 = 0.08; & \sigma_1 = 0.25; & \rho_{1,2} = -0.25; \\ \mu_2 = 0.12; & \sigma_2 = 0.25; & \rho_{2,3} = -0.25; \\ \mu_3 = 0.16; & \sigma_3 = 0.30; & \rho_{1,3} = 0.25. \end{array}$$

    (i) What is the 5–day 95% VaR of $100 million portfolios fully invested in the first asset, fully invested in the second asset, and fully invested in the third asset, respectively?

    (ii) What is the minimal 5–day 95% VaR of a $100 million portfolio fully invested in the first and second asset, fully invested in the second and third asset, and fully invested in the first and third asset, respectively?

    (iii) What is the minimal 5–day 95% VaR of a $100 million portfolio fully invested in all three assets?

Chapter 10

Mathematical appendix and technical results.

Determinants, permutation matrices, orthogonal vectors and orthogonal matrices, quadratic forms.

Multivariable functions.

Lagrange multipliers.

The "Big O" notation.

European options overview.

Eigenvalues of symmetric matrices.

Row rank equal to column rank.

Technical results for Cholesky and LU decompositions.

10.1 Numerical linear algebra tools.

In this section, we give a brief overview to determinants, permutation matrices, orthogonal vectors and orthogonal matrices, and quadratic forms.

10.1.1 Determinants

The concept of the determinant of a square matrix is of little relevance for numerical linear algebra purposes.[1] However, if needed, the determinant of the matrix can be computed efficiently using the LU decomposition of the matrix, which requires $\frac{2}{3}n^3 + O(n^2)$ operations. Using the classical definition of the determinant to compute it would require a huge number of operations, on the order of $n \cdot n! \approx \frac{n^{n+1}}{e^n}$.

A very important use of the concept of the determinant of a matrix is as an equivalent characterization of a matrix being nonsingular if and only if the determinant of the matrix is nonzero; see Theorem 1.2.

---

[1] The condition number of a matrix is much more relevant, since, it indicates not only whether a matrix is nonsingular, as does the determinant of the matrix, but also how far from being nonsingular (i.e., ill-conditioned or well-conditioned) a matrix is; see Demmel [13] for more details.

The determinant of a diagonal matrix D is equal to the product of all the main diagonal entries of the matrix, i.e.,

$$\det(D) = \prod_{i=1}^{n} D(i,i). \tag{10.1}$$

In particular, the determinant of the identity matrix is 1, i.e.,

$$\det(I) = 1. \tag{10.2}$$

The determinant of a lower triangular matrix L is equal to the product of all the main diagonal entries of the matrix, i.e.,

$$\det(L) = \prod_{i=1}^{n} L(i,i). \tag{10.3}$$

The determinant of an upper triangular matrix U is equal to the product of all the main diagonal entries of the matrix, i.e.,

$$\det(U) = \prod_{i=1}^{n} U(i,i). \tag{10.4}$$

Since the transpose of an upper triangular matrix is lower triangular, it follows from (10.3) and (10.4)

$$\det(U^t) = \prod_{i=1}^{n} U(i,i) = \det(U). \tag{10.5}$$

The determinant of the 2×2 matrix $A = \begin{pmatrix} a & b \\ c & d \end{pmatrix}$ is

$$\det(A) = ad - bc. \tag{10.6}$$

Note that the inverse of the 2×2 matrix A is

$$A^{-1} = \frac{1}{\det(A)} \begin{pmatrix} d & -b \\ -c & a \end{pmatrix} = \frac{1}{ad-bc} \begin{pmatrix} d & -b \\ -c & a \end{pmatrix}. \tag{10.7}$$

The determinant of the 3×3 matrix $A = \begin{pmatrix} a_{1,1} & a_{1,2} & a_{1,3} \\ a_{2,1} & a_{2,2} & a_{2,3} \\ a_{3,1} & a_{3,2} & a_{3,3} \end{pmatrix}$ is

$$\begin{aligned}\det(A) = {} & a_{1,1}a_{2,2}a_{3,3} + a_{1,2}a_{2,3}a_{3,1} + a_{1,3}a_{2,1}a_{3,2} \\ & - a_{1,3}a_{2,2}a_{3,1} - a_{1,1}a_{2,3}a_{3,2} - a_{1,2}a_{2,1}a_{3,3}.\end{aligned} \tag{10.8}$$

Lemma 10.1. *Let A and B be square matrices of the same size. Then,*

$$\det(AB) = \det(A)\det(B). \tag{10.9}$$

Lemma 10.2. *Let A be a square matrix. Then,*

$$\det(A^t) = \det(A).$$

10.1.2 Permutation matrices

Definition 10.1. *A permutation matrix is a matrix obtained by permuting the columns (or, equivalently, the rows) of the identity matrix.*

For every permutation matrix P of size n there exists a permutation[2] τ_c of the numbers $1, 2, \ldots, n$ such that

$$P = \mathrm{col}\left(e_{\tau_c(k)}\right)_{k=1:n}.$$

Similarly, for every permutation matrix P of size n there exists a permutation function τ_r of the numbers $1:n$ such that

$$P = \mathrm{row}\left(e^t_{\tau_r(j)}\right)_{j=1:n}.$$

However, the column and row permutation functions corresponding to the same permutation matrix need not be the same, as seen in the example below:

Example: The matrix

$$P = \begin{pmatrix} 0 & 0 & 1 & 0 & 0 \\ 1 & 0 & 0 & 0 & 0 \\ 0 & 0 & 0 & 0 & 1 \\ 0 & 1 & 0 & 0 & 0 \\ 0 & 0 & 0 & 1 & 0 \end{pmatrix}$$

is a permutation matrix.

The row form of P is

$$P = \begin{pmatrix} e^t_3 \\ e^t_1 \\ e^t_5 \\ e^t_2 \\ e^t_4 \end{pmatrix} = \begin{pmatrix} 3 \\ 1 \\ 5 \\ 2 \\ 4 \end{pmatrix},$$

and can be expressed as

$$P = \mathrm{row}\left(e^t_{\tau_r(j)}\right)_{j=1:5},$$

where $\tau_r : \{1, 2, 3, 4, 5\} \to \{1, 2, 3, 4, 5\}$ is given by

$$\tau_r(1) = 3; \; \tau_r(2) = 1; \; \tau_r(3) = 5; \; \tau_r(4) = 2; \; \tau_r(5) = 4.$$

The column form of P is

$$P = (e_2 \mid e_4 \mid e_1 \mid e_5 \mid e_3) = (2\ 4\ 1\ 5\ 3),$$

and can be expressed as

$$P = \mathrm{col}\left(e_{\tau_c(k)}\right)_{k=1:5},$$

where $\tau_c : \{1, 2, 3, 4, 5\} \to \{1, 2, 3, 4, 5\}$ is given by

$$\tau_c(1) = 2; \; \tau_c(2) = 4; \; \tau_c(3) - 1; \; \tau_c(4) = 5; \; \tau_c(5) = 3. \quad \square$$

---

[2] A permutation of the numbers $1, 2, \ldots, n$ is a function $\tau : \{1, 2, \ldots, n\} \to \{1, 2, \ldots, n\}$ which is one-to-one and onto, i.e., a function that assigns to every number i between 1 and n a unique number $\tau(i)$ between 1 and n such that, if $1 \leq i \neq j \leq n$, then $\tau(i) \neq \tau(j)$.

Theorem 10.1. *(i) Matrix multiplication by a permutation matrix to the left results in a corresponding permutation of the rows of the matrix.*

In other words, if $A = \text{row}(r_j)_{j=1:n}$ is a square matrix of size n and if $P = \text{row}\left(e^t_{\tau_r(j)}\right)_{j=1:n}$ is a permutation matrix, then

$$PA = \text{row}\left(r_{\tau_r(j)}\right)_{j=1:n}. \tag{10.10}$$

(ii) Matrix multiplication by a permutation matrix to the right results in a corresponding permutation of the columns of the matrix.

In other words, if $A = \text{col}(a_k)_{k=1:n}$ is a square matrix of size n and if $P = \text{col}\left(e_{\tau_c(k)}\right)_{k=1:n}$ is a permutation matrix, then

$$AP = \text{col}\left(a_{\tau_c(k)}\right)_{k=1:n}. \tag{10.11}$$

Proof. (i) Recall from (1.27) that $e^t_j A = r_j$ for all $j = 1:n$. Thus,

$$e^t_{\tau_r(j)} A = r_{\tau_r(j)}, \quad \forall\, j = 1:n,$$

and therefore, from the matrix–matrix multiplication formula (1.12), we find that

$$PA = \text{row}\left(e^t_{\tau_r(j)} A\right)_{j=1:n} = \text{row}\left(r_{\tau_r(j)}\right)_{j=1:n}.$$

(ii) Recall from (1.26) that $A e_k = a_k$ for all $k = 1:n$. Thus,

$$A e_{\tau_c(k)} = a_{\tau_c(k)}, \quad \forall\, j = 1:n,$$

and therefore, from the matrix–matrix multiplication formula (1.11), we find that

$$AP = \text{col}\left(A e_{\tau_c(k)}\right)_{k=1:n} = \text{col}\left(a_{\tau_c(k)}\right)_{k=1:n}.$$

$\square$

Example: Let

$$A = \begin{pmatrix} -2 & 3 & -1 & 0 & 15 \\ 1 & 0 & -10 & -2 & 4 \\ 5 & -2 & 1 & 0 & 1 \\ -5 & -1 & 2 & -6 & -3 \\ 0 & -1 & -3 & 11 & -9 \end{pmatrix}$$

and let P be the following permutation matrix:

$$P = \begin{pmatrix} 0 & 0 & 1 & 0 & 0 \\ 1 & 0 & 0 & 0 & 0 \\ 0 & 0 & 0 & 0 & 1 \\ 0 & 1 & 0 & 0 & 0 \\ 0 & 0 & 0 & 1 & 0 \end{pmatrix}.$$

Then,

$$PA = \begin{pmatrix} e^t_3 \\ e^t_1 \\ e^t_5 \\ e^t_2 \\ e^t_4 \end{pmatrix} A = \begin{pmatrix} 5 & -2 & 1 & 0 & 1 \\ -2 & 3 & -1 & 0 & 15 \\ 0 & -1 & -3 & 11 & -9 \\ 1 & 0 & -10 & -2 & 4 \\ -5 & -1 & 2 & -6 & -3 \end{pmatrix}$$

10.1. NUMERICAL LINEAR ALGEBRA TOOLS

$$AP = (e_2 \mid e_4 \mid e_1 \mid e_5 \mid e_3) A = \begin{pmatrix} 3 & 0 & -2 & 15 & -1 \\ 0 & -2 & 1 & 4 & -10 \\ -2 & 0 & 5 & 1 & 1 \\ -1 & -6 & -5 & -3 & 2 \\ -1 & 11 & 0 & -9 & -3 \end{pmatrix} \quad \square$$

Lemma 10.3. *The product of two permutation matrices is a permutation matrix.*

Lemma 10.4. *(i) The determinant of any permutation matrix is either 1 or -1. Thus, any permutation matrix is nonsingular.*

(ii) Any permutation matrix is orthogonal, i.e., the inverse of any permutation matrix is its transpose. In other words, if P is a permutation matrix, then $P^{-1} = P^t$.

10.1.3 Orthogonality

Definition 10.2. *Two vectors of the same size are orthogonal if and only if their inner product is equal to 0.*

In other words, two vectors u and v of the same size are orthogonal if and only if

$$(u, v) = v^t u = 0.$$

Definition 10.3. *A square matrix is orthogonal*[3] *if and only if any two different columns of the matrix are orthogonal and the norm of every column is equal to 1.*[4]

In other words, the $n \times n$ matrix $Q = col(q_k)_{k=1:n}$ is orthogonal if and only if

$$(q_k, q_j) = q_j^t q_k = 0, \quad \forall \, 1 \leq j \neq k \leq n; \tag{10.12}$$

$$\|q_i\|^2 = q_i^t q_i = 1, \quad \forall \, i = 1:n. \tag{10.13}$$

Theorem 10.2. *A square matrix is orthogonal if and only if its transpose matrix is also its inverse matrix.*

In other words, the square matrix Q is orthogonal if and only if

$$Q^t Q = Q Q^t = I, \tag{10.14}$$

i.e., if and only if

$$Q^t = Q^{-1}. \tag{10.15}$$

Proof. Let $Q = \mathrm{col}\,(q_k)_{k=1:n}$ be a square matrix of size n. Then,

$$Q^t = \mathrm{row}\,(q_k^t)_{k=1:n} = \mathrm{row}\,(q_j^t)_{j=1:n}.$$

Recall from (1.13) that the (j,k) entry of the matrix $Q^t Q$ is given by

$$(Q^t Q)(j,k) = q_j^t q_k, \quad \forall \, 1 \leq j, k \leq n. \tag{10.16}$$

---
[3] Throughout this book, we require, by definition, that any column of an orthogonal matrix has norm equal to 1. An orthogonal matrix with the properties from Definition 10.3 is also called an orthonormal matrix.

[4] Note that any two rows of an orthogonal matrix are also orthogonal, and the norm of every row of an orthogonal matrix is equal to 1; cf. Lemma 10.5.

Since the identity matrix I has all entries equal to 0 except for the entries on its main diagonal which are equal to 1, and using (10.16), (10.12), and (10.13), we obtain that

$$Q^tQ = I \iff \begin{cases} (Q^tQ)(j,k) = 0, & \forall\, 1 \le j \ne k \le n \\ (Q^tQ)(i,i) = 1, & \forall\, i = 1:n \end{cases}$$

$$\iff \begin{cases} q_j^t q_k = 0, & \forall\, 1 \le j \ne k \le n \\ q_i^t q_i = 1, & \forall\, i = 1:n \end{cases}$$

$$\iff \begin{cases} (q_k, q_j) = q_j^t q_k = 0, & \forall\, 1 \le j \ne k \le n \\ \|q_i\|^2 = q_i^t q_i = 1, & \forall\, i = 1:n \end{cases} \qquad (10.17)$$

From (10.17) and Definition 10.3, we conclude that $Q^tQ = I$ if and only if the matrix Q is orthogonal.

Then, from Lemma 1.6, it follows that $Q^t = Q^{-1}$ and $QQ^t = I$. □

Lemma 10.5. *A square matrix is orthogonal if and only if any two different rows of the matrix are orthogonal and the norm of every row is equal to 1.*

Proof. Let $Q = \text{row}\,(r_j)_{j=1:n}$ be an $n \times n$ orthogonal matrix. Then,

$$Q^t = \text{col}\,(r_j^t)_{j=1:n} = \text{col}\,(r_k^t)_{k=1:n}.$$

From Theorem 10.2, it follows that Q is an orthogonal matrix if and only if $QQ^t = I$. Note that the (j,k) entry of QQ^t is given by

$$(QQ^t)(j,k) = r_j r_k^t, \quad \forall\, 1 \le j,k \le n;$$

see (1.13). Then,

$$QQ^t = I \iff \begin{cases} (QQ^t)(j,k) = 0, & \forall\, 1 \le j \ne k \le n; \\ (QQ^t)(i,i) = 1, & \forall\, i = 1:n. \end{cases}$$

$$\iff \begin{cases} r_j^t r_k = 0, & \forall\, 1 \le j \ne k \le n; \\ r_j^t r_j = 1, & \forall\, i = 1:n. \end{cases}$$

$$\iff \begin{cases} (r_k, r_j) = r_j^t r_k = 0, & \forall\, 1 \le j \ne k \le n; \\ \|r_i\|^2 = r_i^t r_i = 1, & \forall\, i = 1:n. \end{cases}$$

We conclude that the matrix Q is orthogonal if and only if any two rows of Q are orthogonal and the norm of every row of Q is equal to 1. □

Lemma 10.6. *The product of two orthogonal square matrices of the same size is an orthogonal matrix.*

Proof. Let $Q = Q_1 Q_2$, where Q_1 and Q_2 are orthogonal matrices of the same size. Since $Q_1^t Q_1 = I$ and $Q_2^t Q_2 = I$, we obtain that

$$\begin{aligned} Q^t Q &= (Q_1 Q_2)^t Q_1 Q_2 = Q_2^t Q_1^t Q_1 Q_2 \\ &= Q_2^t (Q_1^t Q_1) Q_2 = Q_2^t Q_2 \\ &= I, \end{aligned}$$

and, from Theorem 10.2, we conclude that the matrix Q is orthogonal. □

10.1. NUMERICAL LINEAR ALGEBRA TOOLS

Lemma 10.7. *Multiplying a vector by an orthogonal matrix does not change the Euclidean norm of the vector.*

In other words, if Q is an $n \times n$ orthogonal matrix and v is a column vector of size n, then

$$||Qv|| = ||v||. \qquad (10.18)$$

Proof. Let Q be an orthogonal matrix. Then, $Q^t Q = I$, see Theorem 10.2, and therefore

$$||Qv||^2 = (Qv, Qv) = (Qv)^t Qv = v^t Q^t Q v = v^t v = ||v||^2.$$

□

Lemma 10.8. *Any eigenvalue of an orthogonal matrix has absolute value equal to 1.*

Proof. Let λ be an eigenvalue of the orthogonal matrix Q, and let $v \neq 0$ be the corresponding eigenvector; note that λ could be a complex number. Then, $Qv = \lambda v$, and, from (10.18), we obtain that

$$||v|| = ||Qv|| = ||\lambda v|| = |\lambda|\, ||v||.$$

Since $||v|| \neq 0$, it follows that $|\lambda| = 1$. □

10.1.4 Quadratic forms

Lemma 10.9. *Let $A = (A(j,k))_{j,k=1:n}$ be a square matrix of size n, and let $x = (x_i)_{i=1:n}$ and $y = (y_i)_{i=1:n}$ be two column vectors of size n. Then,*

$$y^t A x = \sum_{1 \leq j,k \leq n} A(j,k) y_j x_k. \qquad (10.19)$$

Also,

$$x^t A x = \sum_{1 \leq j,k \leq n} A(j,k) x_j x_k. \qquad (10.20)$$

Proof. Let $A = \mathrm{col}(a_k)_{k=1:n}$ be the column form of A. Then,

$$A x = \sum_{k=1}^{n} x_k a_k; \qquad (10.21)$$

see (1.7). Since $a_k = (A(j,k))_{j=1:n}$, we find from (1.5) that

$$y^t a_k = \sum_{j=1}^{n} y_j A(j,k). \qquad (10.22)$$

From (10.21) and (10.22), we obtain that

$$
\begin{aligned}
y^t A x &= y^t \left(\sum_{k=1}^{n} x_k a_k \right) = \sum_{k=1}^{n} y^t \cdot (x_k a_k) \\
&= \sum_{k=1}^{n} x_k \cdot (y^t a_k),
\end{aligned}
\qquad (10.23)
$$

where the equality from (10.23) comes from the fact that x_k is scalar (i.e., a number) and y^t and a_k are vectors.

From (10.22) and (10.23), we conclude that

$$
\begin{aligned}
y^t A x &= \sum_{k=1}^{n} x_k \left(\sum_{j=1}^{n} y_j A(j,k) \right) \\
&= \sum_{k=1}^{n} \sum_{j=1}^{n} x_k y_j A(j,k) \\
&= \sum_{1 \leq j,k \leq n} A(j,k) y_j x_k.
\end{aligned}
$$

Thus, (10.19) is proved, and (10.20) follows from (10.19) by letting $y = x$. □

From (10.20), we obtain that

$$
\mathbf{1}^t A \mathbf{1} = \sum_{1 \leq j,k \leq n} A(j,k), \qquad (10.24)
$$

where $\mathbf{1}$ is the $n \times 1$ column vector with all entries equal to 1.

Note that, if $D = \mathrm{diag}(d_k)_{k=1:n}$ is a diagonal matrix, it follows from (10.20) that

$$
x^t D x = \sum_{k=1}^{n} d_k x_k^2, \quad \forall\, x \in \mathbb{R}^n. \qquad (10.25)
$$

Definition 10.4. *Let $A = (A(j,k))_{j,k=1:n}$ be a square matrix of size n. The quadratic form $q_A : \mathbb{R}^n \to \mathbb{R}$ associated with the matrix A is defined as*

$$
q_A(x) = x^t A x, \qquad (10.26)
$$

or, equivalently, as

$$
q_A(x) = \sum_{1 \leq j,k \leq n} A(j,k) x_j x_k; \qquad (10.27)
$$

cf. (10.20).

From (10.27), it follows that the quadratic form $q_A(x)$ can also be written as

$$
q_A(x) = \sum_{j=1}^{n} A(j,j) x_j^2 + \sum_{1 \leq j < k \leq n} (A(j,k) + A(k,j)) x_j x_k. \qquad (10.28)
$$

10.1. NUMERICAL LINEAR ALGEBRA TOOLS

Theorem 10.3. *(i) For any square matrix A,*

$$q_A(x) = q_{A^t}(x),$$

i.e., the quadratic forms associated to a square matrix and its transpose are equal. Moreover,

$$q_A(x) = \frac{1}{2} x^t \left(A + A^t \right) x. \tag{10.29}$$

(ii) If A and B are square matrices of the same size, then

$$q_A(x) = q_B(x) \iff A + A^t = B + B^t. \tag{10.30}$$

(iii) For every square matrix A of size n there exists a unique symmetric matrix M of size n such that

$$q_A(x) = q_M(x).$$

Note that, from (10.30), it follows that different matrices may have identical quadratic forms.

Proof. (i) For any $x \in \mathbb{R}^n$, the value of the quadratic form q_A evaluated at x is a number, i.e., $q_A(x) \in \mathbb{R}$. Then, $q_A(x) = (q_A(x))^t$, which can be written as

$$q_A(x) = x^t A x = (q_A(x))^t = \left(x^t A x\right)^t = x^t A^t x = q_{A^t}(x).$$

Thus, $q_A(x) = q_{A^t}(x)$ and therefore

$$\begin{aligned} q_A(x) &= \frac{1}{2} \left(q_A(x) + q_{A^t}(x) \right) \\ &= \frac{1}{2} \left(x^t A x + x^t A^t x \right) \\ &= \frac{1}{2} x^t \left(A + A^t \right) x. \end{aligned}$$

(ii) From (10.28), it follows that $q_A(x) = q_B(x)$ if and only if

$$\sum_{j=1}^{n} A(j,j) x_j^2 + \sum_{1 \le j < k \le n} (A(j,k) + A(k,j)) x_j x_k \tag{10.31}$$

$$= \sum_{j=1}^{n} B(j,j) x_j^2 + \sum_{1 \le j < k \le n} (B(j,k) + B(k,j)) x_j x_k, \quad \forall x \in \mathbb{R}^n. \tag{10.32}$$

By identifying the coefficients of $x_j x_k$, for all $1 \le j < k \le n$ and of x_j^2, for all $j = 1 : n$, from (10.31) and (10.32), we find that $q_A = q_B$ if and only if

$$A(j,j) = B(j,j), \quad \forall\, 1 \le j \le n; \tag{10.33}$$
$$A(j,k) + A(k,j) = B(j,k) + B(k,j), \quad \forall\, 1 \le j < k \le n. \tag{10.34}$$

Note that (10.33) and (10.34) are equivalent to saying that the matrices $A + A^t$ and $B + B^t$ are equal. We conclude that $q_A = q_B$ if and only if $A + A^t = B + B^t$.

(iii) Let M be a symmetric matrix. Then, $M^t = M$, and, using (10.30), we find that

$$\begin{aligned} q_A(x) = q_M(x) &\iff A + A^t = M + M^t \\ &\iff A + A^t = 2M \\ &\iff M = \frac{A + A^t}{2}. \end{aligned}$$

Thus, the only symmetric matrix M such that $q_A = q_M$ is $M = \frac{A+A^t}{2}$. $\square$

Theorem 10.4. *(i) The gradient and Hessian of the quadratic form $q_A : \mathbb{R}^n \to \mathbb{R}$ associated to the $n \times n$ matrix A are*

$$D(q_A(x)) = ((A + A^t)x)^t; \tag{10.35}$$
$$D^2(q_A(x)) = A + A^t. \tag{10.36}$$

(ii) If A is a symmetric matrix, then

$$D(q_A(x)) = 2(Ax)^t; \tag{10.37}$$
$$D^2(q_A(x)) = 2A. \tag{10.38}$$

Proof. A proof of this result can be found in section 10.2.1; see Theorem 10.5. $\square$

10.2 Mathematical tools

10.2.1 Multivariable functions

The material in this section is adapted from Stefanica [36]; see section 1.6 therein for more details.

Scalar Valued Functions

Let $f : \mathbb{R}^n \to \mathbb{R}$ be a function of n variables $x_1, x_2, \ldots, x_n$ and let $x = (x_1, x_2, \ldots, x_n)$.

If the function $f(x)$ is differentiable with respect to all the variables x_i, $i = 1 : n$, then the gradient of $f(x)$ is the following $1 \times n$ row vector:

$$Df(x) = \left(\frac{\partial f}{\partial x_1}(x) \quad \frac{\partial f}{\partial x_2}(x) \quad \cdots \quad \frac{\partial f}{\partial x_n}(x) \right). \tag{10.39}$$

If the function $f(x)$ is twice differentiable with respect to all variables x_j, x_k, with $1 \leq j, k \leq n$, then the Hessian of $f(x)$ is the following $n \times n$ matrix:

$$D^2 f(x) = \begin{pmatrix} \frac{\partial^2 f}{\partial x_1^2}(x) & \frac{\partial^2 f}{\partial x_2 \partial x_1}(x) & \cdots & \frac{\partial^2 f}{\partial x_n \partial x_1}(x) \\ \frac{\partial^2 f}{\partial x_1 \partial x_2}(x) & \frac{\partial^2 f}{\partial x_2^2}(x) & \cdots & \frac{\partial^2 f}{\partial x_n \partial x_2}(x) \\ \vdots & \vdots & \ddots & \vdots \\ \frac{\partial^2 f}{\partial x_1 \partial x_n}(x) & \frac{\partial^2 f}{\partial x_2 \partial x_n}(x) & \cdots & \frac{\partial^2 f}{\partial x_n^2}(x) \end{pmatrix}. \tag{10.40}$$

10.2. MATHEMATICAL TOOLS

In other words,
$$D^2 f(x) = \left(\frac{\partial^2 f}{\partial x_k \partial x_j}(x)\right)_{1 \leq j,k \leq n}. \tag{10.41}$$

Note that, for all $j = 1:n$, it follows from (10.39) that
$$D\left(\frac{\partial f}{\partial x_j}(x)\right) = \left(\frac{\partial^2 f}{\partial x_1 x_j}(x) \ \ \frac{\partial^2 f}{\partial x_2 x_j}(x) \ \ \cdots \ \ \frac{\partial^2 f}{\partial x_n x_j}(x)\right),$$

and therefore
$$D^2 f(x) = \begin{pmatrix} D\left(\frac{\partial f}{\partial x_1}(x)\right) \\ D\left(\frac{\partial f}{\partial x_2}(x)\right) \\ \vdots \\ D\left(\frac{\partial f}{\partial x_n}(x)\right) \end{pmatrix} = D \begin{pmatrix} \frac{\partial f}{\partial x_1}(x) \\ \frac{\partial f}{\partial x_2}(x) \\ \vdots \\ \frac{\partial f}{\partial x_n}(x) \end{pmatrix}$$
$$= D\left((Df(x))^t\right). \tag{10.42}$$

Lemma 10.10. *Let $C = (c_i)_{i=1:n}$ be an $n \times 1$ column vector of real constants, and let $x = (x_i)_{i=1:n}$ be a column vector of n variables. Then,*
$$D(C^t x) = C^t; \tag{10.43}$$
$$D(x^t C) = C^t; \tag{10.44}$$
$$D^2(C^t x) = \mathbf{0}; \tag{10.45}$$
$$D^2(x^t C) = \mathbf{0}, \tag{10.46}$$
where $\mathbf{0}$ denotes an $n \times n$ matrix with all entries equal to 0.

Proof. Note that
$$C^t x = x^t C = \sum_{i=1}^n c_i x_i;$$
cf. (1.5), and let $f : \mathbb{R}^n \to \mathbb{R}$ given by
$$f(x) = \sum_{i=1}^n c_i x_i.$$
Then,
$$\frac{\partial f}{\partial x_i}(x) = c_i, \ \forall \, i = 1:n; \quad \frac{\partial^2 f}{\partial x_j x_k} = 0. \ \forall \, 1 \leq j,k \leq n.$$
From (10.39) and (10.40), it follows that
$$Df(x) = (c_1 \ c_2 \ \cdots \ c_n) = C^t; \quad D^2 f(x) = \mathbf{0}.$$
□

Theorem 10.5. *(i) Let A be an $n \times n$ symmetric matrix and let $x = (x_i)_{i=1:n}$ be a column vector of n variables. The gradient and Hessian of $x^t A x$ are*
$$D\left(x^t A x\right) = 2(Ax)^t; \tag{10.47}$$
$$D^2\left(x^t A x\right) = 2A. \tag{10.48}$$

(ii) Let A be a square matrix. The gradient and Hessian of $x^t A x$ are

$$D\left(x^t A x\right) = \left((A + A^t)x\right)^t; \qquad (10.49)$$
$$D^2\left(x^t A x\right) = A + A^t. \qquad (10.50)$$

Proof. (i) Let A be an $n \times n$ symmetric matrix, and let $f : \mathbb{R}^n \to \mathbb{R}$ given by

$$f(x) = x^t A x.$$

Let i fixed, with $1 \leq i \leq n$. From (10.20), we find that

$$\begin{aligned}
f(x) &= \sum_{1 \leq l, p \leq n} A(l, p) x_l x_p \\
&= A(i,i) x_i^2 + \sum_{p=1:n, p \neq i} A(i, p) x_i x_p + \sum_{l=1:n, l \neq i} A(l, i) x_l x_i \quad (10.51) \\
&\quad + \sum_{1 \leq l, p \leq n, l \neq i, p \neq i} A(l, p) x_l x_p. \quad (10.52)
\end{aligned}$$

By differentiating (10.51–10.52) with respect to x_i, and noting that $A(i, p) = A(p, i)$ since A is a symmetric matrix, we find that

$$\begin{aligned}
\frac{\partial f}{\partial x_i}(x) &= 2A(i,i) x_i + \sum_{p=1:n, p \neq i} A(i, p) x_p + \sum_{l=1:n, l \neq i} A(l, i) x_l \\
&= 2A(i,i) x_i + \sum_{p=1:n, p \neq i} A(i, p) x_p + \sum_{p=1:n, p \neq i} A(p, i) x_p \\
&= 2A(i,i) x_i + \sum_{p=1:n, p \neq i} (A(i, p) + A(p, i)) x_p \\
&= 2A(i,i) x_i + 2 \sum_{p=1:n, p \neq i} A(i, p) x_p \\
&= 2 \sum_{p=1}^{n} A(i, p) x_p. \quad (10.53)
\end{aligned}$$

From (1.8), it follows that the i-th entry of the vector $2Ax$, where $1 \leq i \leq n$, is given by

$$(2Ax)(i) = 2 \sum_{p=1}^{n} A(i, p) x_p. \qquad (10.54)$$

From (10.53) and (10.54), we conclude that

$$\frac{\partial f}{\partial x_i}(x) = (2Ax)(i), \ \forall \ i = 1 : n,$$

and therefore, from (10.39), we obtain that

$$\begin{aligned}
Df(x) &= \left(\frac{\partial f}{\partial x_1}(x) \ \ \frac{\partial f}{\partial x_2}(x) \ \ \ldots \ \ \frac{\partial f}{\partial x_n}(x) \right) \\
&= \left((2Ax)(1) \ \ (2Ax)(2) \ \ \ldots \ \ (2Ax)(n) \right) \\
&= 2(Ax)^t.
\end{aligned}$$

10.2. MATHEMATICAL TOOLS

To compute the Hessian of $f(x) = x^t A x$, let j and k fixed, with $1 \leq j, k \leq n$. From (10.20), we find that

$$\begin{aligned} f(x) &= \sum_{1 \leq l,p \leq n} A(l,p) x_l x_p \\ &= (A(j,k) + A(k,j)) x_j x_k + \sum_{1 \leq l,p \leq n; (l,p) \neq (j,k); (l,p) \neq (k,j)} A(j,k) x_l x_p \\ &= 2 A(j,k) x_j x_k + \sum_{1 \leq l,p \leq n; (l,p) \neq (j,k); (l,p) \neq (k,j)} A(j,k) x_l x_p, \end{aligned}$$

since A is a symmetric matrix and therefore $A(j,k) = A(k,j)$. Then,

$$\frac{\partial^2 f}{\partial x_k \partial x_j}(x) = 2 A(j,k),$$

and, from (10.41), it follows that

$$D^2 f(x) = \left(\frac{\partial^2 f}{\partial x_k \partial x_j}(x) \right)_{1 \leq j, k \leq n} = (2 A(j,k))_{1 \leq j, k \leq n} = 2 A.$$

(ii) Let A be an $n \times n$ matrix. Recall from (10.28) that

$$q_A(x) = x^t A x = \frac{1}{2} x^t (A + A^t) x. \tag{10.55}$$

Note that $A + A^t$ is a symmetric matrix, since

$$(A + A^t)^t = A^t + (A^t)^t = A^t + A.$$

Then, from (10.47) and (10.48), we find that

$$\begin{aligned} D\left(x^t (A + A^t) x \right) &= 2 \left((A + A^t) x \right)^t; & (10.56) \\ D^2 \left(x^t (A + A^t) x \right) &= 2 (A + A^t). & (10.57) \end{aligned}$$

From (10.55), (10.56), and (10.57), we conclude that

$$\begin{aligned} D\left(x^t A x \right) &= \frac{1}{2} D\left(x^t (A + A^t) x \right) = \left((A + A^t) x \right)^t; \\ D^2 \left(x^t A x \right) &= \frac{1}{2} D^2 \left(x^t (A + A^t) x \right) = A + A^t. \end{aligned}$$

$\square$

Vector Valued Functions

Let $F : \mathbb{R}^n \to \mathbb{R}^m$ be a vector valued function given by

$$F(x) = \begin{pmatrix} f_1(x) \\ f_2(x) \\ \vdots \\ f_m(x) \end{pmatrix},$$

where $x = (x_1, x_2, \ldots, x_n)$.

If the functions $f_j(x)$, $j = 1 : m$, are differentiable with respect to all variables x_i, $i = 1 : n$, then the gradient $DF(x)$ of the function $F(x)$ is the following matrix of size $m \times n$:

$$DF(x) = \begin{pmatrix} \frac{\partial f_1}{\partial x_1}(x) & \frac{\partial f_1}{\partial x_2}(x) & \cdots & \frac{\partial f_1}{\partial x_n}(x) \\ \frac{\partial f_2}{\partial x_1}(x) & \frac{\partial f_2}{\partial x_2}(x) & \cdots & \frac{\partial f_2}{\partial x_n}(x) \\ \vdots & \vdots & \ddots & \vdots \\ \frac{\partial f_m}{\partial x_1}(x) & \frac{\partial f_m}{\partial x_2}(x) & \cdots & \frac{\partial f_m}{\partial x_n}(x) \end{pmatrix}. \qquad (10.58)$$

If $F : \mathbb{R}^n \to \mathbb{R}^n$, then the gradient $DF(x)$ is an $n \times n$ square matrix.

Note that the j-th row of the gradient matrix $DF(x)$ is equal to the gradient $Df_j(x)$ of the function $f_j(x)$, $j = 1 : m$; cf. (10.39) and (10.58). Therefore,

$$DF(x) = \begin{pmatrix} Df_1(x) \\ Df_2(x) \\ \vdots \\ Df_m(x) \end{pmatrix}. \qquad (10.59)$$

Lemma 10.11. *Let M be an $m \times n$ matrix. The gradient of the vector valued function Mx, taking $x \in \mathbb{R}^n$ into $Mx \in \mathbb{R}^m$ is*

$$D(Mx) = M. \qquad (10.60)$$

Proof. Let $M = \text{row}\,(r_j)_{j=1:m}$ be the row form of M. From (1.8), it follows that the Mx can be written as[5]

$$Mx = \begin{pmatrix} r_1 x \\ r_2 x \\ \vdots \\ r_m x \end{pmatrix}. \qquad (10.61)$$

From (10.59) and (10.61), it follows that

$$D(Mx) = \begin{pmatrix} D(r_1 x) \\ D(r_2 x) \\ \vdots \\ D(r_m x) \end{pmatrix}. \qquad (10.62)$$

From (10.43), we find that

$$D(r_j x) = r_j, \quad \forall\, j = 1 : m. \qquad (10.63)$$

Then, from (10.62) and (10.63), we conclude that

$$D(Mx) = \begin{pmatrix} r_1 \\ r_2 \\ \vdots \\ r_m \end{pmatrix} = \text{row}\,(r_j)_{j=1:m} = M.$$

$\square$

---

[5] Note that $r_j x$ is the result of the multiplication of the row vector r_j by the column vector x, and therefore a real number, for every $j = 1 : m$; see also (1.5).

10.2. MATHEMATICAL TOOLS

We note that the result of Lemma 10.11 can be used to prove (10.50). Recall from (10.42) that $D^2 f(x) = D\left((Df(x))^t\right)$. Then, using (10.49) and (10.60), we find that

$$D^2\left(x^t A x\right) = D\left((D\left(x^t A x\right))^t\right) = D\left((A + A^t)x\right)$$
$$= (A + A^t).$$

10.2.2 Lagrange multipliers

Expanded coverage of the Lagrange multipliers method can be found in Chapter 9 of Stefanica [36].

The Lagrange multipliers method is used to find extrema of multivariable functions subject to various constraints.

Let $U \subset \mathbb{R}^n$ be an open set, and let $f : U \to \mathbb{R}$ be a smooth function, e.g., infinitely many times differentiable. We want to find the extrema of $f(x)$ subject to m constraints given by $g(x) = 0$, where $g : U \to \mathbb{R}^m$ is a smooth function, i.e.,

Find $x_0 \in U$ such that

$$\max_{\substack{g(x) = 0 \\ x \in U}} f(x) = f(x_0) \quad \text{or} \quad \min_{\substack{g(x) = 0 \\ x \in U}} f(x) = f(x_0). \tag{10.64}$$

A point $x_0 \in U$ satisfying (10.64) is called a constrained extremum point of the function $f(x)$ with respect to the constraint function $g(x)$. For problem (10.64) to be well posed, we assume the number of constraints is smaller than the number of the degrees of freedom, i.e., $m < n$.

To solve the constrained optimization problem (10.64), let $\lambda = (\lambda_i)_{i=1:m}$ be a column vector of the same size, m, as the number of constraints; λ is called the Lagrange multipliers vector.

The Lagrangian associated to problem (10.64) is the function $F : U \times \mathbb{R}^m \to \mathbb{R}$ given by

$$F(x, \lambda) = f(x) + \lambda^t g(x). \tag{10.65}$$

If $g(x) = \begin{pmatrix} g_1(x) \\ \vdots \\ g_m(x) \end{pmatrix}$, then $F(x, \lambda)$ can be written explicitly as

$$F(x, \lambda) = f(x) + \sum_{i=1}^{m} \lambda_i g_i(x).$$

In the Lagrange multipliers method, the constrained extremum point x_0 is found by identifying the critical points of $F(x, \lambda)$. A necessary condition for using the Lagrange multipliers method is that the gradient $Dg(x)$ must have has full rank at any point x where the constraint $g(x) = 0$ is satisfied, i.e.,

$$\text{rank}(Dg(x)) = m, \quad \forall \, x \in U \text{ such that } g(x) = 0. \tag{10.66}$$

Denote by $D_{(x,\lambda)} F(x,\lambda)$ the gradient of $F(x,\lambda)$ with respect to both x and λ. In other words, $D_{(x,\lambda)} F(x,\lambda)$ is the following (row) vector:

$$D_{(x,\lambda)} F(x,\lambda) = (\ D_x F(x,\lambda) \quad D_\lambda F(x,\lambda)\ ) = \begin{pmatrix} (D_x F(x,\lambda))^t \\ (D_\lambda F(x,\lambda))^t \end{pmatrix}^t. \quad (10.67)$$

Recall from (10.39) that

$$D_x F(x,\lambda) = \left(\frac{\partial F}{\partial x_1}(x,\lambda) \ \ldots \ \frac{\partial F}{\partial x_n}(x,\lambda) \right); \quad (10.68)$$

$$D_\lambda F(x,\lambda) = \left(\frac{\partial F}{\partial \lambda_1}(x,\lambda) \ \ldots \ \frac{\partial F}{\partial \lambda_m}(x,\lambda) \right), \quad (10.69)$$

and note that

$$\frac{\partial F}{\partial x_j}(x,\lambda) = \frac{\partial f}{\partial x_j}(x) + \sum_{i=1}^{m} \lambda_i \frac{\partial g_i}{\partial x_j}(x), \ \forall\, j = 1:n; \quad (10.70)$$

$$\frac{\partial F}{\partial \lambda_i}(x,\lambda) = g_i(x), \ \forall\, i = 1:m. \quad (10.71)$$

Then, from (10.67–10.71), it follows that

$$D_{(x,\lambda)} F(x,\lambda) = \begin{pmatrix} \frac{\partial F}{\partial x_1}(x,\lambda) \\ \vdots \\ \frac{\partial F}{\partial x_n}(x,\lambda) \\ \frac{\partial F}{\partial \lambda_1}(x,\lambda) \\ \vdots \\ \frac{\partial F}{\partial \lambda_m}(x,\lambda) \end{pmatrix}^t = \begin{pmatrix} \frac{\partial f}{\partial x_1}(x) + \sum_{i=1}^{m} \lambda_i \frac{\partial g_i}{\partial x_1}(x) \\ \vdots \\ \frac{\partial f}{\partial x_n}(x) + \sum_{i=1}^{m} \lambda_i \frac{\partial g_i}{\partial x_n}(x) \\ g_1(x) \\ \vdots \\ g_m(x) \end{pmatrix}^t.$$

The following theorem gives necessary conditions for a point $x_0 \in U$ to be a constrained extremum point for $f(x)$:

Theorem 10.6. *Assume that the function $g(x)$ satisfies condition (10.66). If $x_0 \in U$ is a constrained extremum point of $f(x)$ with respect to the constraint $g(x) = 0$, then there exists a Lagrange multiplier $\lambda_0 \in \mathbb{R}^m$ such that the point (x_0, λ_0) is a critical point for the Lagrangian function $F(x,\lambda)$, i.e.,*

$$D_{(x,\lambda)} F(x_0, \lambda_0) = 0. \quad (10.72)$$

To find sufficient conditions for a critical point (x_0, λ_0) of the Lagrangian $F(x,\lambda)$ to correspond to a constrained extremum point x_0 for $f(x)$, consider the function $F_0 : U \to \mathbb{R}$ given by

$$F_0(x) = F(x, \lambda_0) = f(x) + \lambda_0^t g(x).$$

Let $D^2 F_0(x_0)$ be the Hessian of $F_0(x)$ evaluated at the point x_0, i.e.,

$$D^2 F_0(x_0) = \begin{pmatrix} \frac{\partial^2 F_0}{\partial x_1^2}(x_0) & \frac{\partial^2 F_0}{\partial x_2 \partial x_1}(x_0) & \cdots & \frac{\partial^2 F_0}{\partial x_n \partial x_1}(x_0) \\ \frac{\partial^2 F_0}{\partial x_1 \partial x_2}(x_0) & \frac{\partial^2 F_0}{\partial x_2^2}(x_0) & \cdots & \frac{\partial^2 F_0}{\partial x_n \partial x_2}(x_0) \\ \vdots & \vdots & \ddots & \vdots \\ \frac{\partial^2 F_0}{\partial x_1 \partial x_n}(x_0) & \frac{\partial^2 F_0}{\partial x_2 \partial x_n}(x_0) & \cdots & \frac{\partial^2 F_0}{\partial x_n^2}(x_0) \end{pmatrix}; \quad (10.73)$$

10.2. MATHEMATICAL TOOLS

see (10.40). Note that $D^2 F_0(x_0)$ is an $n \times n$ symmetric matrix.

We restrict our attention to the case when the matrix $D^2 F_0(x_0)$ is either symmetric positive definite, or symmetric negative definite, which suffices for the purpose of this book. The general theory of Lagrange multipliers can be found in section 9.1 from Stefanica [36]; see Theorem 9.2 therein.

Theorem 10.7. *Assume that the function $g(x)$ satisfies condition (10.66). Let $x_0 \in U \subset \mathbb{R}^n$ and $\lambda_0 \in \mathbb{R}^m$ such that the point (x_0, λ_0) is a critical point for the Lagrangian function $F(x, \lambda) = f(x) + \lambda^t g(x)$. Let $F_0(x) = f(x) + \lambda_0^t g(x)$, and let $D^2 F_0(x_0)$ be the Hessian of F_0 evaluated at the point x_0.*

If the matrix $D^2 F_0(x_0)$ is positive definite, i.e., if all the eigenvalues of the matrix $D^2 F_0(x_0)$ are strictly greater than 0, then x_0 is a constrained minimum for $f(x)$ with respect to the constraint $g(x) = 0$.

If the matrix $D^2 F_0(x_0)$ is negative definite, i.e., if all the eigenvalues of the matrix $D^2 F_0(x_0)$ are strictly less than 0, then x_0 is a constrained maximum for $f(x)$ with respect to the constraint $g(x) = 0$.

Summarizing, the steps for solving the simplified version of a constrained optimization problem using Lagrange multipliers are:

Step 1: Check that $\text{rank}(Dg(x)) = m$ for all x such that $g(x) = 0$.

Step 2: Find $(x_0, \lambda_0) \in U \times \mathbb{R}^m$ such that $D_{(x,\lambda)} F(x_0, \lambda_0) = 0$.

Step 3: Check whether the matrix $D^2 F_0(x_0)$ is positive semidefinite or negative semidefinite.

Step 4: Use Theorem 10.7 to decide whether x_0 is a constrained minimum point or a constrained maximum point.

The Lagrange multipliers method is used, for example, for portfolio optimization problems; see sections 9.3, 9.4, and 9.5 for details.

10.2.3 The "Big O" notation

In this book, the "Big O" notation is primarily used for polynomials; a formal definition can be found below. More details on the general form of the "Big O" notation can be found in Section 10.5 of Stefanica [36].

Definition 10.5. *Let $f : \mathbb{R} \to \mathbb{R}$, and let k be a positive integer. We write that $f(n) = O(n^k)$, as $n \to \infty$, if and only if there exist constants $C_1, C_2 > 0$ and $M > 0$ such that*

$$C_1 \leq \left| \frac{f(n)}{n^k} \right| \leq C_2, \quad \forall\, n \geq M.$$

In particular, note that

$$\text{if } 0 < \lim_{n \to \infty} \left| \frac{f(n)}{n^k} \right| < \infty, \quad \text{then} \quad f(n) = O(n^k), \text{ as } n \to \infty. \tag{10.74}$$

Let

$$P(x) = \sum_{i=0}^{p} a_i x^i = a_p x^p + a_{p-1} x^{p-1} + \ldots + a_1 x + a_0,$$

with $a_p \neq 0$, be a polynomial of degree p. Then, from (10.74), it follows that
$$P(n) = O(n^p), \quad \text{as } n \to \infty.$$
More precisely, if $a_{p-1} \neq 0$, then,
$$P(n) = a_p x^p + O(n^{p-1}), \quad \text{as } n \to \infty. \tag{10.75}$$
To prove, e.g., (10.75), note that
$$\lim_{n \to \infty} \left| \frac{P(n) - a_p x^p}{n^{p-1}} \right| = \lim_{n \to \infty} \left| \frac{a_{p-1} n^{p-1} + a_{p-2} n^{p-2} + \ldots + a_1 n + a_0}{n^{p-1}} \right|$$
$$= \lim_{n \to \infty} \left| a_{p-1} + \frac{a_{p-2}}{n} + \ldots + \frac{a_1}{n^{p-2}} + \frac{a_0}{n^{p-1}} \right|$$
$$= |a_{p-1}| > 0,$$
and therefore $P(n) - a_p x^p = O(n^{p-1})$; cf. (10.74)

The results below follow from (10.75) and are used in the book:
$$8n - 7 = 8n + O(1), \quad \text{as } n \to \infty; \tag{10.76}$$
$$10n - 7 = 10n + O(1), \quad \text{as } n \to \infty; \tag{10.77}$$
$$n^2 + n - 1 = n^2 + O(n), \quad \text{as } n \to \infty; \tag{10.78}$$
$$\frac{2n^3}{3} - \frac{n^2}{2} + \frac{5n}{6} - 1 = \frac{2}{3}n^3 + O(n^2), \quad \text{as } n \to \infty; \tag{10.79}$$
$$\frac{n^3}{3} + \frac{n^2}{2} + \frac{n}{6} = \frac{1}{3}n^3 + O(n^2), \quad \text{as } n \to \infty. \tag{10.80}$$

Rules for operations with the "Big O" notations can be derived from Definition 10.5 and are as follows:

If k and j are positive integers and $c \neq 0$ is a constant, then
$$c\, n^j O(n^k) = O(n^{j+k}), \quad \text{as } n \to \infty; \tag{10.81}$$
$$c\, O(n^k) = O(n^k), \quad \text{as } n \to \infty; \tag{10.82}$$
$$O(n^k) + c n^k = O(n^k), \quad \text{as } n \to \infty; \tag{10.83}$$
$$O(n^k) + O(n^k) = O(n^k), \quad \text{as } n \to \infty; \tag{10.84}$$
$$O(n^k) + O(n^j) = O(n^k), \quad \text{if } j < k, \text{ as } n \to \infty. \tag{10.85}$$

The following results can be proved using (10.81–10.84):
As $n \to \infty$,
$$\left(\frac{2}{3}n^3 + O(n^2)\right) + 2(n^2 + O(n)) = \frac{2}{3}n^3 + O(n^2) + 2n^2 + 2O(n)$$
$$= \frac{2}{3}n^3 + O(n^2) + O(n)$$
$$= \frac{2}{3}n^3 + O(n^2); \tag{10.86}$$
$$\left(\frac{1}{3}n^3 + O(n^2)\right) + 2(n^2 + O(n)) = \frac{1}{3}n^3 + O(n^2); \tag{10.87}$$

$$\frac{2}{3}n^3 + O(n^2) + n\left(2n^2 + 2O(n)\right) = \frac{8}{3}n^3 + O(n^2) + 2nO(n)$$
$$= \frac{8}{3}n^3 + O(n^2) + O(n^2)$$
$$= \frac{8}{3}n^3 + O(n^2); \tag{10.88}$$
$$\frac{1}{3}n^3 + O(n^2) + n\left(2n^2 + 2O(n)\right) = \frac{7}{3}n^3 + O(n^2). \tag{10.89}$$

10.3 European options overview

The material in this section is adapted from Stefanica [36]; see sections 1.7–1.10 and 3.7 therein for more details.

A **Call Option** on an underlying asset (e.g., on one share of a stock, for an equity option[6]) is a contract between two parties which gives the buyer of the option the right, but not the obligation, to **buy** from the seller of the option one unit of the asset (e.g., one share of the stock) at a predetermined time T in the future, called the **maturity** of the option, for a predetermined price K, called the **strike** of the option. For this right, the buyer of the option pays $C(t)$ at time $t < T$ to the seller of the option.

A **Put Option** on an underlying asset is a contract between two parties which gives the buyer of the option the right, but not the obligation, to **sell** to the seller of the option one unit of the asset at a predetermined time T in the future, called the **maturity** of the option, for a predetermined price K, called the **strike** of the option. For this right, the buyer of the option pays $P(t)$ at time $t < T$ to the seller of the option.

The options described above are plain vanilla European options. An option which can be exercised at any time prior to maturity is called an American option.

Let $S(t)$ be the price of the underlying asset at time t. A call option is at-the-money (ATM) if its strike is equal to the spot price, i.e., if $K = S(t)$. Similarly, a put option is at-the-money (ATM) if its strike is equal to the spot price, i.e., if $K = S(t)$. A call option is in-the-money (ITM) or out-of-the-money (OTM) at time t if $S(t) > K$ or $S(t) < K$, respectively. A put option is in-the-money or out-of-the-money at time t if $S(t) < K$ or $S(t) > K$, respectively.

The payoff of a call option at maturity is

$$C(T) = \max(S(T) - K, 0) = \begin{cases} S(T) - K, & \text{if } S(T) > K; \\ 0, & \text{if } S(T) \leq K. \end{cases} \tag{10.90}$$

The payoff of a put option at maturity is

$$P(T) = \max(K - S(T), 0) = \begin{cases} 0, & \text{if } S(T) \geq K; \\ K - S(T), & \text{if } S(T) < K. \end{cases} \tag{10.91}$$

The Put–Call parity

---

[6]The underlying asset for equity options is usually 100 shares, not one share. For clarity and simplicity reasons, we will be consistent throughout the book in our assumption that options are written on just one unit of the underlying asset.

The no-arbitrage values of European call and put options with the same strike and maturity satisfy a model–independent relationship called the Put–Call parity. The intuition behind the Put–Call parity is that a long call and a short put position in options with the same strike and maturity is the same as a long position in a forward contract on the underlying asset of the options with the same expiration date as the maturity of the options and with delivery price equal to the strike of the options.

More formally, if $C(t)$ and $P(t)$ are the values at time t of a European call and put option, respectively, with maturity T and strike K, on the same underlying asset with spot price $S(t)$, paying dividends continuously at the rate q, the Put–Call parity states that

$$C(t) - P(t) = S(t)e^{-q(T-t)} - Ke^{-r(T-t)}. \tag{10.92}$$

A proof of (10.92) based on the Law of One Price can be found in section 1.9 of Stefanica [36].

The Black–Scholes formulas

The Black–Scholes formulas give the price of plain vanilla European call and put options under the assumptions that the price of the underlying asset has lognormal distribution with volatility σ, the asset pays dividends continuously at the rate q, and the risk–free interest rate is constant and equal to r. The Black–Scholes values $C_{BS}(S,t)$ and $P_{BS}(S,t)$ of a call option and of a put option, respectively, with strike K and maturity T are given by

$$C(S,t) = Se^{-q(T-t)}N(d_1) - Ke^{-r(T-t)}N(d_2); \tag{10.93}$$
$$P(S,t) = Ke^{-r(T-t)}N(-d_2) - Se^{-q(T-t)}N(-d_1), \tag{10.94}$$

where

$$d_1 = \frac{\ln\left(\frac{S}{K}\right) + \left(r - q + \frac{\sigma^2}{2}\right)(T-t)}{\sigma\sqrt{T-t}}; \tag{10.95}$$

$$d_2 = d_1 - \sigma\sqrt{T-t} = \frac{\ln\left(\frac{S}{K}\right) + \left(r - q - \frac{\sigma^2}{2}\right)(T-t)}{\sigma\sqrt{T-t}}, \tag{10.96}$$

and $N(z)$ denotes the cumulative distribution of the standard normal variable, i.e.,

$$N(z) = \frac{1}{\sqrt{2\pi}} \int_{-\infty}^{z} e^{-\frac{x^2}{2}} \, dx.$$

Options Greeks

The Greeks are the sensitivities of the options prices with respect to various parameters, e.g., with respect to the price of the underlying asset or with respect to the volatility of the underlying asset, and are important for hedging purposes.

From the Black–Scholes formulas (10.93) and (10.94) for options on assets paying continuous dividends, the following closed formulas for the Greeks of European plain vanilla call and put options can be derived:

$$\Delta(C) = \frac{\partial C}{\partial S} = e^{-q(T-t)}N(d_1); \tag{10.97}$$

$$\Delta(P) = \frac{\partial P}{\partial S} = -e^{-q(T-t)}N(-d_1); \tag{10.98}$$

$$\Gamma(C) = \frac{\partial^2 C}{\partial S^2} = \frac{e^{-q(T-t)}}{S\sigma\sqrt{2\pi(T-t)}} e^{-\frac{d_1^2}{2}}; \tag{10.99}$$

$$\Gamma(P) = \frac{\partial^2 P}{\partial S^2} = \Gamma(C); \tag{10.100}$$

$$\text{vega}(C) = \frac{\partial C}{\partial \sigma} = S e^{-q(T-t)} \sqrt{\frac{T-t}{2\pi}} e^{-\frac{d_1^2}{2}}; \tag{10.101}$$

$$\text{vega}(P) = \frac{\partial P}{\partial \sigma} = \text{vega}(C). \tag{10.102}$$

10.4 Eigenvalues of symmetric matrices

In this section, we provide an elegant proof of the fact that any eigenvalue of a symmetric matrix with real entries is a real number; cf. Theorem 5.1 and Theorem 10.8.

To do so, we introduce an extension of the inner product (5.3), also called the Euclidean inner product, to vectors with complex entries.

Definition 10.6. *Let $u = (u_i)_{i=1:n}$ and $v = (v_i)_{i=1:n}$ be column vectors of size n with entries complex numbers, i.e., with $u_i, v_i \in \mathbb{C}$, for $i = 1:n$. The complex Euclidean inner product of u and v is*[7]

$$(u, v)_{\mathbb{C}} = u_1 \overline{v_1} + u_2 \overline{v_2} + \ldots + u_n \overline{v_n} = \sum_{i=1}^{n} u_i \overline{v_i}, \tag{10.103}$$

where $\overline{v_i}$ denotes the complex conjugate of v_i, for $i = 1:n$.

Note that
$$(u, v)_{\mathbb{C}} = v^* u, \tag{10.104}$$
where, by definition, $v^* = (\overline{v_1}\ \overline{v_2}\ \ldots\ \overline{v_n}) = (\overline{v_i})_{i=1:n}$ is the row vector whose entries are the complex conjugates of the entries of the vector $v = (v_i)_{i=1:n}$.

The following properties of the Euclidean complex inner product follow from definition (10.103):

$$(u, v)_{\mathbb{C}} = \overline{(v, u)_{\mathbb{C}}}, \quad \forall\, u, v \in \mathbb{C}^n; \tag{10.105}$$

$$(cu, v)_{\mathbb{C}} = c(u, v)_{\mathbb{C}}, \quad \forall\, u, v \in \mathbb{C}^n,\ c \in \mathbb{C}; \tag{10.106}$$

$$(u, cv)_{\mathbb{C}} = \overline{c}(u, v)_{\mathbb{C}}, \quad \forall\, u, v \in \mathbb{C}^n,\ c \in \mathbb{C}. \tag{10.107}$$

Definition 10.7. *The Euclidean norm of a vector $v = (v_i)_{i=1:n} \in \mathbb{C}^n$ is*

$$\|v\|_{\mathbb{C}} = \sqrt{\sum_{i=1}^{n} \|v_i\|^2} = \sqrt{(v, v)_{\mathbb{C}}} = \sqrt{v^* v}. \tag{10.108}$$

---

[7] Note that, if the entries of u and v are real numbers, i.e., if $u_i, v_i \in \mathbb{R}$ for all $i = 1:n$, then the complex Euclidean inner product is equal to the inner product given by (5.3):

$$(u, v)_{\mathbb{C}} = \sum_{i=1}^{n} u_i \overline{v_i} = \sum_{i=1}^{n} u_i v_i = (u, v).$$

Definition 10.8. Let A be an $m \times n$ matrix with complex entries. The hermitian of the matrix A is the $n \times m$ matrix A^* given by

$$A^*(j,k) = \overline{A(k,j)}, \quad \forall\, k = 1:n,\ j = 1:m.$$

Lemma 10.12. *The hermitian of a matrix with real entries is the transpose of the matrix.*

Proof. Let A be an $m \times n$ matrix with real entries. Then, $\overline{A(j,k)} = A(j,k)$, and therefore

$$A^*(k,j) = \overline{A(j,k)} = A(j,k) = A^t(k,j), \quad \forall\, j = 1:m,\ k = 1:n. \tag{10.109}$$

From (10.109), we conclude that $A^* = A^t$. □

The properties below are similar to those from Lemma 1.1 and Lemma 1.2 for the transpose of a matrix, and can be proved similarly:
For any $m \times n$ matrix A,

$$(A^*)^* = A. \tag{10.110}$$

For any $m \times n$ matrix A, $n \times p$ matrix B, and column vector v of size n,

$$(Av)^* = v^* A^*; \tag{10.111}$$
$$(AB)^* = B^* A^*. \tag{10.112}$$

Lemma 10.13. *Let A be a square matrix of size n with complex entries, and let u and v be column vectors of size n with complex entries. Then,*

$$(Au, v)_{\mathbb{C}} = (u, A^* v)_{\mathbb{C}}; \tag{10.113}$$
$$(u, Av)_{\mathbb{C}} = (A^* u, v)_{\mathbb{C}}. \tag{10.114}$$

Proof. Recall from (10.111) that $(Av)^* = v^* A^*$. Since $(A^*)^* = A$, see (10.110), we find that $(A^* v)^* = v^* (A^*)^* = v^* A$. Then, using (10.104), we obtain that

$$(Au, v)_{\mathbb{C}} = v^* A u = (v^* A) u = (A^* v)^* u = (u, A^* v)_{\mathbb{C}};$$
$$(u, Av)_{\mathbb{C}} = (Av)^* u = v^* A^* u = v^* (A^* u) = (A^* u, v)_{\mathbb{C}}.$$

□

We can now prove Theorem 5.1 from Section 5.1:

Theorem 10.8. *Any eigenvalue of a symmetric matrix with real entries is a real number.*

Proof. Let A be a square matrix of size n with real entries, and assume that A is symmetric, i.e., $A^t = A$. Let $\lambda \in \mathbb{C}$ and $v \in \mathbb{C}^n$ be an eigenvalue and a corresponding eigenvector of A. Then, $Av = \lambda v$, and, using (10.106) and (10.108), we find that

$$(Av, v)_{\mathbb{C}} = (\lambda v, v)_{\mathbb{C}} = \lambda (v, v)_{\mathbb{C}} = \lambda \|v\|_{\mathbb{C}}^2. \tag{10.115}$$

10.4. ROW RANK EQUAL TO COLUMN RANK

Since the matrix A has real entries, it follows from Lemma 10.12 that $A^* = A^t$. Note that $A^t = A$, since A is a symmetric matrix. Therefore, we obtain that $A^* = A$. Then, from (10.113) and using (10.107), we find that

$$\begin{aligned}(Av, v)_{\mathbb{C}} &= (v, A^*v)_{\mathbb{C}} = (v, Av)_{\mathbb{C}} = (v, \lambda v)_{\mathbb{C}} = \overline{\lambda}(v, v)_{\mathbb{C}} \\ &= \overline{\lambda}\|v\|_{\mathbb{C}}^2.\end{aligned} \qquad (10.116)$$

From (10.115) and (10.116), it follows that

$$\lambda \|v\|_{\mathbb{C}}^2 = \overline{\lambda} \|v\|_{\mathbb{C}}^2, \qquad (10.117)$$

Note that $\|v\| \neq 0$, since v is an eigenvector of the matrix A, and therefore $v \neq 0$. Then, from (10.117), we obtain that $\lambda = \overline{\lambda}$, which happens if and only if $\lambda \in \mathbb{R}$.

We conclude that any eigenvalue of the symmetric matrix A with real entries is a real number. $\square$

10.5 Row rank equal to column rank

The column rank and the row rank of a matrix A are defined as the largest number of linearly independent columns of A, and the largest number of linearly independent rows of A, respectively. It is important to note that the column rank and the row rank of a matrix are always the same, not only for square matrices, but also for rectangular matrices; see Lemma 10.14.

The author is indebted to Professor Gilbert Strang for the elegant proof below.

Lemma 10.14. *For any matrix A,*

$$colrank(A) = rowrank(A),$$

where $colrank(A)$ and $rowrank(A)$ are the column rank and the row rank of a matrix A, respectively.

Proof. Let A be an $m \times n$ matrix with column form $A = \operatorname{col}(a_k)_{k=1:n}$. Let p be the column rank of A. By definition, there exist p columns of A which are linearly independent vectors and such that every column of A is a linear combination of these p columns. Assume, without any loss of generality, that these p columns are the first p columns of A, i.e., $a_1, a_2, \ldots, a_p$. Then, for every k with $1 \leq k \leq n$, there exist constants c_{ik}, with $1 \leq i \leq p$, such that[8]

$$a_k = \sum_{i=1}^{p} c_{ik} a_i, \quad \forall\, k = 1:n. \qquad (10.118)$$

Let $A_p = \operatorname{col}(a_i)_{i=1:p}$ be the $m \times p$ matrix with columns $a_1, a_2, \ldots, a_p$, and let C be the $p \times n$ matrix given by

$$C = \begin{pmatrix} c_{11} & c_{12} & \cdots & c_{1n} \\ c_{21} & c_{22} & \cdots & c_{2n} \\ \vdots & \vdots & \ddots & \vdots \\ c_{p1} & c_{p2} & \cdots & c_{pn} \end{pmatrix}.$$

---
[8]For $1 \leq k \leq p$, note that $c_{kk} = 1$ and $c_{ik} = 0$ for all $1 \leq i \neq k \leq p$.

Let $C = \text{col}(w_k)_{k=1:n}$ be the column form of the matrix C, where $w_k = \begin{pmatrix} c_{1k} \\ \vdots \\ c_{pk} \end{pmatrix}$, for all $k = 1:n$. Since $A_p = \text{col}(a_i)_{i=1:p}$, we obtain using the matrix–column vector multiplication formula (1.7) that (10.118) can be written as

$$\begin{aligned} a_k &= \sum_{i=1}^{p} c_{ik} a_i = (a_1 \mid \ldots \mid a_p) \begin{pmatrix} c_{1k} \\ \vdots \\ c_{pk} \end{pmatrix} = \text{col}(a_i)_{i=1:p} \begin{pmatrix} c_{1k} \\ \vdots \\ c_{pk} \end{pmatrix} \\ &= A_p w_k, \quad \forall\, k = 1:n. \end{aligned} \qquad (10.119)$$

Then, from the matrix–matrix multiplication formula (1.11) and (10.119), we obtain that

$$\begin{aligned} A &= \text{col}(a_k)_{k=1:n} = \text{col}(A_p w_k)_{k=1:n} = A_p \text{col}(w_k)_{k=1:n} \\ &= A_p C. \end{aligned} \qquad (10.120)$$

Let $A = \text{row}(r_i)_{i=1:p}$ be the row form of A, and let $C = \text{row}(c_j)_{j=1:p}$ be the row form of C. From (10.120) and using the matrix–matrix multiplication formula (1.12), it follows that

$$r_i = \sum_{j=1}^{p} A_p(i,j) c_j, \quad \forall\, i = 1:p.$$

In other words, every row of the matrix A is a linear combination of the p vectors c_1, $c_2, \ldots, c_p$. Then, by definition, the row rank of the matrix A is less than or equal to p, the column rank of A.

We therefore showed that, for any matrix A,

$$\text{rowrank}(A) \leq \text{colrank}(A). \qquad (10.121)$$

In particular, the inequality (10.121) also holds for the matrix A^t, i.e.,

$$\text{rowrank}(A^t) \leq \text{colrank}(A^t). \qquad (10.122)$$

Note that

$$\begin{aligned} \text{rowrank}(A^t) &= \text{colrank}(A); & (10.123) \\ \text{colrank}(A^t) &= \text{rowrank}(A), & (10.124) \end{aligned}$$

since the rows of A^t are the columns of A, and the columns of A are the rows of A^t. Then, from (10.122–10.124), we find that

$$\text{colrank}(A) \leq \text{rowrank}(A). \qquad (10.125)$$

From (10.121) and (10.125) we conclude that

$$\text{rowrank}(A) = \text{colrank}(A).$$

$\square$

10.6 Technical results for the Cholesky and LU decompositions

This section contains the proofs of several technical results related to the existence and uniqueness of the Cholesky decomposition for symmetric positive definite matrices and of the LU decomposition; see section 2.4 and section 6.1 for details.

Lemma 10.15. *Let A be an $n \times n$ matrix with $A(1,1) > 0$, and let $A_{n-1} = A(2:n, 2:n)$. Then,*

$$A = \begin{pmatrix} \sqrt{A(1,1)} & \mathbf{0}^t \\ \frac{A(2:n,1)}{\sqrt{A(1,1)}} & I_{n-1} \end{pmatrix} \begin{pmatrix} 1 & \mathbf{0}^t \\ \mathbf{0} & A_{n-1} - \frac{A(2:n,1)A(1,2:n)}{A(1,1)} \end{pmatrix} \begin{pmatrix} \sqrt{A(1,1)} & \frac{A(1,2:n)}{\sqrt{A(1,1)}} \\ \mathbf{0} & I_{n-1} \end{pmatrix},$$

where I_{n-1} is the $(n-1) \times (n-1)$ identity matrix, and $\mathbf{0}$ is the column vector of size $n-1$ with all entries equal to 0.

Proof. By using block matrix multiplication, we find that

$$\begin{pmatrix} 1 & \mathbf{0}^t \\ \mathbf{0} & A_{n-1} - \frac{A(2:n,1)A(1,2:n)}{A(1,1)} \end{pmatrix} \begin{pmatrix} \sqrt{A(1,1)} & \frac{A(1,2:n)}{\sqrt{A(1,1)}} \\ \mathbf{0} & I_{n-1} \end{pmatrix}$$
$$= \begin{pmatrix} \sqrt{A(1,1)} & \frac{A(1,2:n)}{\sqrt{A(1,1)}} \\ \mathbf{0} & A_{n-1} - \frac{A(2:n,1)A(1,2:n)}{A(1,1)} \end{pmatrix}.$$

Then, using block matrix multiplication once again, we obtain that

$$\begin{pmatrix} \sqrt{A(1,1)} & \mathbf{0}^t \\ \frac{A(2:n,1)}{\sqrt{A(1,1)}} & I_{n-1} \end{pmatrix} \begin{pmatrix} 1 & \mathbf{0}^t \\ \mathbf{0} & A_{n-1} - \frac{A(2:n,1)A(1,2:n)}{A(1,1)} \end{pmatrix} \begin{pmatrix} \sqrt{A(1,1)} & \frac{A(1,2:n)}{\sqrt{A(1,1)}} \\ \mathbf{0} & I_{n-1} \end{pmatrix}$$
$$= \begin{pmatrix} \sqrt{A(1,1)} & \mathbf{0}^t \\ \frac{A(2:n,1)}{\sqrt{A(1,1)}} & I_{n-1} \end{pmatrix} \begin{pmatrix} \sqrt{A(1,1)} & \frac{A(1,2:n)}{\sqrt{A(1,1)}} \\ \mathbf{0} & A_{n-1} - \frac{A(2:n,1)A(1,2:n)}{A(1,1)} \end{pmatrix}$$
$$= \begin{pmatrix} A(1,1) & A(1,2:n) \\ A(2:n,1) & \frac{A(2:n,1)A(1,2:n)}{A(1,1)} + A_{n-1} - \frac{A(2:n,1)A(1,2:n)}{A(1,1)} \end{pmatrix}$$
$$= \begin{pmatrix} A(1,1) & A(1,2:n) \\ A(2:n,1) & A_{n-1} \end{pmatrix} = \begin{pmatrix} A(1,1) & A(1,2:n) \\ A(2:n,1) & A(2:n,2:n) \end{pmatrix}$$
$$= A,$$

which is what we wanted to prove. $\square$

Lemma 10.16. *Let A be a symmetric positive definite matrix, and let B be a nonsingular matrix of the same size as A. Then, the matrix $B^t A B$ is also symmetric positive definite.*

Proof. The matrix $B^t A B$ is symmetric, since $(B^t A B)^t = B^t A^t (B^t)^t = B^t A B$.
Let $x \in \mathbb{R}^n$, where n is the size of the square matrix A. Then,

$$x^t B^t A B x = (Bx)^t A B x = y^t A y, \qquad (10.126)$$

where $y = Bx$. Since A is symmetric positive definite, it follows from (5.17) that

$$y^t A y \geq 0, \quad \forall y \in \mathbb{R}^n; \tag{10.127}$$

$$y^t A y = 0 \iff y = 0. \tag{10.128}$$

Then, from (10.126) and using (10.127–10.128), we obtain that

$$x^t B^t A B x \geq 0, \quad \forall x \in \mathbb{R}^n; \tag{10.129}$$

$$x^t B^t A B x = 0 \iff y^t A y = 0 \iff y = 0 \iff B x = 0 \iff x = 0, \tag{10.130}$$

where the last equivalence follows from the fact that B is a nonsingular matrix.

From (10.129) and (10.130), we conclude that the matrix $B^t A B$ is symmetric positive definite. $\square$

Lemma 10.17. *Let A be an $n \times n$ symmetric positive matrix, and let $A_{n-1} = A(2 : n, 2 : n)$. Then, the matrix*

$$A_{n-1} - \frac{(A(1, 2 : n))^t A(1, 2 : n)}{A(1, 1)}$$

is symmetric positive definite.

Proof. Note that, since A is a symmetric matrix, $A(2 : n, 1) = (A(1, 2 : n))^t$. Then, from Lemma 10.15, we find that

$$A = \begin{pmatrix} \sqrt{A(1,1)} & \mathbf{0}^t \\ \frac{(A(1,2:n))^t}{\sqrt{A(1,1)}} & I_{n-1} \end{pmatrix} \begin{pmatrix} 1 & \mathbf{0}^t \\ \mathbf{0} & A_{n-1} - \frac{(A(1,2:n))^t A(1,2:n)}{A(1,1)} \end{pmatrix} \begin{pmatrix} \sqrt{A(1,1)} & \frac{A(1,2:n)}{\sqrt{A(1,1)}} \\ \mathbf{0} & I_{n-1} \end{pmatrix}$$

which can be written as

$$A = M^t \begin{pmatrix} 1 & \mathbf{0}^t \\ \mathbf{0} & A_{n-1} - \frac{(A(1,2:n))^t A(1,2:n)}{A(1,1)} \end{pmatrix} M, \tag{10.131}$$

where $M = \begin{pmatrix} \sqrt{A(1,1)} & \frac{A(1,2:n)}{\sqrt{A(1,1)}} \\ \mathbf{0} & I_{n-1} \end{pmatrix}$ and $\mathbf{0}$ denotes the column vector of size $n - 1$ with all entries equal to 0. Note that M is a nonsingular matrix, since M is upper triangular and $\det(M) = A(1, 1) \neq 0$; cf. (10.4).

Multiply (10.131) to the left by $(M^t)^{-1}$ and to the right by M^{-1} and obtain that

$$(M^t)^{-1} A M^{-1} = \begin{pmatrix} 1 & \mathbf{0}^t \\ \mathbf{0} & A_{n-1} - \frac{(A(1,2:n))^t A(1,2:n)}{A(1,1)} \end{pmatrix}. \tag{10.132}$$

Recall from Lemma 1.8 that $(M^t)^{-1} = (M^{-1})^t$. Let $B = M^{-1}$. Then, (10.132) can be written as

$$B^t A B = \begin{pmatrix} 1 & \mathbf{0}^t \\ \mathbf{0} & A_{n-1} - \frac{(A(1,2:n))^t A(1,2:n)}{A(1,1)} \end{pmatrix}. \tag{10.133}$$

10.6. TECHNICAL RESULTS FOR CHOLESKY AND LU

Let $x = \begin{pmatrix} 0 \\ x_{n-1} \end{pmatrix} \in \mathbb{R}^n$, where $x_{n-1} \in \mathbb{R}^{n-1}$. Using (10.133), we obtain that

$$x^t B^t A B x \tag{10.134}$$

$$= \begin{pmatrix} 0 & x_{n-1}^t \end{pmatrix} \begin{pmatrix} 1 & \mathbf{0}^t \\ \mathbf{0} & A_{n-1} - \frac{(A(1,2:n))^t A(1,2:n)}{A(1,1)} \end{pmatrix} \begin{pmatrix} 0 \\ x_{n-1} \end{pmatrix}$$

$$= x_{n-1}^t \left(A_{n-1} - \frac{(A(1,2:n))^t A(1,2:n)}{A(1,1)} \right) x_{n-1}. \tag{10.135}$$

Since A is a symmetric positive definite matrix, it follows from Lemma 10.16 that the matrix $B^t A B$ is also symmetric positive definite. Thus,

$$x^t B^t A B x \geq 0, \quad \forall\, x_n \in \mathbb{R}^n; \tag{10.136}$$

$$x^t B^t A B x = 0 \iff x = 0. \tag{10.137}$$

Then, from (10.134–10.137), it follows that

$$x_{n-1}^t \left(A_{n-1} - \frac{(A(1,2:n))^t A(1,2:n)}{A(1,1)} \right) x_{n-1} \geq 0, \quad \forall\, x_{n-1} \in \mathbb{R}^{n-1};$$

$$x_{n-1}^t \left(A_{n-1} - \frac{(A(1,2:n))^t A(1,2:n)}{A(1,1)} \right) x_{n-1} = 0 \iff x_{n-1} = 0,$$

and we conclude that the matrix $A_{n-1} - \frac{(A(1,2:n))^t A(1,2:n)}{A(1,1)}$ is symmetric positive definite. $\square$

We include below a proof by induction of the fact that every symmetric positive definite matrix has a Cholesky decomposition; see also Theorem 6.1.

Theorem 10.9. *Any symmetric positive definite matrix has a Cholesky decomposition.*

Proof. We give a proof by induction. Assume that any symmetric positive definite matrix of size $n-1$ is diagonalizable. We will show that any symmetric positive definite matrix of size n is also diagonalizable.

Let A be an $n \times n$ symmetric positive definite matrix. Then, $A(2:n,1) = (A(1,2:n))^t$, and, from Lemma 10.15, we find that

$$A = \begin{pmatrix} \sqrt{A(1,1)} & \mathbf{0}^t \\ \frac{(A(1,2:n))^t}{\sqrt{A(1,1)}} & I_{n-1} \end{pmatrix} \begin{pmatrix} 1 & \mathbf{0}^t \\ \mathbf{0} & A_{n-1} - \frac{(A(1,2:n))^t A(1,2:n)}{A(1,1)} \end{pmatrix} \begin{pmatrix} \sqrt{A(1,1)} & \frac{A(1,2:n)}{\sqrt{A(1,1)}} \\ \mathbf{0} & I_{n-1} \end{pmatrix} \tag{10.138}$$

where I_{n-1} is the $(n-1) \times (n-1)$ identity matrix, and $\mathbf{0}$ is the column vector of size $n-1$ with all entries equal to 0.

Recall from Lemma 10.17 that $A_{n-1} - \frac{(A(1,2:n))^t A(1,2:n)}{A(1,1)}$ is an $(n-1) \times (n-1)$ symmetric positive definite matrix. Then, from the induction hypothesis, it follows that there exists an $(n-1) \times (n-1)$ upper triangular matrix U_{n-1} with positive entries on the main diagonal such that

$$A_{n-1} - \frac{(A(1,2:n))^t A(1,2:n)}{A(1,1)} = U_{n-1}^t U_{n-1}.$$

Thus,

$$\begin{pmatrix} 1 & \mathbf{0}^t \\ \mathbf{0} & A_{n-1} - \frac{(A(1,2:n))^t A(1,2:n)}{A(1,1)} \end{pmatrix} \quad (10.139)$$

$$= \begin{pmatrix} 1 & \mathbf{0}^t \\ \mathbf{0} & U_{n-1}^t U_{n-1} \end{pmatrix}$$

$$= \begin{pmatrix} 1 & \mathbf{0}^t \\ \mathbf{0} & U_{n-1}^t \end{pmatrix} \begin{pmatrix} 1 & \mathbf{0}^t \\ \mathbf{0} & U_{n-1} \end{pmatrix}. \quad (10.140)$$

Note that

$$\begin{pmatrix} \sqrt{A(1,1)} & \mathbf{0}^t \\ \frac{(A(1,2:n))^t}{\sqrt{A(1,1)}} & I_{n-1} \end{pmatrix} \begin{pmatrix} 1 & \mathbf{0}^t \\ \mathbf{0} & U_{n-1}^t \end{pmatrix} = \begin{pmatrix} \sqrt{A(1,1)} & \mathbf{0}^t \\ \frac{(A(1,2:n))^t}{\sqrt{A(1,1)}} & U_{n-1}^t \end{pmatrix}; \quad (10.141)$$

$$\begin{pmatrix} 1 & \mathbf{0}^t \\ \mathbf{0} & U_{n-1} \end{pmatrix} \begin{pmatrix} \sqrt{A(1,1)} & \frac{A(1,2:n)}{\sqrt{A(1,1)}} \\ \mathbf{0} & I_{n-1} \end{pmatrix} = \begin{pmatrix} \sqrt{A(1,1)} & \frac{A(1,2:n)}{\sqrt{A(1,1)}} \\ \mathbf{0} & U_{n-1} \end{pmatrix}. \quad (10.142)$$

From (10.138–10.142), we obtain that

$$\begin{aligned} A &= \begin{pmatrix} \sqrt{A(1,1)} & \mathbf{0}^t \\ \frac{(A(1,2:n))^t}{\sqrt{A(1,1)}} & I_{n-1} \end{pmatrix} \begin{pmatrix} 1 & \mathbf{0}^t \\ \mathbf{0} & U_{n-1}^t \end{pmatrix} \begin{pmatrix} 1 & \mathbf{0}^t \\ \mathbf{0} & U_{n-1} \end{pmatrix} \begin{pmatrix} \sqrt{A(1,1)} & \frac{A(1,2:n)}{\sqrt{A(1,1)}} \\ \mathbf{0} & I_{n-1} \end{pmatrix} \\ &= \begin{pmatrix} \sqrt{A(1,1)} & \mathbf{0}^t \\ \frac{(A(1,2:n))^t}{\sqrt{A(1,1)}} & U_{n-1}^t \end{pmatrix} \begin{pmatrix} \sqrt{A(1,1)} & \frac{A(1,2:n)}{\sqrt{A(1,1)}} \\ \mathbf{0} & U_{n-1} \end{pmatrix} \\ &= U_n^t U_n, \end{aligned}$$

where $U_n = \begin{pmatrix} \sqrt{A(1,1)} & \frac{A(1,2:n)}{\sqrt{A(1,1)}} \\ \mathbf{0} & U_{n-1} \end{pmatrix}$ is an $n \times n$ upper triangular matrix. Note that the main diagonal entries of U_n are positive entries, since U_{n-1} was assumed to have positive entries on the main diagonal.

Thus, we showed that the matrix A has the Cholesky decomposition $A = U_n^t U_n$. We conclude by induction that any symmetric positive definite matrix has a Cholesky decomposition. □

Theorem 10.10. *If it exists, the LU decomposition without row pivoting of a matrix is unique.*

Proof. We give a proof by contradiction. Assume that the $n \times n$ nonsingular matrix A has two LU decompositions without row pivoting, i.e., assume that

$$A = L_1 U_1 \quad \text{and} \quad A = L_2 U_2,$$

where L_1 and L_2 are lower triangular matrices with entries equal to 1 on the main diagonal and U_1 and U_2 are nonsingular upper triangular matrices. Then,

$$L_1 U_1 = L_2 U_2. \quad (10.143)$$

10.6. MORE TECHNICAL RESULTS

Note that, by definition, L_1, L_2, U_1, and U_2 are nonsingular matrices; see Definition 2.1. Multiply (10.143) by L_2^{-1} on the left and by U_1^{-1} on the right and obtain

$$L_2^{-1} \cdot (L_1 U_1) \cdot U_1^{-1} = L_2^{-1} \cdot (L_2 U_2) \cdot U_1^{-1}$$
$$\iff (L_2^{-1} L_1) \cdot (U_1 U_1^{-1}) = (L_2^{-1} L_2) \cdot (U_2 U_1^{-1})$$
$$\iff L_2^{-1} L_1 = U_2 U_1^{-1}, \tag{10.144}$$

since $U_1 U_1^{-1} = I$ and $L_2^{-1} L_2 = I$.

Recall from Lemma 1.17 that the inverse of a lower triangular matrix is lower triangular, and the inverse of an upper triangular matrix is upper triangular, and, from Lemma 1.15, that the product of two lower triangular matrices is lower triangular, and the product of two upper triangular matrices is upper triangular. Thus, the matrix L_2^{-1} is lower triangular and therefore the matrix $L_2^{-1} L_1$ is also lower triangular. Similarly, the matrix U_1^{-1} is upper triangular and therefore the matrix $U_2 U_1^{-1}$ is also upper triangular. Since the matrices $L_2^{-1} L_1$ and $U_2 U_1^{-1}$ are equal, see (10.144), it follows that they must be diagonal matrices.

Let $D = \text{diag}(d_k)_{k=1:n}$ be a diagonal matrix such that

$$D = L_2^{-1} L_1 = U_2 U_1^{-1}. \tag{10.145}$$

By multiplying $D = L_2^{-1} L_1$ to the left by L_2, we find that

$$L_2 D = L_2 \cdot (L_2^{-1} L_1) = (L_2^{-1} L_2) \cdot L_1 = L_1. \tag{10.146}$$

Let $L_2 = \text{col}\left(l_k^{(2)}\right)_{k=1:n}$. From Lemma 1.10, we obtain that

$$L_2 D = \text{col}\left(d_k l_k^{(2)}\right)_{k=1:n}. \tag{10.147}$$

Recall that all the diagonal entries of the matrices L_1 and L_2 are equal to 1. From (10.147), it follows that the k-th diagonal entry of the matrix $L_2 D$ is d_k, for all $k = 1:n$. Since $L_2 D = L_1$, see (10.146), and since all the diagonal entries of L_1 are equal to 1, we obtain that $d_k = 1$ for all $k = 1:n$, and therefore the matrix D is the identity matrix, i.e., $D = I$.

Then, from (10.145), we find that

$$I = L_2^{-1} L_1 = U_2 U_1^{-1}.$$

Thus, $L_1 = L_2$ and $U_1 = U_2$, and we conclude that the LU decomposition of the matrix A is unique. $\square$

10.7 More technical results

We include here the proof of Lemma 1.17 stating that the inverse of a triangular matrix is triangular of the same type:

Lemma 10.18. *(i) The inverse of an upper triangular matrix is upper triangular.*

(ii) The inverse of a lower triangular matrix is lower triangular.

Proof. (i) Let $U = \operatorname{col}(u_k)_{k=1:n}$ be a nonsingular upper triangular matrix and let $B = \operatorname{col}(b_k)_{k=1:n}$ be the inverse matrix of U. Then,

$$BU = UB = I. \tag{10.148}$$

From (1.11), we obtain that $BU = \operatorname{col}(Bu_k)_{k=1:n}$. Since $I = \operatorname{col}(e_k)_{k=1:n}$, we find from (10.148) that

$$Bu_k = e_k, \quad \forall\, k = 1:n. \tag{10.149}$$

Let $k = 1$ in (10.149). Then, $Bu_1 = e_1$. Since U is upper triangular, it follows from (1.107) that $u_1(i) = 0$, for all $2 \leq i \leq n$. Thus,

$$e_1 = Bu_1 = \sum_{i=1}^{n} u_1(i) b_i = u_1(1) b_1,$$

and therefore

$$b_1 = \frac{1}{u_1(1)} e_1.$$

Note that $u_1(1) = U(1,1) \neq 0$ since U is nonsingular; cf. Lemma 1.16.

We conclude that all the entries of the first column of the matrix B with the exception of the first entry are equal to 0, i.e., the first column of the matrix B satisfies the equivalent definition (1.107) of an upper triangular matrix.

We show by (complete) induction that all the columns of the matrix B satisfy property (1.107).

Let k such that $2 \leq k \leq n$. Assume that the columns $b_1, \ldots, b_{k-1}$ satisfy property (1.107), i.e.,

$$b_i(j) = 0, \quad \forall\, i = 1:(k-1), \quad \forall\, i+1 \leq j \leq n. \tag{10.150}$$

Since U is upper triangular, we also find from (1.107) that

$$u_k(i) = 0, \quad \forall\, k+1 \leq i \leq n. \tag{10.151}$$

Recall from (10.149) that $Bu_k = e_k$. From (1.7) and (10.151), it follows that

$$e_k = Bu_k = \sum_{i=1}^{n} u_k(i) b_i = \sum_{i=1}^{k} u_k(i) b_i$$

$$= u_k(k) b_k + \sum_{i=1}^{k-1} u_k(i) b_i,$$

and therefore

$$b_k = \frac{1}{u_k(k)} \left(e_k - \sum_{i=1}^{k-1} u_k(i) b_i \right). \tag{10.152}$$

Note that $u_k(k) = U(k,k) \neq 0$ since U is nonsingular; cf. Lemma 1.16.

Let j such that $k+1 \leq j \leq n$. Then, $e_k(j) = 0$, and, for any $1 \leq i \leq k-1$, $b_i(j) = 0$ as well, from the induction hypothesis (10.150).

Then, from (10.152), it follows that $b_k(j) = 0$ for any $k+1 \leq j \leq n$, and therefore that the column b_k also satisfies property (1.107).

10.7. MORE TECHNICAL RESULTS

By induction, we conclude that all the columns of the matrix B satisfy property (1.107), and therefore that B is an upper triangular matrix.

(ii) Let L be a nonsingular lower triangular matrix, and let L^{-1} be the inverse matrix of L. Then, by definition,

$$L L^{-1} = L^{-1} L = I. \tag{10.153}$$

By transposing (10.153) and using (1.24), we obtain that

$$(L^{-1})^t L^t = L^t (L^{-1})^t = I.$$

Thus, $(L^{-1})^t$ is the inverse matrix of L^t, which is an upper triangular matrix.

We already proved that the inverse of an upper triangular matrix is upper triangular. It then follows that $(L^{-1})^t$ is an upper triangular matrix, and we therefore conclude that L^{-1} is a lower triangular matrix. □

The result below was used to establish (9.90) in section 9.6:

Lemma 10.19. *If Z is a standard normal variable, then*

$$P(Z \leq -a) = 1 - P(Z \leq a), \quad \forall\, a \in \mathbb{R}.$$

Proof. Recall that

$$P(Z \leq -a) = \frac{1}{\sqrt{2\pi}} \int_{-\infty}^{-a} e^{-\frac{x^2}{2}}\, dx, \tag{10.154}$$

since the probability density function of the standard normal variable Z is $\frac{1}{\sqrt{2\pi}} e^{-\frac{x^2}{2}}$; see (7.109). Using the substitution $x = -y$ in (10.154), we find that

$$\begin{aligned}
P(Z \leq -a) &= \frac{1}{\sqrt{2\pi}} \int_{\infty}^{a} e^{-\frac{(-y)^2}{2}} (-dy) = \frac{1}{\sqrt{2\pi}} \int_{a}^{\infty} e^{-\frac{y^2}{2}}\, dy \\
&= 1 - \frac{1}{\sqrt{2\pi}} \int_{-\infty}^{a} e^{-\frac{y^2}{2}}\, dy \\
&= 1 - P(Z \leq a),
\end{aligned}$$

which is what we wanted to show. Note that, for the third equality above, we used the fact that

$$\frac{1}{\sqrt{2\pi}} \int_{-\infty}^{a} e^{-\frac{y^2}{2}}\, dy + \frac{1}{\sqrt{2\pi}} \int_{a}^{\infty} e^{-\frac{y^2}{2}}\, dy = \frac{1}{\sqrt{2\pi}} \int_{-\infty}^{\infty} e^{-\frac{y^2}{2}}\, dy = 1,$$

since the integral over $(-\infty, \infty)$ of the probability density $\frac{1}{\sqrt{2\pi}} e^{-\frac{y^2}{2}}$ of Z is equal to 1. □

10.8 Exercises

1. Show that
$$\det \begin{pmatrix} 1 & a & a^2 \\ 1 & b & b^2 \\ 1 & c & c^2 \end{pmatrix} = (c-a)(c-b)(b-a),$$
where $a, b, c \in \mathbb{R}$.

   Note: A matrix of the form
$$\begin{pmatrix} 1 & c_1 & c_1^2 & \cdots & c_1^{n-1} \\ 1 & c_2 & c_2^2 & \cdots & c_2^{n-1} \\ \vdots & \vdots & \vdots & \cdots & \vdots \\ 1 & c_n & c_n^2 & \cdots & c_n^{n-1} \end{pmatrix},$$
where $c_1, c_2, \ldots, c_n$ are constants, is called a Vandermonde matrix. The determinant of the Vandermonde matrix is equal to
$$\prod_{1 \leq k < j \leq n} (c_j - c_k).$$

2. Show that any orthogonal matrix has determinant 1 or -1. In other words, show that, for any orthogonal matrix Q, either $\det(Q) = 1$, or $\det(Q) = -1$.

3. Let M_1 and M_2 be $n \times n$ symmetric matrices. Show that, if
$$x^t M_1 x = x^t M_2 x, \ \forall\, x \in \mathbb{R}^n,$$
then $M_1 = M_2$.

4. Show that the quadratic form of a matrix is 0 if and only if the matrix is skew–symmetric, i.e., show that
$$q_A(x) = 0 \quad \text{if and only if} \quad A^t = -A.$$

Bibliography

[1] Carol Alexander. *Market Risk Analysis I: Quantitative Methods in Finance.* John Wiley & Sons, Inc., Chichester, West Sussex, 2008.

[2] Carol Alexander. *Market Risk Analysis IV: Value at Risk Models.* John Wiley & Sons, Inc., Chichester, West Sussex, 2008.

[3] Leif B. G. Andersen and Vladimir V. Piterbarg. *Interest Rate Modeling. Volume 1: Foundations and Vanilla Models.* Atlantic Financial Press, London, New York, 2010.

[4] Leif B. G. Andersen and Vladimir V. Piterbarg. *Interest Rate Modeling. Volume 3: Products and Risk Management.* Atlantic Financial Press, London, New York, 2010.

[5] Kenneth Arrow and Gérard Debreu. Existence of an equilibrium for a competitive economy. *Econometrica*, 3:265–290, 1954.

[6] Philippe Artzner, Freddy Delbaen, Jean-Marc Eber, and David Heath. Coherent measures of risk. *Mathematical Finance*, 9(3):203–228, 1999.

[7] Marco Avellaneda and Peter Laurence. *Quantitative Modeling of Derivative Securities: From Theory to Practice.* Chapman & Hall/CRC, Boca Raton, Florida, 2000.

[8] Stephen Blyth. *An Introduction to Quantitative Finance.* Oxford University Press, Oxford, United Kingdom, 2014.

[9] Claude Brezinski. The life and work of André Cholesky. *Numerical Algorithms*, 43(3):279–288, 2006.

[10] Barry A. Cipra. The best of the 20-th century: Editors name Top 10 algorithms. *SIAM News*, 33(4), 2000.

[11] Les Clewlow and Chris Strickland. *Implementing Derivatives Models.* John Wiley & Sons Ltd, Chichester, West Sussex, 1998.

[12] Biswa Nath Datta. *Numerical Linear Algebra and Applications.* SIAM, Philadelphia, Pennsylvania, 2nd edition, 2010.

[13] James W. Demmel. *Applied Numerical Linear Algebra.* SIAM, Philadelphia, Pennsylvania, 1997.

[14] Frank J. Fabozzi and Harry M. Markowitz. *The Theory and Practice of Investment Management: Asset Allocation, Valuation, Portfolio Construction, and Strategies.* John Wiley & Sons Ltd, Chichester, West Sussex, 2nd edition, 2011.

[15] Jim Gatheral. *The Volatility Surface: A Practitioner's Guide.* John Wiley & Sons Ltd, Chichester, West Sussex, 2006.

[16] George T. Gilbert. Positive definite matrices and Sylvester's criterion. *The American Mathematical Monthly*, 98(1):44–46, 1991.

[17] Paul Glasserman. *Monte Carlo Methods in Financial Engineering.* Springer-Verlag New York, Inc., New York, 2004.

[18] Gene H. Golub and Charles F. Van Loan. *Numerical Linear Algebra.* The Johns Hopkins University Press, Baltimore, Maryland, 3rd edition, 1996.

[19] Nicholas J. Higham. Analysis of the Cholesky decomposition of a semidefinite matrix. In M. G. Cox and S. J. Hammarling, editors, *Reliable Numerical Computation*, pages 161–185, Oxford, United Kingdom, 1990. Oxford University Press.

[20] Nicholas J. Higham. *Accuracy and Stability of Numerical Algorithms.* SIAM, Philadelphia, Pennsylvania, 2002.

[21] Ali Hirsa. *Computational Methods in Finance.* CRC Press, Boca Raton, Florida, 2013.

[22] Roger A. Horn and Charles R. Johnson. *Matrix Analysis.* Cambridge University Press, New York, 1985.

[23] John C. Hull. *Risk Management and Financial Institutions.* Prentice Hall, Upper Saddle River, New Jersey, 3rd edition, 2012.

[24] Jean Jacod and Philip Protter. *Probability Essentials.* Springer-Verlag Berlin Heidelberg, Berlin, 2nd edition, 2004.

[25] Tze Leung Lai and Haipeng Xing. *Statistical Models and Methods for Financial Markets.* Springer Texts in Statistics. Springer-Verlag New York, Inc., New York, 2008.

[26] Peter D. Lax. *Linear Algebra and Its Applications.* John Wiley & Sons, Inc., Hoboken, New Jersey, 2nd edition, 2007.

[27] Peter D. Lax and Lawrence Zalcman. *Complex Proofs of Real Theorems*, volume 58 of *University Lecture Series*. American Mathematical Society, Providence, Rhode Island, 2012.

[28] Harry M. Markowitz. Portfolio selection. *Journal of Finance*, 1(7):77–91, 1952.

[29] Attilio Meucci. *Risk and Asset Allocation.* Springer-Verlag Berlin Heidelberg, New York, 2005.

[30] Salih N. Neftci. *An Introduction to the Mathematics of the Financial Derivatives.* Academic Press, San Diego, California, 2nd edition, 2000.

[31] Salih N. Neftci. *Principles of Financial Engineering.* Elsevier Academic Press, San Diego, California, 2nd edition, 2008.

[32] William H. Press, Saul A. Teukolsky, William T. Vetterling, and Brian P. Flannery. *Numerical Recipes: The Art of Scientific Computing*. Cambridge University Press, New York, 3rd edition, 2007.

[33] David Ruppert. *Statistics and Data Analysis for Financial Engineering*. Undergraduate Studies in Mathematics. Springer Science, New York, 2010.

[34] Yousef Saad. *Numerical Methods for Large Eigenvalue Problems*. Classics in Applied Mathematics. SIAM, Philadelphia, Pennsylvania, 2011.

[35] William F. Sharpe. Capital asset prices: A theory of market equilibrium under conditions of risk. *Journal of Finance*, 3(19):425–442, 1964.

[36] Dan Stefanica. *A Mathematical Primer with Numerical Methods for Financial Engineering*. Financial Engineering Advanced Background Series. FE Press, New York, 2nd edition, 2011.

[37] Dan Stefanica. *Solutions Manual: A Mathematical Primer with Numerical Methods for Financial Engineering*. Financial Engineering Advanced Background Series. FE Press, New York, 2nd edition, 2011.

[38] Dan Stefanica. *Solutions Manual: Numerical Linear Algebra Methods for Financial Engineering Applications*. Financial Engineering Advanced Background Series. FE Press, New York, 2014.

[39] Dan Stefanica, Radoš Radoičić, and Tai-Ho Wang. *150 Most Frequently Asked Questions on Quant Interviews*. Pocket Book Guides for Quant Interviews. FE Press, New York, 2013.

[40] Gilbert Strang. *Linear Algebra and Its Applications*. Cengage Learning, Stamford, Connecticut, 4th edition, 2005.

[41] Gilbert Strang. *Introduction to Linear Algebra*. Wellesley-Cambridge Press, Wellesley, Massachusetts, 4th edition, 2009.

[42] Gilbert Strang. *Essays in Linear Algebra*. Wellesley-Cambridge Press, Wellesley, Massachusetts, 2012.

[43] Lloyd N. Trefethen and David Bau III. *Numerical Linear Algebra*. SIAM, Philadelphia, Pennsylvania, 1997.

[44] Richard S. Varga. *Gershgorin and His Circles*. Springer-Verlag New York, Inc., New York, 2004.

[45] Paul Wilmott, Sam Howison, and Jeff Dewynne. *Option Pricing: Mathematical Models and Computation*. Oxford Financial Press, Oxford, United Kingdom, 1993.

[46] Paul Wilmott, Sam Howison, and Jeff Dewynne. *The Mathematics of Financial Derivatives: A Student Introduction*. Cambridge University Press, Cambridge, United Kingdom, 1995.

Index

Arrow–Debreu model, 87

Backward substitution, 43
    bidiagonal matrix, 46
    operation count, 44
    pseudocode, 45
Big O notation, 303
Black–Scholes formula, 229, 306
Bond
    annual coupon bond, 42
    quarterly coupon bond, 84, 191
    semiannual coupon bond, 73

Call option, 305
Cholesky decomposition, 161, 311
    example, 168
    existence, 162, 313
    linear solver, 174
    operation count, 171
    pseudocode, 170
    tridiagonal spd linear solver, 179
    tridiagonal spd matrix, 177, 179
    uniqueness, 165
Correlation matrix, 25, 194, 197, 212
    sample correlation matrix, 26, 201, 203
    symmetric positive semidefinite, 199, 209
Covariance matrix, 25, 194, 200, 212, 219
    sample covariance matrix, 7, 26, 201, 203
    symmetric positive semidefinite, 199, 209
Cubic spline interpolation, 75, 181
    efficient implementation, 182
    natural cubic spline interpolation, 76, 181
    pseudocode, 77, 185

    zero rate curve, 77, 185

Diagonal matrix, 22
    inverse, 24
    nonsingular, 24
Discount factors computation
    using forward substitution, 41
    using LU decomposition, 73

Eigenvalue, 111, 113, 117, 119
    multiplicity, 117
    strictly diagonally dominant matrix, 149
    symmetric matrix, 140, 307
    symmetric positive definite matrix, 144
    symmetric positive semidefinite matrix, 144
    tridiagonal symmetric matrix, 128, 130
    weakly diagonally dominant matrix, 149
Eigenvector, 111, 119
    linear independence, 117, 118
    orthogonal matrix, 141
    symmetric matrix, 142
    tridiagonal symmetric matrix, 128, 130
European options, 305

Forward substitution, 38
    bidiagonal matrix, 41
    discount factors computation, 41
    operation count, 39
    pseudocode, 40

Gershgorin's Theorem, 124

Identity matrix, 6

column form, 6
row form, 6
Implied volatility, 229
　least squares implementation, 229
　pseudocode for implied volatility computation, 234
Index options one period market model, 100
Inner product, 140

Lagrange multipliers, 301
　maximum return portfolio, 265
　minimum variance portfolio, 259
　minimum variance portfolio no cash position, 271
Law of One Price, 94
Leading principal minors of a matrix, 46, 151
Linear regression, 235, 241
Linear Transformation Property, 207, 221
Linearly independent vectors, 10
Lower triangular matrix, 27
　inverse, 29, 315
　nonsingular, 29
　product, 28
LU decomposition with row pivoting, 61
　discount factors computation, 73
　example, 63
　existence, 62
　linear solver, 71, 72
　operation count, 69
　pseudocode, 70
　uniqueness, 62
LU decomposition without pivoting, 46, 311
　example, 47
　existence, 47
　linear solver, 56
　operation count, 53
　pseudocode, 54
　tridiagonal linear solver, 59, 60
　tridiagonal matrix, 56, 59
　tridiagonal spd linear solver, 180, 181
　uniqueness, 47, 314

Matrix
　banded, 29
　characteristic polynomial, 113, 114
　column form, 2
　determinant, 20, 287
　diagonal, 22
　diagonal form, 122
　diagonalizable, 122
　eigenvalue, 111
　eigenvector, 111
　inverse, 20, 120
　leading principal minors, 46, 151
　lower triangular, 27
　nonsingular, 20, 120
　nullspace, 11
　principal minors, 151
　range, 11
　rank, 11
　row form, 2
　singular, 20, 120
　square, 5
　strictly diagonally dominant, 124, 149
　symmetric, 5, 139
　symmetric positive definite, 142
　symmetric positive semidefinite, 142
　transpose, 4
　tridiagonal, 30
　upper triangular, 27
　weakly diagonally dominant, 124, 149
Maximum return portfolio, 253, 257, 265
　from tangency portfolio, 258, 269
　pseudocode, 257
Min var portfolio no cash position, 271
Minimum variance portfolio, 253, 255, 259
　from tangency portfolio, 256, 262
　pseudocode, 255
Multiplication
　column vector–row vector, 2
　matrix–column vector, 2
　matrix–matrix, 3
　matrix–matrix–matrix, 4
　row vector–column vector, 2
　row vector–matrix, 3
Multivariable functions
　scalar valued, 296
　vector valued, 299
Multivariate normal variable, 215
　bivariate normal variable, 216
　multivariate standard normal, 214

One period binomial market model, 89, 93, 96, 98
One period market model, 12, 87
　arbitrage opportunities, 91

arbitrage–free complete model, 97
arbitrage–free market, 91
complete market, 95
index options market model, 100
non–redundant securities, 88
payoff matrix, 88, 96
replicable security, 90, 94
risk–neutral pricing, 97
state prices, 91, 99
Ordinary least squares (OLS), 227
    for implied volatility computation, 229
    for random variables, 237
    pseudocode, 229
Orthogonal matrix, 141, 291
Orthogonal vectors, 141, 291

Permutation matrix, 61, 289
Put option, 305
Put–Call parity, 230, 305, 306

Quadratic form, 294

State prices, 91, 99
Sylvester's Criterion, 151

Tangency portfolio, 262, 269
Tridiagonal matrix, 30

Upper triangular matrix, 27
    inverse, 29, 315
    nonsingular, 29
    product, 28

Value at Risk, 274
    approximation formula, 276
    subadditivity, 278
Vector
    column vector, 1
    linear independence, 10
    norm, 140
    row vector, 2
    transpose, 4

Made in the USA
Columbia, SC
25 January 2024